Handy
FARM and HOME
DEVICES
and How to Make Them

Hundr

Saving Hir

Publisher's Note:

This facsimile edition has been reproduced from the 1945 edition of *Handy Farm and Home Devices*. In order to maintain the original concept of the book it has been reproduced with a minimum of alterations. **It should be noted, however, that some information contained in this book, particularly in the first aid section, has become outdated and may no longer be considered sound medical practice.**

First MIT Press paperback edition, 1981

This edition published by Angus & Robertson Publishers, Australia, 1980
First published by The Advertiser Printing Office, Adelaide, 1945

Printed and bound by Halliday Lithograph
in the United States of America

Library of Congress Cataloging in Publication Data

Main entry under title:

Handy farm and home devices and how to make them.

Includes index.
1. Recipes. 2. Implements, utensils, etc.
3. Farm equipment. 4. Do-it-yourself work.
I. Bartlett, J. V.
T49.H26   1981   600   81-554
ISBN 0-262-52064-8 (pbk.)   AACR2

Handy
FARM and HOME
DEVICES
and How to Make Them

COMPILED AND DESIGNED BY
J. V. BARTLETT

The MIT Press
Cambridge, Massachusetts

ACKNOWLEDGEMENTS

This book has been published in the belief that one of this nature would be of practical value to every man on the land and to every householder, its purpose being to provide in easily accessible form details of many useful ideas, handy home-made devices and inventions of farmers and others from all over the world on subjects of everyday interest, suitably described and illustrated in such a manner as to be readily available as the occasion may arise.

The above could not be achieved without the assistance and co-operation of those firms who have been only too pleased to give their permission to reproduce so many of the excellent ideas given herein and to those firms, the Publisher desires to express his appreciation and thanks. They, too, will no doubt be pleased and well repaid by the success of this effort on behalf of the Blinded. Each of the Publications named below will be found of great value to every Man on the Land for the helpful information and advice on all subjects which they contain.

The " Chronicle," " Mail," and " Stock & Station Journal " of Adelaide.

The " Weekly Times," " Leader," " Argus," and " Pastoral Review "
of Melbourne.

" Power Farming," the " C.B.S. Gazette," "The Poultry Journal," and
the " Country Press " of Sydney.

The " Western Mail " of Perth.

The " Queenslander " of Brisbane.

The " New Zealand Farmer " of New Zealand.

The Journals of Agriculture of every State.

" The Country Guide " of Winnipeg, Canada.

" Popular Mechanics," " Mechanix Illustrated," and " Popular
Science " of U.S.A.

The " Farmer and Stockbreeder " of England, and others.

We are also grateful to Mr. David J. Farrell, of Sydney, for extracts from his book " FIRST AID IN PICTURES " which is, without doubt, one of the best available on this subject. To Mr. A. C. Duval, of Morphett Vale, S.A., we also express our thanks for some of the ideas shown and to Mr. Fraser Hay, of Adelaide, for many of the drawings and sketches. We also express our appreciation to Mr. G. G. Love, of Adelaide, for advice given in connection with general layout and other decorative work involved in this publication.

To " Advertiser Newspapers Limited," of Adelaide, we also express our thanks for the assistance given in connection with the printing of this book.

To the Schools Patriotic Fund of South Australia, we express our special appreciation for the wonderful assistance given by them in connection with the preliminary costs of this book (including the many drawings and blocks and other expenses), which assistance has contributed in no small measure to the success of this publication.

FOREWORD

The idea for this book originated from a casual remark passed by a farmer who, on seeing the Publisher's collection of ideas, said that, although intentions were often good, very few actually took the trouble to keep a good news cutting book of the many splendid ideas seen in the press and other publications and therefore, when the occasion arose when such-and-such an idea might have been of value and which might have been used, the particulars could never be found. Unless kept in a methodical manner, such valuable hints are apt to be forgotten.

The collection was then shown to many others, all of whom were enthusiastic and considered that, if in book form, it would be invaluable, not only to every farmer and grazier in Australia, but to thousands of other handymen in cities and suburbs also. For this reason, and also because he saw in it an opportunity to benefit to some extent those with whom he has for years been closely associated, i.e., the Blinded Soldier, the Publisher ultimately decided to produce this book in the hope that it would prove valuable and of service to all concerned.

It has been carefully compiled and each idea or useful device is explained in a simple non-technical manner. Many months have been spent in collecting new ideas, sorting and selecting the best and putting them into proper order—ideas of interest to all and of use and value to every Man on the Land—ideas and handy devices which are both time and money saving—all clearly described and illustrated—many of them even making it unnecessary to call in specialised tradesmen.

Each subject has been chosen with infinite care and they are passed on to you in all good faith as they are proven ideas of farmers and others, but naturally no responsibility can be accepted by the publisher for any slight error which might creep in although every idea has been tried out and found satisfactory by someone.

The book is published "as a collection" of some of the best ideas which have appeared in such excellent publications as those enumerated on the opposite page—publications which make a specialty of such ideas and which, in the publisher's experience, are among the best of their kind in the world. It is not intended that this book should take their place—on the contrary, the publisher can recommend any one of them to you as well worthy of your support. This book is merely meant to keep these excellent ideas of theirs alive by reproduction in such a form as will enable them to be always available to you "just when wanted."

The joy of making things will find expression in fashioning useful things shown in this book —emergencies often arise which make certain work necessary or certain ideas or ways of doing things valuable—those given in this book might be the very thing wanted or they might be the means of suggesting something else; any one of which might prove to be both time and money saving.

IT WILL PAY YOU TO LOOK THROUGH THIS BOOK FREQUENTLY—USE THE INDEX FREELY.

TABLE OF CONTENTS

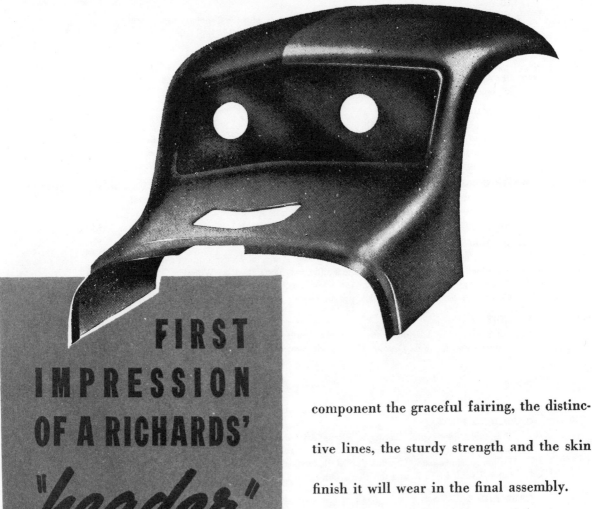

FIRST IMPRESSION OF A RICHARDS' "header"

THIS is the Header and Cowl Top for a Truck cabin, just as it left the Richards' press. One operation of a few minutes' duration has given this component the graceful fairing, the distinctive lines, the sturdy strength and the skin finish it will wear in the final assembly. Unsurpassed experience in making the dies for pressings, and the pressing from the dies is materialised in Richards' proudest achievement . . . . the Safe-T-Steel *"BODY BY RICHARDS"*

IDEAS FOR THE HOME WORKSHOP

MAKING A WORKBENCH

The First Job for a Handyman

A good workbench is the most useful thing any "Handyman" can possess, and the illustrations given are of two different types—enclosed and open—both being quite simple to construct to any convenient size.

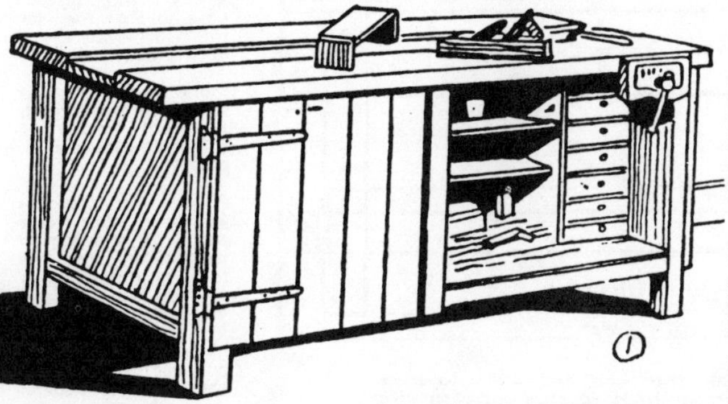

(1)

The first is a small type bench measuring say 3 ft. 6 in. long by 2 ft. deep and 2 ft. 10 in. high and the timber required will be as under, but if a bigger bench is preferred, the length and size of materials will be altered accordingly.

Legs & Frames . 34 ft. of 2x2
Bracings and
Battens. . . . 20 ft. of 2x1
Fillets . . . . . 24 ft. of $\frac{3}{4}$x$\frac{3}{4}$
Shelves, Divisions and
Bottom . . 24 ft. of 6x$\frac{1}{2}$
Tool Racks etc. 20 ft. of 1x$\frac{3}{8}$
Back—$\frac{1}{8}$ ply . 36 in. x 30 in.
End Panels—Tongued and Grooved 25 sq. ft. 4x$\frac{1}{2}$ matchboard.
Top—9x$2\frac{1}{2}$ in. x 7 ft. 6 in. and 7 ft. 6 in. of 7x$\frac{1}{2}$ in.

Rigidity is obtained (fig. 6) by making a skeleton framework, bracing the ends by matchboard panels sloping diagonally from the top front to the bottom back; also by the jointing of the framework, and by the diagonal braces and plywood panelling at the back, together with the arrangement of shelves, etc.

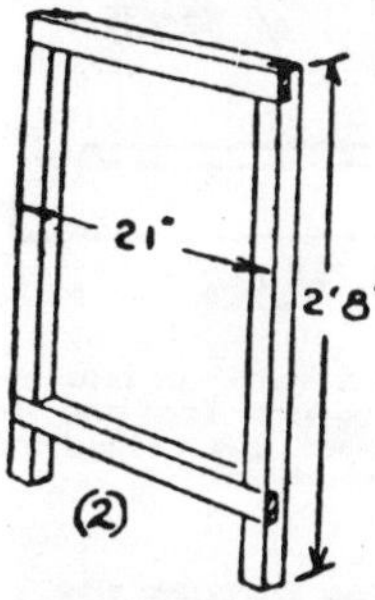

(2)

The End Frames. Two are required (fig. 2)—One right and one left handed. Each consists of two legs 2 ft. 8 in. and two crosspieces, each 21 in. long, the bottom crosspiece having its lower edge 3 in. from the floor.

Connect the parts with simple halving joints—the cutaway parts of the legs being on the inside. Glue and cramp together, and secure with a $\frac{3}{8}$-in. dia. hardwood dowel. **Do not use nails or screws.**

Connecting End Frames. Connect the four crosspieces (fig. 3). Depth of joints, 1 in., or half the thickness of the timber. Mark the timber accurately in order to fit the dovetail close together. THE FRONT TOP RAIL should be $2\frac{1}{2}$ in. from the end of the frame—the TOP BACK RAIL flush with the face of the legs. Fit the lower two rails to the front face of the legs. The lower pair fit so that the top edges are $\frac{1}{2}$ in. below the underside of the lower cross rails (fig. 4). This is to allow for the thickness of the bottom board. Figs. 5 and 6 will also show the position of these crosspieces.

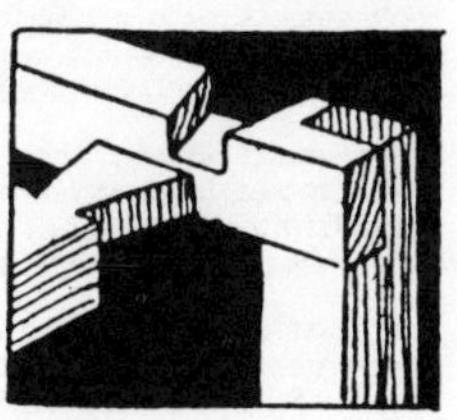

(3)

Mark each piece for identification as it is done; then lay aside.

Panelling End Frames. First place the longest piece of matchboard in the centre of frame from top front corner to bottom back corner (figs. 5 and 6). Cut the board to length; then glue and nail to the inside face of the frame, allowing the surplus ends to overlap. The other pieces of board are then cut and fitted similarly, glueing and nailing each into place and driving the joints into close contact.

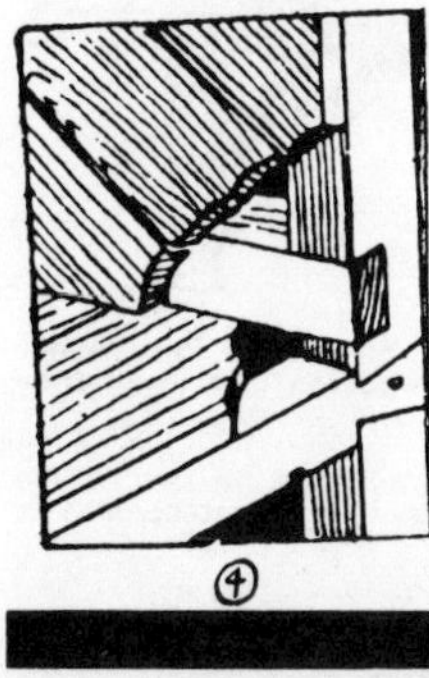

(4)

Spread the glue on the frame, but not on the tongued joints. Cut the ends of the board to fit neatly round the long rails, and when glue has set hard, saw off surplus ends and plane them flush with the edges of the legs and cross rails.

Assembling the Framework. Fit crosspieces by glueing, and fix with $\frac{3}{8}$in. hardwood dowel pegs, taking care that the structure is secure at all internal angles, and that the top is flat, when it will appear as in fig. 5.

Then fix diagonal bracing as shown in fig. 6, using 2 x 1. These pieces reach from corner to corner and are halved together at the centre, the ends being sawn to a double bevel. They should fit snugly and should not be forced. The intersection at the centre is easily ascertained and jointed with a square halved joint.

Glue the joint surfaces. Put the braces into place and secure with a cross nail at each corner, but screwing the centre joint. Cover the back with plywood, glueing same to the frame and diagonal pieces, and nail with 1 in. nails.

Fitting the Bottom Boards. Turn the structure upside down. Cut two or three pieces of $\frac{1}{2}$ in. board to the exact length over the end frames. Then cut the corners out of one board and slide it under the bottom long rail, fitting it very closely around the legs. Then fix it with glue and $1\frac{1}{2}$ in. oval brads driven into the end framework and into the long rail. Then glue and nail the next pieces of plain board; the last piece which comes to the front should be fitted similarly to that at the back, any surplus wood at the edge being sawn off and planed smooth.

After the bottom boards are fixed, cut a piece of 2 x 1 batten to fit closely between the long side rails; glue it in place at the middle of the length of the bench and fix it with two screws to each board.

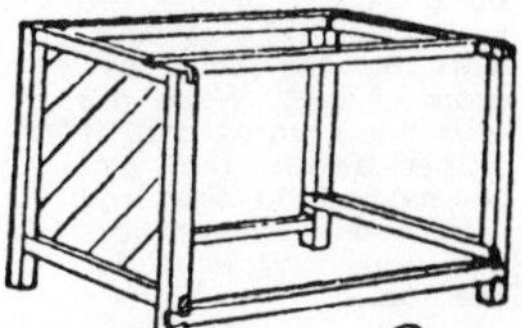

(5)

Making and Fitting the Top. The top consists of two pieces of thick timber set at front and back with a shallow trough in between. This latter can be covered if required, with a loose board (fig. 7), the top surface then being flush. Plane all faces smooth; cut to exact length and lay them in place on top of bench; adjust until top overhangs equally at ends and sides. Then glue and screw the central board into its place. Next drill clearance holes through the top rails to take stout screws. Countersink the holes on the underside; then glue the joint surfaces and screw the boards into place.

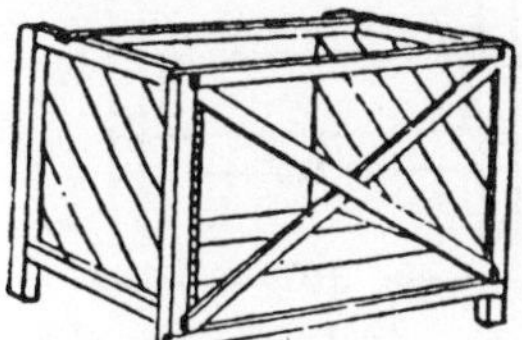

(6)

Drive each piece hard against the central plank. If possible, hold it with a cramp or, failing that, fix the board with a couple of lashings of strong twine while screws are driven home. Screws should be $3\frac{1}{2}$ in. long and must pass freely through holes in frame; smaller holes should be drilled in the top boards so that the screws will take a firm grip. Countersink the holes on the joint faces to counteract any swelling of the wood when the screws are driven in.

Finishing the Bench Top. The bench top is finished off by fitting fillets to the inner edges of the thick boards so that the loose board, when placed upon them as in fig. 7 will be flush with the others.

The ends of the top boards are finished by a strip of wood about $2\frac{1}{2}$ in. deep and $3\frac{1}{8}$ in. thick glued and nailed in place and rounded off on all edges. These pieces also prevent the top coverboard from moving endways. A hole is drilled near one end of the cover so that a finger may be inserted when the board can then easily be lifted out.

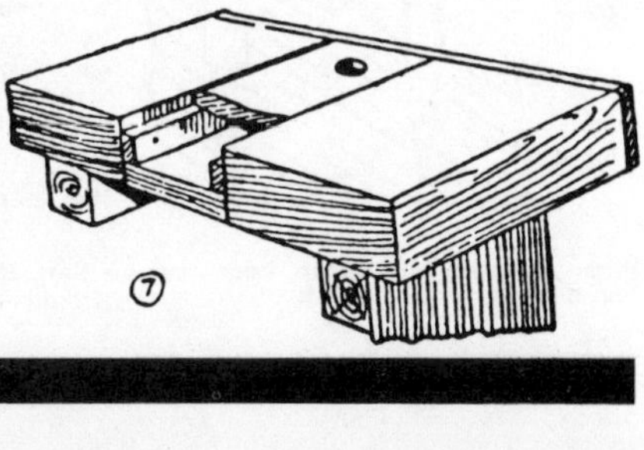

(7)

IDEAS AND HANDY GADGETS FOR THE WORKSHOP

ANOTHER HOME-MADE BENCH

This illustration is of a different type bench, 5 ft. 6 in. long and 2 ft. wide, but any size to suit can be made. Woods usually favoured are oregon and jarrah—oregon for the under frame and jarrah for the bench top, side and vice.

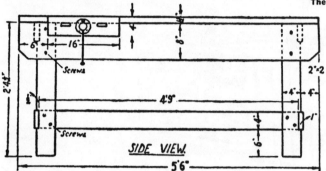

SIDE VIEW.

Make the bench in sections—then bolt and screw together. Commence with the four legs, which are squared and then sawn to length. For the end frames, join each pair of legs with a top and bottom rail, either by a butt joint, or the rails can be housed into the legs. Set the four legs together and mark out the lines for all the grooves at the one time in order to avoid any later error.

The bottom groove should be 6 in. up, whilst the top one finishes level with the top (see diagram of leg). When the rails are squared and of proper length, they can be secured to the legs with screws for the bottom rails and bolts for the top.

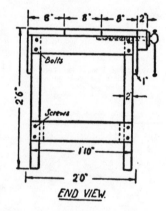

END VIEW.

To complete the frame there are longer rails which connect the end sections. The lower ones are screwed to the inner edges of the legs, and the upper ones are bolted on the outside. The upper rails, being wider than the others, assist in making the frame rigid when they are bolted.

To ensure a square framework, see that the rails are all of correct length and square on the ends. The upper rails are finished with a 2 x 2 corner at the under edge. When fixing rails into position, hold them against the uprights with a cramp while holes are bored for the screws.

Fixing the Top. The three boards for the top should be squared to length and rested in place on the framework. In this position mark and bore the holes for the screws, which must be countersunk.

Boring Holes for Screws and Bolts. Holes for the screws are done in three operations. First bore a hole equal in diameter to the shank of the screw and of the same depth; then a smaller hole for the threaded portion, but not quite the full depth, and finally the top of the hole is countersunk for the screwhead (see illustration).

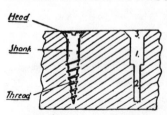

For bolts, the hole is bored to accommodate the shank of the bolt, but if the bolthead is to be sunken, a larger hole for the purpose must be bored first.

When screwing into jarrah, bear in mind that, if the hole is not bored almost to the depth of the screw, trouble will follow.

The screw will probably break off at the thread when attempting to force it. It should be so that the last two or three turns are sufficient to draw the screw firmly into the hole.

The Vice. The horizontal type is worked by a screw, and two runners. Finish the wood for the vice-block to size, 16 in. x 4 x 2 in. Carefully mark the position of the screw-hole so that the vice-screw runs along the underside of the bench top. Continue the hole through the front rail of the bench.

Mark the mortises for the runners and cut them through with a mortise chisel. Also mark and cut these through the front bench rail. The runners, which can be of 2 x ¾ in. material and 16 in. long, are glued and wedged into place.

Fix the vice-screw into the block and secure by screwing on the collar. Screw the bolt to the back of the rail and turn the vice-screw thus drawing the block into place. Accuracy of fit between the jaws of the vice will depend upon the squareness of the runners and mortises.

SKETCH of BENCH.

VIEW of LEG.

This will give a useful, good and strong type of workbench, quite big enough for ordinary purposes but if a bigger bench is required, it is then only necessary to provide for different sized timbers.

A small flush-fitting patent vice can be fitted to either of the benches mentioned, preferably at the left-hand end of the bench, whilst the matter of shelves, drawers, etc., is merely a matter of arrangement to suit individual needs. Other gadgets can also, of course, be added and the following pages will give details and ideas which should be of help in this respect.

A HOME-MADE PORTABLE BENCH FOR OUTSIDE USE

There are many jobs, such as repairs to fences and outbuildings, etc., in and around every farming or grazing property where the tools necessary are needed on the spot and have to be transported there, in which case an arrangement such as that shown here will be found invaluable and very convenient.

As it would have a good deal of rough work, it should be very solidly made, but not too heavy, as one might have some considerable distance to travel at times if the job were well away from the homestead. The wheels, too, should be good, strong ones.

The illustration itself shows the idea, and it could be made from any scrap timber about the place, although, of course, an underframe of iron, bolted to the woodwork, would be ideal. A permanent vice mounted is always an advantage, whilst wood which will stand plenty of wear is necessary.

The arrangement has a special place for tools, with or without lid — the latter being preferable in case it is needed in wet weather. This toolbox provides some place in which any tools likely to be required for outside purposes can always be kept—they are then at hand and not likely to be forgotten just when they are most needed.

The construction of the rest of the bench needs no description —simply a good axle, a couple of old wheels, some scrap iron or timber, and that is all that is needed.

IDEAS AND HANDY GADGETS FOR THE WORKSHOP

ANOTHER TYPE OF PORTABLE WORKBENCH

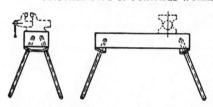

This can be put together at very small cost—it consisting of one main piece of timber with removable supports as indicated. Its main purpose is for mounting the vice, the timber being approximately 8 x 6 x 50 in. The legs can be made of 1¼ in. piping socketed into the timber at an angle of approximately 20 degrees, both side and end elevation. Flange fittings are used to reinforce the timber sockets, these being attached to timber pads which are faced off to the required angle.

If the bench is to be used as a field bench on loose ground, wooden plugs can be inserted in the end of the legs.

HOW TO MAKE HANDY SUPPLY DRAWERS FOR NAILS, ETC.

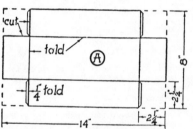

To utilise any waste space hanging shelves can be suitably placed under some workbenches, as shown at "F" in the accompanying illustrations. These can be either of wood or sheet iron but in this article we will assume that the latter is required.

The pieces of sheet iron should be 8 in. x 14 in. Cut the pattern as shown at "A," leaving a ¼-in. lap at each corner for soldering. The lap may be made to fold along either sides or ends. Partitions are shown at "B," thus providing as many compartments as are required.

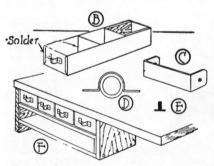

Sheet metal 2¼ in. x 4 are used for partitions which are clamped in a metal vice whilst being soldered in place.

The handles of each drawer are of galvanised iron, ⅛ in. x 2¾ in. The corners are clipped, and a right angle bend ½ in. long is made at each end, as shown at "C." The metal is then bent over a ¾ in. bar or ½ in. pipe, as in "D," and fastened in place with two light rivets, "E." (See articles on sheet metal cutting and riveting.)

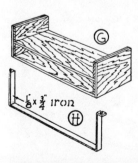

"F" shows the completed shelf arrangement fastened at one end beside the bench, and at the other to an upright fastened to the underside of the bench with angle iron. If preferred, a wooden arrangement can be made of ⅜ in. plywood and hung under the bench top with two light metal straps, as shown at "H."

This idea can also be used where drawers for other articles, such as kitchen furniture, etc., are required. (See also later notes in this book (wooden joints, etc.), which will also help in wooden construction work of this kind.)

A USEFUL SWINGING BENCH DRAWER

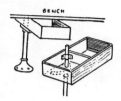

This has many advantages. It can be swung out so that the contents can be got at easily, and it is not in danger of dropping as a drawer is when it is pulled too far out. The support is part of an axle housing. The hole in the bottom of the drawer must fit the support snugly and be reinforced by an extra ply of timber screwed or glued on. The upper support is of 2 in. with the proper size holes bored in it and fastened with screw nails and glue.

ANOTHER IDEA FOR HANDY DRAWER TO WORKBENCH

This drawer can be pulled out to its full length with little effort, because its weight is carried on four pivoted legs. It should be sturdily built and reinforced along the sides where the legs are attached.

A chain fastened to the back of the bench and to the rear end of the drawer limits its forward movements. A block is nailed to the underside of the bench-top to serve as a stop when the drawer is swung back. When the drawer is resting against the block, the legs should slant toward the back slightly, so that it will not fall forward.

GUTTERING BETWEEN WALL STUDS
as Shelves for Small Parts

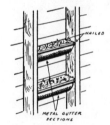

Lengths of guttering nailed between the studs of garage or workshop will provide convenient shelves for nails and small parts, etc.

They can be nailed to the wall and to the studs, the curved sides of the guttering making it easy to pick up the parts wanted.

The illustration will give full details of the idea.

A USEFUL WORKBENCH TRAY

To those who do quite a lot of work on a bench, and especially if there is any dismantling to be done, some partitioned trays such as those shown here will be found useful.

They are ideal for keeping small articles such as screws, etc., handy or to put small articles into as the work progresses. The tray is made of a length of guttering with several partitions of sheet metal soldered into place to provide whatever size partitions are required.

TROUGH ON END OF WORKBENCH to catch small articles.

Extending across the ends of a workbench, short pieces of curved iron will also help prevent small articles such as drills, etc., from rolling off on to the floor and perhaps becoming lost. The ends of these troughs are left open so that sawdust and shavings that collect in them can be easily removed.

11

IDEAS AND HANDY GADGETS FOR THE WORKSHOP

AN EMERY BOX FOR FINE TOOLS

This is quite a good method of caring for small tools, which might often be thrown on the bench when not in use, and therefore become rusty.

Make a box, as shown, and fill it with emery powder, although sand will do. Keep this damp with kerosene and just push the tools down into it. This keeps them bright and does not injure them. Sawdust might be added in small quantities, but this tends to stick to the tool each time it is removed.

A SMALL RACK FOR DRILLS, ETC.

This is a good idea for small tools such as these. A small space can well be set aside either on a shelf just above the bench or on the bench itself for some such small rack as indicated in this drawing.

Its construction needs no description, as the sketch is self-explanatory. This rack will prevent loss and damage, and will also provide a special place for these small items, so that they might be found just when they are wanted.

A Saw Drill or Tool Rack.

TOOL RACKS FROM CLOTHES PEGS

This is very easy to make from a strip of 2 x 1 timber and some old clothes pegs.

A series of holes, the size of the pin body, are bored in the strip, and into each hole a clothes peg is driven until the legs project from one side. These are then secured by driving a wire nail down through them.

HANDY HOME-MADE TOOL RACKS

(1) From Old Hose

Some neat and flexible tool-holders can be made by slitting short pieces of garden hose along the sides and then nailing them to the wall above the workbench, as shown here.

For pliers and narrow chisels, the hose need not be slit, but can be toe-nailed to the wall.

Further, holders for hand-saws may be made by slitting the hose about one-half its length on opposite sides.

2. From Valve Springs

Old motor valve or other types of springs fastened to the back of the workbench will make very handy holders for small and narrow tools, as indicated in the accompanying illustration.

Countersink holes for the eye-bolts and the nuts, and insert the ends of the springs in the eyes, drawing them out to any distance desired.

A HANDY POCKET FOR SMALL TOOLS
Made from Inner Tube

A very handy pocket for spare tools, which may be needed frequently from time to time on any particular job away from the workbench and which may save time to the user by being instantly available, can be made from old pieces of inner tube as shown here.

To avoid the possibility of tools falling out of the pocket, get a small piece of rubber tubing and slip it over the tool as indicated. The tubing is slit in the centre and is impaled on the shaft of the tool and pushed into the pocket, as indicated.

A TOOL BELT EASY TO ATTACH AND REMOVE

This is a useful tool belt which can be donned hastily for jobs away from the bench; jobs which might need two hands to perform.

In this, a leather strap is slit at intervals to provide the loops for the tools, and the ends are cut to the shape of arrowheads for easy insertion through the belt loops on the trousers. This is a very handy arrangement.

A USEFUL CARPENTER'S APRON FROM SACK

A small sack can be quickly converted into a useful apron and it will be found to be a real time saver especially if there is much nailing to be done.

The sack is folded and cut as shown in the illustration, then folded back and sewn to form a belt loop.

The method of sewing to form the two pockets is also shown. It is then worn by slipping the belt through the hem or loop at the top.

A TOOL BOX FROM OIL TIN

This illustration gives an idea for converting an oil or similar tin into a useful portable tool box.

A 5-gallon tin may be used. Cut the tin along the dotted lines as shown in the lower detail and then bend the two halves over, after which a length of wire is hooked under the ends of the bent portion to serve as a handle. For carrying nails and small tools from place to place about the farm, such an arrangement as this will prove a very useful article.

ANOTHER TOOL CARRIER FROM OIL CAN

By removing two sides from a square 5-gallon oil tin and fitting some "V" shaped wooden shelves on the inside of it, as indicated, you can make a good portable tool carrier.

The shelves are nailed in place between the sides of the tin, and a row of nails is provided on each shelf to hold the tools.

IDEAS AND HANDY GADGETS FOR THE WORKSHOP

PREVENTING TOOLS FROM ROLLING

BRASS ROD OR LEAD.

Tools such as screwdrivers, files, etc., have an awkward habit of rolling off a bench unless special means are taken to prevent it.

One way of doing this is by simply weighting one side of the handle of the tools in question as shown in the accompanying illustration.

A hole is drilled into the handle (as shown in lower detail) and it is plugged with a piece of lead or brass rod. This will have the effect of steadying the article.

An idea to prevent Tools rolling.

HANDY NAIL AND SCREW HOLDERS FOR THE WORKSHOP

It is rather a good idea to have special receptacles for nails, screws, etc., near the spot where one is working and yet at the same time out of the way.

One useful method of keeping these small articles close at hand in the shed, garage, or workshop, is to cut the tops from a number of tins, such as tobacco or other suitable tins, and nail these on to the side of the studding or posts in the manner shown.

Place supporting nails a little above the middle of the tin as shown in the illustration, as these will enable the contents to be made easily accessible by merely tipping the tins a little forward.

ADJUSTABLE SHELVING
With Corrugated Iron Sides

Shelves of workshop cabinets can be made adjustable to various levels if they are supported with strips of corrugated iron as indicated in this sketch.

For a neat job, the shelves should be thick enough to fit the sunken parts of the corrugations snugly, and for this reason, the ends should be rounded, which can be done with a wood rasp. This idea can also be used for other purposes round the home.

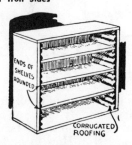

ENDS OF SHELVES ROUNDED

CORRUGATED ROOFING

UTILISING AN OLD TANK FOR TOOL SHED

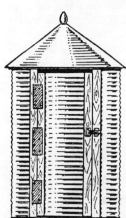

An excellent use for an old tank is to convert it into a useful tool shed; it is then an asset and not a loss.

First, remove a portion of the side—the full height and 2 ft. 6 in. wide. Cut the iron out carefully in one piece to form the door of the shed. Reinforce the sides of the opening with timber and treat the door similarly for rigidity. Take care to overlap the iron with the wood in order to protect the fingers from sharp edges; the said edges being blunted with a rough file.

Hinges made from an old tyre, together with a hasp, staple and padlock, completes the door.

The round hole in the roof for the inlet pipe is filled with a plug of wood and a little tar.

Paint the tank and it will be neat, weatherproof and useful.

A KEYHOLE YOU CAN FIND IN THE DARK

This arrangement is a useful one, especially when there might be an outbuilding containing tools, etc., which should be kept locked.

All that is needed is a little guide made from old scrap around the place and applied to the door without any change in its construction. The device is placed so that the diverging arms form a tapering passage through which the key will be guided to the keyhole.

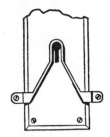

A CONVENIENT PLACE FOR TWINE IN THE WORKSHOP

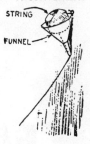

STRING

FUNNEL

In order to have string always at hand it is a good idea to have it in a convenient place which can be done by hanging a tin funnel on the wall in which a ball of twine can be inserted in the manner shown.

If placed just above the spot where one usually stands, it is then always at hand, the end of the twine being threaded from inside of the ball through the spout, and sufficient at a time is then easily pulled out for current needs.

A HANDY STRING CUTTER

SHARPENED

TWINE

This is a good cutter which can be placed handy to the twine itself, whether it is just above the twine as shown here, or set below the twine should the latter be kept in the manner indicated above.

Nail two pieces of wood together as shown, and on the bottom one, drive a nail to hold the ball of twine. On the side place the cutter after sharpening it. The cutter itself is easily made from scrap and can be improvised in any way desired, according to the materials at hand.

ANOTHER USEFUL TWINE CUTTER

Very often a cutter is not quite safe, because the cutting edges are exposed as that shown in the previous article could easily be.

This illustration will give one idea as to how this can be avoided. It will cause no accidents because the blade itself is protected.

In this instance, a very handy place for it is either set in a post or a special cutter can be made and affixed in a position handy to the twine.

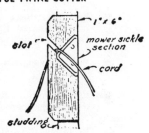

1" x 6"

mower sickle section

slot

cord

studding

ANOTHER HANDY STRING CUTTER

To make this handy string cutter, cut two pieces of 3/16th wood to the size and shape shown in this sketch.

Then get a safety razor blade and clamp it between the two pieces of wood in the position indicated by means of two longish screws, which pass through holes bored in the wood to correspond with the two outer holes on the razor blade.

A Handy String-Cutter made from a Safety Razor Blade.

IDEAS AND HANDY GADGETS FOR THE WORKSHOP

PREVENTING LOSS OF TOOLS

As a means to help prevent loss of tools, and to save time in looking for them, it is quite a good idea to have a definite place to keep them. There are many good ways of doing this, and these illustrations give details of three very useful ideas which can easily be adopted.

The first is an upright wall pattern, with closing doors, which will fit into any part of the workshop and not take up much room. The idea shown in illustration No. 3 can also be adapted to this idea. Shelves can be provided for planes, nails and other articles and, if necessary, can be made in portable form in order to be transported to any place desired.

Illustration No. 2 can be made in cabinet form or in the form of shelves for work-benches. The drawers of this cabinet have been cut out to form recesses or pockets for the various tools. They are outlined in felt.

Each drawer contains its own type of tool, such as drills, chisels, screwdrivers, hammers, etc. One or two compartments can be divided into smaller parts for nails, bolts, screws, etc.

The cabinet shown is 24 x 28 in. with a double tier of drawers 12 x 19 in.

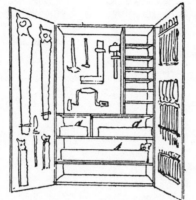

UPRIGHT OR WALL PATTERN of tool chest recommended for the young handyman.

To form pockets for tools, first draw an outline round each tool in pencil on a board about 5/16th in. thick, which can be used as a false bottom in the drawer. Then cut out the pattern with a saw.

Each opening should be a little smaller than the tool itself, so that the latter will set in not quite half-way. A felt lining can then be glued in place.

Another type of cabinet drawer can be made by using a board ¾ in. thick for the bottom. After the outlines of the various tools have been drawn, a gouge is used to cut out the desired form so that each tool rests evenly in a perfectly fitting socket.

No. 3. An excellent place for tools is just over the spot where most of the work is done, and a silhouette board on the wall (as shown) is ideal for that purpose. The place for each tool on the wall serves to remind that it is not there.

This method is far better than throwing the tools in a box, which often causes delay and impatience in obtaining the tool required. To prevent waste, it is also a good scheme to keep an oily rag or handful of waste soaked in oil handy in order to wipe the tools as they are finished with.

A USEFUL TOOL KIT

1 Oilstone
1 Claw Hammer
1 Mortise Gauge
1 Screwdriver
1 Spokeshave
1 Hatchet
1 Wood Rasp, 12 in.
1 Brace, all iron, 10 in.
1 No. 2 Adze
1 Pair Compasses, 8 in.
1 Spirit Level, 24 in.
1 Metallic Tape, 66 in.
1 Nest of Saws
1 German Jack Plane for very rough work, 1½ in.
1 Jack Plane, 2¼ in., for rough work and straightening slightly

1 Pair Pincers, 7 in.
1 two or three ft. Rule
1 Marking Gauge
1 Carriage Clamp
1 Draw Knife, 10 in.
1 Square, 12 in.
1 Square, 6 in.
1 Mallet
6 Bradawls
1 Oil Can
1 Pair Pliers, 7 in.

1 Trying Plane, 2½ in., for making surface perfectly straight
1 Smoothing Plane, 2¼ in., for finishing job smoothly.
1 Rebate Plane, 1¼ in .
1 Rip Saw, 28 in., for cutting "down" the grain
1 Hand or Panel Saw, for cutting across the grain
1 Tenon Saw, for cutting tenons and shoulders for fine work
1 Turning Saw, for cutting circles, etc.
4 Chisels, socket, ½ in., ⅝ in., ¾ in., and 1 in.
6 Chisels, firmer socket, ⅜ in., ½ in., ⅝ in., ¾ in., 1 in. and 1¼ in.
5 Augurs, ½ in., ⅝ in., ¾ in., 1 in., and 1¼ in.
6 Bits, double twist, ¼ in., ⅜ in., ½ in., ⅝ in., ¾ in., and 1 in.
11 Bits, Nails, No. 2 to 12.

A Cabinet Type of Tool Chest, with Special Pockets for each Article

These are but one or two useful suggestions for those who like to keep these articles in a systematic manner. In these, there is a special place for each tool and its absence can be detected in a moment. These and others are very convenient and great time savers.

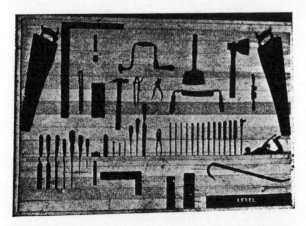

1. View of tool board, showing painted spaces for each tool.

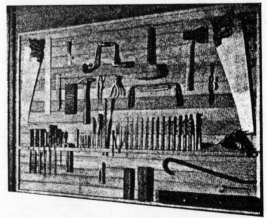

2. View of tool board with tools in place.

IDEAS AND HANDY GADGETS FOR THE WORKSHOP

HOME-MADE ANVILS AND VICES

A LARGE SPIKE TO SERVE AS TINY ANVIL IN WORKSHOP

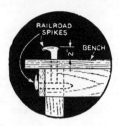

This will be found to be a very useful article when placed in a convenient position. Set in a hole directly over a leg of the workbench, a railway spike makes an excellent anvil for small work.

Saw off the point of the spike, chisel a hole to a depth that it will leave about 2 in. of the spike above the surface of the bench, and cut a hole in from the front of the leg so that another spike can be driven in to support the end of the vertical spike, as shown.

FASTENING A HEAVY ANVIL

To securely fasten an anvil to the block, pass a rod horizontally through the block, so that each end of it will hold a "V" shaped tie rod, which is fastened to metal straps passing along the base of the anvil on each side.

Ideas such as this one might suggest the same principle to readers in connection with some other things as it could easily be applied to quite a number of articles.

ONE METHOD OF CLAMPING ANVIL TO BENCH VICE

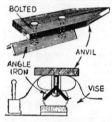

This illustration gives details of one method of converting the bench vice into an anvil. It is often a little difficult to hold a small anvil in a bench vice so that it will not loosen or tip and this may be avoided by bolting it to a short length of angle iron as illustrated.

When inserted in the vice as shown, the jaws will clamp it securely. This idea is especially handy when working on the end of the anvil, as it cannot tip up.

CONVERTING A VICE INTO AN ANVIL

A bench vice can easily be converted into an anvil for light work with this home-made arrangement.

It is cut from a piece of steel to the shape indicated, so that it can be gripped in the vice with the flat surface projecting above to take the various cutting tools.

This is easy to use, easy to convert, and if kept handy to the vice will be found to be a valuable addition to the workshop.

Other suggestions along the same lines are shown under the heading of "angle steel in the workshop."

A USEFUL HOME-MADE ANVIL

A good anvil can be made from a 4 ft. piece of railway iron mounted on a trestle as shown here.

This will stand a lot of heavy work and will be handy in a number of ways. The sketch is self-explanatory; the supporting timbers fitting into the rail as indicated.

A HOME-MADE BENCH VICE

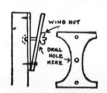

This illustration is of a vice easy to make. It will hold a piece of wood as tightly as an iron one will. Take a piece of 8 x 1½ as high as the table, and another piece of 5 x ¾, two-thirds the height of the table.

A block 4 x 1 x 4 in., is nailed on to the big piece half way up, and a hinge is put on to this and the smaller piece of board. The big piece is then let in at the top, as in the diagram, and is nailed on to "A."

A hole is then bored through all of these, and a bolt is put through with a washer on both ends. A spring is put between the two boards with a nut on the end.

With a spanner, it is an easy matter to tighten the nut. This bolt needs a thread from the outside of the moving jaws when shut to the end.

ANOTHER SIMPLE HOME-MADE VICE

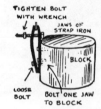

A simple but effective saw vice can be made as indicated here. This one is made from the bridge of an old stove. Drill a hole a little above the centre in both sections. Fasten one to the post with a screw nail through the top hole, first inserting a bolt, the head of which is recessed into the post. Now put the second section on the bolt and fasten with a wingnut. Then fasten the two pieces to the post at the bottom with a long screw, with a washer between. This brings the tops together tightly on the saw when the vice is tightened.

ANOTHER IMPROVISED VICE

Another small vice to hold light parts can be made by taking two pieces of flat iron slightly bent as shown for the jaws. One jaw is bolted to a block or workbench and the other loosely bolted to it at the bottom so that it will open. A longer bolt at the top puts on the pressure when needed.

A VICE FROM TWO CLAMPS

If you have no bench vice, but possess two clamps, you can easily rig up a temporary device in the manner shown in this sketch.

One clamp is used on its side, and is secured to the bench by the second clamp. This is quite a satisfactory arrangement for small work and is an excellent improvised tool for temporary use.

A USEFUL METHOD OF LINING THE VICE JAWS

Finished parts often have to be held in the jaws of the vice and to prevent the steel jaws from marring the surface, a pair of soft jaws is often necessary.

To make such soft jaws, tack or glue two pieces of leather to wooden blocks, as shown. They should be of a length and width equivalent to the dimensions of the vice jaws. The leather should be wide enough to cover the full depth of the vice jaws, and the blocks can then be placed on the jaws so that the leather forms the necessary protection in gripping parts when pressure is applied to the jaws.

IDEAS AND HANDY GADGETS FOR THE WORKSHOP

AN IMPROVISED BENCH VICE

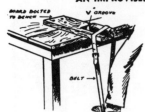

This is an arrangement which will be found quite effective. Any old belt which has outlived its usefulness can be used to provide the tension, while a short length of hardwood bolted to the bench is all the rest that is necessary to make this good emergency bench vice. The sketch will show the idea.

HOW TO PROVIDE A GRIP FOR WORN VICE

Through age and much use a vice may become worn and smooth; therefore it may be difficult to hold certain articles. This can be overcome to a certain extent by inserting an old file between the work and jaw.

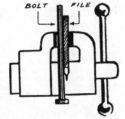

Such an arrangement is specially useful when burring the end of a hard bolt whilst there are many other similar jobs which could be so improved.

PLIERS SERVE AS VICE FOR SMALL ROUND WORK

This is a good arrangement for gripping round work so that any filing, screwing, etc., can be carried out.

A clamp or vice for small round work can be improvised from a pair of slip-joint or gas pliers and a U-clamp. The handles of the pliers are fastened with the U-clamp of the type used to bind wire ropes together. The pliers can then be gripped in the vice or, for some kinds of work, held by hand.

ANOTHER METHOD OF HOLDING ROUND WORK IN VICE

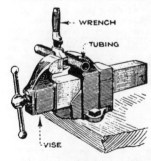

This idea is also useful when cylindrical work is to be clamped. It is the use of a monkey wrench in the manner shown.

Adjust the wrench jaws until the work will rest only on the edges of the jaws; then clamp the wrench and work in the vice in the position shown, the stock will then be held securely as in a pipe vice.

This type of work is often difficult and necessary, but this and the previous paragraph will indicate two very good ways of doing same.

AN IMPROVISED WRENCH

This is a useful wrench, easily made, one that can be improvised at a moment's notice.

Merely run two square nuts on the threaded end of a bolt and adjust them both to fit the desired article to be turned.

The work should be gripped between the two nuts by locking the nuts on to it with a spanner. This idea lends itself to a variety of other applications; it is quickly made and quickly adjusted.

AN IMPROVISED WRENCH FOR AWKWARD JOBS

A very handy wrench for many kinds of work, such as making gates and other things where small bolts are used, is shown here.

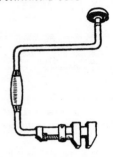

From a small monkey wrench, remove the wooden handle, and weld the metal part to an old stock-bit, as indicated in the drawing. This permits of very rapid work in screwing and unscrewing small bolts.

Where there are so many things to do, as there are on a farm, it pays to do things in the easiest and quickest ways. This is one of the best time-savers.

A WRENCH EXTENSION HANDLE

A useful tool for giving added leverage to double-ended wrenches is shown here.

A piece of flat steel is cut and bent over at the end to hook on the wrench and a pin "B" is riveted into it to bear against the jaw of the wrench as shown. The end of the tool may be made chisel-shaped and is handy for prising such work.

A USEFUL HINT IN SCREW DRIVING

Whenever a little extra leverage is required on the screw driver in order to drive a screw securely, try the idea suggested in this sketch.

The idea is to use a monkey wrench close to the screwhead, and then apply pressure to the driver in the usual manner.

Give the blade a sharp turn with the wrench when it should give just the right amount of extra turn necessary.

AN IMPROVISED LEVEL

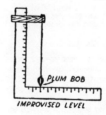

PLUM BOB

IMPROVISED LEVEL

Often the efficiency of one's level may be impaired by rough usage, and the need of it usually becomes apparent in the middle of a constructional job.

This, therefore, is quite a useful idea and well worth trying under such circumstances. First of all, fasten a clamp to the vertical arm of a square and attach a plumb line as shown. When the distance between the string and the vertical arm is equal top and bottom, the surface upon which the lower arm of the square is resting will be level.

MAKING COIL SPRINGS

Take a piece of iron about 12 in. x 1 and ⅛ in. thick; turn up the ends as shown, bore holes for the crank, and bore holes in the crank to receive the ends of the spring wire.

Simple Device for making Springs.

The device can be fastened to the bench with screws or held firm in a vice, and springs of any length up to 12 in. may thus quickly be made; and by having a number of spindles of various sizes handy, springs of various diameters can be made.

IDEAS AND HANDY GADGETS FOR THE WORKSHOP

PLIERS FITTED WITH SPRING TO KEEP THEM OPEN

For turning a bolt or nut which might be in a tight place or for any similar awkward work where it may be difficult to shift the pliers, it will pay to fasten a piece of clock spring to them, as indicated. It is quite an easy job to arrange at a moment's notice.

ANOTHER PLIERS HINT

This idea is a useful one, especially if the objects to be bent are rather hard and there is a lot to do.

Rubber tubing, just long enough to cover the handles is fitted on tightly; this saves the hands and is a safe way of using pliers when working on anything electrical. For instance, if an electric switch is leaking, the insulated pliers are very handy in bringing the switch to the off position.

RUBBER TUBING

RUBBER HOSE KEEPS PLIERS OPEN
For One Hand Work

This is another method of keeping pliers open where inconvenience might be experienced in operating a pair of pliers with one hand.

It will be found that a short piece of rubber hose slipped over the handles helps solve the problem. The hose tends to keep the jaws open when the pliers are not gripped, so that they can easily be manipulated with one hand.

PIECE OF RUBBER HOSE

PLIERS

IMPROVISED TWEEZERS FROM SPLIT PINS

This is rather a good idea for a temporary and quick job in cases where the regular tweezers are not at hand. Quite simple but effective tweezers can thus be made in half a minute from an ordinary split pin as indicated here.

Just take a 3/16th in. split pin about 1½ to 2 in. in length; bend as shown, and you will have quite a handy article. The points can be sharpened.

Such a small and useful tool can be made to carry round in the waistcoat pocket if necessary. It would also pay to make a few to have on hand for emergencies.

IMPROVISED PLIERS FROM COTTER PINS

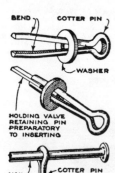

BEND

COTTER PIN

WASHER

HOLDING VALVE RETAINING PIN PREPARATORY TO INSERTING

NAIL

COTTER PIN

REMOVING TIRE VALVE INSIDE IN ABSENCE OF CAP

Some quite useful improvised and handy tools can be made from articles such as these. For instance, for holding and inserting small objects such as valve retaining pins, screws and other small parts in close and awkward places, an ordinary cotter-pin can often be used to advantage.

The points of the cotter-pin are bent as shown in the top drawing, and a small washer, to hold the ends together, is slipped over it.

The centre drawing shows how the arrangement will work, i.e., by pushing the washer forward until the article to be gripped is wedged tightly in place.

In the absence of a valve cap, a cotter-pin and nail can be used for removing the inside from a tyre valve. (See lower detail.)

TWO USEFUL STAPLE PULLERS

Wire staples, when driven down into a post as far as they will go, are often very hard to get out, and the job is found to be a very awkward one.

Illustration No. 1 shows a strong spike bent into a hook at the end, which makes a good tool for removing such staples. The hooked part of the spike is driven under the staple and a hammer and block used to draw the staple out (as indicated in the sketch).

The second drawing gives details of a different idea and is made from an old discarded monkey wrench.

To use it, set the sharp point immediately over the top of the staple, strike it with a hammer and it will easily enter far enough to enable the staple to be pulled when the handle is lifted up.

If no old monkey wrench is available, the same idea can be used with any piece of steel bent into about the same shape.

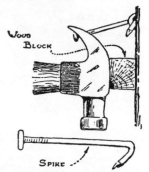

WOOD BLOCK

SPIKE

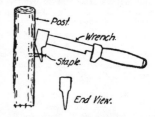

Post

Wrench.

Staple.

End View.

USEFUL HINTS ON HOLDING A COLD CHISEL

HAMMER HOLDS CHISEL

The idea shown in this illustration will assure greater safety in holding a cold chisel when cutting rivets or other steel material.

By attaching the chisel to the end of a hammer, with a strong narrow strap or rubber band around the chisel as shown in this sketch, it will provide the means of keeping the hands well away from the chisel and so it will lessen the chance of injury.

ANOTHER USEFUL CHISEL HOLDER

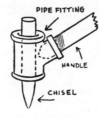

PIPE FITTING

HANDLE

CHISEL

Another excellent chisel holder may be made in the manner shown here.

The holder consists of a 45 degree "Y" type fitting or something similar which may be improvised on the spot. The handle is a length of rod which is threaded to screw into one side of the fitting, as shown. The end of the handle must be bevelled to a cone shape so that it will fit tightly against the chisel. Turning the handle tightens or loosens the chisel in the holder.

A HINT ON USING SLENDER FILES

When using a slender file, the work is often spoiled because the necessary pressure that must be put on the ends of the file to make it cut, bows it slightly in the centre, thus causing the edges of the work to be rounded. To remedy this trouble and enable the work to be done with full strokes and a maximum pressure, the file may be grasped as shown; the pressure of the forefinger and thumb being exerted in the direction shown by the arrows, bends the file to a sweep or curve, thus causing it to file flat across the work.

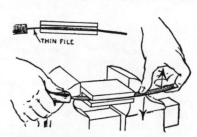

THIN FILE

IDEAS AND HANDY GADGETS FOR THE WORKSHOP

A HANDY DEPTH GAUGE FOR AUGUR BIT

For boring holes by hand to a certain definite depth, simply screw the bit or drill into a cork. This will act as a firm depth gauge. Corks of various sizes can be used for different bits and drills and it will therefore pay to keep several of them in the tool box.

A USEFUL WIRE WINDER

One often has need to wind some fine wire tightly and neatly around an object or to rewind some, and the result is often rather an untidy job; it being difficult to wind the wire nicely and tightly. This small sketch shows how, by means of a stout piece of wood, through which has been bored a few holes, wire and other material can be easily and neatly bound.

A USEFUL METHOD OF CUTTING CIRCLES IN WOOD

One often needs to cut a circle in wood when there may be no compass at hand. This is one simple method, i.e., the use of a pair of scissors and an ordinary paper clamp, as shown in the sketch.

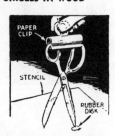

To avoid perforating the paper or other material at the centre, place a small piece of rubber, cardboard or other material under the point of the scissors.

A HOME-MADE TOOL FOR CUTTING CIRCLES IN WOOD

Take a piece of hardwood about 9 in. x ¾ in. wide and ½ in. thick. Then get a broken penknife blade about 1 in. long and file to a sharp edge at one end. Bore a hole in the wood to take the blade and a small wedge (say about ¼ in. square). The wedge can be made from a piece of brass filed to a long " V."

The hole is ¾ in. from the end. Next measure 1½ in. off the cutter, then mark and bore a hole to take a suitable size screw, and then bore one every half inch, 10 in all, leaving about 1 inch to spare. To prevent the wood from splitting, the edge of the wedge should be inserted at right angles to the blade.

Both the foregoing methods are quite simple and accurate methods of cutting or drawing circles and both should be found useful.

FLATTEN & HARDEN.

FILE EDGE. TO ANGLE

DRILLING HOLES IN CEMENT AND BRICK

This is one idea for a home-made tool for this purpose and it will be found useful for a number of jobs. It can be made from an old file or stump of an old woodworker's chisel and constructed as shown. The end is merely filed to a " V " shape.

ANOTHER USEFUL TOOL FOR CUTTING HOLES IN BRICKWORK, ETC.

Take a piece of piping and saw it at an angle of 45 deg.; then sharpen it on a grindstone or with a flat file, as shown. When working, give this pipe drill about a one-sixth turn between each blow of the hammer. Because the cutting edge is broad and supported by metal backing, it is a good tool for ½, ¾ and 1 in. holes as it will cut very cleanly and all particles of brick and mortar should drop down inside the tube when it can be tapped out at intervals.

END OF PIPE SAWED OFF ON 45° ANGLE

GRIND LIP TO SHARP CUTTING EDGE

IMPROVISED TOOLS FROM FORK TINES

Useful tools from old broken forks, etc., can be made by merely heating and bending the tines.

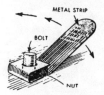

FOR CLEANING OIL HOLES

COTTER PIN TOOL

RING AWL

AWL

That shown for cleaning oil holes is better than a piece of wire and the cotter pin shown will be found useful in many ways. The awls indicated are also useful for making small holes or for scratching lines on metal or tin.

FOLDED METAL STRIP AS IMPROVISED WINGNUT

METAL STRIP

BOLT

NUT

If you have any work where a bolt is employed upon which the nut must be tightened or loosened frequently, and no thumb nut is at hand, a substitute may be made by drilling and bending a strip of tin or other metal in the manner shown here to receive the square nut.

This strip of metal then serves as a self-contained wrench or handle for turning the nut easily.

HOME-MADE TOOLS FOR STUBBORN NUTS

Simple open-ended spanners have a right and a wrong way of use. The open end should always be used so that the jaws are facing the direction of the pull (fig. 1), but a box spanner is better than an open-ended one for most stubborn nuts. Take a length of tempered steel, say 2 ft. x 2 in. wide, from ⅜ to ½ in. thick, if it has a slight curve, so much the better. A hole rather bigger than the tommy-bar holes, must be bored in one end, to take a short pin which then passes through the tommy-bar holes and is secured with washer and nut. A double angle at one end to fit on both sides of the box, with the pin passing right through (fig. 2) makes a stronger job.

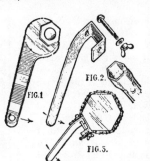

FIG.1.

FIG.2.

FIG.3.

Hub Cap removal can be effected with a chain-wrench substitute made from the attachment just described, and a length of cycle chain. One end of the chain is fixed to the attachment by passing the pin first through one of the wide links. With the end of the attachment close against one of the hub flats, run the chain right round the cap, pull tight, and secure the loose end, by the nearest wide link, to the threaded end of the pin (fig. 3).

A FENCE STAPLE DRIVER

When stapling fences, it may be hard to get the staples "home" without doubling them over, but this should not be so with this simple gadget, unless the wood is so hard that the points will not penetrate.

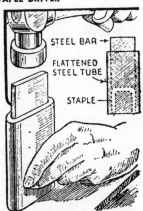

STEEL BAR

FLATTENED STEEL TUBE

STAPLE

It is easily made by using a short piece of tubing of a size to suit the staples being used and flattening with a hammer until it will take a staple freely without much play.

A piece of flat steel bar that is just a sliding fit for the flattened tube serves as a plunger. The staple is tapped into position, the tool is set over it, and the plunger is struck with a hammer.

IDEAS AND HANDY GADGETS FOR THE WORKSHOP

A SIMPLE MASK TO PROTECT THE EYES

ELASTIC HEAD BAND

8" X 10" SHEET

This is a very useful article to have at hand. A sheet of transparent material used thus makes an excellent protective mask for the eyes.

The sheet should be about 8 x 10 in. An elastic ribbon is cemented to the edges, as shown, or the ribbon may also be stapled to the sheet. Such a mask can then be worn for all grinder or lathe work where fragments are likely to fly and injure the eyes. Do not use celluloid or any such highly inflammable material in case it might ignite from flying sparks.

PROTECTING THE SPIRIT LEVEL FROM BREAKAGE

This is a simple and effective way of protecting the glass tube of your wood level from accidental damage.

Just drive two home-made wire staples over the glass as shown in the sketch. If the staples cross the exact centre of the glass, the latter will be easier to read. A fine wire mesh can, of course, be stapled across, but the above method should prove satisfactory enough.

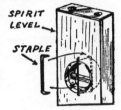

SPIRIT LEVEL

STAPLE

A HINT ON ACCURATE LEVELLING

This is a useful idea for levelling such things as concrete forms and other work where surfaces on which the level must rest are rough.

Merely fit the level with a couple of furniture glides which serve as feet and with this arrangement it would only be necessary to clean a place on the work on which to rest the feet.

LEVEL

GLIDES

HOW TO TEST A CARPENTER'S LEVEL

This sketch will show how anyone can test a level for proper adjustment of bubble. To test, adjust the board until the bubble centres between the bubble marks. Reverse level, and if the bubble centres, the level is true.

BUBBLE MARKS

One of the easiest ways to adjust an inaccurate level is to take very thin shavings off the bottom at the end towards which the bubble moves. Use a very sharp Jack plane and a try-square to keep the bottom true, and check frequently for proper adjustment. Where there is a bubble adjustment, raise or lower the adjustment until the bubble moves half-way back to the centred position, and then check for proper adjustment.

A HANDY HOME-MADE RACK FOR TIMBER, ETC.

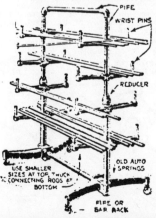

PIPE
WRIST PINS
REDUCER
USE SMALLER SIZES AT TOP, THICK CONNECTING RODS AT BOTTOM
OLD AUTO SPRINGS
PIPE OR BAR RACK

This can easily be made from some piping, a fitting or two, some disused motor springs and old connecting rods in the manner shown. The sketch will explain the construction or perhaps suggest a method of using up some other material from the scrapheap.

It is a most useful and convenient way of keeping various sizes and lengths of various materials, and, if supported on castors, it can be easily moved about from place to place.

A SIMPLE HOME-MADE SCALE FROM CLOCK SPRING

This is a very useful idea for weighing small substances. It is constructed from a clock spring and a couple of wooden blocks screwed to a convenient place on the wall.

The clock spring is screwed to the block so that the free end reaches to the centre of another block or a piece of paper placed within a convenient distance. A small tray is suspended from the spring as indicated. The block or paper is then marked by weighing objects of known weights and marking the positions of the spring end on the block or paper.

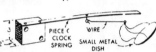

3   PIECE OF   WIRE
2   CLOCK SPRING   SMALL METAL DISH

ANOTHER HOME-MADE SCALE

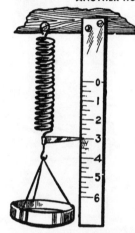

0 1 2 3 4 5 6

A Simple Spring Balance. Mark the Scale with Ounce Weights in the Pan.

An old spring, or a home-made one, can easily be utilised to make a very useful balance for use in the workshop, etc.

First of all, get a good clean, smooth piece of wood for the upright (the construction really needs no description of detail), but do not mark in the weights until it is made.

When the spring is attached and the pointer and pan added, then take some ounce weights and place them in the pan and carefully note the position of the pointer for each weight.

Then mark on the upright the various weights, and it will then be ready for instant use.

A good strong spring is of course necessary, as otherwise the weight in the pan will tend to stretch it and so cause a little misadjustment of weight measure.

TAKING MEASUREMENTS WITH COINS

Coins may be used in emergencies for taking measurements; for one half-penny is 1 inch in diameter; a penny is 1-16th in. thick and 1-10th ft. in diameter, whilst a sixpence is ¾ in., and a half-crown 1¼ in. in diameter.

MEASURING WITHOUT A RULE

At a pinch, the hands, feet and arms can be used as a measuring stick and they will be found surprisingly near the mark in cases where absolute accuracy is not essential. It is quite a good idea to take these measurements of yourself, and either memorise them or put them up in a position where they can be seen at a glance.

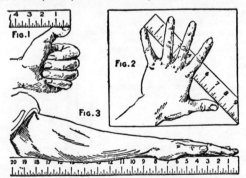

FIG.1   FIG.2   FIG.3

The average thumb is about 1¼ in.; the average span 8 to 9 in., and the forearm to fingertip 20 in. The average "pace" or step is about 3 ft., although this, of course, varies according to stature.

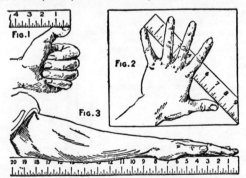

IDEAS AND HANDY GADGETS FOR THE WORKSHOP

A SIMPLE PIPE BENDER

This is a handy tool which does an excellent job. It is formed by combining a tee-piece connected with a length of piping as shown in the accompanying illustration.

The tee and the pipe used for the handle should be of a diameter a little greater than that of the stock upon which it is to be used. By slipping the tee over the pipe and operating as illustrated, a very good job is obtained.

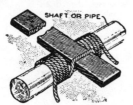
SHAFT OR PIPE

AN EMERGENCY PIPE WRENCH

This is another idea—it can be made from a wooden strip and a piece of rope. Lay the strip across the pipe, as shown, and wind the rope around the pipe and over the strip, so that the latter acts as a lever. The rope, should, of course, be fastened so that the pull is in the desired direction.

ANOTHER HOME-MADE PIPE WRENCH

This is quite simple. The upper jaw is free to swing and is provided with holes for adjustment, although a wide range of pipe sizes can be accommodated in each position of the jaw. With the exception of the bolt, all parts are made from flat steel.

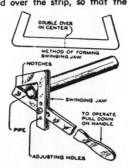
DOUBLE OVER IN CENTER
METHOD OF FORMING SWINGING JAW
NOTCHES
SWINGING JAW
PIPE
TO OPERATE PULL DOWN ON HANDLE
ADJUSTING HOLES

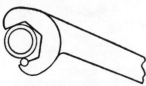
PIPE WRENCHES
HOLES

The jaw is made by bending over the ends as shown, and then bending at the centre; notches are filed in the underside, and if possible this part of the wrench is hardened to minimise wear.

IMPROVISED PIPE VICES

A pipe vice can be improvised from two pipe wrenches. After adjusting the wrench jaws to grip, the handles are set in holes drilled in a piece of wood, which is nailed to the bench.

A Use for old Spanner. One can utilise a fixed spanner and a round file as a pipe wrench. If the spanner is of the right size an excellent grip can be obtained but the difficulty is to keep the file in position until the pipe is gripped, as it may need two hands. This can be overcome by the following.

A notch is filed in one jaw of the spanner, so as to form a seating for a short piece of round file. The piece of file is just slipped into position, and there is no need to hold it while turning the spanner. It cannot slip when holding the pipe vertically, and is easily jammed into position when the pipe is horizontal.

The block on right shows another method used for screwing pipes.

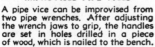

Improvised pipe wrench from old spanner

PIECE OF FILE

Screwing Pipes into Tight-fitting Holes.

A USEFUL WIRE SPLICER

A special tool for this purpose is often found handy around the place and a very useful one can be made from a piece of flat iron, 1 inch wide x 1⅛ in. thick.

First, form two shoulders, ⅛ in. wide, by cutting out rectangular pieces, then bend the top piece into the form of a tube partly closed.

A Wire Splicer.

To use, cross the wires to be joined, hook the tool over the one piece, and let the other wire fit into one of the notches. The tool is then turned until the wire is securely wrapped, the operation being repeated with the remaining end of the wire.

A CHEAP AND EFFICIENT MARKING GAUGE

CLOTHESPIN
SAW OFF ONE LEG

When there is no other marking gauge at hand, quite a good one can be improvised from an ordinary clothes peg as shown here.

One leg of the peg is cut off to form a shoulder to ride against the edge of the work, and holes are also drilled at predetermined distances to take the point of a lead pencil.

By drilling the holes to the distance required, one can draw very accurate lines to suit any particular job and by running the shoulder along the edge of the work, a very straight line is obtained.

ANOTHER HOME-MADE MARKING GAUGE

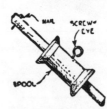
NAIL
SCREW EYE
SPOOL

This gauge will take but a few minutes to make. Take a large spool and trim a stick of hardwood until the spool will slide on it easily.

Drive a small nail in one end of the stick and slip the spool on the other. A set-screw can be made of a small screw-eye screwed into the spool.

Adjustment is made by sliding the spool on the stick until it reaches the position desired, then tightening the set-screw.

It will be best to file off the sharp points of the screw-eye to keep it from scarring the stick. This gauge is very accurate and easy to work.

MAKING A MARKING GAUGE MORE ACCURATE

Every amateur carpenter knows how difficult it is to prevent a marking gauge from following the grain of the wood being marked, thus giving an uneven line.

This is usually caused by the point digging in and thus being influenced out of line by the crooked grain.

The remedy is to set the pin in the stem of the gauge at an acute angle, as illustrated in the drawing at " B," instead of at right angles as shown at "A."

Thus, when the gauge is pushed along the wood with the pin in the new position, it will glide easily and straight through the wood, regardless of the grain.

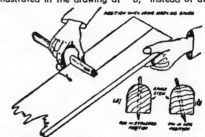

IDEAS AND HANDY GADGETS FOR THE WORKSHOP

REMOVING RUSTY SCREWS BY HEAT

It is sometimes difficult to remove rusty screws without the danger of twisting off the heads.

One way to overcome this is to pour a small quantity of oil over the screw and to heat the screw with a hot iron. After the screw has become heated, it is usually easily removed.

TIGHTENING NUTS WITH FRICTION TAPE

To save time trying to tighten a nut on a round head bolt, which is difficult to keep from turning, a washer cut from friction tape and slipped under the head, as shown in this sketch, can be used.

When the bolt head is held firmly against the tacky surface of the tape, the nut can easily be drawn up tightly.

This will do the job in excellent fashion and should prove a good and lasting way of overcoming difficulties such as these.

TIGHTENING BOLTS

In soft wood, or where a hole has been bored a little too large, it is difficult to prevent a bolt from turning before it is completely tightened up, the square neck failing to hold it into the wood.

This can be prevented if the edge of the head is hammered over as shown in this illustration.

The projecting edges bite into the wood and should offer sufficient resistance to turning to enable the job to be done in a satisfactory manner.

LOCKING BOLT NUTS

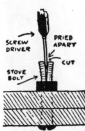

This is quite a useful and effective method of locking small diameter bolts, such as stove bolts. It merely consists of slotting the end of the bolt and prying the halves apart with a screwdriver.

The illustration will give details of the idea and when it becomes necessary to remove the nut, it can simply be unscrewed, and it will force the parts together again.

LOCKING A WING NUT

Next time you desire to lock a wingnut in place, try this idea. Make two staples, such as those shown here, and drive one over each wing at a slight angle so that they will enter the wood just outside the washer as indicated in this drawing.

Although such an arrangement provides an excellent lock, the staples can easily be pried off so that the nut can be turned if necessary.

KEEPING LOOSE BOLTS FROM TURNING

This diagram shows one way to prevent a loose bolt from turning. Simply drill a small hole through the head at such an angle that a nail driven part way will enter solid wood. This is specially helpful when you cannot get to the head and nut at the same time.

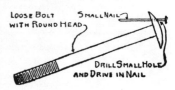

TAPERED THREAD TO CLEAN NUT

Often a nut will become so damaged that the bolt threads will not enter. This shows a simple way to overcome this trouble and to straighten out the threads in the nut.

With the hacksaw, make cuts at right angles in the end of the bolt and draw the parts together in the vice so as not to damage the threads. The tapered thread will enter easily and clean out the threads in the nut.

CUTTING NAILS OR OTHER SMALL MATERIAL

Rubber Guard on Cold Chisel Retains Short Pieces Cut from Nails, Wire and Pins.

Many have had the unpleasant experience when cutting off a piece of nail or wire to find the nail fly off and disappear, so that the work has to be done again.

Half of a rubber ball (used as shown) will make both halves of the nail "stay put." A hole is cut in the half ball large enough to admit the chisel, but without leaving any considerable space around it.

The chisel is set on the work for the cut with the ball raised so that it can be seen and when the hammer has done its work, the pieces of nail will be found under the ball.

NOVEL METHOD OF CATCHING DRILL SHAVINGS

Shavings cut from ceilings or other overhead work are apt to fall into one's eyes or to scatter on the floor, making a mess to clean up after the job is done.

This can be avoided by cutting a rubber ball in half and making a hole in the tip of it, then forcing the half ball over the drill in the manner shown.

This will eliminate any mess on the floor and will keep the dust out of the worker's eyes.

USEFUL METHODS OF GRIPPING SLENDER NAILS AND DRIVING NAILS INTO THIN WOOD

A useful method of driving nails into thin wood is shown on the left. Merely take the bench vice, insert the thin piece of wood into which the nail is to be driven between the jaws of the vice as shown and use the hammer gently.

The second sketch shows the use of a spring paper clip in order to hold slender wire nails whilst driving them in. The nails are gripped as indicated and, besides protecting the fingers, the clip tends to prevent the nails from bending.

IDEAS AND HANDY GADGETS FOR THE WORKSHOP

SECURING LOOSE HAMMER HEADS

This is quite a good way of keeping a hammer from working loose, and flying off. First, see that the handle is tight; then drill a ⅜ in. hole diagonally through the head and handle, as shown.

Then drive through a rivet, nail or piece of wire the proper size and rivet or bend the ends down sharply as illustrated.

PREVENTING AXE HANDLES FROM TURNING

There are, of course, many ways in which this can be done, but one good method is as follows :

To keep wooden wedges from loosening in either axe or hammer handles, nail through the wedge at the approximate point shown in this drawing.

When the wedge is driven into place the nail is bent and embedded in the handle as indicated.

TOOL HANDLES LEADED IN PLACE

This is another method by which tool handles that have a tendency to loosen can be kept tight.

Drill from the centre of the end of the handle diagonally to both sides, trimming the handle down so that it is a very loose fit in the tool.

Then pour molten lead into the holes, wrapping a cloth or piece of rubber around the lower part of the tool head to retain the lead. Be very careful when pouring to avoid air bubbles which might cause the lead to spurt out of the hole and burn you.

USEFUL AID IN PULLING NAILS

This method is a great improvement on those usually adopted and especially over the common practice of using any scrap of wood to push under the hammer when pulling nails, more so if they are in awkward places.

It consists of a slotted wedge-shaped block of hardwood which can be pushed under the head to suit the length of any sized nail.

PREVENTING WOOD FROM FLYING WHEN CHOPPING

This is a good idea where certain types of wood require chopping. There is always a danger of the wood flying from the chopping block and, in the case of kindling wood specially (or other wood in lengths as shown here), a pair of horse-shoes attached to the sides of the chopping block will be found a safeguard and very convenient at the same time.

Nailed securely in place, the horse-shoes also serve as handles if the block is required to be moved from place to place.

Old tyres or loops of wire can also be made to serve this purpose and might easily avert accidents.

AN IMPROVISED WINGNUT

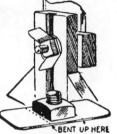

Nuts that have to be tightened and loosened frequently should be replaced by wingnuts, for which a spanner is not needed.

If a regular wingnut is not at hand, one can be improvised from an ordinary square nut by slipping under it a strip of sheet metal with a hole drilled in it to pass over the bolt.

The ends of the strip are bent up, as shown in the sketch, to give finger hold. Galvanised iron of 24 g. will serve for the strip. Sharp corners, of course, should be filed off and rounded.

Wingnut "Dodge"

A USEFUL METHOD OF CUTTING RIVETS

This is one of the best ways of cutting off rivets when it is desired to take them out or cut them off for any reason. To shear them off with a square end chisel is preferable to cutting them with a sharp edge. As a matter of fact, this method is used by many car wreckers in tearing up car frames.

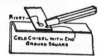

AN IMPROVISED TIN CUTTER

If it is desired to cut roofing or tin of any kind, and the necessary implements are not at hand, a piece of baling wire fastened at one end of a board, as shown, will do. Just notch the tin at one end where you want to cut it. Then lay the tin flat over the wire on the board. Next, stand on the tin and pull up on the wire. This is really easier than it looks.

AN IMPROVISED SQUARING TOOL FROM BUTT HINGE

This is a very useful idea in an emergency and is sometimes much handier to use than a tri-square in marking or squaring narrow work.

The hinge can be used as indicated, but, for accuracy, the hinge pin must be a snug fit so that both parts of the hinge will be in correct alignment.

A CHISEL SHEET-METAL CUTTER FROM FILE

This is a very good article for cutting oil drums, etc., and is made from an old file. It has a half circle cutting edge that makes it easy to grip the work.

Instead of bevelling the cutting edge like that of a cold chisel, it is ground square or at right angles to the surface of the file.

This method makes it easier to follow a guide line as both sides of the cutting edge produce a shearing action. The tang of the file is broken off to provide a good hammering surface.

ANGLE IRON ON BENCH EDGE TO ASSIST SHEARING SHEET METAL

If any sheet metal is too heavy for the hand shears, just screw a length of angle iron to one edge of bench, then use the iron as a shearing edge in combination with a wide shearing chisel as shown. Clamp the work in place with a board or wooden strip screwed to the bench top.

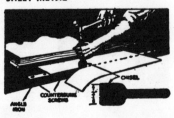

IDEAS AND HANDY GADGETS FOR THE WORKSHOP

USES OF ANGLE STEEL IN THE WORKSHOP

Scrap angle steel can be used in many ways. For instance, if a workbench is covered with linoleum, a beading of angle steel can be screwed along the edge to lap over the lino (fig. 1) to protect the edges and to solve the problem of fixing down the lino.

Angle steel tool racks can also be made as in fig. 2—holes being made in the steel so that on entering the hole can be cut to enable the tool to be withdrawn sideways.

For holding small screwed pieces without damaging the thread, the arrangement in fig. 3 is suggested. Two pieces of angle steel

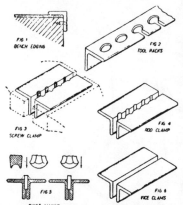

are clamped together back to back with a strip of tinplate between as a separator. Mark off, drill and tap a series of graded holes along the join. Open up, remove the separator and clean off any sharp burrs. The angle pieces hang on the vice jaws and are brought together to clamp the screw. A pin each end could be provided if necessary, to locate one angle with the other. Fig. 4 is a similar type clamp, having plain holes instead of screwed ones, for holding round rods tightly. By drilling blind holes of the appropriate depth, instead of through ones in fig. 4, the arrangement can be used for making rivets. The hole is left plain at the mouth as in fig. 5 for round head rivets, and the stub of metal held in the hole has its projecting end first hammered into a rough dome with a ball hammer, followed by a rivet set to bring up to the correct shape. For countersunk head rivets, the mouth of the hole is countersunk as in fig. 5, the rivet head being hammered into the sinking and finally filed flush with the top of the angle.

As vice jaw protectors, angle steel is useful (fig. 6). They fail, however, when gripping short pieces as the tops splay open. This defect can be remedied by removing the centre top portion of each angle down flush with the vice jaws (fig. 7). To do this, first make two saw cuts (fig. 8), followed by a series of small holes to connect them and finally join the holes with chisel cuts. File the top jagged edges flush with the vice jaws.

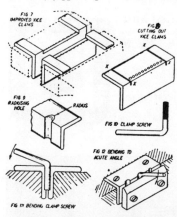

The clamp of fig. 4 is very suitable for gripping rods during the process of bending; it only requires a radius forming on one angle at the mouth of the hole, fig. 9, to give the bend in the rod a definite radius. For making simple lever clamp screws as in fig. 10, this type of jig can be used, but instead of a through hole, a blind one is used (fig. 11) so that the bottom acts as a stop to locate the rod and ensures the right length of bend each time.

To bend rods to an inclined angle less than 90 degrees, the arrangement in fig. 12 is suggested. Here a piece of angle, having a range of graded semi-circular grooves on its vertical face is screwed down to the edge of the bench. The rod to be bent is clamped into the appropriate groove by means of the steel plate and two end screws let into the angle. The top of the plate is radiused and bevelled off to clear the rod coming down.

When bending sheet or strip, angle steel clamps are useful. For ordinary short right angle bends the jaw protectors, fig. 6, are used. Where a number of pieces have to be dealt with, stops can be incorporated in the clamps to ensure that the length of the bend is constant.

PROTECTING HACKSAW BLADES FROM DAMAGE

It is often a little difficult to cut through round work such as steel rods or pipe with hacksaw blades without breakage to the blade, but this idea will show how it can be done neatly and cleanly without the same degree of breakage. As will be seen, the idea is to bind a few rounds of friction tape around the tube to be sawn—this will ensure a nice clean cut without breakage.

MAKING A HACKSAW THAT WILL CUT SHEET METAL

It is difficult to cut sheet metal with an ordinary hacksaw. Take an old handsaw blade and cut it to the shape shown. You should leave lugs on each end which can be rolled into loops and riveted. Ordinary hacksaw fittings can then be used, including the handle. This saw is quite an effective one and will cut even the heavier grades of corrugated iron without pinching.

A USEFUL DEVICE FOR CUTTING GALVANISED IRON

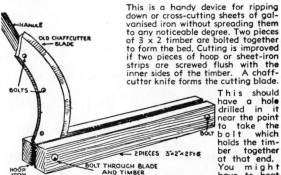

This is a handy device for ripping down or cross-cutting sheets of galvanised iron without spreading them to any noticeable degree. Two pieces of 3 x 2 timber are bolted together to form the bed. Cutting is improved if two pieces of hoop or sheet-iron strips are screwed flush with the inner sides of the timber. A chaffcutter knife forms the cutting blade.

This should have a hole drilled in it near the point to take the bolt which holds the timber together at that end. You might have to heat the blade to drill the hole, but if only the point is heated, it will not lessen its cutting power. A washer on the bevelled side of the knife is an improvement and, when cutting, it is advisable to keep the straight edge of the knife to the material that is to be used, if one portion is merely to be trimmed off as waste.

A HANDY SHEET METAL BENDER

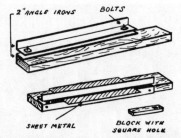

This is handy for making square bends. It is a 2 in. angle 3 to 4 ft. long fastened on to the edge of some longer 2 x 2 wood with heavy flat-headed screws placed in both the top and edge of the board. A second 2 in. angle operates on the first one by using two $3\frac{1}{2}$ x $\frac{1}{2}$ in. machine bolts with heads below the board and covered with hardwood blocks with square depressions to keep the bolts from turning. The metal is placed as at "B" projecting to the line of the desired bend and the nuts drawn tight. The bend is made with hammer or mallet.

S*omething*

he's learning

The boy on the post-war bicycle will learn to respect the strength and lightness of its frame of Reynolds 531 Quality Aircraft Steel Tubes. He'll understand why progressive manufacturers use Steel Tubes to supplant other materials in furniture, fittings, tools and sporting equipment ; for there will be many new applications of Steel Tubes as time goes on and new problems are studied and solved at *British Tube Mills (Aust.) Pty. Ltd., Kilburn, South Australia*

SOME OF THE THOUSANDS OF MODERN USES FOR **STEEL TUBES**

HANDY HOME-MADE WORKSHOP TOOLS

A HOME-MADE BENCH DRILL

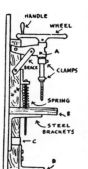

This is a useful drill, easy to make. A casting from a plow (A) is bolted to a 4 x 4 and held rigid by means of two steel braces. A shaft, the size of the hole in the casting, is drilled and keyed to a wheel. A clamp is fitted on below the casting; a small hole having been drilled in the shafting to afford a better grip for the set screw.

A hole is drilled in the end of the shaft and another one into it from the side. Another clamp is then fitted to the shaft and a set screw fitted in this second hole, holds the drill or bit in place. The 4 x 4 slides up and down, being held to the wall by the bench (B) and a steel strap iron (C) bolted to the wall.

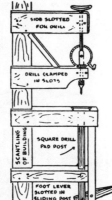

Pressure is obtained by putting weights on the steel bracket.

A CONVERTED BREAST DRILL

This is a light drill made by one farmer and used to advantage. It will be noted that the drill is fixed rigidly in place and that the work is pushed up against it by a foot lever.

The pressure is in line with the drilled hole. In drilling, say, a ½ in. hole, first use a ¼ in. drill, then a ⅜ in. one and finish with one of the desired size.

The idea of making pressure with the foot is a very good one. This method can also be utilised for the following idea.

ANOTHER HANDY HOME-MADE DRILL

This is another way of constructing one's own drill. An ordinary hand brace can, in this way, be made to save a lot of labour in drilling holes, as indicated here.

The easiest way to make the shallow holes to hold the round brace head is to burn them with a red-hot iron doorknob or a large pipecap. A good sized clamp is desirable to hold metal pieces for drilling.

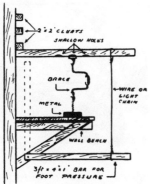

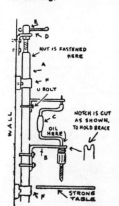

ANOTHER CHEAP PRESS DRILL

This drill was made from scrap, but a little careful work was also necessary.

The parts required are:—A 3 ft. length of 1½ in. pipe (A); a brace with the head removed (C); two pieces of heavy steel (B and D), which can be cut from the corners of an old plow frame; a screw and nut (E) with a sliding handle; and two guides (FF) to hold the pipe and allow it to slide up and down freely.

The unit is bolted to a stout stud. The steel bar (D) must be made very secure.

A HOME-MADE HIGH SPEED DRILL

This sketch shows how to convert an ordinary hand grinder into a high speed wood drill by using a common thread spool.

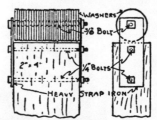

Screw the spool on to the end of the grinder shaft and square one end of the spool hole by pressing the bit shank into it just a little.

Turn the opposite end on to the protruding threaded grinder shaft. While it would not be suitable for heavy work, it gives the high speed necessary for fine, smooth and accurate jobs.

AN IMPROVISED EMERY WHEEL DRESSER

Grinding wheels should sometimes be trued up and the glaze removed by holding a dresser against them whilst they are rotated.

A very handy dresser for this can be made from a set of round washers as indicated in the illustration.

The washers can be hardened considerably by throwing them red hot into water. Fairly good results can also be obtained by holding the end of a pipe against the wheel whilst it is turned.

AN IMPROVISED SPINDLE FROM A GRINDSTONE

This is quite easily made—a piece of ¾ in. rod being used, bent as required and with sufficient space left for the bearings at each end.

Four pieces of ¼ in. flat iron are then required, each of a width sufficient to fit into the centre of the stone, as shown in the sketch. These should be a little wider than the stone in order that they may be affixed to the handle.

Bore these pieces of iron at the end where indicated in order to take a set-screw (see smaller sketch). The shafting should also have small holes bored in it to correspond with the position of the set-screws. Be sure that these holes are very true so that there is no looseness whatever when the set-screws are screwed in. The arrangement is shown here—the set-screws being tightened and adjusted until the whole thing is in true working order. Cotter pins can be inserted in the shaft to prevent any end play if necessary.

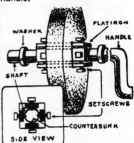

A COMBINED DRILL AND GRINDER FROM OLD CAR GENERATOR

This makes a very handy arrangement. It is merely an old car generator converted in such a way that it provides a very good combined drill and grinder.

The illustration is self - explanatory, although for rigidity the plummer block shown should be placed on the other side of the belt. Very little current will be used and if connected up to say a 6-volt battery or lighting set, it will give good service. "A" is the chuck to take the drills. "B" is a left-hand thread if the motor turns clockwise, but for cars turning anti-clockwise, it should be a right-hand thread. "C" is a nut and washer to hold the emery wheel "D."

IDEAS AND HANDY GADGETS FOR THE WORKSHOP

A USEFUL FUNNEL SUPPORT

This sketch will give details of a very useful funnel support for many jobs, such as that set out below.

A double-tapered spring from a car seat makes this useful support for the funnel when filling bottles, etc.

The spring keeps the funnel from tipping and permits the escape of air.

Electric Light Bulb Stand. Such a support as this could also be constructed so that when not in use for the above purpose, it could stand on the bench as a support for the light.

A USEFUL VALVE STOPPER FOR FUNNEL

When a number of bottles are to be filled by means of a funnel, the work may be accomplished rapidly and without overflowing the containers if this small, finger-operated stopper is employed.

It consists of a cork ball attached to a wire, one end of which is bent into a loop to fit over the index finger of one hand. In filling the bottles, the funnel is held as shown, the finger being raised or lowered to operate the valve.

This should also be quite a useful idea in connection with jam making and other such homely tasks, whilst for filling petrol tanks from bulk or tins, it should be specially suitable.

IMPROVISED LOG TONGS

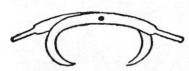

This inexpensive, home-made log tong can be made from 2 in. car springs. Each flat spring is hammered round on the handle end and the round part is made long enough for two hands. Note the handles are curved downwards to enable one to lift the log higher. This is a two-man tong and it makes the lifting of heavy logs much easier.

A HANDY TOOL FOR MAKING WIRE NOVELTIES

These are two tools with forked ends that will be found useful for bending wire when making trellises or anything else in the workshop.

Both tools are made of half-inch steel rod, one consisting of two pieces welded together to form a tee, while the other is bent only at one end to an L shape. A slot to fit the wire is cut in the working end of each (as shown).

By using these tools you can obtain almost any leverage on the wire in order to bend it to any shape. For such things as trellis work, small steel bands may be used to hold the wire together at the joints. One can make one's own netting like this.

A SIMPLE HOME-MADE WORKSHOP HOIST

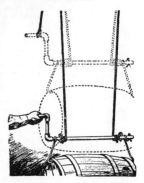

The task of lifting heavy material (especially those containing liquids) to a convenient height, is often rather difficult, but one novel way of doing this is shown here.

If a pair of cables are suspended from the ceiling to support a crank assembly of pipe, as shown here, the work can be accomplished easily. The sliding hooks engage the material in question, which is lifted by turning the crank.

A third rope or cable also suspended from the ceiling is provided with a steel ring, which may be slid over the crank handle to hold the object at the desired height.

USEFUL METHOD OF REMOVING DENTS FROM TANKS

This idea might suggest others to any "handyman" which might be useful in an emergency. For sheet metal tanks, etc., a short rod with an eye in the upper end is soldered to the metal where it is dented, after which the dent is removed by pulling on the rod.

The latter is then removed by melting the solder with a hot iron. In the case of heavy materials, a strong iron rod is welded in the dent, the object anchored to the floor, after which a block and tackle is used to pull out the dent.

HANDY HOME-MADE SCRAPER FROM OIL DRUM

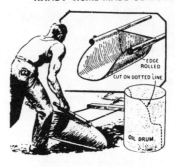

Work on drainage and other excavation jobs may be handled with a scraper improvised from an oil drum as shown.

The drum is cut in half (see dotted lines) after which part of the top edge on each side is rolled to form sleeves for the handles, the latter being held in place with bolts. Large eyebolts near the front ends take iron rods, which are attached to a double tree.

REMOVABLE MOTOR MOUNTINGS

This is a handy portable mounting for a small motor that will permit it to be used for a number of purposes; loose pin hinges, holding the mounting in place, allowing the motor to be adjusted whenever desired. It is fixed to an oak board of suitable size and attached to the edge of the workbench by means of the loose pin hinges. The belt is slipped over the pulleys and suitable weights hung from the edge of the board to keep the belt at the proper tension.

Wherever the use of the motor may be required, hinge pins of the same type are provided, so that they can be readily attached.

USEFUL IDEAS FOR THE GRINDSTONE

RE-SHAPING THE GRINDSTONE

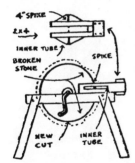

If the grindstone has worn out of shape or has a piece broken out of it, take two pieces of 2 x 4 about 18 in. long, nail them together at one end with a piece of soft wood, leaving clearance enough for the grindstone to turn freely between them.

Bore two small holes exactly opposite each other through the 2 x 4's as shown in the sketch so that they will be inside the broken part of the stone.

The holes should be just large enough so that a 4 in. spike will pass through them freely. Then nail or wire the device on the frame with a 2 x 4 on each side of the stone. Put a 4 in. spike in each hole, and over them tack pieces of inner tubing to give pressure. Start turning the grindstone without using water and soon the nails will shear off the stone to a true circle.

A USEFUL METHOD OF SAVING THE GRINDSTONE

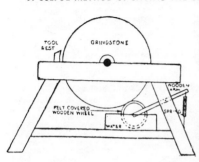

The problem of keeping the grindstone wet during operation can be done in several ways and the two ideas mentioned here provide two different methods in which this can be done whilst either of them might suggest other ideas just as efficient.

The first method indicated is the felt covered wheel which runs in the water and brings the water into contact with the stone as shown in this drawing, thus washing small particles of the stone metal out of the cutting surface and thus leaving the cutting surface sharper.

An old oil tin with the side cut out holds the water. When not in use, one end of the spring is unfastened, allowing the wheel to disengage contact with the grindstone.

AN OLD TYRE PROVIDES WATER FOR GRINDSTONE

A grindstone should be kept at the right stage of dampness. For this, a section of an old motor tyre can be fitted to the underneath of the stand in such a manner that the stone runs inside the tyre section and in constant contact with the water contained therein. This should be fixed so that it can be removed when the work is finished, otherwise if the stone rests in water

whilst idle, the stone will tend to become soft and will wear a lot quicker.

This illustration shows the idea with additions. Enough water should be placed in the trough to keep the rim of the stone dipping in it all the time.

Sharpening is easier and faster when the tool is kept cool in this manner, and the stone is always wet and clean.

A small hole can be bored in the bottom of the trough in order to drain away the water after use. This hole should be provided with a cork to prevent the water escaping whilst grinding.

CASTORS MAKE GOOD GRINDSTONE BEARINGS

A very easy and effective method of supporting the grindstone can be made from ordinary castors as indicated in this illustration. They will work easily and will last well.

Mounted in an inverted position in holes drilled in a grindstone frame, furniture castors make good rollers and permit the stone to be removed without trouble.

The holes in the frame should be reamed to fit the tapering shanks of the castors so that they will not spread apart at the top under the weight of the stone. Frequent lubrication will increase the life of the castors.

OLD BICYCLE TO DRIVE GRINDSTONE OR OTHER TOOLS

This arrangement makes such jobs easy. Belted to the rear wheel, a grinder mounted on the frame of an old bicycle, can be turned at high speed.

The front wheel is removed and the frame fastened on a base as shown, using one support for the fork and one for each side of the rear wheel.

The grinding wheel is mounted on a table, which is clamped to the frame. This idea can also be used for a bigger grindstone or other rotary tool.

HOW TO MAKE A HIGH SPEED FOOT POWER GRINDER

An old bicycle wheel, weighted with lead pipe around its rim, is used to provide a fly-wheel for this bench grinder. The ratchet part of a coaster-brake bicycle hub is used for the axle and ratchet device. The axle is mounted on the end of the workbench, and the support for the grinder is set on the bench in line with the flywheel. A rope is used as a belt, and runs in the grooved rim of the wheel. Holes cut in the top of the bench permit the belt to pass through.

The ratchet device is arranged between the fly-wheel and the brace of the bench, a block being set against the brace to bring the ratchet out sufficiently to make room for the treadle. The latter is pivoted in the rear leg of the bench, and a section of bicycle chain fitted to it as shown to act with the ratchet.

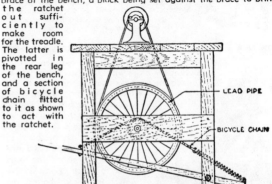

LEAD PIPE

BICYCLE CHAIN

A coil spring is fastened to the end of the drive chain and to the end of the treadle. The high gearing of the belt from the large drive pulley to the small one on the grinder gives great speed, which is desirable in any small grinder.

USEFUL IDEAS WITH SAWS

A HOME-MADE ONE-MAN SAW

This is useful for sawing small trees, etc., into short lengths. It can be rigged up from the ordinary two-man cross-cut saw and can be operated by one man.

Two scantlings, each 8 ft., are driven into the ground about 3 ft. apart, with their upper ends leaning almost together. Two 3 in. strips are nailed across the sides of the tops of posts, through the centre of which is bored a half-inch hole. A bolt of the same size is passed through this hole, and through a hole in a 2 x 2 in. scantling standing vertically—this being on the outside of the cross-strips—providing a free swinging support for the ends of the saw blade. This is shown.

There are several holes in this scantling pendulum for adjusting the blade. One of the handles is removed from the blade, and a small bolt is passed through the small hole in the end of the blade and through the lower end of the scantling. Either a saw-horse may be used or cross stakes may be driven in the ground as shown to hold the logs whilst being sawed. As the saw moves back and forth, the swinging scantling holds the end of the saw steady. It is easily rigged.

STIFFENING CROSS-CUT SAWS FOR ONE-MAN WORK

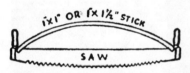

When one man operates a full size cross-cut saw, it is difficult to prevent the blade from "whipping," but if it is stiffened as shown here, it can be easily handled by one man.

A thin slat or sapling 3 or 4 in. longer than the saw blade is notched at each end about ¾ in. deep. The notched ends are placed against the saw handles, and the slat is sprung up in the centre, as illustrated.

ANOTHER METHOD OF STIFFENING A CROSS-CUT SAW

Another similar idea in different form is given in the accompanying illustration. This is done by stringing two wires between the handles and tightening them by a notched stick between the wires and forcing them apart as shown.

This will tend to stiffen the saw so that the handles will have less tendency to wobble from side to side. Some of these ideas can, of course, be used in conjunction with each other.

HOW ONE MAN CAN OPERATE A TWO-MAN CROSS-CUT SAW

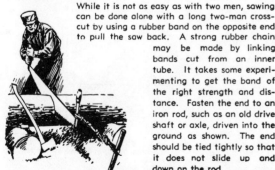

While it is not as easy as with two men, sawing can be done alone with a long two-man cross-cut by using a rubber band on the opposite end to pull the saw back. A strong rubber chain may be made by linking bands cut from an inner tube. It takes some experimenting to get the band of the right strength and distance. Fasten the end to an iron rod, such as an old drive shaft or axle, driven into the ground as shown. The end should be tied tightly so that it does not slide up and down on the rod.

A HANDY HOME-MADE SAW FRAME

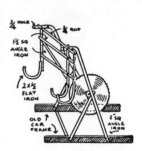

This sketch will show how to make a steel saw frame with a swinging table which will work very well. The frame is made of 2 x 2 in. steel angle iron taken from an old seed drill.

The table is made of 1½ x 1½ in. angle iron. The hooks are 2 x ½ flat steel and they should be made according to the size of the blade used. For a 24 in. blade, the hooks should be about 11 in.

The base is an old car frame about 5 ft. long. The mandrel is made from an old drive shaft taken from an old Chev. car. The frame stands 6 ft. 6 in. high and is about 3 ft. 6 in. wide.

A HANDY SAW-BUCK FROM OIL DRUM

Logs to be cut with a two-man saw can be held securely on a saw-buck made from an old 50-gal. oil drum, as shown in this illustration.

Split it down for about 15 in. on opposite sides, then turn in the edges to leave a V-shaped space. Then sink the drum into the ground in order to make it nice and firm.

This, of course, is useful in that it can be taken from place to place wherever it is most convenient to work.

A USEFUL DEPTH-GAUGE FOR SAW

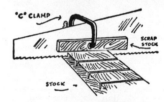

This is a useful article to have on hand for accurate work.

Fastened to the handsaw by a C-clamp, a strip of wood will serve nicely as such an emergency depth gauge. Simply clamp the strip in place according to the desired depth required for the saw cut.

OLD TYRE TO PROTECT CIRCULAR SAW

This is an excellent idea to give protection to any circular saw which might be in the open.

An old motor tyre cut in half and fixed to the bench so that it can easily be taken off is ideal for the saw when it is not in use.

A USEFUL HAND-GUARD FOR CROSS-CUT SAW

This is a very useful device for protecting the hands against injury by striking the objects being sawn.

Screwed to the handle of the saw, as shown, a couple of door pulls will serve as hand guards if too long a stroke is made with the saw.

Guards can also be made from strips of flat iron or portions of tyre covers.

USEFUL SAW-HORSE IDEAS FOR THE WORKSHOP

HOW TO MAKE A USEFUL SAWHORSE

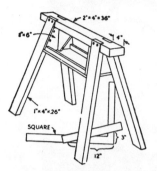

Use 4 x 2 stock for the top of the horse and 4 x 1 for the legs. Cut the legs 26 in. long, bevelling faces and edges on a slant in the proportion of 3 in 12.

Mark sides of notches for the legs by running a pencil along the edges of the legs, and number them to identify them.

Gauge the depth of the notches on top and bottom of the 4 x 2 and saw the sides.

Chisel out the waste. Drill and countersink the legs for $1\frac{1}{2}$ in. flathead screws, and screw to the top-piece. Cut 6 x 1 in. braces and screw inside legs, against top. Fit the angle braces against these pieces and the top, and screw in. A thin shelf with low sides may be nailed beneath the braces to hold tools.

USEFUL IDEAS FOR THE SAWHORSE

Holding Timber on Edge. The first sketch indicates an idea for holding timber on edge for planing by the use of removable stops. This is specially applicable when it is a one-man job as difficulty is often experienced in this connection.

By fitting these removable stops (which are spaced about 1 inch apart) one is able to plane the edge quite easily. The stops are lengths of maple dowels fitted snugly into holes drilled through the sawhorse so that they can be driven down out of the way when not being used.

The illustration will also show the most suitable position for these stops.

An Adjustable Stop. The second illustration is one of a door bolt screwed to the sawhorse in such a way as to provide another type of adjustable stop.

Fitted to the side of the sawhorse as shown, a door bolt provides an adjustable stop against which work can be held firmly whilst sawing or planing it.

When not needed, the pin can be lowered out of the way to provide an unobstructed surface across the top of the horse.

This idea can also of course be used for the same purpose as indicated in the previous sketch and vice versa—either one or two stops being used in either case.

A Support for Wide Work.—Sketch No. 3 is the addition of swinging arms on the top of the sawhorse in order to support wide work. For convenience, one often needs a bench-like surface to support such wide work and therefore a couple of arms pivoted to the sawhorse like that shown in the drawing should prove quite useful for this purpose.

When needed, these arms could be swung around to support the work, and when not in use they are moved round parallel to the top of the sawhorse where they are held by nails dropped through holes in the ends. When the arms are swung to this position, the sawhorse is ready for use in the regular way.

A RESTING PLACE FOR SAW

This idea is one which gives a resting place to the saw which makes it always at hand; it is very convenient and will save much time and trouble in perhaps moving or turning each time the saw is required.

The sawhorse is slotted to hold the saw when not in use, as shown. Cut a long slot in the cross-member of the sawhorse so that the saw can be dropped into it when not using it. Besides being always at hand, it cannot fall and be damaged. If necessary, some soft material slightly greased can be inserted to protect the teeth when putting the saw in or taking it out.

Any of these sawhorse ideas can be used one in conjunction with the other, thus making them doubly convenient and useful.

AN IDEA TO HELP KEEP WORK STEADY

Sawhorse with Slot.

When a number of pieces of wood of about the same width have to be cut off on a sawhorse, it is a good plan to cut a slot in the top bar of the horse wide enough to admit the widest piece, or if it is not desired to cut the horse, build one up by nailing two cleats across at the correct distance apart.

The later is, of course, preferable, as the width of the slot can then be changed easily. The notch enables the work to be held steady with the knee, leaving the spare hand free to hold the end that is to be cut off to prevent it from splintering with the last stroke of saw.

SHOP HORSES MADE FROM PIPE

A pair of heavy duty shop horses that may be found very useful can be made from lengths of one-inch pipe and several fittings.

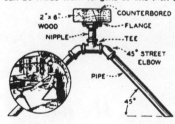

Assemble the legs as shown in the accompanying illustration, sawing off the ends of the pipe at an angle of 45 degrees. The counter-board is a length of 6 x 2 in. stock cut to the desired length and bolted to the flanges.

The use of elbow fittings eliminates pipe bending. This type is very strong, easily made and will last a long time. It can also be made portable and taken from place to place as desired.

ATTACHMENT FOR SAWHORSE

To keep the piece of wood on which the work is intended firm, a stirrup iron attached to a short piece of chain and fastened to the sawhorse, as shown in the diagram, makes a very useful tool.

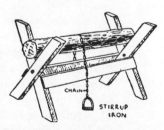

The chain has only to be thrown over the log and the foot placed in the stirrup when the article to be cut will remain as firm as one would wish.

HANDY HOME-MADE FORGES FOR THE WORKSHOP

A HOME-MADE BLOWER FOR FARM FORGE

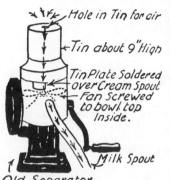

Hole in Tin for air

Tin about 9" High

Tin Plate Soldered over Cream Spout — Fan Screwed to bowl top Inside.

Milk Spout

Old Separator

This is made from an old separator and should give the heat required to do almost any job on the farm.

All that is necessary is to make a fan to fit on the top of the bowl inside the old separator, so that it will spin around inside the milk spout.

Take off the cream spout and solder up the hole.

Get a tin about 9 in. high that will just fit in the cream spout and solder same to make it firm.

Cut a hole about two inches round in top of tin to allow the air to go through. Then attach a piece of water piping to the milk spout long enough to lead to the fire.

A HANDY FORGE FITMENT

This device is useful where heavy pieces of machinery, etc., are to be handled in the forge.

Two pieces of 4 x 4 are mortised and fastened together at the required height, angle iron or straps being used to re-inforce. A shouldered $\frac{7}{8}$ in. pin is driven into each end as suitable pivots, and the ends of the standard are banded to prevent splitting.

A hook on an adjustable link chain could be used to hold the work, or a handle as shown in the sketch would be useful for the lighter articles. This is a length of steel passed through a loop bolted to the arm, the free end being held in position at the required height by placing it under one of the several bolts driven into the standard. Work can easily be swung to and from the forge and anvil with a minimum of exertion.

PIVOT

LOOP

PEGS

PIVOT

SMALL FORGE USING FLOWER-POT AS CRUCIBLE

A burner on a gas stove can be used for any small jobs, such as tempering tools or heating steel for small forgings; but it is not easy to get sufficient heat for some things if the burner is left open and the work merely held over it. In this, half of a common flower pot will serve to keep heat confined and reduce radiation to a minimum.

HALF OF CLAY FLOWER POT

BOTTOM BROKEN OUT FOR LONG WORK

GAS BURNER

CUT HERE

TWO HALVES TO RETAIN MORE HEAT

Gas Stove Crucible.

The half pot is placed so as to cover both work and burner. By using two halves, "double banking" them, it is better still.

To divide the flower pot, it is sawn down the centre with a hack saw. Use an old blade as the baked clay will reduce its sharpness considerably. For long work, break out the end of the pot; for small jobs it is better left in as it keeps the heat from escaping at the back end.

This idea is workable with other types of burners.

A HANDY BLOW TORCH FROM OILCAN AND CYCLE PUMP

A useful blowtorch for light soldering and heating may be made by combining parts of an oilcan and a bicycle pump, in the manner illustrated.

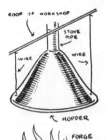

HAND PUMP

BLOW TORCH

SPOUT

4"X12" BASE OIL CAN

The spout of the oilcan is cut off and soldered to the body to form an air nozzle directed just above a wick inserted in the neck.

A piece of air hose is used to connect the pump with the air spout. The whole is mounted on a 4 x 12 wooden base by means of screws passing through an extension soldered to the bottom of the oilcan.

A HOME-MADE FORGE HOOD

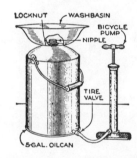

ROOF OF WORKSHOP

STOVE PIPE

WIRE

WIRE

HOPPER

FORGE

This is a useful arrangement and very easily constructed and it will answer the purpose very well.

It can be made from a discarded hopper off a grain binder or put together in any improvised fashion from whatever scrap is available.

It is then hung from the rafters with wire, and a stove pipe or other such pipe is then fitted into it. It will then serve very nicely to take away the smoke of the forge.

The drawing and idea might also suggest some other way of improvising some such similar arrangement to keep the forge clear of smoke.

ANOTHER SMALL FORGE FROM OIL-CAN

LOCKNUT

WASHBASIN

BICYCLE PUMP

NIPPLE

TIRE VALVE

5-GAL. OILCAN

Another very handy little forge that will answer for many small jobs when a regulation forge is not available can be made from an ordinary 5-gal. oilcan, a wash basin, and a tyre pump in the manner shown here.

A round hole is cut in the centre of the wash basin, just large enough to fit over the nipple of the can.

A locknut can be used to hold the basin rigid, but if this is not obtainable, a washer can be slipped over the nipple, and the cap of the can screwed down tight, after the hole of the proper size has been drilled or punched in the centre to allow the air to escape. An ordinary tyre valve is soldered near the bottom of the can and connected to the tyre pump, which furnishes the necessary supply of air.

BINDER WHEEL FITTED WITH LEGS PROVIDES FARM FORGE

This is quite a good and effective forge which is easy to make and which will be found a very handy thing for many jobs.

With an old binder wheel for a start, it is quite easy to make.

BINDER WHEEL

The wheel is supported on flat-iron legs, and the spokes are embedded in concrete, which is covered with fire-clay if this is available.

The hub of the wheel is left open and becomes an inlet for the air blast, which can be furnished by a blower, either hand or power driven.

IMPROVISED LIGHTS FOR THE WORKSHOP

SOME EMERGENCY LIGHTS

These illustrations give one or two other ideas in connection with various home-made emergency lights for sheds, etc., all of which are very easily made.

AN IMPROVISED CANDLESTICK

A piece of candle can be placed anywhere out of harm's way by the use of a pocketknife as indicated here.

This idea could also be used in conjunction with the reflector shown in the next illustration, as an old knife could be inserted through the bottom of the tin (with or without the aid of a wedge) and used in any place where otherwise it would be awkward to place an unprotected light.

A SHIELD FOR CANDLE

This sketch is of a tin cut to shape which is very useful, both as a reflector and as a means of protecting the flame, besides preventing the candle-grease from being dropped all over the place.

It is made from an ordinary tin and cut to any size required and it can be placed either on the bench or hung up.

A SAFE LIGHT FOR A SHED

Quite a cheap and safe lamp can be made as follows:—Obtain a glass bottle and pour about $\frac{1}{2}$ in. of water into it.

Then stand it on a hot stove, and the bottom of the bottle should come away quite easily.

Then make a wooden stand with a hole that will take the neck of the bottle, as shown. The bottle is then well corked and half filled with water. Then take a piece of cork and make a number of holes in it with a large needle. Then soak this for an hour or so in paraffin.

Float the cork in the water in the bottle, and at the part which comes uppermost, bore rather a large hole, so that a small strip of cotton material can be pushed in to act as a wick. The lamp can then be lit and will give out quite a steady light for quite a long time. Even if tipped over, there is very little risk.

AN ADJUSTABLE WORK-BENCH LIGHT

Pivoted on two electrical outlet box covers, the arms of this adjustable work-bench light can be swung to illuminate any part of the bench without sagging.

The two covers, one screwed to the overhead joist, and the other to the extending arm, are held together with a lag screw through the centre.

Proper adjustment of the screw to get easy movement of the arm is found by experiment.

The circular detail on the right shows how the socket is fastened to the arm with $\frac{3}{8}$ in. pipe and lock nuts. The connecting cord, etc., can be so arranged that the lamp can be lowered or raised as required.

SPRING ON WORKBENCH TO HOLD EXTENSION LIGHT

This is one useful way in which a coil spring comes in handy and in this way it can be moved from place to place and stood up anywhere conveniently near the object at which one might be working.

The illustration shows how to support the bulb of such an extension light in any convenient position. Use a coil spring obtained from a discarded car cushion and fix as shown.

Such a spring would also be handy to keep the lamp out of grease and oil when used under a car or on the workshop floor.

COIL SPRING ON WALL TO HOLD EXTENSION LIGHT

Mounted securely on a wall stud convenient to an electric point, a coil spring properly stretched to leave small spaces between the coils makes a handy place to hang up the extension cord of a trouble light.

Strong staples at each end of the spring will hold it taut. When finished using the lamp, loop the cord back and forth, as indicated, between the coils. This will be found very convenient.

A HANDY LAMP SOCKET
With Pull Chain Attachment

A firm mounting for a lamp is obtained by suspending it from a ceiling joint with a wooden arm as shown. This particular sketch shows one with a pull-chain socket.

For this, a hole slightly less in diameter than the small end of the socket is bored near the lower end of the arm, which is slotted right through the hole.

The slot permits the arm to be spread to take the socket, and when released it grips it securely.

Such an idea can also be extended to take ordinary lamps and suspend them from any part of the ceiling for the particular job required. Nails can be placed in a cross beam overhead at several places to fit through a hole in the upper part of the wooden arm; thus the arm can be moved from place to place in the workshop so as to be tight near the particular job being done.

GLASS JARS TO PROTECT OUTDOOR BULBS

Glass jars mounted over bulbs which may be in a position to get damaged, offer good protection. The size of the jar depends upon the size of the bulb.

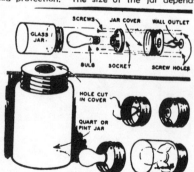

Cut a hole in the cover of the jar to permit the connecting wires to pass through.

Then mount a wall or ceiling socket in the cover.

Mount the cover to the wall and connect to the power source.

The bulb is placed in position in its socket, and the jar is then screwed into its cover.

IMPROVISED LIGHTS FOR THE WORKSHOP

HANDY METHOD OF PROTECTING TORCH

One may often have need of a torchlight for outside work in driving rain at night and this little idea will help protect it from the weather and subsequent damage from moisture reaching the mechanism.

Have an old pickle or other jar always at a convenient spot and on such occasions place the torch in it with the current on; then screw the lid on tight. The jar should be of the large-mouthed variety.

The jar can then be carried or laid down should the hands be required for such jobs as repairing a leak, etc. Perhaps for some purposes a square jar might be best. In any case, this little hint is worth remembering perhaps for camping trips when the torches themselves may not be wholly weatherproof.

A LANTERN HANDLE
Which Will Stay Upright

Annoyance is often caused by the lantern handle falling every time the lantern is put down, but this little hint will ensure that it is kept upright.

By simply attaching a lead weight to a short length of wire, which is in turn soldered to one side of your lantern handle as indicated, the latter will remain in a vertical position.

The weighted wire should be soldered to the handle in such a position that it will clear the lantern frame.

A HANDY CAMP LAMP FROM BOTTLE

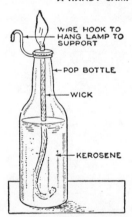

A kerosene lamp is easily constructed from any bottle giving a broad, flat base, to prevent it being easily upset.

If the bottle has been sealed with a crown cap, a $\frac{1}{4}$-in. hole for the wick is punched in the latter. The wick can be made of twisted cotton waste, or a piece of cotton cord, unravelled and loosely twisted.

One end of the wick is passed through the metal cap, so that a small portion projects, and the other end is inserted inside the bottle, which is filled with kerosene. The bottle can be suspended by a wire hook around the neck, as shown in the illustration.

HOW TO LIMIT THE BURNING TIME OF A CANDLE

This can be done with a heated knife blade, as shown here. First warm the small blade of your knife and cut the wick at the desired point. In this way, the upper section of the candle will  burn down to the point where the wick is severed, and fall over, thus extinguishing itself.

A FLOOR LAMP FROM A BUTTER CHURN

A good portable lamp can easily be improvised from an old butter churn or similar arrangement—it being an excellent means of ensuring that the light is nice and high. The churn handle supports the lamp. The cord enters the base through a small hole bored for the purpose. The lid of the churn base can be lifted when necessary and various articles stored in the lamp base.

A LAMP MADE FROM OIL CAN

This will show how the spout of an oil can can be cut (where indicated) and a wick inserted in the manner shown in order to make quite a good emergency light.

There are several variations of this idea (too numerous to give space here), but this one will be found to be as good as most others and will provide quite a useful light for many purposes.

A SELF-EXTINGUISHING CANDLE

This illustration is of a candle which will safely put itself out at any estimated time; it being a very useful device for occasions when one may be called away suddenly from the job for a time and perhaps forget to return, thus leaving the candle burn itself out with the consequent danger of fire.

A small hole is cut in the top of the tin and the candle is forced into it. The bottom half of the tin is filled with water, and, as soon as the candle burns itself down to the lid, it will drop down into the water and so extinguish itself.

ANOTHER AUTOMATIC CANDLE EXTINGUISHER

This is another illustration which will give details of another rather good idea for occasions in which the worker may be called away from the job and forget the fact that a light might have been left burning.

The arrangement is that when the light gets as low as the string, which is passed from the extinguisher through the eyelets to the candle itself, it burns through, and the weight drops on to the flame, thus putting it out. This, too, will save the risk of fire, and is well worth the trouble of arranging.

AN EMERGENCY LIGHT FROM SPARK PLUG

Using only a small-necked bottle, an old spark plug, and a piece of string, an emergency light can speedily be rigged up. Remove the top screw from the spark plug and the wire which runs through the plug, leaving only the bottom with the porcelain base. This is placed in the neck of the bottle and a cotton string is pushed through the hole where the string was. The string acts as the wick. Coal oil is used as fuel. Several of these will give quite a surprising light.

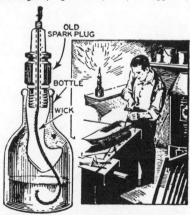

SUNDRY USEFUL IDEAS FOR THE WORKSHOP

AN ARM ATTACHMENT FOR CONVENIENT WORKING

For those who often work by electric light and in difficult places, say on machinery or on the motor car, this little hint might help.

It is a light fastened to the arm in such a way that it will reflect the light directly on to the work and so leave both hands free— it is then always in position. The handle of the light is clipped over the arm, and the bottom fastened to the wrist with a heavy rubber band.

A USEFUL LANTERN HANGER FOR OUTBUILDINGS

This is useful for workshop, stable, or other outbuildings because, when once erected in each place where one is likely to use the lantern, it is always on the spot ready for instant use, and the lantern can then be merely hooked up in a moment. All that is needed is a ¼ in. rod flattened out where

it is spiked or bolted to the joist. At one end is a harness snap to hold the lantern. An ordinary screen door spring furnishes the tension. One end is fastened to the bottom edge of the joist and the other to the end of the bent rod.

ANOTHER METHOD OF HANGING LANTERN IN BARN OR WORKSHOP

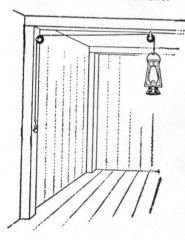

In this, the lantern can be moved as necessary. Get two pulleys with screw stems, and screw one in the beam overhead, the other at the top of the post. Then take a piece of small but strong cord, and at one end fasten a snap and pass the other end through the pulleys.

Put the lantern on the snap and draw it up high enough so that it will be out of reach of forking hay. The end of the cord opposite the lantern may be fastened with a snap, or more length may be allowed for adjusting the height of the lantern, and the cord secured as and where desired.

AN AUTOMATIC SWITCH FOR CELLAR LIGHT

Lights are often left burning in cellar or attic by accident, but with this arrangement they can be turned out automatically when

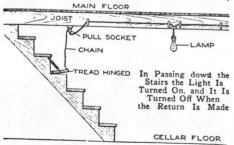

In Passing down the Stairs the Light Is Turned On, and It Is Turned Off When the Return Is Made

a person leaves. For a cellar a pull-socket is fixed to the joist above the stairway. The socket-chain is adjusted carefully and fastened to the edge of a hinged tread, kept slightly raised by a spring. Pressure on the tread will control the light socket.

STACKING ODD TIMBERS, PIPING, ETC.

On nearly every farm there are old tyres lying about. These can be put to profitable use by hanging them on wires in a suitable place and stacking odd timbers, iron or piping in them as shown, instead of leaving them in untidy places on valuable floor space.

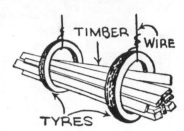

The timber will also last much longer and is much more easily got at when wanted.

TILTED BARRELS FOR EASIER WORKING

This simple prop is easily made by bending a piece of ½ in. or larger iron rod to the shape shown.

"A" shows how the part is to fit the contour of the barrel. The rod is then bent down to a suitable length to give the barrel the desired "tip."

Bend the ends back and form a hook on each end at "C" to prevent the barrel from slipping. Slip the legs on the barrel in the manner shown at "D" and "E" when it may be safely tipped up to the necessary angle at any time and will stay "put."

OVERCOMING SAW-DUST TROUBLE FROM BUZZ SAW

One often has trouble with saw-dust piling up under the buzz saw, and this can be overcome by the device shown in this sketch.

Take, say, a third of an old motor tyre and fasten it so that the draught from the saw blows the dust out into a pile 6 or 8 ft. from the table.

The best angle to fasten the tyre trough can be found by experimenting and the method shown should be such as to eliminate the bother often caused to those who may be working such a saw.

A BUSH SAWHORSE

A handy saw-horse or trestle can be made from a suitable piece of forked bush timber, as shown in the sketch. The forked ends are cut off at the required length, and two holes are bored with an augur to take the other two legs of the tripod.

The ideal fork is about 6 inches in diameter at the heavy end, and is cut to about 2 ft. 6 in. in height.

The augur holes should be bored so that the two supports are wide apart to give increased steadiness. Two of these saw-horses are a great help when sawing wood.

IDEAS AND HANDY GADGETS FOR THE WORKSHOP

IMPROVISED LADDER SUPPORTS FOR HOLDING LATHS, ETC.

This is a good idea for occasions when it is necessary to use laths or other material when working in high places. It is the addition of some side supports as shown in the illustration, in which the laths can be held in a convenient position for easy working.

This will save much tiresome stooping. Four of the laths or other timber are temporarily nailed on to the legs of the ladder, crossing as indicated, to provide the hopper.

The opened bundles of lath are then placed in this so as to be handy to the worker. By providing wheels to the legs of the ladder, the worker can push himself along without getting down. It will take very little time to arrange and will be found most useful.

USEFUL HANDLES FROM WIRE

Good handles for light service can be made from heavy wire, as shown here.

Two pieces of wire about 9 inches long are required. These are held in a vice and twisted, leaving 2½ in. straight at each end. These are bent at right angles to the handle and spread about 2½ inches apart at the outer ends. A small ring is bent on each of the projecting ends for the screws, which can be used in attaching the handle. This has a neat appearance, is strong, and will give good service.

USEFUL METHOD OF OPENING POCKET KNIFE

There are times when a pocket knife is very hard to open and this is a very good way of doing the job should it be found difficult and one does not wish to damage the finger nails.

The idea is to merely slip a piece of good quality paper or cloth under the point of the blade, as shown in this sketch, and then pull steadily. Even if one can manage to get it under the tip of the blade only, it will soon do the job.

NOVEL IDEA FOR GRIPPING WORK TIGHTLY

If there is no vice available or if the vice is not suitably placed, the method shown here will serve its purpose. First of all, holes are set in the bench in a handy position, perhaps in two or three different widths in order to take various sized articles as the occasion arises.

A 6 ft. length of strap or old chain with small hooks attached to the ends is inserted through the holes in the bench and the work is then set between them, as shown in the drawing.

The chain is then brought up through the holes and the hooks are hooked together or direct on to the work in some way.

The necessary pressure is then obtained by placing one foot on the lower part of the chain, and bearing down on it in the manner indicated.

The article can then easily be changed from one position to another by releasing the pressure of the foot and altering the position of the chain. This is a real time-saver, and one easily arranged and adjusted for the many and various jobs for which some such pressure is needed.

NOVEL METHOD OF OPENING TIGHT CONTAINERS

Most people have experienced the annoyance caused by ineffectual attempts to remove tight fitting tops of containers, but this simple method will prevent many broken finger nails or cut fingers. Place a piece of strong string round the tin, just under the lid. Tie the ends, leaving about ⅛ in. of space between the string and the tin. Now insert a pencil, or something similar, under the string and twist, as shown. The top should then be removed quite easily.

A CLOG-PROOF SPOUT FOR OIL CAN

This hint is a very useful one for occasions when it might be necessary to oil out-of-the-way bearings as the spout of the oil can is sometimes accidentally jabbed into grease and dirt, and becomes clogged.

To prevent this, it is a good idea to split the end of the spout and then bend the two sides into a wedge shape as indicated, leaving the spout openings at the sides. The split ends will then clear the obstructions and should be kept quite clean.

A USEFUL HOME-MADE OIL CAN HOLDER

If you experience, at various times, the trouble of the oil can falling off the tractor or other machine on which you are working, it is a good idea to attach a small magnet to the can as shown in this illustration.

The attraction of the magnet to the metal of the machine holds the can fairly firmly against ordinary vibration. The magnet is held to the can by a drop of solder or by rubber bands, or any other suitable means.

A HANDY WIRE SPREADER FOR GLUE

One may often have a small job to do with glue and on many of these jobs a small square of screen wire will make a better glue spreader than a brush.

When dipped into the glue pot, the meshes of the wire fill with glue, which can then be distributed evenly over the work. This sketch will show both the method of construction and the way it should be manipulated.

A GOOD SUBSTITUTE FOR ABRASIVE PAPER

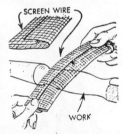

If you need abrasive for an urgent job and there is none at hand, the use of screen wire will be found efficient. As a matter of fact, it will also save a good deal of sandpaper in rough sanding turned work in a lathe. The wire is folded over to provide a strip an inch or so in width and is used in the same manner as sandpaper which, of course, must then be used for the final smoothing.

PORTABLE SHELVES

If space is cramped or one needs the shelf alongside certain work, a strip of heavy wire can be erected against the wall. The shelves are of wood and are attached by hook-shaped pieces of strap iron spaced to fit whatever they are hung on or they can be arranged to hook into certain places on the wall.

USEFUL IDEAS WITH LADDERS

HOW TO MAKE A USEFUL HOUSEHOLD LADDER

This illustration shows a ladder 5 ft. high with 6 steps, but this can be altered to suit. It should be of convenient length, not too unwieldy for women to use and yet not too small for out-of-doors work. Wood should be selected which will wear evenly. White Pine is very suitable but it should be faultless and straight-grained. Use nothing that will warp or twist.

First, and most important, mark everything out carefully, seeing that both sides exactly correspond before starting to groove.

Clamp the two side pieces of the ladder together, and mark along the front edges the positions of the steps as given in the diagram. The width of the grooves will depend on the thickness of the wood, which in this case is $\frac{7}{8}$ in. A sliding bevel is needed to set out the groove lines, the method of determining the angle being given. Notice that when the marking is finished there is waste wood at the bottom.

When sawing these grooves it is wise to clamp a guide strip on the outside of the line each time to prevent any saw slips. The depth of the grooves is $\frac{1}{4}$ in., but the upper line of each groove is cut to slightly more than $\frac{1}{4}$ in. to allow for the spread of the sides, which will make the step fit in a little deeper at the top edge.

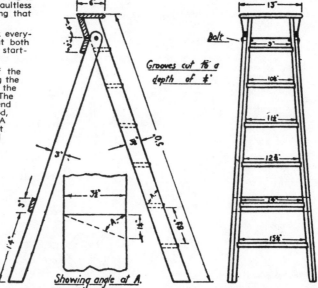

Grooves cut to a depth of $\frac{1}{4}$".

Showing angle at A.

Remove the waste in the grooves. These grooves must not be high in the middle. Holes are bored along the centre line of the grooves at points $1\frac{1}{2}$ in. in from the edges to be used for screwing together the frame later. The top and bottom of each side piece are sawn off along the bevel lines, and can be finished off with a plane.

The steps are next cut roughly to length and clamped together with their centres in line. Measure the lengths of the top and bottom steps, mark them on the wood and connect the points, thus obtaining the lengths of the middle steps. From these edge marks draw square lines across the surface along which to saw each step to its correct length.

These saw-cuts are square, as the spread of the ladder is so slight that any bevelling on the ends of the steps is unnecessary. When the steps are fitted into the grooves, there will be an overlap at the back and front. The front is not altered but the back is planed off before the ladder is assembled, leaving the cleaning up until afterwards.

Next prepare the top piece 13 x 6 x $\frac{7}{8}$ in. and plane it to size, rounding off the front and both ends, which are finished with glass paper. A piece of the same size is needed for the back, and is cut on the ends to the shape shown in the diagram. It is to this piece that the rear frame is hinged.

Assemble the main part of the ladder but, before doing so, clean up all the surfaces with a smoothing plane, and give a thorough glass papering. Hold the frame in position by temporarily nailing the steps until the screwholes are drilled, and the screws driven home.

The top piece can be nailed on, but the back strip is screwed to the side pieces of the ladder, and also to the top to make it more rigid.

Clean along the back edges of the steps to level them up with the sides and pare off the sharp corners on the front edges with a sharp chisel. A final overhaul with glasspaper will complete this section, and the back frame can then be prepared. For this, use 3 x $\frac{7}{8}$ in. wood, and two lengths of about 5 ft. The upper end of each strip is rounded off by sawing the corners and spokeshaving to the line. These two struts or supports are bolted to the ladder sides, and the holes are drilled for this. When they are in position and closed against the sides of the ladder their length can be determined, and the waste sawn off.

To prevent the supports from opening too far a cross-strip is screwed on as at X, the upper edge of which must be bevelled to fit against the back cross-piece of the main frame. The amount of this bevel will depend upon the distance back you open the supports. A second cross-strip is screwed on near the base of the supports to make them rigid.

These parts are cleaned up before being finally fixed in position and screwed. Remember, if necessary, to countersink for all the screw-beds.

A USEFUL HOME-MADE LADDER ON WHEELS

BUGGY WHEELS

A step ladder is a handy thing to have and one mounted on running gear should have additional advantages especially for moving short distances at frequent intervals.

For painting, fruit picking and such-like work, it can be highly recommended as there is no need to pick it up and carry it from place to place.

The only requirements for making this handy wheeled ladder are the front wheels and axle of an old buggy or car and some timber. The height can vary according to requirements. It is also a safe type of ladder and one that does not need to lean up against a tree or anything else for support.

ANOTHER TYPE OF SAFE HOME-MADE STEP LADDER

There should be very little fear of a ladder of this type overturning as it is fitted with special supports which, if correctly adjusted when erecting the ladder, should make it safe for anyone.

One can either make the whole ladder from this drawing or merely make the necessary additions.

The ladder should taper a little towards the top—preferably from a 22 in. base, steps being 1 ft. apart.

This protection against side-thrust is a great advantage on certain jobs.

This idea, and others on the following pages, might suggest other good ideas, any of which can be incorporated in the one ladder.

USEFUL IDEAS WITH LADDERS

A HANDY LADDER FROM ANGLE IRON

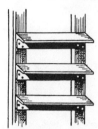

This is a useful type of ladder, easily and cheaply made from odd timber and some angle iron or old tractor fittings.

The way to make this ladder is clearly shown—an advantage being that the material so used for the rungs make excellent foot rests. Both the ladder and the rungs can be made to any height desired.

One or two of such easily made ladders of various heights would be an advantage on any farm or station.

WINDLASS ATTACHMENT FOR RAISING HEAVY LOADS

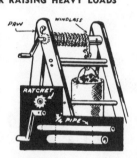

Mounted between the rails of a ladder, this small windlass is very useful when heavy material is to be raised often during the course of a job. Holes in the rails take a length of pipe, over which is fitted a wooden roller for attaching a rope. A crank and ratchet wheel are fastened to one end of the pipe and a pawl is screwed to the outside of the rail to engage the wheel as shown in the sketch.

Another idea is to fit a pulley wheel to the topmost rung for the same purpose.

A HANDY LADDER FOR LOFT

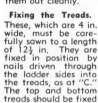

To make the two sides, which are 8 ft. 6 in. long and 3½ in. wide, first mark the sloping lines which indicate the positions of the recess into which the treads fit, as shown at "B." The lines should be 10 in. apart, as at "A," the lowest line being 10 in. from the bottom end. Cut the recesses to a depth of ¼ in. and chisel them out cleanly.

Fixing the Treads.
These, which are 4 in. wide, must be carefully sawn to a length of 12½ in. They are fixed in position by nails driven through the ladder sides into the treads, as at "C." The top and bottom treads should be fixed first.

For the top crossrail, "D," cut a piece of wood 1 ft. 4 in. long and 4 in. wide, round off the top corners, and screw it to the sloping ends of the sides as shown in the sketches. The treads can be planed flush with the back edges of the sides, and the front edges can be slightly rounded.

To give rigidity to the ladder, screw on two struts "E," between the ends of the sides and the back of the bottom tread. These struts, which are 10 in. long and 1¼ in. wide and ½ in. thick, can be cut from planed oak strip.

To prevent the ladder from slipping when in use, two thick iron right-angled hooks are screwed through the top cross-rail and into the ends of the ladder sides as at "F." These hooks engage with the ledge round the loft opening when the ladder is placed in position.

HANDY TOOL RACKS ON SIDE OF LADDER

A useful place for tools to be at hand for instant use is shown here. Nailed to one side of the ladder, a strip of leather or inner tube provides a handy place for them whilst working on the ladder. Besides being always at hand, they are not so likely to be dropped as they would be if laid on top of the work or ladder.

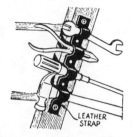

USEFUL WAYS OF KEEPING LADDER FROM SLIPPING

The use of sandbags as depicted here is rather a good idea to keep the ladder from slipping on cement or other hard surfaces.

The sand should be equally divided and the empty middle portion of the bag wrapped with tape or twine. By doing this, it will also serve as a carrying handle.

The second idea shown here is one which does away with the work of dragging or carrying the bags of sand upon which to rest the ladder.

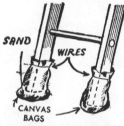

They consist of small bags of heavy canvas, partly filled with sand, which are attached to the legs of the ladder by pieces of wire.

A USEFUL ATTACHMENT FOR STEP-LADDER FOR WORKING IN HIGH PLACES

The useful home-made attachment will be found very handy indeed for all such jobs as painting, etc., when it may be necessary to balance oneself on the top step.

A steel rod slides into fixtures on the side of the ladder whilst there is also an arrangement fixed to the second step on which a bucket can be placed. This could be arranged so that it could easily be changed for a tool box.

A USEFUL TOOL DRAWER FOR LADDER

Suspended from the underside of a step-ladder top, a small drawer would provide a handy place to keep nails, screws and small tools which are so frequently used when working from a step ladder. A catch could be provided for the drawer to keep it closed when the ladder is being moved. If the drawer is partitioned for nails, it will be better still.

DOT
FASTENERS AND FITTINGS
FOR ALL TRADES

For many years the "DOT" line of fasteners have been recognised the world over as the reliable, quick action fastener. They have stood up to the test of Active Service under every climatic condition and in all branches of the Service, on land, on sea and in the air.

Swinging over to PEACE-TIME production

Soon there will be ample supplies for manufacturers of clothing, leatherware, canvas goods and gloves. There will also be the new "GRIPPERS" that do away with buttons on underclothing. Watch for them . . .

When you buy overalls, insist on "DOT" fasteners and you'll do away with Button Bother.

CARR
FASTENER CO. OF AUSTRALIA LTD

ROYAL PARK, SOUTH AUSTRALIA—Telegrams "Carrfast," Adelaide

ASSOCIATE ORGANISATIONS IN ENGLAND, CANADA, AND U.S.A.

SHARPENING AND SETTING TOOLS

SHARPENING AND SETTING WOODWORKING TOOLS

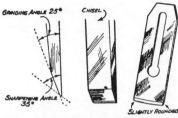

Fig. 1. The correct sharpening and grinding angles for edge tools, i.e., grinding angle about 25 degrees, and sharpening about 35 deg., and details of the edge of a chisel and plane iron.

Correct sharpening or setting of tools is important. It looks quite simple, but it is easily done in the wrong manner.

Edge Tools. Most tools used by amateurs, apart from the saw, are edge tools (chisels, planes, etc.) and if any such tools are examined it will be seen that the end is formed to two different angles, as shown in fig. 1. To sharpen, USE AN OIL-STONE, and, after putting a few drops of thin oil on the stone, run the edge of the tool backwards and forwards over the surface (as shown in fig. 2).

Hold the chisel as shown in that illustration, the tips of the fingers to be within about 1½ in. or so of the edge—the left hand over the right, so that everything is held firmly. Then rub backwards and forwards over the stone, taking care that the tool is maintained at an angle to give the desired 35 deg.

The latter is not easy at first as there is often a tendency to allow the tool to "rock," which results in the edge being rounded as in fig. 3, leaving it comparatively blunt. To prevent "rocking," the wrist and shoulders must be kept rigid, so that movement is from the elbows. The best position is to have the sharpening bench about half the height of the worker.

Fig. 2. How to hold plane iron or chisel to sharpen.

Keep the edge straight and at right angles to the centre of the blade, making certain that the surface of the stone is quite flat. This applies principally to the chisel, for the edge of a plane should be just slightly rounded to keep the corners from digging into the wood (fig. 1). To keep the stone flat, sharpen tools along the sides as well as in the centre, otherwise hollowing will take place on the stone.

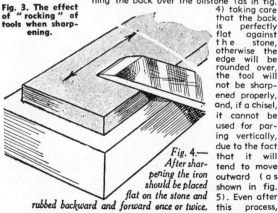

Fig. 3. The effect of "rocking" of tools when sharpening.

Wire Edges. Usually when the edges have been made perfectly sharp, it will be found that they are so thin that there is a very fine strip bent over. This can be removed by turning the chisel over and lightly running the back over the oilstone (as in fig. 4) taking care that the back is perfectly flat against the stone, otherwise the edge will be rounded over, the tool will not be sharpened properly, and, if a chisel, it cannot be used for paring vertically, due to the fact that it will tend to move outward (as shown in fig. 5). Even after this process,

Fig. 4.— After sharpening the iron should be placed flat on the stone and rubbed backward and forward once or twice.

there may be a very slight wire edge which must be removed, preferably by stropping with a piece of soft leather, first on one side and then on the other.

Sharpening Spokeshaves. The foregoing methods are mainly applicable

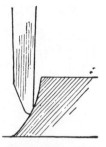

Fig. 5. Chisel which cannot be used for vertical edges, besides which it is set to wrong angles.

Fig. 6. A simple holder for Spokeshave Cutting Iron.

to chisels and plane irons, although it can be applied to blades of metal-framed spokeshaves by making a wooden handle as in figure 6. There is a saw cut in the end of this so that it can grip the cutting iron. The blade of a wooden spokeshave should always be treated in a different way (as in fig. 7), i.e., by standing the oilstone on one edge so that the prongs of the cutting iron overhang each side.

Always wipe over the oilstone with a rough rag after use to remove all oil and fine grains of metal.

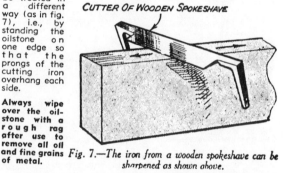

CUTTER OF WOODEN SPOKESHAVE

Fig. 7.—The iron from a wooden spokeshave can be sharpened as shown above.

Figure 8 shown here is a sketch of a metal-framed spokeshave. The cutting iron for the wooden one is of a different type to that indicated in fig. 7.

Grinding.

After continuous sharpening, the end of a chisel or plane becomes "stubby" (fig. 10) and sharpening of "stubby" chisels on an oilstone is a very tedious job, owing to the large contact area. They should then be ground.

Similarly, when the edges become chipped, they should be ground. The chief difficulty in this is to keep the tools at the correct angle to the grindstone, and figure 9 will show quite a useful

GRINDSTONE

Fig. 9.— Grinding to the correct angle is simplified if a block of wood is bevelled and mounted near the grindstone as shown.

LARGE AREA TO BE SHARPENED

PART OF TOOL WORN AWAY BY SHARPENING.

device in this connection. Care should be taken that the correct angle for the bevel on the wood is obtained. If the tool is held firmly against the guide, there should be no difficulty if the stone is kept wet.

SHARPENING AND SETTING TOOLS

SETTING THE PLANE

A plane is by no means easy to set correctly, and there are certain points worth remembering in order to get best results.

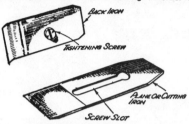

Fig. 11, showing the plane iron, and back iron, which fit together.

Assuming that the plane has a wooden stock, first fit on the back-iron or cap (fig. 11) by passing the head of the short screw through the circular hole at the end of the slot in the plane iron, placing the cap against the flat side of the blade.

Next, the cap is moved along until its edge is between 1/16 in. and 1/8 in. away from the cutting edge, the exact distance depending upon the kind of wood to be used, as well as the variety of plane. For a Jack Plane (normal length about 14 in.) to be used with soft wood, the greater distance may be allowed, and for hard wood, the lesser distance; in the case of a trying or smoothing plane, it is possible to go between the two extremes, again depending upon the hardness of the wood.

Fig. 12. Method of tightening the clamping screw.

Attaching the Back Iron. Having set the cap to the correct distance, the screw can be tightened as in fig. 12. The two irons are held in the left hand with the first two fingers "astride" the threaded brass bush which projects from the cap.

Before the screw is fully tightened, again examine the distance between the edges of the two irons, because this may have been altered. If correct, and the two edges are perfectly parallel, the tightening can be completed.

Tightening the Wedge. Next lay the irons on the inclined bed of the plane with the back iron uppermost; and hold them in place with the left thumb (fig. 13), while the fingers grip the stock. The plane can then be easily turned in any direction.

Turn the plane over and, looking down the sole of the plane with one eye, adjust the irons until the cutting edge projects a suitable distance. Once again the amount of projection depends upon the wood to be treated and the type of plane, but it generally varies between 1/32 in. and 1/16 in.

For a smoothing, trying, or for a jack plane for hard wood, the cutting edge should appear merely as a fine hairline uniformly across the sole. The wedge (fig. 13) can then be inserted, still keeping the thumb in place.

Push the wedge down as far as it will go with the fingers, and then strike it with a wide-faced hammer. When this is tightly

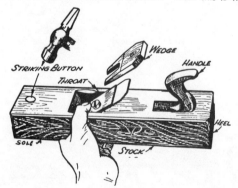

Various parts of a wooden jack plane

in place, check the projection of the cutting edge once again, as it might have been altered by the driving in of the wedge.

HOW TO "SET BACK" THE IRON

If it is found necessary to "take-back" the iron, the method in the case of a plane with a button (fig. 13) is to give the button a quick blow, holding the plane as before, when it will be found that the iron has sprung back.

Fig. 14. The iron of a smoothing plane is set back by striking the head with a hammer.

Tighten the wedge, and examine the projection again, and, if still too great, repeat the process; if it has been made too small, the iron can be driven down by tapping the upper end with a hammer.

When dealing with the other type of plane (fig. 14), the process is similar except that instead of striking the front of the plane to move the iron backward, it is the heel which is struck.

SAVING PLANE IRONS FROM DAMAGE

When not in use a Plane should be laid on its side to avoid Damage to the Blade.

A plane iron will become damaged if stood flat on a bench, as the cutting iron projects slightly beyond the face of the plane, and is therefore liable to catch any projections on the bench.

Always lay the plane-iron on its side so that it cannot catch on anything and thus avoid any unnecessary damage.

Another way is to lay a small strip of wood on the bench and rest the toe of the plane on it, as this will raise the front of the plane, and so create a space between the iron and the bench.

SHARPENING WOOD-WORKER'S TWISTBITS

How to sharpen Woodworkers' Twist-Bits.

One way to do this is to use a fine file as follows: The scoring nibs, i.e., the two prongs which stick downwards on either side of the gimlet point are filed from the inside. The cutting lips are filed on the underside, while the bit is held in the hand, chuck end down.

The scoring edge is shown at "A," and the cutting edge at "B." Use a fine file and take light cuts on the inside edge of "A." If they were taken on the outside, the diameter of the bit would be made smaller at this point.

SHARPENING A GIMLET

First bore a hole in a piece of hard wood, using the gimlet which is to be sharpened; then fill in the hole with a mixture of emery and oil. Insert the gimlet and turn to and fro in the mixture. Change the emery and oil from time to time and, to give a good final polish, bore a hole in soft wood, fill it with flour or brickdust, and give the gimlet a few turns in this, when it will come up like new.

ANOTHER METHOD OF SHARPENING TOOLS

A good, speedy sharpener for tools such as plane blades, chisels, etc., is made from a block of wood, as indicated, and a strip of zinc, 2 in. wide by 11 in. long.

Simple Method of Sharpening Tools.

Place the zinc along the top of the wood and bend over the overlap at each end, when the block should appear as seen in the second sketch.

Nail the zinc on at each end with three nails. Place a small quantity of olive oil on the zinc, also some fine carborundum powder, and the "stone" is then ready for use. This is used in the same way as an oilstone, but cuts very much quicker.

SHARPENING AND SETTING TOOLS

HINTS ON SHARPENING THE SAW

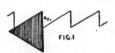

FIG.1

The saw is difficult to sharpen, but these hints might help the amateur. Most ordinary saws have a tooth angle of 60 deg., whether of the ripping type (fig. 1) for sawing with the grain, or the crosscut (fig. 2) for cutting across the grain. This enables them to be filed with an ordinary three-cornered file, as indicated in the shaded triangles. Special files may be required if the teeth are of any other angle.

FIG.2

First, the saw must be supported by a clamp of stout boards, and fig. 3 shows a good home-made article, i.e., two long wooden battens fixed rigidly in a vice.

Sharpening. Starting at one end, carefully observe the angle at which the teeth have previously been filed, and apply the file at the same angle and on the same side. The angle on the file

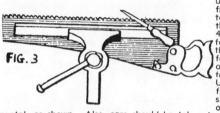

FIG. 3

usually varies from about 60 to 45 deg. to the blade (fig. 4 and 5) the former being the best angle for hardwoods and the latter for softwoods. Usually, the file should be slightly out of the horizontal, as shown. Also, care should be taken to hold the file at the same angle for each tooth, especially after the saw has been reversed, whilst the same number of strokes should be given each.

It will be seen that alternate teeth are filed in opposite directions. Insert the file between the first two teeth and make three strokes backward and forward. Then move the file on to the second space from that,

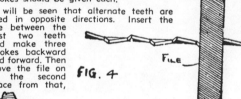

FILE

FIG. 4

FILE

FILE OUT ON HORIZONTAL

FIG. 5

and repeat the process. Thus alternate teeth will be filed.

After doing the whole length in this manner, turn the saw round in the vice, and sharpen the remaining teeth in the same way, bringing all the teeth to the same height.

Setting is the bending of alternate teeth slightly outwards (fig. 6), which gives the clearance for the saw, say 10 deg. (fig. 7). This is best done with a saw set or special pliers (fig. 6). Never bend the teeth more than half way down, and don't give the saw too much set. Any unevenness in setting can be remedied by lightly running the file along the sides of the teeth.

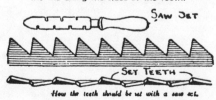

10°   10°

Fig. 7

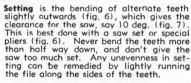

SAW SET

SET TEETH

How the teeth should be set with a saw set.

FIG. 6

CIRCULAR RIPSAWS

A gullet-toothed ripsaw is shown in this illustration and it can be sharpened as indicated. The gullet is ground toward a tooth seventh or eighth beyond the one being ground, as shown by the dotted line at the top.

In filing a circular ripsaw, the fronts of the teeth are filed straight across the saw at an angle (see lines A, B, C and D) which are tangent to a circle drawn half-way between the centre and the rim. Each tooth is bevelled slightly on the back.

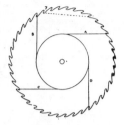

Another type of ripsaw is also shown in the sketch opposite.

Take one precaution. Never let the edge of the file touch the gullet. Notches interfere with the discharge of the sawdust by the saw.

SHARPENING POCKET KNIVES, ETC., ON THE GRINDSTONE

OIL STONE

SHOWING CIRCULAR MOTION OF KNIFE BLADE.

Diagram showing how to sharpen a Pocket-Knife Blade on an Oilstone.

This sketch will show how to sharpen a pocketknife on the grindstone. The position of the blade is clearly indicated on the lower left-hand detail and shows the position it should be kept in whilst circling on the stone. Naturally, a drop or so of oil on the stone facilitates the job.

USING GLASS AS AN OILSTONE

Take a pane of glass and apply some emery powder mixed with machine oil; then rub the chisel too and fro about 12 times and it will be sharpened as well as on an oilstone.

SHARPENING SCISSORS—AN EFFECTIVE METHOD

Some people, in addition to putting the edge at the wrong angle, make a point of grinding the blade all over. The bright finish is deceptive. Instead of sharpening the scissors, the hollow in the blades is often so altered that the blade edges rapidly become dull again.

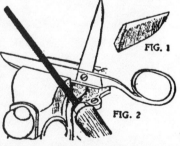

FIG. 1

FIG. 2

It is only when the blades get too thick, owing to frequent sharpening of the edges, that the sides need touching, and then only on the outsides. There is occasionally an exception to this, and that is when the blades have become worn, owing to having been used a lot after they have become dull. In this example (fig. 1), the hollow has to be deepened on an emery wheel. In most cases, however, the blades need sharpening by altering the cutting edge only; this can be done by filing.

The scissors blades are first gripped alternately in the vice (fig. 2), and by means of a file held at the correct angle, the edge is filed sharp by means of curved, sweeping strokes. Starting with the fore-end of the file near the joint, it is pushed forwards and sideways at the same time, so that the back end of the file ends near the point of the blade. This ensures the file being held at the correct angle throughout the stroke, and is much better than taking short, straight cuts, as the edge produced is much more uniform. The smooth cut three-cornered file should be used. The stroke should be taken from as near the rivet end as possible, and when the worn edge has been levelled up and presents an even surface, the burr should be skimmed off lightly with a light stroke of the file.

METAL WORK FOR THE AMATEUR

BENDING AND SHAPING SHEET METAL

Sheet metal offers a material from which one can make many useful articles even if one only has a few simple tools, such as shears or hammers or some of the improvised articles mentioned in this book.   The illustrations given on this page depict many

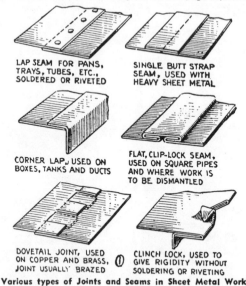

LAP SEAM FOR PANS, TRAYS, TUBES, ETC., SOLDERED OR RIVETED

SINGLE BUTT STRAP SEAM, USED WITH HEAVY SHEET METAL

CORNER LAP, USED ON BOXES, TANKS AND DUCTS

FLAT, CLIP-LOCK SEAM, USED ON SQUARE PIPES AND WHERE WORK IS TO BE DISMANTLED

DOVETAIL JOINT, USED ON COPPER AND BRASS, JOINT USUALLY BRAZED

CLINCH LOCK, USED TO GIVE RIGIDITY WITHOUT SOLDERING OR RIVETING

Various types of Joints and Seams in Sheet Metal Work

of the most common joints and seams which can be easily used and some of them may prove handy to those desiring to do this type of work.   A close study will show the most useful for any particular type of job.

The seams in sheet metal can be joined by soldering, rivetting, or spot welding and information on these subjects is given on other pages in this book. Care, of course, is needed in bend-

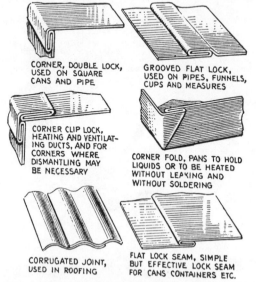

CORNER, DOUBLE LOCK, USED ON SQUARE CANS AND PIPE

GROOVED FLAT LOCK, USED ON PIPES, FUNNELS, CUPS AND MEASURES

CORNER CLIP LOCK, HEATING AND VENTILAT-ING DUCTS, AND FOR CORNERS WHERE DISMANTLING MAY BE NECESSARY

CORNER FOLD, PANS TO HOLD LIQUIDS OR TO BE HEATED WITHOUT LEAKING AND WITHOUT SOLDERING

CORRUGATED JOINT, USED IN ROOFING

FLAT LOCK SEAM, SIMPLE BUT EFFECTIVE LOCK SEAM FOR CANS CONTAINERS ETC.

Other types of Joints and Seams in Sheet Metal Work

ing and forming sheet metal, and dents in the metal should be avoided as they are hard to eliminate.   A rawhide or soft rubber faced hammer should be used gently for all forming operations. If rivets are to be used in this type of work, the holes in the metal should be made with a drill, although perhaps a tinner's rivet set may be used if it is available (see section on rivetting).

A NOVEL METHOD OF BENDING SHEET METAL EDGES USING A BUTT HINGE

Without special tools it is often difficult to bend up the edges of sheet metal neatly, especially when the job to be done is rather awkwardly placed, and this little idea may prove useful in such cases.

Quite a good job can be done by using a large butt hinge and a pair of slip-point pliers, as shown in this illustration.

Gripped in the hinge, which is in its turn gripped in the pliers, the edge can be turned nicely. A hinge used in this manner will also make possible the bending sharp corners and will prevent the marring of the piece of metal.

OTHER METHODS OF SHAPING SHEET METAL

The following illustrations will indicate some other useful methods of going about this work and perhaps at the same time suggest some novel ideas for other work.

Irregular forming of sheet metal is best done over rods and bars supported in a vice. Quite a number of different ways of doing this are shown in figures 2, 3, 6 and 7 on this page.

In **figure 2,** a strip of heavy sheet iron is clamped in a vice and so used to form sharp bends, a piece of angle (or tee iron will do) being used to form the base over which the iron is bent. A good, clean bend is thus made.

Figure 3 will indicate another way in which angle iron can be used for this purpose.

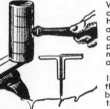

Where shape and size of the work are such that it cannot be handled in a vice as in figure 2, a length of angle iron may be clamped to the metal at the point where the bend is to be made and the same result is then accomplished.

In this illustration, the flat of the angle iron provides a good base on which to gently hammer the iron to be bent.

Sketch marked 6 shows still another method of making small bends in sheet metal. It shows how round bends can be made over such things as iron rods, etc. The rod, of whatever size the bend is required, is gripped in the vice and the strip of sheet metal is then merely bent or gently hammered round it until the desired bend is made.

Similarly, **figure No. 7** indicates how larger bends of the same type can be made, i.e., by using piping of various sizes in the vice.

Again, articles of various shapes can be used in the vice, and, gripped tightly, they should provide good bases upon which to work for almost any shaped article.

The various sketches in this column of course refer to irregular shaping and forming of sheet metal, but, with sufficient care, any of the shapes shown in the opposite column could soon be accomplished with the careful study of the shapes shown combined with one's own ingenuity in making the bend.

METAL WORK FOR THE AMATEUR

VARIOUS OTHER HINTS ON BENDING SHEET METAL, ETC.

The first illustration shows how to form a square section. Place some hardwood to suit the inside dimensions required and form a rebate on the face a little less in depth than the metal is thick, and wide enough to provide sufficient overlap for soldering.

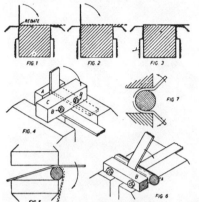

Start bending with the metal in this rebate, clamped in the vice as shown in **fig. 1**.

Fold as shown by the dotted line. Turn the block in the vice as in **fig. 2** and again fold over.

Then repeat twice, finishing with the last side overlapping the piece in the rebate (**fig. 3**). Cut the sheet off flush and solder the joint.

Figure 4 shows how to make a double right-angle bend. The first bend can be made in the vice, but the second is made easier by the addition of blocks "a" and "c" bolted together as shown at "b." The height of "c" should be less than the inside width of the bend. Block "a" is secured in the vice.

The next sketches show the formation of U-shaped bends in two stages. Select a suitable round rod and bend the strip round this in the vice as far as possible (**fig. 5**). This is clamped in the vice flush with the top of the jaws so that the round piece rests on the jaws. Then bend as in **fig. 7**.

Bending a loop at the end of a strip is shown in **fig. 8**. If necessary, cut off the extreme end of the strip as at "a" (after the first bend), as this is often left uncurved. Then continue bending.

Twisting is easy if the length of the twist is not too short, a spanner being used as in **fig. 9**. The top of the vice should be set level with the lower limit of the twist and the underneath of the spanner jaws flush with the upper level.

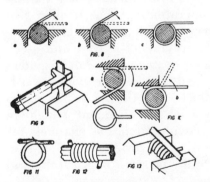

Formation of loops (fig. 10) Grip the end of the rod as at "a," and bend right round into the dotted position to lie over and in line with the starting end.

Move the loop down in the vice so that the jaws grip both sides and bend back the projecting end as per dotted line "b." Cut off the waste end and finish as at "c."

A ring is formed as in **fig. 10** up to stage "b," after which the two sides are cut across with a saw either together at the same point or separately at different points so that the ends can be filed down to give an exact fit (**fig. 11**) when sprung together. When several rings are required, wind the metal round the rod like a spring (**fig. 12**) and squeeze the lot together in the vice for cutting.

These illustrations and methods of doing this type of work are all self-explanatory and may be useful to some who may have to do such work at short notice.

SOAP LUBRICATES SHEET METAL TO HELP CUT WITH SHEARS

If you have some heavy sheet metal to cut with shears, the job can be made easier by marking the line of the cut on the metal with a bar of soap. This will serve as a lubricant so that the shears will cut the metal with less effort.

SOAP LUBRICANT WILL ALSO HELP PUNCHING OF SHEET METAL

The annoyance of a metal punch sticking in the sheet metal when a number of ho'es are punched may be minimised by keeping a bar of soap at hand and pushing the point of the punch into the soap at frequent intervals. In this way, sufficient lubrication is provided to ease the withdrawing of the punch.

MAKING VARIOUS ARTICLES FROM SHEET METAL

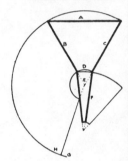

To shape sheet metal to make various patterns, first sketch the pattern to the size required, examples of which are given here. They may appear complicated, but the work is not so difficult.

In the case of a funnel, when drawing the sides B and C, carry on with them until they join at E (as shown); then centre your compass on E and draw a circle which connects with both ends of line A.

Then measure the circle between the points where it touches line A and carry on round to a distance of 3 and one-seventh times that distance to point H. Then connect H and E and you will have the correct pattern for a cone of the same size as ABCD. To make the spout, carry on in the same manner as indicated in the sketch.

The Tray shown can be made in the same way.

It is first drawn and provision is made for folding the sides and for a finishing edge.

Such a tray should not leak, and, if it is likely to come into contact with heat, it should not be soldered.

After having drawn the pattern, cut it out and lay it on the tin; mark round it and then cut the pattern out.

A METHOD OF FLUSH RIVETTING

Assuming that a pin is to be rivetted to a metal plate, the shank of the pin is made a light drive or fit into the hole in the plate. The hole is countersunk to a definite extent, and the top of the pin is turned with a depression so as to leave a thin edge all round and standing above the hole as shown.

After inserting the shank of the pin into the hole, the hollow end portion is either rivetted over in the usual manner so as to fill the countersunk part of the hole,

or is rolled over it in a suitable machine. The volume of metal in the raised part of the rivet should be equal to the volume of the countersink after the rivet is inserted and the flat end of the rivet should be flush with the surface of the plate.

FORGING AND TEMPERING YOUR OWN TOOLS

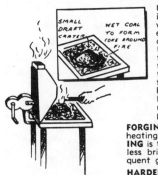

SMALL DRAFT CRATER — WET COAL TO FORM COKE AROUND FIRE

Useful tools are easy to make in the home workshop if the worker understands the essentials of forging, and of annealing, hardening and tempering steels, and the following notes from successful workers may be of value to many. Steel is softest and toughest when **annealed**, hardest and most brittle when **hardened**, and in an intermediate condition when **tempered.**

FORGING is to heat into shape by heating and hammering. **ANNEALING** is to soften, toughen and make less brittle by heating and subsequent gradual cooling.

HARDENING is caused by heating and **sudden** plunging into water or oil, whilst **TEMPERING** is the bringing of steel, after it has been shaped, to a proper degree of hardness and toughness for a particular job. Steel that has been hardened by high heating and sudden cooling usually requires to be gently reheated to a degree dependent upon its subsequent use and it is this latter process that is strictly called tempering. This latter work can be done by blow or acetylene torch and even by the kitchen gas burner for small articles such as screwdrivers, etc.

PLACE FOURTH BRICK ON TOP

For forging, hardening and tempering steel in a forge, "Blacksmith's" coal is ideal, but, lacking this, use any coal but "coke" it up by building up a good mound of fire—open up a small crater in the centre—and thoroughly wet the surrounding coal with water. This will cause the coal nearest the hot crater to form a kind of coke, which is raked into the centre as needed. Always keep the outer part of your coal bed in the forge thoroughly wet whilst working and gradually rake in the newly formed coke to the centre (see fig. 1).

Practically 90 per cent. of all small work on hand tools can be done with an ordinary gasoline blowtorch, and its efficiency is greatly improved if the flame is directed against even a common brick and between two other bricks (as shown), thus confining its heat directly to the work.

Steel should be FORGED at a bright cherry red heat, and light hammering should be continued as quickly as possible as the metal cools. When flattening, tapering or otherwise "drawing" the object to the required form, be sure and forge it on ALL sides and also on the end. In forging a screwdriver or chisel, etc., hammer first to flatten the sides, then on the edges so formed so as to compact and toughen the metal; and when tapering the butt of a cold chisel, first hammer to a slight taper, then strike a few blows against the end, to upset and avoid folding in a hole—then taper some more, and so on (see following illustration). Tools should be forged to conform as near as possible to their finished shape, keeping the grain of the steel following the general shape. For home-made tools, the simple carbon steels are best; they are easy to handle and these notes confine themselves to this type.

ANNEALING. Most tool steel is annealed to working temper, but if using unannealed steel, or old files, first anneal the stock by heating it to bright red, and burying it in a large bed of hot embers until the fire is cold and the steel also. When necessary to forge such stock, rather than cutting it to shape, merely give it one red heat, let it cool to black, then proceed with the forging. DO NOT heat any kind of tool steel to a white heat or you will burn out the carbon content, rendering it useless.

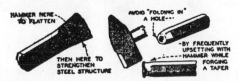

HAMMER HERE TO FLATTEN — THEN HERE TO STRENGTHEN STEEL STRUCTURE — AVOID "FOLDING IN" A HOLE — BY FREQUENTLY UPSETTING WITH HAMMER WHILE FORGING A TAPER

When hardening and tempering a steel tool, if you should happen to get the working edge too soft, do not try and temper it by any further operations until you have first annealed it as above described, and then hardened it again.

In **HARDENING,** you bring it to a bright cherry red, not too quickly, but thoroughly, without over-soaking it, and then suddenly quench it in water or oil. This leaves it very hard and brittle —much too brittle for use—but it is a preliminary to **TEMPERING.**

TEMPERING is really the taking of a little of this brittleness out, leaving it just hard enough for the particular job. The degree of hardness is usually determined by the colour given to the steel at various heats after it has been polished and reheated **following the hardening.**

Before the final tempering, the tool should be brought to a bright "steel" colour by polishing, so that the tempering colours may be seen running from the reheated spot to the point. Polish it, and particularly the cutting edge, with coarse abrasive cloth.

The following table gives the usual run of tempering colours on the polished steel at various heats in their approximate order and, as soon as the correct heat is indicated by the colour, quench the tool instantly in at least 2 or 3 gallons of rain water, mov-

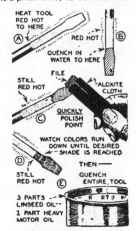

HEAT TOOL RED HOT TO HERE (A) — RED HOT (B) — QUENCH IN WATER TO HERE — STILL RED HOT — FILE — ALOXITE CLOTH — QUICKLY POLISH POINT (C) — WATCH COLORS RUN DOWN UNTIL DESIRED SHADE IS REACHED (D) — STILL RED HOT (E) — THEN — QUENCH ENTIRE TOOL — 3 PARTS LINSEED OIL — 1 PART HEAVY MOTOR OIL

ing it about rapidly in the water. Then test it. It should be "file" proof and hard enough to make a deep scratch on a piece of glass.

Colour		Approx. °F.	Tools
Pale Yellow	approx.	430°F.	Lathe Tools.
Straw Yellow	"	450	Hammer Faces. Razors. Planing and Slotting Tools for Steel and Iron. Wood Engraving Tools. Drills.
Straw Brown	"	470	Leather Cutting Dies. Boring Cutters. Rock Drills. Screw Cutting Dies. Inserted Saw Teeth. Taps. Shear Blades for Hard Metals.
Yellowish	"	490	Punches & Dies. Planing & Moulding Cutters for Hardwood. Penknives, Shears. Scissors. Gauges.
Reddish Brown	"	510	Hand Plane Irons. Wood Borers. Stone Cutting Tools. Twist Drills. Wood Working Chisels. Augurs.
Light Purple	"	530	Cold Chisel Sets for Steel & Castiron. Axes. Gimlets. Needles. Hacksaws.
Dark Purple or Bluish	"	550	Moulding & Planing Cutters for Softwood. Shear Blades for Soft Metals. Circular Saws for Metal & Wood. Screwdrivers.
Darker Blue	"	570	Springs. Hand Saws.

The heat should be evenly distributed over the entire working edge of the tool; chisels and other edge tools should be turned about in the fire to assure even heat and knives, etc., should always be held edge upward in a fire sufficiently large to heat the entire edge at the one time.

TEMPERING may be done in several other ways (see opposite). Heating in a flame (a) does fairly well on some work, but is uncertain in other work. Dipping the work into a pot of melted lead (b) and removing it every few seconds to watch the colours also does well whilst a large pan of dry sand (c) heated over a gas burner, and kept constantly stirred, gives quite good results.

ROUGH POLISH AFTER HARDENING (A) — HEAT BACK OF WORKING EDGE — TOOL — WIRE — MOLTEN LEAD (B) — STIR CONSTANTLY (C) — DRY SAND — GAS STOVE

However, one of the most dependable methods of combining both hardening and tempering on small tools such as chisels, punches, screwdrivers, etc., is as follows (see top right-hand drawings). First, have at hand a piece of coarse, sharp abrasive cloth wrapped round a file; heat about 2 inches of the end of the tool to cherry red (a); dip no more than ¾ inch of the point carefully into water to harden (b).

FORGING AND TEMPERING YOUR OWN TOOLS

Remove, and very quickly rub the abrasive over the hardened point to brighten it (c), then watch the tempering colours run down from the red spot towards the point (d) and the instant the desired colour reaches the point, quench the entire tool in water or oil (e) as indicated by the purpose of the steel.

Another good variation consists of: first, heat and quench the entire end of tool, to harden; next, polish the end of tool with abrasive cloth; finally, heat a small spot about 1 in. back of point to cherry red and when the desired tempering colour reaches the point, quickly quench as above described.

Another way (see above diagram) is to polish the hardened tool, then lay it in close contact with a piece of red-hot iron until the desired tempering colour shows, before quenching. REMEMBER, hardening intended to produce hardness is opposed to tempering, which is intended to remove a portion of this hardness.

CASE HARDENING OR CYANIDING

Repeated grinding and sharpening of chisels, etc., eventually result in wearing away the hardened portions at the working edge and if such tools do not readily respond to rehardening and tempering they were probably made of a very low carbon alloy. To return them to useful service they must therefore be case hardened.

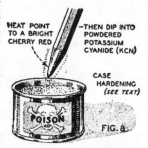

After dressing the tool to the desired shape, heat it to a bright cherry red and dip the point into powdered potassium cyanide which will immediately melt and flow over the surface, giving it a varnished appearance. Replace in fire and reheat to cherry red; again dip in cyanide and reheat. Repeat from 2 to 6 times, according to thickness of tool, finally quenching in water. The result will be a tool that is almost glass hard on the outside but with a soft tough inner core of great strength.

The use of cyanide need not be looked upon as more dangerous than any other chemical compounds. It is deadly if taken internally, but so is tincture of iodine, which we keep in the bathroom.

Hardening tools in this manner is safe and harmless if the workman does not deliberately inhale the fumes.

OTHER HINTS ON FORGE WELDING (from a different source).

1. A clean fire, free of ash and dirt, is required—built from a good grade of soft coal, well coked; that is, with all the oils heated out of it. The fire must be packed down, and all coke broken into small pieces.

2. Both pieces of metal must be evenly heated and both brought to a welding heat at exactly the same time. Welding heat is determined by watching the flame over the fire for "steel" stars seen coming from the pieces being welded.

3. As soon as welding heat is reached, the pieces must be handled quickly before the metal has a chance to cool. Be sure that both pieces are sparking. On way to the anvil, tap both pieces gently to jar off any dirt sticking to them.

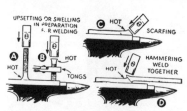

4. Overlap pieces on the anvil in the position in which they are to be welded and tap gently at first with the hammer. As the pieces cool, increase the hammer pressure.

5. Do not use coal until it is thoroughly coked. A smoky fire is not a hot fire. The fire should be a solid, white-hot mass of coals; above this body should be about 1 in. of blue flame.

6. The beginner always forces his blower too much. A low blast is preferable as it forces just enough air through the coal for the fire to consume. Too much blast chills the iron rather than heats it.

7. Do not stick the pieces being welded too low in the fire. There should be at least 1½ to 2 in. of live coals below.

8. Never permit pieces being welded to be exposed to air while heating. They should be covered with at least ¼ in. of coals.

9. There is a tendency for the beginner to burn the metal. A careful watch must be kept of the fire. **At the first sign of sparks or "stars,"** turn the pieces in the fire and then remove for welding.

Whilst forge welding can be accomplished without preparing the metal in advance, the weld is likely to be ungainly unless the pieces are scarfed (bevelled) so that they will overlap. Furthermore, to compensate for any loss of metal due to melting in the fire, the pieces are generally upset or pushed back, thus making them thicker at the spot where they are to be welded.

It is better to heat the pieces (short heats are easiest to work) and upset the ends as shown at A and B, then scarf them as at C. They are brought to the welding heat, fitted together on the anvil, and hammered together as at D. A flux is not essential, but clean sand, borax, or a commercial flux may be used, if necessary.

The completed weld should be somewhat thicker at the joint because it is a relatively simple matter to draw the metal out, but almost impossible to thicken the metal at the welded joint if it is too thin.

FORGING HOME-MADE COLD CHISELS

Tool steel suitable for cold chisels, etc., can be purchased but if one desires to make one's own tools, it can be done. Hexagon

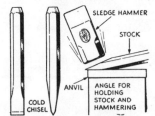

or octagon steel is preferred, although old round or square files make excellent chisels. Tool steel should never be worked when above a bright red heat, nor forged when the heat has dropped below a dull red heat.

Forge the taper of a chisel evenly on both sides by holding the steel at an angle on the anvil as shown. Placing the steel close to the edge of the anvil permits the hammer to overhang the edge of the anvil, which results in a fine point on the chisel. As the point thins, the metal spreads; to remedy this, the chisel is placed on edge on the anvil and forged to size.

HARDENING A COLD CHISEL

1. Place the forged chisel in the fire, bring it up to a bright red colour, and quickly plunge in entirely into a bucket of water (not too cold). Then leave until cold.

2. Grind the edge and do any necessary dressing.

3. Polish the point for about 1½ in. back from the edge with emery cloth.

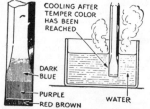

4. Tempering may be done with a blow-torch by heating the chisel about 2 in. up from the cutting edge, or by placing the head of the chisel in the forge fire. Keep the point out of the flame. The heat will travel towards the point until it reaches the polished part. The first colour to appear there is light yellow, then brown, red, purple, dark blue and pale blue.

For metal working, the tip should be dark brown for about 1/16th inch. When the brown colour reaches the tip of the cutting edge, it must be at once plunged into water or oil. Do not dip the entire chisel when tempering, as this would harden the body, which might then break.

METAL WORK FOR THE AMATEUR

FASTENING HEAVY WIRE, ETC., WITHOUT WELDING

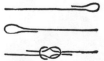

To fasten heavy wire or rods together without the necessity of welding them, bend them into the shape shown in this drawing, and put them together in the form of a knot.

Then get a hammer and hammer this knot closely together. It will be found quite effective and a most useful way of tieing rods, etc. It is also quite a good way to effect a fence repair as the join is quite firm.

HOW TO MAKE SUCH THINGS AS IRON RAILS WITHOUT WELDING

Many amateurs have hesitated to make things like this because of lack of welding facilities, but this handy method does not imply welding and quite a variety of such designs can easily be made.

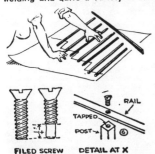

This is a typical example of hand railings erected on a short flight of steps. A point to remember when planning railings is that the materials should be of standard size.

First, make a full size drawing showing the brickwork, and the type of railing desired as shown in the lower of these illustrations. Pay strict attention to the accuracy of the measurements so that the drawing can be consulted for testing when the various parts are cut out.

FILED SCREW   DETAIL AT X

Working from the drawing, measure and cut all vertical pieces, keeping both ends square. Allow 3 in. on the lengths of each piece for setting into the brickwork. Then bend the top rail to shape. For this, use the diagram frequently for testing. Mark on the top rail the positions of the holes to be bored for screwing the nail to the uprights. These holes must be drilled and countersunk at an angle. A wooden guide block will help.

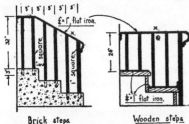

Brick steps   Wooden steps

Burred edges and other irregularities must be filed off. To get an easy start when screwing at an angle, the ends of the screws are ground off as shown above. The frame work can now be assembled.

Mark on the steps the position of the uprights, and proceed to chip out the holes to a depth of 3 in. These holes must be at least ½ in. larger than the iron upright to give room for the setting mixture. The iron work is set in position on the steps and braced to keep it rigid and vertical. Prepare a rich cement mortar and pour this into the holes around the iron posts. Trowel it level on the surface. Molten lead or sulphur are excellent substitutes for the cement mortar.

When the mixture has set, the bracing can be removed. The iron work is then ready for painting. At first a coat of aluminium paint is applied, followed by two coatings of enamel or lacquer.

A USEFUL BENCH SUPPORT FOR WELDING AND SOLDERING

This is a good idea for holding drums or other cylindrical work on the bench when welding or soldering.

The bench is fitted with stops which may be lowered or raised to the desired height as the occasion warrants. The drums are then rotated easily on the stops and are less likely to turn accidentally than they would be if only supported by rollers.

As a matter of fact these stops in the workbench could be used on a number of occasions for other work.

HINTS ON MAKING HINGES FROM SCRAP METAL

Small hinges of odd shape are often troublesome to make and difficult to obtain, but the method shown here will simplify the problem because it makes it possible to use unusually thin metal. The various steps in the construction of the hinge are shown at "A," " B " and " C " In the illustration.

Since each half of the hinge is made by doubling over a rectangular piece of metal, a strong unit is possible. The second part of the hinge must, of course, be made to fit exactly into the first part. Sketch No. 3 is also a somewhat similar arrangement.

A HINGE FROM CAR SPRINGS

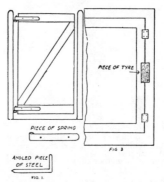

The left-hand sketch shows how the shackle ends of a broken main car or truck spring will make a very good hinge. All that is needed, other than the piece of spring, is a length of round mild steel of the same size as the spring eye. This is bent at the right angle as shown in the small detail. Two holes are then drilled into the spring.

A self-closing device is shown on the right and can be used with this and other hinges shown here. The door is hung on the hinges and a piece of motor tyre fastened to the door frame and door. When the door is opened, the natural resiliency of the rubber will close the door.

ANOTHER SIMPLE TYPE HINGE

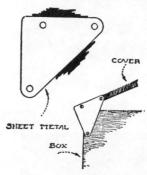

A triangular piece of sheet metal is all that is needed to make this simple hinge.

Three holes are drilled as shown. The cover of the box is attached to the two holes at the top of the hinge and the other hole acts as the pivot upon which the cover swings.

Round-head wood screws are used to attach the hinge. This type can be built to any size to suit the particular box concerned.

HINGES FROM FLAT IRON

This type can be made from flat iron, the gauge of which depends upon the weight to be carried by the hinges. First, cut out four pieces, oblong shape, as shown at (a). Then bend in the centre

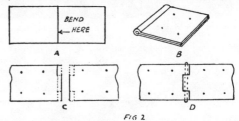

FIG 2

around a piece of heavy gauge wire into the form shown at (b). Then cut out pieces to shape and to correspond one with the other, as at (c). Finally, fit together and pin as at (d), and then drill holes for the screws. Remember that it takes four pieces to make the double sections of two hinges.

SOLDERING HINTS FOR THE AMATEUR

HINTS ON SOLDERING SHEET METAL

Materials required are a soldering iron, a quantity of solder consisting of equal parts tin and lead, a bottle of muriatic acid (spirits of salts) and a block of sal ammoniac.

A handy heater for the irons can be made from a petrol drum by cutting out the top, punching a few holes in the bottom, and cutting a hole within an inch or so of the bottom so that the head of the iron can be passed into the fire.

To prepare flux, pour into a bowl (glass or ware—not tin or galvd. iron) a quantity of the spirits and add a few pieces of zinc to "kill" the liquid—this is excellent for general use. For galvd. iron or zinc, straight muriatic acid is used. Powdered resin is a good flux to use for tin. A lump of sal ammoniac dissolved in water makes a good all-round flux.

Soldering sheet metal requires a heavy, well-tinned iron which should first be heated to a dull red heat, then filed clean as in fig. 8, and this portion (while still at a temperature which will just melt solder freely—a dull red heat) is then dipped in the spirits and then tinned, i.e., coated with solder by turning it over in a little melted solder on the block of sal ammoniac. The work can then commence.

However, before using the iron, clean the JOINT to be soldered with steel wool or sandpaper (fig. 10)—work to be soldered must

be clean—and, with the aid of a brush, coat the joint with a soldering flux (fig. 11), i.e., the "killed spirits." The point of the iron should be placed on the joint to be soldered and moved

slowly along, applying solder as required by placing the end of the solder stick against the iron near the point.

When soldering a loose patch, in order to make it firm, run a drop of solder on to the joint first, then hold the patch firm with the aid of the solder stick while the iron is operated.

The edges of any joints to be soldered should be fitted neatly together and the solder should run freely and adhere almost as if it were part of the tin. Long seams can be tacked with solder in a number of places (fig. 12) before attempting to flow the entire joint with solder. Use a large, heavy iron for this.

SOLDERING TINY ARTICLES BY USE OF HOT WIRE

This is a useful method of soldering tiny things such as small links of white-metal costume jewellery and other such articles. These can be soldered neatly with ordinary soft solder as shown in this illustration.

The 14-gauge copper wire takes the place of the soldering iron, and the heat is regulated by moving the burner. When the end of the wire is hot, soldering paste is applied and a warmed piece of wire solder is touched against it so as to leave enough for joining the parts.

A HANDY DRAWER PULL TO HOLD STEEL WOOL TO CLEAN SOLDERING IRON

This is a handy idea to keep steel wool close by for the purpose of cleaning the soldering iron.

If you screw a drawer pull to the edge of your workbench in a convenient position and pack it full of steel wool, the latter will always be at hand for quickly cleaning the point of your soldering iron.

If the wool tends to work out of the drawer pull, drive a long sheet-metal screw through side of the pull so that the end projects into the wool.

AN ELECTRIC LIGHT AID TO SOLDERING

This is rather a good way to help show up any leak in the article to be soldered.

When soldering a leak in say a bucket, tin or other container, much time will be saved if you place an electric light under the object as indicated in the accompanying sketch.

The light will show up the leak so that a quick soldering job can be done, and it will also show up any other small holes that might be there.

HOW TO COIL SOLDER COMPACTLY

A convenient way to handle wire solder, especially when it is necessary to get it into tight places, is to roll it round a pencil, then pull the pencil out and push one end of the wire back through the centre, as shown. Wind the loose end down round the straight end. As you use up the solder, pull the end out.

LOCKING SMALL NUTS ON TO BOLTS BY DROP OF SOLDER

If you have trouble in keeping nuts tight on any article, just draw them up tightly and put a little solder on the first couple of threads above the nuts.

This will keep them from loosening, and the solder can be removed with a pointed tool if it is necessary to remove the nuts.

SOLDERING HINTS FOR THE AMATEUR

POINTS ON SOLDERING ALUMINIUM

Aluminium solder can be made to adhere to aluminium with ease if the metal is properly cleaned, and a flux is used that will chemically react with the surface film of corrosion or oxide.

First thoroughly clean off all grease and dirt, and then scratch the surface to be soldered with a stiff wire brush, as shown in figure 1. This removes the surface oxide which is always present on aluminium.

① Cleaning ② Applying flux

This must be done in all cases.

Immediately after scratch brushing, special aluminium soldering flux is sprinkled over the cleaned surface (figure 2) and a very large, hot soldering iron is applied.

Electric soldering irons of ordinary available sizes are useless on aluminium, and, accordingly, cannot be recommended for this purpose. The flat surface of the hot iron, which should be heated to 500 deg. Fahr., is used to spread the solder on the work. A blow torch is useful to heat the material. It is important to wait till the flux smokes (figure 4) and then apply the solder. Do not apply it before this happens.

If an iron is used, the solder is applied to the iron and allowed to flow from it to the surface of the metal, without moving the surface of the iron. After tinning, added quantities of solder may be applied in the usual manner to fill up cracks and crevices. If a poor job of tinning results, the fault lies in the cleaning operation, which should be repeated. When a blow torch is used

for the heating, which is preferable on large work, the same general procedure is followed, care being taken to avoid placing the flame in such a position that the aluminium may be melted.

To repair a break in an aluminium casting, the break or crack is filed into a "V" shape as shown in figure 3. This operation provides a crevice into which the solder may flow, and assures complete cleaning. When the surface has been prepared and the parts clamped or wired into position, enough flux is sprinkled over the surface for complete coverage. The flame of a blow-torch is then applied to the back of the seam (figure 5), taking care that the flame does not come into contact with the flux. The soldering is completed as described, and the seam is allowed to cool completely before the clamps are removed. Disturbing the joint before the solder has set, will weaken the joint and probably break it.

If aluminium sheets are to be joined with solder at the edges, a

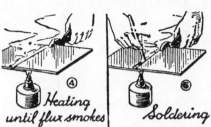

④ Heating until flux smokes ⑤ Soldering

strong durable junction is produced by overlapping the edges, and clamping them together while the soldering is being done. Aluminium soldering fluxes, usually in powder form, take up moisture rapidly from the air

and become useless. Therefore, the container must be tightly closed at all times, except when being used. Flux which has taken up moisture is hard to use and is, in most cases, quite useless. Also, these fluxes are somewhat corrosive if left in contact with the metal, and the finished job should be washed thoroughly after soldering, ordinary water being used for this purpose. After removing the excess flux, the finished surface may be filed flush with the surrounding surface, emery cloth being used to finish the joint. **A good formula used by one man for aluminium solder is 45 per cent. tin, 55 per cent. zinc.**

HINTS ON SOLDERING LEAKS IN PANS, ETC., SHOWING VARIOUS TYPES OF SOLDERING JOINTS

The first essential in repairing small leaks in a kettle or a pan, is to clean the spot thoroughly around the hole inside the

LAP JOINT A

BUTT JOINT B

CRIMPED JOINT C

3 types of soldered joints or seams

dish with emery cloth or some other abrasive until it is quite bright. Place the hot copper under the hole to heat the metal; then rub the upper side with flux, and apply a drop of solder. If one of the solders containing flux is used, then just apply the solder. The solder should not extend below the hole.

Such repairs should be of a permanent nature, provided the kettle does not run out of moisture,

because if it does, the solder will probably melt.

For larger leaks or spots, clean the lower side and cut a small tin patch to cover it with a liberal lap. Solder (tin) the lower side evenly, then apply the tin patch and heat it with the copper until it has been firmly attached or "sweated" in place. Next cover the edges with solder and later file the solder smooth.

The above illustration will give details of 3 types of join which may be found useful. Of course, many leaks in household utensils can be mended by the use of household mending patches which are probably on the market.

SOLDERING UNEVEN SURFACES

SCRUB BRUSH

CORRUGATED IRON

The use of a scrubbing brush will help solder uneven surfaces such as that shown here.

When soldering pieces of corrugated metal together, a stiff brush can be used to apply pressure (in the manner shown); this will hold the parts in place.

The surfaces of the bristles shape themselves to the work so that the parts to be soldered are held in close contact. This idea is not only handy where corrugated surfaces are encountered, but in a number of other circumstances, also.

REPAIRING CHIPPED ENAMELWARE

Once enamelware has become chipped, the metal underneath will rust rapidly unless it is protected in some fashion or other and the following is one good method of overcoming this difficulty.

To protect the metal, rub it with fine abrasive cloth until it is bright and clean. Then use a good flux and give the spot a good coating with solder. This gives added life to the ware and prevents further rusting.

SOLDER

A USEFUL SOLDERING IRON HINT

Many users of soldering irons may appreciate this useful gadget as a rest for the iron.

It is made from a heavy split pin, cut off to a suitable length with the legs spread to an angle of 45 degrees. The shank of the iron should be a loose fit in the eye of the pin. The legs of the iron will always be turned downward when the iron is laid down and should therefore always be in the correct position.

SOLDERING AND OTHER METAL WORK

HINTS ON SOLDERING SMALL METAL TUBING

One may often experience difficulty in holding broken ends of metal tubing in position for soldering, but this can be avoided by running wire slightly smaller than the diameter of the tubing through the pieces before you start soldering.

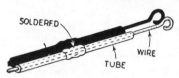

The wire will hold the tubing together and will prevent the solder from obstructing the inside.

Oil the wire to keep the solder from adhering to it. Smooth up the soldered joint and then withdraw the wire. If the solder does not hold, that is the result of incorrect application.

LOOSENING CORRODED TIP OF SOLDERING IRON

This is a useful hint for those who use an electric soldering iron in respect of those occasions when the tip of the iron should become corroded so that it cannot be unscrewed.

The idea is to heat the iron, and then hold it under cold water running from a tap.

This causes a sudden contraction of the metal, which usually will break the grip of the corrosion so that the tip can be removed with a wrench. In doing this, care must be taken not to get water into the heating element of the iron.

NOVEL METHOD OF BALANCING HEATING IRON OF BLOW TORCH

Most blow torches are equipped with a hook that is supposed to go over the shank of a soldering iron to hold it in place for heating.

However, it often takes time and trouble to balance the iron so that it will not fall off on one side or the other. A clip made of an old piece of flat spring metal shaped as indicated will solve the problem.

The clip is sprung over the nozzle of the blow torch and forms a non-slip rest for the soldering iron. When not needed the clip can easily be removed. The arrangement is quite a simple and effective one and well worth the trouble of making.

WELDING THE CORNERS OF A STEEL TANK OR BOX

This useful and novel hint may come in handy at some time or other. It is a method which has been successfully adopted by one man on the land and has proved useful on a number of occasions.

When joining the seams of a steel tank, or the corners of a metal box or pan, try welding the seams and corners on both sides instead of merely on the one side.

While double welding might increase the cost, it makes a strong rigid job which will withstand strains and will prevent the seams from opening and thus causing leaks.

A HANDY HOME-MADE PUNCHING DEVICE

This useful bench accessory will enable the user to punch a hole in $\frac{1}{8}$ in. spring steel which has merely been heated to red heat, and it will make a clean hole with one blow of the hammer on the punch.

The actual punch is made from an old square file, portion of which has been forged to a round shape. A washer is fitted, and a valve spring from a car engine is placed between the washer and the upper plate. The hole in this plate, and the one in the lower plate, must be identical in size, and must synchronise perfectly. The end of the punch should be a neat fit in the holes. Heavy angle iron is used in the making, and should be bolted firmly to a bench or block.

A HANDY HOME-MADE TOOL OILER

This idea will help speed up the job of oiling hand tools and, at the same time, it will make the job less disagreeable. If kept handy, it is always ready for use just when wanted.

The handy oiler shown is made from a small length of 1 in. tubing or pipe and some oiled cotton waste, arranged as shown in the illustration.

The tube is packed with oiled waste, and in use, a portion of the waste is pressed out the end of the tube, as shown.

USING STEEL WOOL AS A METAL POLISHER

This is a useful home-made article which will be found very handy if it is kept in a convenient place ready for use whenever things such as this require attention.

Stuffed tightly with fine steel wool, an empty shot-gun shell that has been fired will provide this very good polisher for metal. The illustration will indicate its use.

The paper of the shell wears away with the wool, so that the latter is always exposed and there is therefore no continual adjustment necessary.

HOW TO BEND HEAVY SHEET METAL

This is one good method of doing this job. For bending heavy sheet metal, mark the work at the point where it is to be bent, and place it in a strong vice with the top of the mark just above and parallel to the top of the jaws.

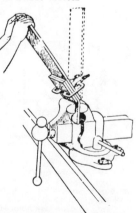

A piece of 4 x 1 in. wood, two or three feet long, is placed on the back, and a smaller piece of sheet metal is placed in front of the work, after which the assembly is securely clamped.

Grasp the top of the piece of wood and pull it forward slowly, and the work will bend at a sharp angle.

This handy little method is well worth knowing, as occasions when it may be required very often arise.

METAL WORK FOR THE AMATEUR

RIVETS AND RIVETING

Rivets are used in many ways, and the following may be useful to some who contemplate doing various jobs around the home.

Figure 1 gives details of three common types of rivet heads.

Figure 2 (usually a copper rivet with a washer) is used for joining wood such as two planks. The rivet is driven through the two planks, and the washer put on and closed up to the work. The end is then riveted over the washer.

Figure 3 is the pronged rivet used in leatherwork, i.e., a rivet with a large flat head, the shank divided into two prongs. When driven into leather of suitable thickness and the job is resting on a metal or hardwood surface, the prongs turn up hook fashion into the lower surface of the leather. Make a hole in the leather before inserting the rivet—if the prongs project at all, they can be prised apart and hammered over into the leather.

Figure 4 — large flathead rivets (tinman's) are used in joining thin metal sheets, and may be made of any material comparable with that for which the rivet is used.

Figure 5 shows the tendency of metal plates to shear the rivet when the latter is not securely fastened. However, if there must be some strain on the work, it should be here.

Figure 6 shows the results of an unusual strain on the rivet, and such positions should be avoided. For thin sheet metal work, rivets from 1/16th to 3/16ths in. are usually employed; the spacing being from ¼ in. to 1 in. Rivets in tanks and steel structures should have a diameter equal to about twice the thickness of the plate. The spacing depends upon the kind of joint and relative strength.

Figure 7 shows a single riveted lap joint, the spacing being five times the single plate thickness.

Rivets less than ⅜ in. diameter are generally driven cold. A single riveted lap joint is only about 55 per cent. as strong as the solid plate.

Figure 8 shows a double riveted lap joint, the strength of which will probably rise to 70 per cent.

Figure 9 shows how sometimes, in larger work (plate 3/16ths or more), although the plates may be drawn together round the rivets, they may not touch each other between them, thus letting in liquids and gases. This can be overcome by caulking and fullering—these processes burring the metal over those places.

Figure 10 shows the use of the fullering tool at " C."

Figure 11 shows how it can be done by blunt chisels of various shapes. " A," the edges of a rivet being caulked over, and " B," the plates of a single riveted lap joint being similarly treated. In a thin metal object, such caulking is not possible, and the joint must be sealed by soldering, brazing or welding.

Figure 12. Forming the Snap Head of a Rivet—In order to drive the plates of the riveted joint together before the rivet is hammered over, a hollow set punch (as shown) may be used. This combination punch has a recess for forming the rivet head.

Figure 13 gives three stages in forming the snap head. "D" indicates that there should be a projection of the shank of the rivet to the extent of 1¼ times its diameter before it is hammered.

" E " shows that first of all the blows should be delivered with the hammer at an angle and the rivet followed round. DO NOT HIT IT HEAD ON IN THE CENTRE. The only exception to this is in the case of a countersunk rivet (fig. 11) where the metal is spread out by direct central blows. "F" shows how the final neat rounded shape is obtained by the use of a rivet snap after the head

has been roughly formed into the conical shape as shown at "E." Holes in plates may be punched or drilled (the latter for preference), as the metal round the hole is stronger. In either case,

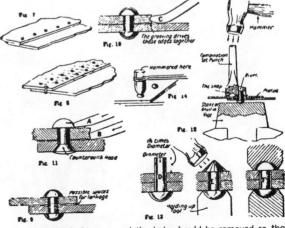

the burr which forms round the hole should be removed so that the edges are slightly rounded.

Rivets for cold driving should always be thoroughly annealed before use. Rivets should be softer than the material being joined. Iron rivets are preferred, as the heads of steel rivets are apt to crystallise when hammered over cold. Copper rivets used in pressure-tight joints to be soldered subsequent to riveting should be tinned before use. They should be first cleaned by dipping in nitric acid.

The use of countersunk or flush rivets should be avoided if possible, especially where rivets are subject to tensional stress. A pan-head or snap (cup) headed rivet is to be preferred. If flush riveting is desired, see previous page. Plain wire should only be employed where both heads are of the countersunk form and where the rivet is a long one.

Figure 14 is another type of punch head used in riveting.

A METHOD OF FASTENING THIN SHEET METAL WITHOUT USING RIVETS

If this type of work should be necessary, it can be done as follows:—

First, drill a row of small holes through both sheets to correspond with each other and enlarge the holes in one sheet to about 3 times their original diameter. Place the 2 sheets together and press the metal around the small holes in the one sheet through the larger holes in the second sheet with a taper punch as shown.

If the holes are in any way objectionable, the two sheets can be bent at right angles and fastened to a third sheet as indicated in these sketches; they can then be flattened again to conceal the holes and also to form a butt joint.

HINTS FOR THE AMATEUR BUILDER

GALVANISED IRON CONSTRUCTION

Standard corrugated iron sheets are made in two widths: 8 x 3" corrugations, which are 2'1½" wide; and 10 x 3" corrugations, which are 2'6½" wide.

The height of the corrugations are ¾". The sheets are made from 6' to 12' in length.

For ordinary roofing purposes and shed work, the Red quality ORB brand is usually used, because it is a harder and stiffer sheet. Use the longest sheets available to minimize the number of end laps.

The average slope of corrugated iron roofs is about 20 deg. pitch (e.g., 4'6" rise on a 12' base), the end lap used is 6" with 1½" corrugation side lap.

For roofs consisting of three or more sheets from gutter to ridge and with slopes below a 10 deg. pitch (e.g., 2' 3" rise on a 12' base), 2½" corrugation side lap and 9" end lap are recommended.

When laying sheets with a 1½ and 2½ corrugation side lap, the two sheets on either side overlap the edges of the one in between, the two outside sheets being reversed, as shown. In order to do this, one edge must be left unnailed until the next sheet on it has been slipped underneath, or over alternatively.

Corrugated iron for walls is usually given only one corrugation side lap, with a 4" end lap.

Secure the sheets to battens with spring-headed roofing nails (or galvanised screws and washers), pierced through the top of every second corrugation at end laps, and three to each sheet at intermediate battens.

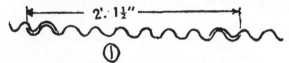

Supports in a roof of 26 gauge Red ORB should not be more than 3' apart if it is subject to walking thereon, as the sag on the sheets would be severe.

If supports are required at a greater distance than 3', heavier gauge Red quality sheets should be used. For upright sections, the supports can be placed up to 4' centres and sometimes more.

Holes are punched on the top of the corrugations to insert the screw or nail, this causes a dent around the hole. A lead washer should be used under the head of the screw, and care should be taken that hook bolts and roofing screws are not tightened down too severely, as this tends to increase the dent by the pressure of the screw. Springhead nails with a **twisted** shank are recommended for their strength and extra gripping quality.

When fixing sheets, first nail through centre corrugation of the sheet 1½" from the bottom. This makes it easier to maintain a straight line from gutter to ridge. If you nail the side laps first, the outer corrugations have a tendency to spread and throw the sheets out of alignment.

To prevent water drifting over the end of the sheet, where the iron finishes under ridge or hip capping or against a parapet use a pair of plyers or the handle of a pair of snips and bend up the hollow of each corrugation.

A galvanised iron roof will last longer if the end and side laps of the sheets are painted before fixing.

It is as well to remember that one should always tread on the nail heads when walking upon any corrugated roof.

RIDGE ROLLS. Edges of all roofs should be finished with a neat ridge roll, ready-made ridge rolls are available where Red ORB sheets are used.

FLASHING. The type of flashing varies according to the requirements of the work, and usually where flashing is in contact with the iron roof, it should be painted and the edges of the flashing beaded very roughly to suit the shape of the corrugations. A 6" overlap is usually sufficient.

TABLE
Approximate area of surface covered by 1 ton, with 1½ corrugations side lap and 6" end lap

8 x 3" Corr. Sheets		10 x 3" Corr. Sheets	
Size. 24 Ga.	26 Ga.	Size. 24 Ga.	26 Ga.
5 ft. 1392 sq. ft.	1979 sq. ft.	5 ft. 1440 sq. ft.	2047 sq. ft.
6 ft. 1418 sq. ft.	2016 sq. ft.	6 ft. 1467 sq. ft.	2085 sq. ft.
7 ft. 1437 sq. ft.	2041 sq. ft.	7 ft. 1486 sq. ft.	2112 sq. ft.
8 ft. 1450 sq. ft.	2062 sq. ft.	8 ft. 1500 sq. ft.	2132 sq. ft.
9 ft. 1461 sq. ft.	2077 sq. ft.	9 ft. 1511 sq. ft.	2148 sq. ft.
10 ft. 1470 sq. ft.	2089 sq. ft.	10 ft. 1520 sq. ft.	2161 sq. ft.
11 ft. 1477 sq. ft.	2099 sq. ft.	11 ft. 1527 sq. ft.	2171 sq. ft.
12 ft. 1481 sq. ft.	2107 sq. ft.	12 ft. 1534 sq. ft.	2180 sq. ft.

OTHER HINTS ON ROOFING SHEDS, ETC., WITH CORRUGATED IRON

Galvanised roofing is usually put on a boarded roof or an open framework. The former has an advantage because of the more normal temperature below. This is not always important, except where used for working under, or for fowls and other animals, or for the storage of anything that will suffer from extremes of temperature.

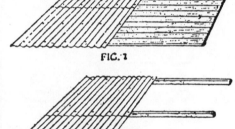

Without boarding, the air below tends to become hot when the iron is heated and cold when the temperature is low. Then there is condensation when the warm air below is chilled by the iron and loses moisture, forming drops of water on the undersides of the iron. If the building is sufficiently open at the sides to keep the atmosphere under the roof the same as that outside, then corrugated iron as a covering is sufficient for most purposes.

If a roof is boarded only and exposed to weather, it is far less durable than one covered with corrugated iron.

Figure 1 (above) shows a large, boarded roof partly covered with corrugated sheets in two lengths, the upper overlapping the lower at the joint, and a line of screws going through both.

Figure 2 (above) shows sheets on an open roof with the sheets resting on and screwed or nailed to horizontal purlins, 4 feet apart.

Figure 3 shows how the iron is attached to the woodwork —nails or screws with convex heads being neater and more suitable than ordinary flat-headed ones. The hole should be through the top of the corrugation, and not in the channel, otherwise the rain will penetrate the building. Holes the same diameter as the nails should first be made and these can be punched.

Figure 4 shows an ordinary centre punch which can be used for the purpose. It is driven in until its tapering body has made a hole large enough for the screw or nail and both top and bottom sheets can be prepared at the one time to ensure uniformity.

HINTS FOR THE AMATEUR BUILDER

ROOFING SHEDS WITH CORRUGATED IRON (Contd.)

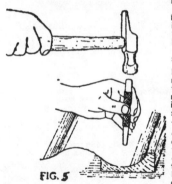

FIG. 5

Figure 5 shows how the punching is done. It is best to lay the sheet of iron on a block of wood, the top side of the sheet being against the block. It will leave a burr which should be filed off.

Figure 6 will show the method of attaching iron to metal, should there be no wood to screw or nail it to. Bolts, such as that shown, are used.

There should be a line of screws near each end of the sheet — the distance from the end being determined by the position of the wood they have to enter, except, of course, in the case of boarding.

In long sheets, there might be one or more intermediate lines of screws. Generally there should be about two corrugations between each screw (as shown in figures 1 and 2), i.e., one screw to every three corrugations.

Ordinary roofs are either of the lean-to type, which has a single slope in one direction, or the span type, which has a pair of slopes meeting at a central ridge.

Slotted curves head

Square nut
FIG. 6

In roofs of the second kind, the corrugated iron needs some kind of cap or covering at the ridge to make it waterproof there. Three varieties of this are shown in figure No. 3 at the right.

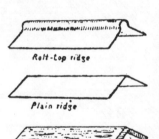

Roll-top ridge

Plain ridge

Wood ridge
FIG 7

They rest on the tops of the corrugations, and screws go through both into the wood beneath. This, of course, leaves space between the channels and the capping, but water cannot run up there.

It is possible to dispense with this capping by arranging the ends of the sheets as indicated in figure 8, but this is rather a rough and ready method.

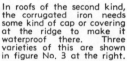

FIG. 8

FIG. 9

In a lean-to roof, the corrugated iron extends a few inches beyond at the highest part, as shown in fig. 9, except, of course, when the back of the house is against a wall, which prevents such an extension.

At the eaves, the sheets project sufficiently to throw water off either into a gutter or to the ground, and at the sides the sheets should overhang by about the width of a corrugation.

A USEFUL METHOD OF CUTTING CORRUGATED IRON

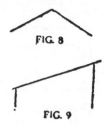

AN EASY WAY

This is a very easy and quick method of cutting galvanised corrugated iron and it will be found quite effective.

In this way, use a cutter or a hatchet or "root topper," shape 1½ in. to 2in. wide, and not a cold chisel.

Cut always upward towards the top of each ridge, as shown here.

Having cut all the "A's" turn round and cut each remaining part "B," also in an upward direction.

A USEFUL METHOD OF REPAIRING IRON ROOFS

The following is a very useful method of doing this work which has been found very satisfactory by some and the idea in question is no doubt well worth passing on to those who might have some such job to do.

It sometimes happens that the nail holes in corrugated iron become enlarged or damaged in some way or there may be some other damage to the sheet, but quite good and effective repairs can be made with the assistance of pieces of lead which can be

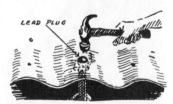

LEAD PLUG

driven into the hole and then flattened out in the manner shown. This serves two purposes, as in addition to filling the holes it makes them waterproof.

In this connection it is better to use lead as it is a substance which does not become damaged under the influence of weather whereas other substitutes may be easily damaged.

As indicated in the sketch, the best way to repair such damage in the roof is to hold the weight under the place where the lead is to be forced into the hole, which procedure will, at the same time, insure that the lead becomes firmly fixed, whilst it will leave a smooth finish. The idea is simply explained in the above illustration.

A HOME-MADE SKYLIGHT

If one has the need of a skylight in any galvanised iron roof and does not want to await the arrival of a ready-made one from the city, the following notes will give a good idea as to how to go about the job.

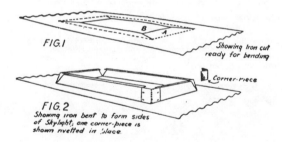

FIG.1

Showing iron cut ready for bending

FIG. 2
Showing iron bent to form sides of Skylight; one corner-piece is shown rivetted in place

Corner-piece

First remove the sheet of iron in which the skylight is to be placed, and on this draw the size of the glass (a); 5 inches in from each side draw another oblong (b); then cut out oblong (b) and also make cuts from the corners to the corners of (a) shown in figure 1.

Bend up the four pieces so formed to make a frame; then bend over a strip 1½ inches wide on the top of each. Solder and rivet pieces over the corners, making sure that they are watertight (2).

Put a good layer of putty on the ledge. Rest the glass on the putty, and put more putty on the edges and the top of the glass. Bend and cut a strip of metal (3) to make a cover (3a) to fit over the frame shown in figure 2.

Press this firmly on to the putty on the glass, and solder to the metal sides.

FIG. 3

Bend on dotted lines.

FIG. 3a

It can then be finished off with two coats of good paint, inside and out, as the latter will hold quite a multitude of sins. The sheet can then be replaced.

It may seem a little complicated, but the job is quite an easy one to any good handyman.

HINTS FOR THE AMATEUR BUILDER

NOVEL IDEA FOR DETERMINING THE APPROXIMATE ANGLE OF ROOF

Occasions sometimes arise when one has the need to determine the pitch of a roof and this can be done with the aid of a pocket-knife, as illustrated here.

As will be seen, the handle of the open knife is held at arm's length so that it is parallel to the side of the house. The blade is then adjusted to the same slant as the roof, when the resulting angle can be measured or estimated.

The foregoing is quite a useful idea, provided absolute accuracy is not required, and it could, of course, be applied to quite a number of other things of a similar nature.

A MORE ACCURATE METHOD OF DETERMINING PITCH OF ROOF

It is actually a simple matter to determine the pitch of a roof with the use of a level and a carpenter's square, as shown here.

Just hold the square on the roof with the tongue, or short side, down. Then place the level against the square so that the underside is at the 12 inch mark on the tongue. The reading on the other part of the square at the underside of the level, when it is held perfectly horizontal, will be the pitch of the roof in inches to the foot. It is quite a reliable method and very simple.

AN IMPROVISED PLUMB BOB

This is a very good emergency plumb bob which will give very practicable and dependable service.

It is simply made from a slip-on pencil eraser and an emergency punch. As will be seen in the illustration, a stout line is knotted and threaded through the eraser, which is then fitted over the end of the punch.

It is then used in the manner shown. It is small and convenient for carrying in the pocket or with other small tools, and is quite a useful and handy article to have on hand.

PLUMB BOB WITH "LONG HANDLE" TO SAVE CLIMBING

This little arrangement with the plumb bob will be found useful on many occasions in building and other constructional work where it is often necessary to establish a plumb line from a high ceiling to a floor, and much time as well as energy can be saved by using the line with a handle, as shown.

The line is tied to the handle, which is then braced between the ceiling and floor so that the line at the handle comes at the desired location.

HINTS ON MAKING GABLE ROOF FOR SHED

Hints such as these are mainly for the amateur and, it is hoped, couched in language which can be followed by any man or boy who can handle a hammer and a saw.

First, always see that a proper plan is drawn up, even if you have to do it yourself. A good scale for roof drawings is ¼ in. to the foot. From this, plan the length of the rafters, etc., which can then be measured off.

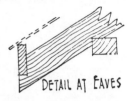

DETAIL AT EAVES

Remember that in case of long rafters, it is necessary to allow a certain amount over length to enable a cutting off of split ends and so on.

In making a drawing for the roof, take care to work in lengths of iron without waste. For instance, the sketch below shows the set of the roof for 9 ft. iron. The overhang of the rafter can be made to suit the iron irrespective of the size of the shed. Anything from 8 inches to a foot is suitable overhang for a small shed. The same overhang should be given the gables.

One chief factor in roof framing is to have the groundwork true and square. In this case it is the top of the shed represented by the top plate. This can be checked for square by means of the diagonal.

The secret of success is to set your work out full size on the ground. In the case of the gable roof, each rafter, whether left or right, is then cut to the same full size drawing and so the roof must go together accurately when it goes up.

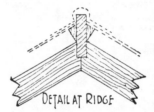

DETAIL AT RIDGE

The drawing here shows all the cuts necessary. There is a bird's mouth on to the ridge up above, the notch for the pole plate and the notch for the fascia. To cut these various notches, pieces of cardboard of **the exact size** of the timber are cut and used as a guide. The notch for the ridge is cut so that the ridge will project just the necessary amount to line the iron up with the tops of the purlins, with the top of the ridge projecting to go underneath the roll of the ridge capping.

If every rafter is cut exactly the same as its fellow (remember that in framing the roof) everything must go together accurately. Do not be tempted into making any alterations in the notches of your rafters in order to correct some other defect. Correct the defect itself. Once you start "faking" the timbers you will get into error and spoil the work. Neither sagging nor hog-backing (which are the chief faults) will occur if the rafters are properly cut.

In framing up, it is necessary to get the ridge up in position first, and held there temporarily, dead centre. Then, if the ridge is long, or in more than one piece, it will be necessary also to strut up the middle, and to take the sag out of it before you start tacking on the rafters. Once the ridge is in position, provided the rafters have been properly cut, it is quite a simple matter to tack them up in position; first the two ends and then the intermediate.

Fascia, purlins, and angle fillet, then follow naturally, after which

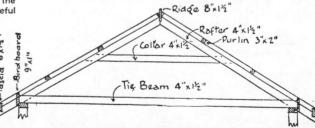

one can put in the bird board which makes the shed bird-proof. The tie beams are spiked across the rafters at the same time as the rafters are put in. This prevents the spreading of the top plate with the thrust of the rafters.

HINTS FOR THE AMATEUR BUILDER

BRICKLAYING FOR THE AMATEUR

To know how to lay bricks is well worth while. To find the number required, take the measurement of the walls in square yards. It takes approximtaely 42 bricks to the square yard. All brickwork must be supported by foundations, usually a concrete base and a brick course known as a footing.

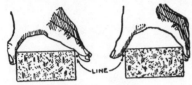

To ensure the bottom of the trench and the surface of the foundation being level, numbers of pegs can be driven into the sides of the trench and, with the aid of a straight-edge and level, they can be fixed to show just where the top surface of the concrete is to come. This is most important.

Mortar Mixture. Mix lime or cement with clean sand, and in a position where it will keep clean. The proportion of lime to sand is 1 and 3, and the heap of lime should be arranged in the centre of the ring of sand.

Fresh lime needs to be broken down from the lumpy state by means of slowly spraying water from a watering can. Do not touch the lime during this process. When the lumps have changed to a creamy paste, it can be shovelled to make sure that it is properly slcked. Then shovel sand over the lime and continue until both are mixed. Add more water if you think it necessary.

Tools required. A shovel for turning the mortar mixture; a bricklayer's trowel; a plumb rule (fig. 1 below) and a carpenter's level (2), both easily made. A large piece of timber (3) is useful for setting out the work. A length of strong string is required, careful use of string and plumb ensuring that the work is kept straight.

1. The First Course is laid either with or without mortar.

2. Extreme care must be taken to put the first layer dead straight on the foundation. Construct the corners first (4), then stretch the line. Then lay all bricks on the first course, working from corner to centre, filling in with broken brick if necessary.

3. Gaps $\frac{1}{4}$ in. between bricks, well filled with mortar. Bricks should be well wetted before use. They should be laid with frogs all facing the one way—up or down—and tapped strongly into bed. Any excess mortar should be squeezed out and cut off.

The sketch at top of this page will give a good idea as to how to hold the brick in setting so that the line on which the work

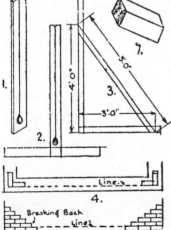

is being done will not be disturbed. A skilful worker will not touch the line even when applying the mortar or laying the brick. Remember, that in laying the bricks to a line, it is very easy to push the line out with the bricks. If you do this, you will finish up with a round wall.

The sketches at top right show how the brick is laid and pressed down (sometimes tapped down) until its upper surface is level with the line.

The secret of good bricklaying is to erect the corners first about 4 bricks high, breaking back the joints (5) until the required height is obtained, carefully plumbing each edge and taking care to get each edge vertical. When both corners are erected, the line is moved up to the second course, and the work proceeded with. If the corners are upright and the rest of the

wall in dead straight line, the wall should be true.

Keep the joints of the brick neat and all of the same thickness; then the tops of the bricks should be level. For vertical joints, the bricks should be buttered with mortar, as in (7), before being placed hard up against its neighbour.

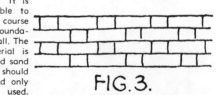

Bricks should be laid on a preconceived plan, otherwise the wall will lack cohesion or bond, and later on will probably develop trouble.

The most popular brick wall (because of its cheapness and damp resisting qualities) is what is known as the cavity brick wall, usually called an 11-in. cavity wall, due to the fact that it is composed of two $4\frac{1}{2}$-inch leaves with a 2-inch gap in between. This latter gap can be made up to 4 inches if necessary.

Now, when a wall is built in this fashion, the bricks in each leaf are laid in what can be described as plain longitudinal bond, shown in figure 1. This exposes the maximum of the brick's surface, with the minimum of joints, and makes a good strong wall, which has not, however, any great artistic merit. It betrays, moreover, that the wall is built as a shell, and is not solid brick.

When solid brick walls are built, two different forms of bonding are adopted. One is known as the English bond (as shown in fig. 2), and one as Flemish bond (fig. 3). It will be noticed that in both these bonds, the ends of the bricks appear.

These bricks are laid as headers, used to tie the wall transversely, and prevent splitting like the sandwich but, although they have a practical value, they also break up the surface of the wall into smaller units and give it a more pleasing appearance.

It is generally said that the English bond (fig. 2) is used where strength is the chief factor, and Flemish (fig. 3) where appearance counts the most. There is no doubt that a wall built in Flemish looks well, and this bond can be imitated in cavity brick walling, the headers in that case being merely dummies cut in halves.

FIG. 1.

FIG. 2.

Plastering. If the work is to be plastered, the joint should be raked out roughly with the point of the trowel before the mortar sets.

A good point for the amateur who wishes to leave his brickwork clean and neat is to rake out the joints neatly when building and then when the work is completed, clean it off with a mixture of 4 or 5 parts of water to one of spirits of salts, after which the work is hosed down and the joints neatly stopped with a good "fat" lime or cement mortar. Do not then stain the brickwork a second time.

Damp Course. It is usually advisable to put a damp course between the foundation and the wall. The cheapest material is made of tar and sand mixed. The tar should be distilled and only clean sand used.

FIG. 3.

There is no exact proportion, because it varies with the grade of sand. The sand should be dry, the tar should be melted and mixed sufficiently to coat each particle. The sand should then stick together in a cake when tamped.

HINTS FOR THE AMATEUR BUILDER

HINTS ON ERECTING A MASONRY WALL

The first stage in building the wall on the foundation is the laying out of the work by means of string lines, accurately set square, and indicating the width of the wall. A simple method is to let nails into the soft concrete of the foundations with the heads just projecting, to which the strings are fixed.

The next step is the erection of the corners, on which the plumbing and straightness of the wall begins. It is usual to carry the corners up 2 to 3 ft. independently, stepping back (fig. 1) and then filling in the space between. For all corners, use a plumb line, or spirit level, with every brick or stone.

Corners are generally erected in brick, though cement blocks and stones, accurately dressed, may take their place. A false guide of about 3 x 1 timber, with two pieces set at right angles, and set accurately plumb in the corner, can be used, and the corner can be built to it (fig. 2).

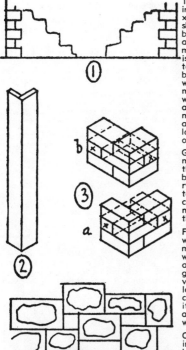

The method of building brick quoins in 14 x 9 in. blocking is shown in fig. 3 ("A" being one blocking and "B" the one immediately above). This is known as a skeleton quoin, and is tied back into the stonework by the bricks marked with a cross, which are headers, and go back into the masonry, and which are tied there by longer stones which overlap them.

Galvanised wire ties may be used between the joints and carried back into the masonry. It is a good scheme to incorporate some cement with your mortar for building these quoins.

Fill in the masonry wall between, hammering the stones well down, and paying attention to both longitudinal and transverse bond (see following article). If the corners are accurate, it is then easy to erect a good strong masonry wall.

One method of building a masonry wall is known as building between boards. This is concrete work, in which large stones are dropped in between the boards and flushed around with mortar.

If the boards are properly fixed, it is easy to build a straight wall this way, but the bond is apt to be weak, and the outside appearance poor. The latter can be camouflaged by roughcasting or rendering up afterwards.

In the orthodox method of building the joints must be well filled with mortar. Do not use an excess of mortar, and where a gap occurs between two badly shaped stones, select a broken piece of stone, jam it into position, and see that it is well flushed up with mortar.

The process of grouting consists of running thinner mortar in between the joints, and is useful for filling difficult crevices. Take care that excess of mortar does not run down over the face of the wall.

It is a good plan to leave the front joints fairly deeply raked out, to allow of subsequent pointing with a richer mortar. Mix a little rapid hardening cement with the lime mortar when pointing. There is nothing difficult in the pointing, and the only thing to watch is that you leave a reasonable amount of the face of the stone exposed. The lining is done while the mortar is still soft with a "graver," which is a piece of steel 3-16ths wide, by means of which a straight line is indented into the mortar, roughly outlining the stones. Horizontals and verticals are kept

true by using a spirit level. After the mortar has hardened, the lines are done out in black paint.

A rough method of finishing off a wall is what is known as flushing up and bagging off. The joints are merely filled up with mortar, and then the whole lot is gone over with a bag, the mortar being wiped over the face of the stone. This class of work does not have a very good appearance, but is suitable for stable or shed.

OTHER HINTS ON BUILDING MASONRY WALLS

In all masonry work, it is always advisable to put a damp-proof course between foundation and wall, otherwise the future stability of the work will be menaced by damp rising from the ground.

There are two chief points to watch. The first is to keep the work perfectly vertical and the other is to ensure bond.

A wall is well bonded when the vertical joints in one course are as far removed as possible from the vertical joints in the next. In brick walls, this is achieved by placing the joints in the centre of the brick below (fig. 1), but in a stone wall this is not so easy.

The term "random rubble" is applied to that work in which a horizontal course appears at regular intervals, which are generally spaced about 3 ft. (see fig. 2). **A wall built random right through is generally stronger than one which is coursed at intervals.**

It is not possible to have a wall of one stone in thickness right through. Generally a wall is built with a face and backing, the largest and best stones being selected for the face, and the backing being made mostly of smalls and broken pieces (see fig. 3). There will be more mortar in the back of the wall than in the front, leading to more shrinkage in the back surface than on the front. This means that the wall will tend to fall inwards rather than outwards, and is a fault in the right direction.

Shrinkage in any part of a wall is kept to a minimum by hammering the stones down into the mortar until they practically touch.

A common fault with inexperienced masons who are careful to preserve the longitudinal bond is to forget the transverse bond in the wall so that the wall splits down the middle (fig. 4).

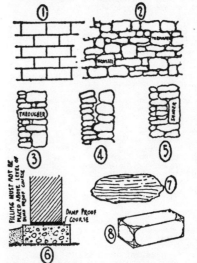

This happens sometimes when the top of a wall is left unprotected in rainy weather.

If rain is threatening see that the top of the wall is covered with bags or by some other method.

Splitting of a wall is prevented by a liberal use of "throughers," or "through stones" which are stones wide enough to go through from the back to the front. It is usual to allow one of these to every yard of wall (figs. 2 and 3).

A "shiner," a stone which is taller than it is thick, is a serious fault in building, especially as it invariably has its strata running up and down, which means that the outer layers will break away easily (see fig. 5).

All stones should be built into a wall with their strata horizontal (fig. 7). Every stone should be trimmed to a rough shape as near as possible to fig. 8. Soft stones can be flaked in the hand by striking with a trowel or with an old tomahawk to knock off any superfluous excrescences. Harder stones are dealt with by placing on a bag filled with sand and trimmed up with a tomahawk or "bolster" (a specie of chisel) and hammer.

HINTS FOR THE AMATEUR BUILDER

WATERPROOFING WALLS

Solid walls of brick or stone are liable to let the water through. Various painting methods are suggested for waterproofing, but none will be effective unless all cracks in wall are first stopped.

This should be done by cutting out the cracks as deeply as possible and stopping with a mortar consisting of three parts of fairly coarse, clean sand to one of cement (fig. 3). If there is any great body of mortar it should not be done in one operation, but should be spread over two or three, so that the mortar has time to stiffen.

Walls of stratified bluestone often allow the water to percolate through the mortar joints. These can be successfully dealt with by raking out and repointing the cement mortar all through.

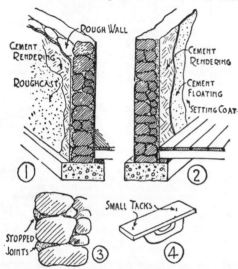

Fig. 1 shows roughcasting method of waterproofing a wall outside. Fig. 2 the cementing method for inside treatment. Figs. 3 and 4 are explained in the text.

It is impracticable to go over any wall and stop up the innumerable hair cracks; therefore, any painting that is done should have sufficient body to close these cracks. There are some paints now on the market which are very effective.

The radical method of waterproofing a wall is to render it in cement mortar and then roughcast. Roughcasting is superior to most other methods of making cement waterproof. All joints should be well raked out, and the rendering done to a level surface screeded off to at least ¾ in. in thickness (see fig. 1). This should be done in more than one coat if necessary, the minimum thickness anywhere on the wall being ¾ in.

This rendering will not assist in the waterproofing unless the sand is reasonably coarse and perfectly clean. Waterproofing compounds can be purchased for mixing with the cement. Hydrated lime is a good waterproofer, and can be purchased in small packets or bags, and may be mixed with cement in the proportion of 9 parts of cement to 1 of hydrated lime. One part of this mixture should be used with 2½ parts of the mixed sand. The surface should be fairly rough from the scratch float; that is, a float with a tack or two projecting (see fig. 4).

The roughcasting is then done with a mixture of 1½ parts of chippings and sand to one part of cement mixed up sloppy enough to enable it to adhere. All this work should be done preferably in the cool weather, and the wall should be well wetted down before the work starts. The more it is kept moist subsequent to completion the more waterproof it will become. The use of bad sand and lack of seasoning constitute the most frequent causes of failure.

All painting methods are best done while the wall is dry. Absolute dryness, however, is **not essential** as long as there is no visible moisture. If it is necessary to paint while dampness is visible, the wall can be dried out piecemeal with a blowlamp as the work progresses.

Internal treatment of walls by painting can be done with a certain measure of success only when the dampness is not of a very bad order. Shellac varnish is a fair water-proofer, but special waterproofing paints can be procured. The newer the wall

the more difficult it is to waterproof with a painting method.

The cementing method should be quite successful. Roughcasting, of course, will be replaced with a smooth coat of about two parts of sand to one of cement, the same precautions as regards seasoning being carried out inside. The setting coat is done with pure Victor Hard plaster (fig. 2). In some places where the exterior of the wall cannot be got at, the internal treatment is best, but the external treatment makes a warmer and drier job.

Too much stress cannot be laid upon the necessity for thorough preparation beforehand whenever cement is put on to a stone or brick wall. If the wall has been previously painted, every vestige of this paint must be hacked off, and the wall left rough, and then well wetted down. In the case of non-porous stone or brick it is a good plan to go over the whole surface with a "soup" or slurry of cement and water.

HOME CONSTRUCTION OF FIREPLACES

A good many farm-built fireplaces do not overcome the smoke trouble. There are four essentials which govern this and at the same time prevent rain from coming through.

The flue must have proper area, it must have a throat correctly proportioned and located; a properly constructed shelf and smoke chamber must be provided and the chimney must be carried high enough to avoid interference with the draught.

In a good chimney air currents travel in two directions, one upward in front portion and the other downward in rear. With a plain chimney these two currents meet at the throat and prevent a free passage of smoke, which will flow back into the room.

These diagrams explain the theory of construction and, although they may be a little elaborate, the general principles should be adhered to. The sloping portion should not begin immediately on top of the fireplace. It should be at least 8 in. above the head of the opening.

Instead of leaving the full opening all the way, a "shelf" should be built out from the back, level with the lower end of the slope. This makes the "throat," which should be of the FULL WIDTH of the fireplace opening (CC).

The depth of "throat" from front to back should be such that the area of the throat is at least as large as that of the flue through which the smoke finds its way to the outer air, and the area of the flue should be ⅛th of the area of the fireplace opening, i.e., if opening is 5 ft. wide and 5 ft. high, viz., 25 sq. ft. in area, the area of the flue should not be less than, say 3¼ sq. ft. Then the throat should be a slit 5 ft. wide and approx. 8 in. deep and the depth from front to back being regulated by the shelf before mentioned.

The action of this shelf in correcting the draught is shown by arrows in sketch "B."

These arrows indicate the current of warm air from the fire flowing up the chimney at front of flue, whilst cool air from outside flows down the back and is deflected by the shelf and then joins the upward current. If down draught is not checked by shelf at throat, it will cause smoke in room.

SIDES OF FIREPLACES should be vertical until throat is passed (to DD in diagram A), and should be drawn in gradually until the flue proper is reached (DE).

If chimney is drawn in at sides as shown in GE, or if width of throat is less than that of fireplace (as shown at F), or if the sloping front began at F or G, the air current would pile up in corners of throat, resulting in smoky fireplaces. A damper is shown open in diagram across throat, but that is not actually necessary.

HINTS FOR THE AMATEUR BUILDER

HINTS ON UNDERPINNING

Some may find it necessary at some time or other to undertake this type of repair job and therefore these few hints might help.

For the amateur, concrete is the easier method, so most of these notes refer to concrete.

The main tools required are:—A post-hole digger, say of 6 or 8 in. diameter; a crowbar and the usual shovel—a long-handled one for preference.

The depth must be decided upon on the spot—it is usually about 4 ft. unless the soil is other than of a solid nature and the piers should be, say, 9 x 14 or 15 in. wide across the foundations and in such a position that they will take the weight of the wall centrally.

For a BRICK pier, the hole to be excavated should be fairly large and in most soils it should not be necessary to retain the sides, but if the walls are in a bad condition or should there be a dangerous corner, something would have to be done to prevent a mishap.

When complete, the earth filling round the pier should be replaced, well rammed and watered in, and the soil above so graded that surface water cannot get in.

To ensure that the weight of the house is taken on the piers steel wedges can be used. These can be driven in at the top of the piers and a cement grout then run in between them.

To make holes for either brick or concrete piers, first clean away the loose soil till the foundations are exposed and then use the post-hole digger to start the holes. This can be done as indicated in these drawings—a good method being shown in the next column, whilst a slightly different one is indicated below.

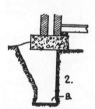

In the former, a crow-bar is then used to remove the soil from between the holes bored so as to make room for shovel work—width, say, about 12 in. Then, when a flat surface is obtained at the necessary depth, the foundations are undercut, keeping the back of the hole as vertical as possible.

In the illustration on this page, the hole is merely sloped down and the foundation cut, keeping the back as vertical as possible. It is also quite a good idea to spread the foot out a little as shown at B. In sandy soil, this idea may not be possible.

For concrete, the standard mixture can be used; say 4 parts of crushed metal, ¾ and ⅜ in. mixed, two parts of coarse sand, and one part of cement.

Make sure that all loose soil is removed from the bottom of the hole before commencing the concrete. The concrete is placed in the hole in stages; first in the bottom as shown in fig. 3, after which boards are roughly fixed as shown at C in fig. 3, although this is necessary only in order to save concrete. There is no objection to filling the whole of the excavation with concrete.

However, if boards are used, the final shape of the pier is something like that shown in figure 4. Some difficulty may be found in finishing the last part of the pier as shown at D in fig. 4. The easiest way of doing this is to allow the concrete in the pier to harden, which it will do in 24 hours, particularly if rapid hardening cement, which is really best for the job, is used.

No attempt should be made to force the concrete up underneath the foundations.

Moreover, as the surface of the concrete will be irregular, it will

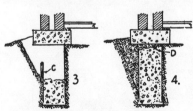

not be practicable to drive a wedge in. It is, however, a simple matter to mix up a mortar of three parts of sand and one of cement, only just moistening it, and then ram it hard with a short rammer in between the underside of the foundation and the top of the pier. This mortar will harden rapidly and will take the weight of the wall almost immediately.

The sketches shown here are merely a slight variation; for instance, the concrete pier in this instance is a little wider and of different shape, whilst the use of "plums" to save cement (stones of about 4 to 8 in. in diameter) is shown.

These should be good hard stones with flat faces, and they should be thoroughly wetted and dumped and rammed into the concrete as the work rises.

There should be very little fear of mishap or failure if the holes are kept vertical. The back may even slope out as shown in fig. 4 in previous column.

It is not a bad idea to place say 4 vertical ⅜ in. rods in the pier to act as reinforcement. Take care to clear away all earth from the underside of the foundations before filling in the concrete. This often means chipping it away and working in an awkward position.

Diagram showing 4 stages of underpinning with concrete. (1) Preliminary post-holes. (2) Hole enlarged. (3) First stages of concrete. (4) Finished job with mortar packing under foundations.

RAISING SAGGING BEAMS

A good way of raising sagging beams is to do so with a plank a little longer than the distance between the beam and the floor, with the aid of a crowbar. Cut a "V" of square notch in one end of the plank, as shown in circle, and place the plank snugly between the floor and the beam, then force it upwards into a vertical position with the crowbar until the beam has been sufficiently straightened.

A notch nailed to the beam at the point where the plank rests will help, and will prevent it from slipping when the strain is put on.

A NOVEL METHOD OF LEVELLING FOUNDATIONS

This sketch will show how a garden hose can be used to find a level for foundations, etc. Use a 50 ft. section of hose, and insert a piece of water glass in each end, fastening them in place firmly by means of friction tape. Now fill the hose with water, hold one glass against the board at one corner and the other glass at the opposite corner or at any desired point. The water lines in the two glasses should then give an exact level. Shorter lengths of hose will do for shorter areas, but the length does not matter, as it can be fixed at various points and brought back to the point desired so long as there is no kink in the hose to force water to one end—the water level will be the same.

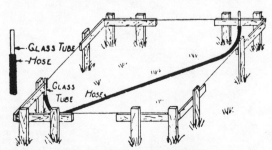

LAYING OUT GROUND FOR FOUNDATION

HINTS FOR THE AMATEUR BUILDER

PATCHING BREAKS IN PLASTERED WALLS

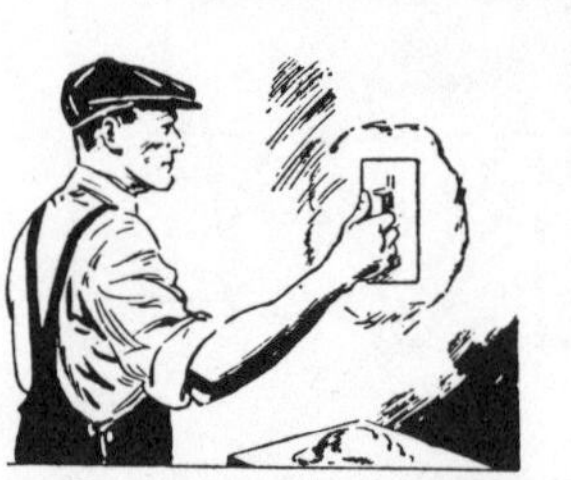

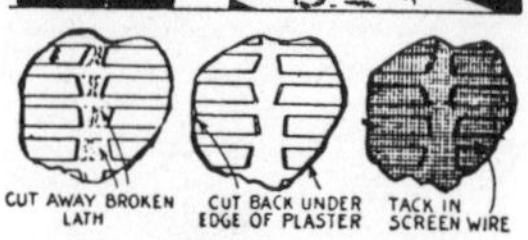

This is quite simple if the following procedure is adopted. If the break is a small crack, remove the crumbled material and undercut the edge of the firm plaster.

If the break is large and the lathes are broken, remove the damaged plaster and cut away the broken parts of the lathes. Then undercut the edges of the firm plaster and tack a piece of screen wire over the lath.

Dampen the edges of the patching plaster so that the patching material will bond to it thoroughly. If a regular patching plaster is not available, a mixture of Plaster of Paris and water will do. Remember one important thing, and that is to always remove all cracked plaster; cut away any damaged lath and then cover with a piece of screen wire.

DRIVING NAILS IN A PLASTERED WALL

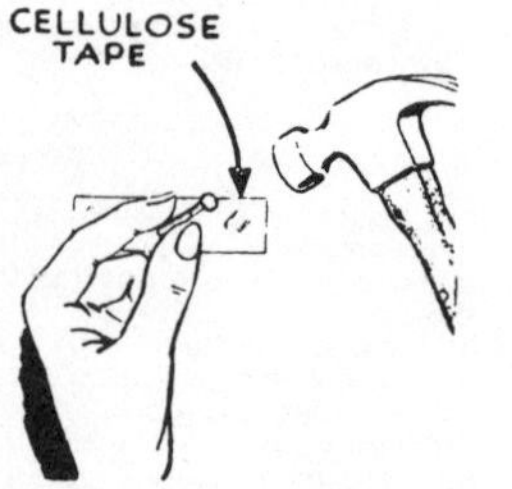

This is rather a handy hint which might save a little annoyance on occasions when one desires to drive a nail into the plaster but is mainly successful in chipping pieces off.

When this job has to be done, try covering the spot with cellulose tape before driving the nail in. You should find that the plaster will not chip anywhere near as easily, with the result that you should have a nice clean job. It is a simple but very effective method not known by very many.

HINTS ON TILING A ROOF

These notes might help those who have a job like this to do.

No. of Rows Of Tiles	Length Of Rafters	No. of Rows Of Tiles	Length Of Rafters
2	2 ft. 2¼ in.	12	13 ft. 2¾ in.
3	3 ft. 3½ in.	13	14 ft. 4 in.
4	4 ft. 4¾ in.	14	15 ft. 5¼ in.
5	5 ft. 6 in.	15	16 ft. 6½ in.
6	6 ft. 7¼ in.	16	17 ft. 7¾ in.
7	7 ft. 8½ in.	17	18 ft. 9 in.
8	8 ft. 9¾ in.	18	19 ft. 10¼ in.
9	9 ft. 11 in.	19	20 ft. 11½ in.
10	11 ft. 0¼ in.	20	22 ft. 0¾ in.
11	12 ft. 1½ in.	21	23 ft. 2 in.

Measurements to be taken from back of gutter to top of rafter.

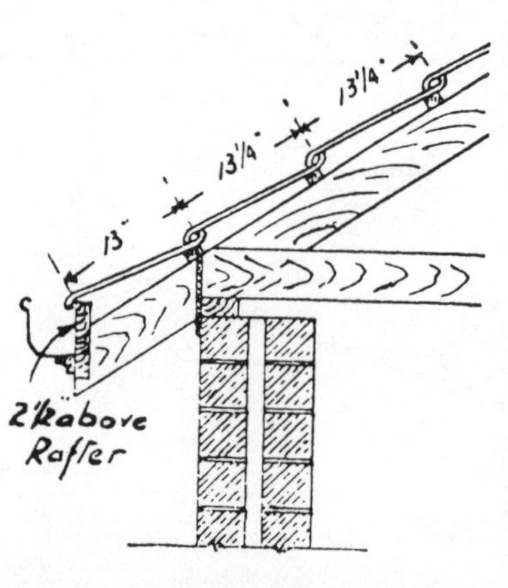

This illustration shows the method of laying tiles, the measurements of each tile, and how they should be affixed to the fascia and rafters whilst, in order to avoid cutting tiles the table given above gives the various lengths of rafters to take the full course of tiles.

The sketch shows **Valley Boards on top of Rafters. Hip Rafters and Ridge flush with Roof Rafters. Tilting Fillet or Fascia to be kept up 2½ in. above line of Rafters.**

HOW TO AFFIX WALL TILES

Things to avoid are mistakes in the bedding mixture, lack of proper preparation of surfaces and failure to soak tiles long enough. Dry tiles weaken the bond.

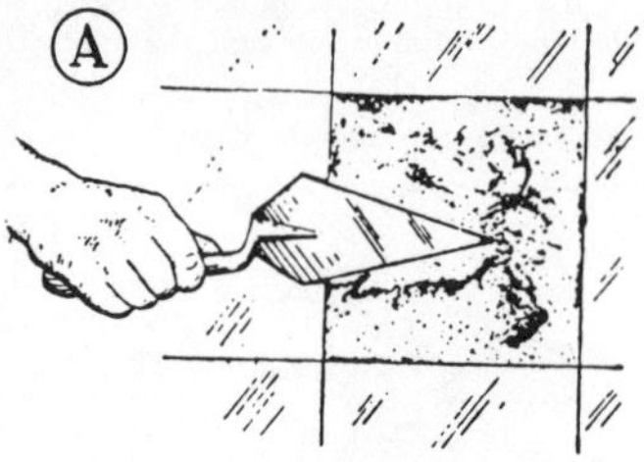

Only prepare sufficient 2 to 1 mixture for an hour's work, otherwise the cement will begin to set, when it should not be worked. Retempering of set cement by further mixing is bad.

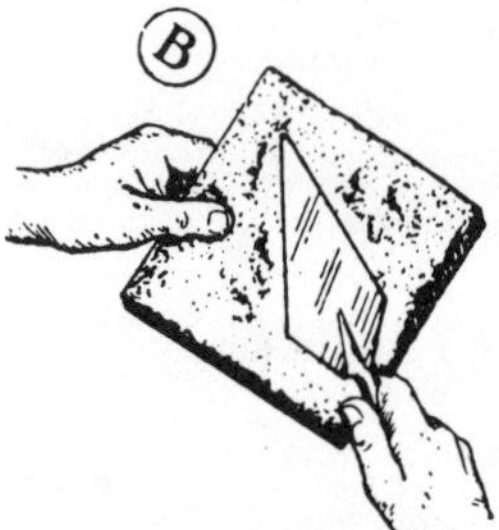

Tiles on Bricks. First clean well by scraping with a blunt trowel. The jointing material between the bricks should be raked out for a depth of about ¼ in. and all loose particles cleaned off.

Then water the brick wall some time before commencing the tiling. Walls should be thoroughly damp but not running with water. Some moisture is required so that the dryness of the wall will not rob the mortar of water, which is needed to harden the cement.

Tiles on Concrete Walls, etc. The same rules apply, but just before "laying on" the setting mortar, dust the damp wall with cement, to ensure a good bond between new and old surfaces.

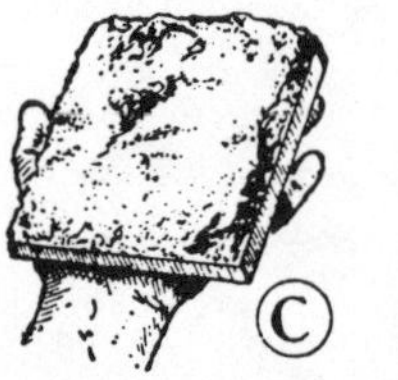

Procedure. The bed of mortar should be about ½ in. thick. For measurements of 4 ft. or more, straight sawn timber ½ in. thick should be set up as temporary guides. To get an even mortar bed, use a long straight edge to scrape off excess material and to show where extra mortar is required.

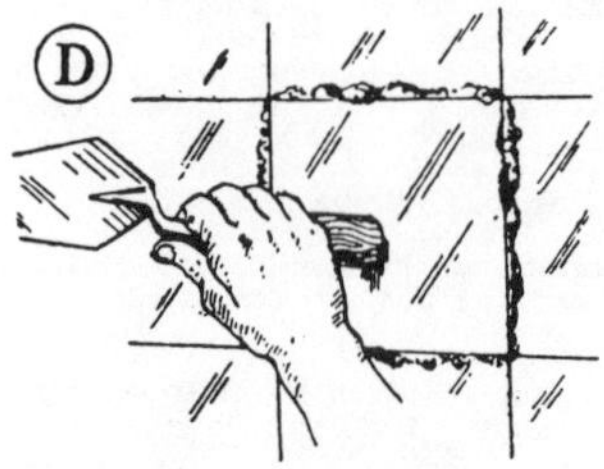

The bottom course of tiles should be fixed first.

Each tile should be soaked in water and a thin coating of mortar then spread evenly on the back. Then, holding the tile carefully with the finger tips, it is put into place and tapped gently with a wooden trowel handle until it is true to line and making a flat surface with the other tiles.

Some excess mortar will squeeze out at the top and the side of each tile; this can be removed with the point of the trowel. A flat piece of board equal in area to about 4 or 5 tiles should be placed over the tiles as they are finished, and gently tapped, to give a uniform surface.

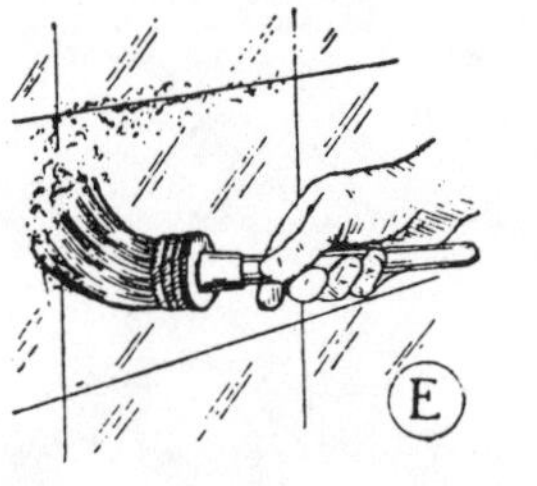

After the cement bedding has set, clean down the face of the job with a damp cloth or old bag, to remove all cement from the face. Do not leave this important operation until next day, because the cement may adhere to the thin film of glazing material in such a way that there is a danger of damage when it is chipped off.

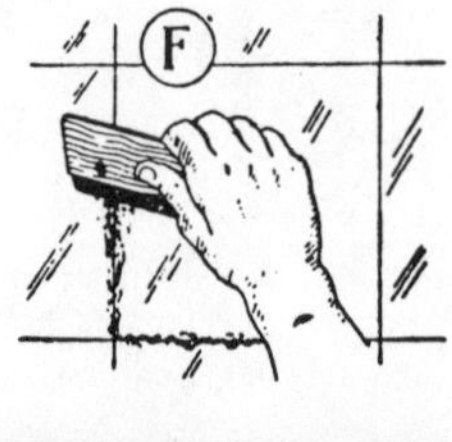

Tile surfaces should be hosed and kept thoroughly wet for several days, to ensure best results. If exposed to the

HINTS FOR THE AMATEUR BUILDER

wind and sun, the job should be covered with wet bags, etc.

Drying Out. After damp curing for about a week, the surfaces may be allowed to dry out slowly. Tiling should not be exposed to high temperatures (as in a stove recess or fireplace) for many weeks after the job is finished. If fires must be lit in less than a month, then a preliminary lighting up of a small fire, 24 hours before, would be advisable. For earlier use than this, special bedding mixtures, using rapid hardening cement and accelerators, would be required. This is, however, a special subject, calling for particular advice to suit each job.

PLUGGING OBJECTS TO WALLS

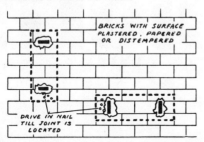

This is a useful method of finding the correct positions in which to plug a wall.

First of all, the object to be fixed must be held in the position desired and a light pencil line should then be drawn round it.

Then, keeping within these pencil lines, feel for the join between the bricks in the manner shown for both horizontal and vertical objects. It should not then be necessary to fill in unsightly plaster holes. When one position is found, one can then find the place for the second plug by measuring of the bricks (the measurement of the bricks being ascertained beforehand). This is a very simple and effective method.

A NOVEL WAY OF SIFTING SAND

When only small quantities of sand or similar substances have to be sifted by hand, a horseshoe placed in the sieve will pulverise the lumps and cause the sand to pass through the screen more rapidly, especially if the sand happens to be mixed with scraps of leaves, twigs or other rubbish.

This idea can also be used for a number of other purposes, including the sifting of flour for cooking, i.e., something heavy being used in the place of the horseshoe as the sifter. It will work well.

SCREENING SAND AUTOMATICALLY BY ITS OWN WEIGHT

Sand screening can be simplified by providing an ordinary screen with a counter-weighted wheeled frame, arranged to slide back and forth over the screen in the manner illustrated.

The sand is shovelled on to the frame, which, when loaded, starts moving downward, spreading the sand uniformly over the entire surface of the screen.

Piling up of sand is prevented by the movement of the frame. As soon as enough sand has been sifted to lighten the frame sufficiently, the counterweight pulls it back to the top.

Then the process is repeated and it is not therefore necessary for the worker to constantly scrape the screen with his shovel to keep the sand going through.

HOME-MADE TOOL TO ASSIST IN TOE-NAILING

When a stud or post has to be fixed to the floor without a mortice and tenon joint, it is usually fastened by what is known as " toe-nailing"; nails being driven diagonally through the stud into the floor.

Care must be taken in doing this so that the first nail put in does not drive the stud out of line. The tool illustrated here will be found useful for this purpose.

It is made from an old flat file with a deep "V" notch ground in the broad end and fitted into a substantial handle. The prongs are pressed into the floor at the foot of the stud, which can then be easily held firmly while a nail is driven in on the opposite side.

A SIMPLE METHOD OF HOLDING FLOORING TIGHT
Whilst Nailing it to Joists

With this block you can drive flooring boards in place and hold them tightly for nailing at the same time.

This is a block that not only allows warped flooring to be driven into place without damage to the tongue or groove, but holds it in place whilst being nailed.

A 4 x 4 block is slotted to slide easily upon a 2 in. joist, and a 4 x 2 block is nailed on to this at one end. In use, the block is slid against the flooring strip and struck with a hammer at the thick end. When the flooring is fitted firmly together, a light blow with the hammer at the opposite end of the block imparts a twist or lock to the device that will prevent the board from springing out of place while it is being nailed to the joist.

HOME-MADE TOOLS FOR KEEPING FLOORING TIGHTLY BUTTED TOGETHER

By rivetting three strips of flat iron to a T-hinge, so that the assembly fits the tongued edge of the flooring, you will have an effective tool to force the flooring boards tightly together.

After the free end of the hinge is bent over slightly, teeth are filed in it to grip the sub-floor.

In using the tool, first push the teeth against the sub-floor and slip the other end against the flooring, allowing the tool to

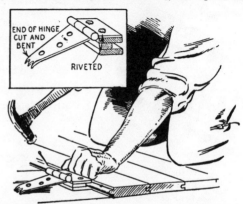

be raised slightly. Then, by pushing it down with your hand or foot, the flooring is forced home snugly, after which it is nailed in the usual way.

HINTS FOR THE AMATEUR BUILDER

WORKING WITH WALLBOARDS

If you are contemplating interior decoration, wallboards are well worth considering, several varieties of which are available, in various sizes.

Besides being widely used in new homes, wallboards are particularly adapted for old houses and they require no skilled labour in application. You can easily do the job yourself.

In most older houses, one of the things most likely to require attention is the plaster, and therefore wallboards overcome that problem, as they can easily be applied over the old wall as indicated in sketch No. 1—the inset showing the corner arrangement for the moulds.

Sizes. The standard size for most wallboard panels is 4 ft. x 8 ft. However, most boards can be obtained in lengths up to 12 ft., and many in narrower widths, and ceiling tiles of various sizes, mouldings and ornaments of the same material are available.

Application. The method depends a lot upon the condition of the walls. If the plaster is badly cracked (as in No. 1), or the walls are uneven and the corners out of plumb, the use of strips is necessary.

Use 2 x 1 pine strips (or other suitable timber) and space them accurately 16 in. apart from centres. They should be arranged also, as far as possible, so that they will come directly over framing members. Cross members should be added also at the bottom and top, also behind the baseboard, as shown in the sketch, to ensure a true nailing base.

Where corners or portion of the wall are out of plumb, the strips should be shimmed (a shim is a thin strip, often tapered, which is used to fill up a space between any part subject to wear) up with thin wood (fig. 1) and it is best to apply these strips just ahead of the board so that adjustments can be made as work progresses.

Wallboard sheets are usually applied in a vertical position, but should you wish to apply them horizontally, a very modern effect can be obtained, in which case the strips mentioned should be arranged as in figure 2.

Softboards usually require conditioning before application. Ordinarily you simply lay the boards singly around the room, allowing them to remain for a day or so until they have adjusted themselves to the atmospheric conditions of the room. In very dry weather or in a heated room, the boards should be sprinkled lightly with water, then piled and allowed to stand for a day or so for conditioning. They should then be taken from the pile as they are used.

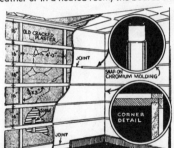

Hardboards are so dense in structure that conditioning is unnecessary, but both plasterboard and plywood that has been conditioned by the above method, are less likely to warp or shrink.

If the joints in softboard walls are to be covered with moulding, space the boards approximately ⅛ in. apart along all edges. Joints which are to be finished by bevelling or rounding are placed in moderate contact, as are sheets or ceiling squares which are already tongued and grooved or rabetted.

A fine saw will cut any wallboard and if the joints are to be covered, a saw cut is sufficiently smooth. For exposed joints, the edges should be bevelled or rounded.

When you are ready to start nailing, the first board on each wall should be checked with a level to be sure it is plumb. It is then nailed along the intermediate strips about 6 in. apart, but nails around the edges should be only 3 in. apart and about ¾ in. from the edges. Galvanised shingle nails 1 in. longer than the thickness of the board are used when they are to be covered by moulding.

All exposed nailing is done with finishing nails of the same length, but driven at an angle and set slightly below the surface, as shown in detail No. 3.

Ceiling squares (or "tiles") in combination with sheets are quite popular and easy to apply if the plaster is sound. The accompanying illustrations show the general procedure.

In putting on the squares over sound plaster, use the adhesive supplied by the manufacturer, applying it in patches near the corners of the square.

On 16 in. squares it will help to apply an additional patch of the adhesive at the centre of each square in addition to the four patches shown, which are sufficient for softboard tiles 12 in. square. Some squares come with tongue-and-groove joints, others are made with a rabetted joint. Edges of both types are bevelled.

In putting up the squares with an adhesive, it is necessary to make sure that each square is pressed firmly into place and that the joints fit true, otherwise the line of the "V" grooves is likely to gain or "run" causing uneven fitting at the finish.

When putting up squares as in the fig. on left, first check the dimensions of the room carefully. If these are even both ways the squares can usually be applied in courses, beginning at one side of the room as shown, but if there are irregularities in size, it is best to work outwards to the walls. On the other hand, if the plaster is badly cracked, it will pay to take it off and fur the joints as in figure at foot of this page.

The furring strips must be spaced carefully, and if the squares are 16 in. filler strips also should be installed, especially if the squares have rabetted joints.

HINTS FOR THE AMATEUR BUILDER

WORKING WITH WALLBOARDS (Continued)

The construction of the building will govern the method of application. Nails, 1¼ in. long, are used to attach the squares to the strips. In putting up tongue-and-groove squares, care must be taken not to force the joints unduly tight.

Sheets whether placed vertically (as in fig. 1) or horizontally (as in fig. 2) are usually applied over furring strips. Manufacturers usually supply directions covering fully the application of their products and it is advisable to follow these carefully.

For handling large sheets on the ceiling, it is generally necessary to provide a "helper" to hold one end of the piece while the other is being nailed.

Finishing. The decorating possibilities of plain softboard panels are many. The material may be painted, stained, decorated with stencils, rough finished with plastic paint, or covered with wall hangings. Water paint, calcimine and other special paints can be applied directly over the unsized board. It is advisable, however, to use a varnish size under calcimine.

Softboards must be sized before oil or varnish paints are applied. Size is available ready mixed and should be applied according to manufacturers' directions. Two coats of any good interior wall paint over the size will produce a good and washable wall. Plastic paint can be applied over most wall boards after the joints have been filled as previously described, without size.

Soft board should be glue-sized for all wall hangings such as paper, canvas, oilcloth, etc. After the size is dry the material should be sanded lightly to remove protruding fibres before proceeding in the usual manner to apply the hangings with wallpaper paste.

Hardboards can be finished with any of the other water paints without sizing but for oil paints and enamels a sizing of shellac, varnish, enamel undercoat or aluminium paint should be used. After applying the size, the surface should be rubbed down with steel wool or fine sandpaper to produce a smooth surface or finishing coats.

Plywood will take stain, varnish, wax or paint and enamel finishes, but it is not suitable for water finishes or wall hangings.

Architectural effect. By the use of a little forethought, some very fine effects can be obtained which add very much to the appearance of rooms. Either " V " groovings or mouldings, which are used to break up large plain areas into pleasing smaller units, are the basis of most of these schemes.

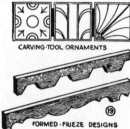

CARVING-TOOL ORNAMENTS

⑲

FORMED-FRIEZE DESIGNS

Almost all softboards are available with bevelled edges for V joints. This type of joint, by the simple addition of intermediate V grooves gives a very fine effect as shown in the small accompanying detail. Note the frieze moulding used which is shown in detail in the sketch below.

The use of wide moulding over joints produces a good panel effect. The wood moulding strips are 2 or 3 inches wide edged with panel moulding to enhance the effect.

The two sides of both hard and soft boards present different textiles and colours, owing to the method of manufacture. The

difference makes a pleasing shaded effect possible by simply reversing the pieces.

Certain tile boards lend themselves to this type of treatment.

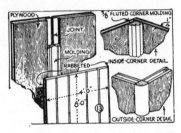

Joints. Plywood manufacturers have solved the joint problem with thin moulding strips set flush with the surface (as shown in fig. 13).

The use of metal mountings for decorative use, and incidentally to hide joints, is specially popular in some countries. These are in chromium, stainless steel and enamel finishes.

For kitchen and bathroom walls, a special hardboard is available which is scored into squares and enamelled to appear like tiles. Metal mouldings cover the joints and corners as shown in the illustrations. These latter represent various types of these joints and mouldings, showing how they are applied.

For canvas or paper walls, the wallboard joints are usually sealed with metal tape and a special putty, making the joint wholly invisible under paper or flat paint.

Whiting mixed with varnish to a putty consistency is excellent for filling nail holes, where the surface is to be finished with a flat oil paint.

Do not use ordinary putty as the oil may work through and cause spots.

Other types of moulds which can be used are many and which give different effects. Most of these moulds are simply nailed over the joints and such spacings as required.

AN IDEA FOR SUPPORTING WALLBOARDS WHILE NAILING TO CEILING

The problem of applying large sheets of wallboards to ceilings when working singlehanded can be solved with this standard which can be adjusted to support the sheet whilst nailing it in place.

It consists of three lengths of 3 x 1 stock, two of which are nailed to a cross of 2 x 1 at the top and telescoped over the third length, which is nailed to a second cross to serve as a base. The 3 x 1 members are slotted lengthwise to take bolts with which the adjustment of the standard is locked.

HINTS FOR THE AMATEUR BUILDER

SUGGESTED PATTERNS FOR TILING, ETC.

These sketches give particulars of some of the very interesting and effective methods of wall and ceiling tiling, whilst the use of the same patterns in floor work is also of ornamental beauty. If in various shades of colour or polished flooring, they will give a very pleasing effect, and will enhance the appearance of any room.

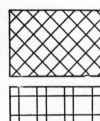

Of course, manufacturers nowadays make some very attractive types of walling and ceiling which can be purchased in very convenient form, but these suggestions are given so that any of our readers might have a choice of patterns should they have reason to undertake this type of job themselves.

It is needless to add that where such patterns are used round objects such as baths, sinks and other fixtures, the material should be carefully scribed to conform with the contours of the fixture in question.

Naturally considerable care should always

be taken before any such job is started in order to lay out the job properly—it pays well in the long run.

Many an ordinary looking room can be made into an attractive one by the use of wallboards, insulating boards or woodwork arranged in a manner such as any one of these sketches suggest.

A USEFUL ALL WEATHER DOOR FOR OUTBUILDINGS, ETC.

By extending the door track as far one side of the doorway as the other, you are able to use two doors.

One is conventional, tight, and when used, completely closes the barn.

The other is merely a frame the size of the first door, but carrying a

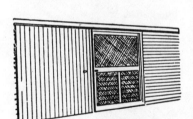

panel gate over the lower half while the upper half is covered with taut woven wire. This door will keep stock in or out, and yet ensures ample ventilation on hot days.

HINTS ON BUILDING WITH MATERIALS SUCH AS ASBESTOS CEMENT AND FIBROUS PLASTER SHEETS

These materials are popular for country homes, milk and poultry houses, sheds, etc., being inexpensive, easy to construct, weather, white ant and vermin proof, and therefore a few general notes will not be out of place.

Walls, ceilings and partitions should be designed to suit stock size sheets and there should be timber supports behind all joints, being spaced at either 2 ft. or 1 ft. 6 in. centres. When fixing horizontally, it is sometimes necessary to let in timber cross-pieces where the joints occur.

Illustrating construction of exterior walls; use of stock sized sheets and spacing of studs (see lower portion)—the wider space being for windows.

Stock sizes are usually 4 ft., 3 ft., 2 ft., and 1 ft. 6 in. wide and up to 12 ft. long, so that practically any convenient size can be cut.

"A"

It is advisable to line both the exterior and the interior walls, using special blunt point galvanised nails at 12 inch intervals and placed about ¾ in. from the edge.

Jointing. The edges are merely butted one against the other, as shown, and cover moulds are used to cover the joints, both inside and out.

"B"

Cover Moulds. Various kinds can be used, ranging from plain strips of various widths to designs such as those indicated here; the latter, of course, adding very much to the attractiveness of the job.

Moulds marked "A" can be used for any joint, whether vertical or horizontal, and to ensure a weatherproof joint, the galvanised strip "B" should be used. This strip should overlap from under the back of the upper sheet down over the front of the lower one, it being covered up by the cover mould.

"C"

If preferred, special combined cover or weatherboard moulds can be used for horizontal joints (see "C"), these fitting under the upper sheet and over the lower, as shown in diagram "D."

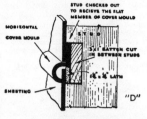

Where these are used, it is necessary to check out the timber studding to accommodate the flat part of the mould (see details in sketch).

"D"

Where horizontal cover moulds intersect at outside angles, it is usual to mitre them. There are quite a number of special moulds for various positions. Internal and external angles are available for any places where the material joins at an angle whilst there are special skirtings for the bottom of the wall and cornices for the joints between walls and ceilings together with various other accessories which help to finish off the job in an attractive manner.

Interior Wall and Ceiling Construction

HINTS FOR THE AMATEUR BUILDER

HOW TO BUILD LOG HUTS, STABLES, OUTBUILDINGS, ETC.

For the building of huts, stables and outbuildings, the "log or slab" hut idea is very often a pleasing variation and one in which construction is quite easy.

Of the two types, the "slab" hut is really more suitable to Australian conditions than the "log" hut, which, owing to lack of the smaller timber in many parts, is not so prevalent.

Slab Huts

The "slab" type is the cheaper form of construction.

The slabs for these may either be obtained by splitting sections of tree trunks round the circumference, so as to have a portion of the "round" of the tree on each slab, or they may be purchased from a sawmill. An advantage of the latter over those split on the site of the job is that they are usually sawn on the inner side, and less trimming has to be done.

In erecting a slab hut, the usual practice in framing a timber building is followed, whilst there are two ways of fastening on the slabs, i.e., vertically and horizontally.

The former has perhaps slightly the better appearance but, for some reasons, the latter has certain advantages.

In horizontal work, there are, say, two ways of attaching the slabs, the simpler one being to nail them on from the outside. Of course, these slabs, then being fixtures, will not take up any shrinkage space as time goes along. Timber will inevitably shrink and so actually the better way is to set the slabs in grooves (not nailed) so that they drop down on to one another and close up any gaps that may form from this cause.

This makes a better waterproof job. The other way is to cement between the slabs, as shown in the sketch herewith.

Nailing. When the slab edges are prepared, lay them on as tight as possible and nail in place. When you come to a corner, mitre the slab ends for greatest neatness. Any corner which protrudes into the room can also be assembled with a reverse mitre.

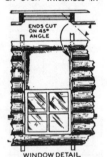

SLAB BEFORE PLANING

SLAB READY TO USE — SIDES PLANED STRAIGHT

Grooving. To erect on the groove principle, nail cleats on to the uprights so as to form vertical grooves in which the slabs cut exactly to fit between the uprights or studs, slide. These grooves or runways for the slabs should be prepared beforehand, taking care to leave the outer cleat about a foot short at the top so that the slabs may be inserted without difficulty. The missing portion is placed in position when the slabbing is completed.

The advantage of this method is not only the facility with which the slabs may be inserted, but when shrinkage occurs, and it may not be for some months—it is a simple matter to fill in the gaps which are left at the top of the slabs through their dropping lower as they shrink, with a narrow slab just wide enough to fill the opening; and as shrinkage continues, wider top slabs can be substituted for the narrow ones.

Cementing. If, owing to irregularities or for other reasons, the slabs are to be nailed into place and chinking used, mix a rather thick mortar of 1 part lime to 3 parts cement and 5 parts of screened gravel, and trowel in place. As the slabs may shrink, put off the cementing for a few days or a little longer if possible.

Trimming. The slabs, either in horizontal or in vertical work, should be trimmed quite straight on the edges, by adzing or otherwise, so that the joints may be close; and for horizontal work, the ends also must be trimmed to an even thickness in order to slide in the grooves (see accompanying illustrations).

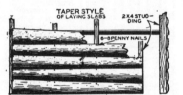

TAPER STYLE OF LAYING SLABS · 2X4 STUDDING · 6-8 PENNY NAILS

Variation in size of slabs. Slabs may vary in width from end to end sometimes—one end, for instance, may be 6 inches wide whilst the other end may be 1 or 2 inches narrower. Laying slabs will then be quite an easy cut and dried job.

The illustrations given above show how slabs with tapering sides can be fitted in one with the other. The other illustration shown is merely one indicating how the windows should be allowed for, etc.

CHINKING BETWEEN SLABS · SLABS LAID EDGE TO EDGE · MORTAR JOINTS · 2 X 4 STUDDING · 6-8 PENNY NAILS

ENDS CUT ON 45° ANGLE

WINDOW DETAIL

Finishing off. The interior of a slab hut may be finished by lining the walls with hessian or strong unbleached calico which may be finished off with strong paper or other preparation. It all depends, of course, as to what use the building is to be put to, and, if a more expensive finish is required, it can be lined with 3-ply or one of the artificial boards obtainable.

The roofing may be made from sheets of bark, galvanised iron, thatching, or tar-impregnated felt; if the latter it is better to cover the whole of the roof with fence shingles or old case timber (as shown in this illustration) which will serve as a foundation for the felt; otherwise it will sag in an unsightly manner.

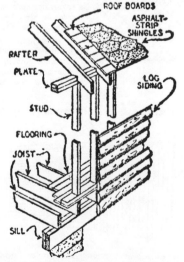

ROOF BOARDS · ASPHALT-STRIP SHINGLES · RAFTER · PLATE · LOG SIDING · STUD · FLOORING · JOIST · SILL

HINTS FOR THE AMATEUR BUILDER

HOW TO BUILD LOG HUTS, ETC. (continued)

The two previous illustrations indicate the difference between horizontal and vertical types of SLAB HUT buildings and the sketch in the centre of this page shows how attractive a LOG HUT can appear.

Log Hut Construction

This is actually buildings made from round timber (or saplings) which have not been sawn to any particular shape and which are used in their original form. In this respect, the logs should have as little taper as possible, and should be about 2 feet longer than the side of the hut required, depending, of course, upon the type of lock joint which is used at the corners. If concrete is not used for a foundation,

Horizontal type of Log Hut

TENON
RIGID JOINING BETWEEN JOIST AND SILL

short stumps may be sunk into the ground for a foot or two, preferably with a large flat stone under the foot of each stump, which, if tarred and treated with white ant repellant will last a long time.

In building the walls, the heaviest logs should be used for the bed logs which should have their upper surfaces trimmed flat (see sketch) and about 3 in. wide, and the other logs would be better hewn flat at top and bottom also, in order to make them lie closer together, otherwise a considerable amount of packing will be needed to fill in between them.

In laying the wall, the butts and tops of the logs should be alternated to keep the wall level. Where the ends are not locked, and every 9 ft. or so, the top log should be fastened to the underneath one by boring a large hole through the upper one and half way through the underlying one and then driving a hardwood pin in. This will secure the logs firmly and make for rigidity.

Where a timber floor is desired, it is best to lay joists and put in a floor of sawn hardwood boards (see illustration at foot of previous page). This is suitable for both types of log hut.

However, joist logs, about 6 in. in diameter for a 12 ft. span, or less, may be laid 2 or 3 ft. apart for a floor foundation, the ends being tenoned and resting in notches on the bed logs. If these joist logs are hewn flat on the top, the floor boards may be laid directly on them.

If the hut is for animals, then a concrete or similar floor is indicated.

Roof construcion is shown on the previous page, but other sketches given below show how ordinary sawn timber can be used or the "log" idea can be carried out right up to the actual roof itself. The top right hand drawing of these two indicates the finished appearance at the corners (with roofing attached) if the idea of the small projecting log is used. Impregnated felt or galvanised iron etc., can, of course, be used as previously indicated.

Other illustrations on this page show various forms of corner and other joints in this type of building and show how to join the logs at right angles. Most of these are self-explanatory and a close study of the sketches will show one how to go about the work.

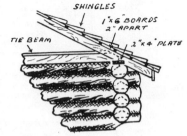

Careful measurements are, of course, necessary, so that each cross section will fit in neatly with its counterpart.

In both " slab " and " log " building, bark improves the rustic appearance, but affords shelter to insects. If the bark is to be left on, the logs should be cut when the sap is down. If it is to be removed, they should be cut in the spring when the sap is up, as they will strip more readily then.

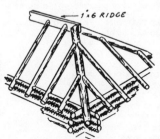

Bark is taken off by making cuts around the tree about every 4 feet and joining them by vertical cuts.

Lining. If a " log " hut is unlined, it is necessary to sop any chinks, otherwise draughts will make their presence felt. Small saplings split or sawn into four, so as to leave a round on one side and an angle to the other, may be nailed into the chinks between the logs with good effect. A brushwood lining or a mud or clay mixture reinforced with a mortar of cement and sand will do, or any other way one may devise himself for such a job.

Earth Flooring. If the plain earth is to do for the flooring, it should be well watered and rammed hard and smooth. One way is to add at intervals, ashes from wood fires, dressing it frequently in this way and by watering and sweeping.

If the floor is earth a drain should be dug all round to prevent water from coming in during wet weather.

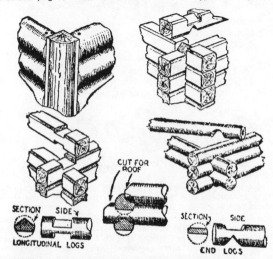
Various forms of Corner Joints in Log Hut Building

Method of constructing a log hut leaving irregular lengths to be sawn evenly on completion of job.

HINTS FOR THE AMATEUR BUILDER

INSULATION

Most heat gets into the house through roof and ceiling. There are several ways of cutting off from the ceiling the heat which is radiated from the roofing iron. Of course, the best way is to use the special preparations which are on the market.

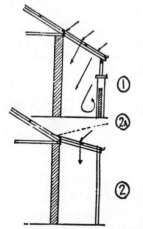

One way is to line the underside of the rafters or purlins with whitewashed hessian. Whitewashing can easily and cheaply be done with a spray paint. The most common method is to pack above the ceiling in between the joists with insulating material.

Charcoal can be used. The smaller the grains the better the insulation. A 2 in. layer of about pea size. It is light and non-perishable. There is also a special non-perishable fibre to be obtained which retains its resiliency and insulating properties for a long period.

Verandahs do not always keep a house cool—they often assist to keep it warm because of the heat radiated on to the walls and verandahs from the iron, which is invariably sloped in such a way that the maximum of radiation strikes the walls.

Fig. 1—This diagram shows how heat is radiated down from a low deep verandah, while a dwarf wall creates a "pocket" to retain the heat. Fig. 2 shows a cooler though less sightly construction, whilst the dotted line 2A gives the style of verandah which would give a maximum of circulation of air and a minimum of radiation on to walls.

This is the coolest verandah, although it is rarely practicable, but where the radiation downwards is unduly severe, it is best to line under the verandah with insulating board. Incidentally, high verandahs give quite efficient protection to walls. Anything over 10 ft. usually gives a thermometer reading a little above shade temperature. The worst verandah in respect of heat is the low pitched deep verandah, partially enclosed with a dwarf wall.

WALLS THAT HELP KEEP OUT HEAT AND COLD

These useful hints come from England, any one of which may be found useful to those who may have occasion to consider this subject.

We are apt to think mostly of roofs when the insulation of farm buildings is under consideration, but walls also have a big bearing on this matter.

Also, as far as animals are concerned, extremes of temperature should be avoided.

The roof is, of course, the first consideration, but when it comes to walls, there are various methods of insulating them such as cavity walls, hollow blocks, timber and iron frames with inner lining, and other features.

Hollow cavity walls are particularly good, and bricks can be used for this purpose. A concrete wall is also improved by a cavity as it is understood that 1 inch of air space possesses the same insulating properties as 4 to 5 in. of concrete. Therefore, cavity construction is a cheap way of insulation.

For a brick cavity wall, the air-space will vary from 1½ to 3 in. in thickness, and metal ties placed between 2 ft. 6 in. and 3 ft. apart in every sixth course serve the purpose of strengthening and tying the two thicknesses together. Also, apart from better insulation, the cavity produces a waterproof wall.

For single story buildings, the cavity should be entirely closed and the wall built solid at openings and at the eaves as still air is a better non-conductor than a moving current.

It is interesting to note that a six-inch hollow block possesses approximately the same insulating properties as a nine-inch solid

wall so that it enables, at the same time, a saving of 6 inches to be made in the overall width of a building.

There are different forms of hollow blocks, and these are particularly suited to steel-framed buildings and offer a quick means of construction.

The illustrations given on this page also include the multivent brick which is used in some parts—this is a 9-inch double cavity block made of concrete and introduced with the object of saving in mortar and time as compared with a brick cavity wall.

There is also the cellular brick, although having the normal brick dimensions, is shaped so that a considerable air space in the wall is obtained when the brick is laid.

WALL INSULATION

BRICK CAVITY WALL

PLAN OF CAVITY WALL CONSTRUCTION IN REINFORCED CONCRETE SLABS & POSTS

Then there are, of course, the cheaper forms of construction, i.e., galvanised iron and timber, which, when lined, are very good insulators.

Where stock is concerned this style is better for the upper portions of buildings than the lower.

A concrete base is desirable for timber framed walls and should be carried up above the floor line with the lowest member of the framing secured to the concrete by means of rag bolts built into the walls at intervals.

A damp proof course is also desirable. Any weather-boarding used should be either the rebated-and-moulded type, or, better still, the tongued and grooved variety.

A form of pier and panel construction applied to a concrete wall may be so arranged that an air space is obtainable in the wall. The slabs should be precast and placed in position from above with the joints filled in with cement mortar.

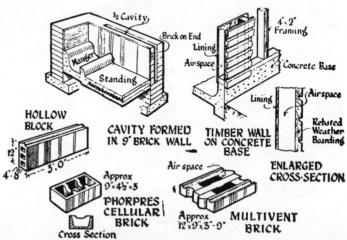

HOLLOW BLOCK

CAVITY FORMED IN 9' BRICK WALL

TIMBER WALL ON CONCRETE BASE

ENLARGED CROSS-SECTION

PHORPRES CELLULAR BRICK Approx 9"×4½"×3 Cross Section

MULTIVENT BRICK Approx 12"×9"×3"-9"

The advantages of insulation outweigh any extra cost and further advantages are to be gained by the use of close fitting doors and windows.

The form of insulation adopted will be governed by the purpose for which the building is intended; for instance, a cavity wall in brick or concrete to a height of 4 ft. 6 in. in the cowshed and 2 ft. 6 in. in the piggery combined with timber framing lined on the inside for the upper portion combines the advantages of cheapness with durability.

HINTS FOR THE AMATEUR BUILDER

HOME-MADE SCAFFOLDING FOR HOME REPAIRS

FIG. 1

Necessary repairs often require a temporary staging and the erection of safe structures of this type is of importance.

Where the entire exterior is to be painted or attended to in some way, stationary or built-up scaffolding is best. For instance, where repairs along the whole side of a house are required, a built-up scaffold with well braced uprights such as that shown here is best used.

The uprights should be 4 x 2, and the cross-pieces upon which the planks rest, approx. 7 x 1¼. The upright bracing should be 3 x 1. Planks 9 x 2.

For more foot room and greater safety, use two planks side by side and cleated underneath, as in fig. 1 above.

When nailing, leave heads sticking out a little to facilitate easy removal. The 3 x 1 braces are nailed to the uprights and to stakes driven into the ground. Wherever the braces cross each other, a nail is driven through to prevent them from vibrating back and forth, and to make the scaffold a much stronger unit.

The boards which the planks will rest upon are secured to the uprights with not less than 5 nails at each point of nailing, as in figure 3. On soft ground the uprights are prevented from sinking into the earth by means of short squares of board, as shown. Double uprights should be not more than 12 ft. apart, since a greater distance allows too much spring to the planks.

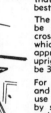

The 4 x 2 uprights should be not less than 3 feet above the highest plank on the staging. At this level, a 3 x 2 guard rail should be nailed on horizontally, if it can be arranged. This is important, as it takes very little to throw a person off balance when working above ground.

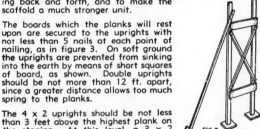
FIG. 3

A built-up scaffold, with double uprights connected by boards, is quite good because it does not require fastening the boards directly on to the house. However, figure 4 shows how single uprights can be used by nailing the inner end of the boards to vertical supporting boards nailed to the shingles.

When working alone on a hard surface where stakes cannot be driven into the ground, you can erect the uprights by bracing them against a couple of big stones, otherwise you should use stakes as illustrated in figure 5. This gives a good steady scaffold for this purpose.

FIG. 4

Another good type of scaffolding, using the push brackets of figure 6, is shown (see lower corner of page). This is easy to erect and is specially adaptable for use where work is to be done at one particular spot on the house or other outbuilding.

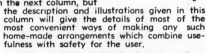
FIG. 5

There are, of course, other methods of erecting scaffolding and a few novel ideas are given in the next column, but the description and illustrations given in this column will give the details of most of the most convenient ways of making any such home-made arrangements which combine usefulness with safety for the user.

FIG. 6

In each case, the methods shown are those which have been well tried and which are the most simple to erect—the timber sizes given need not necessarily be adhered to if one has not the particular size about the place, but they are those most suitable for the safety of the job.

NOVEL AID FOR REPAIRS ON ROOF

This is rather a good method of working or painting on a roof which will make the work much easier and lessen the risk of falling.

It is simply a matter of tossing a sandbag across the peak of the roof to the opposite side. From webbing surrounding the bag, a good strong rope leads back to the worker, ending in a loop of adjustable size that encircles the waist. With the aid of friction, the outfit thus forms a perfect counterbalance, and still allows the user complete freedom of movement.

When he reaches the end of his tether, the bag is easily hitched along. This idea is specially useful where the house-top is of a slippery or steep nature.

A QUICKLY IMPROVISED SCAFFOLD FOR WORKING IN HIGH PLACES

This handy arrangement can be quickly made from some rope and a few pieces of wood and is a very convenient one if one wishes to work in a fairly high place as it allows one to do a very wide stretch at a time.

Just take two lengths of 4 x 2 and some rope. Drill the timber at one end to take the rope, which is knotted on the underside to keep it from slipping through the hole. Then nail woodblocks at the other end, as shown, spacing them to straddle the ladder rungs. Then raise from rung to rung as desired.

A HANDY HOME-MADE SCAFFOLDING
Adjustable for Height

For those who wish to build, paint, plaster, or do any such overhead work, a pair of adjustable horses, such as shown here, to hold the scaffolding, will be of considerable use.

The top members are made of 2 x 6, or 4 x 6 stock, and two rectangular holes are cut for the extension uprights, which are drilled at 2-inch intervals to receive pins. A cross-piece is nailed to the top of each set of uprights to support the scaffolding.

AN INVISIBLE HOUSE CHIMNEY

This little sketch shows how a house can be constructed, if necessary, so that the chimney does not protrude into any of the rooms.

Another idea would be to have the chimney placed in the same position but across the corner as it would then throw the heat out into the room more and permit more persons to sit around it.

CHIMNEY

The idea is, of course, mainly for small four-roomed places where simplicity is the keynote or for outbuildings or week-end places.

HINTS FOR THE AMATEUR BUILDER

HINTS ON HOME DRAINAGE AND UNDERGROUND DRAINS

EARTHENWARE PIPES are best for this; they last longer, especially where corrosive liquids are concerned, and laying is simple.

In laying a drain, cut the trench reasonably true to grade and lay pipes firmly in sand or fine loam. The grade is kept true by means of "boning" rods which must stand on pipes and not on sockets (fig. 1). As you go down grade, bone in one length of pipe ahead of the one to be jointed, and then lift it away

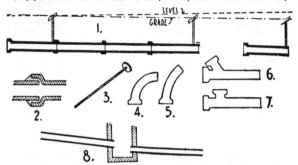

whilst the joint ahead is being made to allow insertion of a leather disc of the diameter of the pipe (fig. 3). This disc is pushed beyond the joint being made, and then when the joint is completed, it is drawn out so that any loose bits of cement are cleared away.

JOINING—Use 2 of fine sand and 1 of rapid hardening cement. Pipes should be properly centred, true to grade and firmly bedded, with hole scooped out under the joint to permit of easy working. Then work cement paste into joint with finger and bevel all round with trowel (fig. 2). Pack sand carefully back round joint and fill trench to about half depth of drain. Water carefully but do not ram—then continue. When whole drain is done, inspect for any disturbed joints, then fill whole trench.

FITTINGS 4, 5, 6 and 7 can be procured—usual sizes being 2, 3 and 4 inch diameters. **NEVER CHANGE** from a steep grade to an easier one, as silt will deposit at the change of grade. If a change is necessary, put in an inspection pit as per fig. 8 and if the drain is of any length, put in fittings (fig. 7) say every 15 feet or so and at every change of direction for inspection purposes, and to prevent deposit of silt in pipes.

SURFACE DRAINS

These are essential to carry water away from house or foundation. Again, do not change grade of drain as silt will collect. "Boning" rods are also used for grading (see fig. 1).

Fig. 2 shows a cheaply made drain, called the three brick drain. First dig trench 12 in. wide x 7 in. deep—level the ground for the centre brick, bed it firmly in position—spread sand evenly in

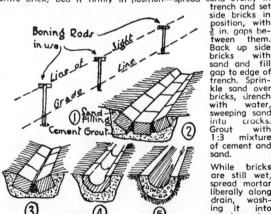

trench and set side bricks in position, with ⅜ in. gaps between them. Back up side bricks with sand and fill gap to edge of trench. Sprinkle sand over bricks, drench with water, sweeping sand into cracks. Grout with 1:3 mixture of cement and sand.

While bricks are still wet, spread mortar liberally along drain, washing it into opening between bricks with clean water, trowelling it down and along. Do not stint mortar and fill every crack. Keep covered for few days with wet bags.

If an extra cheap drain is required, try 2 bricks (fig. 3), but this is a little more difficult to lay. The neatest and best

drain is the half-round tile (fig. 4). It should be bedded in sand and grouted in with cement in the same manner as before mentioned. These, together with junctions, can be purchased.

Then there is fig. 5—a drain fashioned out of cement concrete with a half round billet of wood to provide the sunken portion which can be removed an hour or so after being laid and the surface of the drain treated with cement mortar before the concrete has had time to get properly hard.

OTHER HINTS ON SUB DRAINAGE

Whilst on the subject of drainage, these hints might be found useful, especially in parts where there is a high rainfall or where salty conditions in the soil make it essential to keep the "salt table" below the level to which roots naturally penetrate. Sub-drainage is especially suitable in hills areas.

A sub drain should have a clear outlet either on to a slope, into another drain, or into a deep pit which can be pumped out when level reaches that of the drain.

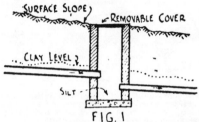

In garden work, depth is determined by the depth of clay. As a rule the drain should go into the clay, not just along the surface of it. The depth is determined by the outlet. 2 ft. will be better than nothing, but 2 ft. 6 in. is an average for the garden.

Where the grade is almost flat, they should run as straight as possible so as to make the most of whatever grade there may be. Anything up to 1 ft. in 20 ft. is permissible. After that, come down in steps, with inspection pits at each step.

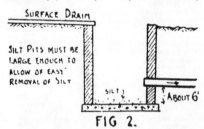

In the upward slope of the drain, you may change from a flat grade to a steeper one, but not from a steeper grade to a flat one, or silting will take place.

If this is necessary, put in an inspection pit (fig. 1). Gradual changes of direction are permissible, but use an inspection pit here also.

Surface water should be rigidly excluded from a sub drain, but if, as in a garden, it is desired to use one drain to act as a sub drain and a stormwater drain, silt pits (similar to fig. 2) must be built where the water enters the sub-drain. Clean water, as from a roof, can be led straight into a sub drain, either via a pit or via a very gradual angle only, if possible.

Drain pipes are made in 1 ft. lengths (fig. 3b) and are laid without collars. The holes, if any, should be placed downwards, and the joints placed as closely as possible. Three inch pipes are general, although 4 inch ones can be purchased for large drains where silting is feared. For larger orchard drains, the ordinary socketed pipes (fig. 3c) can be used, with "dry" joints.

In ordinary garden work, instead of an elaborate inspection pit, a 4 in. pipe length can be used, going down to a sump built underground (see fig. 3a).

If any stoppage or silting does occur it

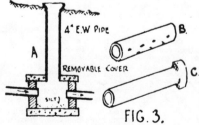

is an easy matter to dig down at or near the pipe and refill when the trouble has been rectified.

Subsidiary drains can be laid going into the main drain, either by means of an inspection pit, or a Y junction.

HINTS FOR THE AMATEUR BUILDER

CHEAP DRAINS—SOME HOME-MADE TYPES

The provision of proper drainage is an important part of farming and other work on the land. Some are fortunate enough to have land that is naturally drained; some lands require draining if any good is to be done with them.

Two 6 inch hardwood boards or slabs nailed together at right angles makes a cheap drain; or if sawn timber is not available, three logs laid in the bottom of the trench are a serviceable substitute.

Where stones are plentiful they may be used to form what is known as a rubble drain. The fascine type of drain does its work

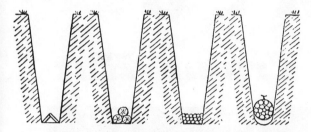

very well, and should last from 15 to 25 years if the bundles are bound with wire. Saplings of ti-tree swamp, oak, or even mangrove, if a tidal stream is accessible as a source of supply, are used. The brush is trimmed off, and the sticks are bundled together, and bound with wire.

The bundles should be a little larger in diameter than the bottom of the V-shaped trench in which they are to be laid, so that they will stand a little above the bottom, as shown in the diagram. The first bundle is laid along the trench with the butts towards the outlet, starting from the beginning of the drain; the next bundle is laid so that the brush end overlaps the butts of the first bundle, and so on.

Earthenware pipes should be inserted at the end and allowed to project a little beyond the outlet of the drain, as the timber will rot at these places if exposed to the air. The brush trimmed off the saplings is laid on top of the bundles, forming a layer which prevents silt entering the bottom of the drain. **The four types of drain described are illustrated in the sketch.**

HOW TO HALVE A DRAIN PIPE

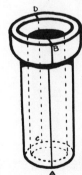

It is sometimes found necessary to halve some drain pipes which may be on hand and this is a good description of a neat method of halving a glazed earthenware drain pipe.

The pipe is stood in a vertical position, with the funnel end uppermost, and filled with dry earth or sand, which is lightly rammed down. It is then struck a succession of medium blows one or two inches apart, according to the thickness of the pipe walls, with a light hammer in an ascending direction along opposite sides, for its full length (along the lines A, B, and C, D in the accompanying illustration), taking care to strike more lightly at the wide end, where the earth is loose.

When the point D is reached, the pipe should fall apart; if it does not, then the blows struck were not heavy enough. The break will follow the lines where the blows were struck. The whole operation can be completed in a few moments.

It must be emphasised that the break is caused entirely by the pipe being struck with a hammer. If an empty pipe were struck it would be shattered, but because of the resistance offered by the sand or earth, the pipe splits open in a similar manner to a log split by wedges driven by a maul.

AN EMERGENCY LEVEL EASY TO MAKE

You can improvise a good level to any size desired in this way. With 3 wood strips, or poles if a large level is needed, form a triangle. The angles do not have to be exactly the same; rigidity is the main thing. Drive a nail into the lower end of each leg of the triangle, letting the heads project about 1 in. Then attach a plumb bob from the top of the triangle.

Now set the legs on two solid objects and mark the position where the plumb bob crosses the horizontal bar of the triangle.

Next, reverse the positions of the legs, being sure that the nail heads rest in the same locations as before, and again mark the position of the plumb bob on the horizontal bar. You will now have two marks on the bar. Measure one half the distance between the two and mark as before. When the low leg is raised so the plumb bob cuts this centre mark, the nail heads are resting on the same level plane.

A NOVEL METHOD OF LEVELLING SITE FOR SILO, SHED OR TANK

Accurate levelling of the ground is the foundation of success for building the above and a very simple method is suggested here.

First of all, made-up ground should not be used. The site should be perfectly level without any qualifications; no-one by looking at a piece of ground can say whether it is level or not, and the only sure way of ascertaining same is for a spirit level to be used. Extra time spent is well worth while. Take a silo, for instance, unless it is set on a level base, it cannot be expected to hold upright a mass of silage weighing a considerable tonnage.

With this idea, except for a spade and mattock, the only tools required are a wooden peg; a 2 in. nail; an 8 ft. length of 2 x 1 in. wood with a $\frac{1}{4}$ in. hole bored 2 inches from one end; a brick and a spirit level.

Having decided where, say, the silo wall will stand, place a brick on the ground at the lowest point. Drive the centre peg into the ground until the top of the peg is level with the top of the brick. Test this by laying the wooden arm, with the spirit level tied on the top, as shown, across both peg and brick.

Drive the nail into the top of the centre peg through the hole in the arm so that the arm can swing round in a circle. Keep the brick at the correct distance from the centre peg and move it about 2 feet. Now sink it into the ground until it is level with the peg. Level the space between the original position of the brick and its subsequent position, so that there is a level strip of ground 2 ft. wide and 2 ft. long. Move the brick a further 2 ft., sink it into the ground till level with the peg, and again level the path to its new position.

By continuing in this way, a circular path 2 ft. wide forming a level foundation for the silo wall is formed. The soil inside this path should be dug out and the ground levelled. It is well to level a distance of at least 6 in. outside the silo wall, and

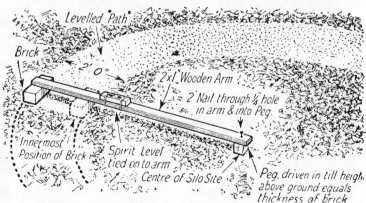

above all, to level down to solid ground and never use a made-up site.

The same principle can be adopted for small sheds, etc., if the "handyman" can extend and adapt the idea to his particular needs.

CEMENT AND ITS USES

CEMENT AND ITS USES

This is the age of concrete. Its uses are many and varied, and it is economical. For Farms, Homes, Garages, Sheds, Tanks, Pavements, Fencing Posts, and countless other things where structural strength is required combined with resistance to fire and moisture, wearing quality, low first cost and effectiveness against vermin, it is ideal.

There are certain simple rules which must be strictly observed, and the object of this section is to set out the main principles of concrete making, showing suitable illustrations from which anyone, even though inexperienced, can make many useful things if they base their work on the methods shown herein.

Factors for Good Concrete Work

(1) Correct tools.
(2) Clean, hard, well-graded aggregate.
(3) Correct proportioning of ingredients.
(4) Thorough mixing.
(5) Using the right amount of water.
(6) Placing concrete immediately after mixing.
(7) Ramming sufficiently to consolidate the mass.
(8) Subsequent watering.

First of all, calculate how much finished concrete will be required for the job and ascertain how much cement, fine and coarse aggregate, and timber for the forms will be required (see the following notes). Construct the forms in a convenient position and see that they are clean and well greased (see section "Forms and Moulds.")

Concrete Terms, etc.

"Fine" aggregate means sand which will pass through up to ¼ in. square mesh.

"Coarse" aggregate is the pebbles or stone used, i.e., from ¼ in. up to 1½ or 2 in., according to the nature of the work.

"Mixture"—A 1 : 2 : 3 mixture means 1 cubic foot of cement, 2 cubic feet of "fine" and 3 cubic feet of "coarse" aggregates.

The first figure is the cement, the second is sand, and the third the coarse material.

A 1 : 2 mixture is called a mortar, and means 1 part of cement and 2 of sand.

AVERAGE PROPORTIONS for various purposes

This is governed by the particular purpose for which the concrete is required.

1 : 2 : 4 Mixture. This is usually for ordinary average purposes: Building, Pavements, Retaining Walls, Tanks, Troughs, Tennis Courts, together with certain foundations and machinery bases.

1 : 2½ : 5 or 1 : 3 : 5. Where medium quality concrete is required, such as most foundations, walls, sheds, barns, and unimportant large masses, except where the ground is bad, when it would be safer to use 1 : 2 : 4.

1 : 2½ : 3. This is used where very good concrete is required for, say, water tanks or important reinforced work.

1 : 2 : 3. Used for gate and fencing posts, and, if any ground is uncertain, use this for heavy machinery, together with a reinforcement.

1 : 3. Used for topping, but for heavier wear (sheds, etc.) use 1 : 2.

1. For finishing the topping on floors, etc., a little neat cement may be lightly dusted on the surface.

Tools to use

These are simple and are mainly a mixing platform, water barrel and bucket, steel wheelbarrow, sandscreen for grading aggregate, a square nosed shovel (say 10 in.) for turning and mixing, a wooden float for finishing, a measuring box, tampers and spading tools, with the addition of perhaps an edging tool and trowel.

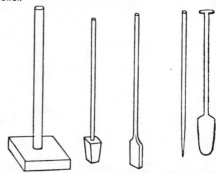

The first two illustrations on this page give details of the ready-made variety of tools which can be purchased, but, if the job is an urgent one, and there is any one or more tools which might be needed and which are not available, the lower right-hand sketches will show how they can be made.

HOME-MADE TOOLS FOR CONCRETE WORK

These can easily be made from scrap material. There is the mixing platform, another of which is shown on the following page.

However, the sketch below shows the addition of a wheel, making it a portable platform almost in the shape of a wheelbarrow. Such a handy arrangement could then be used for many purposes.

Ordinary mixing usually is done with a shovel, but a good mixer can be made by bolting a 12 inch square of heavy gauge iron or steel on to a length of ¾ in. piping, and notching two sides as shown—see upper left hand part of sketch whilst the lower right-hand will show the particular tool in action.

Wooden floats of various sizes can be made as indicated, also other forms of trowels, although these are cheap enough at any store. One or two sweep levels will be useful when it is necessary to rapidly surface the concrete. The derby float is also useful in this respect.

A scoop can be made from an old bucket or drum (see centre of illustrations) and kerosene tins can be used for measures, as sand and other aggregates are measured by bulk and not by

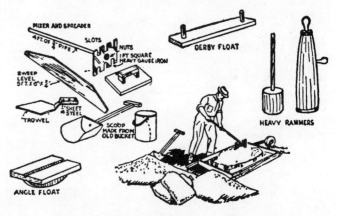

weight. Rammers are also needed—samples of these are shown.

An angle or corner float is also useful where an external angle has to be made smooth or rounded off.

Only clean hard aggregate should be used, varying in size from the largest which the character of the job permits to coarse sand (larger sizes predominating).

CEMENT AND ITS USES

MATERIALS TO USE

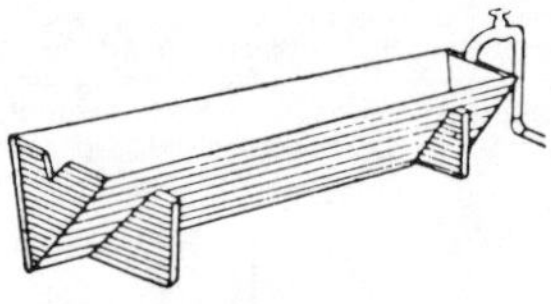

Do not use finely powdered sand, as such material interferes with the action of cement in hardening — the strength of concrete depends upon adhesion of cement to clean surfaces of hard particles of sand or stone.

If uncertain as to whether sand is clean or not, one way of ensuring same is to make a small trough out of plain boards 8 or 10 ft. long, as shown. Put the sand in the trough, and while gently stirring, let water from the tap or hose run through it. Water will overflow at the lower end, carrying away any dirt, and clean sand will remain.

MEASURING BOX

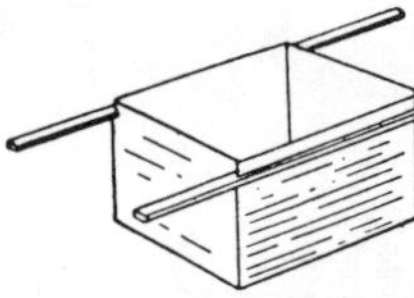

The best way for correct measuring is a home-made box of 1 cubic foot capacity, for determining each exact batch, proportions 12 x 12 x 12 in. Do not guess at quantities. Use such a measuring box, or, if lesser quantities are required, use a bucket to proportion contents, i.e., a 1 : 2 : 3 batch of concrete would be 1 bucket of cement; 2 buckets of "fine"; and 3 buckets of "coarse" aggregate.

MIXING PLATFORM

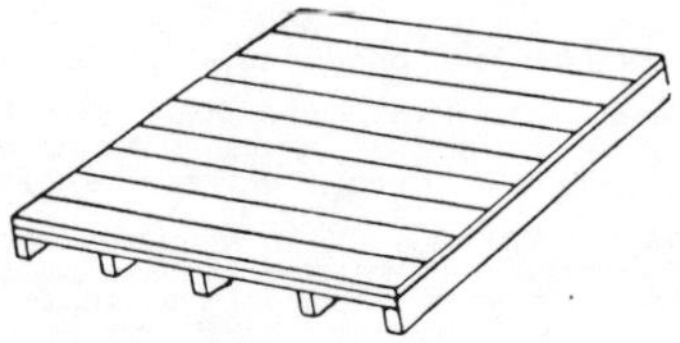

This should be watertight, say 7 ft. x 12 ft. or 8 x 10 ft., substantially made of boards 1½ in. thick, tongued and grooved so that the joints will be tight and platform rigid. These planks may be nailed to three or more 4 x 2's set on edge. A good idea is to have two sides and one end of platform finished with a strip nailed along the edge projecting two inches above the mixing surface to prevent materials from being washed or shovelled off whilst mixing. A slab of concrete can be used, either on floor or in a corner of yard.

MATERIALS REQUIRED FOR 1 CUBIC YARD OF CONCRETE

(Average conditions.)

Proportion.	Paper Bags	Cub. ft. Sand	Cub. ft. Coarse	Approx. water per bag Cement
1 : 2 : 3	6¾	14	20¾	4½ galls.
1 : 2 : 4	5⅞	12	24	5 galls.
1 : 2 : 5	5	10½	26¼	5¾ galls.
1 : 2½ : 5	4¾	12½	24½	6 galls.
1 : 3 : 5	4½	13¾	23	6¼ galls.

QUANTITIES REQUIRED

1 part cement; 2 parts "fine" and 4 parts "coarse" do not make 7 cub. ft. of concrete, as the fine only fills in the voids in the coarse, and the cement fills in the voids in the "fine" sand. The volume of finished concrete is very little greater than that of the coarse aggregate.

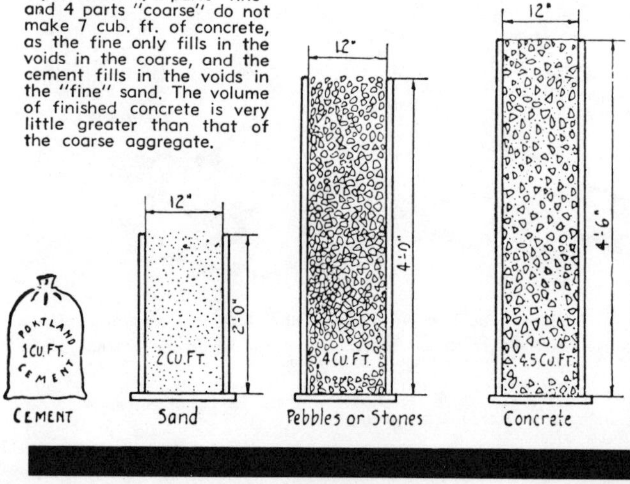

WATER

It is essential that the correct amount of water should be used. A good procedure is to add about ¾ of the amount required, say about ¾ gallon to each cubic foot of concrete. Add water evenly and slowly, mixing all the time. Add water whenever dry spots appear. Use only clean water. The mixture should not be wet enough to flow easily or to be soupy—too much reduces strength; too little does likewise, besides making it porous.

HOW TO MIX CONCRETE

There are two ways — Hand and machine, the latter being best.

Every pebble or stone should be completed coated.

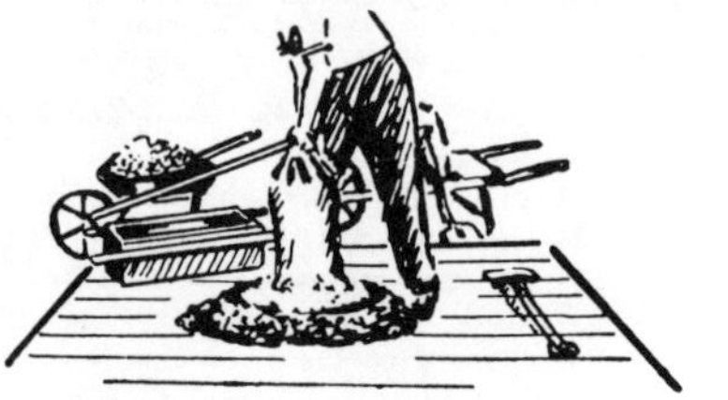

1. Measure the required quantity of clean sand in a measuring box and spread on a mixing platform evenly say about 4 in. deep.

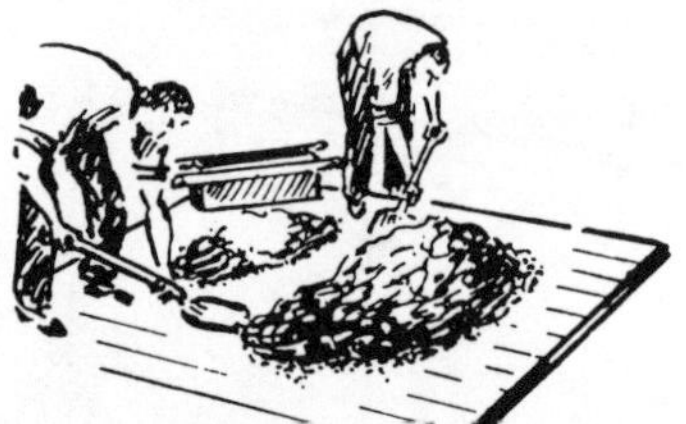

2. Then spread the right amount of cement evenly over the above—do not guess at quantities.

3. Mix these two thoroughly by turning over with shovels until color is uniform, free from streaks. Streaks indicate that the sand and cement have not been thoroughly mixed.

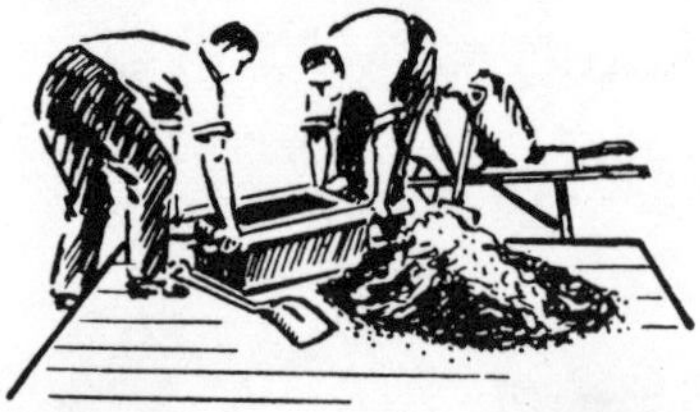

4. Measure the coarse aggregate, spread it on top, and repeat the mixing process until the colour is again uniform.

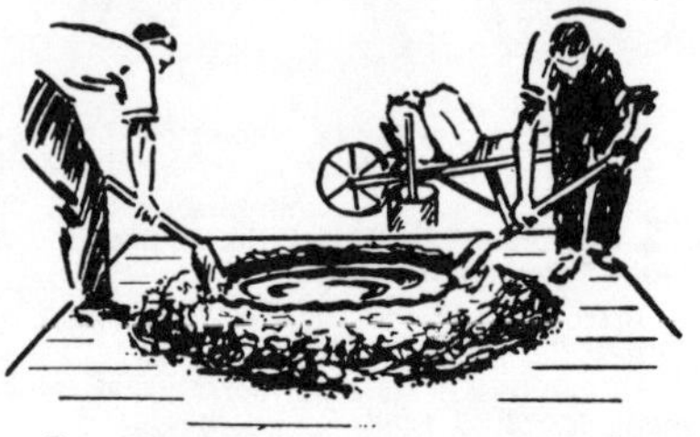

5. Then form a depression or hollow in centre. Mix whilst adding water until the mixture is of a quaky jelly-like consistency. Do not use too much water.

Mix in proportion. Do not make the heap too big that it cannot be conveniently handled.

FORMS AND MOULDS

Forms should be made of timber or steel. They should be greased with either soft soap, linseed oil, lard mixed with kerosene or crude oil—to prevent particles of concrete from sticking to the forms when removed. Forms should NOT be greased when it is intended to plaster the surface of the concrete, but should be thoroughly wetted down immediately before placing the mix. The smoother the wood used, the better will be the finished job.

PLACING AND JOINING

Place the concrete in the required forms as soon as thoroughly mixed. Do not mix more than can be placed in 1 hour. Where concrete cannot be finished in one operation, the surface where it is to be joined should be left as rough as possible. Again, before concrete operations are resumed, the surface of the concrete already set should be wetted, and a ¾ in. layer of 1 : 1 cement and sand mortar applied as the fresh supply of concrete is being joined up. Tamp the lot well. Except when making floors, concrete should be placed about 6 in. deep in forms.

Each layer can then be tamped down in order to expel air pockets and solidify the material.

CEMENT AND ITS USES

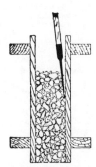

Spading

Concrete next to the walls of the moulds should be well worked with a spade or wedged stick, so that the coarse aggregate is forced a little back to allow mortar to flush in and form a smooth, even surface to the outside of the finished work.

Ramming

Ram sufficiently to consolidate; the damper the concrete, the less ramming required.

Finishing

Should a finely finished surface be required, the concrete first laid down should not come quite to the tops of forms and should not be smoothed off.

Whilst the concrete is still green (within 24 hours of laying), a finishing coat of one part cement and either two or three parts sand should be applied and finished off with a wooden float.

Avoid excessive floating or trowelling or hair cracks will result.

A little neat cement may also be dusted on the surface.

Curing

Keep work as damp as possible—protect the fresh cement from loss of moisture due to burning sun or drying wind. As soon as it is set hard (hard enough to resist finger impressions), it should be cured by sprinkling and later covered with wet bags or a layer of wet sand or earth, which should be kept saturated for at least 7 days more.

Do not use until well hardened. Footpaths, 2 or 3 weeks; paths for heavy traffic and floors for cowyards, etc., from 1 to 2 months. Stable floors longer if possible. Don't make floors of stables or cowsheds, etc., too smooth, owing to the danger of animals slipping.

AREA WHICH CAN BE COVERED BY 1 CUBIC YARD OF CONCRETE								
(Calculated in thickness of inches.)								
Thickness	$\frac{1}{2}$"	$\frac{3}{4}$"	1"	$1\frac{1}{2}$"	2"	3"	4"	6"
Area (sq. ft.)	648	432	324	216	162	108	81	54

HOW TO LAY A BETTER CLASS CONCRETE FLOOR
For Verandah or Inside of House

Firstly, make a good foundation of sand or good gritty material. Do not lay concrete on natural surface of ground.

Secondly, insert a damp-proof course between this foundation and concrete with end turned up against wall. This also checks whiteness which sometimes appears.

Thirdly, use 1 : 2 : 4 mixture with up to $\frac{1}{2}$ in. and $\frac{3}{4}$ in. coarse material and lay about $2\frac{1}{2}$ in. of this. Screen off roughly and then lay some reinforcement (preferably special welded fabric), but wire or pig netting can be used. See that reinforcement does not bulge. Then lay final $\frac{1}{2}$ in. of concrete to make it 3 in. thick.

The surface should be level but rough, and on same day, say in about 3 hours, the finishing coat should be put on. A good wearing coat is 1 of cement, 2 of coarse sand, and 2 of $\frac{1}{4}$ in. metal.

Then spread over and level with a wooden float.

A mixture of 3 parts cement and 1 part Red Oxide can then be dusted over evenly through a sieve and worked in with a wooden float, then allowed 2 or 3 hours for setting.

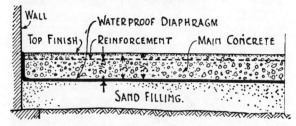

WALL
TOP FINISH
WATERPROOF DIAPHRAGM
REINFORCEMENT
MAIN CONCRETE
SAND FILLING.

It is then trowelled up hard without any further dusting. If the trowel brings up water, discontinue until water dries out, but do not add cement in order to dry. It should then be of good even colour, and for ultimate best results, waxing or painting should not be done for 12 months.

A USEFUL AID IN MIXING CEMENT

It is sometimes a difficult job to water and mix cement single-handed, and this idea from one man might help.

To facilitate adding water at the same time as mixing the cement by himself, he used a short piece of wood, as shown, having three holes drilled through it to take the hose in the manner shown.

A pair of iron brackets screwed to the inside of the mortar box supported the wood vertically, and permitted it to be removed quickly when not needed.

DISCARDED OIL TINS USED AS CONCRETE FORMS

Where the ends of concrete pillars for foundation and centre support posts extend above ground level, handy forms can be improvised from oil tins. These are adapted by removing both ends and then slitting each down the side.

The cut sides are nailed to blocks of wood, after which the supporting cross-pieces are attached as indicated, to provide a means of adjusting the forms to proper height with wood blocks or stakes driven into the ground.

If the inside surfaces of the tins are well oiled before pouring the concrete, the forms will separate from the concrete easily as the nails can be pulled through the tin. In loose soil, it may be advisable to use additional tins as the hole is dug to prevent cave-ins.

MOISTURE-PROOF CONTAINERS FOR SMALL QUANTITIES OF CEMENT

Moisture proof containers in which to keep cement so that it will not harden can be made by slightly altering the heads of steel oil drums.

With a sharp hacksaw, cut the crimped edge, as shown in the circular detail, and then drive out the lower piece which has been sawed loose. The head can now be lifted and, when replaced, will effectively protect the contents of the drum.

A weight placed on the drum will prevent any tendency of the head to rise up.

A STRONG CONTAINER FOR MIXING MORTAR from old Oil Drums

A mixing tin that can be made to stand hard use and at the same time be an inexpensive one, can be made by cutting off the ends of a steel oil drum, as indicated in this sketch.

Such a container will not warp or crack, as it can be pounded with a hammer to help remove dried mortar. It is best to file or grind the edges of the drums, after cutting them, in order to smooth them.

It can then be placed on a stand at a convenient height for working.

CEMENT AND ITS USES

GENERAL PRINCIPLES OF CONCRETE CONSTRUCTION WALLS AND FOUNDATIONS

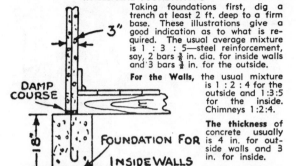

Taking foundations first, dig a trench at least 2 ft. deep to a firm base. These illustrations give a good indication as to what is required. The usual average mixture is 1 : 3 : 5—steel reinforcement, say, 2 bars ¾ in. dia. for inside walls and 3 bars ¾ in. for the outside.

For the Walls, the usual mixture is 1 : 2 : 4 for the outside and 1:3:5 for the inside. Chimneys 1:2:4.

The thickness of concrete usually is 4 in. for outside walls and 3 in. for inside.

Steel Reinforcement for walls ⅜ in. diameter 12 x 12 in. All reinforcement bars for walls should be inserted in squares not less than 12 x 12 in. Some

prefer them smaller, but for general purposes, the above s sufficient. Similarly, some prefer extra reinforcement bars in foundations, but these notes are all based on minimum requirements.

FORMS FOR CONCRETE

The following diagram shows one face timbered whilst a firm earth bank acts as the other side.

Where both sides are to be tim-

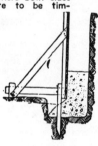

bered, the same method for both sides should be used as shown on the timbered side of the sketch, i.e., the supporting stakes being driven into the ground for the support of the form, whilst the concrete at the base should be wider than at ground level.

For the "form" for work above ground level, one side should be first of all lined up and plumbed—then braced by diagonals driven into the ground, as shown below. The form for the opposite side should then be fixed likewise and secured to the first by braces and ties.

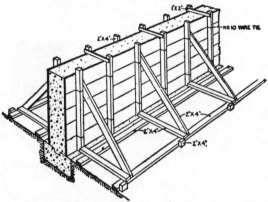

This prevents the wall from bulging as concrete exerts great pressure. It is easy to make these spacers (details herewith).

Ties also, as shown, should extend through the walls from one side to the other. No 10 fencing wire is passed round the posts on opposite sides in a loop and then twisted by means of a rod or stick. Spacers should be exactly equal to the thickness of the wall. These also prevent the walls from being drawn too closely together, and they should be placed near each tie when it is being twisted up. They should be removed before they are covered by the concrete mix as it is being placed.

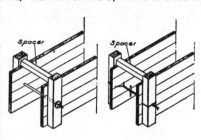

After the concrete is set, the tie wires may be cut and the forms moved along the wall to be used again, any protruding wires being clipped close to the surface of the concrete. Another method is to use bolts (greased) which can be withdrawn easily (see sketch).

The layers of concrete should be of 6 in. to 10 in. at a time, well tamped and spaded. When building upwards, move forms further up walls and reassemble as each section is placed and set, i.e., when it resists finger pressure (see previous article on curing, etc.).

CONCRETE STEPS

Wooden steps decay. Only a simple form is needed to make good concrete steps, and this sketch shows how they ca be made with only a small amount of material.

1 in. material is used which is braced and staked as shown to prevent bulging when the concrete is poured

in. This type of form can be used for any number of steps, as it is really a series of separate forms, one upon the other, each being shorter than the one below.

HOW TO CONSTRUCT ODD FORMS FOR CONCRETE FROM CARDBOARD

For odd-shaped concrete forms not more than a few inches high, such as a circular or other such foundation (as shown here), heavy corrugated or other cardboard from grocery boxes will be found quite satisfactory.

Such material will bend easily and it can be held in place with bricks or other heavy material as indicated.

WHEEL RIM STEPS
Ready Made Forms of Concrete

One ingenious farmer who had a number of old motor car wheel rims on hand utilised them to make forms for a set of steps.

He laid one rim at the bottom, filled it with concrete, laid another on top, far enough back to leave width for a step, filled it with concrete and so on to the top.

The result, as shown, was a substantial, good-looking, and permanent stairway, which could be used anywhere where there is an uneven path, or where an ornamental step is needed.

CEMENT AND ITS USES

CONCRETING A CHIMNEY CAP

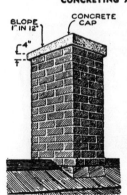

The life of a chimney is lengthened if it is given a concrete cap. It holds the chimney in alignment, prevents the top bricks from becoming loose, acts as a watershed, and gives it a better appearance.

First clean any loose bricks at the top and set them in fresh mortar before concreting. The concrete cap should project 1 in. beyond the brick on all sides of the chimney. On top it slants, with a fall of 1 in. to the foot, the concrete being 4 in. thick at the inner edge. The cap should be made by tamping a rather dry mixture—1 part cement and 4 parts sand—into a form made the proper size for the chimney.

When dry, it is set on the brick with ordinary mortar.

LAG SCREWS FOR CONCRETE FLOORS

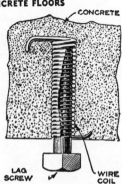

A good way to arrange for the fastening of machinery, etc., to concrete floors, consists of a coil of wire being inserted in the concrete flush with the surface, into which the screw or bolt may be inserted at will, and as easily removed.

This device is very useful and enables objects to be moved—a peg being inserted when not in use to prevent dirt from collecting in it.

Similarly, a wooden peg can be inserted loosely into the coil while the cement is drying, so that the inside will not be filled with dirt or concrete.

USEFUL METHODS OF ANCHORING BOLTS IN CONCRETE

The accompanying sketches indicate some of the various ways of anchoring machines or timber to concrete floors or walls. "A" shows one method of fastening with ordinary machine bolts. This shows the head embedded either in the fresh concrete or in

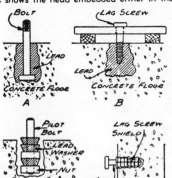

the holes filled with lead or other substance. Be sure there is no water or oil in the holes to make the hot material spatter.

Machines are often fastened to concrete floors by drilling an irregular hole ("B"), setting in a lag screw, and then pouring lead or babbit or other material in around it. The lag screw can then be unscrewed and tightened as desired.

Timbers and machines can also be fastened to concrete floors, etc. ("C") by using lag screw expansion anchors put into a hole in the concrete and expanded as the lag screws are turned into them or ("D") by putting an ordinary nut on the end of a pilot bolt, slipping lead washers over the bolt and spreading them with a loose nut and a short piece of pipe until firmly wedged. Then the pilot bolt is turned out and a machine bolt of the desired length screwed in.

ANOTHER USEFUL IDEA FOR ANCHORING BOLTS IN CONCRETE

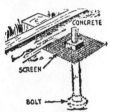

When it is necessary to anchor a bolt in freshly poured concrete, one contractor supports it in position with a piece of screen wire as shown here.

First, the bolt is placed in the concrete in the desired position, then the wire is slipped down over the threaded end and the nut is then started, as indicated.

In this way the wire serves as a float to keep the bolt in a vertical position until the concrete has set.

NOVEL IDEA FOR MAKING HOLES IN CONCRETE FOR RAILINGS, ETC.

When making anything such as a concrete stairway which is to be fitted with a metal railing, you can make the holes for the railing supports by merely sinking some bottles in the wet concrete in the positions desired.

After the concrete has set and the railings are ready to be installed, it is only necessary to break all the bottles out. This will leave the holes in the concrete ready for erecting the post—the holes being clean and uniform to any depth desired.

BUILDING A MOTOR GARAGE OF CONCRETE

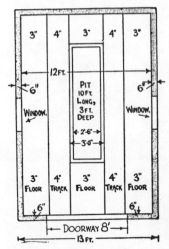

This makes a durable and fireproof garage. The floor should be at least 4 in. thick, walls 6 in. thick, with ¼ in. reinforcements in a 12 in. mesh. Door opening 8 ft. Inside width 12 ft.

The length inside is 18 ft., door 7 ft. high. Pit is deep enough for a man to stand upright, and long enough to be able to reach all parts without having to push the car to and fro. A length of 10 ft. x 2 ft. 6 in. and depth of 3 ft. is recommended. Walls and floor of the pit should be 3 in. thick.

Roof. For any moderate span, flat roofs are as cheap as those with timber frames. Steel reinforcements for a 4 in. thickness can be made by using ⅜ in. bars spanning between the side

walls and placed 4 in. apart, with ⅜ in. bars 6 inches apart in the other direction. Steel reinforcement can be purchased in rolls if required.

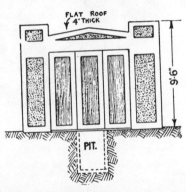

The timber framework for the walls and flat roof should be assembled complete and the concrete poured in one uninterrupted operation so that the walls and roof become one solid mass. Flat roofs are safer from fire.

CEMENT AND ITS USES

A HANDY HOME-MADE CONCRETE MIXER FROM OLD MOTOR PARTS

If you have much cement work to do and can obtain some old motor parts (as indicated), this home-made machine will be well worth while.

Motor parts and a 60-gal. drum or barrel will comprise this rotary mixer, which has a geared hand crank. The car or truck frame is cut as shown.

A section without shackle ends forms the sled, and a similar section with shackles upturned, and suitably braced, supports the mixer frame, which is pivoted as shown in figure 1. The top illustration will show the frame in the mixing position where it is held by means of a sturdy iron prop, as shown.

This is pivoted to the frame and attached to a slotted handle, which slides back and forth on two bolts, so the prop can be moved on or off a small metal block welded to the inclined brace.

To disengage the prop, first push down on the tilting lever, which is a pipe that can be slid under the drum when not used.

A cut off rear end is mounted concentrically in line with the drum.

The cut-off drive shaft has a squared end to take a crank for turning the drum which rests on two ball-bearings at each end. These are not shown here, but any handyman can fix them in position to enable the barrel to be turned easily. A chain or prop can be used to hold the drum

in position; the prop, however, being an improvement on the chain.

This idea could also be applied to such things as grain picklers, whilst a grain pickler shown later in the book could be adapted to a cement mixer.

ANOTHER IDEA FOR A HOME-MADE MIXER

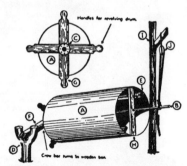

This sketch will indicate another method of using a drum as a home-made mixer.

This is easily transported from place to place and can be hitched to a tree or post by block and tackle at one end to whatever height is desired and supported at the other end as shown.

The detail gives particulars of the ends which can also be used as handles for carrying. The mixing can be done at the appointed place and then the mixer can merely be lifted to the spot where the concrete is required or the concrete can be mixed on the site of the job and the end of the mixer merely lowered in order to pour out the concrete.

A HOME-MADE CONCRETE MIXER

To fit on to rear wheel of truck (wooden spokes)

First, saw a barrel exactly in half. Make the end cover a little larger than the barrel and cleat it for two-thirds of its width, leaving 6 inches for a door (or the last board). Make these a close fit, and hinge the door board with two good heavy " T " hinges.

Then get 3 long bolts with hook at one end, and nut and thread at the other; these to be the length of the half barrel, plus the depth of hub of the wheel. They go through the barrel and hook on to the spokes, and also hold the lid of the barrel in place, the nuts being screwed up to make all tight. An iron staple keeps the lid shut with a wedge driven through it. In the middle of the lid is a hole to insert hose, so that water can be added.

TO USE, take the truck to the site of the job, jack up the back axle, then place the platform under the rim of barrel to catch the mixed cement. Turn barrel with door to top and shovel sand, cement and metal into it in proportion. When the door is shut and wedge driven in, start engine and engage in lower gear. This turns barrel and mixes it in a few minutes. Then insert hose and add the required water. Revolve again. With door at bottom, knock out wedge and cement will come out.

While one batch is being laid, the operation can be repeated, and so much time saved.

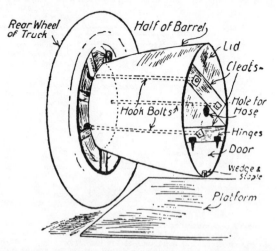

Keep hooks as near the centre of the wheel as possible and avoid undue strain on the spokes. If a truck is not available, a dray wheel can be used and turned by hand, but thicker spacing pieces will be needed.

CEMENT AND ITS USES

CONCRETE PATHS

Concrete paths are not only attractive, but for lasting qualities, structural strength, cleanliness and resistance to fire and water, are ideal. They are simply constructed—cool weather being preferred.

Unless the ground is sandy, or perfectly drained, remove the earth to a depth of 10 in. and fill with 6 in. gravel or cinder filling, then ram and level. Ordinarily 4 inches of concrete is sufficient unless

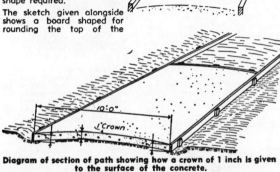

Tamper

1"x4" straight edge.

Wooden float.

motors or waggons will cross the path, when 6 in. thickness will be required.

Block off the paths in sections, with partition strips 4 x 2's, or, for the thicker concrete, 6 x 2, using sufficient pegs to ensure that the sides do not bulge. Place the concrete in alternate sections, as shown, and after these have hardened sufficiently to be self-sustaining,

Form for stretch of path showing an improvised tamper made of square timber for compacting the soil, a straight-edge and method of striking off surplus material preparatory to finishing with a wooden float.

remove the strips and concrete the intermediate spaces. When filling in the JOINTS in the alternate sections, put a few layers of tarred paper in between to provide for expansion and contraction.

After the concrete is placed in the forms, level off with a strike board, which can be rested on the edges of the forms and operate with a saw-like motion. To secure a non-slippery surface, finish with a wooden float. Avoid too much trowelling. CURE as shown in concrete notes.

Rapid hardening cement is excellent for this work.

Allow for drainage of surface by sloping $\frac{1}{4}$ in. to the foot in the required direction, or, if slope is required both ways, shape the striking board accordingly. If a gutter is desired, press say a piece of greased 3 inch pipe into the wet concrete before the initial set. If weather is very dry, it is advisable to tamp soil, thoroughly wet it and allow surplus moisture to drain away before placing the concrete.

ROUNDED SURFACES FOR CONCRETE PATHS

The main principles are given in the foregoing article and the accompanying illustrations merely serve to show how to construct boards which will give any particular shape required.

The sketch given alongside shows a board shaped for rounding the top of the

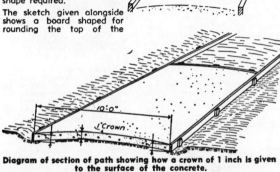

Diagram of section of path showing how a crown of 1 inch is given to the surface of the concrete.

lower-course of concrete whilst the sketch at the top of the next column shows how the board should be shaped for finishing the rounded surface of the upper-course of concrete.

One and Two Course Work

The directions given for preparing a concrete mix for a **one-course** construction of pavements apply also for the **two-course** as regards foundation, drainage, materials, forms, mixing, placing, finishing, curing and joints. However,

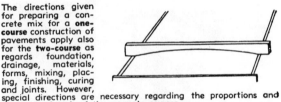

special directions are necessary regarding the proportions and thickness of each of the separate courses.

The average two-course pavement should consist of a base not less than 4 in. thick, composed of one part cement, two parts of fine aggregate and four parts coarse aggregate. The top coat or wearing surface should be not less than 1 in. thick and composed of mortar in the proportions of one part cement and three parts fine aggregate.

The first course or base should be deposited on the foundation and thoroughly compacted by tamping. The surface of this base should then be levelled off by a template or board which should leave it nowhere less than 1 inch below the finishing surface.

AN IDEA FOR TAMPING PATHS
so that Clay or Concrete will not stick

This is a useful idea and one well worth knowing.

The tendency of wet clay or concrete to adhere to the bottom of a tamper can be avoided by giving it a slight twist as it is lifted each time.

The twisting action tends to clean the surface of the tamper and break the vacuum that exists between it and the wet material.

To facilitate twisting the tamper, a hand grip is provided (as shown in the illustration) by a small length of pipe and fitting.

HOW TO PROVIDE SAFE FOOTING FOR SLOPING PATHS

It is often necessary to roughen the surface of a concrete path in order to provide a safer footing in wet weather and this is quite a good idea although, of course, an ordinary rough surface would suffice, this type will, at the same time, provide an attractive pattern.

SECTION OF RUBBER MATTING

Get a wooden roller and cover it with a rubber matting and then run it over the concrete while it is still soft. This leaves the impression of the matting on the concrete.

Any design of matting will do.

If the concrete has a tendency to adhere to the rubber, coating it with cylinder oil at frequent intervals will prevent this trouble. The idea might hardly seem worth troubling about, but the little extra work is well worth while, as it leaves a permanent and attractive job.

CEMENT AND ITS USES

COLOURING AND MARKING FOOTPATHS

Spreading color mixture

The use of coloured concrete for driveways and footpaths is very popular in some parts and it is very attractive. Concrete can be coloured by adding pigments, but it is usually best to purchase cement already mixed. For economy, the colour may be confined to a thin top layer.

The dust-on method of applying colour to a concrete slab is to mix one part of cement with 1 to 1½ parts of dry aggregate and the required amount of colour.

Materials are proportioned by weight, and are mixed dry until the colour is uniform.

The dust-on mixture is applied at the rate of at least 125 lbs. per 100 sq. feet of area, and it is floated or worked into the concrete as shown in illustrations 1 and 2.

Floating on the color

Usually two applications of colour are required to make it a good job. Possible colour schemes are endless. The surface is finished by trowelling or otherwise treating the slab to get the desired texture.

The other two illustrations show a method of marking off any desired pattern, and the colour can also be worked in in one or in a variety of colours to suit any particular requirements.

Laying out the pattern

Some people like to have a variety of colours, as it gives a very good effect and it can of course be done by merely giving each slab or section a separate colour to its neighbour and so on.

The concrete should be allowed to set until it becomes stiff, but can still be worked.

Troweling smooth

Then smooth the surface, preferably with a wooden float, as wood produces a surface about the correct roughness whilst metal floats make the surface too smooth from a non-skid standpoint.

Don't forget the expansion of joints as indicated in previous pages.

CEMENT PENETRATION PATHS

Another method of making pathways is that of cement penetration. In this, the coarse aggregate is spread evenly over the area beforehand, without sand or cement. The screenings are rolled or tamped tightly into place, so that there is a minimum of space between them. Then the sand and cement mixture, which is known as grout, is poured over the surface, and fills the small spaces. This grout should be mixed to form a fluid of the consistency of thin cream, so that it will pour easily and find its way into the small spaces between the screenings or gravel.

The first essential is to devote some time to the preparation of the foundation. Carefully mark out the area to be treated, and with the aid of pegs, a long straight-edge and a spirit level, the surface can be excavated to a depth of 3 in. Over this spread a light layer of sand. When preparing foundations, it is usual to allow for a fall of 1 in. in 3 or 4 ft. to carry the water away from the house.

Then fill in with coarse screenings, gravel or broken asphalt to the full depth, but do not use any material finer than ⅜ in. Dusty screenings or gravel will interfere with setting.

These screenings must then be rolled or tamped down as tightly as possible. Add extra material to fill in the holes formed by rolling. It is then ready for the cement grout, which can be mixed in a bucket or tub. It is a good idea to have helpers so that one man can keep pouring while others are mixing.

Mix in the proportion of 1 of cement, 2½ of fine, clean sand, and 1½ of water. Put the water into the bucket first, then slowly stir in the sand, and then lastly the cement, until it is of a uniform colour and an even flowing mixture is obtained. It can then be poured on to the screenings. Before doing this, wet the screenings by sprinkling with water, so that they will not absorb the moisture from the cement mixture. It must be poured on so that it penetrates the layer of screenings and floods over the surface. Then it is trowelled. This trowelling will bring the water to the top and press down the small pieces of screenings to form a smoother surface.

Pouring grout from a bucket in which it was mixed, into the stones which have been spread uniformly over the path and rolled or tamped into place.

If a slab formation is desired, thin strips of wood 3 × ⅜ in. are let into the screenings before pouring on the cement. When the latter has set sufficiently, these strips can be removed. Use rather a rich cement mixture to fill in these spaces and to surface the area, say, 1 cement, 2 sand and 1 water well mixed, roughly trowelled over the surface, and worked down into the divisions made by removing the wooden strips.

In about an hour this mixture will have set sufficiently to trowel over the surface, and to finish off with edging tools, if available. Before doing this, to make sure that the slabs are well separated, cut along the dividing lines with a thick knife or trowel. These divisions allow for expansion and contraction and help to prevent cracking.

Do not let the finished surface dry out too quickly. To prevent this, it should be covered over with bags and kept damp for at least a week.

CEMENT AND ITS USES

A HANDY TOOL FOR CLEANING CONCRETE

This is a very useful home-made tool for cleaning concrete floors, paths and other work, as it simplifies the work to a great extent. It is made by merely pivoting a long stiff handle on to a disc from an old disc-harrow. It literally shaves off the dirt and other matter from the surface. The illustration will show the manner of construction and suggestion as to how to use it.

A NOVEL METHOD OF USING SPIRIT LEVEL WITH STRAIGHT EDGE

If it is desired that a path be perfectly level, a spirit level attached to a straight edge as shown here will ensure that it is so.

This enables one to span the space between the forms and save time in getting both sides of the forms to the same height. The level is attached by putting two dowels in this straight-edge for insertion into the two holes drilled in the edge of the level in the manner shown in the above illustration.

ANOTHER LEVEL IMPROVISED ON STRAIGHT-EDGE

This illustration will show how a plumb bob can be affixed to a straight-edge if nothing else is available for the purpose. A block 16 in. long and say, 4 x 1, is nailed exactly at right angles to the straight-edge as indicated in the drawing and the plumb bob is suspended from a screw eye at the upper end of the block, as shown.

After marking the exact centre of the block near the lower end, it is then easy to tell when an object is level by bringing the line of the plumb bob directly over the mark on the block.

Another good idea for an ordinary straight-edge is the use of a piece of angle iron as it makes a very good implement for finishing off concrete paths and floors. The weight of the iron helps to hold it firmly and ensures a good clean job.

Another good substitute for a straight-edge is a piece of steel or wood used as a bow with a length of 18 gauge wire in place of the cord.

A HANDY STRAIGHT-EDGE WITH SHOVEL HANDLE

To provide his 10 ft. straight-edge with a convenient handle by which it could be readily manipulated, one farmer attached a broken shovel handle.

This allowed the worker to lift the straightedge from a standing position, which eased the usual task of kneeling to test the work. Low spots in the concrete can be detected easily from a standing position simply by noting the marks left in the soft cement.

CEMENTING AN OLD TANK

An old tank made good in this fashion will be useful for many years. It should not be cemented unless it is on a reasonably solid foundation, as timber is liable to rot.

First build up stand of 4½ in. brick in cement (C), taking care it rests on solid earth. Then fill the inside with stone or old bricks (B) well bedded in sand and watered down. Then level off top with cement mortar. Lift tank on to this while mortar is still soft, placing nothing between iron and cement. Rapid hardening cement is good for this.

See that a flushing plug is put in, 3 in. (D). The outlet for the tap should be extended upwards (F), screwed into the existing socket (A). This is to prevent silt entering tap. Half inch wire netting (E) is then fixed round inside of tank. This should be bent round to lock with bottom.

Reinforcement in the bottom (G) is not necessary, but advisable.

The bottom of tank should be 3 in. thick 1-2-4 concrete well rodded in around the wire and left with a rough surface. This should be graded slightly towards the flushing plug, which facilitates cleaning.

The first coat of cement is thrown on between the wire netting and the sides, until it is covered and the flutes filled. This and the subsequent coat should be of mortar of three parts clean sand to one rapid hardening cement. Throw the cement on with some force; it should stick easily enough. Leave no air pockets.

Always use sharp sand. Leave this coat a day before proceeding with the next.

The second coat is of the same—mix ⅜ in. thick. See that there are no large particles of sand which might get in the way when finally trowelling. Before putting it on, wet the first coat thoroughly by going over it with a sloppy mixture of cement and water. This helps to make it waterproof, and ensures a good adherence.

Put the second coat on as quickly as possible, using long strokes of the trowel. Do not work on it too long at the start, or bubbles will form under the cement, which will then fall off in patches.

If this happens, cut out the loose sections with trowel and replaster, taking care not to overdo it again.

Use a steel trowel to apply the cement. A wooden float is used to consolidate it. Exercise a fair pressure, keeping an eye open for bubbles. Small ones can be cut out with trowel.

The second coat is put over the bottom as well, working it well into the weak spots such as where the flushing plug or the outlet

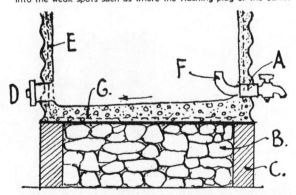

comes. When the bottom has been done, place pieces of board down to stand on or to rest bottom of ladder. This second coat will begin to stiffen after an hour or so, and is then ready for the final trowelling, which is done with a steel trowel. When finished, get out of tank as carefully as possible, drawing up ladder behind you. The pieces of board can be fished out when tank is full.

Keep the tank closed for two days, after which let in about 6 in. of water very carefully. After four days the roof water may be let in. There may be some seepage in places for some weeks, but these gradually disappear. If there are any bad leaks near the bottom, run some cement down a length of downpipe to the spot, and they will soon tighten up.

Dependable
Service

AUSTRALIAN
APB
PLYWOOD BOARD

in
Plywood

Not only the Tradesman but the Handyman and Home Carpenter will find **PLYWOOD** to be the ideal material of unlimited uses.

In a recent American " Designs for Post-War Living " Contest, 85 per cent. of the entrants, including 7 out of the 8 winners, specified **PLYWOOD.** Many designed all-Plywood structures.

Others used this miracle wood for interior or exterior walls, floors, ceilings, shelving, cupboards, and many other purposes.

To the Furniture Industry **PLYWOOD,** with its remarkable versatility and adaptability, is proving to be truly a miracle wood.

IS NOT A SUBSTITUTE NOR AN IMITATION OF ANYTHING ELSE. IT IS GENUINE IN ITS OWN RIGHT BECAUSE THE BEAUTY OF WOOD IN THE FORM OF PLYWOOD IS UNSURPASSED

HANDYMAN JOBS IN AND AROUND THE HOME

WOODEN JOINTS AND HOW TO MAKE THEM

Joints present a fascinating study as they are more than a means of fastening pieces of wood together. There are a number of ways of joining two boards edge to edge, but there is usually one way better than others, and therefore it is a good thing to know how.

First, mark the face side or edge with a knife; saw in the waste (see centre sketches),

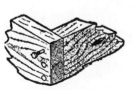

No. 1. This is known as the butt joint, and is the simplest to make. It is used in making boxes, small cabinets, etc.

No. 2 is what is called the rabeted joint, i.e., the two ends being held together with glue and nails as shown.

No. 3 is what is termed the corner butt with reinforced cleat. This is actually stronger than the plain butt joint.

No. 4 is the half-lap, which can be either at the end or anywhere in the piece. It is used chiefly for jointing two members of a cross frame.

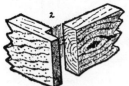

No. 4a is another of the No. 4 type, but is called the half lap slice, being used to join the ends of straight or curved pieces to lengthen them.

No. 4b is the mitred end half lap, being somewhat similar to the end half-lap, but with the corner mitred instead of cut on the square.

No. 4c is a cross half-lap, used as a joint where square edges of two pieces cross each other, as in the dividing sections of a drawer.

No. 4d is the end half lap. It is used as a corner joint on a wide variety of frames, screens, etc.

No. 5 is the doweled edge and corner joint, used for joining two or more narrow boards when making table tops and fine cabinet work. The dowels are centred lengthwise along a gauge line and are flattened very slightly to permit the escape of surplus glue and air when the dowels are driven home.

MARK WITH KNIFE

WASTE

MARK DEPTH WITH MARKING GAUGE

When setting out the pieces to be joined, **first plane up one face, then one edge, and mark them; the face with a mark like a comma, and the edges with a cross** (as indicated). Measurements should be done on these edges. Then mark with a knife rather than a pencil. Thirdly (and important) always saw or cut in **the waste**, i.e., the part that will be cut away.

No. 5a is of the same type as fig. 5, i.e., usually known as the dowelled corner joint.

No. 6 is a spiral groove — useful for dowels. This admits glue to portions which would perhaps be bare. It forms a channel which permits escape of air.

No. 7 is a mitre joint with corrugated fasteners, being a quick method of joining wood together for corners or cross bars. All one has to do is to draw the parts together tightly and drive the fasteners across the edges.

No. 8 is a housed mortise and tenon joint used for joining rails to legs and posts, etc.

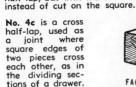

No. 9 is a pinned mortise and tenon used for the same purpose as No. 8. This is more often used to hold the lower rail to the leg in certain styles of furniture.

No. 10 is a bevelled corner joined with clamp rail which makes a very quick and good joint. It is driven into a saw-made cut on the two parts; it also draws the parts together as it is driven into the wood.

FACE & EDGE MARKS

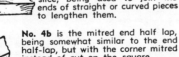

| WASTE | WASTE | WASTE |

WRONG   RIGHT.

the correct form. "B" may easily split because of the sharp angles.

No. 11. These are dove-tail joints and are the attainment of real skill. The larger shows the finished job. "A" shows

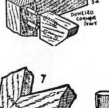

DOWELLED CORNER JOINT

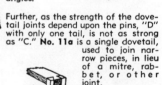

| A | B |
| C | D |

N 11

END   FRONT

Further, as the strength of the dovetail joints depend upon the pins, "D" with only one tail, is not as strong as "C." **No. 11a** is a single dovetail, used to join narrow pieces, in lieu of a mitre, rabbet, or other joint.

No. 11b is a dovetailed half lap.

HANDYMAN JOBS IN AND AROUND THE HOME

WOODEN JOINTS AND HOW TO MAKE THEM (continued)

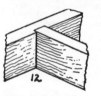

The following are a few additional wooden joints which are well worth knowing, as they may prove useful at any time for some particular purpose.

No. 12 is what is known as the Dado joint—used a lot in building shelves. **12a** is the stopped Dado

joint, i.e., for places where it is desired to conceal the groove from the front.

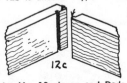

No. 12b is another type of Dado

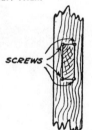

Joint. **No. 12c** is an end Dado or box corner. It is a good, strong joint.

No. 12d is a rabeted and grooved drawer front.

LOOSE TENONS—HOW TO TIGHTEN THEM

SCREWS

Quite often tenons in framed work become loosened through shrinkage, causing the structure to become shaky and out of alignment. Glueing is, of course, one remedy, but it is really only of temporary benefit, especially in exposed work.

One simple remedy is to drive a stout screw into each corner of the joint, as indicated here; it is much easier than wedging, and in some cases more effective. Further, it is a very quick and easy method of overcoming this difficulty.

EXTRA CUTS AID IN WASTE REMOVAL
When Making Half-Lap Joints

WASTE

EXTRA SAW CUT

GAUGE LINE

When making a wide half-lap joint or when cutting long tenons by hand, you can remove the chips to uniform depth with ease if you make one or more extra cuts in the waste stock as shown in this illustration.

As many as two or three additional saw cuts down to the gauge lines will be found specially helpful when the wood is at all cross-grained.

THE ART OF VENEER DECORATING

Veneer is the art of decorating a timber surface by overlaying it with figured woods, cut very thin, and glued to the thicker piece. Veneer is really a thin sheet of wood which has been cut from a larger log. The name plywood is given to two or more layers of veneer glued together. There are two varieties of veneer—knife and saw-cut—the former being the more modern and economical.

Laying veneer is not difficult, and few tools are required. A veneer hammer, as shown in the next column, is usually home-made, consisting of a piece of sheet metal 3/32 in. thick and 4

ing long. The lower edge is rounded and then mounted and fitted with a handle. A housewife's old-style flat-iron will also be needed and a toothing plane which has a blade with a grooved back, giving a serrated edge similar to saw teeth. An old hacksaw blade could be used instead.

The foundation, or base timber, well planed and seasoned, is roughened on the surface, working the blade with criss-cross and up and down strokes. This surface is then sized with thin glue water applied by brush.

Select and cut a piece of veneer slightly larger than the surface to be covered, using a chisel and straight-edge to cut it out. Allow the sized surface to dry and then dampen the face of the veneer with hot water. Apply a coating of hot, thin glue. Place the veneer in position and bring the veneer hammer into use. It is worked over the surface from the centre outwards in zig-zag movements to bring all the surplus glue towards the edges.

Now re-dampen the surface slightly and pass the flat-iron previously made hot, over the surface with light and rapid strokes. The heat from the iron turns the moisture into steam, which re-melts the glue, drawing it up into the veneer. A final rub-over with the hammer completes the laying.

Veneer Hammer

Note that the iron should be just hot enough to hiss when touched with a dampened finger. After glueing the narrow strips of veneer round the edges, the work is turned face downwards on a flat board and the edges trimmed off with a sharp chisel. Some prefer a razor blade or a fine-edged pocket knife.

You may wish to decorate the surface by cross-banding, glueing to resemble a frame. The grain of these strips run the short way of the piece, and so is at right angles to the outer edges.

Set a sharp cutting gauge to the required width of the banding and cut round through the surface veneer.

Remove the waste veneer by lifting with a chisel. This should be done as soon after veneering as possible and before the glue sets. If you decide to cross-band after the glue has set, the gauging is carried out as before. Warm water and a hot iron are used to remelt the glue, taking care not to disturb the surface.

Make your banding by cutting strips of the required width across the grain of the veneer. These strips are damped on the top surface, glued on the underside, and rubbed down in position with the hammer and hot iron.

If the strips are very narrow, an ordinary bench hammer can be heated to take the place of the flat iron. When you reach the corner, allow the two pieces to overlap, draw through the mitre line, and cut along it with a razor blade. After removing the waste pieces, the bands can be ironed into place.

It is not usual to attempt any planing with veneer, so the cutting on the edges should be clean and true. When the cross-banding is finished, cover all joints with strips of adhesive paper to check undue shrinkage.

Built-up Pattern with Cross-banded Edges

If a more decorative finish is desired, two veneers can be joined and paired to form a pattern, or perhaps four pieces could be used. These pieces are cut from the log consecutively, and so have the same grain marking. This pattern is built up from several pieces which are held together by strips of adhesive paper. The whole is then veneered as with one piece.

If a patch of veneer shows a tendency to lift it can be dampened and ironed down. To clean up the surface after veneering, the paper is carefully dampened and removed with a cabinet worker's scraper. This is followed up with several applications of glasspaper to produce the desired surface for polishing.

HANDYMAN JOBS IN AND AROUND THE HOME

PANELLING AND HOW TO MAKE JOINTS

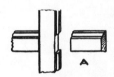

The appearance of a panelled room is enhanced by neat panelling strips which are used to cover the joints, or to break up the panelling sheets into sections, and these sketches might therefore be of assistance to anyone who might contemplate doing their rooms in this way.

There are several types of these cover joints which may be used— plain ones of approximately 2 in. x ½ in. being most commonly used, but other strips with, say, a moulded edge are very effective, whilst a combination of plain and moulded strips present a very nice appearance.

Illustration A shows how the joints are made when moulded strips are used throughout, whilst B will show how the joints are made when a combination of plain and moulded strips are used—this sketch showing the plain horizontals and moulded verticals.

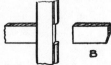

This latter combination would be just as pleasing if the verticals are plain and the horizontals moulded—it does not matter which way they are placed.

PANELLING A HALL OR ROOM

Panelling will beautify a hall or room and can easily be done by the amateur handyman. First of all, select the plywood required, as it will determine the height of the dado. The usual size of sheets is 6 x 3, whilst some are 4 x 3 or 7 x 3.

Next comes the height of the dado. Four-foot sheets are generally used about 4 ft. 6 in. high. Six-foot sheets can be used to their full height or cut in halves. Low dados are surmounted with a dado rail, usually about 3 in. x 1 in., but the taller dados are usually finished with a specimen shelf about 4 in. or 5 in. wide x 1 in. thick, supported by small brackets (as shown).

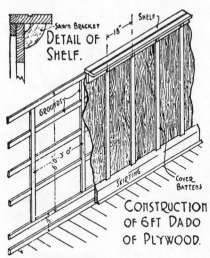

DETAIL OF SHELF.

CONSTRUCTION OF 6 FT DADO OF PLYWOOD.

The usual way of fixing plywood is by means of what is called "grounds" (see diag.), i.e., light pieces of timber fixed to the walls.

This can be 2 in. x 1 in. oregon or pinus radiata.

They should be fixed at intersection of sheets, and horizontally about every 18 in., one at the top and one at the junction of the dado with the skirting. Another at the foot of skirting is advisable. This should be thicker than the others by

the thickness of the plywood. The plugs are located in the seams of the brickwork. The vertical grounds are fixed to the plugs, but the others can be cut in between, as shown, and securely nailed with fine brads.

The plywood is then fixed by use of 1 in. flat hard nails where the nails will be covered with battens, or with 1 in. fine brads, where they are in the open, the brads being carefully punched below the surface.

Where the figured plywoods are concerned, stand them up around the room before fixing, so that the best effect can be secured. Doubtful sheets can be placed behind doors, etc.

After skirting, battens and specimen shelf have been fixed, the work is sandpapered off and stained, or merely oiled with raw oil, after which all brad holes are stopped with putty, coloured to match the timber. One coat of shellac varnish, one coat of hard oak varnish, and one coat of eggshell flat makes a good finish.

WORKING WITH PLYWOOD

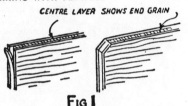

CENTRE LAYER SHOWS END GRAIN

Fig 1

Chisel off corner before trimming edges with plane

Plywood has many uses; it is reliable, free from warping and shrinking; it is cheap, light and can be obtained in various widths, and it has beautifully grained surface veneers in oak, walnut, mahogany, and other finishes. The most common size is 6 ft. x 3 ft., with a thickness of 3/16 in. having one side sanded.

Cutting down waste. Always bear in mind the size of the sheet when planning a job, i.e., if making a cupboard, it is an advantage to work on a width of 18 in. or slightly less, so that a sheet cut down the centre will do for the two sides.

Fig 2.
Triangular block glued in to strengthen butt joint.

Cutting the Wood. Use a fine-tooth saw, as those with large teeth often cause splintering on the underside layer of the plywood. If this is not available, use a tenon-saw, holding it at a fairly acute angle to the sheet when cutting, and placing little or no pressure on the saw. This lessens the risk of damage.

Care is needed in finishing the cut, as this is the time when most damage is caused. On the thinner type of plywood, a chisel drawn along a straight-edge will often be suitable. Use an ordinary fret-saw for cutting curves and other small shapes. They are best suited for the job.

Planing. The edge is the only part which really needs the plane. It is risky to plane right through to the far end of the pieces, as the grains of wood are at right-angles, and some might be liable to split. Therefore, it is better to take the plane along first from one end and then from the other. Failing this, it is advisable to chisel off a corner as in sketch No. 1.

Fig 3.

Joints. Owing to the thinness of the wood, ordinary butted joints are not often used, except in very light work. In such cases fine nails should be used, and should be driven into the centre

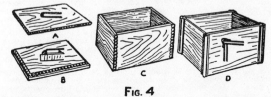

Fig. 4

Showing the use of mouldings to conceal the edges of plywood.

layer only, making sure that they do not enter the joint between the layers, where they might cause a split. It is advisable to glue in triangular blocks as shown in figure 2 to strengthen any such butt joints.

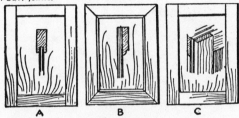

Fig. 5.

(a) **Plywood panel in grooved frame.** (b) **Mitred moulding round plywood panel.** (c) **Battens used to form framework of door**

Figure 3 shows how it is possible to use the dovetailed joint, especially where thicker types of plywood are used, but good use can be made of grooved mouldings to conceal the edges of the wood.

HANDYMAN JOBS IN AND AROUND THE HOME

CUTTING GLASS IN THE HOME WORKSHOP

CONVERTING A BOTTLE INTO A FUNNEL

SMOOTH EDGES

OLD GLASS BOTTLE

To know some of the best ways to cut glass to any desired shape is very useful as many people hesitate to do the job.

A useful article such as a combined scoop and funnel can be made from a bottle by cutting off the bottom to the angle indicated in this drawing. The edges should be smoothed down with a fine file or on a grinding wheel, taking care, of course, not to break the glass.

Such a funnel will be found very handy where a metal scoop or funnel is not desirable. You can scoop up the material with it, using the bottle-neck as a handle, and then turn it over to let the contents turn into a small-mouthed container.

HINTS ON CUTTING GLASS

Cutting Bottles, etc. A good clean cut without ragged edges can be obtained by taking a piece of string, dipping it in kero or petrol and tying it once round the bottle at the point where the cut is desired. Hold the bottle sideways, with the knot at the bottom, so that the string will not fall off when you light the ends of the knot.

When the string has burnt out, tap the bottle around the line where the string was, and the top should come off cleanly.

Another method is to pour lard oil into the bottle up to the mark where the break is wanted, then heat an iron rod to red heat, and plunge it into the oil. The glass will crack round the edge of the oil, and the top may be lifted off.

You can also cut bottles or glass with a red hot poker or piece of metal by just tracing it slowly over the line of cut. Tap the glass carefully along this line.

Trimming under Water. Glass can be trimmed under water (but not cut) as, for instance, this method is not applicable to cutting a large pane in half. The water really serves to dampen the vibration.

The cutting medium is usually a large pair of tinner's shears (as in fig. 2) and the whole operation is carried on under water. In cutting such things as glass discs and shield instruments such as headlights, it is not necessary to have an absolutely smooth edge, as the glass is usually held in place with a frame or bevel.

The simplest way is to trim such glass under water with large shears.

Be sure to turn the cut edges away from you, and when the disc is cut, you can smooth off the job by grinding.

Getting a smooth edge. As an alternative to the water method, rough lines can be cut outwards to the edge of the glass from the circumference of the scribed circle (see fig. 3 on top of fig. 5). If you scribe the circle, cut the rough lines and tap the glass; it will break, but it will leave a ragged projection at every point where the lines join the circumference, and this must be ground off.

However, if you tap the glass round the circumference immediately after scribing the circle, and then cut the radiating lines, you should get a circle with no projection.

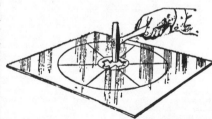

To cut a circular hole, scribe the circle with a circular cutter, but do not try to break it out at once or you will spoil the piece of glass through its cracking past the scribed circle. Just carelessly scribe a few radial lines from the edge of the circumference to the centre, and then scribe a small circle at the centre. Break out this small circle first by tapping, and then continue tapping to break out the segments, and you will have a neat circular hole.

Drilling a hole in glass is really very easy. First, take a round head screw and clamp it by the shank in a bench vice. Hold the glass to be drilled over the head of the screw and tap it with a light hammer round this point. This tapping will merely break the hard surface of the glass, roughing it so that the drill point can take hold. An ordinary hand brace will do, but when it comes to the drill, that is another story.

Take any ordinary three-cornered file and sharpen the triangular end to a point so as not to lose temper by excessive heat.

This sharpening should be done by grinding on a wet grindstone. If a grinder is not available, a wet flat stone will do.

Now chuck the file in your drill and go ahead. The size of hole will depend upon how far you drill into the glass.

TAPE

Saving the Cut-out. If you want to cut an opening in some glass already installed, but not accessible from the inside, and you do not want the piece to fall inwards and perhaps damage something inside, the use of adhesive tape will suffice. Start your cut in the regular way, but put a few pieces of tape across the scribed line as you progress (fig. 5). Then put one piece at bottom. Tap the glass around the circle, using the lower edge of the tape to lift the glass out.

Another method is with the aid of a wooden bushing as shown (cemented on to the glass with liquid solder to steady the drill). The counterboard section of the bushing acts as a reservoir for holding an ample supply of turpentine. If a carbon steel drill is used, it pays to heat the point to a bright red, dip it in sulphur, and then quench it quickly.

How to Repair Broken Window Panes

Smashed window panes are easy to repair. The numbered illustrations given here show, step by step, how to fit in a new pane of glass.

① USE CONCENTRATED LYE TO SOFTEN OLD PUTTY AND REMOVE GLASS

Oftentimes old putty is difficult to remove, even with knife. Apply a concentrated lye solution with an old paint brush to soften putty. Do not get any lye on hands.

FRAME GROOVE

② SCRAPE CLEAN GROOVE OF FRAME

Scrape off all old paint and putty adhering to the wood. Waterproof groove with coat of linseed oil or thin paint.

③ PAINT GROOVE WITH LINSEED OR THIN PAINT

PLACE HANDLE UNDER GLASS—PRESS GENTLY AND BREAK

-d-

KNIFE

-E-

④ MEASURE ALL SIDES FOR LENGTH AND IRREGULARITIES

CUTTING ⑤-a TAKE TO HARDWARE MAN

USE STRAIGHT EDGE AND MARK LINE WITH CRAYON ON GLASS

CUT DEEP ENOUGH TO MARK ONLY

-C-

To get correct size of glass required, cut cardboard to exact size, or measure all four sides of the window.

CUT PIECE OF CARD BOARD TO TRY FOR EXACT SIZE

It is best to have glass cut to exact size at hardware store. Place thin layer of putty all around in groove, then put glass in place, and fasten with glazier's points. Knead putty well before using, adding a little oil if necessary, to soften.

⑥ LAY IN LAYER OF PUTTY IN GROOVE

IF PUTTY IS HARDENING MIX IN LINSEED OIL

⑦ ROLL PUTTY INTO STRIPS FOR EASE IN SPREADING

SET IN GLASS— HOLD IN PLACE WITH GLAZIER'S POINTS USING HAMMER OVER KNIFE BLADE TO DRIVE IN

⑧

GLAZIER'S POINT

Roll putty into long strips, place over groove, and spread with a putty knife. Work putty back and forth until uniform bevel is obtained all around the window. Wipe off oil stains with gasoline or turpentine.

TO REMOVE PUTTY STAINS USE GASOLINE OR TURPENTINE

AFTER ONE DAY PAINT SAME COLOR AS FRAME

After putty has set, apply a coat of paint. If glass is held in place with wood or metal strips as shown below, apply thin coat of putty before nailing or screwing strips in place. Then proceed as usual.

⑨ SPREAD PUTTY STRIPS WITH PUTTY KNIFE

PUTTY BED

⑩ PUTTY PAINT

METAL FRAME USING PUTTY

←GLASS

PUTTY

PUTTY GLASS

WOODEN STRIP FRAME WITH PUTTY

METAL FRAMING

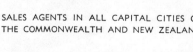

THE HANDYMAN ROUND THE HOME

USEFUL HINTS FOR AMATEUR PAINTERS

Unless paint is properly mixed before it is used, it cannot be expected to give good results. Stirring round and round in the manner shown on the left-hand side of the first illustration (below) will not mix paint thoroughly, and attempting to stir a full tin will generally result in the spilling of a good deal of oil.

Before stirring paint, dip or pour some of the oil from the top. Stir the remainder by starting from the bottom and bringing the paddle to the top with a twist as shown on the right-hand side of sketch No. 1. Pour the oil back little by little, and stir gently. Finally, pour the paint back and forth from one can to another.

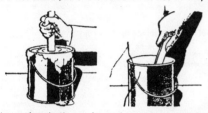

Do not leave paint uncovered when not in use, as shown on the left-hand side of illustration No. 2. Always replace the lid as indicated on the right.

Besides getting dirty, paint left uncovered will also 'skin' over. If the cover cannot be replaced, tie a piece of newspaper or cloth over the top.

Where paint has been left uncovered, the skin should be removed

in one piece by cutting round the edge with a putty or mixing knife, and by lifting it off. If the skin is broken up it will not dissolve, and it will make the paint lumpy. Pieces of skin can be removed from the paint by straining it.

BRUSHES

Generally speaking, there are certain correct ways of holding a brush. Never grasp it as shown on the left of the following drawing, but rather hold it as indicated on the right, or, especially where larger brushes or kalsomine brushes are concerned, as per the larger illustration on the top centre of this page.

The brush should be held lightly between thumb and fingers, and applied with an even movement of the wrist in a manner so as to wear the bristles to a chiselled edge. If the brush is used sideways it will wear to a point, and will in consequence be

spoiled. Jabbing a brush into a corner will also spoil it by making it stubby.

Use long, continuous strokes always exerting an even pressure, and, whilst holding the brush lightly at all times, yet paint vigorously into the surface.

Care of Brushes. If left lying around (as in left-hand detail of this sketch), brushes will become hard and unfit for use. They should be cared for after each job. One of the simplest methods, if you intend to use the brush within a day or so, is to suspend it from a wire in linseed oil.

Brushes to use. For mouldings and all small work, a 2" or 2½" wall brush for wide work. For interior work, i.e., sashes, doors and skirtings, a 1" and 2" or 2½" flat are the most useful. For outside painting use 1" flat for sashes,

Another good method is to fold a sheet of paper freshly painted with some of the paint, over the bristles to form a water-tight jacket, and stand the brush in water.

When the job is done, clean the brush in a suitable solvent and wash it with soap and water, without letting the bristles become watersoaked. It should then be dried thoroughly.

Should the bristles become hard owing to neglect, soak them in a liquid paint remover that can be purchased, and when the bristles are soft, wash in benzol, finish with soap and warm water. Never use your Kal-brush in oil paints.

PAINTING

In painting clapboards, do not start painting the flat part first as shown on the left of above sketch. The proper way is to paint the underneath edges first as shown on the right. Brush along several edges at a time for a space of a few yards.

Then coat the faces of the board.

If the edges of the boards are not painted, they will be without a protective coating, and the moisture from the rain will get into the wood and cause the formation of blisters under the paint. If the flat portions are painted first, some of the paint will be wiped off when the under edges are coated.

DIP LESS THAN HALF THE LENGTH OF BRISTLES

USEFUL PAINTING HINTS

Before using a new brush, strike it smartly across the edge of a board several times to throw out the dirt particles. Then work out any loose bristles with the fingers. Finally, dip the brush in turpentine and work it on a clean board or piece of paper. Careful painters also use a dusting brush for cleaning dust and dirt off first.

In applying paint, the brush should always be dipped into the liquid only about one-third the length of the bristles (see illustration) and excess paint slapped off against the pail as shown. When carrying the brush from the pail to the work, keep the loaded bristles down. This prevents the paint running into the bristles.

SLAP OFF EXCESS PAINT TO PREVENT DRIPPING

Lift the brush lightly from the surface at the end of each stroke.

When painting into corners, set the loaded brush into the corner as shown, then draw the paint right away with a light, quick stroke.

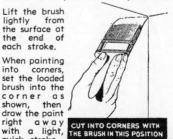

CUT INTO CORNERS WITH THE BRUSH IN THIS POSITION

CARRY THE LOADED BRUSH WITH THE BRISTLES DOWN

HANDYMAN JOBS IN AND AROUND THE HOME

VARNISHING

When varnishing, enamelling or lacquering, the material should be "flowed" on with a full brush, the flowing stroke made first with the grain of the wood.

FLOW ON VARNISH WITH LONG STROKES

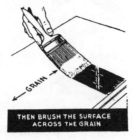

THEN BRUSH THE SURFACE ACROSS THE GRAIN

The varnish will level to a fairly smooth finish of its own accord. It should then be stroked lightly across the grain and, as a final touch, with the grain (see examples).

SERVICEABLE HOME-MADE BRUSHES

Some serviceable and cheap home-made brushes which will do quite a good job in an emergency can be made as follows.

Just get some horsehair, a short length or two of copper pipe, and some short pieces of wire. The length of wire is put through the pipe and hooked round some horsehair as shown in the sketch No. 1.

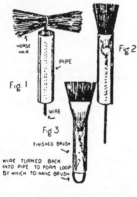

The wire is then drawn down through the pipe in the manner shown, drawing the horsehair with it to a certain distance. The completed brush is shown in sketch 3.

Such brushes are extremely useful for countless jobs on the farm and in the milking shed, etc.

SKINLESS PAINT

A useful strainer. This is a handy article to keep near the paint pots.

When particles of the skin that form on the top of a tin of paint that has stood for a time accidentally gets mixed with the paint, and is likely to get picked up by the brush and spoil the paint, just suspend a perforated tin inside the paint tin with wires.

The holes will permit the paint to pass through, but will keep out the pieces of skin. The paint brush is dipped into the inner tin.

MAKING A CLEAN JOB

When painting from small tins, the paint often creeps down the side of the tin and drops on to the floor or on to the work.

This can be avoided by making a holder from a larger tin as shown here, as the dripping is then prevented.

The guard is made by cutting away the upper part of an empty tin of suitable size, leaving only a strip a little over an inch wide, which is rolled to form a handle (see dotted lines on left-hand sketch for procedure in cutting).

A HOME-MADE STIRRER FOR PAINT

A metal paddle made like the one illustrated here is much more efficient than the ordinary plain stick.

It is, of course, necessary to clean the stirrer before putting it aside after use.

BENT UP AND SHARPENED

The material may be a strip of galvanised iron at least 24g., stouter if possible. If thin iron is used, it will be necessary to turn over a seam along each edge to make it stiff enough for thick paint. The lower end of the paddle is bent over at right angles, say $\frac{1}{2}$ in., and the edge sharpened. This provides a handy scraper for loosening the pigment which has settled into a mass at the bottom, also a flat surface for mashing the lumps that have loosened. The holes help in blending the pigment with the oil.

A USEFUL HOME-MADE PUTTY KNIFE

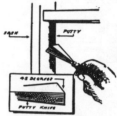

Amateurs often finish puttying with ragged edges. By making this putty knife, the work will be found much easier. All that is required is a piece of sheet steel, not thicker than 16 gauge, 5 or 6 in. long, and cut into triangular shape, 1 in. wide at the larger end. This is gripped in a vice, and bent lengthwise down the centre at right angles, so as to make it trough shaped.

The two wings at the broad end are now filed at an angle of 45 deg. from the centre outwards, and the edges made smooth on the inside. The pointed end of the tool is driven into a handle of convenient size.

To use the knife, a strip of putty is laid in the rebate of the window sash (the glass being already in position), and the knife, being held so as to "straddle" the rail, is drawn almost perpendicularly along the rail so that one corner of the bevelled point bears against the glass. It will be found that the putty will spread in a nice even strip with a straight edge. One or two trials may be needed before the operation is satisfactory.

If thicker steel is not available, a piece of flat galvanised iron of 24g. may be used as the raw material for the knife.

THE USE OF PUTTY

In filling holes or cracks with putty, do not use a stiff putty knife, as shown on the left, for it will push or pull the putty away from the hole.

Good practice is shown on the right. Roll out a little of the putty between thumb and forefinger, press it down firmly into the hole, and remove the excess with a downward twist of the thumb. For long cracks which cannot be readily filled in this manner, a flexible putty knife, used in much the same manner as the fingers, will serve. For large openings, stuff paper, rags or oakum into the hole before applying the putty.

AN ADJUSTABLE BRUSH FOR ANGLE PAINTING

This brush will help paint in inaccessible corners. Saw off an ordinary brush about two-thirds of the way up the ferrule. Drill corresponding holes in the metal ends, and join the two parts with a screw and

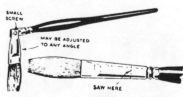

nut, as shown. Set at the most convenient angle and then tighten the nut. It will make an awkward job much easier.

HANDYMAN JOBS IN AND AROUND THE HOME

HINTS ON USING THE BLOW LAMP

The blow lamp is not necessary very often, but if the old surface is badly cracked or blistered, it may be required, otherwise a good rubbing down is all that is necessary. When using the blow lamp in hot weather, keep a wet bag handy in case of fire. Hold the flame of the blow lamp close to the wood until the paint starts to blister, when it can be lifted off with a stripping knife —the flame being slowly moved up with the stripping knife following it close underneath as indicated.

For working in corners, pieces of blunted stick will do, but the shave hook is very useful. After burning off, one treats the timber exactly as new work, the process being to cover the knots with knotting; then priming, rubbing down, stopping with putty, and then painting 2 or 3 coats with the selected colour. The ideal surface for repainting should be slightly chalky.

PAINTING GALVANISED IRON

Galvanised iron is rather difficult to paint, but with good paint and certain precautions, a good job can be done. New iron must first have its hard glaze roughened up with a steel wire brush, particular attention being paid to the joints which have been soldered. It should then be allowed to "weather" for some time—the longer the better—but if this is not possible, brush well on a coat of 5 lb. of bluestone to a gallon of warm water, which will turn it black, but will not do it any harm.

Let it dry thoroughly.

A good priming is made from red lead with a gallon of boiled oil and a quart of turpentine. Add a little more turpentine if needed for easy working. This use of red lead is one of the few exceptions to the rule that a dry pigment mixed with boiled oil should never be used as a primer. The red lead must be pure and fine. The mixed red lead will soon set and harden, so figure out and mix just the quantity required, and on the day before using mix the dry red lead with three-quarters of the oil. Next morning add the rest of the oil and the turpentine. Stir well and keep stirred during the work.

To calculate the quantity required, reckon that the addition of 30 lb. of dry lead to a gallon of oil and a quart of turpentine will bring the liquid up to 2 gallons and $2\frac{1}{2}$ pints. A gallon of this priming will cover about 800 square feet of galvd. iron. When thoroughly dry, apply a good oil paint.

REPAINTING GALVANISED IRON

This, of course, will depend on the condition of the old surface. If merely faded, brush or broom clean, and lay on a single coat with enough turpentine to penetrate and using just enough paint to cover. If not in good condition, two coats may be necessary. It may need brushing with a wire brush or scraper; then bare places touched up with red lead covered with a uniform coat.

If peeling badly and evidently not bound to the iron, scrape the entire surface and treat as new iron, or rather iron that has been weathered, and give a priming and a covering coat.

Several paint manufacturers market a paint specially prepared for galvanised iron, and it is advisable for amateurs to use one of these, following closely the directions on the tin. **Never use** paints containing lead or other poisonous pigments on roofs where the catchment water is used for domestic purposes. Oxide of iron is the only paint you use for such roofs.

A USEFUL HANDLE FOR CARRYING PAINT POTS

If one has several paint pots to carry or if one wants to have 2 or 3 on the ladder at a time, this arrangement should suit admirably. One can then carry several pots in one hand.

The hooks which support them are movable and are held by set-screws at any position desired. If the pots contain different quantities of paint, balance may be maintained by moving the pots nearer to or farther from the handle. This is easily made from pieces of scrap iron.

HANDY METHODS OF KEEPING PAINT POTS FIRM ON LADDER

The first illustration shows a very handy way to prevent small paint tins from sliding off a step-ladder.

It consists merely of a couple of pieces of weather stripping to hold the tins in place. Both strips are tacked on at an angle so that the tins can be wedged between them.

Such an arrangement will be found useful for various size tins.

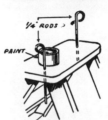

The second sketch shows another way of keeping paint pots near at hand and in a firm position. This idea will also enable one to keep the pots from sliding off when moving the ladder from place to place.

Rods are inserted through the top, as indicated. Bend two lengths of $\frac{1}{4}$ in. rod as shown at left, and then slip them into holes made in the top step. In use, the rods are merely lifted and dropped so that the extending hooks engage the rims of the tins, holding them nice and firmly in place and near at hand.

USEFUL BALANCING POLE ON LADDER

This little arrangement will help considerably when working on high places either when painting or on other jobs.

As everyone knows, it is often very awkward working on the top rungs of a ladder (and specially so when wielding a paint brush) as one is inclined to overbalance.

This pole solves this problem, and it is made from a length of broom handle with a wooden collar near one end, which is inserted through a hole in the top of the ladder, a block being nailed underneath to reinforce it.

HOW TO REMOVE PAINT SPOTS FROM BRICKWORK

If you accidentally drop paint on to some brick surface, an easy way to remove it is shown here.

Mix a solution consisting of caustic soda, $1\frac{1}{2}$ lbs. with 1 gal. hot water.

Apply this solution to the paint to be removed and then wash it off with clear water, repeating the operation until the paint disappears.

In handling this solution, be careful that none of it gets on your skin, as it causes severe burns. Also, it is a good idea to use an old brush, as the solution is hard on the bristles.

HANDYMAN JOBS IN AND AROUND THE HOME

THE ART OF SPLICING

JOINTS AND SPLICES IN ELECTRICAL WORK

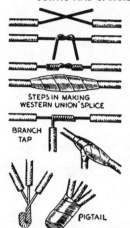

STEPS IN MAKING
WESTERN UNION SPLICE

BRANCH TAP

PIGTAIL

These sketches should be of help to any who may have occasion to joint or splice such articles as electrical wires.

The first joint shown is an end splice for extending a wire. The second is the joint required for tapping a branch at right angles.

Both are used in open wiring.

The third is the pig-tail joint, commonly used in all junction boxes, at fixtures, and in motor terminal boxes. It is constantly utilised in conduit and similar wiring. Approved solderless connectors may be used on pig-tail joints if preferred to solder and tape.

The ends of the wires must be scraped absolutely clean and far enough back to allow enough turns to make a mechanically tight joint. Solder well and wrap tightly with both rubber and friction tapes. Loosely made joints, especially if left unsoldered, can become a fire hazard.

SPLICING ROPES

In hemp splicing, the strands are tucked **against the lay** of the rope. A splice weakens a rope by about one-eighth.

Whipping a Rope. The end of a rope should always be secured or it will fray out—the commonest method being an ordinary whip. A length of twine should be placed along the rope (fig. 1) and some turns taken **against** the lay round both rope and twine, commencing at a point furthest from the rope end. The twine is then placed in the form of a loop (fig. 2) along the rope and over the turns already taken. Then take the part of the loop marked "a," and continue turns tightly round the rope and the part marked "b" of twine until the loop is almost used up; pull through the remainder snugly by part "c," and cut off short when no end of the twine will be visible (see fig. 3).

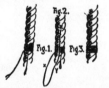

The Eye Splice. After first opening the strands, bend the rope to the desired size with strands placed as shown. Then tuck the middle strand under a strand of the rope and against the lay

(as shown)—then force the left-hand strand under the next to the left. Then turn the rope round to the left so as to bring the remaining strand on top, tucking it from right to left under the third strand on the rope. Each strand should then be tucked alternately over and under a strand of the rope—then split the strands, taking half of each, and tuck them a third time and so on—finally cutting the ends off.

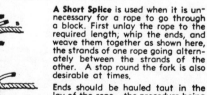

A Short Splice is used when it is unnecessary for a rope to go through a block. First unlay the rope to the required length, whip the ends, and weave them together as shown here, the strands of one rope going alternately between the strands of the other. A stop round the fork is also desirable at times.

Ends should be hauled taut in the lay of the rope—the procedure being along somewhat similar lines as indicated in the Eye Splice, "a" rope into "b" and "b" into "a"—the centre drawing merely serving to show how one strand should go over one of the opposite and under the next, etc.

If it is intended to serve (bind) over the splice, put the strands in 1¼ times, take a few of the underneath yarns from each strand to fill up the lay of the rope and marl them down for **serving.**

The Long Splice is one used for a rope which passes through a block, an illustration of which appears on another page.

The Cut Splice is made by laying two ropes in the position shown here. The ropes between "aa" form an oblong loop and the strands of one rope are tucked into the other as in the eye splice.

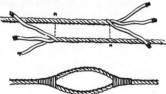

Splices are often wormed, parcelled and served as indicated in the lower drawing.

WIRE ROPES

Steel flexible ropes are reasonably easy to splice if a little care is exercised. **Tucks should be made WITH the lay** of the rope and special care must be taken to avoid kinks.

Details of one or two of the most important of the splices are given below and others will appear in later issues, but space here does not permit of more.

Whipping. When cutting wire rope, it is desirable to whip the rope very tightly on each side of the place to be cut (see the figure 1 in the above drawing) and then further whipping can be applied before unlaying the strands at the points where splicing is to commence (see point marked "2" above).

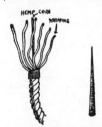

Further, when the strands are separated their ends should also be whipped as indicated on the left of this para. At the same time, the hemp "core" should be cut out close to the whipping on the rope.

Splicing Tool. A home-made marlin-spike can be made somewhat to the shape shown here—it should be fairly long and tapering and, after placing it under a strand, it should not be withdrawn until the tuck is made and all the slack of the strand drawn through.

The Short or Long Splice "Marry." The illustration on left shows one method of what is termed "marrying" a splice. As will be seen the core has been cut out—the ropes whipped and drawn closely together, previous to tucking the strands in (see below). When any such splice is completed, the rope should be stretched before removing the strand ends.

The Short Splice. This is very reliable for joining broken wire rope and a good method is given here. Tuck the first strand under two strands and all the **rest** under one strand respectively. Tuck the whole again and this time each strand under one strand, then halve the strands and tuck again.

SHORT SPLICE

To make a neat splice, do not haul the part of the rope that has been unlaid too close to the neck of the splice, and in tucking the strands, do not take a short nip but take long lays.

The Long Splice is made for occasions when a rope goes through a block. If the rope is, say, 1 in. in

circumference, the length of lay should be at least 6 feet. Always unlay 2 strands simultaneously to keep the rope in its original lay. Unlay the strand of one rope and fill up the gap thus caused by twisting in the opposite strand of the other rope. Then do the same with 2 more strands and so on and after 3 pairs of strands are in their places, single them and continue to unlay and lay-in until the 6 meeting places of the strands are equal distance apart. The rope should then appear as in the sketch. To finish off, tuck in the ends by using 2 marlin spikes to force the ends of the strands into the place previously occupied by the core.

HANDYMAN JOBS IN AND AROUND THE HOME

USEFUL HINTS ON HANGING WALLPAPER

Rooms can be made attractive by the use of nice wallpaper, and the job is quite an easy one if certain rules are followed.

Tools. Fig. 1 shows the most useful plus, of course, a stepladder or two, a couple of planks and a light table, together with trestles (see fig. 2); these trestles being hinged in the centre if necessary for stacking for future use. Some like a zinc strip fastened along one edge of the table for trimming purposes, but a good wood surface is sufficient.

Wall Preparations. Fig. 3 (in 3 sections). Always strip any old paper from the walls before re-papering; this is best done by soaking with hot water. Use a white-wash brush and go right round the room at the one time, wetting the paper until it will absorb no more.

③ PREPARING THE WALL . . . . . .

3ʳᵈ PATCH ALL CRACKS   2ⁿᵈ REMOVE WITH SCRAPER

Often a little baking soda, borax, sal soda, or ammonia added to the water will help soften the old paste. After the old paper has been removed, sponge the walls down and let them dry (fig. 4). Then fill in smoothly with a prepared patching compound any defects or cracks in the walls. Plaster should be glue-sized preparatory to papering—this should be rather thin and applied hot, using a large brush to apply quickly before it jells (fig. 5). One coat will suffice.

If the walls to be papered have been previously painted it will be necessary, in order to make the paste stick, to kill the gloss and oil in the paint by first sanding with rough paper and then washing with a weak solution of sal soda and water (fig. 4). Follow this with a size of plain vinegar. If the walls are very rough, first cover them with a lining paper and use a fairly stiff paste. Also use a wide, stiff smoother brush and paper down hard to assure a firm bond.

Estimating Material. Figure 6 gives the number of rolls required for walls of various sized rooms. The procedure is: first find the height, then the measurement round the room.

For instance, a room 56 feet round the walls and not over 10 ft. high should take nine pieces. For ceilings, the usual method is to take the measurements of each wall and find the number of square feet and then divide by 60.

Most wallpaper is 12 yards long x 21 in. wide, containing approximately 63 sq. ft., but for the purpose of estimating quantities, it is usual to work on 60 sq. ft. These figures are based on the ordinary single rolls, but there are now double rolls on the market, in which case only half the number of rolls would be required.

Making Paste. There are excellent preparations on the market, but if none is available on the spot at the time, the following is a good formula to use (fig. 7). Mix the flour with cold water until it has the consistency of thick cream. Be thorough in beating the batter smooth. Remove any lumps by straining through a fine sieve.

Add alum to make the paste firmer and easier to spread. Place the mass over a flame and boil, stirring continuously, then remove and add cold water until like cream.

Let the paste stand until perfectly cold before using.

A tablespoonful of turpentine to a pail of paste, added while the mixture is hot, will increase its adhesiveness. If lightweight paper is to be used, make paste thin, if heavy paper, thick.

⑤ APPLYING GLUE SIZE   ④ WASHING THE WALL

Fig. 7. Flour 4 lb. Alum 1 oz. mixed with cold water.

No. of Feet Round Room	Height from Skirting to Cornice			
	8 ft.	9 ft.	10 ft.	11 ft.
32	4	5	5	6 pieces of paper
40	5	6	7	7 " "
48	6	7	8	9 " "
52	7	8	9	9 " "
56	8	8	9	10 " "
60	8	9	10	11 " "
68	9	10	11	12 " "
72	10	11	12	13 " "
80	11	12	13	14 " "
88	12	13	14	16 " "
100	13	14	16	18 " "

FIGURE 6

HANDYMAN JOBS IN AND AROUND THE HOME

USEFUL HINTS ON HANGING WALLPAPER (continued)

Cutting the Paper. First study the pattern in order to cut it with the least waste. There are two types of paper, i.e., the straight and the drop-figure

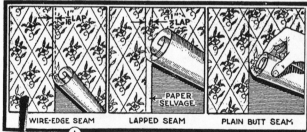

Fig. 9

papers as shown in fig. 8. The latter is usually a floral design which will not match immediately opposite, and therefore must be dropped or moved downward to match the opposite strip. This drop measures one half the full figure, and must be cut accordingly, so that if your pattern is 18 in. long, the opposite length of paper must be lowered 9 inches. The pattern is often marked where it is to be cut.

You should cut from two rolls in the case of a drop-figure pattern, cutting on the marks from one roll, and between the marks from the other. A straight figured wallpaper matches immediately opposite and all lengths are cut on the marks.

Pasting and Trimming. Fig. 9 shows 3 types of joints or seams, i.e., the butt, lap and wire edges. The lapped seam is the simplest to use as it only requires trimming on one edge. Some papers are ready trimmed, and they are only suitable for a lapped seam. For a butt seam, both edges must be trimmed by hand, regardless as to whether the paper may be ready trimmed. This joint is preferable, and it makes a neater job.

The wire edge seam is more or less a lapped joint which resembles a butt joint, with less skill required

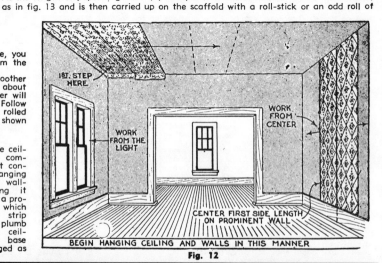

in keeping the joint closed. Trimming is done after the length has been pasted. Here the pasted ends of the paper are temporarily folded over midway, as in fig. 10—keeping the edges perfectly even, after which the straight-edge is laid parallel to the paper to guide the knife in trimming the selvage (fig. 11). When only one edge of the paper is to be trimmed, first make sure you are trimming the right edge. In pasting thin and delicate papers, you will have to work a little faster, otherwise, if left too long, the paper is apt to tear whilst hanging. Above all, get the habit of wiping your paste-board off each time; otherwise there will be stains on the paper.

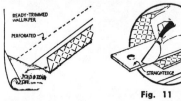

FIGURE 8 (lower)—Straight and drop figure papers.

FIGURE 14 (upper)—Showing how to roll seams down.

Fig. 11

wallpaper. If the angle of the ceiling is not true, you first strike a guide line about 16 inches in from the wall and hang to this.

"Tack" the end of the strip in place with a smoother brush, allowing it to extend down to the side wall about ¼ in. As you continue across the room the paper will unfold. Brush it out smoothly and avoid blisters. Follow this strip with succeeding ones. The seams are rolled down firmly, as shown in fig. 14.

Fig. 13

Walls. After the ceiling has been completed, the first consideration in hanging the first side wall-strip is having it plumb. Select a prominent wall on which to centre the strip (fig. 12), a plumb line from the ceiling to the base board is arranged as

Hanging the Paper—Ceilings. The whole secret is in the manner in which the paper is prepared prior to hanging. With a butt type seam, it makes little difference whether the paper runs the length or width of the room, but with a lap seam, it is important to work from the lighted side of the room (fig. 12), because, if not done, shadows will be cast from each seam, making the ceiling very noticeable upon entering the room.

As the length of paper is gradually pasted, it is folded back and forth in loose folds, as in fig. 13 and is then carried up on the scaffold with a roll-stick or an odd roll of

Fig. 12

HANDYMAN JOBS IN AND AROUND THE HOME

HANGING WALLPAPERS (continued)

Fig. 15

shown in figures 15 and 15a. The starting length of the paper is hung to this line, keeping the edge of the paper exactly level with the plumb line, working each way from this centre strip.

If a lap seam is employed, it is not necessary to trim either edge of this first strip.

Use your trimming knife in cutting the paper to length at the base board.

At the window and door cornices, crowd the paper around the moulding with the smoother and trim carefully with a knife as shown in fig. 16. In entering a corner, do not continue a full width strip around the angle as shown in the left hand detail of figure 17. Instead, cut a "fill-in" strip of the proper width, as shown on the right hand side of the illustration.

Finally, the border is hung, commencing in an obscure corner of the room as indicated in figure 18 at the foot of this column.

Fig. 15a

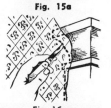

Fig. 16

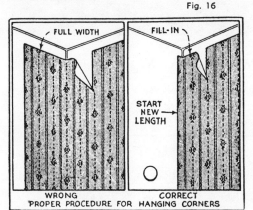

WRONG | CORRECT
PROPER PROCEDURE FOR HANGING CORNERS

Fig. 17

START THE BORDER IN AN OBSCURE CORNER

Fig. 18

Keep the pasted side off the lower side wall while hanging the bordering, in order to avoid staining.

By following these notes, one should be able to make quite a good job of this type of work; jobs which are often put off from time to time because of the lack of a little knowledge.

It is a job which can be done by any "handyman" in his spare time and done quite effectively. It only needs a little care and knowledge as to the best way to go about the job.

A QUICK REPAIR FOR WINDOWS

Sometimes a pane of glass becomes badly cracked, but none of the glass is knocked out, and, with a little attention quickly, the glass will be quite useful for quite a long time.

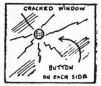

This can be fixed quite easily by using two buttons, one on each side, at the point where the cracks converge. The buttons are then simply sewn together as shown in the illustration.

REMOVING PAINT FROM GLASS

This is a very handy and quick method of removing paint and other transparencies from glass.

It consists of merely rubbing a coin over the glass a few times and then following it up by cleaning off with a damp rag.

The main point about this idea is that the glass should not become scratched in any way.

CUTTING SAFETY GLASS

First score the glass across one surface with a glass cutter. Then lay the glass on a table with the scored line on top and directly above the table edge.

Place one hand on each side of the scored line, and press down on the overhanging part until you see or hear the glass crack along the cut.

Then turn the glass over and score a second line exactly opposite the first. Then repeat steps 2 and 3 to break the layer of glass on the other side. Work the glass back and forth to break the plastic sheet in the centre. If it doesn't part readily, lay the glass over a small stick or rod, weight down two sections to spread the cut, and separate the plastic sheet with a thin razor blade. To cut "chicken wire" glass, simply score one surface and break in the usual way. The embedded wire snaps off readily.

SOFTENING PUTTY WITH BLAZING FLUID

One way of removing hard putty from frames is to pour a little inflammable liquid over the putty and ignite it. The fluid will burn out rapidly and leave the putty soft enough to be easily removed.

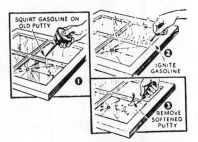

If using an old oil tin, keep it well out of the way before setting fire to the liquid.

CUTTING PUTTY FOR SASHES

By tacking a sheet of corrugated tin to a board, one may roll putty over it into convenient strips. A bottle is used to roll the putty, and the strips, being of the size and shape to fit against the sash, will smooth easily into place when a putty knife is applied in the usual way.

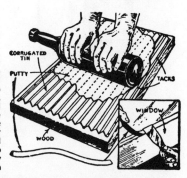

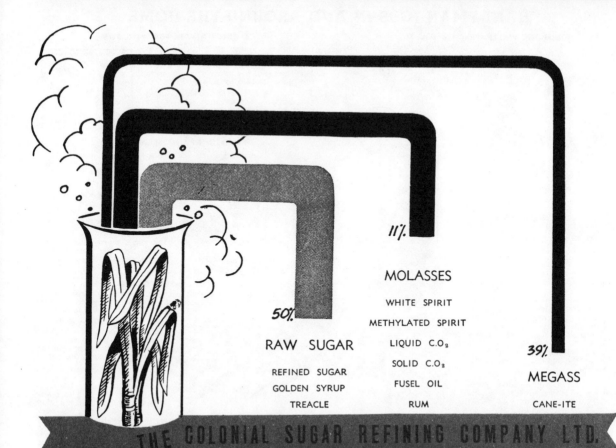

50%.

RAW SUGAR

REFINED SUGAR
GOLDEN SYRUP
TREACLE

11%.

MOLASSES

WHITE SPIRIT
METHYLATED SPIRIT
LIQUID C.O$_2$
SOLID C.O$_2$
FUSEL OIL
RUM

39%.

MEGASS

CANE-ITE

THE COLONIAL SUGAR REFINING COMPANY LTD.

BUILDING MATERIALS DIVISION

| FIBROBESTOS ROOFING | ★ | CONCORD PLASTER | ★ | ASBESTOS, SLAGWOOL | ★ | "GYPROCK," GYPSUM, WALLBOARD |

Sugar-cane—one of the most versatile raw materials that Australia produces.

Dozens of growing secondary industries are calling more and more for sugar products, by-products and their derivative.

In the post-war world these materials will enable Australian manufacturers to compete with confidence, both in the home and export markets

SYDNEY ★ MELBOURNE ★ BRISBANE ★ ADELAIDE ★ PERTH

NEW ZEALAND AND FIJI

HANDYMAN JOBS IN AND AROUND THE HOME

THE SIMPLE ART OF RECANING FURNITURE

There are often articles of this type to be renovated. When a cane seat breaks, the way to repair it is to cut out all the old cane and start at the beginning. If there are no holes in the frame, new ones must be bored, usually about ½ in. from the inner edge, according to size of seat and size of cane used.

Try and use the same size cane as used before, but if none is available as a sample, work on the following measurements: If the holes are 1-8 in. or 3-16 in. diameter and 3-8

BEGIN STRINGING FROM THE FRONT CENTER HOLE

in. apart, use what is termed as superfine. If holes are ½ in. apart, use fine-fine; when 5-8 in. apart, use fine. Quarter-inch holes ¾ in. apart require medium. Those mostly used are fine and medium. Then there are also the narrow and wide binders.

Cane usually has one glossy surface easily recognisable, and this side should be kept face upwards. A 1,000 ft. bundle will reseat 3 or 4 average size chairs. The only tools needed are 5 or 6 tapered pegs.

Another drawing showing weaving under and over with second horizontal

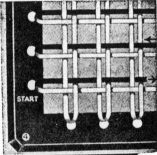

THE WEAVING BEGINS — UNDER ONE STRAND AND OVER THE NEXT

Weeving Begins. The next step (fig. 4) is the actual weaving; this is done from left to right, each horizontal strand (shown in black) is passed under one vertical and over the next. Make the return trip along the next line from right to left; this time weaving over and under, instead of under and over. In weaving, frequently draw the entire strand up taut.

The Diagonals. This is the next step (fig. 5). Starting at the left front corner hole, work the strand under the double row of horizontals and over the double row of verticals, continuing in the same manner on the return trip also. Some prefer to work with one hand above the frame and

Showing how the first diagonal goes under horizontals and over the vertical pairs.

Keeping Cane Moist. To make the cane more pliable and easy to work, each new strand should be immersed in water for a few moments just prior to use. Too much soaking makes it too limp. Dipping the hand in water occasionally will keep it sufficiently moist.

Square Seats Easiest. When weaving **round** seats you must skip several holes, so that the strands will run parallel. For **square** seats, first run the strands vertically from front to back, starting with the centre hole, as in fig. 1. Insert the strand, letting the end extend about 3 in. below, and hold in place with a peg.

Run the entire strand between the thumb and forefinger to keep it from twisting, glazed surface uppermost. From the centre front hole, pass the strand through the centre back hole, drawing it firmly, but not too taut to break, and fasten with a peg.

Then bring the end up through the adjacent hole side, shift the peg to this hole, and, running the cane through the fingers, draw it to the front, parallel to the previous strand. Insert into hole and fasten with peg. Continue this until all vertical strands are in place, omitting the corner holes.

START THE DIAGONAL. STRANDS IN ONE DIRECTION

THEN FINISH IN THE OPPOSITE DIRECTION

CROSS STRANDS ARE STRETCHED FROM LEFT TO RIGHT

Step No. 2 is a repetition, except that the strands run across and over the tops of the first ones, as in fig. 2.

Strand ends. When a strand is nearly used up and is too short to reach across again, peg the end and start a new strand.

Do not join strands.

Before starting the **third step**, fasten the free ends of the strands thus far in place by tying to the underside. To do this, wet the ends of each strand, pass it under one of the loops of cane between the holes, and bring it round in a knot. A knife blade will help in slipping the strand under the loop. Some prefer to fasten all the loose ends as they go.

Third step. This is a repetition of step 1, a second layer of vertical strands being laced over the horizontals, as in figure 3.

ANOTHER LAYER OF STRANDS GOES OVER THE FIRST ONE

one under, and to carry the cane the full distance before pulling it tight, if that distance is not too great.

In the next step (fig. 6), make a diagonal weave in the opposite direction, using the reverse procedure, passing over the horizontals and under the verticals. When this weave is complete, all loose ends are tightened and tied on the underside.

Applying the Binding. Figure 7 shows how the binding provides a neat finish by covering the holes around the border. Fix the binder to the chair with a strand of the same size cane as has been used on the seat by securing it at every alter-

nate hole around the chair by a loop around the binder, the loop being made by passing the strand up from the underside, over the binder and then down through the same hole.

If the strand cannot be passed twice through any hole, enlarge the hole.

Keep the binder tight at all times. Square corners may be turned by thorough soaking and manipulation and a coat of lacquer will make it impervious to moisture. If the seat, when thoroughly dried, rings when struck sharply with the hand, you will have done a good job.

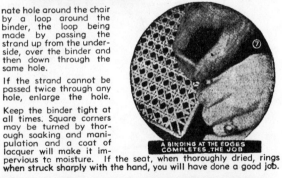

A BINDING AT THE EDGES COMPLETES THE JOB

HANDYMAN JOBS IN AND AROUND THE HOME

HINTS ON REPAIRING FURNITURE

These few hints are drawn from various sources and may be helpful, but, owing to lack of space, they refer mostly to chairs, etc. as they are most likely to be concerned.

Repairs to all furniture should be done as soon as possible as otherwise extra wear and tear will accentuate the damage and make it more difficult to repair.

Chairs often get broken by children standing or jumping on them and they do not therefore last very long when treated in such a manner. One good method of repairing them is to use a fairly heavy piece of sheet metal as a reinforcement for the new seat and place it in the position shown. Then cover it with some suitable material and it will then be as good as new again and children can jump on them to their hearts' content without breaking through the seat again.

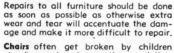

SHEET METAL

Chair supports also often break in the manner shown in this illustration, in which case one method of repairing them is by the use of a metal plate through which has been drilled suitable holes for sufficient screws to make a good solid job.

If it is at all possible for the broken pieces to be taken right out of the chair, it will be quite an easy job to fit the plate on to the broken pieces by working on the bench.

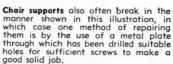

The break can then be glued into position and the plate fastened when the rails can be glued back into position on the legs of the chair.

If the break is a long one such as that shown in the sketches on the right, the only attention needed might be merely the use of glue and screws, with no necessity for the metal plate. The lower drawing shows the combination of both methods of repair.

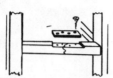

If, however, one does not wish to take the broken piece out in order to repair it, it may be necessary to use a clamp of some sort in order to hold the legs together for the metal plate to be fixed in place.

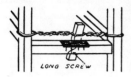

LONG SCREW

An improvised clamp is shown in this illustration and it is very easily made.

A stout piece of twine or wire is fixed as indicated when it can be tightened by twisting a short length of wood as shown. This will force the pieces into place.

REPAIRING CHAIR RUNGS

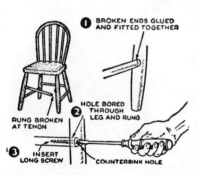

① BROKEN ENDS GLUED AND FITTED TOGETHER

RUNG BROKEN AT TENON

② HOLE BORED THROUGH LEG AND RUNG

③ INSERT LONG SCREW — COUNTERSINK HOLE

These often give way at the point where the tenon enters the leg and repairs might be difficult, as the broken piece has to be dug out.

The method of repair is shown here. The broken ends should be coated with glue, pressed back into place and allowed to set. Then drill a hole and drive a long screw endwise into the rung, as shown. Cover the screw-head with plastic wood.

OTHER METHODS OF REPAIRING BREAKS

Breaks may occur in other ways and can be quickly repaired in the manner shown here. In the first instance, dowelling can be used, in which case two dowels are better than one, if they are possible.

These dowels can be arranged by driving nails in where the dowels have to go—they are then cut off and filed sharp, projecting about $\frac{1}{4}$ in. Then fit them together so that the nails will leave marks to indicate where the holes are to be bored.

NAILS CUT OFF AND POINTED

Then pull the nails out and bore the holes. Groove the dowels so that excess glue can escape. The leg should then appear as shown in the sketch on the left—they are then glued and forced into place.

If the break is a long one, it may be repaired merely by the use of screws and glue as shown on the right hand side of these two illustrations.

However, if the lower end of the chair legs have become badly damaged or perhaps lost, repairs can be effected in quite a different way as shown in the accompanying sketches.

In these, the pieces are cut, glued and screwed as indicated and they provide a very neat and effective job.

The use of brackets to repair any loose joints is also shown. Chair joints have a bad habit of becoming loose, and it is a good idea to pull them apart and glue the joints again keeping them clamped tightly while the glue is setting. **Metal brackets** can also be used in addition as indicated. One illustration shows the single bracket holding one support to the chair leg whilst the other is fixed so that it will hold both supports. In this instance it will be necessary to chisel a little from the leg at the joint of the bracket so that the bracket will fit flush against the rails. This makes a very neat and strong job.

HINTS ON RENOVATING FURNITURE

Owing to lack of space, this is confined to table tops and the method has been found very successful. First clean the table with warm water in which a small piece of soda has been dissolved. Do not use too much soda or you will strip off the existing polish.

Having cleaned the table go over it again with clean warm water, then set aside to dry. When dry, smooth down the surface with some fine glass-paper, and rub well with clean duster. A bottle of french polish is required and a rubber consisting of a pad of wadding wrapped round with a piece of soft linen rag, as at "A." The pad is then held as shown at "B," and with a little polish on it, is rubbed over the table with small circular movements. Always follow the instructions printed on the bottle of polish. A bad crack or hole can be filled with plastic wood with a knife blade as at "C" and when hardened, it can be cut away level with the wood and then polished or painted just like ordinary wood.

HANDYMAN JOBS IN AND AROUND THE HOME

FIRST AID FOR FAVOURITE BOOKS

Home repairs are not difficult—the first book is easily the worst and thereafter it is easier. No special press is necessary, but one can be made from 1 inch board, say, 12 x 9, with two bolts and nuts 6 x $\frac{1}{4}$. All that is needed is even pressure.

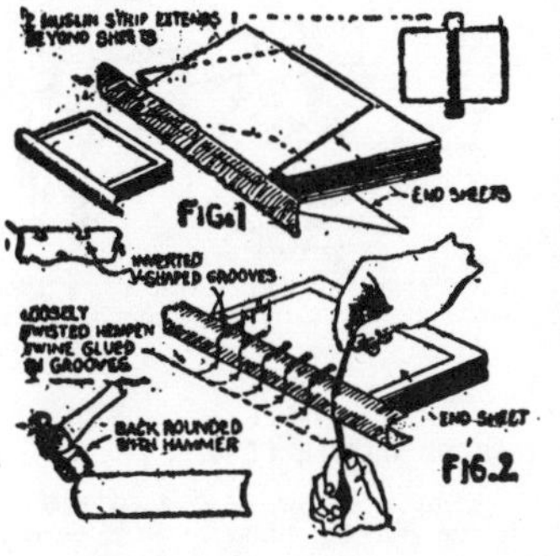

Torn pages can be mended by gumming over with strips of strong transparent paper. Loose leaves can be reinforced at their back edges. When all pages are in order, they should be knocked up evenly to the back. This is important.

Then press the book well to flatten the back folds —the back projecting about $\frac{1}{4}$ in. Cover the back with a thick flour paste to which a little liquid glue has been added—say a teaspoonful to a cup of paste; also a teaspoonful of sugar. Work this well into the edges of the leaves and rub the back smooth with a piece of round wood and leave 24 hours to dry.

These illustrations then show the procedure. **Fig. 1.** Two pieces of tough paper are cut a trifle smaller than the size of the pages (these are called "end sheets"). Join these with a strip of muslin or calico (extending 1 in. beyond the sheet at each end) and so that the space between the sheets is about $\frac{1}{2}$ in. less than the thickness of the book. This is pasted to the back of book and left to dry.

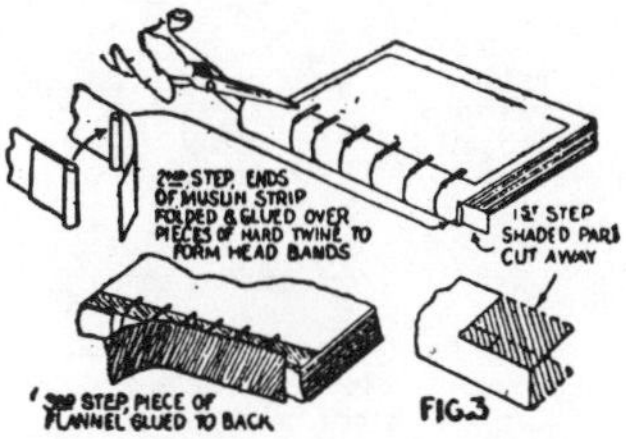

When dry, the book is pressed again and grooves, as shown, cut in the back for cords (**fig. 2**) when loosely twisted twine is glued in—projecting about 1 inch on each side. When the glue is nearly dry, lay the book down and tap lightly along the back edge as indicated in order to slightly round the book. Then clamp the book again with the back in the rounded position; apply a coat of paste, rub it down and leave to dry.

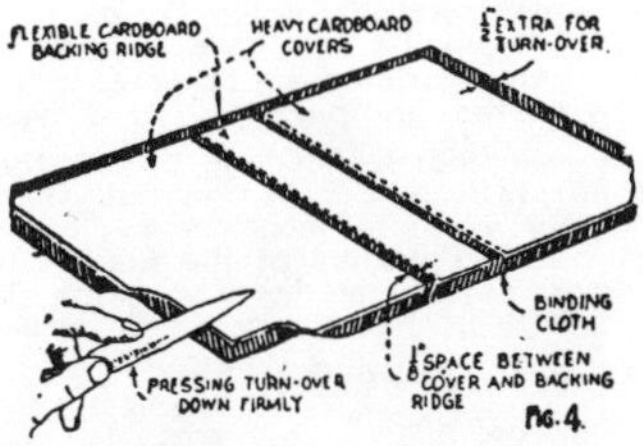

Fig. 3. Cut the extending ends of the calico, glue them and double them over a short piece of hard twine (see illustration) to form the " head " bands and glue them down to the back of the book. An extra strip of flannellette or similar material is then glued to the back projecting an inch on each side; then a piece of strong brown paper is glued over the cloth, this being the same width as the book but $\frac{1}{4}$ in. shorter than the length.

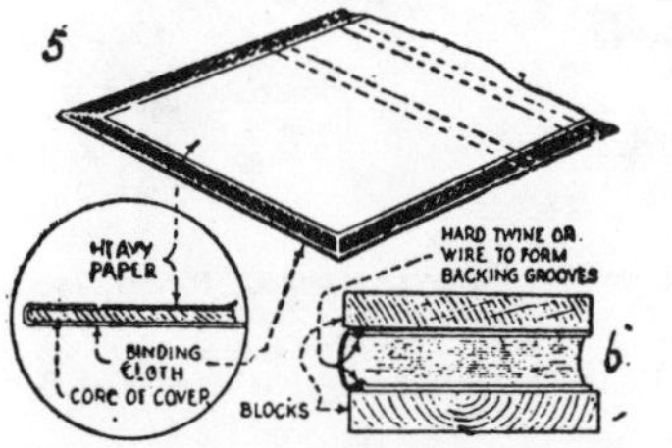

If new covers are to be made, they should project $\frac{1}{8}$ in. on 3 sides and allowance must be made for $\frac{1}{8}$ in. space between the covers and the backing ridge—the latter being cut to the same size as the back of the book.

The covers (**fig. 4**) are now laid down on the binding cloth with the backing ridge between them, leaving a space of fully $\frac{1}{8}$ in. on each side. The cloth is cut to allow $\frac{1}{2}$ in. on all sides for turnover. Mark the positions with pencil as a guide, then coat the inner surface of the binding cloth with glue; place the covers back and press into place.

The projecting cloth is then carefully turned over and pressed down tigthly. Avoid wrinkling at corners—this can be done by cutting a small square piece out of each corner, taking care not to cut in quite to the corner of the cardboard.

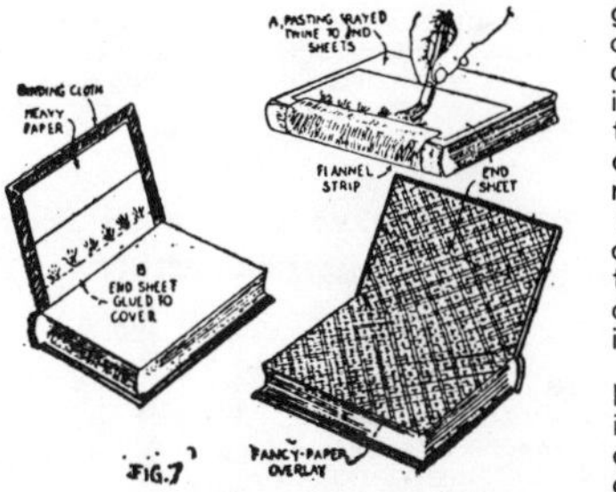

After this has all been done, and before the glue on the cloth has dried, cut two sheets of heavy paper to fit inside the covers and to butt against the cloth all round, but not overlapping it (see left-hand sketch of **fig. 5**) and paste them down—this is done to check warping.

Next, the book is laid in place on the back cover and the front cover is brought over so that the backing ridge is in line against the back of the book. A piece of hard twine is tied loosely round the book, in the position shown in the sketch, and so that it lies over the $\frac{1}{8}$ in. space between covers and backing ridge (**fig. 6**).

It is then put in the press in the manner shown so that the back can be rubbed well against the book. This shows how to form a "backing groove" which will help the book to open well. Press till covers are dry (12 to 24 hours).

Putting covers on. Remove the books from the press, open the covers and fray out in fan shape the ends of the cords which are in the grooves and paste the frayed twine to the "end sheets," being careful that none of the strands cross (**fig. 7**).

Then paste the flannellete strip and the " end sheets " to the inside of the covers. If desired, this operation can be done before the previous one of pressing in the " backing groove " when both glueing jobs can be done simultaneously. To prevent wrinkles, the " end sheets " must be stretched towards the front edge of the covers.

Before putting in the press to dry, put a piece of oiled or waxed paper between the end sheets and the pages in order to prevent them from sticking.

The overlaying material can be glued into place and a further pressing with oiled sheets in between will finish the job.

OTHER HINTS ON BOOK REPAIRS

To clean dirty pages, use pieces of stale bread, crumbled, and rub it over the soiled pages with a rotary motion. Soap and water, if applied sparingly with a soft sponge and dried off immediately with blotting paper, will do also. Difficult grease will respond to similar treatment with benzine.

Covers can be freshened up by rubbing over with benzine and recolouring with a pale watercolour. Leather books can be done in the same way or with a mixture of equal quantities of milk and the white of an egg. Apply with rag and, when dry, polish with a piece of silk.

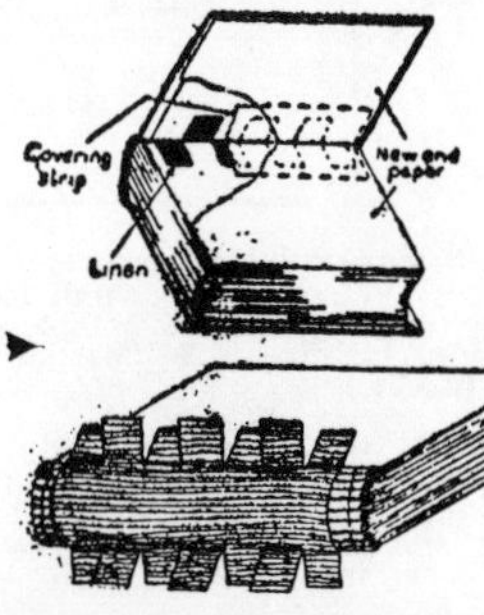

The sketches below give another method of repairing covers, hinge strips and corners being fitted. If the book has parted from its cover this method is quite satisfactory. A strip of linen about an inch shorter and twice the thickness of the book in width is cut and glued to the back of the book.

The overlaps are divided into 7 or 9 equal parts, the book is inserted into the cover, and the alternate strips glued to book and cover as shown. When the glue has set a strip of paper is folded down the middle and glued over the linen to strengthen the joint. New end papers finish off the job.

USEFUL HINTS FOR THE HOME

A SIMPLE HOME-MADE SHOWER BATH

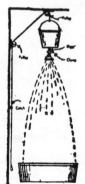

This is a very simply constructed type of shower. It consists merely of a bucket, a wash-tub, a shower-head or sprinkler, a short piece of hose, two small pulleys, a short piece of rope, a clamp to go over the hose and a catch on which to tie the rope.

Be sure to use rope and pulleys strong enough to support the sprinkler bucket. If a wash-tub is not available, the shower may be built over a concrete floor with sufficient drain.

ANOTHER HOME-MADE BUSH SHOWER

This is another very useful idea for country homes where there is no water laid on.

The illustration given is of an idea used by one farmer with very satisfactory results, and for those who might contemplate such an arrangement as this, the following details will no doubt be of interest.

It is made from a 40-gal. drum into which is inserted a length of $\frac{1}{2}$ inch pipe, as indicated. This pipe would need to be screwed in, say, through one of the bungs or the pipe could be threaded at the point where it enters the drum and suitable nuts and washers are then screwed on tightly to keep it in place and to keep it airtight. The shower is then fixed to this pipe.

A hole can then be bored in the other bung in order to insert a motor tyre valve, which is soldered into position in the bung. The bung is, of course, still able to be unscrewed and taken out as it is necessary to fill the drum through this bung. It must be replaced tightly in order to be airtight. The shower is then operated by means of an ordinary tyre pump as sufficient pressure is provided to make the shower operate.

Instead of the tyre valve, a semi-rotary pump might be installed by any handyman in order to make the pumping of water to the shower an easier job.

A DIFFERENT TYPE OF HOME-MADE SHOWER

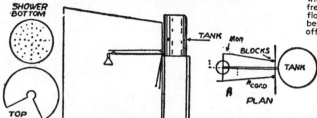

This is an inexpensive arrangement and the material for it can be found on any farm. A small tank or oil drum is sufficient. The materials required are a tank or drum; 4 ft. of $\frac{3}{4}$ in. pipe; an ordinary tap to fit; $2\frac{1}{2}$ feet of $\frac{1}{4}$ inch iron; and two small running blocks.

The piece of iron is bent as in fig. "A," 6 inches at each end, in opposite directions and fastened to the handle of the tap with tie wire tightly twitched (or drilled or riveted.) A cord is tied at each end and taken over the running blocks, which are screwed into the wall, the free ends being allowed to hang down within easy reach.

The right angle bends in the iron enable the tap to be turned full on and off. The dotted lines indicate the position when turned on. The spray can be made from an old kero tin and soldered to the top.

NOVEL IDEA TO CLEAN WASTE PIPE

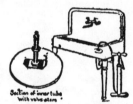

When the sink, bath or lavatory becomes stopped, a plumber's bill may often be saved by the use of a motor tyre pump.

Take an old inner tube having the valve intact. Cut from this a circle around the stem, leaving 2 or 3 inches of rubber on all sides. Wet the rubber and hold it firmly over the drain while someone else applies the pump. This will be found to be quite effective and a very useful standby, whilst the same idea can be applied to other jobs where there is any stoppage in pipes.

HINTS ON KEEPING DRAINS FREE

To clean drains, remove the strainer or grating, take out as much dirt as possible, then clean out the bend or trap with a

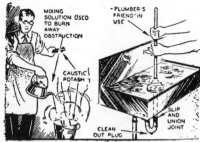

hooked wire or some coil spring (see next page for similar idea).

A pail or two of hot water should complete the job or a hot solution of caustic potash poured into the drain will remove any greasy material.

On the right of this sketch is also shown what is called the "plumber's friend," which will help clear a clogged drain (a rubber ball cut in two will suffice). To use this, fill the sink about one-third full and place this cap over the drain. Then push the cup down rather suddenly, and just as suddenly allow the cup to regain its original shape. If this will not clear the drain pour in potash.

REPAIRING A FLUSHING CISTERN

A few hints on these adjustments may be useful. If the ball valve which controls the supply of water to the overhead tank is sticking, it may be due to the copper float scraping on the sides of the cistern, or on other portions of the flushing mechanism, or it may be that the plug "E" is not sliding freely in its cylinder.

If the ball float is not able to fall, the cistern will empty and will not refill whilst, if the ball float falls and cannot rise freely, the water will continue to flow into the cistern until the float rises. The stem of the float is a soft brass rod, and by bending this slightly downwards, the flow of water can be cut off when it reaches any desired level in the cistern.

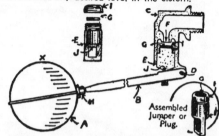

A. Copper ball in two halves soldered together. B. Soft brass holder. C. Body of valve. D. Pivot pin. E. Plug or jumper, with rectangular hole for lever. G. Rubber washer, held into place by cap, 1. Note the "knife edge." J. Upon which lever, B bears.

By removing the pin "D," it will be possible to take out the ball and arm, so that examination of the plug and cylinder is facilitated. Before doing this, the water should be turned off at the main, or at the tap above the cistern.

USEFUL HINTS AND IDEAS FOR THE HOME

ONE METHOD OF CLEANING UNDERGROUND DRAINS

This is a useful method of cleaning drains which are awkward to get at. It comprises a length of spring cable with one end unwound slightly to form a hook. Such a cable could reach either along the level drain or up the other one if necessary.

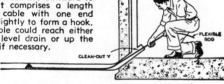

A HOME-MADE SEPTIC TANK

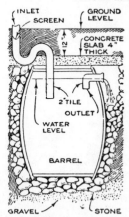

This improvised tank may be found useful where it is not possible to build a standard one. For disposal of kitchen water, it will certainly prevent surface accumulation, which is often so unsightly.

An empty oil barrel can be used; a sack of cement, 3 short lengths of 2 in. tile or galvd. gas pipe and an elbow is all that is necessary, apart from the rock and gravel.

First, a hole about twice the diameter of the barrel is dug to the desired depth. If the water level permits, it should be dug deep enough to provide good drainage in gravel or rock.

Next, two holes are drilled in the barrel, as shown, and the inlet and outlet pipes are inserted. This being done, a few large rocks are thrown into the hole, and the barrel is put into place; the space between the outside of the barrel and the hole is filled with rocks, care being taken to place them in such a way as to provide the greatest possible amount of open space between them. The pipes are then sealed into the openings in the barrel with mortar; the top is covered with boards or heavy paper, to prevent the wet concrete from running down and filling the voids in the rock. Then the reinforced concrete slab is put in place, covering the barrel and the stone. It can now be connected to the kitchen drain.

If properly installed, with the pipes ending below the surface of the liquid, as indicated, the sewerage will be completely decomposed in the two compartments and will seep away in the form of a fluid. This type of tank should serve for years as the barrel will resist decay as it is constantly saturated.

ANOTHER CHEAP SEWAGE SYSTEM OR WATER DRAIN

This is also a useful arrangement. It is composed of a pipe leading from, say, the kitchen sink underground to an oil barrel or box buried in the ground which, in turn, stands upon several feet of rocks.

Rocks are also piled around the barrel for part of its height. The barrel is covered with earth and some sacking or paper placed on the rocks before the hole is re-filled.

The pipe should be buried about 5 ft. deep on a slope, with the lower end resting on the top of the barrel or through a hole near the top.

The barrel should have no bottom and the stones beneath should be covered with coarse gravel. The short piece of pipe from the sink connects with the horizontal pipe, which should be 12 ft. long x 4 in. diameter.

Use a T-piece connection so that the plug can be removed and the horizontal pipe cleaned out. This system should be used to dispose of liquid waste only.

A NOVEL CHIMNEY CLEANER

This is an idea well worth knowing. It consists of a piece of logging chain, 4 to 6 ft. long, fastened to a flexible wire like a piece of clothes line and it will make a very good chimney cleaner easy to manipulate.

It is quite simple and effective. All you have to do is to work the chain up and down along the sides and in the corners of the chimney and this will loosen the soot.

If this little arrangement is always kept on hand, it will simplify the job and thus enable the work to be done often and easily.

HINTS ON CURING SMOKY CHIMNEYS

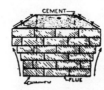

When the wind strikes the edge of an ordinary straight chimney, it often curls over and enters the chimney, forcing the ascending smoke back again.

This can be overcome by topping the chimney, as shown, as it causes all air currents to move upwards. A chimney so built need not be so high as the ordinary type, especially where roofs pitch up and away from it.

In repairing old, broken chimneys, it is worth while using a few bricks and cement to make them conform to this shape. A chimney should have 1 ft. of draught to every square foot of open fireplace, in order to draw properly.

Illustration No. 2. In order to create a good draught in a chimney that is smoky, it is a good idea to deepen the hearth 7 or 8 inches below the floor level, and cut a narrow trench 4 or 5 in. deep across the floor to the outside wall; then place some round spouting in the trench reaching to the outside of the wall, and level the floor again with cement.

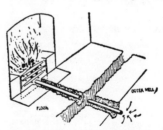

If the ground outside the building is above floor level, dig a hole a little deeper than the spouting and bank the soil back with a little wall; then place a piece of fine mesh netting over the end of the spouting to prevent rats from entering the house. As the hearth bottom is lower than the trench bottom, ashes will not clog the mouth of the spouting. This idea should create a good bottom draught.

Illustration No. 3 is a contrivance made by one farmer who had a smoky chimney. By making this grate, he made his rooms smoke free. It is the full width of the fireplace, and being well made, it was by no means unsightly.

The two main supports can be made from angle iron, and two bars threaded to take two nuts at each end, can easily be made.

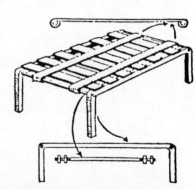

Two straps running lengthwise and wrapped round the ends of the spacing bars are made from flat steel as used on cornsack bales, and the cross-pieces are made from the same material. By tapping the long straps towards the side frames when the cross straps are in position, the latter will be tightened.

USEFUL HINTS AND IDEAS FOR THE HOME

A HANDY WARNING AGAINST FIRE

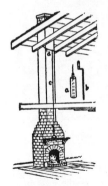

A handy home-made fire alarm in case the chimney or roof near the chimney catches alight is indicated here.

Stretch cords between the rafters in any position desired so that if there is fire, the cord will burn off and release the weight attached to it, which, in its turn, will drop on to any object placed there for the purpose of warning.

An electric push bell with dry battery is one idea. Place this on a shelf and, to keep the whole thing from swinging, get a piece of heavy wire (b) about 10 inches long and fasten it to the wall or chimney for the weight (a) to slide on. The weight need be suspended only an inch or two above the bell.

AN IDEA FOR CELLAR STEPS

Accidents are often caused when descending cellar steps in the dark, not knowing just when the bottom steps are reached.

This idea should make the bottom steps visible and so enable one to know when the bottom is reached.

Merely paint the lower two steps white, and you will be surprised to find how convenient it will be.

INEXPENSIVE FILTERS FOR CISTERNS

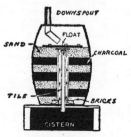

Anyone can make the accompanying filter at very little cost. It will be found very efficient for cleaning water from a roof before it enters the cistern.

It consists essentially of a keg or other receptacle filled with alternate layers of sand and charcoal, through which the water must pass. The illustration will give the idea. An outlet pipe in the bottom of the keg projects well up into it and is covered with a tile.

Water first passes through the sand and charcoal, then it flows up inside the tile where it enters the outlet pipe. This tile-and-pipe serves as a trap to keep sand from entering the cistern. A wood-disk float placed on the top layer of sand under the downspout from the eavetrough serves as a splatter shield to prevent the sand from disturbing.

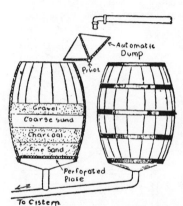

The second illustration shows how two barrels can be arranged near the house and filled with sand, gravel and charcoal.

There is also a bucket that automatically dumps the water from the down-spout first into one barrel and then into the other.

This is placed between the tops of the barrels and the sketch will give details as to the manner in which it works.

MAKING A CONCRETE MAIL BOX

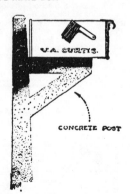

A well-made and well-lettered mail box should be an asset to any farm. One mounted on a neat post that stands straight is a big improvement on those very often seen; those which lean over so crookedly and which often have the top missing altogether. The concrete post shown here is easy to make and will last indefinitely, besides always having a neat appearance.

Only a simple form is needed—made of 6 x 1 boards. This is laid on a level floor and no top or bottom is required on the form. Reinforcement rods and a good mixture of cement should be used.

In order to show whether any mail has been left or not, a small arrangement can be inserted on the side of the box for the postman to manipulate. This is a great convenience.

A USEFUL TROLLEY MAIL BOX

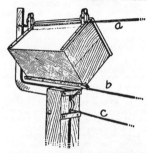

This is an idea which will be found useful for places where the house stands some distance back from the road; such an arrangement can be rigged up to and from the mailbox. The latter is hung on two pulley door hangers, as shown in the sketch.

A strong post, with a bent arm, is set next the highway, (a), and a line is suspended between it and the house, on which the box runs.

A pulley is fastened in or to the post, and over it runs a cord (b) and (c) to pull the box back and forth between the house and the road. The box is sent down to meet the carrier, who places the mail in it, and then it is quickly pulled back to the house.

A SUBSTANTIAL FLAGPOLE FROM PIPING

This is quite simply constructed. A neat, substantial pole can be erected of 12 ft. of 2 inch galvanised piping; a 2 in. to $1\frac{1}{2}$ reducer; 8 ft. of $1\frac{1}{2}$ in. pipe; a $1\frac{1}{4}$ to $\frac{3}{4}$ in. reducer; 6 ft. of $\frac{3}{4}$ in. pipe; and a $\frac{3}{4}$ in. cap, put together in the order named.

Through the centre of the cap, a $\frac{1}{4}$ in. hole is drilled for the bolt which holds the small galvanised pulley to the top of the pole. A galvanised hook for the rope is clamped to the pole 6 ft. from the lower end, with a strap of galvanised iron.

A $\frac{3}{8}$ in. rope of the best quality should be threaded through the pulley. The staff is set upon a rock in the bottom of a hole, $2\frac{1}{2}$ ft. deep and 2 ft. in diameter, and is braced temporarily. Around it is poured a rather wet mixture of 1 part cement,

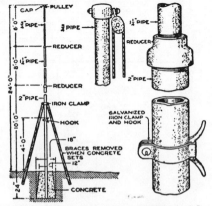

A Flagpole Made of Iron Pipe and Fittings, and Set in Concrete, Is Durable in Construction and Graceful in Appearance

2 parts clean river sand, and 3 parts crushed rock. This should be rounded up above the surface of the ground. When the base has set firmly, the braces may be removed.

USEFUL HINTS AND IDEAS FOR THE HOME

A HOT WATER SYSTEM FOR THE FARM

The average household needs much hot water and for those who are prepared to put a few pounds into the making of a simple system in which operating costs are "nil," the idea given here will be found quite practical. It has been tried with success.

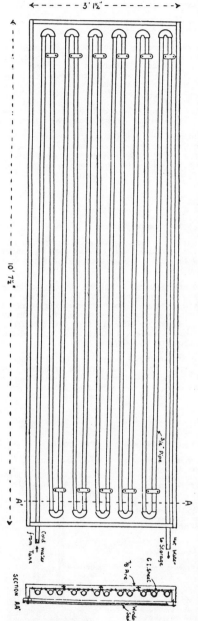

It depends for its success on the ability of an exposed metal surface, when protected from the wind by a glass frame, to absorb heat from the sun's rays.

If the metal surface is a continuous coil of piping, the heat thus absorbed may be transmitted to water circulating in the coil, and if the heated water can be removed to a storage vessel and replaced by cold, the process may be continued so long as the sun is shining.

These diagrams describe the layout (1 and 2). In No. 1 is shown the plan of the heating coil, together with a section "AA" through the box. The latter is 10 ft. 6 in. x 3 ft. internal dimensions, and is constructed of ¾ in. timber. The sides are 3 in. high.

A sheet of galvanised lines the bottom. On this is clamped a coil constructed as shown from ¾ in. piping. Both galvanised iron and piping should be painted dull black.

The lid of the box consists of glazed window sashes, which prevent air currents from cooling off the pipes, yet allows free penetration of light.

This box is set on the roof at such an angle as to afford maximum exposure to the sun's rays, with northern exposure and tilted at an angle of 30 deg. with the horizontal.

The free ends of the coil pipe are led to the water storage tank (No. 2) which is either placed between the ceiling and the roof or in a specially made chamber in the roof. Care should be taken to provide a tank of ample proportion—one of 50 to 60 gallon capacity is generally suitable. This should be placed in a wooden box which will allow of a thick insulating layer of fine cork, sawdust, or fine dry material all round. This is most important in keeping water at a high temperature.

A cold water supply from a high house tank or water main should be brought into the storage cistern, as shown, while the hot water connection for the household supply may be taken off from any convenient point near the top of the cistern.

A tee on the pipe from the top of the coil across to the storage tank will prove satisfactory.

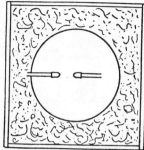

TOP VIEW

For those who wish to alter the dimensions of the installation suggested, it may be taken as a useful guide that under normal conditions, one square foot of surface area should be allowed for each gallon of water to be heated at a temperature of 150 deg. F.

It may also be of interest to point out that some heat is absorbed by this system even on hazy or cloudy days.

Naturally the solar heater would be best suited to those districts which enjoy a high proportion of clear, sunny days, but its usefulness should also be considerable in the higher rainfall areas, particularly during the rainy season.

Although it may look a little complicated, the arrangement is a very simple one and easily constructed, and it has been found quite effective where installed.

ANOTHER TYPE OF HOT WATER SYSTEM

A very good hot-water system for farms and other homesteads where there is no water laid down, can be made as shown here.

The force pump should be the type having an extra discharge outlet in addition to the spout. When the faucet on the spout is turned on, cold water can be pumped directly from the cistern.

When this faucet is turned off, however, and the pump is worked, water goes up through the pipe "A" and into the bottom portion of the hot water tank.

In so doing, it displaces hot water from the top of the tank. This water is forced through pipe "B" until it comes out directly over the sink. A hot-water jacket in the kitchen range is connected to the boiler in the usual way.

It must be remembered that no hot water is obtained unless the faucet is closed and the pump worked.

The range boiler is in no danger of running dry if the pump is not used, for no hot water leaves it unless the pump is worked. The only other outlet from which water can be drawn is the drain at the bottom of the tank, which is used only when it is necessary to clean it out.

USEFUL HINTS AND IDEAS FOR THE HOME

ANOTHER USEFUL HOT-WATER SYSTEM

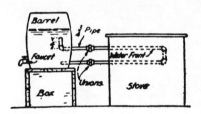

This simple arrangement can be very cheaply made and it will keep quite a lot of hot water readily available. It can be attached to the kitchen stove and should be found quite useful to many.

Most stoves are made in such a manner that this idea can easily be adapted. Use ¾ in. pipe and a barrel with a faucet. The unions can be secured at any hardware store.

ANOTHER SIMPLE HOT-WATER SYSTEM FOR TOWN OR COUNTRY

This particular system consists of a furnace or heater, a storage cylinder, in which hot water is stored until required, and a cold water supply tank situated at such a height that the water from it will gravitate to any place where hot water is needed.

In a single storeyed house, the cold water tank is usually situated 5 to 6 feet above ceiling level. This tank is supplied with water from the ordinary main, the water level in it being maintained by means of a ball-cock. The usual average size for an average house is 40 gallons.

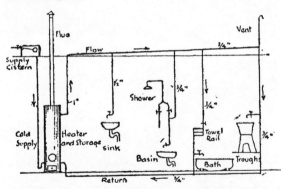

The usual type of boiler or furnace is of cast iron, which is generally lagged or covered with an asbestos compound to prevent heat losses. The storage cylinder is also lagged, sometimes with cork, but generally with hair felt. The better the quality of lagging the less the heat loss, and the longer the stored water will remain hot without the furnace being fired.

The storage cylinder is usually close to the furnace, and is connected to it by large size copper pipes, through which the water circulates.

A Smaller Domestic Plant

In many of the smaller installations, the storage cylinder and the furnace are combined, the fuel being consumed in a tube which is contained in the storage cylinder itself (see illustration). A flue leads away above roof level, to take away the gas products of combustion.

This latter type of combined heater and storage cylinder is very efficient, as there are practically no heat losses and, as the water is in direct contact with the heating surface, and does not have to circulate through pipes, the recovery from cold is very rapid.

Moreover, as the water does not come into contact with any metal other than copper, there is no corrosion; the water remains clean and, if the mains service is reasonably pure, there should be no staining of basins and baths.

The pipes between the boiler and the storage cylinder, when these are separate, are generally of large bore, 2 in. being a not unusual size. The pipe from the supply system to the furnace, which can be of ordinary galvanised iron, should be at least 1 inch diameter.

The supply pipe from the hot water system out to the points where hot water is required should be at least 1 in. to the first branch. This pipe can run along the top of the ceiling joists, where it can be heavily lagged without being unsightly.

The drop pipes, as they are called, to basins and similar points can be at least ½ in., but to the bath the pipes should be ¾ in.

In order to keep water circulating so that cold water does not have to be drawn off every time water is required at one of the points, a return pipe is fitted. This should be at least ¾ in. back to the storage cylinder. The whole system should be heavily lagged with hair felt wired on to the pipes to prevent heat losses. Where pipes are visible, lagging with felt is unsightly. Kitchen or bathroom pipes should be chromium or nickel plated. A polished pipe radiates less heat than a dull one, and this is the only provision that is made in such places against heat losses.

The less unprotected pipe there is, however, the better. Furthermore, the shorter the drop or lead from the flow pipe in each case, the less wastage of hot water there will be, as invariably one has to draw off the cold water that remains in the drop pipe before the hot water flows at the point required.

For Country Homes

In country homes, or other places where wood or coal fuel is used for cooking, it is a usual practice to do away with the special heater, and instead to have a special heating coil fitted into the furnace of the kitchen range.

Most kitchen ranges are so adapted that the coil can easily be fitted. The amount of hot water such a system will supply will depend upon the length of time the fire is going during the day. A 20-gal. storage cylinder is a small size suitable for supplying a bath and sink. A 30-gal. cylinder is usually the size for a bath, with sink and basin, whereas a 40-gal. is a fairly liberal size for an ordinary household installation.

In calculating the quantity of hot water required, allow about 15 gallons for each bath. This, mixed with the necessary cold water, will make a bath about 9 inches deep, but if your ideas of a bath are more luxurious, you will necessarily require a large storage cylinder and, consequently, a larger heat as well.

HOW TO KEEP DRINKING WATER COOL

To make provision for the supply of cool drinking water during the summer, build an underground tank of concrete as shown in this drawing.

Place the tank, say, 12 inches below the surface of the ground in fairly close proximity to the outlet tap.

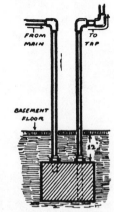

There can either be an inlet pipe from the water main or the water can gravitate from an outside tank.

The line to the tap should be inserted into the tank as indicated but where there is no pressure from the main, it may be necessary to use a pump or some such thing to pump the water to the tap. If there is a basement or cellar under which the tank can be placed, so much the better.

An arrangement such as this is well worth while, especially in hot districts, where the provision of nice cool drinking water is a problem. Cool water can be a luxury sometimes and well worth the trouble of making something like this.

USEFUL HINTS AND IDEAS FOR THE HOME

AN INDOOR WATER SUPPLY FOR THE HOUSE

Those who would like to have running water in any room desired can do so at small cost and can also have it handy for garden purposes near the house. Such a system will give great satisfaction and be extremely useful.

One way to do this is to instal a water system, with a pressure system as shown in this sketch. The pressure tank is so arranged that by pumping it full under strong air pressure, the water is forced all over the house and distributed by means of galvanised pipes.

The installation and operation is simple. Any pipe fitter or plumber can put the

HOUSE WATER SYSTEM

plant together so that it should work perfectly. All that is needed for operating is to keep the tank pressure up to the designed point. This may be 20, 40, 60 or 100 pounds. A few strokes of the pump is sufficient, and if the water is used as economically as possible, the matter of pumping will not be very great.

The most satisfactory way of pumping is, of course, by the windmill or engine. If either of these two methods are adopted, there will be no need to be so economical with the water. Any waste water can be run off.

As will be seen, it is very simple. Note the hand force pump tank in the basement to hold the water under pressure. Where preferred, this system could, of course, be altered by having the tank just under the roof, and the taps and bath in the house fed by gravity. The pressure developed in the tank is sufficient to force the water anywhere wanted, and can also be extended to cover stock tanks and water troughs in the stalls and elsewhere if desired.

HOW TO PROVIDE MORE HEAT FOR A LARGE ROOM

A room in which there is a fireplace is usually quite warm close to the fire, but is likely to be cold further away. There is much waste heat in a fireplace, and to utilise it, the installation of a radiator and hot water system as shown here is quite a good idea. ¾ in. piping is used connected with standard fittings.

The grate in the fireplace is made of pipe and fittings as shown to fit into the opening which will, of course, vary, hence no dimensions are given.

The cold water supply is arranged in some place adjoining, and the pipes are connected to the radiator and the grate underneath the floor. Circulation of water is indicated by the arrows.

KEEPING RAINWATER TANKS CLEAN

All rainwater tanks are liable to pollution by dust, bird droppings and other debris from roof surfaces, etc. This is specially so in summer when rain is interspersed with long dry spells, during which the gutters become particularly soiled.

One of the best ideas we have seen and one well worth illustrating is that of the Department of Public Health in N.S.W., i.e., what is known as the "interceptor," which automatically collects the first run off from the gutters, and diverts into the tank only the later water, which should then be reasonably clean.

This interceptor deals with dust, sand and finer particles which cannot be excluded by means of a sieve.

This interceptor (see sketch) consists of a cylindrical vessel "A," 1 ft. 6 in. in diameter and 4 ft. high, which terminates at its top ends with a 3 in. inlet, and cone shaped reducing sides. A hollow composite or wooden ball, 5 inches in diameter, is inserted loosely in the cylinder before fixing on the bottom.

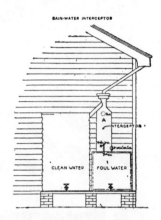

This ball should be so fitted that, when it is pushed upwards by the rising water, it fits snugly in the cone sides, and prevents further water from entering the interceptor.

At the bottom of the interceptor chamber is a pipe ¼ in. in diameter and 6 in. high, which is fitted inside the cylinder with a tee connection.

The interceptor is stood on a smaller tank, and this small pipe "B" should be let down into the smaller tank.

For cleansing purposes there is an inspection disc or hand-hole cap at the side of the interceptor. Until this cap is opened there will always be up to 6 in. of water or mud in the base. After a spell of dry weather this cap should be removed and the interceptor cleaned out.

The apparatus works as follows:—When the rain first starts, the first water from the gutters is taken directly into the interceptor and, although a small quantity escapes by means of the ¼ in. pipe, the interceptor gradually fills up, until the ball rises to the conical top, and closes the inlet. The water will then pass direct from the down pipe into the clean water in the tank itself.

When the rain stops, the water gradually escapes through the small pipe "D," down into the foul water tank, leaving the interceptor empty and ready for the next rain. The latter is not lost as it can be used for garden purposes from the foul water tank.

This idea is specially useful in country districts of low rainfall.

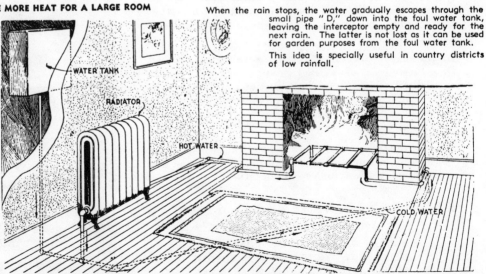

Piping built into fireplace is made part of a hot-water system by which parts of the room remote from the fire are heated.

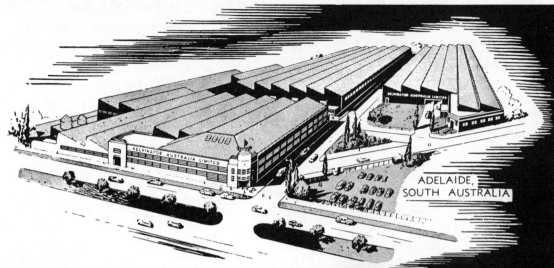

ADELAIDE, SOUTH AUSTRALIA

Kelvinator

A Brotherhood of 4 Nations . . .

The great Kelvinator factories of America, Great Britain, Canada and Australia—each an independent self-contained organisation—are allied in the resolve to maintain the Kelvinator tradition . . . First in Refrigeration.

It is the constant free interchange of data, information and discoveries between the Kelvinator factories that keeps Kelvinator ahead, always ahead, in the field of Electric Refrigeration.

In the war years, the Kelvinator factories devoted their resources of skilled manpower and highly specialised plant to war production. But much of that production has involved experiment and new developments that will bring great benefits to post-war Refrigeration.

The millions of users in the four great English-speaking Nations share in the benefits and prestige created and maintained by Kelvinator co-operation.

KELVINATOR AUSTRALIA LIMITED

Anzac Highway, Keswick, S.A.

AND AT WILLIAMSTOWN ROAD, PORT MELBOURNE, VICTORIA, AND EUSTON ROAD, ALEXANDRIA, SYDNEY, N.S.W.

USEFUL HINTS AND IDEAS FOR THE HOME

HOW TO BUILD A LARGE COOL SAFE
Suitable for use in Country Districts

This is an idea which might be of considerable use to any who care to try their hand at making something of this sort in order to improve the comfort of their homes. The principle is somewhat similar to the drip safe and other ideas on these pages, where air passing over wet surfaces evaporates the water and evaporation cools the inside.

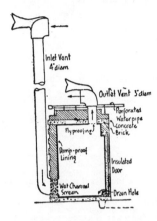

It is thus possible to apply the same principle to the construction of a permanent larger storage chamber—details of which we give here and which could be made by any handyman.

For such a chamber, porous brick or porous limestone is most suitable, put together with a comparatively poor mixture of either lime and sand, or cement and sand no richer than 4 parts of sand and 1 of cement.

Construct the outside surface to give as much evaporating space as possible. If limestone, the surface can be cut into flutes resembling the air-cooled motor cycle engine and, if brick, it can be built with alternate courses projecting, or the outside surface of the bricks can be roughened with a chisel. Build the top of this chamber of the same porous material as the walls with a concrete slab or bricks as shown and stepped up to an apex or arched over.

Inside. Plaster with the same class of mortar and, because the interior of the storage chamber will always be slightly damp, the next step is to line it with galvanised iron. This iron should come right up against the mortar and should not be insulated from it in any way.

The storage chamber should be airtight and the door tight fitting, as in an ordinary ice chest. The door need not be of porous material but should be heavily insulated.

The floor should be solid, preferably of concrete, built right on to the ground with no airspace between, although it may have a damp-proof course between the earth and the floor.

The storage chamber should, of course, be in such a place that the sun will not shine directly on it at any time of the day. A shed of brush or a brush covering could easily be made.

A good deal of water will be used, because if the cool safe is operating properly all the water will be evaporated, and it cannot be recovered. The system of pipes should be so arranged that the water drips slowly enough over the roof and down the walls so that they can be kept properly damp without any water running away underneath.

Galvanised lining prevents the air inside from becoming overcharged with moisture, and to prevent condensation provision should be made for a dish or depression in the floor containing material such as common or butcher's salt, which can be renewed from time to time when it has absorbed all the water that it can. Open the door as little as possible during the day, as otherwise hot air will enter and take time to cool down.

Ventilation, if desired, can be provided by means of a bell-mouth ventilator facing into the air, with a wet charcoal screen interposed between the ventilator and the inside of the cool safe. In such a case, it would be necessary to provide an outlet, preferably another bell ventilator facing away from the wind.

An arrangement such as the above should present no difficulty and all classes of food could then be stored together, provided the articles with any contaminating flavour be stored near the outlet and the corners nearest the inlet. It may seem a little complicated, but for one used to handling tools and thinking things out a bit, this should be the means of making one of the most useful of cool safes.

ANOTHER USEFUL COOLING SYSTEM FOR FOODS

This is another very useful home-made arrangement which will be found quite effective, easy to construct, and well worth while in any house which has not already some place where foods can be kept cool and appetising.

This cooler, built into a corner or side wall of the house, is a really excellent idea for keeping vegetables and other perishable foodstuffs fresh and sweet, especially if it is on the side of the house facing the direction from which most breezes come.

It consists of nothing more than a simple cupboard, fitted with screen wire shelves, with a small screened opening in the house wall, near the bottom, and another at the top.

Fresh air enters through the lower opening, and passes out of the upper one; the constant current of air being a good factor in keeping the food fresh and cool. If the house is built up at all, the lower screen can be underneath, or it can be at any point desired in the wall, being best, of course, at a spot just underneath the first section of the cupboard.

If in districts where the outside air is often very hot, the cooler should be so arranged to take cool air from the cellar, and to make it pass through fairly quickly.

From the top, a sheet metal or wooden flue is run above the roof (as shown on left hand side of drawing). This is better than cutting a hole in the side wall, as when the flue is heated by the sun the air within it rises more rapidly, drawing the cool air in from the bottom. The vent is usually of 4 in. diameter.

The shelves are easily made with frames to fit and with flywire and rest in cleats screwed to the inside of the cupboard. A trapdoor, say about 12 in. square, is cut in the bottom or side as indicated above, and should be covered with fly-screen wire, and if a door is required on the outside for any purpose, it should also be fitted with screen wire and spring hinges.

In cool weather the trapdoor is kept closed, and the air taken from the outside. When the outside air is too hot, the bottom trapdoor is opened and the side screen door filled with a piece of wallboard or thin wood which has been cut to fit nicely for such occasions, thus keeping the cupboard closed.

If such things as milk bottles, etc., are wrapped in wet cloths and set in such a cooler, the current of air will keep them quite cold. Fresh meats kept in closed containers and wrapped in wet cloths also keep nice and cool, but, of course, other things such as vegetables can be left as they are.

Slight variations of the above to suit circumstances will readily suggest themselves to the handyman. Also, some insulation materials as walls would add to its efficiency.

USEFUL HINTS AND IDEAS FOR THE HOME

AN EMERGENCY THERMOS JAR

Water for drinking and other purposes can be kept warm or cool for a considerable time by putting it in a jar which is then placed in another larger container, such as a pickle jar, with the space between the two packed with sawdust or other insulating material.

If you are going for a picnic, the inner jar can be completely surrounded with the insulation and removed when it is needed.

A HOME-MADE ICELESS COOLER

One means of keeping food cool is shown here. It is of wood, any size to suit; this being dependent upon capacity required.

A narrow wood slip is nailed across the top, and on either side 3 pieces of wood are nailed to serve as shelf-rests. This will give 2 shelves for placing food to be kept cool. The top and bottom shelves are reserved for the cooling apparatus, which consists of a pan on the top shelf half filled with cold water and a similar one on the bottom shelf.

A white cotton cloth is draped over the top bar "B" and small stones should be placed in pockets sewn at the end of the cloth, as these assist in keeping the material down in the water. This cloth then passes over the bar and hangs down behind the shelves into the water in the lower pan; the cloth being weighted to keep it submerged in place similar to the top shelf.

The two food shelves "SS" and the top cooling pan shelf are about 1 in. less in width at the back than the sides of the cooling case so as to permit easy passing of the cooling cloth from top to bottom pan. Strong white muslin is tacked over 2 holes cut in either side of the cooling-case as in sketch. These are to admit a passage of air over the food shelves.

The door is hinged and has a pair of fastenings in order to keep it tightly closed and care must be exercised in making the door in order to ensure a fly-proof fit. The door is made of batten frame-work with a centrepiece for strength, and the whole then covered with muslin tacked to the framework.

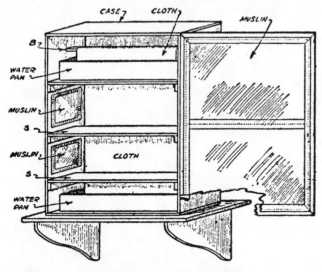

If you are able to procure ice to place in the cooling pan, so much the better, but this is not essential. Ordinary salt may be added to the water to assist coolness. The water must be replenished when necessary.

The food is placed on the top shelves "SS," the process of cooling being through the evaporation of the water—the arrangement should, of course, be kept in a shady spot or it may be placed on a shelf or fastened to the wall with brackets.

Although not so effective as a real ice-refrigerator, it will answer the purpose of keeping food wholesome for a longer spell than an ordinary safe. If one pan is not large enough, use two or more, seeing that each has a cloth draped over the bar to hang down into the pans on the shelf.

A constant supply of clean, fresh air is an important factor in keeping food fresh. For appearances, finish off this cooler with white enamel.

A HOME-MADE WATER COOLER

It is a nice thing to have cool water within reach, whether in the house or in the barn. A simple and effective arrangement can therefore be made by using a barrel and a large stone jar.

Place the jar inside the barrel and surround it with charcoal, sawdust or chaff, if nothing else is available. With a tight lid and a wet cloth spread over the top, water will keep cold for some considerable time.

The uses of such a cooler may be multiplied to include many things in the house.

ANOTHER HOME-MADE BUTTER OR MILK COOLER

In this, you make use of the cooling effects of evaporation.

Small objects, such as butter, can be kept cold by means of a flower-pot, a cloth, and a dish of water, as shown.

The dish is filled with water, and an empty tin or block of wood is placed in the middle. A plate holding the butter is set on the block and a porous pot then inverted over the plate.

Then cover the above with a piece of loosely woven cloth, the edges of which dip into the water, and a hole is cut in the cloth just over the hole in the pot.

The water soaks up into the cloth and, in evaporating, cools the pot and its contents.

ANOTHER TYPE OF USEFUL COOLING BOX

It is a simple matter to make an arrangement like this, which will be found very effective and useful. Two boxes will be needed, one about 6 in. longer and wider than the other.

The smaller one is put inside the larger and the space between them is packed with sawdust, powdered cork, wool, charcoal, or some other insulator. A thick insulated door is also provided.

Some cooling agent must be put in this box with the food, and, if no ice is available, a freezing mixture of equal parts of ammonium nitrate and water may be used. When the nitrate dissolves in the water, it has a very great cooling effect.

The freezing mixture is put in a tray at the top of the box. When the solution is complete and the cooling effect has stopped, the water may be evaporated and the nitrate recovered to be used over again.

If the inner case is lined with zinc, and a zinc container

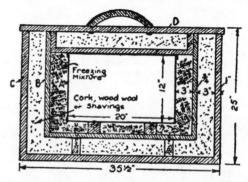

is provided for the food, the freezing mixture may be placed between them with better effect. A section on view of such a refrigerator is shown.

USEFUL HINTS AND IDEAS FOR THE HOME

A HOME-MADE FIRE GRATE FROM OIL DRUM

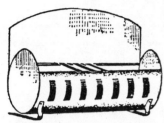

This useful fire grate can be made from an oil drum. Cut the drum down the seam and part of the way round the ends, the loose portion then being folded back and trimmed to a curve for a back to the grate.

Inch-wide slits are cut in the front portion of the drum to form the bars, and two pieces of hoop-iron are bent to shape and riveted in position to act as legs and to enable the drum to stand firmly. A bar of iron with a few cross-bars riveted to it will be useful for boiling the kettle, etc.

A USEFUL STOVE FROM OIL DRUM

If heat is required in an outdoor place or in the workshop or other place, this is one that will be useful and inexpensive to make, it being a slow-combustion arrangement which will give good heat.

The sketch is self-explanatory and its objects will be quickly seen, whilst the actual sizes given need not necessarily be adhered to.

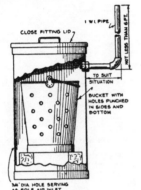

The outer casing is a ten-gallon paint or oil drum which is fitted with a lid, and two firebricks or similar to support the bucket.

The fire must, of course, be lit in the open air and then transferred to the container.

A FIRELESS COOKER

This is a good fuel-saving device. Food ordinarily cooked in a saucepan can be placed in this cooker after it has been heated to boiling point by the usual means. Food to be cooked in this way will never burn but will take three times as long to cook as compared with a fire.

Make a suitable box for the outside container of suitable dimensions according to the number of saucepans you wish to use.

For 1 saucepan, a wooden box measuring, say, 15 x 15 x 15 in. will be suitable, and one measuring 24 x 18 x 16 in. high will take three saucepans. Allow a 6 inch space all round each and make the box airtight by puttying up the corners. Fit the lid carefully and hold it down with a clasp.

Put a good amount of clean dry hay on the bottom of the box, and press it down to make a 5 or 6 in. layer. Pay attention to the corners. Then stand the saucepans in position on the hay, and pack with hay in the form of weaving the spaces left between the saucepans—the latter should have the lower part of handles covered with hay when in use.

Next, make a cloth bag of exactly the same measurements as the inner dimensions of the box. Fill the bag with hay to make a cushion that will completely fill the space left between the top of the saucepans and the lid of the box. It is important that there should be no air spaces left for the escape of heat.

When you take the cushion off and lift out the saucepans without disarranging the hay, the cooker will be ready for service. It is only necessary to bring the food to the boil and transfer it, while boiling, to this cooker.

A BUILT-IN BRICK COPPER

The first thing, of course, is to know how to go about the use of bricks, which is dealt with earlier in this book. The arrangement of bricks is called the "bond," and a row of bricks is known as a "course." The main object is to see that a joint between two bricks never coincides with a joint in the next course.

The bond to be used in this idea is called a garden wall bond, and is clearly shown. Presuming the copper is to be built in under cover, there is no need to bother about weather conditions.

A lime mortar is recommended, as this will expand with the heat of the fire, a quality not possessed by cement mortar. Lime mortar is 1 of lime to 3 of clean sand. The heap of lime is arranged in the centre of a ring of sand. Fresh lime is lumpy, and needs to be broken down or slaked with water. Do not touch the lime during this process as it has a decided burning action.

When all the lime has softened to a creamy state, it can be shovelled into the sand to give a well-mixed mortar of even consistency. This mortar can be left for a day or so and still be fit to use after good mixing.

When building in a copper, the correct system of ventilation must be adhered to, otherwise all the heat will make directly for the chimney and the water will take a long time to boil. The heat must be carried round the copper at least once—twice if possible—before it finally makes its escape through the chimney.

The simplest way to explain the construction of the passage for the distribution of heat is to consider the arrangement of each course or layer of bricks. There are 8 such courses. The first course covers the complete area, which is 36 in. square and is built on a level surface to act as a foundation. In the second course, provision must be made for the ashes space, this being 9 in. wide and going back a distance equal to the length of the grating, about 15 inches. This grating can be purchased. A cast iron one stands up to heat very well.

In the next two courses a fire door and fireplace must be worked in. The fireplace goes back about 27 inches (see side view).

It is in the second of these two courses that the ventilation system is started.

The bricks are built right in against the edge of the copper, leaving only a half-brick space at the back for the draught to rise to the next course. In this course (No. 5) the bricks are built back about 3 in. from the copper all round, allowing a free passage of heat.

For the sixth course the bricks are again built in to the copper, leaving a half-brick space at the front through which the heat rises to course No. 7. Here again the bricks are built back for about 3 in. all round. An opening is made in course No. 8 to allow the draught to escape through the chimney.

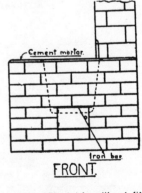

This may be placed anywhere along the back edge, but usually in the corner.

With these two courses where the bricks (or half-bricks) are arranged in circles the spaces between them and the outer walls can be filled in with broken bricks mortared in position. The bricks will not fit perfectly against the copper, but fairly close fits are possible, especially if half-bricks are used.

When the top is reached, a rich cement mortar, one of cement mixed with two of sand, can be used to finish it off. The chimney is made by building the bricks on their edge as shown.

HINTS WITH BELTS AND LEATHERWARE

HINTS ON SEWING, REPAIRING AND CARE OF LEATHER

These few hints may be of use to those who may have occasion to do this type of work at short notice, as they are the experience of one who has had a good deal of it to do.

The life of leather may be multiplied many times with proper treatment and a little care in this direction will be well worth while. Leather should be "fed" at frequent intervals with oil or grease (preferably a recognised dressing) if it is desired to obtain the maximum service.

In spite of care, however, leather will become dirty, and a wide variety of leather articles, such as belts, etc., may be cleaned by washing with water and saddle-soap, castile or any other similar mild soap, then rinsing well and drying.

However, the drying of leather calls for a word of caution. A quick way of ruining same is to try and dry it rapidly with heat (for instance, say a pair of boots in front of a fire) or by direct sunlight. Such heat causes stiffening and cracking.

The safest procedure, therefore is to place a wet article where a draught of air strikes it, i.e., in an open doorway or in an airstream from a fan. After drying, or after cleaning leather by washing or any other process, it is a good idea to polish it or give it some other dressing at once.

Footwear. In the event of no recognised dressing being available, a good lubricant for making them water resistant is neat's-foot or sperm oil. The leather, particularly the soles, is well impregnated with one of these oils; then the shoes are set aside until the oil dries, after which they are polished. Neat's-foot oil dries a little more slowly than sperm oil.

When two pieces of unlubricated leather rub against each other, they cause a squeaking noise—in shoes it is generally between two layers of leather forming the soles. One remedy is to make a small opening at the edge of the layers and introduce through it a mixture of castor oil and powdered soapstone. The opening is then closed by cementing or sewing.

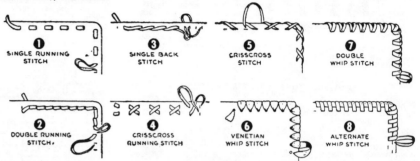

① SINGLE RUNNING STITCH
② DOUBLE RUNNING STITCH.
③ SINGLE BACK STITCH
④ CRISSCROSS RUNNING STITCH
⑤ CRISSCROSS STITCH
⑥ VENETIAN WHIP STITCH
⑦ DOUBLE WHIP STITCH
⑧ ALTERNATE WHIP STITCH

Sewing and Repairing Leather

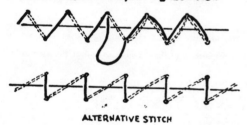

ALTERNATIVE STITCH

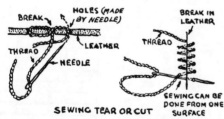

BREAK. HOLES (MADE BY NEEDLE) BREAK IN LEATHER
THREAD LEATHER THREAD
NEEDLE
SEWING CAN BE DONE FROM ONE SURFACE
SEWING TEAR OR CUT

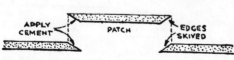

APPLY CEMENT PATCH EDGES SKIVED

MAKING AN INVISIBLE PATCH

Mending and Patching Leather. The illustrations given above will show how a leather article may often be given a new span of life by mending and patching. Should the damage be a mere slit, sewing with linen may be all that is required. For a larger

hole, a cemented patch that can be made almost invisible, may be used. It is done as follows:—

First, cut a paper pattern to cover the spot; then lay out a patch about ¼ in. larger all round. It should be of the same kind of leather as the article being repaired. Then, with a sharp knife, bevel the edges of the patch. Then lay the patch over the hole and dust around it with dressmaker's chalk or talcum powder. Remove the patch, and, following the chalked outline, skive around the hole, bevelling the leather to match the patch.

This is shown at the foot of the illustration on the opposite column.

Use waterproof leather belting cement or a good rubber cement to fasten the patch in place. If a hairline shows around the edge, use ink of appropriate colour to cover it. Then finally polish in the usual way.

Belt Lubrication—home-made substitutes. The secret of good belt performance is proper lubrication to keep the leather soft and supple without making it slippery. A soft, pliable belt, combined with good pulley design and belt tension, requires no sticky, friction-producing dressing, to make it efficient. Heat generated by pulley friction dries out a belt—hence the necessity of lubrication.

If one has no recognised dressing on hand, one can be prepared on the spot, consisting of about equal parts castor oil and neat's-foot oil. It should be applied to the outside of the belt and permitted to soak through to the pulley (hair) side of the leather.

Another dressing sometimes used is a mixture of about 7 oz. of tallow and 3 oz. of cod-liver oil, by weight. Rub this on the pulley side of the belt.

Should a belt slip because it has become coated with oil, etc., it should be dry-cleaned—this can be done by washing in a dry-cleaning fluid or in a mixture of gasolene-turpentine (about twice as much of the former as the latter). When belt is dry, apply a dressing.

EDGE LACING. Edge lacing will greatly improve the appearance of many leather articles. Quite a number of designs are shown on this page and need very little explanation. The simplest form is the Whip Stitch (particulars of which are given below).

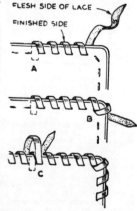

FLESH SIDE OF LACE
FINISHED SIDE
A
B
C

All edges should be cemented, trimmed, thonged and dyed, and 3/32nd inch lace should be used for small articles, and one-eighth for the large ones. Cement one end of a 3 ft. length of lace to the flesh side of the leather as at "A" in the illustration. If there are two or more thicknesses, cement in between them. Also, point the loose end of the lacing.

Use an awl to open the thong slits so that it will be quite easy to insert the lace through the slits made in the leather.

Holding the finished side of the work towards you, lace from left to right, drawing up all stitches with an equal tension. The corners should be laced as at "B," going through the same slit twice, while to join a new length, skive both ends back for ¾ in. and cement them together.

Finish the lacing by going through the first slit again, as at "C." Put a little cement on the flesh side of the lace before tightening the last stitch, and then cut off the surplus.

HANDY HINTS WITH BELTS AND LEATHERWARE

BELT LACING (RAWHIDE OR LEATHER)

The first illustrations given below deal with lacing a belt with leather or rawhide, and is termed the **DOUBLE ROW METHOD.**

There are quite a number of varying conditions under which belts operate, and therefore there are also various methods of joining but the following are some of the best approved ways of doing this.

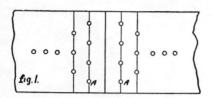

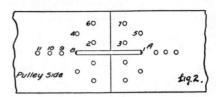

up 4, down 5,
up 6, down 7,
up 6, down 7,
up 4, down 5,
up 2, down 3,
up 8, down 9,
up 10, down 11.

Figure 1 indicates how the ends to be jointed should be cut perfectly square and the first row of holes should be punched ¼ in. and the second row 1 in. from the cut ends—the first hole in the first row (marked "A") being 3-8 in. from the edge.

Figure 2 shows the pulley side with the first two holes laced together.

The holes are numbered, and the order of working is as follows—Down 1 and 8, then from end "A" up 2, down 3,

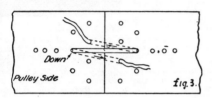

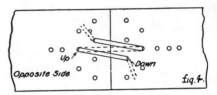

Figure 3 indicates the first stitches from each holes 1 and 8, placing the thong through the centre holes in each second row and drawing the ends of the thongs even on the other side.

Figure 4 shows the opposite to the pulley side. Lace from second row on one belt to first row of the other, then back to second, etc.

Figures 5 & 6 show the appearance of completed lacing on both pulley and outside sides.

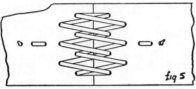

Outside of the completed lacing

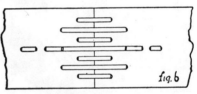

Pulley side of the completed lacing

THE FOLLOWING IS THE SINGLE ROW METHOD

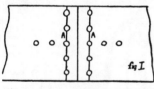

Again, cut the ends to be laced, perfectly square. Draw lines "AA," 5-8 in. from the ends and punch 5 holes 13-16 in. apart; outside holes 3-8 in. from the edge (see figure 1).

Commence as at "BB" and lace each way, making sure to keep the lace from twisting.

The lace should be double on the pulley side and end at "CC" (figures 3 and 4).

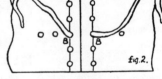

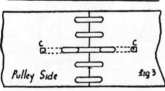

Draw thongs through the centre holes and bring the ends up tight (see figure 2).

Cut the lace after passing through holes "CC" and nick with a knife so that it will not slip out.

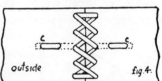

NOVEL IDEA WITH CROCHET HOOK TO HELP LACE BELT

This is rather an ingenious method of lacing a belt which one farmer uses and it will save quite a lot of time.

With small belts in particular, this novel method will simplify things quite a lot, especially if a metal crochet hook, as indicated here, is used to pull the lace ends through the holes in the belt.

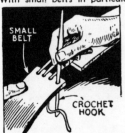

In this connection, it is necessary to use rather a large hook, and, if a suitable one is not at hand, one can be improvised from a small brass rod which any "handyman" should be able to make.

The idea shown might also indicate its usefulness in connection with other things which need sewing and which might be a little difficult under ordinary methods.

A USEFUL BELT FASTENER FROM HINGE

This sketch shows a useful improvised belt fastener that can be used successfully with little expense. All that is required is an ordinary butt hinge, just a little narrower than the belt to be joined.

The ends of the belt should be squarely cut off and the hinge affixed to the outside of the belt by means of copper rivets and washers, which are passed through the holes in the hinges.

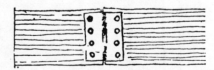

This means is specially suited where the working belt pulleys are small, for it provides a very flexible joint and will not break as a solid fastener will. It should never be attempted to join a belt with a hinge which is wider than the belt. If it projects over the side of the belt, it will be dangerous when it is travelling.

HANDY HINTS WITH BELTS AND LEATHERWARE

HOME HARNESS AND LEATHER REPAIRS

Frequently, for want of a little care, expensive gear is allowed to deteriorate quickly, and " a stitch in time " for minor repairs will save much trouble and expense later on.

Equipment required. Figure 1 gives details of a home-made clamp which will act as a form of vice to keep two or more pieces of leather together for stitching. In this the jaws are automatically tightened as the user sits on the seat.

Figure 2 is a simple form made from two barrel staves for the same purpose.

FIG.1   4"×30"×1½"   6"×20"×1½"

FIG.2

A pair of pliers, assorted awls and handles, saddler's needles, compasses, hand-knife, half moon knife, punches of various sizes, a palm, and an edge tool is used to remove the sharp edges from the leather after cutting. A curved awl is used when stitching has to be done from one side only, as is often required in collar repairing.

Awls for ordinary stitching are diamond shaped. Punches are used for making various holes.

Special hemp is needed for stitching saddlery, a ball of which can be kept in a tin with the end passed through a hole in the lid.

The thread may be used in various thicknesses, according to the type of work, by twisting two or more strands together.

The strands are pulled out, passed over a hook, and carefully broken off by unravelling with the right hand, and gently pulling with the left, so that the thread ends in a finely-tapered point.

When sufficient strands are pulled out, they are twisted together by holding one end in the !eft hand and rolling the thread on the knee with the right hand.

They need not be doubled before

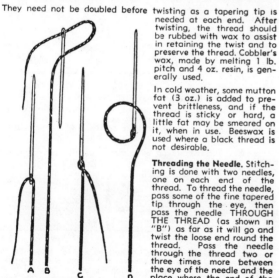

Using the half-moon knife: Above, cutting a strap; below, shaving or bevelling.

twisting as a tapering tip is needed at each end. After twisting, the thread should be rubbed with wax to assist in retaining the twist and to preserve the thread. Cobbler's wax, made by melting 1 lb. pitch and 4 oz. resin, is generally used.

In cold weather, some mutton fat (3 oz.) is added to prevent brittleness, and if the thread is sticky or hard, a little fat may be smeared on it, when in use. Beeswax is used where a black thread is not desirable.

Threading the Needle. Stitching is done with two needles, one on each end of the thread. To thread the needle, pass some of the fine tapered tip through the eye, then pass the needle THROUGH THE THREAD (as shown in "B") as far as it will go and twist the loose end round the thread. Pass the needle through the thread two or three times more between the eye of the needle and the place where the end of the tip is twisted round the thread

and smooth off with the finger and thumb.

Stitching. Grip the two pieces of leather in the clamp as shown. A wheelpricker is sometimes used to mark the leather as a guide to the stitcher so that the stitches will all be the same size, and in correct line.

Stitching should be commenced at the end furthest from the stitcher and worked towards him. The awl is pushed through at a slight angle. When the first hole is made, the needle is passed through and the thread pulled through until there is an equal length on each side.

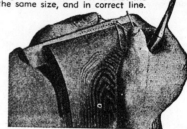

The next hole is made with the awl, and the left-hand needle passed through the thread a few inches; then pass the right-hand needle through the hole, trying to keep the left-hand needle and thread in the angle nearest the first stitch, and the right-hand needle and thread in the upper corner of the diamond-shaped hole. On completing the stitching, a stitch or two is turned back, using a round awl, and the threads are cut off flush with the leather.

HOME-MADE VICES FOR QUICK HARNESS REPAIRS

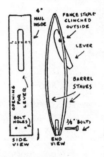

Here are three useful hints, any one of which might be found useful where no other harness vice is on the spot and emergency repairs are needed.

The first handy device is made from barrel staves. The two ¾ in. bolts at the bottom should be tightened until the staves fit tight on the 4 × 1 between, giving pressure on the jaws. In one stave there is a slot into which a lever is hinged. A 4 in. nail is fastened on with staples, forming a pivot. The lever spreads the jaws for inserting the work.

The second is also from a pair of barrel staves. This, as will be seen, can be held between the knees in

a convenient position and will securely grip heavy straps and traces.

As indicated, a steel hoop is bent to form a sort of oval loop and this is slipped over the staves in order to lock them together and so provide a tight hold for the straps or traces.

The third is another barrel stave idea.

When using this clamp, hold it between the knees, using a block of wood and a horse-shoe in the manner indicated. The shoe will help keep the pressure up.

A USEFUL HARNESS OILING STAND

A very effective stand which will make this type of work easy can be made from an old barrel and a saw-horse.

The illustration is self-explanatory and shows how the job can be quickly and effectively done without much trouble.

If kept close at hand and ready for use, the job of harness cleaning can be attended to more often to advantage.

HANDY HINTS WITH BELTS AND LEATHERWARE

A USEFUL LEATHER KNIFE FROM OLD HAND SAW

This very useful little leather knife can be made from a piece of the blade of a discarded hand saw.

It is cut out with a cold chisel and then worked to the shape shown with a file. The cutting edge is ground with an emery and the edge finished on an oil stone. It makes a very useful article for cutting and trimming leather and for harness, etc.

A QUICK REPAIR FOR BROKEN STRAPS

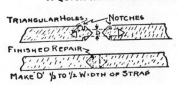

Often a strap will break at a very inconvenient moment, but a satisfactory emergency repair can be made as shown. If the work is neatly done and the finished splice tapped gently to smooth down the parts, it does not look bad at all. Of course, it should be sewn or riveted as soon as possible.

BUCKLE REPAIR JOBS

When the buckle breaks away from a strap owing to the leather wearing through at the loop, it is an easy matter to refit the buckle if the strap is long enough to allow the worn portion to be cut off.

Cut an oblong in the centre of the strap about an inch from the end, large enough to admit the tongue of the buckle and running lengthwise of the strap. Now slip the tongue through the hole from beneath. If rivets are at hand, the bent-over piece may be fastened; otherwise it may be left loose (see sketch).

It is better to rivet the end if possible, however, to prevent the buckle from falling off when the strap is unbuckled.

The illustration on the right is self-explanatory.

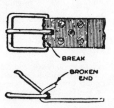

A new Buckle Bar may be made from a Split Pin.

SPLICING A TRACE

This is an excellent method of repairing a broken trace. Cut the broken ends of the trace square; then place the square ends together. Next, mark on the trace the points for the rivets to correspond with the holes in the trace splicer. Then make the

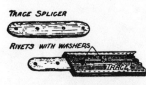

rivet holes and place the splicer (metal or leather) in the centre of the trace as shown. Place the job on the anvil; place the rivets in the holes with a washer on the rivet, and rivet into place. Rivets should be flat-headed, and placed with the head on the horse side of the trace, and then smoothed as neatly as possible. To make a good job, sew the edges as shown.

Any piece of metal will do approximately ⅛ in. thick x 1 or ¾ in. wide, and from 6 to 8 inches long.

ONE WAY OF SPLICING A STRAP

This illustration shows one way of splicing a strap.

First cut each end square. The smooth side is stronger than the flesh side, therefore in bevelling always cut away the flesh side as shown in the upper figure in the cut shown, with the straight side of one strap placed in contact with the bevelled side of the other.

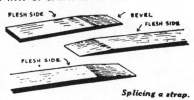

Splicing a strap.

The cross-over.

The lower two pieces are put together as

The following sketch will show how the stitching is done, with the two ends of strap held in place by a clamp. After marking with a spacer or ruler, the holes are punched with an awl, puncturing from the smooth side towards the flesh side.

The stitching is done by passing both needles through the holes from opposite sides and drawing each stitch very tightly. When the last stitch through both straps is made cross-over as shown, whichever method is preferred, then reverse the splice in the clamp, with the smooth side still to the right, and stitch the other edge of the splice. To finish the stitching, place the left needle and thread through as usual; then place the right needle in the hole and wind the left thread twice around the right needle and draw both ends tight. The winding will lock the threads in the leather. Make another small hole ⅛ in. below the next to last one on the splice and put in another locking twist. Then cut off both threads.

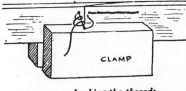

CLAMP

Locking the threads.

The finish is shown in the illustration alongside.

MAKING A BUCKLE

This illustration is given merely as an example in working with leather, showing the procedure adopted. Place the strap on the bench, rough side up, and from about 2 inches from the end make a wedge shape. Then taper the end with a round knife—punch two holes in the belt about 1 inch apart, the first being about 2½ in. from the outside edge of the strap.

Then proceed as per "C," "D," and "E," cutting an opening in the folded end to receive the tongue of the buckle.

SKIVE AND CUT END TO A TAPER OF ABOUT 2" ON ROUGH OR FLESH SIDE
A
STRAP
HOLES
B

CUT WITH JACKNIFE HERE TO BOTH HOLES
FOLD AND GRIP FIRMLY WITH LEFT HAND HERE
C

PLACE STRAP IN RIVETING MACHINE THUS PLACE ANOTHER RIVET HERE
E

TUBULAR HARNESS RIVET

Put the buckle in the strap as shown at "D," and then rivet—the first one being close to the hole, the second near the end of the strap as shown at "E." In placing the second rivet, do not let the buckle end of the strap down, or it will not fit tight against the strap in the finished job.

PLACE BUCKLE ON STRAP AS SHOWN HERE
D

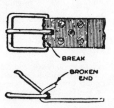

BREAK
BROKEN END

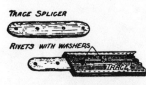

TRACE SPLICER
RIVETS WITH WASHERS
TRACE

STITCHING
THE FINISHED SPLICE

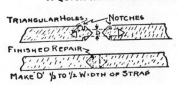

TRIANGULAR HOLES — NOTCHES
FINISHED REPAIR
MAKE "D" ⅓ TO ½ WIDTH OF STRAP

CUT HERE

HANDY HINTS WITH BELTS AND LEATHERWARE

MEASURING A BELT

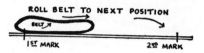

ROLL BELT TO NEXT POSITION

1ST MARK   2ND MARK

This is an easy and accurate way of finding the exact length of an endless belt.

Place the belt on the floor, bench or any other smooth surface. Then mark both the belt and the floor in the manner shown in the above illustration.

Then roll the belt along the floor until the mark on the belt again touches the floor. The distance between these two points on the floor will be the length of the belt.

BUTTING BELT ENDS

When it is found necessary to cut a belt in order to shorten it, be sure that the ends are cut at a right angle. This is done by placing a square along the edge of the belt and cutting accordingly.

If no square is handy, employ the method shown in the above drawing. Double your belt, then twist one end so that it is reversed, and cut both ends at the same time. This will ensure a straight belt.

It is important that the ends should be quite square, and this is one of the best and quickest ways of ensuring that it is.

A NOVEL METHOD OF KEEPING THE BELT TIGHT

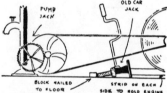

PUMP JACK   OLD CAR JACK

BLOCK NAILED TO FLOOR   STRIP ON EACH SIDE TO HOLD ENGINE

This illustration will show one good method adopted by one farmer in order to keep the belt tight on his pump engine.

Just put two strips of 2 x 1 for the engine to slide between when it is properly lined up with the jack, and use an old car jack to push it tight. This can be slackened off each night, if desired, quite easily. The arrangement might appear a little complicated, but it is quite simple and at the same time quite effective.

TWO BELT IDEAS THAT WILL HELP

These ideas come from good sources and might prove of use to someone. The tendency of a belt to sag when driving a pulley on a vertical shaft with a large one on a horizontal shaft, such as deep well installations, can be taken care of by adjusting the centre of the face of the vertical pulley so that it is lower than the top of the horizontal, as at "A" and "D."

The distance that the pulley is lowered should be equal to 1-8 in. for each foot of distance between the pulley shafts. In most installations, this should not be less than 25 ft.

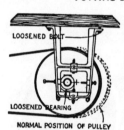

On belt drives of this type, the stretch of the belt will be uniform on both edges if it is given a half-twist on the slack side, as at "B" and "C." Without the twist, the belt will stretch along one side.

SET DRIVEN PULLEY SO THAT THIS LINE WILL BE TANGENT

NOTE-HALF TWIST ON SLACK SIDE OF BELT

DRIVER   DRIVEN

CENTERS NOT LESS THAN 25 FEET

THIS END GIVEN HALF TWIST WHEN SPLICED

A HOME-MADE LEATHER MARKER

A very useful leather marker can be improvised from an old clothes peg and a gear from an old clock, or similar thing.

WOODEN CLOTHES PIN

GEAR FROM OLD CLOCK

LEATHER

Leather marker.

The teeth can be filed to any size required. As a matter of fact, one could make such a tool from other scrap material which would do the job quite well.

Also, a small tool such as this might be useful for a number of things other than the marking of leather.

A HANDY HOME-MADE POWER JACK

This handy power jack can be used for reducing the speed by running the engine belt on the large pulley and the belt to the machine on the small one, say, for a grindstone, concrete mixer, or reciprocating pump, etc., or for increasing the speed by reversing the belt, as for a centrifugal pump, etc.

The speed ratio is about 4 to 1, and a 12 or 14 inch pulley on the other end of the shaft would give a still greater choice of speeds. With good bearings and lubrication, the loss of power will be quite small, and the fly-wheel effect of the pulleys help a good deal in sawing wood and similar work.

PUTTING BELTS ON PULLEYS

LOOSENED BOLT

LOOSENED BEARING

NORMAL POSITION OF PULLEY

It is not good practice to put on a large belt by forcing one edge over a rotating pulley, as this stretches one side and is likely to ruin the belt. This may be avoided, where conditions permit, by loosening one of the adjusting bolts on the shaft hanger, as shown, so that the belt can be slipped over the pulley, after which the bolt is tightened.

Before loosening the bolt, the position of the hanger should be marked to avoid tedious work in re-aligning the shaft after the belt has been put on. The sketch shows the idea.

A USEFUL BELT TRIMMER

By tacking four pieces of wood of suitable size to a board clamped to the workbench, and driving the point of a sharp knife, as shown in the diagram, a jig can be improvised for trimming belts.

It will trim them quickly and accurately. The two bottom pieces of the jig should be a little bit thicker than the belt and they are laid against the edges of the belt. The belt is then drawn through the jig, and the trimming is complete. It is quite easy.

MAKING LEATHER BOOT LACES

This is a very good way of making strong home-made boot laces for heavy workboots.

Take a piece of leather, as shown, and a good strong knife and board.

Drive 2 nails into the board as indicated and then drive the knife right through the leather into the board; then draw the leather along, taking care to keep it perfectly even.

Method of making Leather Boot Laces. Pull the leather against a knife stuck in the bench.

HANDY HINTS WITH BELTS AND LEATHERWARE

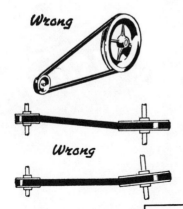

Wrong

Large pulleys provide greater driving pull with normal belt tension. The extra tension needed to prevent slippage on small pulleys overheats a belt

Right

Right

Be sure that both shafts and pulleys are aligned. Improper alignment of either causes excessive side wear on a belt and will result in a rupture

Wrong

Right

Wrong

Never put too much load on a belt. Two machines driven simultaneously at full load always require an extra primary belt

Longer Belt Life

These few hints may be found of value to some who may have much work to do with belting. Economical use of belts means longer service from them and considerable saving in money and material.

Always run belts at the recommended speeds. All belting-and-sheave combinations have a specific speed at which centrifugal force tends to throw the belt away from the groove, causing loss in transmitted horsepower.

It will pay also to use a sufficient number of belts on each drive to meet the power requirements of your machines. You will find it far better to overbelt than to underbelt. For example, using four belts on a drive requiring five reduces belt life about 60 per cent.

These sketches show various other points to watch.

Wrong

Run belts cool and dry. An unventilated guard, excessive moisture, or heat makes the rubber in a belt hard and brittle

Wrong

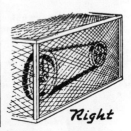

Right

Wrong

Prying a V-belt over a pulley rim may rupture it. If required tension does not permit the belt to be put on by hand, a slotted mount will allow the motor to be slid in for installing the belt

Right

Wrong

Lubricate bearings, but keep oil off belts, and don't use dressing on a V-belt — adjust tension instead. Dirt in grooves wears away belt rubber

Right

USEFUL IDEAS FOR FARM AND STATION

A LABOUR SAVING HAND TRUCK

This is a real labour saver, easy to make. The full length of the handle-piece is 3 ft. 9 in. cut from 2 x 1½ material. At the top end the handle is marked and the shaping is done with a rasp, spokeshave, file and glasspaper. Give these handle grips a good smooth finish.

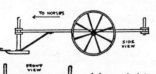

The sketch shows 3 cross-rails at equally spaced intervals along the side pieces.

These are mortised into the sides, and in addition to glue, each joint is pegged for added strength. Use waterproof glue.

Note that the layout of the frame shows a difference in width at top and bottom, which means that the mortises and tenons are cut at an angle. This angle is very slight and can be overlooked if the tenons are wedged in addition to pegging. Do this during the glueing and clamping stage. For further rigidity in the frame, there are two ladder bolts fitted through the sides and bolted firmly as shown at "B."

The amount of projection of the foot iron depends on the load. From 4 to 6 in is usual, although where loads are bulky rather than heavy, up to 12 in. is allowed. This iron attachment is provided with arms 1 ft. 6 in. long for the purpose of securing it to the frame with either bolts or screws.

Blocks must be fitted at the base end of the handle pieces for attaching the axle and wheels—the size depending on the diameter of wheels. Secure these blocks with ¾ in. bolts. Use the same size bolts for attaching a metal plate over each wheel to act as a guard to keep the load off the wheels. A satisfactory size wheel is 6 in. diameter. Use a fairly heavy type of iron wheel—some prefer a solid rubber-tyred one, which has the advantage of being silent. One can vary the width of truck up to 20 in. wide at the top and 15½ in. at the bottom if needed. Iron legs can also be used so that the truck can be stood up in a horizontal position.

A HANDY HOME-MADE CART

This is made from the axle and wheels of an old mower. A flat bottom 10 ft. long and just wide enough to fit the wheels, is made of 2 in. timber with two 6 x 2's spiked across each end and projecting 5 in. past each side. Two-inch holes bored through both crosspieces will hold stakes firmly in place.

The shaft is clamped to the two outer planks 6 ft. from the front end.

A heavy bolster brace is bolted beneath the front end; and another flat-iron strip about 3 ft. long is placed at right angles to the brace to take the draft and bolted to the centre of the flat bottom. A 6 x 3 wooden runner, 1½ ft. long and shod with the mower shoe, is bolted to the centre of the brace and the end of the iron strip with a 1 in. bolt. When a strong hook is attached to the front end of the runner the cart is ready for use. When empty it can easily be drawn by hand and can be turned in its own length.

A HANDY HOME-MADE TWO-WHEEL TRAILER FOR HAY OR HEAVY LOADS

This is a very handy two-wheel trailer which is very easily constructed and which should be an asset on almost any farm—it being capable of hauling up to ¾ of a ton of hay or other material. It would also be very easy to use as a trailer as it would not whip from side to side at high speed.

The materials needed would be based on the following sizes, etc., but almost any other material which might be lying about the farm would do. Those shown here are the rear axle and wheels from an old car; two 14 ft. of 4 x 4 timbers; two bolsters from an old wagon; an 8 ft. length of 4 x 4 for a hitch; and a few bolts and clamps to hold it together.

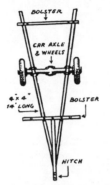

The springs were taken off and the timbers clamped directly on to the rear axle so as to make it lower and to avoid pitching and swaying.

The axle is put about 14 inches back of the middle of the long timber so as to put part of the load weight on the rear wheels of the car to increase traction.

The 14 ft. timbers are tapered to fit on each side of the 4 x 4 hitch, and the front bolster is also fastened rigidly to the rear end of the hitch timber as well as to the 14 ft. stringers.

Any heavy trailer hitch can be used, provided the connection is secure and the pull is thrown on the car frame rather than on the bumper.

The originator of this idea used a 14 ft. hay rack and the trailer was found to be easily strong enough to hold 50 to 60 bushels of wheat.

ANOTHER IMPROVISED TROLLEY FOR CARTING SUPER, SEED, ETC.

Some old cultivator or any other wheels are the basis of this very useful home-made article and it could easily be hitched up to the tractor or other implement and taken from place to place as required. Quite heavy loads could be transported easily—the weight depending, of course, upon the size of the vehicle and the strength of the timber used.

The most suitable size timber for the main supports would be of, say, 3 to 4 in. thick with the main centre one a little heavier in order to take the main strain. The flooring of the trolley could be of, say, 6 x 1, with, say, 2 x 2 or 3 x 2 around the outer edges.

The sketch will show the arrangement of the wheels and how the larger ones can be let into the framework —the latter opening being constructed just wide enough to take them. Any scrap iron will provide any protection needed for the wheels.

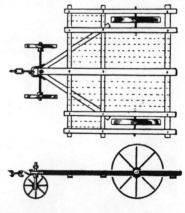

The axles and their fittings can be improved according to materials available.

Stub axles could be used with a bolt through the hole in the end and plates under the inside ends.

Groovers may also be cut in the wood in order that the axles will not slip back or forward. The inside groove should be ½ in. or so deeper than the outside to give the wheels a slight tilt in at the bottom. An arrangement can be added to the junction of the main rail and the two smaller wheels to enable it to be raised or lowered as desired.

To prevent the vehicle from tipping up, the main axle should be two-thirds back from the front end and there should be an iron fixture on the end of the main rail for traction purposes.

USEFUL AND NOVEL DEVICES FOR FARM OR STATION

USEFUL HOME-MADE CART FENDERS

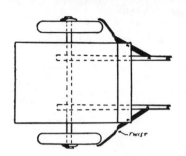

Fenders fitted on each side of a vehicle (especially a rubber-tyred one) will prevent it from severe damage from collision or from gate posts should, for any reason, the side collide with any such object.

These consist of pieces of steel of suitable length fixed to the body and shafts and then twisted a short distance from the end, as shown—leaving the steel projecting beyond the tyre.

If they are so fitted, the vehicle should not receive a "full on" blow and further, in the event of a bolting horse, there is always the chance of the steel being bent against the tyre, and thus acting as a brake. There is, of course, the possibility of the fender puncturing or damaging the tyre, but the damage in this respect will probably be easily offset by the saving gained from greater damage.

A SPECIAL CARRIER FOR HEAVY OBJECTS

This is an arrangement which can be very handy round the place for carting any heavy objects such as petrol drums, bales or bags or any other material which might be impossible to lift, and which can only be moved by a horse drawn or other vehicle.

Such a handy cart can be pushed along easily by anyone from place to place in very little time, it being so constructed as to distribute the weight evenly and in such a manner as to facilitate easy running.

Its construction is self-explanatory, and, if strongly built, the crane arms shown will take quite a heavy lift and will last a lifetime. Extra hooks for lifting bags and other objects can, of course, be added.

Such a vehicle will also do away with the necessity of rolling such objects as petrol and oil drums (thus saving damage to them) besides doing the work so much easier and quicker.

AN UNDERSLUNG CART TO CARRY HEAVY LOADS WHICH IS EASY TO LOAD

This is another type of useful cart which will be found very handy for handling heavy articles such as those mentioned in the previous illustration; it being raised only a few inches from the floor, which makes loading very easy indeed.

The wheels, like those shown in the previous article, can be taken from an old buggy or car (car tyres can be used for either).

In this instance, the wheels are attached to a dropped axle, which supports a 3 x 4 platform.

The handles are made of 2 x ¼ flat iron and extend about 1 foot in front of the wheels, where they are bolted to the platform which is supported at the rear end by vertical flat iron pieces extending down from the handles.

TIGHTENING LOOSE WAGON TYRES

When a tyre becomes loose and you have not the time at the moment to get it reset, you can tighten it by this simple method.

Take a strip of flat iron an inch or so longer than the width of the tyre, and cut V-shaped slits near each end. Then slip it under the tyre. The V-shaped tabs are bent over the edge of the tyre and the ends of the strip down over the felloe of the wheel.

LOOSE TYRES—ANOTHER SIMPLE CURE

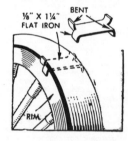

This is another simple and effective method. The idea is to remove the outer tyre and insert a length of hoop iron between it and the rim as shown in this sketch.

Then make the whole arrangement tight enough by driving it in with the hammer, not over-doing it in case the tyre bursts. Any surplus iron can then be cut off. Holes can be drilled or punched so that the tyre bolts can be replaced. Such a wheel should be useful for a long time.

TYRES KEPT ON WAGON-WHEELS BY SIMPLE TWO-WAY CLIPS

When the wooden felloe of a wagon wheel dries and shrinks so that the tyre will not stay in place, use clips bent from flat iron as shown here.

First the metal is cut to size and then slit back from the ends in the centre with a hacksaw to form tabs. Then the metal is driven between the felloe and the tyre, after which the two tabs at each end are bent in opposite directions, one over the tyre and the other down over the felloe. Three clips evenly spaced around each wheel are usually sufficient.

USEFUL METHOD OF GREASING A WAGON WHEEL

It is sometimes a little difficult to grease a heavy wagon wheel, but this suggestion might make the job a little easier.

First cut a notch in an 18-inch piece of 4 x 2 timber, and place it on the inside of the wheel against one of the spokes. Lift upward on the opposite side of the wheel and it will slip out quite easily. The process may be reversed for replacing the wheel.

SETTING BUGGY TYRES

Sometimes buggy tyres may need setting. Take an iron about 12 in. long and 1 in. wide and about 1-8 in. thick and rivet two studs into it near each end as shown at A-A.

Now use one of the holes in the tyre to slip over one stud. For the other stud, you have to drill a hole. Measure out the amount of set needed and bore the hole accordingly—that is, wider apart than the studs are. Now bring the holes together just enough to fit over the studs by bending the tyre up at B. Make the tyre red hot at this point again and hammer the projection down flat and the tyre is ready to put on the wheel.

USEFUL AND NOVEL DEVICES FOR FARM OR STATION

HINTS ON TYRES

HOME-MADE RUBBER TYRES FOR PLOUGHS

CUT THIS SECTION OUT

HOLES BORED FOR BOLTS

On some occasions, farmers might consider that easier running could be obtained by the use of rubber tyres on their ploughs, and, should their particular plough not be so equipped, perhaps the following idea from one user might be of interest.

Any discarded truck or other tyre can be taken and clamped on to the furrow wheels of, say, a 10-disc sundercut plough for instance. Easier running should certainly result, and, in many cases, it might be possible to work in a higher gear, which should cut down fuel cost.

As shown, a section is cut out of the tyre with a strong, sharp knife, using also a hacksaw to cut through the beading. Using an ordinary five-eighths bit, bore holes through the tyre from side to side as far away from the cut as the construction of the wheel will permit.

Pass 8-inch cup-headed bolts of ½-inch diameter through from the outside and screw on the nuts.

BOLTS

WHEEL WITH TYRE BOLTED IN PLACE

The bolt should have long threads to permit of the tyre being pulled in tightly.

The accompanying sketches will explain the whole operation and perhaps the same idea can be applied to several other things.

It should certainly suggest other uses for tyres which might be partially worn out as far as the car or truck is concerned as there is often quite a considerable length of useful life left in a tyre after it has been discharged from the car.

ANOTHER METHOD OF MAKING RUBBER TYRES FOR WAGONS, ETC.

TYRE

WIRE TWO BEADS TOGETHER

Another handy way of converting old rubber tyres into useful tyres for farm wagons, etc., is shown here.

An arrangement such as this will make a vehicle with iron wheels run much smoother, as these old car tyres can be put on the wheels to absorb the shock of bumpy roads.

The tyres can easily be wired on as indicated in the sketch. If the tyre is not large enough to cover the circumference of the wheel, a section can be cut out of another tyre and put on to fill the gap. Besides absorbing the shocks, it will also mean longer life. As will be seen, it is a very simple arrangement and very effective; a method which has been tried with success by one man over a long period.

A REPAIR HINT FOR SPLIT TYRES

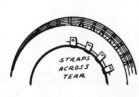

STRAPS ACROSS TEAR

This useful hint might help keep certain damaged tyres in service, especially if they are for use on an old truck or horsemobile.

It refers mainly, of course, to tyres that may have cracked badly or which might have split inside the beading.

All that is necessary is to get some strips of leather or rubber and attach them in the manner shown. Gutter bolts are used to attach these to the tyres after the latter have been punched to take them. It is also advisable to make the job watertight, etc., by sticking a patch of rubber or other material over the place on the inside. An ordinary gaiter could also be used. Both the latter will reduce friction as far as the inner tube is concerned.

This idea could also be used to help keep old tyres on the rims of rough knock-about vehicles—say when the beading has become worn and yet the tyre itself has quite a lot of life left in it. Almost any type of tyre can be so mended and still give quite a lot of useful service.

A HOME-MADE WHEEL SCRAPER

This illustration shows how to use discarded discs to make handy scrapers for the wheels of farm and other vehicles.

The edges of the disc may be shaped on an emery wheel in order to fit the particular wheel rim desired.

The disc is then bolted on to a piece of 4 x 2 fastened to the implement frame as indicated, when a good, strong and long-lasting scraper will be found very effective and useful.

USEFUL WAGON SEAT FROM OLD TYRES

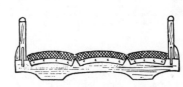

PIECE OF TYRE

This illustration gives details of an excellent wagon seat which is very easy to make and which is very comfortable to ride on. It is made from a short piece of board and some pieces of old tyre, arranged in the manner shown.

The two sections of the tyre shown are cut and nailed the necessary distance apart for the particular vehicle concerned.

In this direction, it is better to use heavy duty or six-ply tyres if it is possible to obtain some as they will stand up to the job much longer than the lighter tyres will.

The illustration will show how the end of the tyres should be hollowed out in order to make a good fit over the sides of the wagon and the sketch will at once illustrate how much more comfortable such an arrangement would be when compared with various other methods.

OLD TYRES MAKE GOOD WAGON SILENCERS

This is another use for small sections of good strong tyres.

Quite a number of wagons make a lot of noise when travelling without a load, either on the rougher tracks around the farm or out on some of the metal roads.

Such old tyres if cut as illustrated here will help eliminate this noise as they can be used as shock-absorbers and silencers. In this connection the tyre are partly cut through in several places and nailed to the bolster or any other place desired as shown in this illustration.

A NEW USE FOR OLD WAGONS

On many farms, there are some old wagons standing around which are practically useless, but they can be put to good use as this one has. It has been made into a portable sheep shade. A little timber, thatched with straw, or cyclone wire, completes the arrangement.

It covers a space of about 20 x 18 feet, which will shade from 50 to 60 sheep and it can be moved about the paddock, thus forming a moveable sheep camp, helping to distribute the drop-

pings and, under the practice of rotational grazing, can be used to provide shade in small fields which otherwise would have none.

To move, it can merely be hitched on behind a horse or tractor or other vehicle and taken to the place desired.

USEFUL AND NOVEL DEVICES FOR FARM OR STATION

WATER IN TRACTOR TYRES

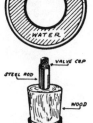

Some farmers like to inflate their tyres with water, claiming increased traction, better riding, reduction in bounce, less wheel slip and sidewall breaks, and less general attention necessary.

If this is desired, the sketch will show a good way of doing it. A valve cap is bored through the end without damage to the thread, and soldered or otherwise fixed into a piece of steel or other tubing. This is then inserted into a wooden plug, which fits tightly into the hose, as indicated. The hose can then be connected to the water supply.

The valve plunger is removed, the cap screwed on, and, when all is ready, the tractor wheels are turned until the valve is a little higher than the hub or at the height required for the water.

When this is done, the tyre can be inflated with air to the usual pressure.

As it is being filled, it is necessary to let some of the air out by removing the wooden plug occasionally.

GRAVITY FEED FOR TRACTORS

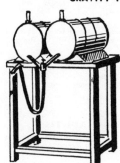

Some farmers like to keep their drums of tractor fuel and oil well above ground to facilitate getting the contents into the tractor tank and crankcase when needed.

This little idea should prove a convenient one in such cases.

These drums are mounted on a make-shift platform 5 ft. high and cleats hold them firmly in place. Pipes and a rubber hose run out the contents of either when a valve is turned. Note inlet pipes at the top of the drums for use of the tank car when it makes its rounds.

AN ADAPTABLE TRAILER FOR FUEL, SUPER, ETC.

This can be used for haymaking or for the carriage of wheat bags or super and then converted to service a tractor. 40-gal. drums can be placed on the platform, on wooden brackets shaped as shown to keep them from rolling and secured by iron bands passing over the drums and bolted to the platform. A good way to fill the tractor tank is to use a 1 in. semi-rotary pump and a short length of paraffin-resisting flexible hose, mounted on top with an iron suction pipe long enough to reach nearly to the bottom of the tank.

A locker can be mounted on to the trailer platform to hold spares, lubricating oil and water, and a chain, etc. A drawbar should be made so that a plow or other implement can be hitched on. Everything can be made detachable so that it can be quickly re-converted to a flat platform type.

ANOTHER USEFUL METHOD OF TRANSPORTING TRACTOR FUEL

This is another simple arrangement to keep fuel handy. A cart or buggy frame is used with supports to hold two fuel drums. The frames should be of good, strong material and a short piece of strong timber should be provided, hinged to the frame where shown, to act as a prop. This can then be hitched up when moving the vehicle.

Either separate outlet pipes or a central one, as shown, can be fitted. If the latter, either fuel or oil can then be drawn from either barrel through this central outlet which is made of tin tubes, soldered and shaped and connected as shown.

A NOVEL TRAILER HITCH PIN

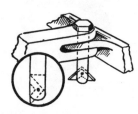

A very useful trailer hitch pin may be made with a steel bolt and a triangle key, as shown here. The bolt is slotted, and the triangle key held in place by a pin.

The shape of the triangle key causes it to hang in a horizontal position, with the ends projecting from either side of the pin to stop the bolt from bouncing out of the hitch. This saves a lot of time hooking up and unhooking.

PIPE SPACER TO PREVENT "BUCKING" OF TRAILER HITCH

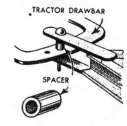

One farmer prevents the hitch clevis of a heavy two-wheeled trailer from "bucking" when travelling loaded over uneven ground by inserting a spacer cut from iron pipe between the top half of the clevis and the tractor draw-bar. The clevis pin passes through the spacer as shown. This arrangement allows free sidewise movement, yet prevents the pounding caused by up-and-down movement of the clevis.

A HANDY BINDER HITCH

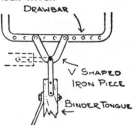

This is a simple attachment to the tractor drawbar for hooking up the binder which is very convenient and which has saved many split binder tongues for one man. The V-shaped attachment makes possible a sharp, right-angled turn, and a neater job of cutting the field. The attachment is made from scrap iron a little lighter than the drawbar, such as a heavy wagon tyre.

A USEFUL CULTIVATOR HOOK FOR SINGLE DISC DRILL

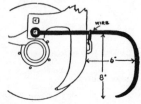

This hook is bolted to the side and it rips up the strip between the discs and thus eliminates cultivation before drilling. They are set to run 2 in. from the disc blades at the same depth. They take out weeds between the discs and they cover the groove generally left by the disc and they lift the lumps to the surface. They can be made from ½ in. iron.

The points are flattened out like a chisel 1 in. or more wide and should be kept sharp. They do not plug up if the back row is kept 6 inches from the front row and the front row 6 in. from the drill discs or boots.

USEFUL AND NOVEL DEVICES FOR FARM OR STATION

OILED PAPER PROTECTS PLOW AGAINST RUSTING

Experiencing the usual trouble in removing heavy grease used to protect a plow against rust, one farmer adopted the method of coating the polished surface with a light machine oil and then pressed sheets of oiled paper into contact with the surface.

The paper will adhere tightly to the metal and yet it is easily stripped off when the plow is to be used again. This is an idea which might also be used in connection with other materials.

NOVEL METHOD OF CUTTING DEEP ROOTS

In some parts, and especially where it is necessary to turn over new ground or ground adjacent to trees, hedges, etc., trouble is experienced with the deeper roots inasmuch as many of those which one would like to cut, simply glide along the underside of the plow without being severed.

To overcome any difficulties in ploughing through old and deep-rooted plants or roots of trees, a row of notches filed on the underside near the heel of some plowshares will help considerably. The large roots are thereby sheared off readily by the short serrated edge formed by the notches. The latter should be about ⅜ to ½ in. deep and 1 in. apart.

A USEFUL MALLEE ROOT PULLER

This is a very useful implement which will do a very good job for the above purpose.

It is easily made and is particularly useful where one has to deal with deep-rooted stumps as it will

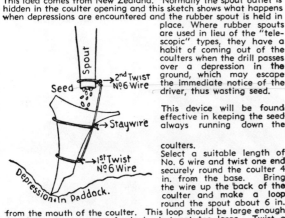

hook under them and pull them out quite effectively. It is shaped as shown in the drawing—a ring or other circular hitching arrangement being inserted on one end in order to hitch it to the tractor whilst a handle is fitted and attached to the hook end in order to facilitate easy handling.

USEFUL DEVICE FOR DRILL SPOUT IN UNEVEN COUNTRY

This idea comes from New Zealand. Normally the spout outlet is hidden in the coulter opening and this sketch shows what happens when depressions are encountered and the rubber spout is held in place. Where rubber spouts are used in lieu of the "telescopic" types, they have a habit of coming out of the coulters when the drill passes over a depression in the ground, which may escape the immediate notice of the driver, thus wasting seed.

This device will be found effective in keeping the seed always running down the coulters.

Select a suitable length of No. 6 wire and twist one end securely round the coulter 4 in. from the base. Bring the wire up the back of the coulter and make a loop round the spout about 6 in. from the mouth of the coulter. This loop should be large enough for the spout to move freely in, but not too large. Twist a short piece of wire round the top of the coulter to hold the device in a rigid position and you will then have the spout always over the mouth of the coulter no matter how rough the paddock.

IMPROVISED CULTIVATOR BOOTS

This idea might be useful in an emergency, as it may, at any time, become necessary to replace some boots for the tynes of a cultivator, perhaps just at some time when one has none of the standard article at hand.

This drawing will, therefore, show how some squares of heavy gauge galvanised iron can be arranged and made to the shape required—fastened on by bolts, as illustrated in this sketch.

These can be fixed to the tynes in any position required; at the same time being so that the flow of seed or super is not out of sight. If fixed as shown here, they should not clog. To prevent delay at an awkward time, it would be well worth while having two or three of these always ready at hand for an emergency.

It is quite a simple arrangement, easily made, and found very useful by one who has tried it in an emergency.

A COMFORTABLE SEAT CUSHION

This is another good use for an old motor inner tube or an ordinary sack will do.

It will make a very comfortable cushion which will remain in place on a farm implement seat with little or no attention. The tube is opened out and sewn together to resemble a sack, or, if an ordinary sack is being used, it is first filled half full with hay or straw and when the latter is in place, the sack is sewn across the middle to hold the filling.

Then turn the remaining portion of the sack inside out. The pocket thus formed is slipped over the implement seat, with the cushion part on top. The arrangement is clearly shown here and the smaller sketch will indicate in detail how the sack (or cushion) is cut and sewn.

ONE METHOD OF RENEWING DUCKFOOT POINTS

Worn points from duckfoot cultivators can be reconditioned from old discs from implements and a job such as this is a good one for spare time moments.

The old worn points are drilled in two places, a hole being bored on each side of the centre rib, below the bolt hole. After boring one or two sets, these can be used over and over again, as it is easy to punch out the rivets and attach new points.

Cut out a template of tin, triangular in shape, and the size of the points to be renewed. Mark out the discs by means of the template, using a cold chisel, or else a crayon, which will not be effaced when the disc is heated.

Heat the discs and cut out the points, using a sharp cutter. Whilst the triangles are hot, bend them to fit the worn points already bored. This can be done by placing them on a log of wood from which a piece has been scooped out.

A blow with a hammer will bend the piece to the correct shape.

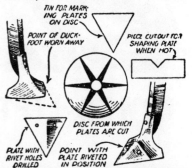

They are then bored to synchronise with the holes in the worn points and riveted into position. These reconditioned points give excellent service and last as long as new ones.

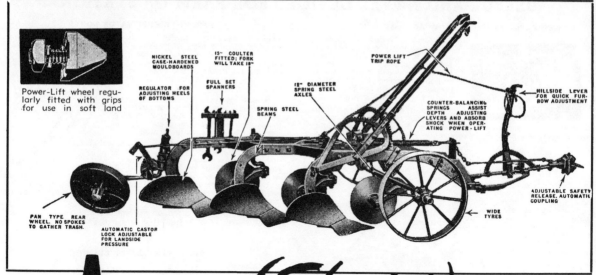

Power-Lift wheel regularly fitted with grips for use in soft land

NICKEL STEEL CASE-HARDENED MOULDBOARDS

15" COULTER FITTED; FORK WILL TAKE 18"

REGULATOR FOR ADJUSTING HEELS OF BOTTOMS

FULL SET SPANNERS

SPRING STEEL BEAMS

12" DIAMETER SPRING STEEL AXLES

POWER LIFT TRIP ROPE

COUNTER-BALANCING SPRINGS ASSIST DEPTH ADJUSTING LEVERS AND ABSORB SHOCK WHEN OPERATING POWER-LIFT

HILLSIDE LEVER FOR QUICK FURROW ADJUSTMENT

PAN TYPE REAR WHEEL. NO SPOKES TO GATHER TRASH.

AUTOMATIC CASTOR LOCK ADJUSTABLE FOR LANDSIDE PRESSURE

WIDE TYRES

ADJUSTABLE SAFETY RELEASE, AUTOMATIC COUPLING

An *(Shearer)* AUSTRALIAN PLOUGH HELPED BRITAIN BEAT THE U-BOATS . . .

In the dark days of the European War, Germany's U-Boats attempted to starve Britain into submission. The threatened island had to produce — or perish. In response to Britain's S.O.S. for farm equipment, 2,000 Shearer Prince Ploughs were rushed to British farmers.

This was the largest single order placed, and the " Prince " plough was so honoured because of its proved efficiency in turning wastelands and moorlands into productive food-growing areas. To plant the land turned by the " Prince " ploughs, Shearer's sent England 2,250 12-row Disc Drills.

Shearer "Prince"
POWER-LIFT MOULDBOARD PLOUGH

MADE BY

JOHN SHEARER & SONS PTY. LTD., KILKENNY, SOUTH AUSTRALIA

USEFUL AND NOVEL DEVICES FOR FARM OR STATION

A HANDY FARM CRANE
Made from Material Usually at Hand on Farm

It is not difficult to build a crane that will enable one man to do such work or unload heavy goods without assistance. Most of the material required is usually at hand.

The main post of the crane is a strong tree trunk, at least 6 in. in diameter when barked, and with a branch in the right position to form a strut for the "jib" or horizontal member of the crane. This jib may be made either of round timber or a piece of suitable sawn hardwood 8 ft. long and about 4 in. x 2 in. or 3 in. x 3 in.

It is pinned firmly in a notch cut in the top of the post and bolted to the diagonal strut. The outer end carries an eyebolt fitted with a pulley block.

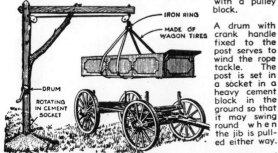

A Handy Crane for Farm Use is Made of a Forked Tree Trunk Thus Simplifying Construction and Giving Great Strength

A drum with crank handle fixed to the post serves to wind the rope tackle. The post is set in a socket in a heavy cement block in the ground so that it may swing round when the jib is pulled either way.

A piece of ordinary iron stovepipe makes a good lining for the socket; if the post is too large for this it must be reduced to fit, but not enough to leave much play or the contrivance will be rickety. A section of hollow log, smoothed inside, also makes an excellent socket. The post should be deep enough to prevent it from wobbling.

A second pulley, of course, must be attached to the post just under the jib to serve to guide the rope to the winch drum. It is possible to make one pulley—that at the end of the jib—do, but the second pulley keeps the rope out of the way of any vehicle that may be under the crane, and distributes the strain on the jib.

A hook will be needed at the outer end of the tackle for attaching to the load to be lifted. For wagon racks and similar lifts, a grab may be made of four old iron wheel tyres bent into hooks and joined together at one end with a ring. By lowering the hooks and attaching them to the corners of the rack or body a boy can easily raise the load with this gear.

This description should enable any handyman to construct the crane.

Where the material specified is not available the resourceful handyman will soon find some effective substitute.

There are three separate ideas on this page, all having a bearing on this subject, and any idea in one may easily be incorporated into the other.

For instance, a crane of rough timber such as that shown in the first illustration can be combined with the swinging attachment and collar of that shown on the bottom right-hand corner.

They are all simply constructed and are based upon the timber being found on the spot, and, further, if by any chance there is a handy tree near at hand, same could be used by rigging some similar arrangement as that shown in either of these sketches.

Every farmer should have a crane or something to help lift heavy weights because, with its aid, any machine can be quickly hoisted when wheels, axles, etc., need to be changed or when perhaps heavy weights are required to be loaded on to any vehicle.

A USEFUL GENERAL PURPOSE HOIST

This is a very simple but useful lifting arrangement for loading and unloading many things on any farm or station or in any workshop.

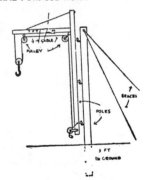

The first thing wanted is a good, stout post which is let 3 feet into the ground and well braced with wire.

The arm, which is 7 feet long, is mortised into the upright and it is also braced with wire.

The upright is swung on three hinges so that the loads can be swung around to either side out of the way.

A HOIST FOR LIFTING HAY OR GREEN MATERIAL

This is a good type of hoist for those who require something which can be used for raising meadow hay or green material on to a stack. The following details of a one-horse hoist will therefore be of value and the accompanying illustration will give full details as to its construction, viz.:—

Poles. The upright pole is 20 ft. long, of which 18 feet is above ground level. The pole should be at least 8 inches thick at the base. The arm should be at least 12 feet long and not less than 4 in. in diameter. The arm is attached to the upright pole by means of a collar and swinging attachments as illustrated about 12 feet from ground level.

Pulleys. Four 4-inch pulleys are attached as shown. A swivel and hook or grab arrangement is on end of hoist rope.

Collar and Swinging Attachment. A six-inch collar of wound wire is fitted around the pole to hold an "eye" attachment. This attachment, which is let into the pole, is made from 14 in. x 2½ in. x ¾ in. iron, shaped as illustrated in "B" enlarged. A one-inch hole is drilled to take the hook, which is made from 1 in. round iron. The end of the hook is flattened, and a 5-8 in. hole is

Explanation of sketch is as follows:—

"A," Pulleys; "B," Swivel; "C," Hook; "D," Rope for raising or lowering the arm according to height of stack; "E," Collar and Swivel (see enlargements); "F," Stays or Guy Ropes; "G," Rope Tie; "H," Rope to pull material over stack.

Enlargement—"A," Collar; "B," Eye enlarged; "C," Hook; "D," Pin and Eye; "E," Straps.

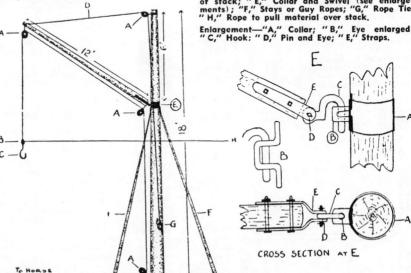

CROSS SECTION at E

drilled to take the pin which holds the two iron straps on the arm.

The two iron straps are made of 15 in. x 2½ in. x ¾ in. iron with holes drilled through for the pin and bolts, the iron being shaped as shown in cross section "E."

USEFUL AND NOVEL DEVICES FOR FARM OR STATION

A HOME-MADE PORTABLE HEAVY HOIST

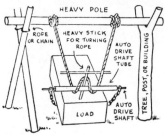

This can be set up against a building or forked tree, using two poles chained or roped together as the other support.

The heavy rope or cable is twisted around a motor drive shaft or heavy pipe; through which a drive shaft or crowbar is placed, with a log chain looped around the projecting ends and under the load to be lifted. The twisting is done by a bar or heavy stick, with a rod dropped behind it to hold at any desired height. If it is well greased, a ton or more can be lifted.

A SIMPLE WAGON BOX HOIST

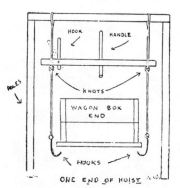

This is a simple device for raising or lowering. The windlass pole should not be too big, i.e., not more than 4 in. in diameter and at that it will raise the box two feet for each turn.

The cable or rope passes through the pole. The hook is mortised into the pole and can be slipped over to catch the cable as shown. This holds the box after it has been raised. The handle should be loose in the hole so that it can be slipped through from one end to the other. This sketch only shows one end of the device as four ropes and hooks are needed. It has been found to be a very effective arrangement.

OTHER HANDY HOME-MADE FARM HOISTS

These are simple but effective types of home-made hoists for raising heavy loads or for lifting things like an engine from a car or tractor.

The smaller illustration is one made from the front axle of a car, a cable or chain about 6 feet long, and a fence stretcher or block and tackle.

It can then be swung from a tree, a heavy pole, or the frame of a building. It also has plenty of side swing to make it convenient.

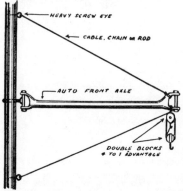

The method of making needs no explanation as it is clearly shown in the sketch, and with a little alteration it could be made to swing in a circle.

In the second illustration, a discarded car axle is also used and converted into a crane of a slightly different type—this could also be made to swing in a complete circle if it were fixed to a rounded pole, as suggested in the accompanying sketch.

ANOTHER TYPE OF GOOD STRONG HOME-MADE HOIST

A good hoist that will lift a beef carcase or other heavy object can be made by sinking two good strong posts into the ground, bracing them firmly, and placing a roller on the top, as indicated in the sketch.

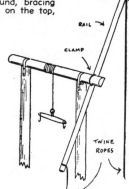

This roller could be of any material and the top of the posts should be hollowed out to take this roller whilst two strong pieces of strap iron are carried over the tops in order to hold the roller in place. These are clearly shown in the sketch.

The rail is then fastened to the roller with a clamp and a piece of twine or rope attached to the ends. The weight can be held at any height by giving one of the ropes a hitch around the post.

An old swingle-tree works well as a spreader.

AN EASILY-MOVED DERRICK

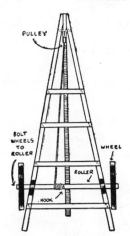

This is a very handy arrangement, since it has wheels instead of a crank, and by lifting the small end it can be moved from one place to another on the wheels.

The wheels are pinned through the roller shaft so that both revolve together. A small hook takes the end of the rope when the derrick is at work and the rope can be slipped off when moving so that it will not wind up.

A hook of ⅜ in. iron rod or a bit of rope can be used to fasten one wheel to a leg and hold up a load after it has been lifted by the derrick.

ANOTHER HOME-MADE PORTABLE DERRICK

The following is a very handy portable derrick suitable for many jobs. The axle and wheels can be from some old implement.

In this instance, the bottom of the swinging post is pivoted to the cross-piece while a stub shaft and a piece of strap iron make a bearing at the top. A pulley is attached to the outer end of the swinging arm, a second is put between the members of the upright post at the top, and a third one is fastened close to the axle at the bottom.

The location as shown is intended for the pull to be on the side away from the weight to be lifted, but the pull can be made from any desired direction by properly locating the lower pulley. The upright is about 10 ft. high, and the arm is 12 ft. long. Loads up to 1,000 lbs. can be lifted easily and swung to either side.

In this one, an old separator axle was used but a heavy car axle could be used by turning the drive shaft straight up, putting a pipe or shaft in the tube to serve as a turning post, and clamping a heavy wood frame to the axle with diagonal support for the anchor part. The boom could be two 4 x 2's clamped to the turning pipe, and the boom brace could be fastened loosely at the bottom with a band round the drive shaft tube.

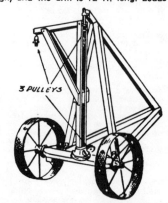

USEFUL AND NOVEL DEVICES FOR FARM OR STATION

A SIMPLE ONE-MAN LIFT

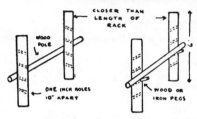

There are many one-man lifts, but although this may not be the quickest, it is very simple and quick.

All that is needed is 4 posts, about 6 in. dia. and 7 or 8 ft. long, together with two 15 ft. poles. Holes about 10 in. apart are bored in the posts at an angle. Bolts or hardwood pins may be used to support the poles. One corner is lifted at a time. This could be used for lifting hay, or almost anything, and, if erected in a convenient out-of-the-day spot, it would prove its worth.

A HAND HOIST FOR BARRELS

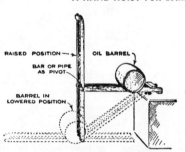

The top arrangement is useful for lifting motor lubricants and tractor kerosene to a point where the tanks need to be filled.

Only 4 lengths of 4 x 2 timber and a few braces are needed; two of the 4 x 2's are placed parallel as a support for the oil barrel; the other two are pivoted to them, as shown in the drawing, and serve as levers to raise the shorter lengths to a horizontal position after the barrel has been rolled into

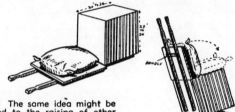

place. The same idea might be applied to the raising of other heavy objects, such as wheat and super bags, other examples of which are shown on various other pages in this book.

Another type of hand hoist is shown above and can also be made by the use of a box, as indicated. All that is required for this is a good strong box of suitable size, with two light, strong handles.

The sketches explain themselves, and either of these hoists could be transported to whatever place required, i.e., out in the fields when drilling super or when harvesting or into the work shop where something might be required to be lifted.

A SIMPLE HOME-MADE HOIST FOR BALE HANDLING, ETC.

Hay and straw are being baled more and more on many farms as this method of fodder conservation not only assists storage, but greatly assists the proper proportioning of food to stock, etc.

In many cases, the stacking of baled hay and straw may have its difficulties, especially if labour is a bit short, but this simple device should be of assistance as it is a simple but effective method of handling the bales. The loading tool is also quite a good one, simply constructed and easily made to serve its purpose.

The device consists of a 24 ft. length of 1½ in. piping or other material, swinging from a suitable point as shown in the sketch. In this instance, strap-iron is used, suspended from a pole or tripod as indicated.

The piping is strengthened by a chain supporting each end on the cantilever principle. Into one end is fitted a short length of 1 in. piping to form a handle grip.

To the other end is attached a jaw grip for holding the bales.

This consists of two pieces of angle-iron loosely bolted together and cranked towards one another at their lower ends, to which are attached the working ends of two old dung forks with the tynes bent inwards.

Two coiled springs, attached from the end of each angle-iron to the bend of its opposite keep the jaws open. A small amount of pressure enables them to be closed into the bale, and the weight of the bale when suspended keeps them in position. A jerk on unloading is usually sufficient to make the springs open the jaws.

AUTOMATIC UNLOADING

The illustration given here is of a very useful method of automatic unloading of silage or hay, etc. Both this and the following idea are somewhat similar in operation in many respects.

This particular sketch is one that is particularly useful for pit silage. By laying ropes along the car, truck or wagon body before loading, the labour of unloading can be greatly reduced, if it is done in the manner suggested.

Besides being useful for pit silage, it would also serve the purpose of unloading material at the foot of an elevator or cutter-blower. The idea is clearly shown and quite simple in operation.

A USEFUL AUTOMATIC ROLL-IN STACKER

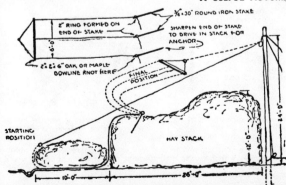

The illustration on left is of a useful device tried out by one farmer. In this, three men are required to operate it, one to do the stacking, one to drive the team and arrange the slings, and the other to operate the sweep rake.

The material needed for building this equipment is as follows:— 80 to 100 feet of one-inch rope; 3 pieces of half-inch rope, 35 to 40 feet long; three iron stakes made of ¾ in. iron bent to form a ring at one end and pointed at the other. One piece of 2 x 2 hardwood, 6 feet long; 3 rings 3 inches in diameter, made of half-inch iron, and two single block pulleys and a telephone pole 25 to 30 feet long. The rope is held in place with guy wire.

The illustration will give the method of operation quite clearly, showing how the load is driven to and taken from the stack.

USEFUL AND NOVEL DEVICES FOR FARM OR STATION

LIFTING AND LOADING UNSEWN BAGS

The following are some very practical suggestions. It is often necessary to load unsewn bags in transporting wheat to and from the paddocks and to lift bags of super into drills, etc., and the following home-made arrangements might prove useful to any who find this sort of work difficult; in fact, any one of them will minimise labour and thus help in the day's work.

A ONE-MAN LOADER FOR TRUCK

This is a one-man loader. It consists of two pieces of timber, with about four rollers and a platform about 3 inches wide, one foot from the lower end.

It is placed against the side of the truck, and, by using two bag hooks, the bag of wheat can be lifted on to the platform. The extra foot from the ground brings the top of the bag about level with the truck body.

ANOTHER SIMPLE TRUCK LOADING HELP

Procure a piece of board, about 1 inch thick, and 12 to 14 inches wide, and long enough to reach the level of the truck body when

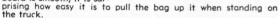

placed at about a 20 to 25 degrees angle. Plane the face of the board very smooth and on top of the board fix two small iron brackets made to go over the side rail of the truck, with a small flange bent over the top to grip the side.

At about 8 to 12 inches from the bottom of the board attach a shelf. With the aid of two bag hooks, any ordinary man will have no difficulty in placing a bag of wheat on this shelf; and, as the board is smooth, it is surprising how easy it is to pull the bag up it when standing on the truck.

By pulling up to a well-built dump where the bags are, say, three wide, the bags are then always near the boards. By moving the boards along the body of the truck, as required, loading can be done quickly.

A BAG LIFTER FROM BUSH TIMBER

This is quite a good home-made bag lifter, the fork being 1 ft. longer than the height of the cart.

A cross-piece is bolted across the single end.

In use, this rests on the tail of the cart and stops the wobble when the fork is lifted.

Across the opposite side of the form (22 in. from the ground) is a 4 inch wide platform, or step bolted to each leg by a long bolt.

Rest the crosspiece against the back of the cart, then upend a bag of super against the step; then lift its lower end. Heave the bag on to the step, then upend the fork, bag and all, and dump the bag on the cart. It calls for much less effort than a straight-out lift of 3 ft. 6 in. does.

A HANDY ARRANGEMENT FOR LIFTING BAGS ON TO TRUCK

The following illustration will show the general idea and construction of this handy home-made gadget, which will be found very easy of operation. It should be made of light timber so that it can be shifted round the truck from place to place without much trouble, as required.

First make an oblong frame of suitable length, making sure that it is somewhat longer than the depth of a bag of wheat, whilst it should also be wide enough to allow the bag to swing freely in its holder when in place.

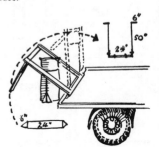

The frame cross-piece at the truck end should not be flush with the side pieces as, in order to prevent the frame slipping, it should be such that it will engage the beading around the edge of the truck.

This frame has what is termed a "push-pole"— this being a fixture to enable the user to control the lift after the top of the frame has risen out of his ordinary reach.

This is fixed to the frame by some means to enable it to be flexible—or the top cross-piece could be so inserted into the frame that it will move as required.

The bag holder (see inset) is made U-shaped from, say, $\frac{3}{8}$ in. iron, so fitted to take the bag. This should be 24 in. across, 30 in. high, with two 6-inch lugs, which are used to swing the bag at the point where it is pivoted to the frame.

The bottom section of this U-piece bag holder should be of strong material (sheet metal for preference) 1 ft. wide and 2 ft. long with an additional 6 inches on each end cut to a point on each side (see small detail at foot) and bent upwards at right angles. These are fixed into position with U-bolts on both top and sides; the nuts, of course, being on the outside.

A chain is used to encircle the bags—this being fixed at the centre to one side of the bag holder, whilst there should be two hooks on the other side leg of the holder to take the ends of the chain after the bag of wheat has been placed on it. The bag-holder should be fixed to the frame about 2 ft. 8 in. from the cross-frame on the truck edge—U-bolts can be used as bearings and fastenings for the supporting lugs.

To use this gadget engage the cross-piece of the inside edge of the truck beading—lay the push-pole on the ground—place a bag in the holder and hook the chain around it to hold in position.

Then lift by means of the push-pole until it is upright, when the bag can be easily taken off on to the lorry.

A TRIPOD ARRANGEMENT FOR LOADING BAGS

This is quite a simple arrangement as all that is necessary is three lengths of scrap timber for the legs which fit into a socket previously made in another piece of timber which is to act as the loading arm. This socket should carry a king-pin and the tripod should be fixed in position in the manner indicated, although the loading arms are not shown in their true proportion in the sketch.

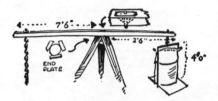

The height of the legs should be in accordance with the lift required. Other measurements are shown in the drawing and the bag holder itself can be made from any scrap material—the centre of the bag being supported by a ring of hoop iron, chain or other material, which could be hooked round and shifted up and down as required.

An arrangement such as this is very easy of operation. The small upper inset will show the arrangement of the connection between the legs and the loading arm, whilst the other smaller inset shows the arrangement of the end plate and legs.

USEFUL AND NOVEL DEVICES FOR FARM OR STATION

A USEFUL LIFTING HOOK FOR SIDE OF TRUCK

This is quite a good idea, but, of course, the idea of hooks is one to be improved upon. A U-frame with chains (as shown in other illustrations) would be an improvement, but the method of lifting is quite good.

Such an arrangement could be fastened on to the side of the truck instead of on a tripod, and up to 10 bags or so could be loaded before having to stack them.

A PORTABLE GRAIN LOADER FROM MOTOR PARTS

Parts of old machinery from three different motors went into the making of this very useful portable grain loader.

Although, of course, it is not everyone who might have three old cars to work on, nevertheless the idea might be a good one for some who might desire such an arrangement.

For a frame, a Chevrolet axle was used, in this instance, on which an Overland motor was mounted, and it was conected to a radiator from a Whippet.

By mounting an elevator from an old threshing machine separator, the machine was completed that would load 250 bushels of wheat in 20 minutes. Although this particular one is made to take loose wheat, it could be improvised to take filled bags also.

Such a useful adjunct to any farm could be taken into the field by merely hitching it on to the rear of the truck or other vehicle.

A GOOD LIGHT PORTABLE RAMP TO ASSIST LOADING

For those who prefer to wheel instead of lift bags on to the truck, this idea will be found of use. The wheels in this should track with the truck and should be at least 3 ft. in circumference. The ramp is in two sections, as shown, fitted with hooks at the top end which engage with something suitable on the truck end.

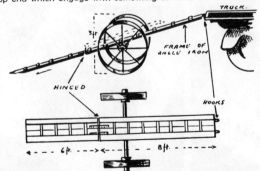

It will be seen that the two sections are hinged together to enable it to be folded when moving about. The framework should be of not less than 2 x 1-8 angle iron and the hinge should be of very strong material to stand up to the weight passing over it.

If such a ramp is made (and it is very simply made) the bags can be simply wheeled from the ground straight up on the truck and placed into position without any double handling at all.

HOME-MADE ADJUSTABLE BAG HOLDERS

Difficulties are often experienced when a number of bags have to be filled and the following are a variety of hints which might be useful.

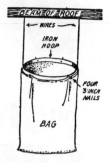

FILLING CHAFF BAGS

This hint may be useful if your chaff-cutter has no bagger attached to the elevator. Make a strap of iron, which will fit inside the mouth of a chaff bag. Punch four holes at intervals round the hoop and put in 3 in. nails bent into the shape of a hook. The hoop is suspended from a beam at a height which just permits a bag placed on the hooks to reach the ground. Using a heavy rammer, it is easy to put a good weight of chaff into the bags.

ANOTHER USEFUL SACK HOLDER

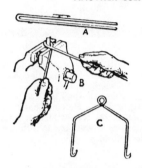

A supporting hook is often useful for this purpose. To make one, take a 4 ft. length of No. 6 or 8 wire or ¼ in. iron rod. Bend it in the centre to the shape of a hairpin. Put the loop round an iron rod, chisel or similar tool held in a vice, and cross the ends so as to make a ring or eye, as in fig. B.

Make the shoulder bends as at C and bend the ends of the wire up to form hooks. A piece of strong cord through the loop enables the sack to be hung from a rafter at the correct height, so that the weight of the full sack rests on the floor and not on the hooks.

ANOTHER ADJUSTABLE BAG HOLDER

This one is quickly adjustable to fit any sack and hold it taut. Horizontal arms riveted across the lower ends of two vertical pieces, which are bent as shown, and pivoted at the upper ends, fit inside the sack mouth.

A third piece, pivoted to one of the vertical irons, has teeth cut in the lower side to engage the end of a slit made in the other vertical piece. By pushing this arm the vertical pieces are spread to draw the sack mouth taut. It will not tear the cloth when being inserted.

A DIFFERENT TYPE BAG HOLDER

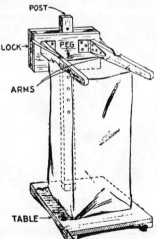

This is a simple holder for keeping bags open for refilling.

Adjustable in height, it has two hinged hardwood arms which carry sharp-pointed nails bent upwards to engage the mouth of the sack. Strong rubber bands attached to the arms and to the post pull the arms outward to keep the mouth of the sack taut.

The table or base, post and arm carrying block are made of any stock available. A peg inserted through a hole in the block and post takes care of the height adjustment.

USEFUL AND NOVEL DEVICES FOR FARM OR STATION

USEFUL HINTS FOR TRACTOR OWNERS

AN IDEA FOR SMOOTHER RIDING

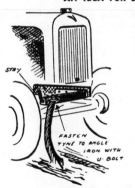

This is a very simple gadget which should help eliminate much of the jolting and shaking which is often the case when the tractor is traversing fallowed or other rough ground.

The illustration shows the suggested arrangement and how it can be fixed in front of the wheel which does not run in the furrow—it clearing away any unevenness which causes much jolting.

This enables both wheels to run in some sort of furrow and it should thus eliminate to a certain extent side skid of the front wheels, whilst it should also assist in a straight course being maintained.

A USEFUL FURROW GUIDE

Where one is operating a big tractor it is often a little difficult to maintain proper position, and therefore this little hint might help.

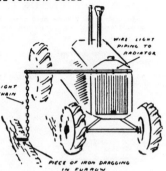

It is a handy furrow guide made by fixing on to the tractor in the manner shown, a length of steel, piping or other material so that a light chain or anything else suitable can be suspended into the furrow.

If it is the same height as the tractor, the driver can keep it well in view.

A REAR VIEW MIRROR

This little arrangement will enable the driver to keep a constant watch on the trailing implement or on the work being done.

Attached to the tractor as shown, this truck-type rear view mirror enables one to do these things without constantly turning round or keeping your head in an uncomfortable position.

This is specially helpful when plowing ground or in any job where you must keep your eye on the implement behind the tractor.

AN ADJUSTABLE HITCH FOR TRACTOR

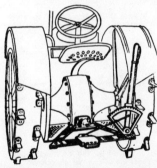

This adjustable hitch was fitted by one farmer to his Fordson.

He has found it a wonderful help when plowing as it enables him to keep perfect control of the front plow on either two or three furrow plows.

It is also of considerable use on hillsides, whilst it enables one to run the front furrow out to straighten the work up.

Another advantage is that it prevents the implements from damaging tractor mudguards, etc.

AN IMPROVISED REAR LIGHT FOR A TRACTOR

This is quite a useful idea for those who may wish to improvise a light for this purpose.

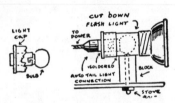

A very useful rear light for a tractor can easily be made by cutting an ordinary flashlight down in the manner shown in this sketch.

A hole is made through the flashlight cap where a car tail light connection and bulb is soldered on (see illustration).

The light is mounted to the rear of the tractor by means of a wood block and stove bolt, which is first pushed through from the inside of the light case.

Such a light will give quite a considerable illumination at a minimum cost and with very little power.

ONE METHOD OF PULLING OUT A BOGGED TRACTOR

This illustration shows one very useful method of getting a tractor out of a muddy or sandy patch. In this manner a lot of time and fuel will be saved.

The idea merely consists of making two pieces of 4 x 4 hardwood blocks as shown, four eye-bolts and two short lengths of chain, the latter being just long enough to reach around the tyre and through the blocks as indicated in the accompanying sketch.

This arrangement can be carried on the machine and easily put on at any time.

The sketch is self-explanatory and shows how it is affixed to the tractor.

ANOTHER WAY OF PULLING OUT A BOGGED TRACTOR

This sketch illustrates a sure, safe and simple way of pulling a tractor out of a bog. As will be seen, two wires or wire ropes are tied to the two rear wheels of the tractor and led forward over the front axle to an anchor of some kind in front.

It will be seen from the sketch that as the tractor is driven forward, the wheels wind the wires around themselves and so the tractor is edged forward.

In order to prevent any "bucking" the wires are led over the front axle. The tractor or truck as the case may be is then started up and the action of the wheels moving round and causing the rope to wind around will gradually force it out of the bog.

This method can be used for backing also whilst lorries and cars could also be pulled out of bogs in the same way, provided there is no danger of the rope being jammed anywhere as it wound round the axle.

131

USEFUL AND NOVEL DEVICES FOR FARM OR STATION

WHEN TRACTORS PULL HORSE IMPLEMENTS

The following are a few ideas from one who emphasises the importance of the hitching arrangements in the conversion of horse-drawn implements and carts for use with tractors. Whilst the details must be left to the individual, a few illustrations and notes of these modifications may be helpful.

HORSE MOWER AND TRACTOR

One farmer found this outfit a simple and fast way of mowing with a rubber-tyred tractor. The drawing will explain the method of coupling.

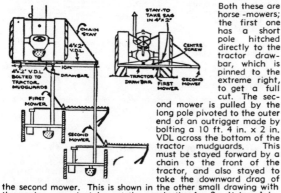

Both these are horse-mowers; the first one has a short pole hitched directly to the tractor drawbar, which is pinned to the extreme right, to get a full cut. The second mower is pulled by the long pole pivoted to the outer end of an outrigger made by bolting a 10 ft. 4 in. x 2 in. VDL across the bottom of the tractor mudguards. This must be stayed forward by a chain to the front of the tractor, and also stayed to take the downward drag of the second mower. This is shown in the other small drawing with the centre screw to take out the sag in the 4 x 2. It is a $\frac{1}{2}$ in. iron stay bolted to both ends with this screw in the centre. The farmer concerned also has fitted tilting platforms to the mowers for cutting short grass seed for clover. This outfit is capable of cutting 3 acres an hour in good going.

CONVERTING OTHER IMPLEMENTS

It should always be borne in mind that the substitution of tractor power for horses may put severe strains upon the implements as the tendency will generally be to work at higher speeds.

The hitching arrangements must therefore be well and strongly attached to the implements, allowing, at the same time, for the difference in height between the horse and the tractor drawbar

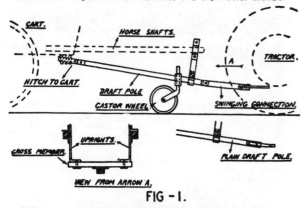

FIG - 1.

Side views of a hitch for a cart when it is not desirable that the shafts be shortened.

as well as maintaining the correct disposition of the implement under working conditions.

The illustrations on this page are all diagrammatic and, as pointed out, must be adapted to suit each individual make and type.

Figure 1 illustrates an arrangement of tractor hitch for a cart where it is not desirable that the shafts be removed or shortened.

This shows a castor wheel fitted to the draft pole and a swinging connection between the pole and tractor drawbar, thus taking the weight of the cart and allowing for flexibility between tractor and cart.

Where lighter work is required (small drills, etc.), the castor wheel and the swinging connection can be dispensed with. The draft pole should in every case be substantially fixed to the framework of the cart or implement.

An arrangement of a hitch for a wagon is shown in **figure 2** In this case, the shafts have been shortened and a draft pole, suitably supported and coupled up to the shafts, has been fitted.

An alternative, where it is desired not to remove the shafts, is to fit the arrangement shown in figure 1 (without castor wheel

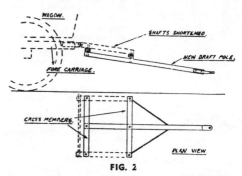

FIG. 2

A side view and a plan of tractor hitch for a wagon where the shafts have been shortened and a draft pole attached.

and swinging connection), the hitch to the cart in this case being fastened to the forecarriage.

Harrows, cultivators and similar implements present little difficulty for conversion, as the central pin and whippletree arrangement is readily adaptable.

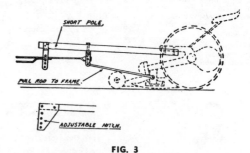

FIG. 3

A simple means of attaching a tractor to a horse-drawn mowing machine.

Figure 3 shows an arrangement of hitch for a horse-drawn mower, the draft pole and whippletrees being substituted by a short pole. A pull rod to the frame is also fitted, although in some cases no provision is made for the pull rod and either an adjustable hitch plate (as shown) can be fitted, or the pole can be set at an angle to suit any particular tractor.

In the case of binders, the existing draft pole and whippletrees can be replaced by a shorter pole and an adjustable hitch plate can be fitted. Where the binder is fitted with a forecarriage, the existing pole should be shortened and a plain eye fitted for the drawpin.

Height of Tractor Draw-pin. Where it is permissable to shorten the shafts in a good many implements a draft pole can be fitted as shown in the illustration given below at right, allowance being made in the hitching-up arrangement for the correct height on the tractor draw-pin.

If the implements are fitted with a horse pole, this can be shortened and well supported on the implement, with suitable provisions for the tractor drawpin.

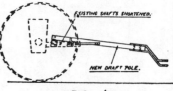

FIG - 4

How to hitch when the existing shafts or draft pole can be shortened.

USEFUL AND NOVEL DEVICES FOR FARM OR STATION

HORSEMOBILE AND TRAILER HINTS

These few hints are from an English source and show how iron cart or motor wheels can be converted and tractor trailers made.

When converting a cart, two old motor wheels should be mounted on a straight axle. Sometimes it is possible to use the old cart axle by merely having the ends turned down in a lathe, or built up by welding, to fit the bearings of the motor car wheels. More often a new axle has to be made up and usually it has to be placed at greater distance below the floor of the cart than was the original axle. Motor car wheels are smaller than old cart wheels; therefore, unless the axle is made lower the cart will ride too low, with the shafts at the wrong angle for the horse. Cranked iron bearers can be used to lower the axle, or solid wooden blocks can be used for packing. The axle can be held by U-bolts big enough to embrace the wooden blocks.

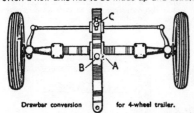

Drawbar conversion for 4-wheel trailer.

A 4-wheeled tractor trailer can be made from a car chassis. Any blacksmith can make up a drawbar to be connected to the front axle and the steering track-rod so that a side pull on the drawbar will cause the front axle to turn in the same direction.

Strip off the steering gear and steering arms, leaving the track rod in place. Use a piece of iron for the drawbar pole about 4 in. wide and ½ in. thick. Clamp a bracket, marked "A" in sketch, to the middle of the front axle. This is to carry a vertical pin for the drawbar to swivel in, at "B." Clamp another bracket in the middle of the track rod—this carries a vertical pin "C."

In the drawbar, drill a hole for the pivot pin "B," but make a slot instead of a round hole for the pin at "C." This slot is to allow for the fact that the distance "BC" does not remain constant when the vehicle turns a corner.

Let the pin "C" be long enough to allow the drawbar at that point to move up and down an inch or so before it touches the head of the pin or the platform of the bracket. At "B," the drawbar is firmly pivoted, but at "C" it can move the length of the slot horizontally and the length of the play between the head of the pin and the platform of the bracket, vertically. The draw bar pull is taken at the axle and not at the track rod.

The drawbar may have to be cranked to bring it to the right height for the tractor hitch; if so, a clevis or U-shaped iron should be made at the end of the drawbar, to enclose a tractor-hitch, so that a plain drawbar pin can be used. A hole in the end of the drawbar will serve; though a nut and bolt should be used for a drawbar pin.

U-bolts with blocks of wood as packing can be used to secure the body to the chassis. If the steering arm is locked by a clamp, the front wheel brake connections come in just at the right place to make an easy link with the over-run brake control. Make provision for final adjustment of the brake cable as they should come on automatically whenever the trailer tends to over-run the car.

If nicely adjusted, the trailer will begin to slow up almost as soon as the car.

ANOTHER CONVERTED TRAILER OR BUGGY

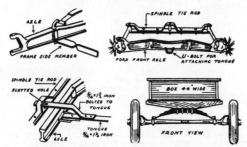

In this, the hind axle is an old buggy axle turned down to fit Ford front wheel bearings. Buggy springs are also used on the rear axle. There are two reaches connecting the rear and front axles, made of flat iron 1½ x ¼ in., and given a half-turn at both ends, see upper left-hand drawing. The front view shows that the box is 44 in. wide, and that the front assembly of the running gear of the car is used, including the spring. Therefore two sets of front

wheel bearings and wheels are used as the rear assembly. The front axle is shown at the lower left. A U-bolt inserted in the axle takes the tongue.

A piece of flat iron, suitably bent, is bolted to the tongue and passes over the axle to the spindle tie rod.

A piece of flat iron, bent saddle fashion, takes this iron, which has a slotted hole to engage the bolt and allow for play. Both the tongue and the iron fastened to it are of 5/16 iron, 1½ in. wide.

The same assembly could be made the basis of a horse-drawn buggy, but it would need a different box, with suitable seating arrangements, and the tongue would be made to use with horses, otherwise the general construction would be the same, with adjustments to take either one or two horses. Instead of one iron bolted to the tongue and connecting with the spindle tie rod, two could be made, one for each shaft.

A ONE-MAN LOADING TIP DRAY

This little hint might be useful to some, it being one method of loading a heavy object into a farm cart single-handed.

The idea is to leave the tailboard in, tip the cart right back, roll the object on to the tailboard and tie it there if necessary.

Then put a strong pole through the spokes at the rear of both wheels and start the horse forward. The pole lifts the tail of the cart with the object inside. Then replace the tip pin, remove the pole and drive on.

ONE METHOD OF FITTING A TIP TO A DRAY

This is a very useful idea if one desires to fit a tip to a dray or a rather large cart, and it will be found such that it will save

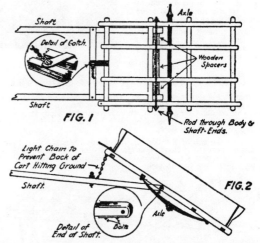

FIG. 1

FIG. 2

quite a lot of time. The method can, of course, be used by any "handyman" with a suitable vehicle or it can be allowed for when making a conversion from one type of conveyance to another.

It does not need much explanation as the type of catch is shown and is one which can be very quickly and easily made. The sketches show in detail the pivoting arrangement, but allowance should be made for the tailboard, so that it can be taken out prior to tipping.

USEFUL AND NOVEL DEVICES FOR FARM OR STATION

ONE METHOD OF MAKING OIL DRUMS EASY TO HANDLE

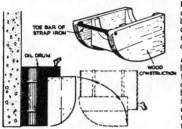

Drums of all types can be easily handled by one man if he uses a tilt-like type of stand like the one indicated here.

After the drum has been placed in position with the oil cock at the top, it is tilted back a little and the stand is then pushed against it with the toe bar under the front edge of the drum. When the stand is rocked forward, it will pull the drum with it and lay on its side. In this horizontal position, the drum can then be readily pushed about until it reaches the desired location.

ANOTHER HANDY RACK FOR OIL DRUM

This sketch shows a handy rack for any sized oil drum. It is made of hardwood and fastened together with bolts. The rockers are from wagon tyres and the braces are heavy strap iron.

The rack is made so that the barrel or drums stand upright until petrol or oil is needed, and it is then tipped over on to the rockers. This eliminates all lifting and is a one-man job.

A RIGID STAND FOR OIL DRUMS

There are many farmers and others who keep oil and kerosene, etc., on hand in drums which they would find more convenient if they had a stand of some sort on which to keep them.

A rigid stand can easily be made from old car rims. The latter are merely cut in half and bolted together as indicated in this drawing, two horizontal braces of angle iron being bolted or riveted to the rims, which serve as legs for the stand.

It is then always ready for instant use and in a convenient position for filling the necessary containers.

A SIMPLE METHOD OF STRAIGHTENING BALING WIRE

This method is simple and quick. There is a vice on most workshop benches, and this is used. Grip about half an inch of the plain end of old baling wire in the teeth of the vice, then take an old piece of $\frac{1}{2}$ in. iron bar about 2 ft. long and put this through the looped end of the wire.

Now catch the end of the bar against a wood block nailed to the bench and apply sufficient leverage to straighten the wire. Withdraw the bar and with a small cold chisel and hammer, cut off the half inch held in the vice.

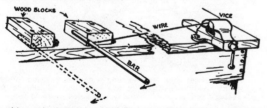

By this method one man and a boy can straighten a large quantity in a short time, with the added advantage that if there is any weakness or flaw in the wire, then it will break in that weak spot and must be discarded.

AN ACETYLENE GAS GENERATOR

A Simple Home-made Plant

One ingenious farmer has put together a very useful type of acetylene gas generator which he has used for some years with very satisfactory results.

A water container 15 inches in diameter is made from 24-gauge galvanised iron. An upper portion to act as a gas container which measures 14 inches in diameter is made to slide up and down inside the water container. Depths of the two containers are three feet and two feet six inches respectively.

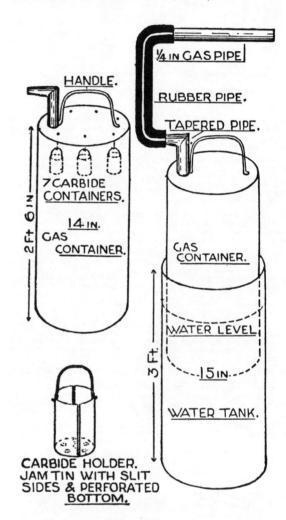

The gas container is fitted with a handle to facilitate lifting, and has a tapered nozzle to take a $\frac{1}{2}$-inch rubber pipe. Inside the gas container are hooks to take the carbide containers, which are jam-tins with perforated sides and bottoms, and wire handles. The tins should be about a third full of carbide.

The method of operation is to lift out the gas container, hang the carbide tins in position, and replace in the water tank, having first disconnected the rubber tube. The gas container will sink down as the air escapes through the nozzle, and will commence to rise as soon as the carbide comes in contact with the water and generates the gas. Place the thumb over the nozzle and slip on the rubber tube. It will slip on easily if the nozzle is wetted.

There should be ample pressure for house lighting, but if necessary, this can be increased by putting a weight on the top of the gas container.

It is advisable to have two sets of carbide containers.

USEFUL AND NOVEL DEVICES FOR FARM OR STATION

HOME-MADE TUMBLE SWEEPS FOR CLOVER, ETC.

These are very useful little implements and very handy to have round the farm, etc., where there may be clover, hay or other grasses to be raked up and gathered.

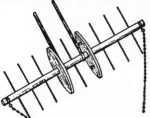

Design No. 1—This is very simply constructed, and it will take the place of a hay rake for making windrows, or for sweeping hay up to the stacks. It is pulled from the ends, and the handiest method of using it is to have a boy riding the horse, so that the man behind the sweep has both hands free. The skids, which are in the shape of ellipses, can be made in two halves, if desired, and secured to the main bar as fixtures. As soon as the sweep turns over, it is ready immediately for the next load. The handles are attached to the main bar by means of loose rings, which will allow the bar to rotate freely. Projecting bolts, or studs, are placed on the inside faces of the ellipses, and when it is desired to tip the load, the handles are placed beneath the projections, and turned so that the points of the tynes strike the ground, and the sweep turns over and rides on the other half. It is advisable to put strips of hoop-iron round the skids to prevent wear.

Loose rings running in grooves are provided at the ends of the main bar for the attachment of the draught chains, which require to be about double the length of the ordinary plough chains. The teeth should be about four feet in length, passing through holes bored in the main bar, so that about two feet will protrude at each side of the bar.

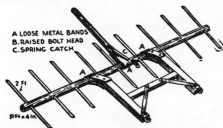

A LOOSE METAL BANDS
B. RAISED BOLT HEAD
C. SPRING CATCH

Design No. 2 is also practically self-explanatory. It is another type of tumble sweep. The pegs are two feet long, and are made of wood or light pipe. In action, the sweep handle is raised until the spring catches on the bolthead, which forces the pegs into the ground, and the sweep tumbles over.

Metal bands are let into the beam at points marked "A," and these are a loose fit to allow the beam to revolve. "B" is the raised bolthead, and "C" is the piece of spring metal.

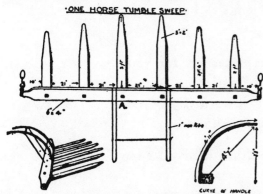

·ONE HORSE TUMBLE SWEEP·

CURVE OF HANDLE

Design No. 3 is practically self-explanatory. The main beam is a length of 6 x 4 hardwood, 12 ft. in length. The teeth are 3 x 2 timber from two to three feet in length sunk ½ inch into the main beam.

Iron skids of ⅜ x 3 inches metal are attached to the centre teeth. Curved handles of piping are fitted as shown in the sketch, and loose collars at the ends of the beam carry links for chains.

HOME-MADE IDEAS FOR HANDLING COCKY CHAFF

These are three excellent ideas, each of which is different in construction.

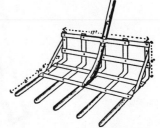

The first is a very handy implement; very simply made. The fork is made of ordinary 1 in. hoop iron and has five prongs, each being pointed, and with the last 8 in. hammered to a fluted shape to make for added strength.

The centre prong is made longer than the others and continues past the second cross-piece at the back, running about 12 inches up the handle for extra support. Another piece is riveted across the front of the handle with further reinforcement running vertically up the handle.

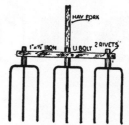

HAY FORK
1"x⅜" IRON   U BOLT   2 RIVETS

Illustration No. 2 is a sketch of another device that is ideal for the job and which is not too heavy.

It is made, using an ordinary hay fork with either a 6 ft. or an 8 ft. handle, and two other fork-heads—the rest of the construction being self-explanatory.

The cross-piece joining the fork-heads is shown in detail, joined to the centre one by a U-bolt.

No. 3 is another idea. Take the ends out of a kerosene case; nail them together at right angles and tack a piece of tin (triangular) on each side to form a box.

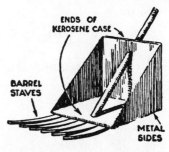

ENDS OF KEROSENE CASE
BARREL STAVES
METAL SIDES

For tynes, get some staves from a small keg. Saw them down the centre and taper them to a sharp point on the other end, with the curve upwards, and nail under the bottom board, allowing the back of the prongs to overlap most of the way under the bottom and about 9 inches out. A mallee or other stick will make a good handle.

These will also suggest other ideas, i.e., perhaps there may be some old car springs available for the tynes in this latter arrangement or perhaps some other material.

A ONE-HORSE MANURE SCRAPER

The job of raking up manure for transportation to the manure pit is anything but a pleasant job.

However, the scraper shown in this sketch was made from a piece of sheet iron, 10 in. by 3 feet, curved for its whole length and bolted to an ordinary plough stock.

The bottom edge of the scraper was sharpened for removing manure closely compacted with the earth. A horse is then hitched to the scraper, and the animal is merely driven over the ground to the manure dump.

Such an implement could also be used as a scraper for paths or a tennis court or for cleaning up weeds.

USEFUL AND NOVEL DEVICES FOR FARM OR STATION

STORING BINDER CANVAS

This is an idea of one farmer for storing binder and combine canvases in order that they would be out of the way of mice.

This very simple and effective method is to thread the canvas on a rope, as shown in the illustration, and then thread a disc of tar paper as indicated.

Mice will not crawl beyond this barrier. This should also be a good idea in connection with any home-made belts one may have such as those indicated on this page. It should then help to keep them mouse and ratproof, and would save the annoyance of finding them full of holes when they were required for use.

A LIGHT ROOF FOR A PORTABLE ENGINE

This is an easily made arrangement which should be found very useful to many.

It is a removable roof, for protecting a portable engine from the weather should it be necessary to leave it in the open.

The illustration is self-explanatory. The roof is made of iron, over a light but strong wooden frame, which should be designed to rest on top of the engine when in place. Such a covering provides shelter and protects the engine from the elements wherever it may be on the farm. It is, of course, made to slip on and off at a moment's notice, but it should also be made so that it is secure in a high wind.

A NOVEL PORTABLE CHAFF SHED

This is an idea for a shed on wheels so that it can be pulled along the stack for easy feeding, and which can also be hauled close to the stable when filled. It is self-explanatory as regards its construction.

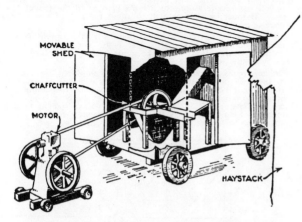

The cutter is at the front end of the shed, and there is a door at the stack side so that the sheaves can be thrown on to a platform within reach of the feeder. The engine is of the semi-portable type, and the belt runs to the cutter through the door shown in the illustration.

A HOME-MADE CHAFFCUTTER ELEVATOR

This illustration shows a cheap elevator for a two-knife chaffcutter for carrying chaff to the shed from the cutter. As long as this type is erected not more than 4 ft. high at the delivery end, it should be found satisfactory.

Materials required are:— Two old wooden rollers from a binder, which

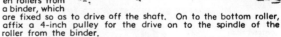

are fixed so as to drive off the shaft. On to the bottom roller, affix a 4-inch pulley for the drive on to the spindle of the roller from the binder.

Now procure some good wheat bags; open them at the sides and join at the ends. This will form your conveyor belt, and it will drive the top roller at the delivery end, as shown in the accompanying sketch.

ANOTHER USEFUL CONVEYOR FROM WHEAT BAGS

This is another cheap and useful home-made conveyor belt for chaff and other material—the sketch indicating how it can be arranged to lift the chaff to, say, a higher floor or to a position high up in the chaff shed where it can then be deposited on top of the heap.

All that is needed is two rollers, some good strong straps and a pulley. One roller is suspended from the ceiling or any other spot desired, by two iron hangers as indicated in the sketch, whilst two straps connect these with the other side of the shed or to some other fixed object. The other roller is mounted on bearings, affixed to the chaffcutter in the manner shown. The pulley is then attached and it is driven in the usual way.

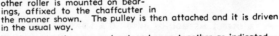

The bags are then opened out and sewn together as indicated— it being a good idea to turn the edges in to form a 3 or 4 inch selvedge. This latter is then put on to the rollers and adjusted to the proper tension by tightening the straps which are attached to the upper roller. These straps are so fixed that they can be easily tightened should the conveyor tend to sag at any time.

ANOTHER TYPE OF HOME-MADE EXTENSION CHAFF ELEVATOR

The following is an improvised elevator made from scrap and used with success by one man. Bags can also be used, as above, and an old oil drum or drums can be used as rollers if necessary.

In this instance, the top roller was a 5-gal drum with wood fixed to the ends in order to form bearings for a spindle. A wooden frame is then used and it can be suspended to the roof beams from eye bolts, or in any other improvised fashion, in such a way that it can be moved to and from different positions in the shed.

The other roller is a piece of rounded timber (about 5 in. dia. x say 3 ft. long) which is driven by a 4in.

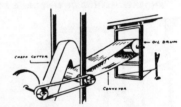

pulley, fitted on the main spindle of the chaffcutter, as shown in the illustration. This section is held in place by two uprights of timber as shown. If the cutter is portable, these can be made to fix on to various places on the roof if necessary. The bags are cut and hemmed as per sketch No. 2, whilst a tightener can be improvised to the top elevator in any manner desired.

USEFUL AND NOVEL DEVICES FOR FARM OR STATION

A HANDY STACK PROTECTOR

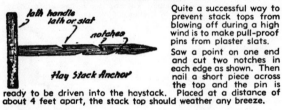

lath handle
lath or slat
notches

Hay Stack Anchor

Quite a successful way to prevent stack tops from blowing off during a high wind is to make pull-proof pins from plaster slats.

Saw a point on one end and cut two notches in each edge as shown. Then nail a short piece across the top and the pin is ready to be driven into the haystack. Placed at a distance of about 4 feet apart, the stack top should weather any breeze.

HOME-MADE BELGIAN STOOKING FORK

This is a very simple contrivance which will save much stooping while stooking.

It is particularly helpful to older men who like to go out and give a hand at harvest time. The middle tyne is taken out of a three-pronged fork and the outer two are bent to form hooks. A short handle is used. Very little time and trouble is therefore needed to make this useful tool.

A HAY KNIFE FROM OLD DISC

To make this hay knife, cut an old 15-in. plow disc into the V-shape shown. Heat and pound it out until it is flat and fairly sharp, when it can be finished on a grindstone.

FOOT REST

SIDE VIEW

The hardwood handle is $1\frac{1}{4}$ in. thick and 32 in. long, and is tapered at one end to approximately the same thickness as the knife.

The footrest is 4 inches of $\frac{1}{2}$ in. pipe with a bolt through it and supported by a piece of strap iron. The "D" handle is taken from an old spade. It costs nothing to make and is far superior to most other knives.

A USEFUL METHOD OF BINDING A LOAD OF HAY

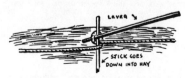

LEVER

STICK GOES DOWN INTO HAY

In binding a load of hay, a long pole can be roped over the top from front to back, but when such a pole is not to hand, this simple device will accomplish the same result.

A 4 ft. stick is pushed down into the hay in the middle of the load and a rope is stretched from the front standard to the rear of the wagon. The rope is then tightened by twisting it around the stake by means of a stick, as shown. After the rope is tightened the stick is tied to it to prevent untwisting.

ANOTHER METHOD OF BINDING A LOAD OF HAY

SLIP STICK

This is one good way of securing a load of hay on a wagon. It is a method somewhat similar to that used for a tent; a rope and a slip-stick being used.

The rope is tied to the front of the rack, passed over the hay and fastened to the rear end of the rack.

The slip-stick is then used to tighten the rope as indicated in the drawing. It is quite a simple idea but very effective.

A METHOD OF REPAIRING BINDER KNIVES

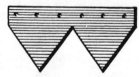

Binder knives are often broken and several of these home-made articles will be found handy on many occasions. They can be made from any suitable material such as old drill discs and riveted on to the knife where it has been broken. A few made in one's spare time might be well worth while.

A USEFUL SLING FOR UNLOADING HAY

Getting hay into a large barn without slings is tedious work and a little trouble to provide slings is well worth while. An iron rod about 6 ft. long with a ring at each end, and 40 ft. of rope are all the materials required.

ROD

In operation, this sling is laid across the bottom of the wagon with the rod hanging over one side and the rope over the other. The hay is then piled on top.

For a big load, a second sling is laid on the hay when the wagon is half full, and the same procedure followed. On arrival at the shed, the loose ends of the rope of the upper sling are threaded through the loops on the opposite side which pass through the rings on the ends of the rod and the bundle is hoisted to the loft or deposited in the shed where required. The second half of the load is then disposed of in the same way.

A HANDY FEED BOX ON HAY WAGON

A feed box placed on the end of a wagon makes it easy to give the team a full feed of grain as well as hay when working away from home.

The team can then be tied behind the wagon, the lid raised and fastened. It is easily made because the bed members form the sides and there remains only the closing of the bottom and end. The cover is hinged.

Such a box can also be used to carry tools, nails, etc.

A HOME-MADE HAY PRESS

The skids are 6 x 6 and about 24 ft. long. The uprights are of the same size. The lever extends 10 ft. beyond the fulcrum to permit the counterweight to lift the plunger to the top of the box. It must be stiff enough to stand the pull of the team, doubled by the use of a block.

The size of the box can vary. If it is 18 x 24 in. inside, it will make a handy size bale. It is 8 ft. high. For convenience in getting out the bales, it may be made 23 in. at the back and 24 in. at the front.

Ordinary planks are used vertically and are so placed that cracks at the back and front are left sufficiently wide for wiring. The front is cut half-way up and the lower section hinged at the bottom to provide a door for the removal of the bale. The sides are left open for 2 ft. at the top with sloping shelves to aid feeding. Lining the box with tin greatly reduces friction. An unyielding fastening for the door must be provided.

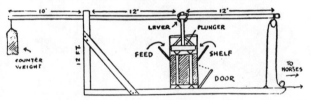

COUNTER WEIGHT
LEVER PLUNGER
FEED SHELF
DOOR
TO HORSES

The plunger is 6 x 6 and 6 ft. long, fastened to the lever with a piece of chain. The head of the plunger should fit loose in the box and be well braced to the plunger. The procedure is to put as much hay into the box as possible, give a good steady pull, then back the team up and fill again as often as is necessary. As the team backs up the counterweight will lift the plunger.

USEFUL AND NOVEL DEVICES FOR FARM OR STATION

A USEFUL HOME-MADE HAY STACKER

This is an idea from Canada which might also be applied here. The base is a pair of 6 or 8 x 12's, 24 ft. long, held apart in front by a cross piece 4 x 4 x 12. There is no crosspiece at the

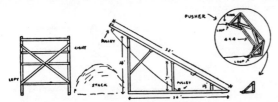

back as it would interfere with the stack. They are braced with two diagonal pieces of 2 x 6, bolted to the runners at each end and to each other in the middle as shown.

The uprights for the framework at the rear or stack end are two pieces 4 x 4 x 14 ft., and three or four crosspieces are bolted on as shown. For these, 2 x 6's 12 ft. long are used, braced diagonally with two 2 x 6's x 16 ft. For rigidity, the pieces are bolted to the uprights and bolted or nailed together where they intersect.

For the side view as shown in sketch, there is a pair of centre posts 7 ft. high (braced), with a piece across the top, to support the slide up which the hay is drawn.

Near the front there is also a pair of short posts, 18 in. high, of 4 x 4, with a crosspiece. This latter carriers the lower ends of the floorboards, and the upper post to the crosspiece which is located on the frame as shown. Note that these two braces meet at the upper end in the middle of the crosspiece. This gives greater rigidity.

The main timbers of the sloping side, which carry the load, are 32 ft. long of at least 6 x 6. Between them are 5 crosspieces to carry the floor, each 12 ft. long, bolted on under the timbers so that the timbers form sides for the slide.

At the top of the sloping timbers a 2 x 6 crosspiece is firmly bolted. It projects out on the side on which the horses pull. To it are attached the two top pulleys, the one on the projection keeping the rope on that side clear of the framework.

Inch flooring is nailed on top of the crosspieces between the timbers. The load falls through the space between the end of the floor and the 2 x 6 crosspieces at the top end of the timbers, which carries the pulleys. The lower end of the floor ends in the middle line of the crosspiece supported by the short 18 in. posts.

From the lower edge of the flooring to the ground is a hinged apron, also made from inch material. This can be folded back when the stacker is being moved or is not in use. Two or three heavy strap hinges are used. When the load of hay is brought in with the sweep it is drawn upon this apron, which extends a foot or two beyond the lower end of the main frame.

The pusher is 14 ft. long of 4 x 4 with triangular end frames of 2 ft. bases and uprights, thoroughly braced. Two ¾ in. ropes are used, one 80 ft. long is on the side away from the horses and is fastened to the pusher with a wire loop. The shorter one, 68 ft. long, carries a hook at the bottom, so that it can be unhooked from the pusher, and when the latter is empty, it enables it to be swung out of the way of the sweep.

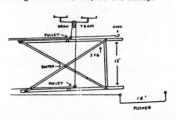

The ropes are carried from the pusher up through the pulleys attached to the top crosspiece. The long one is on the top of the frame and the short one, on the pulling side, is clear of the frame. This allows the ropes to come down to the lower pair of pulleys clear of the framework.

The sweep of hay is swept up on to the apron—the pusher is swung round behind it—the go-ahead signal is given—the team moves away sideways from the stacker—the load is pulled up the slide and dumped on the stack.

A SMALL IRON COVER FOR HAYSTACK

Much damage can be done to hay if rain should fall when the stack is being constructed and if some covering is at hand when the rain starts, much hay can be saved. If a tarpaulin is available, that will suffice.

If this is not at hand, there are usually some old galvd. iron tanks about the place which form ideal covers. These should be cut in two and the tops and bottoms removed. If the curved iron is not wide enough to cover the stack, it should be flattened somewhat in order to spread it.

ROOFING A HAYSTACK WITH GALVANISED IRON.

Good thatchers are sometimes scarce, and this idea is worthy of attention as it ensures complete protection, time saved in stack building and it is a permanent asset gained.

For the stack shown in fig. 1, the floor is made of 12 in. logs laid crossways 5 ft. apart. Saplings are laid along these at 6 in. intervals. A mouseproof platform is well worth while if it is intended to keep the stack for some years. 24g. galvd. curved corrugated iron is used. This curve can be formed by bolting two 10 ft. sheets together end to end. This forms an arch with a span of approximately 15 ft. and a height of 3 ft. 6 in. When ordering iron, have every sheet curved the one way, so that the edges are down, as it is easier to put on. It is necessary to punch the bolt holes and assemble the roof on the ground before building it on to the stack.

For this, a convenient stand can be made by fixing a rail (stout

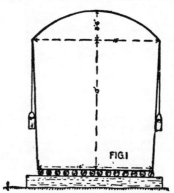

FIG.1

enough not to bend) parallel to the ground at a height of 3 ft. 6 in. and long enough to carry 3 pairs of sheets bolted together, and to leave a few feet over at either end for working room (say 12 ft. long). The pairs are then bolted (as shown in single pair in fig. 2), and each pair is also bolted to the adjoining one.

When 3 pairs have been assembled, the rear (or first) pair is unbolted, and the sheets are numbered 1 and 1a, care being taken that the lettered figure is always on the same side. Another pair is then fitted on the working edge, and the same procedure gone through until the whole roof has been assembled, numbered, and taken apart ready for building on top of stack.

When fitting, a 6 in. overlap is given at the top of the arch. Three bolts hold this join, the outside ones also holding the overlap of the neighbouring pairs down. Two additional bolts are inserted down each side of each 10 ft. sheet, so that each complete arch is jointed to its neighbour by 5 bolts.

The prepared sheets are hauled up singly in a suitable rope sling, and the builder bolts the first pair together with the outside centre bolts at top of the arch. He then joins the next pair by the centre bolt only, before joining the set to its neighbour.

To secure the roof, a permanent anchorage should be provided. Cables can be passed right over the roof in the middle of every alternate pair of sheets. Do not pierce the iron at the edges and attach the wire as it will tear out in a gale. Weights can be suspended from the ends of the wires, allowing for settlement of stack. Additional rigidity may be necessary in windy localities by bolting a 3 x 1 hardwood batten 6 in. up along the edge of the roof. It is also wise to pass an extra wire over the two end pairs of sheets and secure them to the bed logs. These should be tightened as the stack settles.

FIG. 2

USEFUL AND NOVEL DEVICES FOR FARM OR STATION

MAKING ROPE FROM BINDER TWINE

"Tie it with binder twine" is almost a proverbial phrase on most farms and twine can also be used at a pinch to make quite good rope. With this simple home-made appliance, it is quite easy.

The wooden frame shown in the sketch is about 18 in. high and about 20 in. wide, whilst the three cranks are made of ⅜ in. iron and are fixed as shown. The centre one has a second crank to form the turning handle. On the opposite side, all three cranks extend about 6 inches from the frame work and each terminates with a hook. All three are connected together by a connecting rod made of a flat piece of iron with three holes

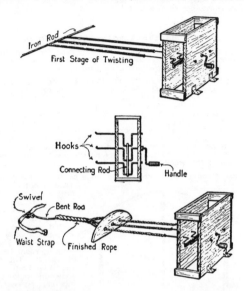

drilled in it. (See centre illustration.) When the centre one is rotated by means of the handle, the other two also rotate.

To get the right length. One man takes a straight iron rod about 2 ft. long and holds it horizontally a certain distance away from the appliance. It is important that the distance he stands away should be rather more than the length that the finished rope is required to be.

The second man now takes the binder twine, and, by means of a slip knot fixes the end to the hooked end of one of the cranks. He now walks along to the other man and puts the twine over the rod and then back over the hook and then back again over the rod until there are 8 or 10 strands or more according to the desired thickness of the finished rope.

The first stage. The twine is now cut and the ends tied to the hook. The second man then turns the handle and all 3 sets will twist. The turning is continued whilst the other man holding the 2-ft. piece of rod pulls it while holding. When the 3 sets of twine are firmly twisted along their entire lengths, the turning is stopped and the handle secured by a short piece of cord.

The second man now takes a piece of wood having three 1 in. holes bored in it. The distance between the holes is equal to the distance between the hooks of the cranks. One by one he slides the 3 lots of twisted twine (now three cords) off the rod and passes each through a hole in the board and all three ends on to a single hooked end of a piece of bent iron rod, which the first man now holds instead of the straight 2 ft. rod.

This bent piece has the hook at one end and a swivel at the other and attached to the swivel is a strap long enough to go round a man's waist and all is ready for the final operation, which consists of both men twisting in opposite directions, the one by turning the handle of the appliance and the other by turning the bent rod.

On one side of the board the three cords now merge into one and the board is pushed along just in front of the point of merging. When it is within about 6 inches of the end the turning is stopped, the short ends unhooked and plaited together. The result is a good rope made cheaply and when and where it is wanted.

OTHER USEFUL GADGETS FOR MAKING ROPE FROM BINDER TWINE

The following are other simple and easy ways of converting twine into rope. **The first** is very simple; a brace being used in the manner shown with a cone-shaped piece of wood to help keep the strands apart.

In the second, instead of the box-like device for turning the 3 hooks at the same time, this has two boards, one about 15 x 8 which can be nailed to a post and the other 8 x 8. Each board should have 3 holes bored to correspond exactly one with the other in the shape of a triangle—these are for the iron rods as shown which should be bent and threaded to take a nut as indicated.

The handle should be placed exactly in the centre of this triangle in the smaller board. This board is then rotated and the twine will twist to the desired thickness. In this also a cone-shaped piece of wood is used and the same procedure is adopted as in column one. If two men are working it would be advisable to have a strap buckled around the waist to give tension to the rope whilst turning. Any one of these ideas singly or in conjunction with each other will be effective.

TWISTING FENCING WIRE INTO A WIRE CABLE

Extra thick wire is often required for, say, anchoring fence posts, etc., and it can be obtained in the following manner:—

Cut as many lengths of wire as you wish strands in the cable, and attach one end of each wire to one of the spokes of the wagon wheel. Attach the other ends of the wires to any heavy, but moveable object, such as a bag of cement or sand. Then jack up the wheel, and turn it slowly. This will twist the wires into a firm cable, due to the tension produced by the weight at the opposite end, which is pulled towards the wheel.

A SIMPLE WINCH FOR TWISTING HAY OR STRAW INTO ROPE

One often sees a load of hay secured by ropes made of twisted hay or straw. This is a simple home-made winch for doing this.

The construction and operation are clearly illustrated so that no detailed description is necessary for making such an arrangement.

USEFUL AND NOVEL DEVICES FOR FARM OR STATION

COW RUGS FROM CORNSACKS AND SUPER BAGS

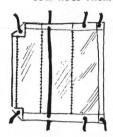

Some very useful cow rugs can be made from old super bags and cornsacks, various methods of making same being shown here.

In this instance, 3 bags are used in the manner shown — this giving double thickness but if only lightweight rugs are required, 1½ bags will do.

The sketch will show the arrangement of the bags—straps or rope is used to go through the holes shown; one advantage being that one strap goes right across and round the body just behind the forelegs and shoulder so that the rug will stay in place. In both this and the following idea, the straps or ropes would be more easily and quickly handled if some small coupling arrangements were fixed to the ends so that they could be quickly fastened.

ANOTHER COW RUG FROM SUPER BAG

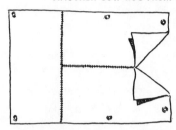

This is somewhat similar—3 bags being used, but this time the two sides are sewn only as far as indicated in the sketch; the balance of the sacks being turned down as shown in order to fit round the neck and chest.

Straps, cord or rope is tied through the holes indicated—the middle ones going right round the girth—the back ones connecting across the hind legs and the other two meeting across the chest. One way of keeping the rug in place is to fix extra wide straps or material round the girth, whilst other straps could be added where necessary.

COW RUGS FROM WOOLPACKS

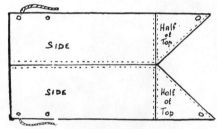

This sketch shows one way of doing this; one pack making two rugs.

The best way to cut the top and the bottom of the pack is to make one cut of each, straight from corner to corner and then to fix as indicated. This type is quickly and easily made and will be found quite serviceable for all normal requirements.

NOVEL METHOD OF STACKING BAGS

This is rather a useful hint for occasions where bags are required to be stacked in high places.

The risk of falling is much lessened if strips of canvas or hessian are placed between the various tiers as indicated in this illustration.

The stacking of any material such as super-phosphate, etc., even if stacked on different principles to the above, could be well improved by the application of the same method to keep them from falling.

HINTS ON JOINING BALL TO TWINE SUPPLY

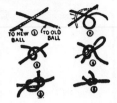

This is one useful way of joining a new ball of twine to the twine supply in the binder.

If you are not used to this method just try practising the knot illustrated in figures 1 to 6 in these drawings.

It is quite a good procedure and one found very successful by quite a number of farmers—it being quick and very effective.

KEEPING YARN IN THE EYE OF A NEEDLE

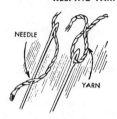

The annoyance of having yarn or twine pull from the eye of a needle and so cause frequent rethreading may be avoided by first pulling the yarn through the eye and then spreading the strands near the end that was pulled through and then inserting the needle as shown.

This will make a smooth tie without a knot and its use will be found very convenient on many occasions. It also helps to avoid losing quite a number of needles.

HOME-MADE BAGGING NEEDLES

Home-made needles can be made as shown here—this particular one being made from an ordinary sardine tin opener.

The handle of the tin-opener is straightened out, then hammered almost flat, after which it is filed or ground sharp and bent to the desired curve. At the opposite end, the slot to form the eye will need to be opened slightly with a chisel.

TEMPORARY REPAIRS TO GRAIN SACKS

This gives one very handy method of closing holes which have appeared in full grain sacks. It is a disc of rubber from an old inner tube, shaped as shown, which is forced in through the openings of the bag, using the end of a broom.

When inside the sack, the discs should flatten out and they are then held in place by the pressure of the grain. One soon gets into the knack of inserting this so that it will spread as mentioned.

TALLOW SLOWS UP ROPE WEAR

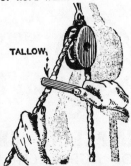

This is a very useful idea to obtain the maximum wear from rope. Tallow rubbed into any manila, cotton or linen rope at points which get the greatest wear, will do wonders towards lengthening the life of the rope as well as making it easier to handle, especially in wet weather.

Genuine mutton or sheep's tallow is best and will not tend to rot the fibres.

USEFUL AND NOVEL DEVICES FOR FARM OR STATION

HINTS ON THE USE OF EXPLOSIVES

To those who contemplate clearing stumps, etc., with explosives, the following suggestions of a general character may be of help.

Success in stump blasting depends to a large extent on proper location of the explosive charge.

In blasting tree stumps, 12 or 16 oz. of explosives per foot of diameter of the tree should be sufficient for stumps up to 3 feet in diameter at ground level—this, of course, would vary with different conditions; 16 oz. per foot for larger stumps, but for very large trees, a very much greater quantity of explosive may be found necessary.

For small stumps, or where there are only short, spreading roots (not vertical), as in sketch no. 1, the charge should be placed as near as possible directly under the centre of the stump and a single hole should be sufficient. If possible it should be located 18 to 24 inches below the main part of the stump so that the explosion will radiate as indicated in sketch No. 2.

A charge will blow at almost a right angle, as indicated by the dotted lines in sketches 2 and 3, so that if the trees are evenly rooted, the charge should be so placed and at such a depth that this cone will include the body of the stump as well as the largest roots.

If the roots on one side of the stump are larger than the other place the charge under the stronger side as shown in sketch No. 3. The two latter sketches will also show the arrangement and placing of the charge and how it should be tamped.

For average-size trees, sketch No. 4 shows the best arrangement. The roots can either be severed or otherwise as desired and holes can be bored into the earth with an augur at intervals under the main roots (or into the stump roots themselves if preferred) in

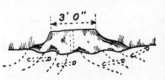

such a manner as to permit the charges being grouped in a circle as indicated in this illustration.

A two-inch augur should prove satisfactory and the bore-holes in the soil should be of sufficient diameter to permit of the concentration of the charge at the bottom of the hole. It is also a good idea to insert the tamping stick into the bore-hole before placing the dynamite in order to make sure that there are no obstructions which might prevent placing the charges at the bottom of the hole.

For stumps of say 5 ft. or more (sketch No. 5) holes should be bored under the main spreader roots and also down the centre of the stump, the latter continuing into the soil at the foot of which a chamber should be formed by firing a small preliminary charge.

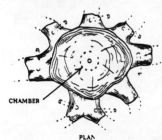

CHAMBER

PLAN

For a tree with a **decayed centre,** arrange the charge as shown in illustration No. 6 —say two or three holes under the main roots each finishing, say, just under the outer circumference of the tree or a little inside, as indicated in this illustration—the charges being inserted from each side of the tree as indicated.

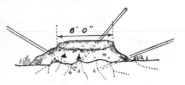

The best idea for trees with **heavy tap roots** is that shown in this illustration, the charge for which can be laid by making two or three holes round the tap root, as indicated. These should be made at an angle.

When a stump is **half buried** in a bank or hillside, the most suitable method is shown in the next sketch—the number of vertical holes necessary depending upon the size of the stump; their purpose being to split it.

Tamping. Care should be taken in this respect— figures 2 and 3 will show the arrangement of the charge, tamping, etc.

After the charge is in place, the borehole should be tamped, i.e., filled to the top with earth and the first 5 or 8 inches should be gently pressed down without exerting any considerable force; then the rest should be packed in as hard as possible and should completely fill the hole. **Tamping should be done with a wooden stick** and care should be taken to keep stones from falling into the bore hole.

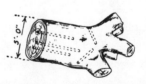

Log Splitting. These illustrations indicate the best methods of doing this work. First bore the holes in the wood with a wood augur, as shown—the size of the logs, of course, being the deciding factor as to how many charges are to be inserted. Then load the charges, tamp suitably, and fire.

Post Holes. When the ground is soft, a hole should be punched to the depth required, say, up to 4 feet and charged with about 6 oz. of explosive. In hard rock, shot-holes about 18 inches deep should be drilled and charged with 4 to 6 oz. of explosive and the procedure repeated until the required depth is reached.

In case any farmer should attempt stump blasting with blasting powder, gelignite is suggested as the most suitable explosive.

To those who contemplate work of this description, we can recommend a useful booklet which is published by Messrs. Nobel (Australasia) Proprietary Limited of Melbourne, which is free on application to anyone who may be interested.

STORAGE OF EXPLOSIVES

The following sketch is a good illustration from a farmer's point of view. Places of storage should be dry and well ventilated and with an even temperature of about 60 to 70 degrees. Detonators should be stored separately. The receptacles to be strong, closely jointed wooden boxes, covered externally with galvd. iron, with doors, good locks and hinges.

USEFUL AND NOVEL DEVICES FOR FARM OR STATION

A HOME-MADE BLASTING TOOL

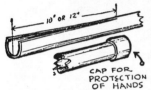

This is a tool made by one farmer with satisfactory results. It is made from a piece of 1¼ in. pipe and it was found very effective for digging holes under stumps for blasting powder.

Take a piece of pipe not over 1¼ in. inside dia. and split it back on one side with a hacksaw for 10 or 12 inches, then spread the split edges apart. The pipe used in this instance was 5½ ft. long and was found excellent for getting holes under stumps where the roots were too close together to dig between them with a larger tool. The other end of the pipe should have a coupling on it to protect one's hands, or gloves.

USEFUL HINTS ON SINKING SHAFTS

These few notes are based on the successful experience of one man in sinking a 5 x 3 well which had reached solid rock. In such cases, it is usually hard to keep the corners straight, and to know how the holes should be drilled to obtain best results.

Two holes were put down, as shown in figure 1, one being about 18 in. in depth and the other 2 ft. 6 in., the charge in the short hole being fired first.

After the second charge has been fired, there should be a conical shaped hole as shown in fig. 2 and the next task will be to put down a hole parallel with the wall at one side, so that it leaves a "bench" which is afterwards removed by another parallel charge.

These are, of course, only general instructions, as the type of country makes it hard to apply any hard and fast rule. Naturally the charge will leave the hole in a rough condition, and the corners will have to be made, and the walls trimmed. However, by working a series of "benches," it should be possible to accomplish the task with little difficulty.

A HOME-MADE WOOD SPLITTER

This useful type wood splitter devised by one man has done good service and saved much time and labour. He got a pulley from an

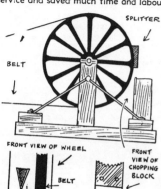

elevator which had a 12 in. face. To the rim on one side is riveted a wedge, faced with two leaves of an old car spring, brought to a sharp edge in front.

The splitting block is made as shown, with a notched iron plate. The belt from a 3½ h.p. engine runs on the other side of the wheel. The stick of wood is held on its side and pushed in so that the wedge shaped splitter comes down on it. If the splitter sticks, it simply throws the belt and no harm is done. As fast as a man can feed the blocks to the machine it will split them. The idea itself might be of value to many even if another type of wheel has to be used.

RING-BARKING TREES

To prevent suckering, it is preferable to merely bark ring trees and not to sap ring them, as the former will produce a much slower starvation effect as the latter forces the top of the tree to die quickly, leaving a reserve of plant food in the roots and the butt of the tree, which will then find an outlet through the dormant buds and therefore growth will continue through the suckers formed from those buds.

There is far less likelihood of suckers if the tree is bark rung as the whole tree gradually dies out at the same time.

This is briefly explained by the fact that certain substances are drawn from the soil per medium of the roots and pass upwards through the sapwood to the leaves, which, in combination with other substances drawn from the air, produce the tree's food which then passes down to the roots through the moist portion which is just on the inside of the bark.

If the bark is knocked off, it exposes this moist surface, which will then dry and so the tree slowly starves.

One good method of ring-barking is to frill a tree as shown in the above illustration, which speaks for itself. In this connection, substances such as sodium arsenate (calcium chlorate has also been used with success) is sometimes poured into the cut to assist in the killing—there are also certain special preparation used in the same way. Care must of course be taken in the use of sodium arsenate, as it is dangerously poisonous and stock should be kept away, but full instructions in its use can no doubt be obtained from the Forests Department in each State.

There is also another method which has recently been tried out and which is proving most successful in killing trees without the risk to animals which is the case when arsenical compounds are used.

This is to frill around the trunk of the tree, as shown, and to place in the open frill a slightly damp mixture, consisting of two parts calcium chloride, one part copper sulphate, and two parts soil, instead of pouring in a solution of other compounds as is often the case. This produces a sort of pug and has proved very successful in some parts; it is cheap and is perfectly harmless to stock and the operation can be carried out without removing the animals from the paddocks.

BURNING STUMPS

One good suggestion for a method of treating stumps of recently felled trees in order to prevent them from sending up shoots is to apply kerosene to the stump, as shown here.

Some ¾ in. augur holes are bored downward through the top of the stump and kero poured in.

The effect of the kerosene is said to be to kill the roots, and at the same time to assist in burning the stump much earlier than is possible under other conditions.

One augur hole and one application is sufficient for a small stump up to 3 in. in diameter, but for larger stumps it is necessary to make several holes and to repeat the filling once or twice a week for a month, owing to the more extensive spread of the roots.

USEFUL AND NOVEL DEVICES FOR FARM OR STATION

ALIGNING RELATIVE POSITIONS ON ROOF AND FLOOR

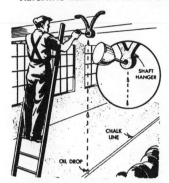

This is a very novel and useful idea for occasions when it is necessary to judge the exact relative positions of objects on roof and floor.

For instance, to adjust overhead shaft-hangers to the relative position of any machine which may be set on the floor beneath them, draw a chalk line on the floor to indicate the desired location of the shafting and then drop oil from the hanger to determine when it is in proper alignment.

If there is no air current to deflect the drops, this method is very accurate and can be used for quite a number of other occasions when relative positions on roof and floor are required.

HOME-MADE TOWER FOR WIND-CHARGER

To make a tower for a battery charger, take some boiler flues from an old steam engine and get them acetylene welded, making four pipes each 16 ft. long. Other material such as piping can, of course, be used, but the materials mentioned here are those used by the farmer concerned who erected this type of tower.

A piece of 4 x 4 about 6 feet long and three old wheel rims were used, one from a drill wheel, one from a plow wheel, and a third about 12 inches in diameter.

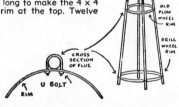

Four long bolts were used, two about 10 inches long for the top of the flues and two about 14 inches long to make the 4 x 4 secure in the small rim at the top. Twelve U-bolts were used, four to fasten each rim in its place between the upright flues.

This makes a tower 18 ft. high and one that will last a long time. It can be made secure to the ground by means of iron stakes or cement blocks. Such a tower would therefore be quite easy to make from scrap material and, if no wheel rims were available, something else could be devised to do in their place.

NOVEL METHOD OF ANCHORING A FEED GRINDER

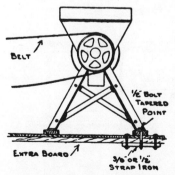

Nail an extra board lengthwise of the joints underneath the floor, and under it bolt a piece of $\frac{3}{8}$ in. strap iron. Tap it to take a one-half in. bolt tapered at the point so that it will centre itself in the hole.

In this way, you can line up the hole in the grinder support with the one in the floor.

Drop the tapered bolt into the hole and screw it down. You can do this without having to crawl under the granary to screw nuts on to the bolts.

AFFIXING FARM MACHINERY TO CONCRETE BASES

This makes removal for repairs, etc., easy, whilst two ways are shown for setting bolts into concrete foundations, the upper method being particularly adaptable to pumps. (See also page 89.)

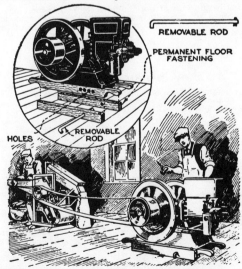

Take 4 pieces of flat iron about 18 in. long and bend into U-shape, as shown. Drill holes large enough to permit entrance of bolthead in each piece, and from this hole cut a slot a trifle wider than the shank of the bolt and about 1 1-8 in. long.

Suspend these U-pieces in the mould with slots pointing to the centre in such a position that the centre of the slots will be in line with the holes in the pump base. Make sure these are not moved out of alignment when concrete is placed.

As soon as concrete has set sufficiently to prevent flowing, the bolts are placed in position and worked back and forth in the slots to remove some of the cement and form a cavity for the bolt heads. The one difficulty in setting the bolts is to space them properly so as to enter the holes in the engine base.

For the other, take bolts or pieces of $\frac{1}{2}$ in. rod about 12 in. long threaded on one end. Bend the other end 3 in. at right angles.

Suspend bolts from stationary wooden strips laid across form in a position corresponding to holes in engine bed. Before cement is poured in, wrap the shank of the bolts with heavy pasteboard or corrugated cardboard to make cylinders about 1 in. dia. After cement has hardened, these cylinders will still be soft from moisture absorbed and can be easily removed, leaving holes in the base that permit a fair range of movement of bolts.

MAKING THE FARM ENGINE MORE CONVENIENT

The problem of holding down an engine without resorting to the usual method of bolting it to the floor, is solved by this portable and adjustable base. Two heavy wooden beams are bolted to the underside of the engine, their ends projecting far enough to be used as handles. Two similar beams, somewhat shorter, are permanently attached to the floor so that those on the engine will fit between them. A removable rod is then pushed through the holes drilled in all four beams, to lock them together and hold the engine down securely. One hole is drilled through each outside beam and a series of holes through the inner ones so that the two base members can be locked together at different points, to obtain

proper belt tension. Floor beams of the same type are attached near every engine-driven machine so that, to attach the engine, it is only necessary to slide it into place and slip in the rod.

USEFUL AND NOVEL DEVICES FOR FARM OR STATION

A HANDY TORCH FOR SCRUB BURNING

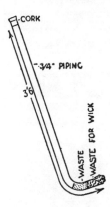

The idea illustrated here representing a handy torch for scrub burning has been successfully used by one ingenious farmer and some such implement (or a number of them) might be well worth having by some who may be in districts where such a thing is often needed.

It consists of a piece of pipe of convenient length, bent around at the end as shown (somewhat the shape of a hockey stick).

One end is plugged with old rag or cotton waste tightly enough to prevent oil soaking through in excessive quantities; a second piece at the end being left somewhat looser to act as a wick.

The top end is closed with a cork. The length of pipe is then filled with the kerosene, or with any waste oil that will soak through the wick and burn easily.

It is more convenient to use than the usual method of trailing around burning branches, and can be used for the rapid burning of firebreaks during bushfire weather.

A USEFUL FIRE EXTINGUISHER

This handy tool or "fire flap" is a most useful one for extinguishing grass fires. It is far more efficient than the usual twig as it does not spread the sparks but stifles the flames, and the rubber does not catch fire.

As seen in the sketch, two rubber flaps are cut from old 6 inch motor inner tubes; each flap should be, if possible, 14 to 15 in. square, with an extra length in the middle of each flap of about 3 in. wide and 4 in. long.

The flaps are laid one on top of the other, the extra centre bit is folded round a wooden handle of 4 to 5 ft. in length. Broomsticks might be used but a little longer handle is preferable.

The centre pieces of the flaps are firmly nailed to the handle, then bound with wire and the wire is then covered by rubber binding.

One user of this type of fire-flap has used them periodically for several years with much success. It might therefore be advisable for any who live in fire danger areas to make several of these in their spare time to have handy in case of need.

A USEFUL SMOTHER FOR GRASS FIRES

This is another quite useful idea for extinguishing a grass fire as it has been used with success by one farmer, and in districts where grass fires are likely, it is well worth while keeping a few old

tyres handy for use as suggested, as grass fires can be fairly quickly extinguished by dragging the tyres over the grass as shown here.

The tyre is wired to the end of a light pole and it is pulled over the burning grass as indicated.

It is quite effective and there is very little danger of the rubber igniting, if the tyre is moved fairly rapidly, which would of course also be better in order to put the fire out.

ERADICATING BRACKEN

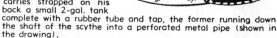

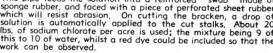

This is an idea from Scotland and consists of applying drops of saturated solution of sodium chlorate to the cut of a broken stem whence it travels down to the rhizomes and destroys the buds at the base of the fronds.

In this case a scythe is used and the operator carries strapped on his back a small 2-gal. tank complete with a rubber tube and tap, the former running down the shaft of the scythe into a perforated metal pipe (shown in the drawing).

This pipe feeds the solution into a reinforced "swab" made of sponge rubber, and faced with a piece of perforated sheet rubber which will resist abrasion. On cutting the bracken, a drop of solution is automatically applied to the cut stalks. About 20 lbs. of sodium chlorate per acre is used; the mixture being 9 of this to 10 of water, whilst a red dye could be included so that the work can be observed.

OTHER IDEAS FOR ERADICATING BRACKEN

There are various useful ideas in operation such as stock trampling and eating; top-dressing and sowing sub-clover is also of value. There is also, of course, the Gippsland hook, which is

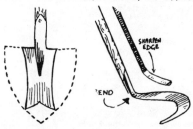

very effective, and in this connection, some find it an advantage to bend same over as shown in this sketch.

A good implement can also be made from an old shovel — the illustration showing how it should be cut—the dotted lines showing the original shape and the firm lines the finished shape of the "slasher." The fish-tail end will also be noted. It should, of course, be sharpened, and, if necessary, the handle can be altered to suit.

Another idea is to always carry a bent stick whenever walking through bracken infested country and, if a collection of these sticks is kept in a handy place, they will be found of very great use. A sample stick is shown in the sketch.

ANOTHER METHOD OF ERADICATING BRACKEN

This also comes from Scotland, and experience has shown it to be very effective—good results being obtained by bruising, which can be done with this home-made implement in preference to cutting.

It can be cheaply made but the drag bars must be heavy and, if possible, with concave facing or edges. The sketch shows two drags attached but three or four could be used if the ground is not too rough or hilly.

The scientfic idea behind bruising seems to be that bleeding of the underground rhizomes continues over a long period, causing impoverishment at the roots, whilst the damaged fronds allow disease and parasites to interfere with the root system.

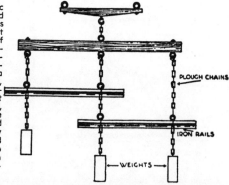

USEFUL AND NOVEL DEVICES FOR FARM OR STATION

NOVEL BIRD SCARERS

Most scarecrows are inefficient because they show no " life." That shown in this drawing is made to swing on a post, and is actuated by the wind. Sink a flat piece of timber into the ground, allowing it to project about 3 ft. Then pivot a similiar piece to it with a loose fitting bolt, as shown. Saw a slot across the top end of the second piece at an angle as shown in the detail; fasten it to a horizontal piece for the arms, and nail shingles, cut to represent hands, in slots on the ends of the arms.

Nail a piece of lead or other metal to the bottom end of the pivoted piece, for a counter-weight. After the frame is finished, dress the scarecrow, allowing plenty of play at the pivot.

If the arms are at a considerable angle from the direction of swing, and the gusts of wind strong enough, the upper half of the scarecrow will move backward and forward, causing a bobbing motion that is a sure fright for most feathered pests. The counterweights must be heavy enough to bring the figure upright when the breeze abates, but must not, of course, be heavy enough to prevent the figure from swinging.

ANOTHER NOVEL TYPE OF BIRD SCARER

This type is quite effective and if many are required they can easily be done at the one time as one could then make the various parts collectively and they can then be assembled all at the one time. To prevent rust a coat of aluminium would be a good idea.

Better still, the arrangement could be made with material not quite so conspicuous as far as the support is concerned, i.e., piping, etc. The moving portion is a bright tin plate which acts as a mirror either in the day-time or by moonlight and they will work with wind from almost any direction.

The vanes themselves can be made from a six-inch circle of tin plate by arranging them in the manner shown and soldering them to some heavy tinned wire—the other wire stays being added, as shown, to make the structure a firm one.

In the above instance, the base and side arms are of wood and the axis is pivoted in sockets which are drilled into the ends of brass wood screws as shown in the smaller detail in the top left hand corner. This method is quite a good one, as it admits of any necessary adjustment from time to time and it also ensures a minimum amount of friction. The vanes as will be seen are at right angles to each other.

A REFLECTOR SCARECROW FROM BROKEN MIRRORS

A box wider at the bottom than at the top, so that the sides will flare, is made with broken pieces of glass affixed to the side.

It is then suspended by a piece of cord so that it can swing freely.

Although it will rotate with the wind at almost any angle, it is advisable to set it up with the axis pointing in the direction of the prevailing wind. A spike in the bottom will enable it to be put in the ground anywhere and at any distance from the ground.

A USEFUL WASTE CONTAINER

The accompanying sketch shows one way in which one can make a handy, moveable waste container in a very few minutes. This is a very useful contrivance to put within easy reach so that it will not necessitate running outside to throw away rubbish every time some is gathered up.

Merely nail a few inch boards together in a complete rectangle; this will provide the holder; then screw in a hook on each side, turned upwards, on which the sack may be suspended and kept open.

Such an article as this will be found very convenient.

GATHERING CLOVER OR OTHER SEEDS IN A SMALL AREA

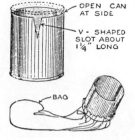

Gathering seed when the area of the land is small, is a tedious task.

To save time, use an ordinary fruit tin,. with a slot in the side, as shown, and if a larger quantity of seed is needed, cut a large hole in the bottom of the tin, and attach a bag to catch the seed as it falls through.

When using it, catch the stalk in the slot, with the head inside the tin, and pull outward. The edge of the slot will detach the seed, which will fall into the tin.

A DANDELION ERADICATOR

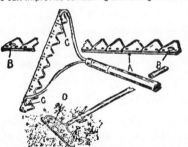

One can take a short piece of an old mowing machine sickle, or he can improvise something else along these lines, and make a very good dandelion eradicator. To do this, get a piece of sickle with the sections on slightly longer than the width of the yoke of an old worn-out garden rake. Now take the old rake and cut off the head, leaving the yoke prongs only, and bend each of these, as shown at C.

About 1½ inches should be bent then mark and drill a hole in the end of the sickle piece at B so that the ends of the yoke that have been turned down can be set in the holes and riveted lightly on the under side. The bar should be down so that the section is uppermost as shown.

The method of using is shown at D. This eradicator also cuts other noxious weeds, but does not pull the grass even if used when the grass or turf is wet.

HOW TO DEAL WITH THISTLES

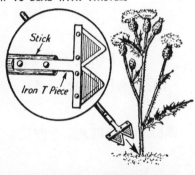

The following is a well tried suggestion and is also a use for old mower blades. Two blades are bolted or riveted on to a stick so that the edges overlap slightly. This tool is easily handled and is light.

The cutting action combined with the squeezing action of the "V" gives quick and excellent results.

USEFUL AND NOVEL DEVICES FOR FARM OR STATION

HOME-MADE FUMIGATION PLANTS
Useful methods of combating Weevil and Fumigating Trees, etc.

The home-made arrangement shown here would be quite a useful adjunct to any farm; besides being convenient it would also be quite a money saver and something well worth having for quite a number of jobs. For fumigation against weevil, etc., it should be particularly useful.

There is scarcely any necessity to enlarge upon the sketch itself as it is comprised mainly of an old galvanised iron tank supported on a timber fixture in the manner shown—the lifting gear being fixed to a piece of good, strong timber which is attached to the tank itself by 2 or 3 thicknesses of fencing wire running round the tank and hooked over the ends of the said piece of timber. A block and pulley (or some other home-made hoist as indicated in other sections of this book) is used so that the tank can be hoisted or lowered over the bags or trees to be fumigated.

The location of such a fumigator should be in some out-of-the-way corner but in the sun as there should be a certain amount of heat in order to do the job properly.

A method of stacking the bags would have to be evolved so that they would keep upright and would not fall over; otherwise there would be difficulty in enveloping them when the tank was to be lowered. This can be done by sinking some stout timber or posts in the centre, sufficiently high to enable the bags to be stacked two high—the bags can then lean against this timber in an upright position—a chain or rope being tied around them in order to help keep them upright.

This arrangement should, of course, be airtight, and to help in this direction, some mud should be ready mixed and placed so that the gas cannot escape around the bottom of the tank. The fumigator should be left on for about two days for best results and to avoid the mud cracking during that time through drying out, some damp bags should be placed on top of the mud.

Before refilling the fumigator, raise it about 3 or 4 feet and leave it for a couple of hours to let the poisonous gas escape.

It will be noticed that there are containers placed on top of the bags which should contain between them a cupful of carbon-bisulphide, which should be sufficient for 18 to 20 bags. In this case, a 1,000 gallon tank is used.

The smaller sketch shown here is one which could be used for a few bags at a time (as well as for trees, as indicated in the sketch), and no special lifting arrangement would be needed.

A tank could be cut in two halves and used as shown—the halves being fitted together and made airtight in some way so that the gases would not escape via the join in the iron.

Citrus and Other Trees. Although most sprays used nowadays are sprayed on to the trees, there may be occasions when they need fumigating in this manner and therefore, whilst the trees are small and easily got at, some such arrangement as this would prove a very useful standby.

If the trees were small enough and there was plenty of room for a vehicle to be driven alongside, an arrangement such as that shown at the top of this column could be used—it being operated from an improvised support fixed to a dray or other vehicle, but if the trees were close together, it would be rather difficult to do so, and therefore something along the lines of the lower drawing might be possible.

However, it would, of course, be only suitable when there are only a few trees to do, say, in the farm or station house garden, and not on the larger orchards, and then again, it would hardly be possible to make such a fumigator big enough for the larger orange and other trees, but where small and young trees are concerned, the idea should be well worth while. Its main use, however, would be for small quantities of bags and such like articles which need fumigating.

A HOME-MADE WHEAT PICKLER FROM CASE OR DRUM

For any farmer who does his own pickling, but who has not sufficient to do to warrant a big plant, he can easily make one which will do the job, either from a case or petrol drum. If a box is being used, it should be well made and the top removed and used as a lid. On the underside of the lid, fit and nail two crosspieces 2 x ½ in. from each end. Attach 1½ in. butt hinges, also 2 hasps to fit tightly over D's, as shown.

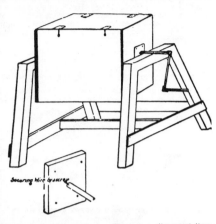

Each edge should be dust proof. Thick flannel can be used on the underside of lid where it comes into contact with the edges of the box. The outside edges can be strengthened and made dustproof by bands of hoop-iron. Draw two diagonal lines on each end of the box and bore holes at the intersections to admit of the spindle passing right through the box.

Prepare two blocks about 3 in. square of ½ in. material to strengthen the end of the box and to allow the spindle to be secured to permit of rotating the box. Bore both blocks with a similar sized augur bit to that used for boring the ends of the box. Secure with 4 wood-screws in each. A piece of ¾ in. galvd. piping, long enough to act as a spindle, will then be needed, one end of which should be threaded to carry a ¾ in. elbow. A crank can then be made from two pieces of ¾ in. piping each 9 in. long; one to be threaded at each end, and the other at one end for the necessary elbow.

OTHER HOME-MADE SEED DRESSING MACHINES

These are quite good for mercurial seed dressings—all that is needed being a rotatable container which has a tightly fitting lid so that the powder will not fly out and hamper the operator.

An old butter churn can be improvised by fitting baffle plates as shown in sketch No. 1. An ordinary wooden barrel can be adapted as in 2. Spindle and handle can be made from piping and elbow joints. A door is cut in the side of the barrel (using keyhole saw at an angle of 45 deg.) so that the door and opening are bevelled. The spindle can be keyed to each end of the barrel by a large nail, passing through holes bored in the pipe and secured to the wood by staples. Baffles can be added as in sketch No. 1.

Another mixer is shown in sketch 3, together with mounting.

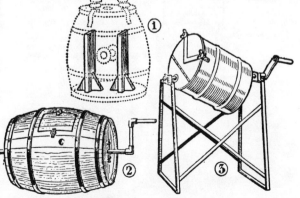

With welding, an oil drum can be made very efficient. A section of one end of the drum is cut out and replaced by a hinged lid, fastened by means of brackets with wing nuts.

USEFUL AND NOVEL DEVICES FOR FARM OR STATION

CHECKING RATS—AN EFFECTIVE SCHEME

It is not easy to keep rats out of farm buildings, even where the floors are made of concrete. Rats have a habit of burrowing beneath and providing themselves with at least two outlets.

One remedy for this is to stop all the holes that can be found leading under the concrete. This can be done with a mixture of cement and sand or fine gravel, mixed to a softish paste with water. A simple way of putting this mixture into the holes is described by a contributor to "The Farmer and Stockbreeder," who wrote:—

"Most people are familiar with the method confectioners employ in icing cakes; the icing paste is pressed out of the pointed end of a cone-shaped packet. The principle of the home-made 'grouter' is the same, although, of course, made on a larger scale.

"The container is made of good quality hessian, and the pointed end contains an ordinary tin funnel of fairly large bore. If a second funnel is forced over the first, so as to trap the hessian material between them, it makes a better job and prevents leakage of the grouting mixture when pressure is applied to the bag.

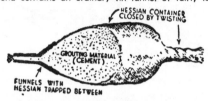

Device for squeezing a cement grout into rat holes

"With this simple apparatus the stopping material can be forced right into the tunnel. It is a good plan, however, to squirt some strongly smelling liquid into the hole first—a little turpentine or carbolic disinfectant serves. When the hessian grouter is finished with for the time being it should, of course, be rinsed, otherwise the cement, on hardening, spoils it for future use."

This measure should be accompanied by some scheme for killing the rats thus entrapped. One effective method is to stop all the holes but one and drop a handful or two of carbide of calcium, broken into small pieces, into this hole, following it up with a liberal drenching of water, using a hose. As soon as enough water has been poured down, the hole is stopped up to retain the gas. No rat will survive gassing with acetylene. Ample water should be applied in order to ensure the complete saturation of the carbide, otherwise trouble may ensue. **This treatment should not, of course, be applied under inhabited buildings.**

A HOME-MADE FUMIGATOR FOR RAT DESTRUCTION

This home-made gas producer idea may be of value where it is not wise to lay poison. Take an old paint drum about 12 in. long and 8 in. diameter, and fasten the lid to the side by means of a link hinge. Then punch a hole in the lid to admit the point of a pair of bellows. In the case of the drum punch a 2 in. hole, and solder a short length of metal tubing around the hole as shown.

Rivet or solder a strip of metal about 2½ in. wide to the inside of the drum to prevent cotton waste and sulphur, which is later put into the drum, from clogging the pipe. In use, the drum is opened and some oily cotton waste is placed inside and ignited.

If necessary, the lid may be closed and the cotton waste fanned with the bellows to get a good glow.

Usually, however, the waste will burn readily if the lid is removed. While smoking well, place the pipe in the mouth of the burrow, preferably to the windward side of the other holes.

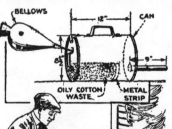

All holes from which smoke issues should be plugged tightly. Then the drum is opened, and some sulphur is sprinkled on the cotton waste, after which the cover is replaced and the bellows operated to force the fumes into the burrow. Sulphur dioxide is generated and this will kill the vermin if they cannot get out.

AN EFFECTIVE SPARROW TRAP

An effective sparrow trap is indicated here. It is made of plain fencing wire and netting. 20 ft. of the former and 6 ft. of ¼ in. mesh x 2 ft. netting is all that is needed. First make three triangles, 1 ft. 6 in. each way, with plain wire, and wire them together with three 2 ft. lengths, one at the top and two at the bottom. The two end triangles are shaped at the base as shown, to take the funnel-like entrance which is made of wire and fastened in position.

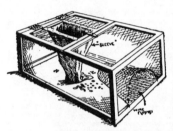

The funnel should be 6 in. high at the entrance, tapering to a hole no larger than a penny, to prevent the sparrows from getting free once they are inside. Having made the framework, the wire netting is cut to shape and wired on securely. The "floor" is left open. The sparrows "sense" a trap if they walk on to the netting just inside the entrance.

The door to enable the trapped sparrows to be taken out is cut out of one side of the netting, threaded with a piece of wire and fastened back again. A wire handle completes the job. To set the trap, throw down a little corn, and stand the trap over it.

As many as 50 have been caught in this way in one day.

ANOTHER SPARROW TRAP

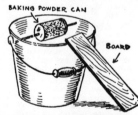

This is somewhat similar, except that it is made with a box-like frame which enables the whole thing to be taken up when the birds are in it and plunged into a pond or trough to drown them.

It also has a sleeve-like arrangement so that one can insert the hand in order to catch the birds easily if need be.

Just put the bait on the floor and leave the door open, and then when the birds are in, close the door and dispose of the birds as desired. The sleeve is a good idea as the birds cannot escape and are easily caught.

A MICE TRAP THAT IS ALWAYS SET

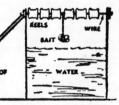

This idea is on somewhat similar lines to the next one. Use a pail or the bottom half of a square oil tin. Insert a round tin of some description in the manner shown—grease it well and roll it in crumbs, wheat or seeds until it is well coated. In the bottom put a few inches of water. The mice jump from the board to the tin, which turns round and dumps them into the water from whence they do not easily escape.

ANOTHER WATER TRAP FOR MICE

This device has been successfully used and is easy to make. Requirements are a kerosene tin, a few cotton reels, a piece of fencing wire, a section of board 2 or 3 in. wide and sufficiently long to provide a runway for the mice leading from the ground to the top of the trap; a small piece of thin wire and some bait. Holes are then punched through two opposite sides of tin near the top; the wire is passed through half a dozen reels, and out of the tin at the other side.

Slightly grease the fencing wire to make the reels move quickly. It should be set up as indicated.

USEFUL AND NOVEL DEVICES FOR FARM OR STATION

A HOME-MADE SUPER SPREADER FOR BIG AREAS

This is a design constructed by a New Zealand farmer with successful results. The basis of the machine is an old motor car chassis, a "T" model Ford being used in the original model. Upon this is built a table-top body, and an improvised turntable allows full-lock draught. A pole is fitted, making a useful light lorry or "horsemobile," which will be an asset on any farm.

The distributor box is 20 ft. in length, and made from 12 x 1 dressed timber. The width at the top is 6 inches, and at the bottom 1¾ in. Removable extension sides give added capacity. A plate of 1-16 iron in the bottom of the box has a series of 5-8 holes drilled at 3 in. intervals.

Another place similarly drilled is fitted over this in such a manner that it will slide and bring the two sets of holes in or out of register, thus reducing the sizes of the openings and regulating the quantity of manure sown per acre.

Supports of strap iron hold the box in position, and one of these is made to swivel so that the box can swing round parallel with the side of the lorry when the implement has to be taken through a gateway.

An Ingenious Drive. The drive is obtained through the differential via the tail-shaft and through a return shaft mounted on a cross-member on the underside of the decking.

This intermediate drive is obtained by mounting the ends of the tail-shaft and return shaft to a cross-member and fitting them

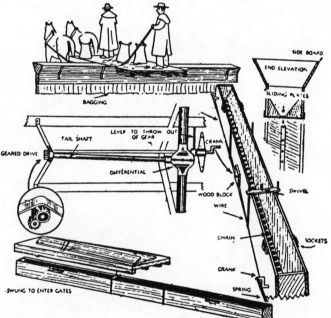

with meshing pinion from an old binder. A lever is pivoted to the decking, and this is used to throw the drive out of mesh. The rear end of the return shaft is fitted with a crank.

The 1¼ in. square link binder chain is laid over the top plate in the distributor box and attached to cranks at each end. These cranks protrude through the sides of the box and are connected by a rod or wire in the centre of which is a hardwood block, which is recessed to take the crank on the end of the return shaft.

In operation the rotary motion of the crank causes the chain to move to and fro at each revolution, a spring being fitted to assist in the return movement, if necessary.

The actual details of the transmission are not shown very clearly in the diagrams illustrating the original article. It should be possible to evolve a little better method, such as an endless chain operated by a sprocket, and, no doubt, the average farmer will be able to evolve some minor modifications of the principle, according to materials available.

A HOME-MADE SUPER BROADCASTER FOR HILLY COUNTRY

This is quite a useful idea for those who may have some country which is too rough or steep for a machine to operate. With this bag, one should be able to broadcast 12 to 15 bags per day—both hands being free for the work. It is also better than a box as it does not press so heavily and it is much more convenient.

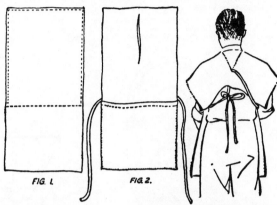

To make, lay a wheat or super bag flat and cut as shown by the dotted line in diagram 1. The selvedge forms a handy tie to secure the bag. The front portion of the bag is cut away and the rough edge is turned over and secured by a few stitches. The back of the bag has a slit through which the operator's head is thrust and the selvedge is passed round the back, through the lower portion of the slit, and tied. They thus keep the weight distributed on the shoulders instead of the neck. The idea will also be useful for seed distribution, grasshopper baits and other things.

A HOME-MADE MARKER FOR TOP-DRESSING

This is a very useful little arrangement for occasions when one has the need of a marker to show which portions of the fields have been top-dressed and which are still to be done—it sometimes being rather difficult to tell under some circumstances.

The idea is to get a piece of steel which is springy enough for the job, and make it into the shape of a cultivator tyne. Then, take one end and drill it in order to take a cultivator point for use as shown in the illustration. The other end is then attached to any convenient part of the vehicle to be used.

The sketch will also show how the necessary tension may be maintained—it consisting of a spiral spring attached as indicated. There are, of course, other methods which may be used for this purpose, such as bolting a perpendicular rod to the tyne, loaded with any old scrap.

When the marker is not needed, it can be operated from the driver's seat by a lever which is easily fixed to, say, a light chain and hook arranged so that it will lift the marker out of action, at a moment's notice.

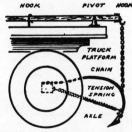

No actual explanatory details are shown here, as such an idea can be adapted to any old scrap which might be about the place and if there are any old cultivator tynes handy, they would be ideal.

USEFUL AND NOVEL DEVICES FOR FARM OR STATION

A HOME-MADE SUPER DISTRIBUTOR

This is a drawing of a super distributor made by one farmer from odds and ends round the place. It is of the horizontal disc type, and will spread over an expanse of 40 feet at 1,000 revs. per minute, travelling at an ordinary walking pace of 2¾ miles per hour. The distributor wheel is of the fan blower type with the bottom disc dished like a plough wheel, thus giving strength with lightness, and enabling a better distribution of super to be made.

It has six blades, which are straight and radial, and these are riveted to a strengthening ring 3 in. wide on top of the blades.

On the under side of the dished wheel are three blades. The distributor wheel runs in a casing which encloses it for about 5-8ths of its circumference, and without these three blades the super

The gearing is constructed from a worm wheel and spiral from a Ford truck (T. Model), and this is enclosed in a casing which was made and arc-welded. This casing permits the parts to rotate in an oil bath, and has ball-bearings at the top and bottom, giving durability, silence and easy running. Hand holes for making adjustments, and testing plug for inspecting the oil are provided.

The distributor wheel is 20 in. in diameter, and about 3 in. deep, allowing ample space for the hand to be inserted for cleaning. A dome is placed in the centre of the wheel to cover the holding nut and washer, and to assist in guiding the super to the blades. A form of universal joint is provided at the junction of the wheel spindle and the agitator spindle, and the latter extending upwards about 10 in. to a supporting bar running diagonally across the hoppers, where it has a covered bearing to keep it free of super.

The agitator spindle is made so that it can be removed, and a short archimedean screw substituted if it is desired to use the machine for sowing oats or other grain. The machine can be placed in the

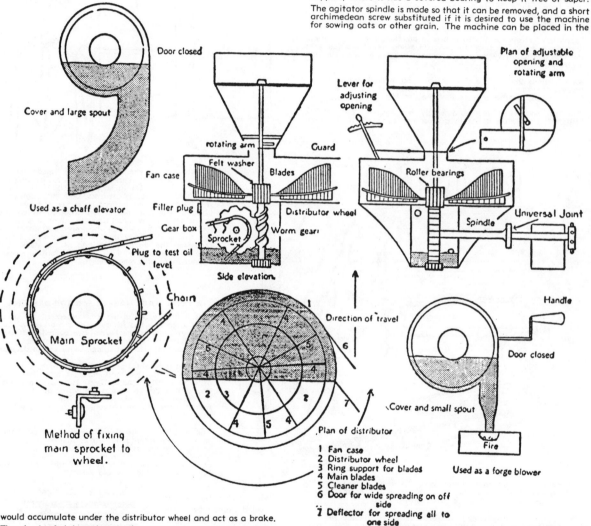

Used as a chaff elevator

Method of fixing main sprocket to wheel.

Side elevation.

Plan of distributor

1 Fan case
2 Distributor wheel
3 Ring support for blades
4 Main blades
5 Cleaner blades
6 Door for wide spreading on off side
7 Deflector for spreading all to one side

Plan of adjustable opening and rotating arm

Used as a forge blower

would accumulate under the distributor wheel and act as a brake.

The wheel is fed through a circular central aperture from a hopper, and an agitator in the hopper breaks the lumps and keeps the super running evenly. To assist in breaking large lumps, a rod is placed diametrically across the hopper, 1 in. above the agitator, whilst the aperture edge also serves to break small lumps.

A small door on the distributor wheel casing permits the super to be distributed at a wide angle, and in addition, there is a deflector that can be adjusted to permit distribution of the super on one side of the machine only, an innovation that will be found particularly useful when broadcasting along fences or in wind.

The fan case supports the hopper and also the quantity regulator, which consists of a narrow, straight slide without slots or holes, operated by a lever working on a notched quadrant.

bottom of cart or truck, or suspended under the vehicle. It is chain driven from a large sprocket attached to the off-side road wheel. The sprocket was made by bending a piece of iron into a circle and boring it to take small bolts which act as the teeth of the chain. The chain runs to a ratchet or clutch sprocket on the shaft that passes through the centre of the worm-wheel. This type of sprocket permits the wheel to continue to revolve and thus clear itself when the vehicle is stopped, and saves throwing any strain on the machine if the vehicle comes to a sudden stop.

A friction disc is provided for use with a truck or with a horse that starts suddenly.

The worm-wheel shaft is divided and provided with a universal joint, and the whole machine can be dismantled and assembled.

USEFUL AND NOVEL DEVICES FOR FARM OR STATION

A USEFUL HOME-MADE SUPER DISTRIBUTOR

This is a rough sketch of a very easily made distributor used by one man with success, which was made from various old parts of a car and other implements, using the chassis, axle, springs, etc.

In the first place, the chassis was converted by cutting it in such a manner that only the front wheels were used—the drawing giving some idea as to the position in which the cut should be made.

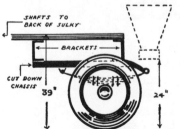

The broadcaster is then fixed in a position which was previously the front part of the car and the rest of the cart is made to carry the bags of fertiliser.

The distributor being in the position which was formerly the front of the car, means that the newly made job is drawn along from what was previously its rear end—this arrangement appears to be the best method, but, of course, this can be arranged to suit the individual needs, having in mind the material available at one's disposal.

The above broadcaster can be driven from whichever wheel is most convenient to the driver—the off-side for preference. Also, there should be some means of keeping the chain from running off if the wheels should get out of alignment. This might be arranged by clamping the steering arms to the axle.

A HOME-MADE SMALL FERTILISER DISTRIBUTOR FOR GARDEN, ETC.

For distributing super in rows before the planting of crops, the home-made arrangement shown here, attached to an ordinary plowstock, has a great advantage over the usual hand methods.

A wooden box hopper for carrying the fertiliser is pivoted in a U-shaped support; the vibrator irons are fastened to the sides of the box at an angle and engaged with vibrator pins. The disc in which the vibrator pins are inserted is 12 in. in diameter, and is attached to the plowstock in the manner indicated in the above sketch, by iron straps.

A small square hole is cut in the bottom of the rear end of the hopper as an outlet for the fertiliser, which is guided into the furrow by a small stationary trough made of tin.

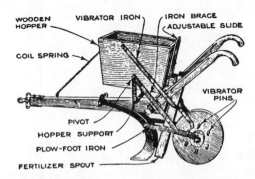

The size of the opening in the hopper is controlled by a thin piece of board that slides up and down and is held in place with a thumbnut and screw.

A stiff coil spring is provided and attached to the hopper and plowstock, in the position indicated, so as to bring the hopper back to the level position after it has been tipped up by the vibrator irons when they make contact with the pins.

This is a very useful arrangement, and well worth the time and trouble in its construction—it will save time in the long run.

A SELF-DUMPING MANURE BOAT

This is a labor saving device for throwing off a load of manure without using a fork and is especially good where heavy, wet manure from cattle pens or yards is concerned.

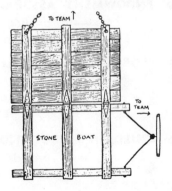

Attach two chains to the side of the boat A-A, one on the front and one on the rear end, 18 inches from each end, and lay the chain across the boat with one pole, B-B the length on top of the chains.

Put the load of manure on this as usual, and then bring the loose ends of the chains, C-C up and over the top of the load.

When ready to unload, hitch the team to C-C so that the pull over the top of the load will roll the manure off the boat. The pole on the chains is to raise the manure without missing any. The chains can stay attached until the job is done.

An arrangement such as this, or the following idea, can be used for almost any similar work, and will be found most convenient.

ANOTHER TYPE OF MANURE BOAT

This is another useful idea to save labour.

The floor is constructed as shown and is hinged to the framework of the sled, as indicated.

The chain, only parts of which are shown, is attached to a swingle-tree. When the boat is loaded, chain and swingle-tree are thrown over the load.

To unload, the horse is unhitched from the swingle-tree in front of the boat and hitched on to the other one. With a light pull the load is dumped.

A HOME-MADE HARROW OR PASTURE RENOVATOR

This home-made implement is suitable for most ground, and especially old pastures. Its construction consists of two pieces of channel or some similar shaped iron connected by some heavy timber, such as a couple of sleepers, or some heavy flat iron. The channel iron is put together in V formation, say about 8 ft. wide at the end.

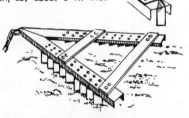

The teeth are formed of old pieces of iron or broken car springs —say 9 or 10 in. long, bent as shown in the sketch.

One edge of each of these teeth are then sharpened to a fine edge and twisted so that the sharp edge faces the direction of travel (the sketch does not quite show this as it was difficult to do so). A couple of bolts are used to attach each piece of spring or iron (as indicated in the sketch) whilst a piece of heavy chain, with ring attached, will complete the job.

USEFUL AND NOVEL DEVICES FOR FARM OR STATION

PREPARING SKINS FOR MARKET

A few notes on this subject might help some to save money by adopting the correct procedure in handling and marketing.

Sheepskins. Kill on a clean floor, keep pelt sound and wool clean.

When drying, always do so under cover, protected from rain and sun. Hang the skin lengthwise on a rail, neck to tail, pelt out, and with neck and other points opened out. Squeeze blood from neck.

To help stretch the skin, leave trotters on when drying, but cut off before sending the skin away.

When the skin is quite dry, sprinkle with weevil preventative, not forgetting the edges and points. In bundling, fold the skin over once, side to side, wool out, then fold the neck well over. Do not turn it in on the pelt.

See that the skins are quite dry before packing. If the skins are brittle through drying too quickly, they might crack, in which case do not fold the skin, but pack pelt to pelt and tie with three wires across and two lengthwise.

The illustrations given herewith show the right and the wrong way of handling such skins, and it is well worth while going to the extra trouble in order to get best results.

Hides. Proper care in flaying is necessary. Appearance is everything. The use of a little salt will pay handsomely. Leave as little fat and flesh on as possible.

Keep the hide as clean as possible and salt it well with clean salt as soon as it is taken off. To salt, spread the hide out squarely on a clean floor, and salt well half-way across from one side, making sure not to forget the edges, neck and legs.

Then fold the other half over. See that the hair side, which is generally dusty, does not come into contact with the flesh side. Turn the lower edges over together and fold the ends into the centre, then roll up from each end.

Use plenty of salt; it is cheap and does not allow the hides to dry out so rapidly as they otherwise would. They are sometimes hard to open up when dry.

THE RIGHT WAY.

THE WRONG WAY

Rabbit Skins. These sketches show the right and the wrong way to stretch them and are well worth studying.

The heads should be removed and the skins stretched from belly to back as indicated in the illustration (not from side to side).

They should not be baled before they are dry, and to prevent weevil damage they should be well sprinkled with weevil wash before they are baled.

The appearance of skins such as these goes a long way towards best prices being obtained.

Kangaroo, Wallaby and Fox Skins. Peg these out squarely and evenly. The chief cause of damage is weevil. Use weevil wash on them. Always dry in the shade if possible and do not use salt. Bundle pelt to pelt, fur to fur.

A USEFUL RACK FOR DRYING SKINS

This is a sketch of a useful rack for drying sheepskins which has been tried out with excellent results. The rack assists in the even drying of the skins, and dogs and crows are unable to damage them, especially if it is some distance off the ground. Skins that are evenly stretched look far more attractive when opened up for sale.

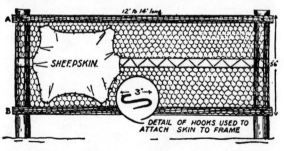

DETAIL OF HOOKS USED TO ATTACH SKIN TO FRAME

"A" and "B" are pieces of oregon or other timber 12 to 14 ft. long, bolted to the shed posts about 5 ft. 6 in. apart. Heavy-gauge wire netting 2 ft. 6 in. wide, and as long as the parallel timber, is stapled to the top and bottom rails "A" and "B," and is laced together at the inner edges with soft clothes-line wire, and drawn tightly together.

A few dozen wire "S" hooks with one end sharpened, and measuring about 3 to 4 inches in length, are used to stretch the skins flat on the netting. The shanks and feet can be cut off and the skins will dry quickly and evenly, looking much better than those which are stretched on a rail.

TRAPPING RABBITS—A USEFUL METHOD

The netting trap described here has been found very successful if the warren is watched each day or so in order to see that the stoppings are not interfered with by outside rabbits.

(1) Make the cylinders about 40 inches long, by 6 or 7 inches across, of rabbit proof netting.

(2) Make a ring of stiff wire 2 inches less in diameter than the cylinder. Fasten this inside a few inches from one end of the cylinder, with the plain wire so that it is equi-distant all round from the walls of the cylinder. This is the swing-door stop.

(3) Make a second stiff wire ring one inch larger than the "stopping," and cover neatly with wire netting. Hang this with wire ring ties, inside the door-stop, so that it can swing freely one way, and so let the rabbits pass into the cylinder but not back again.

(4) Press the far end of the cylinder flat and lace shut with a wire skewer. Several of the straps are required for a warren.

Place them door-end first into the most frequently used holes, then plug up all trapless holes as follows:—

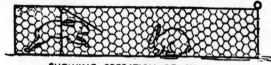

SHOWING OPERATION OF TRAP

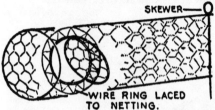

SKEWER

WIRE RING LACED TO NETTING.

DETAIL OF TRAP-DOOR

Rabbits are afraid of rustling paper, so first push a large bundle down the hole; nearly fill up the hole with earth and then near the outside put another large ball of crinkled paper to scare off the outside rabbits. When all the holes are blocked by either traps or paper, the warren is set. Nothing much will happen for the first 48 hours, but after that numbers of rabbits will be found in the traps each day until the warren is empty provided that the paper filled holes have not been interfered with.

USEFUL AND NOVEL DEVICES FOR FARM OR STATION

A HANDY SKINNING DEVICE

This device makes it easy for one man to skin small animals such as rabbits, etc., either for meat or fur. After opening the pelt, the hook with the long strap (about 18 in.) is fastened into the skin and then the strap is looped to a post. The hook on the short 8 in. strap looped round the belt is fastened to a leg or to the carcase and the desired pressure is put on while the hands are free to work the skin loose. If the flesh tears easily, a loop of stout cord can be doubled and put around the carcase and the hook fastened into the looped end.

AN EMERGENCY WINDLASS

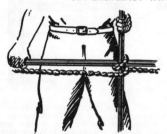

This sketch shows an improvised windlass, useful in an emergency. A rope is fastened securely to the two objects between which the force is to be applied.

Two heavy rods or pipes are held by the side of the rope, one vertically and the other horizontally and a hitch is taken around the two as shown. Considerable force can be exerted by turning the horizontal rod, winding the rope around the vertical one. This method may be used also to pull a car out of a mud hole provided there is a sturdy fence or pole handy for use.

SIMPLE DEVICE FOR HOLDING CUT ENDS OF WIRE UNDER TENSION

If a suspended wire is not held securely before cutting it, the ends will drop and whip around in a dangerous manner.

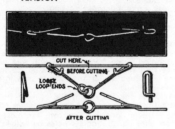

This little device will hold the cut ends securely. It is made of two short lengths of heavy wire looped at one end into each other, the other ends being bent as shown, to slip over the wires to be cut. It is important that they must be a spring fit on the wire. Before cutting the wire, the gripper is snapped over it on each side of where the cut is to be made.

When the wire is cut, the weight of it pulls the gripper out straight and it tightens up as shown in the upper drawing, the sudden jerk bending up the cut ends, which are then held securely. To bring the long end of the wire safely to the ground, the gripper is pulled at one end and the short end of the wire removed.

AN IMPROVISED SPRING SEAT FOR VEHICLES

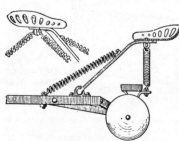

This is a comfortable home-made seat for horsemobiles or any implement, made from an ordinary implement seat.

It is shock absorbing and will protect the driver from severe jolting. The seat is fixed as shown and held in position by three coil springs.

Two of these springs extend diagonally to either side, connecting the seat and frame whilst the other spring is fixed in the manner shown. The arrangement prevents undue movement in any direction and supports the seat without its having any rigid connection.

EMERGENCY REPAIRS TO CHAIN

This is a very handy little idea worth knowing and it may come in very useful at a time when a chain may be broken at a very inconvenient time.

It is an idea for repairing a broken chain in an emergency by the use of a nail, bent as illustrated in this drawing.

The drawing needs no explanation; a nail can usually be found nearby and the arrangement suggested will be found very easy to make. Also, it will stand a good deal of rough usage and will make a very good stop-gap until the chain can be repaired.

A NOVEL WAGON GRIP FOR REINS
For Use When Team is Unattended

This handy arrangement has been found most successful by one farmer who has occasion to leave his team unattended from time to time.

It is an eccentric clamp which can be nailed to the side of the wagon box within instant reach of the driver when he has ocasion to dismount and temporarily release the reins.

As will be seen, the clamp is made from a couple of wood blocks, made into the shape indicated. Furthermore, the action makes it very easy indeed to attach or remove the reins.

AN EFFECTIVE HOME-MADE WAGON BRAKE

This is a very simple but effective home-made brake. Its construction is such that a slight pull on the lever causes the brake blocks to press tightly against the tyre. The lever is quite short, occupying only a little space. No pole projects upwards above the level of the top of the cart to get in one's way whilst loading or otherwise working.

A rope, tied to the rear end of the lever, extends to the front end of the wagon, where it is accessible to the driver. The rope is tied to the right hand standard, to keep it at a point handy to the reach.

The materials are all easy to obtain. The hardwood is 3 in. x 2 in., whilst four iron bars $\frac{3}{8}$ x $1\frac{1}{2}$ in. are required, two of them being used on top and two beneath, to keep the brake-block holders in position.

Two thin iron bars, bent to the shape shown, are used as a support for the brake lever, and also to connect the brake-block holders, and they provide a sort of rack for the lever when it is idle.

These pieces are attached to the short block-holder by means of a U-shaped bolt, and to the longer one with a lag screw. The timber into which the lag screw is driven is banded at the end to prevent it from splitting.

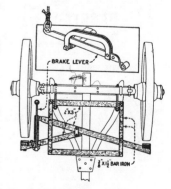

The block-holders are further connected by means of two bolts and two short straps at a point near the centre of the wagon.

Pieces of an old casing should be nailed to the brake blocks, to prevent wear of the wood.

The sketch does not show the detailed construction of the brake, although a few dimensions are given but one should be governed by the size and kind of wagon, when determining the size parts to be used. The brake can be made adjustable by drilling more than one hole near the front end of the lever, where it is given a quarter twist.

USEFUL AND NOVEL DEVICES FOR FARM OR STATION

HANDY LAND MEASURES

Accurate measurement of land is a difficult task when working with a tape line, but if done with a measuring wheel or other home-made contrivance, it can be a much easier job.

A USEFUL HOME-MADE MEASURING STICK

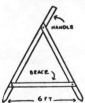

Wooden dividers, as shown here, are a very useful help in measuring acreage. One man can undertake the work alone almost as fast as he can walk.

The handle is held in the right hand, and the stick is swung over and over as the operator moves along.

The points are brought down each time at approximately the same distance from the fence or line of measurement. A convenient distance is 6 feet, but some might prefer 8 feet 3 inches which equals one half a rod, 80 of which would measure the length of the side of a square one acre plot. This is a very easy and reliable method.

A LAND MEASURE FROM A BICYCLE WHEEL

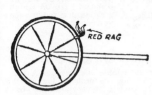

The front wheel of a bicycle makes a useful measure to enable one to operate single-handed. Such a wheel makes 10 revolutions to the chain.

A piece of red rag attached to the rim at one point renders accurate counting of the turns of the wheel quite simple. This type of land measure has been found very dependable.

A LAND MEASURE FROM OLD BUGGY OR OTHER BIG WHEEL

This is a somewhat similar arrangement. An old buggy wheel can be converted in the manner shown and can be turned by a convenient handle made in the hub in any manner devised from material on hand. Ordinary building lathes could be used, supported by spokes made from light timber (this is actually shown in this illustration).

A small automatic counter near the hub will keep a record of the revolutions, thus enabling the operator to check the distance, or the method mentioned in the previous sketch can be used.

This latter arrangement will enable one to count the number of turns of a wheel, and, if the circumference of the wheel is previously known, the distance could easily be calculated and the desired results obtained.

A SMALL HOME-MADE MEASURING WHEEL

This is another somewhat similar arrangement on a smaller scale; it indicates the use of a small wheel and a forkstick which can be improvised at a moment's notice.

In this instance a light cultivator wheel is set between the limbs of the fork and held in place by a bolt, after which a piece of cloth is tied to one of the spokes.

Counting the number of revolutions of the spoke and multiplying this by the circumference of the wheel will give the measurements required.

A HOME-MADE FARM LEVEL

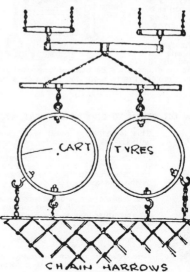

This useful device can be made from 2 pieces of ½ in. glass tubing, about 5 in. long; a foot of pipe, ¾ or ½ in., and 2 elbows; with clamps to fix the pipe firmly to the stand.

The elbows are screwed on to the ends of the pipe as shown, and the lot fastened to a board, elbows pointing upwards.

The glass tubes are cemented into the elbows with anything that will act watertight. This needs care. First the paste used is rubbed well into the threads of the elbow, then the end of the glass is wrapped with string, which is also covered with the paste. The glass is set in place, and more paste packed round it. A stand is made and plumb bob suspended. The level is prepared by filling the pipe with water, coloured for preference, until it rises about 3 in. in each glass. Adjust the plumb bob so that its point just touches the ground. It is then a simple matter to measure the elevation of the water above the ground.

By sighting along the level of the water in both glasses, any distant point seen in line with both water surfaces will be at the same level. The stand should be adjustable in height.

A HOME-MADE LAND LEVELLER

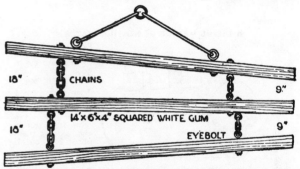

Old cart tyres joined together will make a useful implement for levelling cultivated land or for spreading manure. This illustration will show how easily one can be made, and, with chain harrows attached, it will do splendid work.

ANOTHER USEFUL LAND LEVELLER

This is a good idea. The first bar should not be parallel with the team, the idea being that clods will slip down the bar and break up gradually. If a solid obstacle be encountered, it will minimise the jar on the horse's shoulders. For a

six-horse job, timber 6 x 4 x 14, squared up, is used. Ten five-eighths bolts and 4 lengths of stout chain are all that is necessary.

USEFUL AND NOVEL DEVICES FOR FARM OR STATION

AN OIL DRUM AS REFUSE BURNER

An old oil drum makes a very useful and easily made rubbish burner, as illustrated in this sketch.

Simply bolt or rivet four strap iron legs to it to keep it off the ground, or it can be placed up on stones or bricks. With a small axe or hatchet, cut a few gashes through the sides near the bottom to provide some air intakes.

The iron rims from old truck tyres also make excellent rubbish burners—3 iron stakes being driven into the ground inside them to keep them from moving.

REDUCING COKE CONSUMPTION BY DRIP-FEED USED OIL

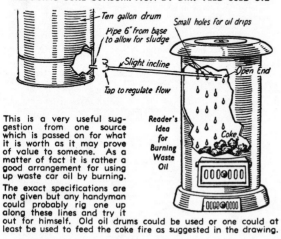

This is a very useful suggestion from one source which is passed on for what it is worth as it may prove of value to someone. As a matter of fact it is rather a good arrangement for using up waste car oil by burning.

The exact specifications are not given but any handyman could probably rig one up along these lines and try it out for himself. Old oil drums could be used or one could at least be used to feed the coke fire as suggested in the drawing.

NOVEL STOVE FROM OIL DRUMS TO GIVE EXTRA HEAT, ETC.

This is rather a novel idea tried with success in one quarter as it will give extra heat to a room or it will provide quite a lot of extra hot water if a system of pipes is connected from one drum to the other as shown in the illustration.

The drawing will suggest ways and means of doing this and perhaps suggest other uses to which such an arrangement could be put.

Further, a drum could perhaps be attached to the kitchen stove in the same manner in many instances in order to give extra heat to a room.

A USEFUL METHOD OF HEATING WATER

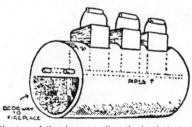

First take an empty drum and at one end cut a good large hole for a doorway.

Then get two ¾ in. pipes, and run them through the centre of the drum from end to end, placing them about 6 in. apart.

Next, cut three square holes in the top of the drum to allow the buckets to come down and rest on the pipes. A good fire can then be placed beneath the buckets of water which will rapidly come to the boil.

OLD TYRES ASSIST EASY TRANSPORT ON AWKWARD ARTICLES

The first sketch shows how old tyres can be utilised to transport barrels or even square objects from place to place without much difficulty. In the case of barrels this might not be so necessary, but if they contain anything that might be damaged by jolting along the ground, this idea should prove useful.

TYRES WILL HELP ROLL HEAVY LOGS, ETC.

Two old tyres mounted on rims having valves in the inner tubes that do not project beyond the rims will save work when moving heavy logs, etc.

The ends of the logs are inserted through the tyres, as shown. By gripping the tops of the tyres one can keep an upright position and roll the logs very easily.

A HOME-MADE FOOT POWER CIRCULAR SAW

The illustrations given below should enable one to make a first-class circular saw. The legs "A" are the ordinary legs of the bench at the end (figs. 2 and 3); and to prevent vibration, as is very necessary where it is desired to produce good work, another pair of legs should be made and fixed in position as shown at "B" (figs. 2 and 3).

The bottom rails must be prepared and fixed between the legs as shown at "C" and "D" (figs. 1 and 2). A simple method of doing this is to screw four angle brackets as indicated at "C" (fig. 2). The objects of these rails is to prevent the legs from spreading, and to hold the crank-shaft in position.

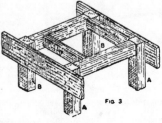

The two cross-rails "E" (figs. 1 and 2), to carry the centres of the crank-shaft, should be dovetail halved into the legs as shown. The arrangement of the woodwork will be clearly understood from fig. 3.

The circular saw spindle shown, about 10 in. long, is of the simplest form.

It should have a grooved pulley, which may be of wood; the spindle works between centres as shown. The treadle board may be a piece of 1 in. x 11, and hinged at the back to the rail "D" (fig. 2), the attachment of the connecting rod being shown by "F" (fig. 2). A suitable wheel and crankshaft can be purchased.

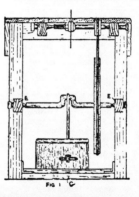

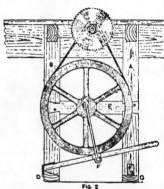

USEFUL AND NOVEL DEVICES FOR FARM OR STATION

UPROOTING SMALL TREES WITH CAR JACK

Small trees can often be uprooted quite easily with the aid of a motor car jack and a long beam, say, about 4 inches square.

The beam is chained to the trunk of the tree, as shown, and it is then jacked up at one end. The jack is then lowered, the beam loosened and chained to a lower point on the tree, and the operation repeated.

It will assist if a board is put under the beam where it will rest on the ground.

ELBOW STRAPS HELP CARRY AWKWARD LOADS

Carrying heavy baskets of feed or other produce is very often a back-straining task if the basket is carried by its two handles in the normal manner.

If a person is reasonably muscular, it would be much easier and more convenient to carry the basket by one arm with the aid of an arm strap with a hook, in the manner shown here.

ANOTHER USE FOR OLD TUBES

Many uses can be found for a strip of rubber from old inner tubes, and this is one of them. Hands are apt to get sore when digging, hoeing, and doing other such jobs which call for constant friction. Just cut two pieces of rubber, as shown, so that they will slip over and protect the fingers and palms, while being held in place by the loops formed to grip the back of the hands.

Also, rings cut fr   a tube, slipped over th   et and up the legs keep   e trouser bottoms from coming   into contact with wet soil much more comfortably than the usual piece of string.

Two or more rubber bands carried in a handy place will also come in handy in many ways when working about the farm or garden, taking the place of string, wire, and nails on many occasions.

ANOTHER WAY OF KEEPING CLOTHES DRY WITH OLD MOTOR TUBES

Two lengths of inner tube pulled over the legs, as shown here, will keep one's clothes dry below the rain coat in wet weather. A slit cut at the bottom with a "V" strip cemented in it will flare the tubes and keep the water from running into the shoe.

HOW TO USE OVERSIZE CORKS

It is often necessary to use corks which are oversize. Also, a cork which is trimmed to proper size with a knife will rarely seal a bottle correctly owing to the difficulty in making smooth cuts

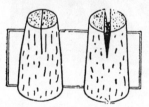

on the corks, no matter how sharp the knife may be.

A method which will avoid this difficulty is to cut out a V-shaped piece from the centre of the cork, as shown in the right-hand sketch. When the cork is pushed into the bottle-neck, this V-opening will close, as on the left, thus permitting an airtight joint.

USEFUL METHODS OF FILING KEYS

The tools needed are a vice, a few files, and sometimes a hacksaw and an awl. A 4-in. flat warding file is useful for cutting rectangular notches in the ordinary tumbler lock key, and the lozenge file, such as is used for sinking dies, is convenient for filing the V-wards of a pin tumbler key.

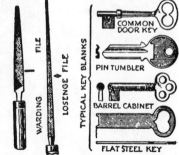

In purchasing a blank key, choose one as nearly the size and shape of the original key as possible. If the original key is available, the making of an exact duplicate merely requires that one mark and file the blank carefully and check frequently. A ward cut too deep will sometimes ruin the key.

If the key is of the pin tumbler type, clamp the blank and the original key together in proper alignment in the vice and file the notches in the blank with a lozenge or other suitable file as shown. The original key will serve as a template.

When the original key is missing and the lock is of the common variety, hold the blank over a lighted match or candle until it is blackened, insert it in the lock and turn it hard, pressing tightly. Remove the key and file where the soot has been removed. It is impossible for the amateur to fit a key of the pin tumbler type to a lock, so a copy must be made by copying an existing key.

LENGTHENING A PIPE, SHAFT OR ROD

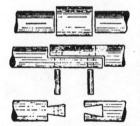

If it is necessary to lengthen a piece of pipe or rod, one simple plan would be to weld or braze it, but neither of these processes can always be readily applied.

One simple method is to use a sleeve as shown in the upper drawing. The sleeve should be made a snug fit over the broken part, and then pinned in position. If a sleeve is not available, the joint shown in the centre sketch can be used. In this case a lap joint is formed and then held together by means of pins or rivets. The lower sketch shows a pinned dove-tail joint. This is a stronger joint but more difficult to make. In making these joints, fit the parts together carefully for maximum strength.

SMOKING MEAT WITH BARREL AND STOVE PIPE

Those wishing to smoke only a few hams or sides of bacon will find this idea useful. The tunnel ensures cool smoke and eliminates the danger of overheating the meat. Dig a trench about 12 in. deep and twice the length of a piece of stove pipe. Bury the pipe in the middle of the trench. Over one of the open ends place a barrel upside down and bore a few holes in the top of it. Hang the meat with cords looped over small sticks. In the other end of the trench build a fire with chips, etc. Regulate the draught with a piece of sheet metal.

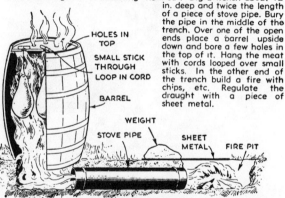

HOLES IN TOP
SMALL STICK THROUGH LOOP IN CORD
BARREL
WEIGHT
STOVE PIPE
SHEET METAL
FIRE PIT

USEFUL AND NOVEL DEVICES FOR FARM OR STATION

TREE PULLING AND LIFTING WITH TACKLE

Some Useful Hints for the Amateur

These sketches and ideas are from the experiences of those who do quite a lot of this type of work and therefore they might be of value to those who may have to deal with such problems as they may arise.

Most of the hints given are those which can be used quite effectively by one man working alone or by one man working with one horse.

To begin with it is shown how extra power is gained by the use of different methods; for instance, there is no extra power at all gained from a single block such as that shown in illustration No. 1, but double power would be gained from a rope through two single blocks, as shown in figure 2.

Again, a runner, such as that indicated in illustration No. 3, adds an additional power to any purchase it is used with.

Figure 4 is of another type of lifting tackle, known as the "luff" (this one showing a double and single block). The "luff" will also give extra power as will figure 5, which is known as the "double luff." Further illustrations are given in the next column.

Then there is also the three and four-fold purchase which are on somewhat similar lines to that shown in figure 6, and which will give anything from six to nine times the extra power that would be gained from the single block shown in illustration No. 1.

No. 7 is a different type again, giving 3 times the power, and Nos. 8 and 9 are other arrangements one using 3 single and the other one double and 2 single blocks, giving 5 times the power.

The following hints and examples in connection with log rolling and tree pulling are the methods used by one man with success and are quite a good basis to work on.

Wire rope can, of course, be used in lieu of a hooking-on chain, but he prefers a chain with a grab or shortening link as it does not slide down the trunk of the tree as a wire rope often will. Also, it is his custom to always use heavy trace chains as otherwise the harness may often break and the pull is always arranged so that the horse either walks on level ground or down hill when pulling as it saves a lot of energy.

How to get more than 1 roll with 1 pull

Without cant hook

With cant hook

Stump and Log Rolling. The methods shown here are of various ways of rolling logs with and without canthooks, either of which may be useful to those desiring to do this type of work.

Tackle rigged up on the same principle as that shown in the top sketch is quite sufficient for most short pulls, whilst the method shown in the lower drawing is also very good for rolling or even dragging or hauling big logs up to 3 ft. in diameter.

This can be done by rolling the log on to some green saplings which have had the bark bruised off and placed in such a way as to allow the log to slip along easily.

Single Block Tackle. This is one suggested arrangement of single block tackle which indicates how one block pulls off the other, giving extra power with each additional block. Blocks and tackle next to the stump take double the strain of that next the horse, so they must be the stronger set.

Also, the weakest rope should be $1\frac{1}{2}$ times the power of the horse, and if the latter can pull, say, 1 ton, the weakest rope should be $1\frac{1}{2}$ tons breaking strain, the stump pulling rope double, and the block and chain quadruple in order to take a 10 ton strain. It should not take more than a 10 ton strain to roll or pull a tree up to, say, 18 in. in diameter. It is a good idea in such cases to use, say, two heavy and two lighter blocks with 5-8 in. and 3-8 in. flexible cables.

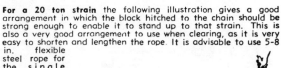

For a 20 ton strain the following illustration gives a good arrangement in which the block hitched to the chain should be strong enough to enable it to stand up to that strain. This is also a very good arrangement to use when clearing, as it is very easy to shorten and lengthen the rope. It is advisable to use 5-8 in. flexible steel rope for the single blocks and 3-8 in. for the double purchase blocks.

The rope or hooking-on chain should be put on as high as possible, in order to obtain the maximum leverage, and the larger the tree the higher it is necessary to go.

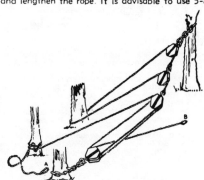

Running Tackle. The running tackle shown in some of these sketches has a big advantage over the single in that it is not then necessary to back the horse several times in order to take in the slack—one loose end being anchored to a stump or log. This is also useful to use with two single blocks as the running tackle has its own leading end. The loose end can, if necessary, be anchored by winding the rope round the anchor and clipping the bight under the coils.

Double Purchase Running Tackle. This sketch shows how either end can also be anchored to allow lengthening without the horse having to walk back in order to take in the slack.

Triple Purchase Tackle. The last sketch indicates probably one of the handiest methods for most general work which may, with experience, also be worked as running tackle with a long length of rope—the sketch showing one end hooked to the heel of one block —12 in. triple blocks and 3-8 in. flexible cable being best. It can also be used in conjunction with single blocks for pulling trees, etc., and is good for rolling logs as indicated in the previous para.

There may, of course, be occasions when these ideas are not quite so simple, as in the example on next page. However, these notes will give a good general working knowledge.

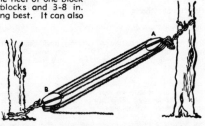

USEFUL AND NOVEL DEVICES FOR FARM OR STATION

TREE PULLING WITH TACKLE (Continued)

This useful idea of one user is based on different lines to those shown on the previous page, but it has certain advantages should sufficient anchors not be available, and which also, under some circumstances, would require quite a lot of rope.

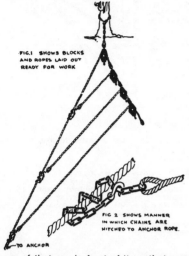

FIG.1 SHOWS BLOCKS AND ROPES LAID OUT READY FOR WORK

FIG 2 SHOWS MANNER IN WHICH CHAINS ARE HITCHED TO ANCHOR ROPE.

TO ANCHOR

In this arrangement there is only one main anchor rope needed—the additional blocks being attached to this rope by short lengths of rope or chain in the manner shown and which can be added or dropped at a moment's notice as required.

To avoid any damage or slipping of the rope, note the manner in which the extra ropes are hitched on, as this is the main idea which makes for success.

To work on this method, a little preparation is required because each block will travel double the pace of that one in front of it, so that one will require twice as much rope, which should, of course, be cut accordingly.

These sketches will indicate the system of attaching these small lengths to each other—the lower sketch showing the manner in which they are fastened to the main rope. This comprises a small length of about 2 ft. 6 in. of 3-8 in. iron chain to one end of which a hook is attached by welding or otherwise; the other end being spliced or otherwise to the piece of rope itself.

For the main anchor and second block flexible steel rope of say ½ in. should be used with 3-8 in. for the third and fourth block, that is to say, if one horse is used, and up to 4 blocks required.

A USEFUL HOME-MADE BUSH PULLER

Many farmers clear bush land with chains and even by digging the bushes out. Both methods take much longer than is necessary. The following method has been used successfully for many years by one farmer and is therefore well worth recording here.

In this case a small hook was used with a Fordson tractor or other tractor of the same or lesser power.

The material is 3½ x 1 1-8 in. steel. The hooks are made two at a time in order to save wastage of material.

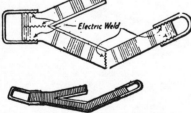

Electric Weld

The large hooks, as shown in the illustration, are for steam tackle and very large crawler tractors.

They need oxy-acetylene cutting and electrical welding equipment. The angle of the "V" is very important and must be between 35 deg. and 40 deg., i.e., at 9 in. up the legs of the "V," 6 in. across.

The advantage of making the large hook composite is that the gripping angle can be cut with oxy-acetylene and ground before welding together. The angle reduced from each side is ¼ in. to each inch of thickness, i.e., about 15 degrees.

The hole for pulling is in line with the centre of the "V." The hook should be attached to the tractor with a cable as this is much lighter for strength than a chain.

HOW TO USE A LASSO

To be able to lasso successfully is to a farmer a definitely useful accomplishment.

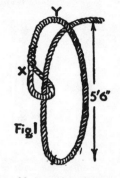

Fig 1

5'6"

The practical uses to which the lasso can be put are numerous, but on most farms its chief use would probably be found in the stockyard when horse-breaking is in progress.

Usually the method of catching a young horse is to drop a loop over his head by means of a long stick pronged at the end. However, when it has been mastered, the lasso will soon be found preferable, as it is quicker and safer.

In choosing a rope for a lasso, the one selected should be strong enough to hold a young horse, and at the same time fairly heavy, so that when thrown, it will carry well. About 20 to 30 feet of medium to heavy rope will be found satisfactory, but, if it is available, an untanned hide rope is one of the best.

Having selected a rope, the running attachment at "X" in the first diagram is made. It is best to splice the join of the rope here, as a knot would tend to unbalance the noose. It is only a matter of interweaving the strands and is well worth the trouble.

Taking up the first position, the noose should be extended until its length is about 5 ft. 6 in. Then the noose should be turned until the running knot "X" is half-way down its length, as in figure 1.

Then take the top of the loop at "Y" in the right hand, keeping the noose forward of the rope. The end of the rope is then taken in the left hand between the thumb and forefinger in such a way that the hand can be firmly closed around the rope when the animal has been lassoed.

Then proceed to coil the remainder of the rope into loops of about 1 ft. in length, resting them on the middle finger of the left hand in such a way that they are free to follow the noose when it has been thrown. This is shown in the second sketch above.

Some people find it easier if they coil the rope first on the right hand and then transfer the coils to the left hand.

The lasso is now ready for throwing, and with practice proficiency in the art will soon be attained, enabling one to use it with confidence in the stockyard.

When swinging, the rope should be held about 12 inches below the loop, as shown in this drawing, and, when swinging the rope around the head, the size of the noose can be altered as might be found necessary, but one of the reasons for holding the rope as indicated in these sketches is that it enables the noose to open in a circle as far as it will go.

It is simply whirled above the head two or three times and thrown when it is open.

A right-hand thrower will find it helpful if he turns his left shoulder towards the object which is to be lassoed. The whole procedure may sound a little complicated, but it is really much easier than it sounds, and a little practice will soon enable one to do this job with ease. The above notes are from quite a reliable source, and are passed on in the hope that they might prove useful.

USEFUL KNOTS AND HITCHES

USEFUL KNOTS AND HITCHES

A knowledge of suitable knots, etc., often arises and a selection is given here, any one of which may be useful on occasion.

No. 1. The Square Knot. A common knot, but some have difficulty with it. To tie, take your rope and tie an ordinary right hand over-hand knot, and follow this with the left hand form of the same knot.

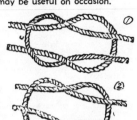

No. 2. The Granny Knot. The square knot is a good one to use when tying two ropes together, but do not mix it with the granny knot. This is the ordinary hard knot. It slips easily unless very tightly tied and then it is hard to untie.

No. 3. Weaver's Knot. This can also be used for tying two ropes or straps together.

It is easily untied, and never draws tight. If you are driving a four-horse team it comes in handy when you have to tie the lines together.

A little practice will find it quite easy.

No. 4. Figure 8 Knot. This is often used at the end of a rope to keep the strands from untwisting or to prevent the rope from slipping through a hole or pulley.

No. 5. Sheepshank Knot. This knot will help you on occasions, such as if you wanted to haul something with a rope, after the team has been hitched up and you find the rope too long. It can be tied in a minute, unties easily, and will hold as long as the rope is tight. To keep it from untying when the rope is loosened, fasten the loops to the main part of the rope.

No. 6. The Bowline Knot. This is one of the most useful.

You often want a loop that will not slip or pull, and the bowline is the easiest way to tie it. If you have no neck strap or halter for the horse a rope will do for the time being if you can tie a bowline. The sketches will show you how. It is the best way to form a non-slipping loop on the end of a rope.

A loop is first made by throwing the end of the rope over to the left in front of the standing part, and then passing the end up through the loop. This is the stage which must be carefully followed. Next, carry the end round behind the standing part, then bring it back to the front from the left and through the loop. When tightened, it will be found that the knot will not give, no matter what strain may be put upon it.

No. 7. Blackwall Hitch. This is one of the simplest of all hitches to make. It does not look very safe, but it really is so long as there is a steady pull on the rope.

A big advantage is that a shake of the rope loosens it. It sometimes comes in handy when descending from a tree or other high place.

No. 8. Half-hitch. The half hitch is another good temporary fastening.

So long as there is a fairly steady pull, it will hold, and, like the Blackwall hitch, it is easily loosened. It is simply a loop around the standing part with the short end of the rope pinched beneath the loop.

No. 8

Nos. 9 and 10. Half and Timber Hitches. The timber hitch is more secure, and, as the name suggests, it is often used in hauling logs and timber.

It is really very much like the half-hitch, except that the short end is wrapped around part of the loop one or more times instead of simply being pinched under it.

Timber Hitch.

The combination of these two hitches is much more secure than either one alone, and sometimes you will have use for it. It comes in handy if you have to lift long timbers or pipes out of a well, for instance, where there is a straight pull. The illustration shows the combination.

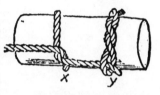

No. 11. The Clove Hitch. This is a much used temporary fastening for boats, or even for hauling timbers, although it is less secure than the combination mentioned above.

It can be made by having two half-hitches opposite each other and dropping the loops thus formed over the end of the timber or post.

A KNOT THAT WILL NOT TIGHTEN

In hauling heavy objects by means of a rope, knots are often drawn so tight that they are difficult to untie. To eliminate this, slip a small stick through the knot before drawing it up.

By removing this stick, the knot can be untied with ease, no matter how it tight it seems to be.

THE HARNESS KNOT—IT DOES NOT SLIP.

The sketch shows this knot in 4 stages. It is made by first tying an ordinary over-hand knot and drawing a bight through it (fig. 1).

Pull the loop of the overhand knot, which is on the top of the standing part, of the rope through the bight (fig. 2), and draw it tight (fig. 3). This knot

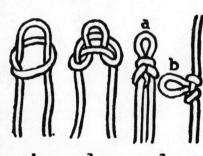

will not slip when a load is applied at the loop with both ropes or on one rope (a) or the ropes in opposite directions.

USEFUL KNOTS AND HITCHES

HOW TO MAKE AN END AND CROWN KNOT, ETC.

When the hay rope breaks, and you have two ropes instead of one, it is just as well to know how to put them together, end to end.

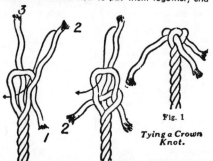

Fig. 1

Tying a Crown Knot.

The life of the rope will therefore be lengthened. However, you should first learn to make the knot on the end of the rope, and these hints will help.

Fig. 2

Crown and Wall Knot.

To make a crown knot, bring strand 1 in figure 1 down between strands 2 and 3, pass strand 2 across the loop as shown and pass strand 3 through the loop. Then pull each strand until they are all tight.

The crown knot can be made more secure by adding the wall knot as shown in figure 2.

THE HAY KNOT

The hay knot is one which gives a decided advantage when pulling lashing ropes tight. The complete knot is shown in fig. 1, and it is made by forming a loop in the rope where it hangs down from the top of the load. This loop should be made as high as possible. Hold the loop in the left hand and double a portion of the rope in the right hand and push it through the loop as in fig. 2. The loose end of the rope is then passed through the ring of the cart or truck or under any suitable tieing point,

FIG. 1

FIG. 2

FIG. 3

and then carried up through the lower loop, as in figure 1.

By pulling down on the loose end a kind of pulley effect is obtained, and the lashings can be hauled taut. The loose end is secured by doubling it and passing it between the load and the lashings and securing it with a simple knot. This is somewhat like the "sheepshank" knot for shortening, and will hold as long as a strain is kept on the rope. If a more secure knot is required, the first loop should be drawn up further and be made to take a half-hitch round the rope as shown. If there is a risk of it loosening, draw out the top loop and take a half-hitch round the taut rope as in figure 3.

TYPES OF CATSPAW KNOTS

Here are illustrations of two different types of knots, which are often termed "catspaw" knots.

That shown at the top of the sketch is also called the "rocking hitch." As indicated, two bights are made in a rope, and these are turned over from the operator three or four times and the loops so formed are then put on the hook.

To make the other (see lower half of the illustration) make two equal bights; taking one in each hand and rolling them along the standing part until they have three turns round the standing part. Both loops are then brought together and passed over the hook, as shown.

These are good, strong and serviceable knots for purposes such as that shown here.

CATS PAW OR RACKING HITCH
FINISHED

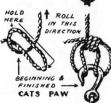

HOLD HERE   ROLL IN THIS DIRECTION

BEGINNING & FINISHED
CATS PAW

HOW TO MAKE A LONG SPLICE

To mend, say, a hay rope, or other, quickly and efficiently, it is a good idea to make a long splice. The illustrations below show

1 Untwist strand A for about 3 feet. Replace strand X with A.

2 Tie overhand knot at G. Cut off X, leaving about 6 inches. Replace strand Y with B.

3 Tie knot at H and cut Y as you did X. Replace Z with C.

4 At I, tie the knot and cut Z. String indicated by arrow is starting point of splice.

5 Now weave into rope the ends at points G, H and I. To taper off, remove a yarn from strand each time you tuck it under.

6 Cut off the yarns. Singe with match, roll splice under foot. Your job should now resemble a new rope.

the necessary steps. The black rope in the sketches represent one end of the broken rope, and the white rope represents the other end.

The first thing you do, of course, is to cut off the frayed strands at the point of the break. When the splice is correctly completed, the rope should be as good as new, and there will be no enlargement at the point of the splice.

USEFUL KNOTS AND HITCHES

A GOOD ROPE LADDER

This illustration will give details of a very useful and simple type of easily made rope ladder, one which can be seen at a glance is both easy and quick to erect and quick and easy to dismantle.

The rope is merely looped round the rungs, as indicated in the sketch. The rungs may be of any timber sufficiently strong enough for the purpose for which it is desired.

This idea is really preferable to that of boring holes in timber through which the rope can be threaded; first, because it is a quicker job, and, unless the timber is fairly strong, it may split.

It can also be made to any size required, and then dismantled when the particular job is finished.

OTHER USEFUL IDEAS WITH ROPE

A rope is constantly of service, and many are the uses to which it can be put, and therefore a hint or two in connection with sailors' knots may be helpful.

How to sling a plank for painting or other purposes is shown in **figure 1**; bring it entirely round the plank in order to prevent its turning and letting the user down. Half or three-quarter inch rope is usually sufficient.

A useful way to sling a can or pail from the end of a rope is shown in **figure 2**. Prepared in this way the article is secure so long as the rope is not slipped off from the bottom. Secure the knot firmly at the top to allow of no slipping and so that the pail may not become lop-sided.

Scaffolding may often be erected by tieing poles together as shown in **figure 3**. This sort of lashing will not slip if made tight.

In many cases, a chain may be used as shown in **figure 4**, in which case the weight should be on the side of the upright where the chain is lowest.

All of these lashings must be drawn very tight so as not to allow any play, which may result in disaster.

An excellent hitch is shown in **figure 5**, readily made, easily loosened, and valuable for many purposes. This knot is readily untied by slackening up the drawing strand. It does not become tight and hard as many ordinary knots after heavy usage.

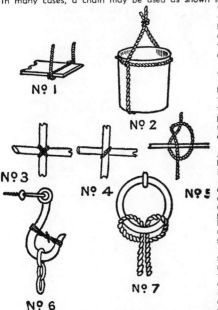

No. 1

No. 2

No. 3

No. 4

No. 5

No. 6

No. 7

In many cases where heavy hooks are used they are liable to become unfastened unless a cord is affixed, as in **figure 6**. A few turns of heavy twine or light wire in the middle will frequently prevent any loosening of the chain.

A ring hitch, as shown in **figure 7**, is a very effective and safe method, which may be made at short notice. The loose end of the rope is allowed to hang free or may be tied with a slip knot to the drawing strand.

A WET STRING KNOT THAT WILL HOLD TIGHT

This is quite a useful idea when tops of sacks or other articles are required to be tied with a knot which will remain tight.

Knots tied with wet string as indicated, will not become loose. It is wrapped round the mouth of the sack twice, and the twine is twisted in the manner shown.

If made in this fashion, knots are hard to remove, unless they are cut with a knife.

A SHOW SHEAVE KNOT

The N.S.W. Agricultural Gazette gives this very useful way of sheaf tieing. In the complete cord "A-D," an overhand knot is tied at "B" about 2 in. from the end. This knot is pulled tight.

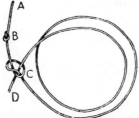

The string is now passed twice round the sheaf and the knotted end of the cord is tied in a loose overhand knot "D." When "D" is pulled the knot "C" will slip up to knot "B" and grip the cord until the ends "A" and "D" are tied. Sheaves may be tied very tightly by this method.

KNOTS TO HELP CLIMB HIGH TREES, ETC.

ROPE

Two rope slings can be used, as shown. The rope should be strong and pliable, and the sling should be large enough to loop about the pole.

In use, place one foot in the lower one, then throw your weight on this one; hang to the pole with one hand, and raise the other loop as high as you can reach with the free foot.

With your foot in this loop and your weight on it, change hands on the pole, slide the lower loop up with your foot until it is just below the other; throw your weight on it and then move up the other loop. Continue this procedure until you reach the top.

USEFUL KNOTS WITH RINGS AND STRAPS

These sketches are of knots which are useful yet quickly arranged at any time when it may perhaps be desired to attach a strap to anything like a ring or a "D."

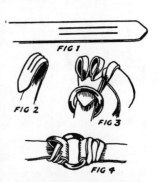

FIG 1

FIG 2

FIG 3

FIG 4

Figure 1 will show how the strap should first of all be split—the length of the split being about 3 times the width of the strap.

Sketch No. 2 shows the split strap doubled over so that the ends of the split will come together—when each of the loops is given a twist to the right.

The procedure is then as per figure 3, whilst figure 4 shows the strap drawn tight.

RAIN GAUGES, ETC.

HOME MADE RAIN GAUGES

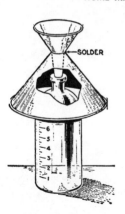

This sketch indicates how a good rain gauge can be made from a graduated bottle and two tin funnels. First remove the spout of the larger funnel and insert that of the smaller one into the opening and solder where indicated. Then place the spout of the small funnel in the neck of the bottle.

In order to determine the amount of rain, the bottle should be marked in fractions of an inch. This can be done with a file or by marking a scale on paper and gluing it to the glass; then coating it with varnish.

The diameter of the funnel should be the same as the inside of the bottle and the sides of the bottle must be parallel.

Bearing this in mind, any straight-sided bottle or receptacle will do, no matter whether round or square, provided the funnel is the same shape as the bottle or tin.

Of course, if an accurate measure is required, it is better to fix a small upright band around the outside edge of the upper funnel in order to prevent the rain-drops from splashing out.

The above gauge will give a rough estimate of the fall, but if a finer estimate is required, obtain a piece of 1 in. glass tube as shown in the right hand diagram, in which to pour the water from the other gauge.

25 inches in a one-inch glass gauge (inside diameter represents 1 inch of rainfall. It is then an easy matter to divide up this 25-in. tube into separate parts as shown. This scale can be marked by painting a strip of enamel down the tube and cutting the marks with a knife.

Measuring Glass

Another method of measuring is to obtain an ounce medicine glass with a funnel four and seven-tenths in diameter, as this will be needed in order that 10 points of rain on this surface will equal 1 ounce of water.

There is actually no necessity for the inverted funnel as shown in the accompanying sketch as a funnel inserted into the bottle or tin will do provided of course it is a good fit and allows no outside water to run into the bottle.

Also the object in having a funnel at all is mainly to prevent evaporation between showers. To read the gauge, hold the bottle between thumb and first finger with the water at the level of the eyes.

A HOME-MADE BAROMETER

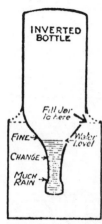

This will tell you roughly before you leave home in the morning what the day is likely to be. Take an old jam jar, and a clear glass pint bottle, with a tapering neck, and you will have all the apparatus necessary to make a fairly reliable weather glass.

Fill the jar to the brim with clear, cold water, then invert the bottle into the jar and the barometer is ready for use.

The water will rise up in the bottle neck, and this water level indicates the probable weather conditions—the higher the water, the better the prospects of fine weather.

When the water level falls near to the bottom of the bottle neck, much rain or a gale may be expected.

A sudden rise or fall in the water level means a quick change in the weather; a slow rise or fall a gradual change.

Place the weather glass in a cool spot outside the house, unaffected by the rays of the sun.

FINDING DIRECTION

TRUE NORTH—AND HOW TO FIND IT.

For surveying purposes, or if one desires to erect a weathercock or sundial, it is necessary to find the true north; therefore select a position where the sun shines for an hour or two both before and after 12 o'clock (noon).

First mount a piece of knitting needle or some other piece of straight steel vertically in a block of wood. Then on a piece of white paper, strike three or more concentric circles (shown as "a," "b" and "c" in the diagram), and fix the paper on the wood block by sticking the needle through the true centre of the circles.

Some time before noon lay the block, with paper in position, on a perfectly level table or box in the position selected, and fix it so that it cannot shift. Now watch the shadow of the knitting needle, and when it touches one of the circles, make a mark there with a pencil. After noon, watch the shadow of the needle again, and when it touches the same circle a second time, make another pencil mark.

This completes the observation. Connect the two marks with a line "A"-"B," bisect this line exactly and through the centre of it draw a line cutting through the common centre of the circles. **This is the true North** line at that particular locality, and it should be indicated by some permanent mark, such as two pegs in the ground, before the gear is removed.

A USEFUL METHOD OF OBTAINING DIRECTION BY DAY

Provided meticulous care is not necessary and one merely desires to obtain a general idea as to direction, a simple but very effective way of ascertaining the North can be made by holding a watch horizontally in front of one and then turning it so that the numerals denoting 12 o'clock are pointing directly at the sun.

North will be found by the direction indicated if an imaginary line be drawn from the centre of the watch to midway between 12 o'clock and the hour hand whilst the watch is being held in the position given above.

The illustration will better explain the idea and it can be relied upon at all times.

HOW TO FIND THE SOUTH BY NIGHT

There are several ways of finding the South (in the Southern Hemisphere) by the aid of the stars, and some of these are shown in the accompanying illustration.

(1) They form a rough semi - circle, the centre of which is the South Pole.

(2) South is also the centre of a line drawn from "Achernar" to midway between the two pointers.

(3) It is found by extending the long axis of the Southern Cross as indicated 4½ times from the lowest star on the Cross.

(4) It is also at the intersection of the lines drawn for the previous two methods (see sketch).

Do not mistake the Southern Cross—the two pointers are always in the same position.

TENNIS COURTS

HINTS ON MAKING A TENNIS COURT

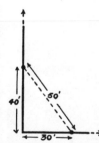

The size of a court is indicated below and plenty of room round it should be allowed for play. To make sure that the side lines are perfectly parallel, mark a point 40 ft. along one side line and one 30 ft. along the back line, when a line drawn between these two points should measure 50 ft.

To get the levels, use pegs and a spirit level mounted on a straight-edge, and when level at sides and ends, some tightly stretched string can be run across and the foundation levelled accordingly, making allowance for drainage. A good getaway for drainage would be, say, 3 to 4 in. to sides and ends, whilst any soakage should be intercepted or diverted to a good depth, especially near the back lines. Drainage is important when making a court.

Gravel Courts. About 3 in. of unsifted gravel should be levelled and allowed to settle down, then an inch of gravel sifted through 1-8 in. mesh should be laid down and spread with straight-edge (not rake), working from centre outwards. Leave till rain falls, then roll first with a light then a heavy roller.

Clay Courts. The preparation is the same as for gravel, but hard subsoil or cinders can be used instead of unsifted gravel. Cinders should be bound together with a clay mixture and rolled, then the clay topdressing must be dressed, pulverised and sifted evenly when dry. Allow to lie till rain falls, then when dry roll and fill in till ready for use.

Bitumen Surfaces should have solid foundations with 2 or 3 in. of screened gravel on top—watered well and left till damp. When the bitumen has been put on (say 2 parts bitumen to 1 part water) and well soaked in, about 1-8 in. of clean sifted sand should be spread over the surface, rolled with a heavy roller and left to dry. The surface can then be sprayed again (1 bitumen to 2 water); sift on more sand, mix well with stiff broom, making sure to leave no lumps or hollows. This coat should be at least ½ in. thick. Then sift on more sand as soon as possible until the surface is covered. It should then be rolled well after 2 or 3 hours and the surplus sand can be swept off after the preparation has been dried off for a week or so.

A HANDY SCRAPER FOR A TENNIS COURT

This sketch is of a very effective home-made scraper, made by one man from scrap, and is one which, if made, will save a lot of time each season when re-scraping is required.

The illustration will show how perhaps any scrap material could be used for the purpose, provided one has a couple of old wheels

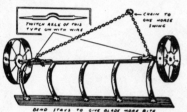

with a couple of axles, etc. The axles are bolted on and to give extra firmness some wire can be twitched round them as shown in the sketch.

This, or some similar arrangement, could be made quite easily with a little trouble, but it would be well worth while as it could be used for a number of purposes round the place, such as a manure scraper, etc.

To add weight when scraping, one could affix a bag or bags of earth or other material to the implement or someone could sit on the back of the blade.

HINTS ON MARKING A COURT

These are a few hints for the tennis court after the "rough" has been taken off and the time for marking has come :

(a) Clean gypsum, after being burnt in a vessel in the forge and powdered, is an ideal line marker and very cheap.

(b) Lines will last a long time if a shallow trench 1¼ in. wide and ½ in. deep is dug on every line and filled with a mixture of superphosphate made into paste with water.

(c) A cheap "gadget" for marking courts is made from a large kettle with the spout hammered in.

AN IDEA FOR A TENNIS COURT MARKER

This is a lime duster with which a tennis court can be easily and quickly marked off. It is an octagonal shaped container, the width of the line required, and is shaped somewhat like a wheel as indicated.

Pushed along the desired line, the bumping action of this container shakes out the lime, thus making it unnecessary to go over the line more than once. It can be fitted with a handle by using a heavy piece of wire as a fork at the container end, fixed to a length of broomstick.

Some such useful arrangement could perhaps also be combined with the ideas shown in other parts of this book under the heading of fertiliser distributors. (See pages 173 and 295.)

ANOTHER HANDY MARKER FOR TENNIS COURT

This is simple, cheap and effective. A large tin acts as a reservoir for the whitewash; a vertical slot 2 in. wide and 7 in. deep being cut in the front, 1½ inches from the bottom, to take a portion of the large wheel.

Pieces of wood bolted on at the sides and bottom of the tin are used to strengthen and to carry the two small wheels. Suitable handles are attached at the upper corners of the tin.

Two wheels to distribute the white-wash are cut from timber.

The large one is 12 in. diameter and 1½ in. thick and is secured by brackets of strap iron fastened to the tin with gutter bolts and bored near the ends to carry a small spindle. The spindle should be about 5 in. from the top of the tin, so that one inch of the wheel is through the slot.

The smaller wheel is 6 in. in diameter, and revolves upon an axle running through the tin from side to side.

Some arrangement for keeping the wheels in close contact will be found necessary, and the simple device shown will be sufficient. Stout wire bent in a "U" with the ends hooked through

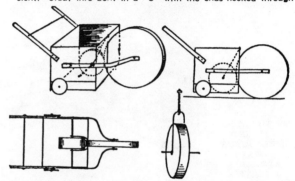

the axle, is fitted with an eye-bolt and nut. The fitting from the back wheel of a bicycle does the job well. If necessary, the edges of the wheels can be covered with felt.

HANDY GATES AND FASTENERS

USEFUL TYPES OF HOME-MADE GATES

The following are sketches of a few types of home-made gates which give a variety of ideas. The first type (see first 4 illustrations) is simple, effective, and rather an improvement on

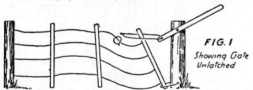

FIG. 1
Showing Gate Unlatched

the usual gate of this variety. The bottom catch is the same as in most of these gates, but instead of the customary lever used to keep the wires taut and the gate shut, the one used in this gate swings on the fence post, being attached by a bolt (see fig. 1).

One end is longer than the other.

To the shorter end (which, when the gate is shut, is at right angles to the post and on the opposite side to the gate) a long loop of wire is fastened and passed over the end support.

To shut the gate, the lever is pulled downwards on the loop and secured with an ordinary wire loop to the top wire of the gate (see figs. 2, 3, and 4, which will give details of the full movement).

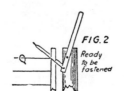

FIG. 2
Ready to be fastened

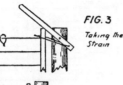

FIG. 3
Taking the Strain

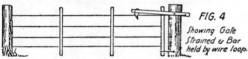

FIG. 4
Showing Gate Strained & Bar held by wire loop.

ANOTHER SIMPLE HOME-MADE GATE

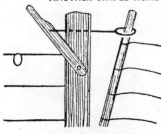

This sketch is a slight variation of the same idea except the latch is different. In this, the lever has a pivot bolt at the end and the loop is attached as indicated.

The wire is passed through a hole in the gate post before forming the loop for the gate; this helps to hold the lever steady, and a quarter move attaches it to the fence wire. The loop is merely passed over the gate post, the lever is pressed down and the handle inserted in the loop, when a good tight gate is obtained.

ANOTHER SOMEWHAT SIMILAR GATE FASTENER

The difference in this gate is in the attachment to the fence. "A" is a metal ring big enough to fit over the gate upright. From the ring a chain or length of twisted wire passes through a hole in the strainer post to an eyebolt "B" fixed in the strong lever "C."

When the lever is pressed down the gate is drawn taut.

Another eye-bolt "D" hangs on a length of chain when not in use, and is plugged into the hole "E" to keep the lever down when the gate is closed. It is quite a useful and efficient arrangement.

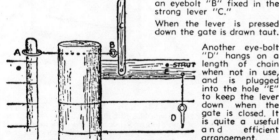

A PIVOTED HORSE-SHOE MAKES A GOOD GATE LATCH

This is a useful idea for almost any type of gate. The difficulty of locking or latching or holding the gate tight so that it will not swing or give easily may be overcome by the use of an old shoe as indicated here. It is bolted on to one section of the gate so that it may be swung over to engage a large staple in the opposite section. If it is a wire fence, the staple can be in the gate portion and the horse-shoe pivoted on to the strainer post.

A GATE FASTENER FROM OLD TYRE

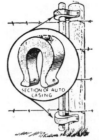

This sketch shows a piece of old motor tyre put to use as a fastener. Instead of wire loops, two cross-pieces of tyre are nailed to the gatepost in the positions shown.

They should be at such a distance apart that when the top of the sapling is pushed up through the upper loop as far as the wire will allow, the bottom of the pole will just slip into the lower loop when it is pressed down a little with the foot. The flexibility of the tyre allows this to be done, whilst such tyre loops last indefinitely in all weathers.

GATE FASTENER FROM PRONGED STICK

This is a slight variation, but a good one. It is made from a small forked sapling and an old iron bolt or rod. The sapling is shaped to fit round the gatepost, allowing sufficient space in the fork for the gate upright. The fastener is held to the post by means of the bolt through fastener and post.

To hold the fastener so that the cattle cannot lift it, a sliding loop of wire is fitted round the top wire of the gate, and is slid over the end of the fastener when the gate is closed, thus holding it securely in place.

ANOTHER WIRE GATE TIGHTENER

This is yet another way to make a wire gate fastener. The piece of wood on top is 4½ inches wide and approximately 20 in. long.

Just fasten it to the gatepost by means of a hinge and it will give a good purchase in tightening the gate. A hole in the wood would, of course, be quite a good idea as the gatepost could then be fixed that way.

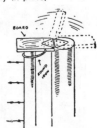

ANOTHER WAY OF KEEPING GATE TAUT

This is an excellent idea. Merely fix an old cart or motor spring in position as shown. The main leaf, with the eyes for the shackle bolts, should be used. Holes are bored through the post in line with the eyes of the spring, and a rod, having one end bent to a hook is slipped through each hole, after which the other end is bent at right angles to engage the eye of the spring.

When the gate is closed, the inner ends of the rods are pulled inwards against the spring and hooked around the sapling of the gate. The tension of the spring will hold the gate firm.

HANDY GATES AND FASTENERS

HANDY TYPES OF BIGGER GATES

A NEAT GATE MADE OF BATTENS—With details of Wooden Latch

This is easily made, being bolted together throughout. All the material used is 3 x 1 in. battens, except the top rail and back stile, for which 6 x 1 is used. The sketch shows the method of construction.

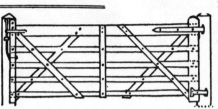

The rails are sandwiched between the front and back stile boards, double battens, of course, being employed for these uprights. A bolt is put through each joint, making the rails secure. The cross-braces are fixed as shown—3 on each side, the centre pair vertical.

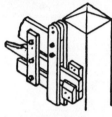

The latch shown is a "shop" one, but this expense may be saved by building one of odds and ends left over from the main job—this latch is shown in the smaller sketch.

A block should be fitted below the latch above the second rail in order to keep it level.

The gate is 9 ft. wide overall, but for an existing opening it must, of course, be dimensioned to suit. Four feet six inches to 5 ft. is quite a suitable height. The timber required for a gate 9 ft. x 5 ft. is as follows:—3 x 1—4/9ft. long; 4/5 ft. 6 in.; 2/4 ft. 6 in.; 2/5 ft.; 6 x 1—2/5 ft.; 1/9 ft. Total, a little under 30 superficial feet.

Wooden Gate Latch.

OTHER HANDY TYPES OF BIGGER GATES

A cheaply made 12 ft. double gate is indicated first of all. All the timber is 3 x 1 hardwood, bolted together. The rails are bolted between double ends. The gate is light, and one of the chief points is

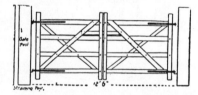

that separate gate posts are provided. It is not good practice to hang a gate on the straining post of a wire fence unless it is very big and so stayed that it does not give.

The second sketch is of a different type, 11 ft. wide, relatively light and rigid. A solid gate post is essential, because the gate

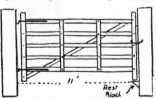

cannot swing freely unless the post is immovable. Hinges should be of the hook and eye variety.

Another point worth mentioning is to hang the gate with a slight swing into the closed position, and to put a sliding block under the hanging end of the gate close up to the post. The gate should clear this block, but it becomes useful if the gate should sag a little, particularly in wet weather. One end should be 4 x 4 hardwood, and the other 4 x 2, whilst the rails can be 4 x 2 oregon, mortised into both ends. The two uprights are also of the same material.

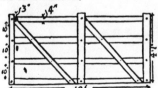

No. 3 illustration is another type of swinging gate, 10 ft. wide. The timber is 4 x 1, and every joint is bolted with 3-8 in. bolts.

The three main uprights 4 ft. 1 in. high are doubled and the four cross-pieces put in between, 10 in. apart, the top one being 3 in. down. The two stays need only be single pieces. Given a coat of white lead and oil, this will last for many years.

A HINGELESS GATE

A block of wood about 2 ft. long is sunk in the ground next to the gate post, with 3 in. left above ground. A lag screw is screwed into the block and the square head cut off.

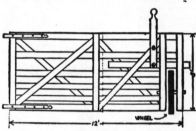

A hole is drilled into the bottom end of the gate, so that the headless screw fits into it. The gate is hung from the top by boring a hole in a piece of 6 x 2 board nailed across the gate post. Another lag screw is screwed into the top of the stile through the hole in the board (as shown).

A USEFUL ROLLING GATE

This shows an easy way to swing a heavy gate and it can be fixed to any gate. Take a fair sized wheel and set it under the free end of the gate, as shown. For this particular gate, about 52 ft. of 4 x 1 x 12 timber is required. This includes a spring latch that allows a rider to open the gate without dismounting. An ingenious person can make his hinges out of old car springs, or to make it easier, an old car wheel can be used at the end of the gate, as shown. This will carry the weight of the gate and, at the same time, prolong its life.

HINTS ON HANGING A GATE

All gate posts should be set and braced. For position, and before the gateposts are actually set, hang the gate on the posts after the holes are dug and before they are filled in. Adjustments can then be made and when they are made and the gate is in the right position, brace the gate and posts as shown, supporting the gate from beneath with blocks. Leave it supported until the holes are filled and the concrete is sufficiently set.

Fig. 1 shows open holes and gate braced.

Another way of providing proper distance is to get the "width of opening" from manufacturer's catalogue then cut two straight boards to the exact length and use these to brace the posts correctly apart in their open holes as in fig. 2. The twisted wire brace will hold the spacer

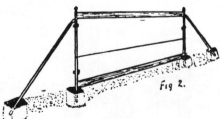

boards in place against the two posts. Then fill the post holes, and let the concrete set. Some like this plan best because it eliminates the necessity of handling and propping the gate and avoids the possibility of moving the posts before the concrete has actually set.

HANDY GATES AND FASTENERS

A SELF-CLOSING GATE

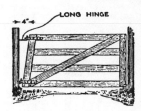

A good self-closing gate can be made like any other gate, except that the top bar should be 4 in. shorter than the bottom; also, the upper hinge pin is longer than the lower by the same length.

It will be seen that whenever the gate is swung open, the latch end will be elevated, so that it will swing shut of its own weight, no matter how much or how little it is opened.

A SELF-CLOSING HOUSE GATE

This is an excellent idea for a gate which is near the house and often used. A hole is bored in the centre of each cross-piece so that the gate can be swung on an iron pipe held at top and bottom.

Chains, from the top cross-piece, support the gate at the proper distance from the ground. When pushed open they raise the gate slightly, and its own weight causes it to close rapidly.

A strong cross support at the top will keep the fence tight and make bracing of the gateposts unnecessary.

ANOTHER SELF-CLOSING GATE

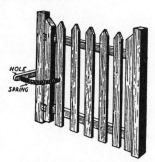

The sketch is self-explanatory. There is a curved rod inside the spring which should be about one-quarter of a true circle, but if the workmanship is not very precise, a slotted hole in the buffer piece will do very well instead of a round hole.

The spring can be made of anything which may be available, such as fencing wire, etc. The posts should be solid and the gate as heavy as desired. A double spring so built will, of course, make for extra strength and springiness.

A USED BED FOR A GATE

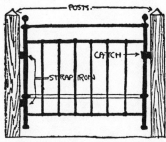

Articles such as an old iron bed, which has passed its usefulness, can be made into a very good gate. A coat of green enamel makes a world of difference to its appearance, and it will last a long time.

With loops made of scrap iron for hinges, it answers the purpose admirably.

An ordinary latch can be fitted. **This idea suggests other novel** ways of making gates. For instance, a pair of wheels could well be fitted to the side posts on a swivel to provide quite a good swinging type of gate.

AN INGENIOUS HINGE FOR A SELF-CLOSING GATE

This is rather a good idea. The necessary gadgets are made from hoop iron. There are no springs needed, and although one can be fitted (as shown at "D") to stop the gate from swinging, if necessary.

The upper hinge is of the ordinary staple type, the closing being done by the lower hinge, which causes the gate to hang out of plumb when it is opened.

It will swing open either way, and is particularly handy when both hands are occupied. The portion "A" is screwed to the gatepost, the other section "B" being clamped to the gate itself. It is very simple to construct and will be found quite effective.

AN AUTOMATIC GATE

This is an idea for anyone who wishes to avoid opening and shutting gates every time they enter or leave. To make this swing gate, the following is needed:—Outside uprights, 4 in. pipe, 16 ft. above ground; middle uprights, 6 in. pipe, 16 ft. above ground; cross beam, 2 in. x 8 in. timber, chains crossing at centre post.

When the front bumper of a car strikes one side of the gate it is swung open. The chains wind about the centre post, causing the gate to lift. It closes by its own weight.

The gate is attached to the centre post with U-bolts, so that it will turn freely. The larger the centre post, the harder the gate will be to open, and the quicker it will close.

To prevent the gate from swinging too far one could easily erect a small stopper or strut from the main pole, or get into the habit of just touching the gate sufficiently to give it the correct momentum.

ANOTHER WAY OF KEEPING DOORS OR GATES SHUT

This is specially useful for any gates over 6 feet high. The pulley is made from some round wood, shaped to suit, and secured, by means of a spindle, to one of the door or gate posts.

Actually the sketch needs no explanation. A strap or cord is used, from which a weight is suspended, and this is attached to one corner of the door or gate post and then passed over the pulley. The door must, of course, be well hinged, so that the weight will be able to close the door easily.

One other method of attaching the pulley is to use an ordinary eye-bolt standing out, say, about 3 inches from the post.

HANDY GATES AND FASTENERS

WOODEN DOOR LOCKS
Some Simple Concealed Types

The wooden door fastening, as usually seen, is a crude affair, incapable of keeping out intruders. However, a little trouble can make them so that they can be operated only by those who know the secret.

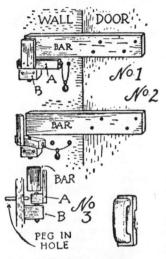

Numbers 1, 2 and 3 show a secret lock that few people could open unless they happened to know how. The bar fastened to the door is held by a swinging lever "A," which is bolted to a heavy block "B." The block "B" is fastened securely to the wall.

In No. 2, the lock is shown open. This is accomplished simply by pushing a small peg through a hole in the wall; the point of the peg pushes the lever away from the bar, and the door swings free.

There is a cord tied to a screw-eye at the end of the lever which passes through a second hole beside the first one. The other end of the cord is fastened to a ring on the other side of the wall. A pull on the ring locks the door. On the inside the slack of the cord is taken up by a small weight which keeps the ring on the outside pulled tight against the wall.

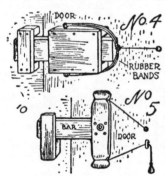

The small diagram alongside **No. 3** shows a handle for the outside which can be placed to conceal the holes in the door. This handle is fastened to a block, and the block is held to the outside by a single bolt near the upper end, so that it can be swung to one side. If the string which comes through the hole is fastened to a ring, the bottom of the block should be hollowed slightly to make room for this.

The lock shown in **No. 4** has a sliding bolt held in place by two stout rubber bands. These bands are looped over screw-eyes. A string is tied to the screw-eye in the end of the bolt; the other end goes through a hole in the door some distance away and is tied to a ring on the outside. The ring can easily be concealed under a wooden handle.

Lock No. 5 is one of the easiest to make. However, few people will be able to work it if the end of the string on the outside of the door is concealed.

When this upper string is released, the lower string, which passes through a screw-eye and has a weight on the end of it, closes the lock. The bar swings on a bolt passed through the crosspiece.

AN ANIMAL PROOF GATE LATCH

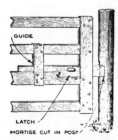

Another simple latch proof gate against animal intelligence consists of a notched wooden bar, fitted against a similar notch in one of the rails of the gate. This is indicated in the accompanying sketch.

This bar is provided with a hand hole, and the end slides into a mortise cut into the gate post. The latch is held in position by guides fastened to each side of the gate.

It is remarkable how many gates horses and cattle learn to open, which is so often very inconvenient, but the use of any of these ideas should help prevent same.

OTHER ANIMAL PROOF GATE LATCHES

The "Pastoral Review" set out a number of sketches of various fasteners which have been found satisfactory by many farmers.

No. 1. "A" represents a piece of stout iron with both ends driven into the gate-head somewhere about half-way between the top and the bottom. "B" is a similar piece of iron, but it only has one end in the gate or post, as the case may be. "C" is the iron link which connects the two.

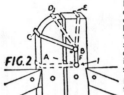

Of course, "A" must be threaded through "C" before being driven in. The link must be sufficiently loose to lie flat against the wood when the gate is closed, and also to slip over the top of "B."

No. 2. This, if a little more elaborate than the above, is neater and quite as effective. The only drawback to it is that it may be puzzling to strangers. This is quite compensated for by the fact that horses and cattle find it impossible to manipulate. It is as effective on a single as a double gate.

Instead of the clasp being fixed in the usual way, a slot is cut, as shown at "F," 3 in. x $\frac{3}{4}$ in. through the gate or post, so that the $\frac{1}{2}$ in. bolt will slide freely up and down when lifted by the hand. The clasp will not rise further than "A" unless the bolt end is lifted as far as "B," which will allow the clasp to make the circle C, D, E, and permit the gate to be opened.

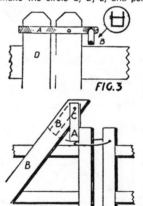

No. 3 is a simpler fastener. The fastener "A" is fixed to the right hand head by means of a bolt. "B" represents the locking apparatus. It is made of flat iron like "A," and is hung very loosely from the end of "A," quite close to the top rail. When "A" is lifted to open gate, "B," unless moved with the other hand, is brought down on to the rail, and makes an effective lock. When the gate is being opened, it is a simple matter to toss "B" on to the top of "A," where it will stay until put down again.

No. 4 is a simple device, which can be attached to a single or double gate; it is fastened by a loop at the top of the head, as shown. A short bar "A" is hung from the bar by means of the bolt "C." This bolt is a shade smaller than the augur hole through the two bars, and so allows "A" to swing freely. "A" must be sufficiently heavy to always drop into place automatically.

ANOTHER TYPE OF STOCK-PROOF GATE LATCH

This is a familiar type with the addition of a bolt working in a groove in one of the cleats in which the sliding bar runs. The small diagram shows an end view of the cleat, with the bolt in position. The bolt is simply a plain piece of iron rod bent into a right-angled hook at top end. A notch in the top edge of the sliding bar just opposite where the bolt comes when the slide is fastened, receives the hook of the bolt. The bolt projects an inch or so beyond the bottom of the cleat, so that it can be held up by the finger until the bar is slid back. When the bar is pushed into the latch again, it automatically drops into place.

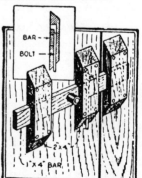

HANDY GATES AND FASTENERS

A SIMPLE AUTOMATIC GATE

This sketch shows a simple self-closing gate, useful for giving access to a paddock or milking yard. It consists simply of a piece of 4 x 2 timber or a fairly stout sapling, with a suitable length of chain.

It can be pushed open from the house side without using the hands. The wooden bar is pivoted to the bottom of the gatepost and held in position by the chain, as shown, so that it projects diagonally; the top end resting against the upper part of the opposite post.

A bolt or peg near the top of the pivot acts as a stop to prevent the gate from being thrown back too far.

The bar must, of course, be pivoted on the side of the post on which the stock are located, so that they cannot push it open.

EASY METHOD OF KEEPING GATE OPEN

One way of saving quite a number of steps is shown here. Any farm gate can be kept open by a hook which slips into the eye bolt which is fastened to the gatepost on which the gate is hinged.

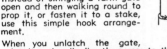

Instead of swinging a farm gate open and then walking round to prop it, or fasten it to a stake, use this simple hook arrangement.

When you unlatch the gate, swing it and walk directly across to the other post and slip the hook into the eye bolt. The hook is attached to a bar clamped on to the gate.

GATES WHICH ADMIT PEOPLE BUT BAR ANIMALS

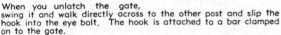

This gate is a useful one and it will permit a person to pass through easily, but animals cannot get through.

On each side of the fence, and about 3 ft. apart, drive two posts approx. 6 ft. high. How this is done is shown in the illustration.

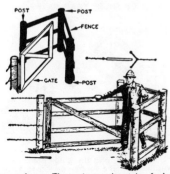

These posts should be placed so that when the gate is open, it will come right up to the posts, but will not go past them. Either wire or boards will do as a fence. The gate need not be fastened, for it cannot be left open.

MAKING A FIRM GATEWAY FOR MUDDY PATCH

There is very often a very muddy patch in the gateway which is always unsightly and a cause of annoyance. This little idea will help get over this difficulty. It has cured the trouble on the farm where one farmer tried it.

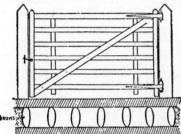

It is another use for old oil drums. Obtain a few of them, then dig a pit between the gateposts and, after knocking out the tops and bottoms of the drums for the water to run through, place them on cement, in the pit, and then cement over the top, using medium gravel and cement. Such a gateway should last for ever.

TWO ADDITIONAL POSTS MAKE STOCK-PROOF GATE

This is just another idea showing how to make a gateway which will stop horses and other large animals from going through and yet it will permit the quick and easy passage of people.

The illustration will show how the mere addition of two posts will give this advantage, the chief advantage being that one does not have to bother about stopping to open and close the gate as one goes through. The arrangement of posts is clearly shown.

A HANDY GAP IN FENCE ALLOWS PEOPLE TO PASS, BUT PREVENTS ANIMALS FROM GOING THROUGH

This type of opening in the fence also does away with the necessity of a gate. Cut such a gap in the fence about 2 ft. long, then 18 in. from this, and on the pasture side, build a fence panel about 8 ft. long so that it laps by the gap about 3 ft. at each end.

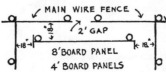

A short panel across the end of the 18 in. passage, as shown, will effectively turn horses, cattle and calves and will still allow anyone to slip through easily. To turn pigs and sheep, a board partition can be nailed into the turn of the passage as shown in later illustrations (see pig section).

AN EASY-TO-BUILD NON-SAGGING GATE

This can be easily made. It is constructed of only 4 pieces of 2 x 4 stock, yet it is unusually strong. Woven or barb wire is stretched between the end pieces, the gate being swung by means of a hoop and strap hinge.

A HORSEBACK GIRL'S GATE

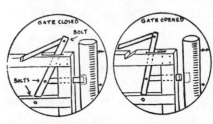

This gate enables one to open it without getting out of the saddle. The only iron on the gate is 3 bolts and a piece of strap iron for the upright. It may be opened and closed from the saddle and it will be found much handier if the gate is made to swing both ways.

A GATE OF VARIABLE WIDTHS

This is a very handy type of gate for any farm. It is a wooden gate which can be made of variable length which will swing to close either of two openings of different width. Such a gate is easy to make.

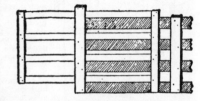

If unplaned 6 x 1 boards are used in the main gate, which closes the smaller opening, the slide extension illustrated here may be of planed boards 4 in. wide and 7-8 in. thick. Pieces of lath laid under one of the cross members at the back of the extension will give slots between the cross members that will clear the main gate boards and make the extension slide easily. Wheels on the bottom might also assist.

HANDY GATES AND FASTENERS

A USEFUL DOOR HANDLE

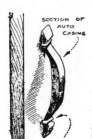

This illustration shows how a section of tyre casing can be utilised to make a very useful door handle.

The casing is cut in pieces as indicated and then fastened on with wire staples with the ends twisted at the rear.

HAND HOLE TO ENABLE DOOR TO BE LOCKED FROM EITHER SIDE

This is a useful idea for any door which is required to be locked from either side. The hole should be cut directly under the lock and should be just large enough  to take the hand. Being this size it will not permit anyone to manipulate it with tools or to break the lock.

AN IDEA FOR HOLDING GATE OPEN

A piece of board about 1 ft. long is notched as at "A." Pivot it loosely to the side of a stake by means of a bolt. Drive a nail into the stake at "B" to act as a stop and to keep it horizontal. A small spiral is hung at "C." This serves to keep the arm up against stop "B." It also allows the catch to be depressed. The bottom bar of the gate should strike the latch just above the bevelled point.

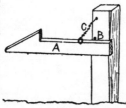

A BURGLAR PROOF BOLT

Some bolts are not burglar proof, and anyone with a little skill can insert a hacksaw, turn the bolt, and slide it out of its socket. One way to make them burglar-proof is to fix a block of wood in the space behind the bolt, as shown here.

Making a Bolt Burglar-Proof.

A MOVEABLE CENTRE POST FOR WIDE GATE

Where implements of unusual width have to be moved from paddock to paddock, ordinary gates are often not wide enough, but the necessary width may be secured by having two ordinary gates with a centre post between them.

This centre post, instead of being planted immoveably in the ground, is so fitted that it can be easily taken away as required, and replaced quickly after the implement has passed through.

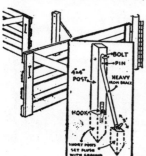

One way is the sunken oil drum filled with concrete with a socket moulded in the concrete to receive the post.

Another way is to plant two stub posts with the tops flush with the surface of the ground, as shown. The centre post is squared off at the bottom and fitted with an angle hook, which hooks into an eye on the top of one of the stub posts. A heavy iron brace is fastened to the top of the moveable post, and a bolt and a steady pin, the other end of the brace being curved to fit into an eye on the top of the second stub post. When the gate is to be opened to the full double width, the bolt is unscrewed, when it is easy to bend the post over and unhook it from its supports.

A USEFUL DOOR CATCH

This easily made spring catch will save time in opening and shutting many doors and gates, as it can either be merely pushed or pulled open as the case may be.

Its construction is clearly shown. The circular spring indicated should be made from springy steel.

Spring Catch for door.

A DOOR STOP FROM HORSESHOE

A very efficient door stop for any door may be made from an old horseshoe from which the toe calk has been worn off or removed.

Although serviceable without alteration, the shoe may be made more secure by fitting a couple of sections of hose over the heel calks so that this portion of the stop rests on the rubber.

HANDY GATES FOR THE SHEEP YARD

This is just an ordinary gateway with certain additions as shown. Preferably, some rounded timber with a diameter of approximately 4 in. are used and these are supported by strong wood or iron pivots. In some cases rubber or other material is used braced firmly into position.

When fixing, see that this addition is of a lesser diameter than the gate posts, otherwise the gate will be difficult to hang and it will not swing right back against the fence as it should do.

OTHER HANDY TYPES OF SHEEP YARD GATES

It is very often rather difficult to handle swinging gates when there are many sheep to be handled, and therefore types of gates as shown here will help in this direction.

One gate lifts on a pivot and the other slides across the opening.

The lifting gate is pivoted at the bottom corner of one of the gateposts, and the guide post is set a foot or two back and parallel with the fence, serving to keep the gate in line when lifted. Some method should then be devised to keep the gate firmly in position when shut; one simple method being to erect a second post parallel with the other so as to form a sort of slot for the gate to drop into.

For the sliding gate (below), the top and bottom rails run through two hoop-iron guides fixed on to the posts as shown, and the gate is supported on two rollers, one being attached to the post under the centre bar of the gate, and the other to the gate itself, running on the bottom rail of the fence. To keep the

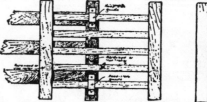

gate firmly shut when not in use, an ordinary catch can be used or a loop of wire or any other fasteners mentioned in other sections of this book. Either of these gates will be found very handy indeed.

HANDY GATES AND FENCING HINTS

OPENINGS IN THE FENCE

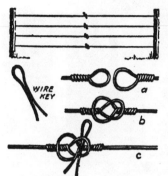

It is often useful to be able to get through a fence in a paddock with a team and implements when the gate is some distance away, or rather narrow for the harvester, etc.

Sketch No. 1 shows how, by leaving out a post, thus making a longer panel, the wires are cut in the middle of the panel; loops are put in the ends of all the wires and keys made from odd ends of wire.

The wire strainers are then employed and the loop of one strand is slipped through its opposite number and the key inserted. The sketches show the closed fence and the various stages in closing the gap after it has been opened.

An opening can be made in this fence in a few seconds and secured again just as quickly.

Sketch No. 2 gives the same idea with a different knot. The desired strain having been put upon the wire, it is cut at its centre between the grippers, leaving two loose ends. At the ends of one wire make a small loop, the size of which varies according to the gauge of the wire.

In 8 gauge wire, the loop should be about 1 in. long (inside measurement), a smaller loop being required for finer gauges of wire.

In the other wire, make a bend as shown, at a point about a quarter of an inch short of the loop. By pulling on the lever, the bend is brought opposite the loop, and is then inserted into the loop and prevented from coming out again by putting a short piece of wire through the bend and across the loop.

The reason for making the bend one quarter of an inch short of the loop is so that the wire, when joined, shall be at full tension, no slack being allowed to go back.

IDEAS FOR FENCE OPENINGS—WIDENING A GATEWAY

Where it is necessary to move wide machines from one paddock to another, much time is often lost in unyoking, etc. It is a good idea have a removable panel of fence at the latch side of the gate so that a wide opening is always available when needed, and this method will be found suitable.

A section of piping or a length of hollow log is sunk into the ground to a depth of about 2 feet, below the spot where the post should stand, and the butt of the post is adzed down to fit fairly

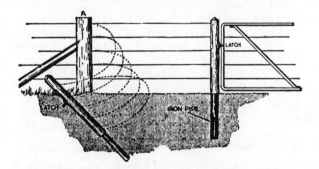

tightly into it. By this means it is possible to have an extra width of, say, 10 or 12 feet. The strainer post would, of course, be placed at "A" instead of at the side of the gate.

A USEFUL LOOPHOLE IN FENCE

This is a useful idea which will prevent one's clothes from being caught up in a barb wire fence when trying to get through.

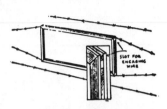

It is a double frame, which slips in between two strands of the wire and through which a passage can be made from one enclosure to the next without engaging the barbs.

One precaution seems necessary. It should not be placed opposite any tempting mouthful of green feed or the old cow, reaching for the green feed, and finding she was also protected, might put on enough strain to wreck the fence.

GATE MADE IN FENCE WITHOUT CUTTING WIRES

Farmers often loosen the wires of a fence from a few posts and weight them down to make a temporary opening and one like this can easily be made into a permanent gate which the casual observer would hardly notice.

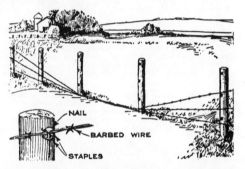

Instead of fastening the wire to the posts in the usual manner, staples are driven horizontally on each side of the wire. The staples are set into the post far enough to leave an eye through which a nail is inserted to hold the wire to the post.

The wires are kept down by hooking them over nails driven into the posts near the bottom.

A HOME-MADE MOTOR BY-PASS

A handy gate always open to motors yet closed to animals can be made as follows:—At a place where drainage is available, dig a pit 7 ft. long, 6 ft. wide, and 18 in. deep.

Lay two rail sleepers or their equivalent across the pits as indicated at one end by "A." Lay five 2 x 6's—"B" in the illustra-

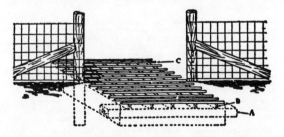

tion—on edge along the pit; notch them into the foundation timbers at each end and spike them solidly, so as to make a strong and durable framework.

Across these 2 x 6's, nail 13 or more poles as shown at "C." Leave space enough between these so that animals will step through if they attempt to pass.

HANDY GATES AND FENCING HINTS

SIMPLE GATE REPAIRS

Time will be profitably spent if you periodically check up to see that all cracks are filled with putty, and all surfaces are well painted or oiled to prevent the entry of moisture into the joints with its resultant distortion and rot. Once a gate has dropped it is difficult to effect a permanent repair just by nailing, but a satisfactory solution to the problem will be found in the idea presented.

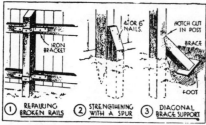

The gate should be taken off the post and laid on a flat surface, so that all joints can be knocked together and the gate squared up. Then you can stretch and bolt down a 1 in. strip of heavyweight galvanised hoop iron, diagonally from corner to corner on both sides of the gate. Fig. 1 shows the back view. It will be necessary to drill ¼ in. holes about 1 in. from each end of the hoop iron and at a point where it crosses the centre rail, so that ¼ in. bolts can be driven through the iron strip and the gate to brace it rigidly. The nuts on the bolts, with washers underneath, should be placed on the inner side of the gate. If it is not practical to arrange an iron brace on each side of the gate, you should place two strips X-fashion on the inside surface.

Fig. 2 shows the correct position for a T-hinge on a gate. Stand the gate in its position with small blocks underneath to keep it the desired distance above the ground, and then you can screw on the hinges with the knuckle placed centrally over the space between the gate and the post. If a gate post is so decayed that it will not hold the hinge screws, the damaged part can be cut out with a chisel, and the recess filled in with a new piece of wood.

If it becomes necessary to replace a gate post, the construction for the bracing as shown in fig. 3 will be ideal for the resistance of strain in all directions. There is no need to smooth the surfaces, but the construction should be carefully carried out to make a strong job, when the braces are nailed in position on the post and the foot.

PUTTING YOUR FENCES IN ORDER

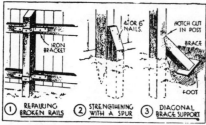

Fig. 1 shows a very simple but effective method of repairing a broken or rotted fencing rail.

Bend a substantial piece of sheet iron to conform to the shape of the post, and then fix it on the rail and the post with a few screws. The iron should be painted to prevent it from rusting.

If a post rots off near the ground level there is no need to replace the post, as a repair can be easily effected by digging a hole at least 2 ft. deep at the back of the damaged post to take a spur. Generally a 3 or 4 ft. x 4 in. x 3 in. spur, with a long tapered bevel, as shown in fig. 2, will be ideal.

The bevel, as well as casting off rain, simplifies the driving of nails to make a secure job. You should use nails at least 4 in. in length, or, if you wish, bolts can replace the nails. After fixing the post and spur together, the hole can be gradually filled with earth, which is rammed down tightly round the spur with a square-ended piece of wood, or else you can use concrete for the filling.

The diagonal brace of 4 in. x 3 in. redgum, footed with a wooden block (fig. 3), is very useful for supporting a post which persists in tilting over. The upper end should fit and be nailed into a notch in the post some inches above the ground level, and the lower end should be sunk into the ground 15 in. or more away from the post.

It is a wise precaution to coat all sunken timber with tar or creosote to resist decay.

IDEAS FOR FLOOD-PROOF FENCES

Fences across creeks, etc., are often damaged by floating debris during flood weather. In the **first sketch** it shows how this can be overcome by an anchor post in the centre of the ditch or creek where the fence wires might tend to lift.

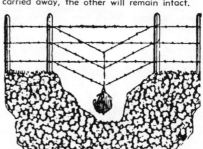

The wires are strung in the usual manner and an extra wire is then stretched from the adjacent posts as shown. Better still would be this idea with all wires ending on a separate post which is placed on the bank alongside the regular fence post, i.e., two posts on each bank —one for the regular fence and one for the small section over the creek. These posts should be set close together—if then, by any chance, the one in the creek is carried away, the other will remain intact.

In the **second sketch,** the main fence wires of the are run straight over the top of the gully and a temporary fence is built across and anchored to an extra post on each side and with a heavy stone attached as shown. When there is a heavy rush of water during heavy rain, one of the posts may go, but usually one remains, and the wire and the rock that weighs the fence down is usually found along the bank. The actual fence is unharmed.

A SPECIAL WIDE GATE FOR SHEEP

The "Pastoral Review" gives details of this excellent gate, which is easy to make and simple in operation. It can be made to any width (18 ft. being the popular size), and, if well built, it should be useful on a main receiving yard, especially when handling ewes and lambs. It is different from others in its method of opening and closing, and it easily replaces itself as part of the yard fence.

If the top wire is 3 ft. 6 in. from ground, the gate uprights should be 7 ft., i.e., the length of the uprights should be double the height of the top wire. This wire runs through a hole in the centre of each upright without being tied to same—it remains the continuous top wire of the yard. Wires A, B, C and D are secured to the uprights in the usual way. If netting is not used, more wires will be required.

E and F are diagonal wires which keep the gate square and taut. At G, a few links of old hobble chain, with the swivel link intact, is a good idea, as this acts as a hinge. Then a strong wire, or 2 strands of lighter gauge, is taken from the chain through the top hole of posts H and I and strained to the bottom of the next yard post.

At J on each upright a small length of light chain is fastened, to hook on to the fence post at K, thus allowing the sheep to pass underneath as the gate is parallel to the ground when opened.

Uprights are spaced in accordance with the fence posts and drop

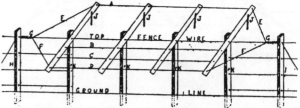

alongside these when the gate is lowered. The gate closes on the inside of yard and the uprights are secured at the bottom of the fence posts to avoid any yielding to pressure by sheep. A tie of soft wire is preferable for this as chains rattle and frighten sheep when contacting in yard.

HANDY GATES AND FENCES

ORNAMENTAL GATES AND FENCES FOR GARDEN AND HOME

To those who contemplate erecting something a little different from the usual, the following designs will probably be of help.

The first type is more suitable to the larger type of home—it consisting of concrete, brick or stone pillars supporting the gate itself. An ornamental effect on the top of the pillars puts the finishing touches to it.

Hinges can be set in concrete as shown on page 179, whilst the gate itself can be made to any pattern desired.

The second type is merely a quaint and attractive gate with a boxed tree or shrub decorating each post —the latter being of stone.

This also suggests many designs which can be made from plain wooden boards nailed together and cut as desired.

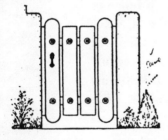

The third is another design and is a sample of one of many patterns that can be worked out by almost any handyman and which should not be difficult to copy.

It can be made of timber or of iron fashioned on the spot. This particular one is of plain appearance and inexpensive to make but the idea suggests other and more elaborate designs if so desired.

The fourth illustration is of another pattern easily made and at very little cost.

It would suit a house with a low fence almost as well as any other type of fence.

The last is a novel and very useful fence or gate for any spot that is required to shelter any plants, etc.

It is also ornamental and simple to construct, and it is adaptable to fences of low design or for any height which might be required.

Its construction does not need any detailed description, as the sketch will show the method of procedure quite plainly.

This column indicates some useful and ornamental types of fences which may prove of interest to those who contemplate such fencing. They are all a departure from the ordinary and any of them might suit one's particular needs.

The first is a good type of light fence with plenty of strength to withstand stock, etc.

The different height of the alternate pickets gives a very pleasing appearance — the crosspieces, besides giving extra

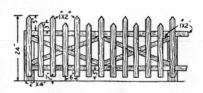

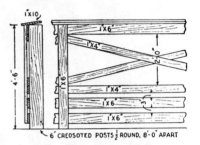

6" CREOSOTED POSTS ½ ROUND, 8'-0" APART

fence, with end section of post also shown.

This fence has three horizontals with pickets of alternate heights reaching above the centrepiece, and when seen in length presents a good-looking and very strong type of fence, somewhat similar to sketch 1, but with

the extra top rail. **Number 4 illustration** is one type of lattice fence— this one being of alternate wide and narrow pieces which can be built to any height, whilst the top of the fence can, of course, be built to any shape.

The left hand section shows the finish of the end pieces and the side section of the post.

Sketch No. 5 is that of a very light fence nevertheless, it is quite effective.

GROUND LINE

strength, adding to its neatness.

No. 2 is an open type of fence which looks well with a background of shrubs in a nice garden. Its construction is strong and simple — and when seen in length, it has a very pleasing appearance. This sketch, of course, only shows the end detail at the post.

The third sketch indicates a small section of a good, strong

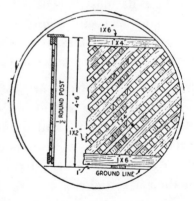

GROUND LINE

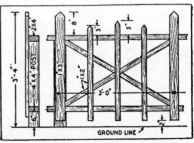

GROUND LINE

FENCING HINTS

HOW TO MAKE CONCRETE POSTS

Concrete posts are a paying investment. Their first cost is their last; their appearance is neat and uniform, whilst the simple moulds required for making them can be made by anyone. Average about 18 bags of cement to each 100 posts.

A 1:2:3 mixture is best, using $\frac{1}{2}$ to $\frac{3}{4}$ in. coarse aggregate, not heavier. They are usually of 3 types, i.e., square, tapered on two, or tapered on four sides. Tapered posts give the best appearance.

Consructing the Mould. This should be made of 2 inch timber (dressed on both sides) for the sides, and the end with 1 in. par-

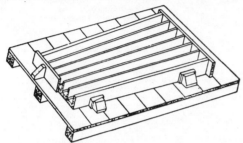

A mould for making tapering posts

titions. A square mould is simple to make, and this illustration gives a simple method of constructing a mould to take tapering posts 5 at a time, tapering from 5 in. square at the bottom to 4 in. x 5 in. at the top. Length of post is 7 ft. The posts should be 2 ft. to 2 ft. 6 in. in the ground and the soil well tamped into the hole. The mould should be greased before use with soft soap or linseed oil, etc.

Holes for Wires. These are formed as shown in the following illustration by using, say, 6 pieces of 3-8 in. or $\frac{1}{2}$ in. bars which should be well greased before use to prevent sticking.

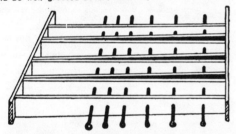

A mould for making 4 posts with iron rods for the holes.

Reinforcing. Diagrams are given showing the position of reinforcements (note the black dots in the larger sketch and also those in the smaller drawings). The larger drawing also shows an effective method of fixing the wires to the fence.

Posts should be reinforced with 3 or 4 mild steel bars 3-8 in. or $\frac{1}{4}$ in. to give them rigidity. Correct placing is important and the types shown herein give the best position—reinforcement in the centre is useless. The rods should be near the corners where the greatest tensile stress occurs. They should be $\frac{3}{4}$ in. from the surface. Scrap fence or barb wire is not good enough as concrete does not stick to same properly. Again, wire in coils is difficult to straighten and will not stay in the correct position while placing the concrete.

Placing. Some people place reinforcement in position in the mould before the concrete is poured in by forming a framework and suspending it from bars laid across the upper edge.

The easiest way is to first place the concrete 1 in. deep in the moulds

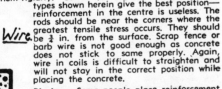

PROPER POSITIONS FOR REINFORCING RODS IN VARIOUS TYPES OF POSTS

then the reinforcing rods $\frac{3}{4}$ in. from the sides and bottom, and put firmly into place to within 1 or 2 in. from each end of the mould.

Then half fill with concrete; then pass the rods through to make the holes in the post. Then add more material to within $\frac{1}{2}$ in. of the top and put the other two reinforcing rods in similar position to the first. Fill, then tamp and trowel. The concrete should also be spaded and protected for a week or ten days.

CONCRETE BASES

Concrete bases or footings are sometimes needed, in which case you should excavate to at least 3 ft.

Then fill the hole with concrete to ground level, taking care to insert proper reinforcing rods so that they will extend from the top of the post to at least 2 ft. below ground level.

The forms for the post can then be placed directly over the fill already made and the filling completed.

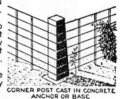

CORNER POST CAST IN CONCRETE ANCHOR OR BASE

GATE AND CORNER POSTS

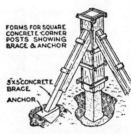

FORMS FOR SQUARE CONCRETE CORNER POSTS SHOWING BRACE & ANCHOR

5"x5" CONCRETE BRACE

ANCHOR

These are subject to great strain and should be larger than the others. The same principles apply except that they are better done on the job in a simple box held together with clamps, as shown here.

They must have increased reinforcement along the sides as well as the corners. 8 x 8 in. or 10 x 10 in. makes good corner posts.

This sketch includes braces and anchor and also illustrates how the clamps may be fixed on without the braces being there.

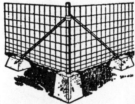

The second sketch is of another type or corner post and bracing.

It shows an iron post set in concrete and double braced; it being a particularly neat method of treating a corner.

A corner so braced will never get out of plumb. The main post is 21 in. square at the base, 18 in. at the top, 3 ft. deep.

The smaller ones are 18 x 20 at bottom and tapering to 14 x 16 at top, 18 in. deep. The reason for the taper is to prevent any tendency of the block to lean over or rise when a strain is put on.

AFFIXING BOLTS, HINGES, WIRE HOLES, ETC.

This can easily be done by placing them in the mould in their relative positions and, when the cement hardens, there should be no sagging. The article to be inserted can easily be arranged by merely securing it on to the reinforcement bars or by inserting it exactly in the correct position in the concrete while the latter is still in a moist condition. The rods (for the holes) can be pulled out several hours after the concrete has been deposited.

Leave 30 days to harden before the wiring is done.

SOLID CONCRETE, ANCHORED IN BASE OF CONCRETE MORTAR & FIELDSTONE

FENCING HINTS

FENCE BRACING

End corner and gate posts need bracing against the pull of the fence; the bracing should be in line with and from the direction of the fence.

One good way is to bear against the post about 2-3rds of the distance from ground level to the top, although there are, of course, other methods as shown in these illustrations.

If concrete braces are cast with the post, the reinforcing rods should extend well into the main post. If done separately, insert triangular wooden blocks into the moulds before the concrete is put in.

CORNER POST & BRACE R ILS
CAST IN FORM SHOWN BELOW

Another method of bracing is shown in sketch 4. This is a well tried idea and consists of joining the strainer post to the next one with a rail placed firmly into position.

Two wires are then run from the top of one post to the bottom of the other, as shown, and the

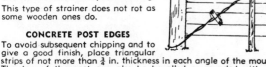

CORNER POST   FENCE-LINE BRACING

strain is taken by inserting a rod into them where shown, and twisting.

This type of strainer does not rot as some wooden ones do.

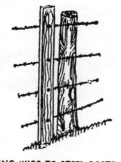

CONCRETE POST EDGES

To avoid subsequent chipping and to give a good finish, place triangular strips of not more than ¾ in. thickness in each angle of the mould. The top of the post can also be bevelled or rounded with an edging tool after the concrete is placed.

ONE WAY OF SPACING WIRE

If a spacing stick such as this is used, a neat job will result. It will also save much time

A piece of 4 x 4 about 5 ft. long is a useful size. Drive a 3 in. nail through the board as far from one end as you wish the bottom wire to be from the ground. In using, the stick is set upright against a post; the wires are slipped on to the nails (the points, not the heads), and the wires are held in place whilst the stapling is being done. By pressing a knee or thigh against the board, the wire is held snugly against the post.

FASTENING WIRE TO STEEL POSTS

These are two improvised methods of affixing wire to steel or wooden posts. In **the first,** cotter pins are used to advantage, being even more useful than short tie wires.

The keys are spread and slipped over the fence wires, after which they are inserted into the holes in the posts. The keys are then clinched tightly, as shown

COTTER KEYS

COTTER PINS

STAPLES

In **the second** illustration, cotter pins are again used with wooden posts. This is handy where it might be necessary to remove or allow stock or vehicles to pass through.

Drive two staples, one on either side, and place the wire between them, locking it in position by dropping an improvised cotter pin made of strong binding wire through the loops of the staples. The ends of the cotter pins should be bent over to prevent them from being bounced out by vibration. The wire is held quite securely yet it is easily released.

A HOME-MADE STITCHER AND WIRE SPLICER

This is a useful article in fencing.

The stock is a piece of ¾ in. rod of convenient length, with a ¼ in. hole drilled through near an end to receive the wire to be spliced.

The other end is flattened and has a 7-16 hole to take the cross-bar of 3-8 in. rod with an eye turned on each end as shown.

One of the loops, of course, must be made after the handle has been threaded through the bar.

SPLICING WIRE

This is one of the best ways of splicing wire. First pull both sections together (the cut ends of the wires overlapping) until the first stay wire in either section lies alongside the first stay wire in the other.

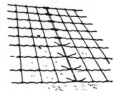

Then take the overlapping ends of the wires and wrap them tightly together with pliers or a splicing tool.

If the overlapping cut ends on the fence sections to be spliced are not long enough for effective wrapping, it may be necessary to cut out one stay. When cutting off a section always make the cut half way between two stays to provide overhang for future splicing.

A HANDY METHOD OF WIRING CONCRETE POSTS

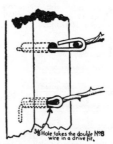

3/8 Hole takes the double No 8 wire in a drive fit.

This method is one used successfully by one large farm — they having made hundreds of concrete posts and tried many systems of wire holding, but this was found to be the cheapest, quickest, and neatest, and, above all, the strongest.

Another good feature of this fastener is that when any repair work has to be done, all that is required is to straighten the staple that is knocked down at the back of the post, push the staple out, insert the new wire, drive the staple home, and bend it down again at the back of the post.

In casting the posts they put an extra hole in every post just below the ground level, then, should the post come to a place where it has to be footed, the hole is there ready to receive the wire that is attached to a buried foot.

The staples are made from No. 8 fencing wire.

USEFUL METHODS OF ERECTING POSTS
Showing Use of Plumb Bob

Fence posts have a better appearance and are more durable if set up truly vertical. Plumb line enables this to be done. **That on the right** gives a very simple method—a "V"-shaped notch being cut in the end of a board about 5 feet long, and a hole bored about 6 in. below the notch. Fix as shown with the length of line adjusted so that the bob will just clear the ground. The line should then hang vertical.

The second is a length of wire bent into a loop, one end of which is bent inward so that it rests against the post as a support, and the other end has a hook to attach the plumb bob.

This can easily be turned to plumb the post from any angle.

WIRE HOOP

SPIKE END

PLUMB BOB

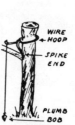

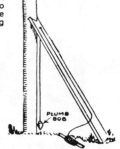

PLUMB BOB

FENCING HINTS

REPLACING POSTS IN A PERMANENT FENCE

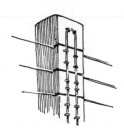

This idea has been a great success with one farmer, who has had to replace many broken posts in a permanent fence.

After a new post has been dug in, mark where the fence wires are to go. It is advisable to have the flat side of the post next to the wires.

Next, get a cross-cut saw and saw an inch deep groove for each wire. Slip the fence wires into the cuts. Now staple two lengths of wire up and down the post. This helps to hold the wires in place. There must be two staples between each fence wire as shown.

A POST ANCHOR TO PREVENT HEAVING

Where a line of fencing runs along uneven land, the posts in the depressions are always apt to rise or "heave" owing to the lifting action of the wire in rising to higher ground. This is specially noticeable after any very wet weather.

Posts in such positions can be anchored by nailing pieces of stout wood, say 3 x 2 or 1½ in. across the post in the positions indicated in this sketch. This will resist the tendency of the post to rise.

AN ANCHOR FOR CLOTHES POST (or any other high post)

This sketch shows a good method of fixing a clothes post so that it will not pull over when a line is attached to it, even if in soft ground.

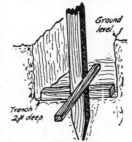

Two pieces of wood, 3 ft. in length, are nailed across the post as indicated. A trench is dug about 1 ft. deep at either end and two feet deep in the middle (as seen in he sketch), one of the cross-pieces resting on the side. The post is then placed as shown and the earth filled in around it.

Where the post is supported on two sides, as in the case of a fence, one cross-piece only may be needed, but where it has to take the full strain, as in a clothes-line, then the double piece is best.

HOW TO STAY A POST IN AWKWARD GROUND

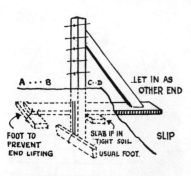

Some fences are confronted with problems which often appear to have no solution.

This is one of them. It is an example of a suspended stay on some ground which has fallen away or where there is an awkward bank.

To take the fence lower down the hill might be impossible, and to bring it up nearer the road might also be impossible.

The distance between C and D is to too narrow for a stay. The illustration will therefore offer a solution for any such difficulties and the idea given might also suggest other ideas for other such difficult problems.

HANDY DRIVING CAP FOR POSTS TO AVOID BUCKLING

Difficulty is sometimes experienced, owing to buckling, when driving small rods or posts.

This is caused by the vibration set up in the rods when struck with a driving hammer. Most of this trouble can be eliminated by using a weight on the end of the rods, etc., when driving them.

The weight is merely a piece of iron or steel shafting drilled part way through to the proper shape in order to slip over the ends of the rods.

WATERPROOFING POST TOPS

This is a good way of preserving posts by keeping the water from penetrating the top. Square or hexagon shingles, or scraps of roofing compound provide very good caps for this.

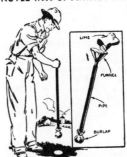

The protecting piece is nailed to the top of the post, after which it is trimmed to fit. If the blade gets too sticky, try using a pair of tin snips.

Posts will last much longer with some such arrangement as the water failing on top of the post usually soaks down and causes gradual decay.

The illustration will indicate the idea and, of course, any suitable material will suffice.

NOVEL WAY OF FIXING POSITION OF POSTS WITH LIME DUSTER

Quite a lot of time and labour can be saved by the use of this lime duster instead of the usual method of putting down stakes in order to fix the position of fence posts.

The duster merely consists of a length of pipe with a piece of burlap tied tightly over one end to form a small bag.

In use, the pipe is filled with lime, and the workman walks along and taps the ground where a post is to be set. The lime sifts through the cloth and leaves a white spot on the ground.

HANDY METHOD OF MAKING CEMENT ANCHORS FOR POSTS

This is a novel way of making ready-to-use cement anchors for posts when quite a number can be done at the same time. They make the post more firm than if merely stuck in the ground.

For those who prefer steel posts to be anchored in this fashion, this method also does away with the need for carrying the cement, sand, etc. to the fence line itself as it is possible to attach such anchor pieces to the posts before taking them to the fence site.

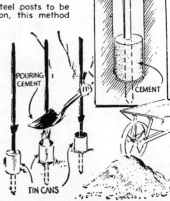

To make these, a number of posts are driven into the ground say a few inches through large size tins, and the cement poured in. They are then complete and can be taken direct to the fence line, inserted into the hole and tamped down.

FENCING HINTS

DIGGING POST HOLES

There is a certain art in this. On the left is shown the correct finish, with sides plumb and bottom square and flat so that the

post can get a good footing on it.

Alongside and on the right is seen the wrong way, with the hole tapering inward as it goes down and the bottom round so that the post is wobbly from the start, with the consequence that there is a hollow under it when the dirt is filled in, and the post will settle out of line after a short time.

HOME-MADE POST HOLE DIGGERS

Quite a good post hole digger can be made from two old shovels, and a piece of heavy strap iron, as shown here. This will enable a hole to be made by merely revolving the tool with some downward pressure.

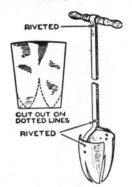

It should be strongly made if to be used in clay or stony soil.

If working in clay or any sticky soil, much time can be saved if the blades of the digger are dipped in a bucket of waste oil at regular intervals. The oil film prevents sticking and makes the soil slip off easily when the digger is lifted from the hole.

POST HOLE DIGGER FROM MOTOR SPRINGS

Another good and easily made post hole digger can be obtained from the use of short leaves of old motor springs. They are quickly constructed and will give good service.

First, cut from a block of wood, about 6 inches square, a pyramid of the shape shown in the drawing. A slot the width of the springs is then cut on all sides as shown by the dotted lines. This takes the leaves of the springs, which have previously had their edges ground to a sharp cutting edge.

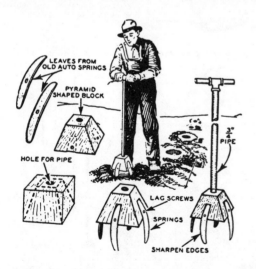

Then fasten the cutters in place with screws. A handle is made by taking a couple of pieces of ¾ in. pipe, assembled as shown. A pin run through the sides of the block holds the pipe firmly in place.

A HOME-MADE TOOL FOR STRAIGHTENING WOVEN WIRE FENCING

This is a very useful and easily made tool for straightening woven wire fences which may have been bent or have become sagged. The details of construction are shown in the sketch.

It can be adjusted to the height of the fence and the wire can be held in place with the notched end whilst stapling the wire to the posts.

HOME-MADE POST HOLE DIGGING TOOLS

These are some very good home-made combined spades and crowbars which should prove very handy indeed.

The first is made from 1 in. piping and an old head of a spade. A hole can be dug very easily with an implement of this weight and length, especially if the end of the piping is pointed.

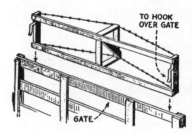

The second is a crowbar converted into a spade—the latter part being from scrap steel flattened at one end and riveted on.

The third is another type with a different fastening for the spade end. The edges of these spades can be turned up or left flat as desired, whilst they can be riveted to the bar or, if an acute angle is required (as in 3) metal straps can be heated and bent.

NOVEL WAY OF PROTECTING WOODEN GATES FROM DAMAGE BY CATTLE

Wooden gates are often damaged by cattle trying to reach over them for fodder in the next field. This can be prevented by hooking a barbed wire protector over the gate, as shown here.

It is merely a wooden frame, with wire applied as indicated, with two pieces of flat iron bent to form hooks, which are slipped over the gate.

It is placed on the side of the gate where the cattle are, and it will effectively prevent them from reaching over. An electric wire for the same purpose would also be effective.

ANOTHER HOME-MADE TOOL FOR TIGHTENING WOVEN WIRE FENCING

This useful tool is not hard to make and it embodies an excellent idea for temporary repairs for this class of fencing. If such a fence has begun to sag between the posts the wire can be tightened quickly by re-crimping the horizontal wires with a tool of the shape shown.

Usually it is only necessary to crimp the top, centre and bottom wires, but be sure to crimp all three as you go along the fence as otherwise it will stretch unevenly.

FENCING HINTS

LIVE-WIRE FENCING

The use of the electric fence has become increasingly common in many parts during the past few years, and, although it was originally designed to check the prowling of pests, it is now recognised as useful in connection with stock.

The electric fence in its most simple form is a single barbed or plain wire supported by light stakes—the wire being mounted on insulators. A special controller, operated from a battery, is used to send electric charges along the wire.

There is one distinct advantage in the electric fence and that is that it can be readily moved from place to place and can be used to fence off small areas temporarily. Care should be taken to prevent grasses and weeds from coming into contact with the electrified wire as such contact may neutralise the desired effect.

The charge unit is operated by a battery, but the current used is only slight. A fully charged 6-volt car battery should last from 6 to 8 months, but makers generally advise recharging about every 3 months for best results. The battery should, of course, be housed in a weatherproof box.

Educating Stock. All stock should be educated to fear this type of fencing. Bulls are fairly easy to control, but pigs are very much more difficult. Pigs can be trained by tying something tasty to the electric fence within easy reach. Another way is to stretch a wire across a gateway and leave the gate open.

Also, it is a good idea to wet the ground in the gateway in order to make a good earth for the pigs' feet when they should receive a shock as they attempt to cross the wire.

Horses are easily educated with a breast-high wire across an enclosure as a shock or two is usually sufficient. Cattle have the habit of running their heads under wires and they should have all long hairs on necks and shoulders clipped before introducing them to the electric fence, in order to get best results.

As regards sheep, a low two-wire fence should be run across the corner of a well-grassed paddock, and the sheep placed in the corner because, after eating out the corner, they will turn their attention to the grass in sight just outside the wires. They will then make contact and receive a shock and will not again very often attempt to pass under any wires resembling those used in their training. Soon after shearing time is the best time to train sheep.

Methods of Fencing. For horses and cattle, one wire 3 feet high is best; for pigs, two wires, one 6 inches and one 14 inches above ground. Barb wire stretches a little so that posts used for barb must be closer than those used for other wire—say a chain apart at the most.

Most important is the insulation of the wires. A button type should be nailed to every post, one for each wire, with the wire securely fastened to the insulator. The shackle type of insulator is best for corner posts. In the next column, we also show some very handy types of emergency insulators which can be used at a pinch.

In summer, when the ground is dry, the shock from the fence is much weaker and may encourage stock to get over the wires.

This may be rectified to some extent by using iron posts and driving them deeply into the ground, insulating the two electric wires from the posts and then running another wire between the two and fixing it securely to the bare post.

Gateways may be made by stretching two wires across an opening but a proper iron gateway is preferable as there will then be no

trouble in driving the pigs out as some difficulty may be experienced with wire gates as the pigs might be scared to go through the opening even though they can see that the wires have been removed.

Space does not permit of a full explanation of the various component parts of an electric fence, i.e., the induction coil, interrupter, and the condenser, etc., but the illustrations given will indicate some of the methods of fixing.

AN UNBREAKABLE HOME-MADE INSULATOR FROM TYRE CASING

Owners of electric fences who have trouble with broken porcelain insulators, especially at fence corners, may find this a very useful idea.

They can be replaced with some pieces of old motor tyre casing in which some of the grooving is still present.

The bead is cut off all round the tyre on both sides, and then the tyre is cut up into sections from 6 to 9 in. long and nailed to the posts so that the wire can be fastened in the centre groove by means of small wires in the casing. Short wires passed through holes in the casing secure the electric wires.

ANOTHER HOME-MADE INSULATOR

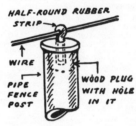

HALF-ROUND RUBBER STRIP
WIRE
PIPE FENCE POST
WOOD PLUG WITH HOLE IN IT

In order to move an electric fence to change pasture location with little effort and time, one farmer uses half-round rubber strips as insulators on the posts.

Pipes are also used as posts, as shown, as they can easily be driven in and taken out.

Each pipe is fitted with a wooden plug, drilling a hole in it just large enough to retain the rubber strip.

To drive the post, make a cap to fit over it in order to prevent damage.

A BOTTLE AS EMERGENCY INSULATOR

EMERGENCY INSULATOR
ELECTRIC FENCE

If an insulator on an electric fence becomes broken, and one to replace it is not immediately available, it is a good idea to slip an empty bottle over the top and attach the wire to this as indicated in the sketch.

Extra length of fence may be added by using such insulators when regular equipment is not available.

This is quite a simple but very effective arrangement, often used in an emergency with satisfactory results by one farmer

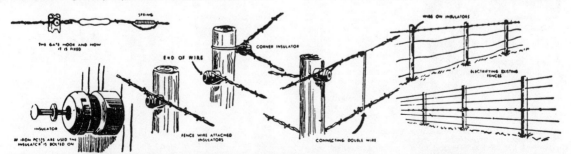

SPRING

THE GATE HOOK AND HOW IT IS FIXED

END OF WIRE

CORNER INSULATOR

WIRE ON INSULATORS

ELECTRIFYING EXISTING FENCES

INSULATOR

IF IRON POSTS ARE USED THE INSULATOR IS BOLTED ON

FENCE WIRE ATTACHED INSULATORS

CONNECTING DOUBLE WIRE

This sketch shows that there is nothing complicated about erecting an electrified fence.

FENCING HINTS

A HOME-MADE POST PULLER

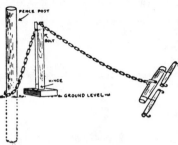

This useful post puller is simple and easy to make. It is merely a heavy piece of wood about 1 ft. square together with a piece of hardwood about 3 ft. long.

This is fastened to the square piece by a strong hinge and the stick is notched at the top. A bolt is put through it to keep it from splitting.

Fasten the chain to the post just above the ground and pass it over the upright in the notch.

Then drive ahead and the post should come out quite easily. One farmer improvised another such post puller from an old wagon tongue, taking about 3 ft. of it to use as the puller, a notch being cut in the top to take the chain. The same procedure was then adopted.

ANOTHER USEFUL HOME-MADE POST PULLER

This post puller differs from the ordinary type in as much as it has a flexible connection between the stand and the post. The triangular stand or support is made of either angle or flat iron, the former for actual preference.

A 10-inch link is pivoted to the end of the lever, and two pins extended from one side of this link to grip the post. The pins may either be welded to the link or may be short bolts, and are spaced just far enough apart to allow them to slip over the post when the link is held horizontally, but will securely grip it as soon as the link is forced up at an angle.

This type is specially useful for steel posts and when fences are to be moved.

The same type of arrangement may also be used and in which a chain can be used in place of the link. In this instance, bolt a short piece of chain with a hook at one end to the short end of the lever. To operate, hook the chain around the post loosely and pry. As the post comes out, let the chain slacken and slide down the post. Then pry again.

ANOTHER POST LIFTER

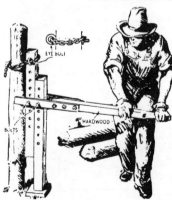

This hand jack makes short work of the tedious job of pulling up old fence posts. It is made of three hardwood parts; a handle, a moveable or lifting member and a stationary piece. The last two are cut to the same length, and an equal number of holes are bored in each.

Two pieces of flat iron are bolted to the handle, and holes are drilled in these for heavy bolts which pass through the holes in the stationary and lifting pieces.

A short length of chain, run through an eye bolt at the top of the lifting piece, is looped about the post. This will exert a very powerful lift and will enable one to pull up quite large fencing posts.

HANDY PORTABLE POSTS FOR FENCES

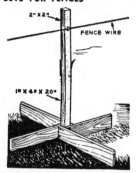

This is an idea which can be used in quite a number of cases and especially where an electrical fence is concerned.

It can be used for such things as changing the feeding ground for pigs and other stock, as it will not need permanent posts and therefore it can be taken from place to place as desired.

Its construction is clearly indicated and a good number can be made at a time. The uprights are 2 x 2 timber and the base pieces 4 x 1, each about 20 in. long or as is necessary to meet each particular occasion.

ANOTHER HANDY PORTABLE FENCE

This fence also needs no holes dug and is a good temporary arrangement which can be moved without loosening the wire. Such a fence is especially handy when desiring to pasture a portion of a small field and it is desired to move the fence back occasionally.

For poultry, netting can be tacked on to the posts.

ANOTHER STYLE OF TEMPORARY FENCE

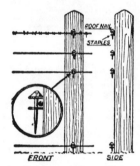

This type of fence is very handy when it is required for the same purpose as the above or to run a piece of netting round some green crop or other spot.

Staples are driven into stakes or posts, and the wire or netting is pressed against the post when a roofing nail is dropped through the staples to keep it in place.

In winter, when the stakes can easily be driven in or pulled out of the ground without much difficulty, this type of fence would be an excellent form of "lightning" fence which would be found useful in more ways than one. The whole arrangement is very simple, yet very effective for the purposes mentioned.

A QUICK CHANGE PANELS FOR PENS WHICH CAN BE EASILY MOVED

This is a very useful arrangement and one which does not take much trouble to erect from any scrap which might be around the place.

The quick-change panels shown are set between posts set in rows and are specially useful where small pens of lambs or poultry are concerned.

The panels consist of a wooden framework covered with netting and fitted with metal clips on each end, which slide along the sides of the posts. If the posts were portable posts any size pen could be moved to any spot very quickly indeed.

FENCING HINTS

HINTS ON UNROLLING WIRE, ETC.

These hints on rolling and unrolling wire may be useful, and in this connection, quite a number of different ideas are included.

Careful attention should always be given to uncoiling or unreeling as the life of any wire, wire rope, or cable, etc., is very much reduced by kinking.

When once a wire has become kinked and is again straightened, it is nearly always weakened and therefore it is advisable not to use wire on some jobs which has once been kinked. The drawings given here show wrong ways and right ways of handling wire.

A CROWBAR AID TO UNROLL BARB WIRE

This is one useful way of unrolling barb wire from 1 cwt. reels, and it will be found to be a very useful and convenient one.

The wire should be drawn out from underneath the coil for preference, otherwise it spins too fast and is inclined to tangle. It is also an advantage to have the augur hole slightly tilted, as shown.

The flat end of the bar prevents the coil from slipping off.

It is advisable to have an attendant at the coil while the wire is being drawn so that he can hit the wire close to the coil with a short stick if the barbs jam.

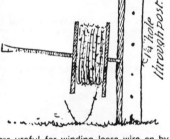

The empty wooden reels are useful for winding loose wire on by the same method. The crowbar idea is quite a good one and can be used in several other ways, as indicated in other drawings.

UNROLLING BARB WIRE FROM WAGON

This is another useful method of unrolling barb wire especially when there is only one man to do the job. It is a good, safe and easy way and is fully set out in the illustration—very little extra explanation being necessary.

A plank is first fitted in front of the rear end gate cleats, after which a hole is bored in the centre of this to take a length of 1 in. pipe, or other material.

In use it is a simple matter to fasten the wire end to a corner post, slip the spool on the pipe spindle, and drive down the fence row. Friction between the plank and spool serves as a brake which prevents the wire from unrolling too fast and becoming tangled.

If desired, an additional hole can be bored in the plank, making it possible to unroll two spools of wire at the same time.

A SAFE HANDLE FOR CARRYING BARB WIRE

This is a very good method of carrying and unrolling a spool of barb wire and unrolling without help is facilitated by slipping the spool on such a post in the manner indicated in the accompanying sketch.

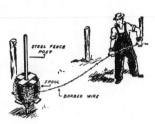

This makes carrying easy, as the cross blade keeps the spool from sliding off, and, when driven into the ground temporarily, the post also provides a handy holder for the spool whilst being unwound.

A USEFUL DEVICE FOR UNWINDING WIRE

This is another easily made device for unrolling barb wire.

It really does not need any explanation as the drawing itself is sufficient.

It consists of a stout piece of wood fashioned in the manner shown with a steel prong for use as indicated in the lower detail.

This anchor hook is specially used when it is necessary to halt for stapling.

To hold the wire taut for stapling, the handle is pressed down, and the anchor hook, attached to the handle, is forced into the ground. This arrangement could also be affixed to the device shown at the foot of this column.

UNROLLING BARB WIRE IN WHEELBARROW FASHION

Quite a good method of unrolling barb wire is also shown here. It is the provision of a pair of handles, properly spaced and fitted with two cross-pieces for rigidity as shown in the illustration and slipping an iron rod through two holes at the lower end and through the roll of the barb wire.

To prevent the rod from slipping out, it should fit rather tight in the handles or, if desired, it may be threaded for a washer and nut.

Improvised Reel Holder Pushed Along Single-Handed, Unwinds Barb-Wire Fencing

FENCING HINTS

A HOME-MADE JENNY FOR WINDING WIRE

This is a spinning jenny for pulling out plain wire. An old plough disc, a wooden cross made of 6 x 2 timber and five broken drill wheel spokes are required.

Put about four inches of thread on each spoke, place them through the ends of the cross, and put a nut on top and below the timber. Slope the tops of the spokes in slightly to allow the coil of wire to slip over them easily.

The fifth spoke is driven down through the wooden cross and then through the plough disc into the ground.

The jenny spins very easily, but it is an improvement to have two ends of the cross about a foot longer than the width of the coil of wire in order to prevent the wire slipping over the ends and getting caught on the nuts underneath the wood.

HANDY HORSE-DRAWN WIRE RACK

If much fencing is done, the use of a home-made horse-drawn un-winding rack, whether for netting, barb or any other type of wire fencing material, would eventually save much labour and time.

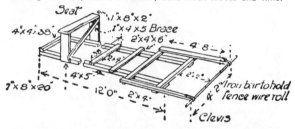

To construct one like the sketch there would be :

Two pieces 4 x 4 or 4 x 5 x 12 ft.	One piece 4 x 4 x 38 in.
One piece 2 x 4 x 46 in.	One piece 2 x 4 x 38 in.
Two pieces 2 x 4 x 56 in.	Two pieces 2 x 4 x 50 in.
Two pieces 1 x 8 x 20 in.	One piece 1 x 4 x 45 in.
Thirty 4 in. spikes	One piece 1 x 8 x 42 in.
Two 5 in. clevices	A handful of nails.

The two 4 x 5 x 12 ft. are laid down and the 4 x 4 38 spiked to the front end. The 2 x 4 crosspieces are then spiked on, the two 50 in. lengths nailed about 28 in. apart, and the 56 in. lengths spiked to the ends of these as shown. Two spikes are driven at each joint. The seat and support are made from the 1 x 8's braced with the 1 x 4, and securely nailed to the rack. About 3 in. from rear end of the two 56 in. lengths of the 2 x 4 frame, holes are drilled to receive clevis pins. Clevises are then attached, and through these a 5 ft. length of iron pipe is passed.

When completed, load it on a wagon chassis. Place the 46 in. lengths of 2 x 4 just in front of the rear wagon stakes to keep the rack from slipping back. Back the wagon to the roll of fencing, and raise the front end of the rack to lower the rear end, which then makes it an easy matter to slip the pipe through both clevises and through the wire. If the wire is heavy, it may be necessary to keep the front end down to the wagon with rope.

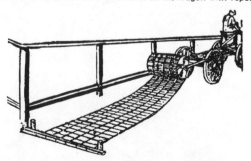

When in position in field, stake one end of roll to the ground and drive the team forward. For barb and other wire two or three rolls can be unwound at once. This can also, of course, be pulled along by hand.

A SIMPLE WIRE WINDER

A simply made winder or unwinder is shown here, although it may not be, of course, as mobile as some. AA is a length of ⅜ in. round iron or ½ in. water piping bent to measurements given.

BB is an empty wooden barb wire reel, which slips on to the end of rod A. C is a cord of wire to tie the

reel to the crank, and D is the wire to be wound up off the fence. To use the winder, first undo all the ties round the wire on the fence posts. Then staple wire to the centre of the reel or poke it through the slats. One man carries the left end and winds with his right hand, his mate carrying two-thirds of the weight on the long end of AA.

OLD TYRES USED AS REEL TO WIND BARB WIRE

This is a handy idea for winding wire. The big wheel shown will make it easy to take up wire from temporary fences. Two old tyres and 4 pieces of wood about 1½ x 1 x 25 in. are needed.

First cut holes for the wood in one wall of each tyre, then assemble these walls facing each other, and secure the sticks by driving nails into them

through both outer tyre walls. This will provide a fast moving and easy method of doing this job and it can easily be managed by one man. The sketch should need no explanation.

A USEFUL MOBILE WIRE WINDER OR UNWINDER

This illustration explains itself; the reel being mounted on old buggy or other wheels with short shafts, when the cart can be drawn along by man or horse, while somebody helps steady the reel to

keep it from unwinding too rapidly.

This can also be used for winding wire, the machine being pushed just fast enough to keep up with the wire as it is wound, or, if the wire is loose, it can just be wound up by turning the crank.

WIRE WINDER FROM OLD BUGGY WHEELS

This is another idea for winding barb wire without danger to hands or clothing.

It is two old buggy wheels fastened together by a large bolt slipped through the axles. The bolt is tightened, drawing the wheels together so that they roll as one wheel. Cross-wire spokes serve as a base for rolling. The sketch will give details as to its use.

FENCING HINTS

MENDING A BREAK IN THE FENCE
How to Use Hammer As Wire Strainer

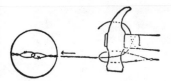

To use a hammer as an impromptu wire strainer connect on a new piece of wire to the broken strand and remove the barbs if it is barbed wire.

Make a loop in the broken wire and pass the new length round the hammer, as shown.

Wind up the wire tightly round the head of the hammer by rotating it with the haft as a lever, then pull strongly against the loop and wind some of the wire from the hammer-head round the strand.

ANOTHER TYPE OF HANDY WIRE STRETCHER

Simply take a piece of 4 x 2 about 3 ft. long and bore a hole about 6 in. from the end D. Shape off a handhole at the other end at B. Make a saw cut centreways from the square end to the hole as shown at C.

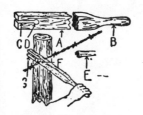

Now make a wooden pin slightly tapering E that will slip into the hole and the stretcher is ready for use. To use, simply push the saw cut notch over the wire, as shown at G till the wire is in the hole. Then push the pin into the hole against the wire as shown at F and with the end of the stretcher against the post pull on the handle.

USE OF CAR JACK IN STRETCHING SHORT LENGTHS WHEN REPAIRING

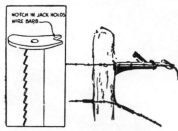

An auto jack will quickly stretch short lengths of barbed wire when repairing a fence

This illustration shows the use of a motor lifting jack which is quite a handy article for small fencing jobs, especially when repairing a broken wire, where a little stretching is necessary. A notch can be cut in the edge of the jack lift place to engage the wire. Our sketch does not show any support to the lifting jack, but merely illustrates the position in which it should be used.

HOW TO USE A CROWBAR

The sketch reproduced here illustrates how a crowbar or a short sapling can be used as a makeshift wire-strainer.

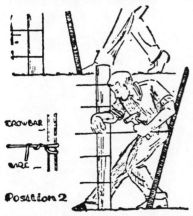

Using a crowbar as wire strainer.

A turn or two of the wire is taken round the bar and over the standing part. The point of the bar is driven into the ground, and using it as a lever the wire is pulled back as far as necessary. The operator then sits against the bar to hold it while he drives the staple into the post to secure the wire.

With plain wire the staple would be set in place before straining, so that it would only have to be driven fully home.

A HANDY WIRE STRETCHER

An old cart or buggy axle can be used for stretching fencing wire. For this, the wheels are firmly anchored by a chain or otherwise to a strong peg driven into the ground.

One end of a rope is also fastened to the peg and the other end is passed through a single pulley block with hook and tied to the axle so that it cannot slip round when the axle is turned.

A hole is driven through the axle in a convenient position and an iron rod inserted. When the axle is turned by means of the rod, a strong pull is obtained on the rope, and the fencing wire being looped over the pulley hook, a good strain can be exerted. The wheels and axle can also be used for pulling posts, as well as for short lifting.

ANOTHER HANDY WIRE STRAINER FROM CART

If there is no wire strainer handy, a spring cart can be used as shown. If the horse is reasonably quiet, there is no need to take him out of the shafts. First tie a chain from the axle to the post in front to act as a brace; next jack up the wheel a few inches off the ground. Tie the wire to a spoke where it joins the hub, then turn the wheel by hand.

When the wire is tight enough, push a piece of timber through the spokes, then under the cart to act as a brake. You can put in a few staples to hold the wire whilst it is being tied to the strainer.

The lower sketch is one of a very light but handy jack which would do for this and quite a number of other jobs round the farm. Note the arrangement of chain to keep it steady and also the notch in the end of the cross-piece in order that anything to be lifted has a firm grip.

A HOME-MADE NETTING STRETCHER

Fixing netting to fencing is sometimes difficult and if not tightly stretched does not last nearly as long. The illustration here consists of a length of 4 x 2 hardwood, or a stout sapling of equal strength equal in length to the width of the wire to be handled. Several heavy iron hooks are fixed in the bar to grip the netting. A heavy iron ring is joined to the bar by 3 lengths of strong rope, hemp or wire. This is to attach the tackle or straining mechanism in which the wire is pulled taut. Straining posts should be well braced.

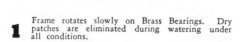

HINTS ON WATER CONSERVATION

HOW TO CONSTRUCT CONCRETE STOCK TANKS

These have many advantages and are cheap and easily built. They do not decay or rust or become leaky if water is left in them, and there is no upkeep.

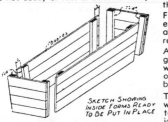

SKETCH SHOWING INSIDE FORMS READY TO BE PUT IN PLACE

First, level the site; then excavate the ground to a depth of 6 or 8 in. to reach a solid foundation. Avoid spongy spots. A good idea is to then fill with 5 or 6 in. of cinders or gravel, which should be well tamped down.

The illustration shows one way of making a concrete tank and it is a sound idea to construct a concrete platform about 6 ft. wide all round the tank, to prevent the ground from becoming boggy. Make the centre platform the exact size of the tank, 6 in. thick, the rest of the platform sloping away. Allow the platform to harden first and then set the outside forms in position directly over the centre slab. The uprights should project a few inches above the top of the boarding and cross bars nailed thereto and to the inner form to hold them in position.

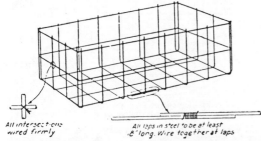

All intersections wired firmly

All laps in steel to be at least 18 long. Wire together at laps

The other sketches show how to make the inner and outer forms, placing of reinforcement, cross-pieces, braces, etc. In reinforcing first place a layer of concrete in the bottom equal in thickness to the distance desired for the reinforcement. The latter should be bent in U-shape so that it will reinforce the sides as well, and where the wires join, they should overlap 18 in.

The ideal reinforcement is shown, indicating the way in which all insertions should be wired firmly together and how each end of steel wire should overlap and be wired together. Place concrete in layers of 6 to 8 in. at a time, spading or rodding it thoroughly to prevent the formation of stone pockets or voids. Place the concrete in one continuous operation to avoid joints, but if this is not possible, be sure and get a good bond between the fresh concrete and that placed previously by cleaning the joints thoroughly and placing a 1:1 mixture (cement and sand) on the joint. Keep the concrete covered and damp for the first 10 days

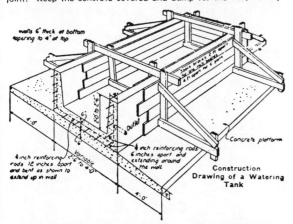

walls 6" thick at bottom tapering to 4" at top

½ inch reinforcing rods 12 inches apart and bent as shown to extend up in wall

½ inch reinforcing rods 6 inches apart and extending around the wall

Concrete platform

Construction Drawing of a Watering Tank

The materials used should be clean, hard, and well graded, varying in size, the sand from fine to that which will pass through a No. 4 screen, and the coarse from ¼ to 1 in. in diameter. Mixture should be 1 cement, 2 sand, 3 coarse, with about 5 gallons water per paper bag of cement.

ANOTHER EASILY MADE SHEEP DRINKING TROUGH

Actually the preparation of the wooden framework is the main thing to consider after the site has been chosen and ground levelled off. A good idea is to construct same to serve, say, two or four paddocks by erecting at intersections of, say, four fences as shown in the small sketch. The trough, of course, should then be made sufficiently wide and long.

An idea is to erect the outer framework lined with either plain or galvd. iron, this representing the outer wall surfaces of the trough. Then make 4 frames to act as supports for the inner wall surfaces. These should slope from 5 in. at the base to 4 in. between frames at the top (see sectional view).

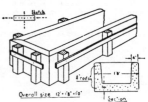

Overall size 12' x 8' x 10'

Section

When the framework is in position, concreting can proceed.

Mixture 1:2½:4 is quite good; clean aggregate being used (see cement construction). When the outer frame is in position, the trough can be laid to a depth of 4 in. and levelled off. Allow about two hours for concrete to set and then fix inner frames in position by props and strips nailed temporarily.

Reinforcement is needed, either say ¼ inch rods or steel mesh fabric—wire netting not being so good. When the reinforcement is wired into position, a start can be made with filling the sides.

When the top is reached, the work should stand for two days before removing the inner frames. Always keep covered with wet bags when not at work. The surfaces should be finished with a fine mortar to a depth of ½ inch, carefully finished off with a steel float. Remove the outer frames and finish with mortar.

Note the rounded finish for top of walls. When the surface will stand water, carefully fill the trough to a depth of 3 to 4 inches. Keep the surface damp for 7 days and then fill the trough and keep the outer surface damp for another 7 days.

Build a strong post and rail fence round the outside as a protection and if possible surround the trough with flat stone to prevent the ground from being torn away.

ANOTHER RECTANGULAR TANK

The two shapes most commonly used for tank making are the round and the rectangular. The latter are easier to build as far as preparatory forms are concerned, but the round tanks use less cement for the same holding capacity, and require less reinforcing. Large tanks are therefore usually of the round type and the small ones rectangular.

This illustration shows another method of construction—without platform—the concrete in which, of course, as in the others,

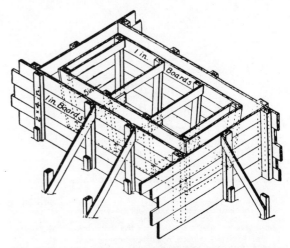

1 in. Boards

should be of correct proportion and mixed to the right consistency. The floor should be placed and well compacted, after which the side forms should be filled. Special care should be taken to work the concrete round the blocks used for supporting the side forms, and to see that no dirt falls into the concrete.

WATER CONSERVATION AND OTHER HINTS

The thickness of a wall for a tank is governed by the depth but as a rule it is never less than 6 inches, increasing to, say, 14 inches thick where a tank is, say, 12 ft. long by 12 ft. deep.

Forms Required: The timber should be 4 x 2 for uprights, and boarding planed to 1 inch in thickness for the sides. These should be true to shape, and not warped in any way. Twelve 4 x 2's are wanted. The face boards are then cut to the measurements of each side of the tank and nailed to the 2 in. face of three of 4 x 2 posts. Each side of the rectangular form is constructed in this manner, and the four sides are joined together by raising them into a vertical position parallel and opposite to each other with the posts on the outside.

Our illustration shows forms ready for constructing this tank, after the foundation has been prepared, the forms are placed exactly on the prepared foundations. The sides are either nailed or screwed together so that the corner joints are made thoroughly tight in order to prevent the escape of any of the cement grout. Struts should then be fastened to the posts and held in place by stakes. The method of reinforcement is along the same lines as per previous pages.

Connections. These should be inserted at a proper height for a pipe to the house pump, for a leader from the downspout and for an overflow.

CONSTRUCTING A CIRCULAR TANK

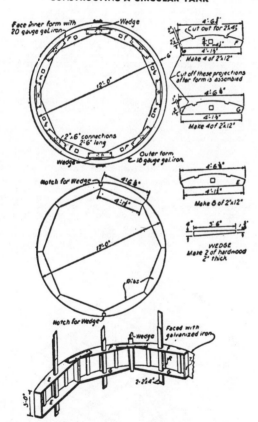

Forms required for construction of Circular Tanks

Although the forms for this class of tank are more difficult to make, the extra trouble taken will be well repaid in the fact that circular tanks present a more attractive appearance and have a greater holding capacity for the same amount of material.

If used for stock tanks, a surrounding pavement is useful to prevent stock from forming mudholes and will ensure a dry footing.

As an example we give details of a circular tank, 12 ft. diameter, the floor thickness of which should be to the scale as shown at the top of the following column.

Depth of Tank Feet	Diameter Feet	Floor Thickness Inches	Holding Capacity Imperial Galls.
6	12	7	4227
8	12	7½	5640
10	12	8	7200
12	12	9	8455
14	12	9½	9867
16	12	10	11200

Forms for Circular Tanks. To secure the curve for the inner forms mark out on a level floor a circle 12 feet in diameter or any other diameter which may be desired. Two sets of 8 ribs each are cut to fit the circle. For a tank of 12 ft. diameter

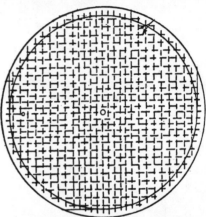

the ribs are usually made of 2 in. material, and are 4 ft. 6½ in. long. The ends of the ribs are cut so that they will butt together tightly.

Each set of 8 ribs is then fastened together to form a complete circle by nailing or bolting 2 in. x 6 in. pieces of timber about 30 inches long across the joints. For the particular tank under description, a number of 4 x 2 battens 32 in.

Plan of reinforcement of floor for Circular Tanks, 5-8 inch rods being used.

long are notched into the ribs, thus spacing the two ribs one above the other and making forms 32 in. high. Extra pieces, as shown by "T" and "R" in the drawing, are nailed between the upper and lower ribs to give greater rigidity.

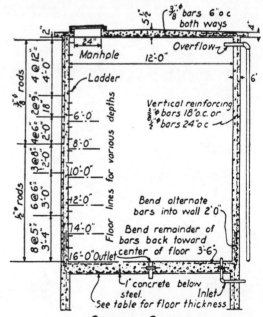

CROSS SECTION

Cross-section of water-supply tank, showing position of manholes, overflow, inlet and outlet pipes, with floor lines for various depths, diameter and number of horizontal reinforcement rods. The spacing of these rods decreases as the depth of the tank increases.

WATER CONSERVATION AND OTHER HINTS

Cement required for Circular Tanks. 3-8, ½ and 5-8 inch rods for floors. The following illustration shows a tank of 12 ft. diameter with depths varying from 6 to 16 feet, showing where the rods of various thicknesses are used. Holding capacities are shown on the previous page.

The same principles for mixing and making forms as already shown, and where any joins in the concrete are made, the same principles are observed as in rectangular tanks. If the forms will allow it, the tank should be built in courses about 28 inches high. In the case of a tank 12 feet deep, the lower 2 ft. 6 in. should be reinforced horizontally with ½ in. bars spaced 8 in. apart, the next 2 ft. with 3-8 bars 6 in. apart, the next 18 in. with 3-8 in. bars 9 in. apart, and the top 4 ft. of tank should be reinforced with 3-8 rods 12 in. apart.

Thickness of floor and amount of reinforcement vary according to depth of tank. Vertical reinforcement for walls consists of 3-8 bars at 18 in. intervals. Reinforcing steel is located in the outer portion of the wall and in lower portion of floor slab in each case with not less than 1½ in. of concrete between the steel and the surface.

A SQUARE TANK

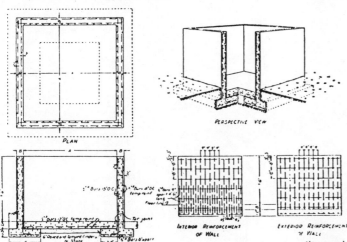

Method of constructing a square water storage tank

The square tank shown in this illustration is a valuable type for the storage of water, oil, etc. These can be built to any capacity. The following table gives a few details.

Approx. Capacity Galls.	Inside Length ft.	Inside Depth ft.	Thickness Walls ins.
670	6	3	6
1200	8	3	6
2700	12	3	8
4800	16	3	9
5400	12	6	10
10800	12	12	14

These sketches show the plan, together with the end view of the concrete (top right), indicating the work below the ground surface, the reinforcement of walls (lower right).

The construction details given for rectangular tanks can be readily applied to this type of tank.

CONSTRUCTING CONCRETE WELLS

Underground water supplies can be easily protected from contamination by rodents, vermin and polluted water from all sources by the use of concrete.

Spring water can be protected by constructing a concrete wall several feet deep or to the depth at which the water bearing stratum is reached. This, of course, will not prevent contamination at the source of the spring, but it will exclude small animals and surface water. A concrete cover is a desirable addition; this should be made heavy enough to prevent accidental removal (see latter part of this article).

Well Construction. The earth wall of the excavation will generally be found sufficiently firm to act as the outer form for

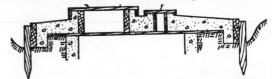

moulding the concrete. If the earth walls are not firm, forms will have to be made and the excavation enlarged to provide room for them. A convenient collapsible interior form may be made in sections by following the directions given relative to forms for circular tanks. One by 4 in. material for facing the forms is generally found suitable. A coating of oil applied to the forms will prevent concrete from sticking to them. For small wells, a wall thickness of 4 inches is sufficient, but for large wells, 6 inches is recommended.

It will be found advantageous to construct the walls of wells in courses of 3 to 4 feet at a time, beginning at the bottom and working upwards. Usually concrete is allowed to harden 24 hours before forms are removed and reset for the next course.

A concrete platform surrounding the well is almost indispensable. For wells of a diameter of 6 feet or less, a platform 4 inches thick at the edges is adequate, provided that it is reinforced with rods not less than ¼ inch diameter, and spaced 5 inches apart in both directions. The rods should be embedded about 1½ inches above the lower surface of the concrete. If reinforcement rods are not obtainable, wire mesh may be used instead.

The platform should extend well over the edges of the wall of the well, and should be at least 1 inch higher in the centre than at the edges to ensure good drainage.

The bottom form for the cover slab is made by building a tight board platform which can be braced in position from below or attached to the previously placed wall. Before placing the concrete, provision should be made for a manhole in the cover and for an opening for the pump. Bolts are often set in the concrete for attachment of the pump base.

A simple expedient for providing a manhole is to set a large dishpan on the platform form. Removal of the pan will leave an opening with sloping edges in the concrete, for which a close fitting concrete cover can be made by casting it in the interior of the pan. The cover slab forms can be dismantled and removed through the manhole. Do not remove the platform forms too soon; in warm weather allow a week, and in cool weather even longer.

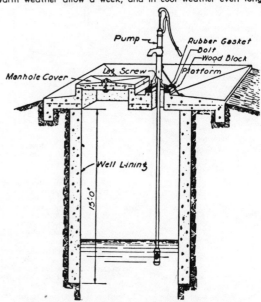

Recommended method of constructing concrete wall, curb and platform

WATER CONSERVATION AND OTHER HINTS

HOW TO MAKE GALVANISED CORRUGATED TANKS

24 gauge iron is used. For a tank of 200 gallon capacity, two sheets 10 feet long are necessary, curved to a full circle and joined by a 4 in. lap (see fig. 1).

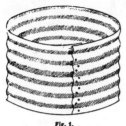

Fig. 1.

To rivet the seams clamp a small hand vice at the top and bottom, then put in a couple of rivets at each end, after which remove the vices. Small galvd. roof bolts can also be used to hold the iron in position.

Punch the holes for the rivets from the outside, holding a piece of hard wood on the inside as a "dolly"; rivets about 2 in. apart, or one to each corrugation. Put the rivets in from the outside, an iron dolly being held to the heads, the washers placed in position, and the rivets hammered down and snapped on the inside.

The second cylinder of the tank is fastened at the top, and then placed over the first cylinder (see fig. 2), and lowered until the required lap is reached; 1 or 1½ corrugations should be sufficient in a small tank. A rope is then passed round the body of the tank, with a short piece of pipe to form a tourniquet or twitch, and this is tightened until the seam is in position (fig. 3).

Punching or riveting are then proceeded with.

A tank that consists of two sections only should have the vertical seams on opposite sides.

Taking the line of the corrugations as a guide the joint round the centre of the tank is easily adjusted, and should have a single line of rivets about 8 in. apart.

The next operation is to turn a flange on the body of the tank in preparation for the fitting of

Fig. 2.

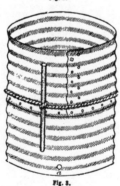

Fig. 3.

the bottom. This is done as shown in figs. 4 and 5.

As the tank now stands, the top or outside cylinder will be that to which the bottom is fitted. A line is drawn ½ in. from the top edge, and the flange beaten over on a "handstake." Where this tool is not available, an ordinary laundry flat-iron makes a good substitute.

For the bottom, one sheet of 24 gauge galvd. flat iron, 72 x 36 in. will be required. As this sheet will not be wide enough for the full diameter of the tank, it will need to be cut and joined together by a grooved seam (fig. 6).

For the seam, a 5/16th seaming tool or groover is used, the raised side of the seam being kept on the top to go inside the tank.

To ensure a neat fold round the bottom it is necessary that the grooved seam be thinned down at each end (fig. 8).

Fig. 4.

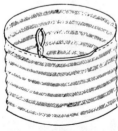

Fig. 5.

The tank is then turned over, and the flanged end laid on the sheet of iron, and scribed down with a small pair of compasses (fig. 7) a margin of 3-8 in. being allowed for the turn-up.

This method of striking out a tank bottom is usually adopted when compasses sufficiently large are not available. Care should

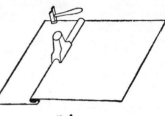

Fig. 6.

be taken in its operation, as if the measurements are not fairly accurate buckling and distortion may occur later.

The bottom being cut out, it is now placed on a bench, and flanged to the line previously marked. This is done by placing the flat iron on the line, and beating the marked margin up to nearly a right angle, as shown in fig. 8.

Then the body is fitted to the bottom as in fig. 9, and the flange closed down as in fig. 10.

A hole should be punched for the tap near the bottom of the tank (fig. 17), large enough to allow a ¾ in. water pipe socket to enter.

A 2 in. hole is also cut close to the top for an overflow outlet (fig. 17). The top edge of the tank may now be flanged over, as was previously done for the bottom.

For the lid, one sheet of 26g. galvd. iron 72 x 36 in. will be needed, and this should be cut and joined with a grooved seam as with the bottom (fig. 6), or riveted as in fig. 11.

The lid is marked out as in fig. 7, and a 15 in. circle is struck for the mouth or manhole; this can be placed in the centre or near the side as required. The flange is then beaten up as in fig. 8.

Around the mouth a good strengthening

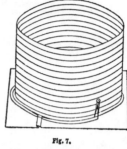

Fig. 7.

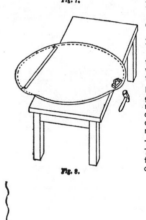

Fig. 8.

Fig. 9.

collar is usually placed. This is made by taking a strip of plain galvd. iron about 2 in. wide, and of a length sufficient to circle the opening and allow of a 1 in. overlap, and cut as in fig. 12.

The above is not turned up as in fig. 13, and a rod of ¼ in. round iron of similar length is enclosed (fig. 14), three-quarters of an inch of the round iron being left protruding at the lap end to strengthen the joint.

Next, round the collar up as shown in fig. 15, and secure with a small rivet. Insert the collar in the mouth, and beat the flange over, as in fig. 16.

In fitting the lid to the tank, the same procedure

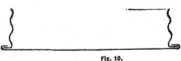

Fig. 10.

Fig. 11.

192

WATER CONSERVATION AND OTHER HINTS

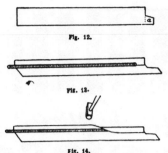

Fig. 12.

Fig. 13.

Fig. 14.

is followed as with the bottom. Fig. 17 shows the lid in position. A moveable strainer is usually let into the mouth of the tank (fig. 20).

Research work on the life of tanks has shown that an open or well ventilated top will result in longer life than is the case when a flat top is fitted.

Where insect pests are prevalent or dust, or falling leaves renders a top necessary, the life of the tank will be lengthened

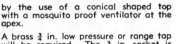

Fig. 15.

by the use of a conical shaped top with a mosquito proof ventilator at the apex.

A brass ¾ in. low pressure or range tap will be required. The ¾ in. socket is now inserted about a quarter of its length in the hole already made, and soldered firmly into position.

The socket is supported by a boss (fig. 18) which is easily made from a piece of plain galvd. iron, 9 x 4 in.; cut a hole 1¼ in. in diameter, and then shape as shown in fig. 19, by bending along the dotted lines. The boss will then have a rough resemblance to a funnel, the small end being made to fit tightly around the end of the socket, and the other end trimmed to the contour of the tank (fig. 17). Then solder the boss securely to the tank, also along the joint, and around the socket.

Fig. 16.

There now remains only the soldering to complete the tank.

For this, a fairly heavy soldering iron, weighing not less than 2 lb. should be used. All rivet heads and seams on the outside of the tank must be carefully soldered, extra care being taken with the bottom. Finally, the tap may be screwed into its right place.

About 4 lb. of solder will be required for the above tank, and 4 lb. of rivets and washers. The foregoing details can be applied in making tanks of all capacities.

Fig. 21 will show the tools required. In addition, a riveting hammer and a 2 lb soldering iron will also be necessary.

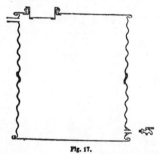

Fig. 17.

Fig. 18.

Fig. 20.

When building tanks of more than 4 ft. high the vertical seam on the third cylinder should be over that of the first cylinder and so on (see fig. 22).

The practice of tarring galvd. iron tanks and troughing should be regarded with suspicion. Some tars contain acids which promote the rusting of galvanised iron and, unless local experience has definitely shown the particular tar available to be strongly protective, it should not be used.

There are special preparations which do the job well.

Materials Required. The following are necessary for tanks up to 1,000 gals.—the 200 gal. tank having already been dealt with. A ¾ in. tap and socket is required for each or 1 in. for larger tanks.

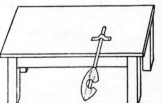

Fig. 19.

400 galls.
Size
3 ft. 9 in. dia. x 6 ft. high. 6 sheets G.C. iron 6 x 24g., each curved to half circle, 1 sheet galvd. plain iron, 6 x 3 x 24g. 1 sheet galvd. plain iron, 6 x 3 x 26g.

About 6 lb. solder, 6 lb. rivets and washers.

600 galls.
Size
4 ft. 4 in. dia. x 6 ft. high. 6 sheets G.C. iron, 7 ft. x 24 gauge, each curved to half a circle. 2 sheets galvd. plain iron, 6 ft. x 2 ft. x 24 gauge. 2 sheets galvd. plain iron, 6 ft. x 2 ft. x 26 gauge. Together with 6 lbs. solder, 6 lbs. rivets and washers.

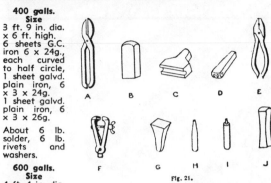

A   B   C   D   E

F   G   H   I   J

Fig. 21.

800 gallons
Size, 5 ft. 3 in. dia. x 6 ft. 3 sheets G.C. iron, 8 x 24 g., each curved to half circle. 3 sheets G.C. iron, 9 x 24 g., each curved to half circle. Note.—Join one 8 ft. sheet and l 9 ft. to form a circle. 1 sheet galvd. plain iron 6 ft. x 2 ft. 6 in. x 24g. 1 sheet galvd. plain iron 6 ft. x 3 ft. x 24g. 1 sheet galvd. plain iron 6 ft. x 2 ft. 6 in. x 26g. 1 sheet galvd. plain iron 6 ft. x 3 ft. x 26g. 7 lbs. solder, 7 lb. rivets and washers.

1,000 gallons
Size, 6 ft. dia. x 6 ft. high. 3 sheets G.C. iron, 9 ft. x 24g., each curved to half circle., 3 sheets G.C. iron 10 ft. x 24g. each curved to half circle. Note.—Join one 9 ft. sheet and one 10 ft. to form a circle.

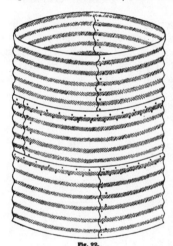

Fig. 22.

2 sheets galvanised plain iron 6 ft. x 3 ft. x 24g. 2 sheets galvanised plain iron 6 ft. x 3 ft. x 26g.

A GALVANISED IRON WATER CATCHMENT

Where it is difficult to direct rain into an excavated tank, a special catchment as indicated here is very useful. This consists of a roof of galvd. iron, built on a hillside or slope, sloping towards a central point, thus enabling the water to run along and into the storage tank. With a known average rainfall one can gauge the storage capacity needed. A roof 120 x 100 ft. in a rainfall of 20 in. would equal about 9

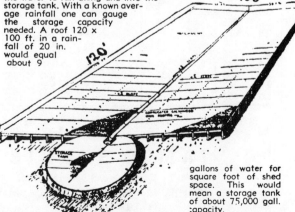

gallons of water for square foot of shed space. This would mean a storage tank of about 75,000 gall. :apacity.

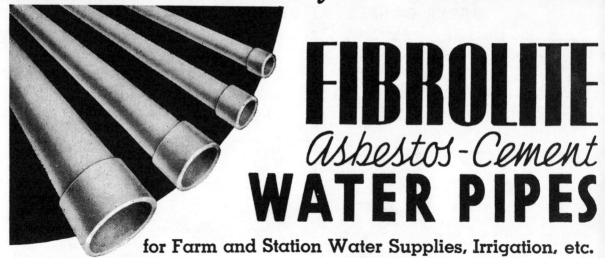

WATER CONSERVATION AND OTHER HINTS

SOME USEFUL WINDMILL AND PIPING HINTS

The following are a few ideas on various subjects connected with windmills, etc., which are the result of experience, any one of which might be useful to someone or other at some time or other.

PUMPING FROM A SHALLOW WELL OR CREEK

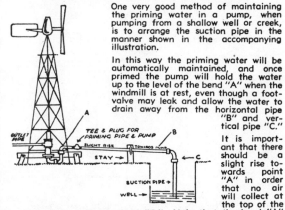

One very good method of maintaining the priming water in a pump, when pumping from a shallow well or creek, is to arrange the suction pipe in the manner shown in the accompanying illustration.

In this way the priming water will be automatically maintained, and once primed the pump will hold the water up to the level of the bend "A" when the windmill is at rest, even though a foot-valve may leak and allow the water to drain away from the horizontal pipe "B" and vertical pipe "C."

It is important that there should be a slight rise towards point "A" in order that no air will collect at the top of the bend just above where marked "C." Note that the bend "A" should be just below the level of the top of the pump and outlet pipe.

NOVEL METHOD OF UTILISING MILL AWAY FROM STEEP BANKS OR DEEP WELL

This sketch shows one very good method. If the sides of the creek or well are at all dangerous, or the well is too wide for the mill tower or if there are any other circumstances which may make it desirable to have the mill placed at a little distance away from the sides, a beam system such as that shown here can be used.

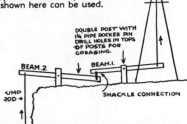

As windmills are constructed to work on the up-stroke, two beams should be used in order that the up-stroke of the pump will synchronise with that of the mill. Two beams of equal length are balanced on two supports which are slung between double posts. One end of beam No. 1 connects with the mill rod—the other end to beam No. 2. The other end of beam No. 2 connects to the pump rod.

HOW TO USE A MILL TO PUMP TWO TYPES OF WATER

If a bore should contain water which is not wholly suitable for use and circumstances permit of the partial use of other nearby water say from a creek or dam the two waters may be pumped by the one mill or engine and proportioned as desired.

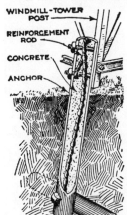

The sketch shows the idea.

If the two supplies are near each other the bore water is delivered as usual into a tank whilst a second pump rod is connected to work another pump, fixed on the ground alongside

side the bore. Should the supplies be so spaced, that it is impossible to draw water by means of a pump alongside the bore, other ideas as described here may be used.

NOVEL WAY OF USING A WINDMILL WHEN WATER IS IN GULLY AWAY FROM EFFECTIVE WINDPOWER

An arrangement like this would be useful to those who may have water in some spot where little or no wind reaches it and therefore it would not be of any use erecting a mill there.

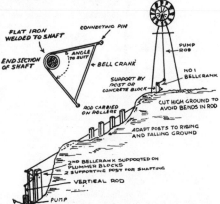

A mill can then be erected on a hill or distant spot where there is good wind and two bellcranks made and fixed in position as shown. No. 1 bellcrank is fixed under the mill, with one arm connected to the pump rod and the other to an inclined rod leading down to the pump. The sketch will better explain the idea. The connecting rod from the mill to the pump must be suitably supported so that it does not bend and thus lose length in the stroke. Galvanised piping makes the best rod.

Bellcrank No. 2 is then fitted to the lower end of the inclined rod, thus converting the rod to vertical which then leads direct to the pump. The two supporting posts at foot of the sketch are not in true perspective, but are meant to convey the idea of support for the bellcrank.

A HANDY REINFORCED ANCHOR POST FOR MILL

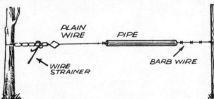

Where windmill anchor posts may have rusted away, or where a good lasting post is required, the following idea will be found both useful and everlasting.

First, place ¾ in. reinforcing rods in each post at one side of the anchor bolts. Then fill the pipes with a free running mixture of sand and cement.

The concrete should be thoroughly tamped, and of a mixture in the proportion of two parts sand to one of cement, and of a quaky consistency.

A 3 inch or 3½ inch pipe would be best for strength.

This little idea could, of course, be applied to other uses, especially where strength is required, say, in connection with fencing, etc., or in other forms of building.

HOW TO CLEAN THE INSIDE OF RUSTY PIPES

If piping gets rusty or corroded inside, thread through it some plain wire to which is attached some barb. Then tie both ends tightly to two posts or trees. The pipe can then be slid to and fro over the barbs when they should be scraped fairly clean. The barbs will wear with use, but can be replaced from time to time. Various size wires can be used for various size pipes—a very small barb being used for, say, ¼ in. pipe. A wire strainer will also facilitate changing the pipes when necessary, and a little paint drained through the cleaned pipe is a good idea.

WATER CONSERVATION AND OTHER HINTS

AN AUTOMATIC WINDMILL SHUT-OFF

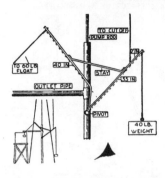

Here are two or three home-made ideas for switching the mill out of the wind when the tank is quite full enough.

In the first illustration, a wire from arm B runs over a' roller on the top of the tank and is fastened to a float in the tank.

This float is 60 lbs. in weight. Arm B is 40 ins. in length. Arm C, which is almost at right angles to Arm B, is 35 ins. in length, and has a 40 lb. weight hanging to the end by wire, with the mill pull-out wire arranged 7 inches from the end.

Weights and measurements may have to be varied for different mills.

The principle is that the weight in the tank must lift the 40 lb. weight on the end of arm C as the water level drops in the tank. When the water level rises, the float also rises, and the weight on the opposite end must be sufficient to pull the mill out of the wind.

THE BALL TAP METHOD OF WINDMILL SHUT-OFF

With this method, the mill is always· definitely "off" or "on."

A ball tap is fitted to the end of the outflow pipe, which has been fitted with a T-joint, from which a length of hose runs to a flange in the bottom of an 8-gal. drum attached to the shut-off wire.

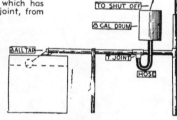

As the tank fills, the ball tap closes the end of the out-flow pipe, and water is pumped into the drum which, when full, pulls the wire and puts the mill out of the wind. As the water-level recedes in the tank, the ball tap opens and the water drains out of the drum, allowing the mill to swing into action again. When in its lowest position, the drum should still be above the out-flow pipe.

THE FORK AND LEVER METHOD

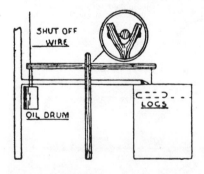

This is also a simple and effective method for an automatic shut-off for the windmill, one that has been tried with success.

Its construction is clearly shown, indicating the use of an oil drum in conjunction with the fork and lever method.

If the tank is 6 or 8 feet away from the mill, one needs a piece of timber to go from the middle of the mill to two feet inside the tank and a fork to carry same with bolt through fork and lever, as shown in the smaller detail.

Get an 8-gallon drum and tie on mill end and fill with dirt or stones to pull the mill off, and then cut logs of wood for a float. When the tank is full the logs will float, and when the tank gets empty or low, the float should be heavy enough to lift the pull off the mill.

ANOTHER SIMPLE WINDMILL SHUT-OFF

In this arrangement, a beam is pivoted on a forked stick and a heavy weight is hung on each end, say, something in the nature of some blocks of cement in kerosene tins being a very good idea.

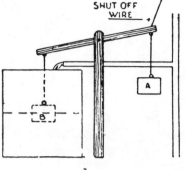

Block "A" is attached to the shut-off wire at one end of the beam, and block "B" hangs in the tank.

By adjusting the weights, either by chipping them or by moving them further along the beam, it will be possible to arrange them so that when the tank is full, the density of the water will allow block "B" to rise and the weight of the block "A" will pull the shut-off wire and put the mill out of the wind.

As the water recedes in the tank, block "B" exerts a greater pull, and lifts up block "A," allowing the mill to operate again. This method should not fail, and should last without attention until the iron rusts or the wood rots.

WHEEL SHUTS OFF DISTANT WINDMILL

This is quite a good idea, and it is arranged by mounting an old hay rake wheel on a pipe and supporting the end by posts. In

this way one farmer was able to turn on or off a windmill which was far distant in the pasture, and he found it a very convenient arrangement indeed.

A galvanised wire, supported occasionally by a pole, with a hole in the top, runs from the mill to the wheel. For the portion which winds about the wheel shaft, a chain is substituted.

Since the ratio between the wheel and the shaft on which the chain winds is about 35 or 40 to one, it is only necessary to weight one side of the wheel and it will not permit the mill to turn off or on without someone turning the wheel by hand. Yet a single vigorous spin of the wheel will do either.

HOME-MADE BALL-TAPS

We have several very good ideas for home-made ball-taps, but space does not permit of their inclusion in this issue. However, this one is an idea for a very cheaply made ball - tap which should act very well where low pressure water supplies are used.

The outlet pipe from the tank is fitted with an elbow or bend, downwards as indicated.

A piece of hoop-iron is doubled and clipped over the pipe to form a hinge on which the float-arm operates. The float-arm is a length of 1 in. flat-iron to which is attached a float or ball. A tarred tin of suitable size makes a good one. At the hinge end, the flat-iron is given a half twist.

Just below the outlet pipe, a small plate of flat-iron covered with rubber is riveted to the float-arm, so that it is pressed against the outlet as the float rises. If it is boxed in to guard against damage by the stock, a ball-tap of this type will give good service for years.

WATER CONSERVATION AND OTHER HINTS

A BUSH WINDMILL

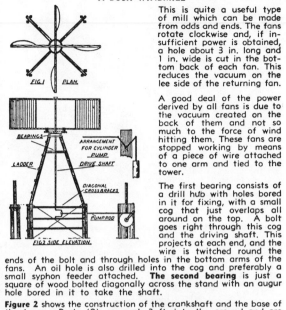

FIG.1   PLAN

BEARINGS

LADDER

ARRANGEMENT FOR CYLINDER PUMP

DRIVE SHAFT

DIAGONAL CROSS BRACES

PUMP ROD

FIG.2 SIDE ELEVATION.

This is quite a useful type of mill which can be made from odds and ends. The fans rotate clockwise and, if insufficient power is obtained, a hole about 3 in. long and 1 in. wide is cut in the bottom back of each fan. This reduces the vacuum on the lee side of the returning fan.

A good deal of the power derived by all fans is due to the vacuum created on the back of them and not so much to the force of wind hitting them. These fans are stopped working by means of a piece of wire attached to one arm and tied to the tower.

The first bearing consists of a drill hub with holes bored in it for fixing, with a small cog that just overlaps all around on the top. A bolt goes right through this cog and the driving shaft. This projects at each end, and the wire is twitched round the ends of the bolt and through holes in the bottom arms of the fans. An oil hole is also drilled into the cog and preferably a small syphon feeder attached. **The second bearing** is just a square of wood bolted diagonally across the stand with an augur hole bored in it to take the shaft.

Figure 2 shows the construction of the crankshaft and the base of the tower. Posts (9) are sunk 3 ft. into the ground and are nailed round the outside, and two poles are bolted diagonally about 3 ft. from the ground, and wires twitched from the top to bottom to top of the opposite posts. On the left is the built-in ladder. The idea of the posts is to enable mallet poles to be used for the tower. The long poles are not erected until the posts are strutted and tight (the front rail is left out of the drawing). **The Pump Rod** is of mallet and the connecting joints are made of hoop iron with old hose tighteners on the handle and crankshaft.

Figure 4 is an arrangement for working a cylinder pump; the power is taken over a bearing, and changed to vertical. If the fans are closer to the driving shaft, great speed results, but less power, and if the fans are less than 2 ft. out, the wind would curl around in them and create a back pressure and stop them.

The fans should be at right angles to the driving shaft, and no set at all. Before the mill is connected to the pump it should be let run on its own in order to work in, plenty of oil being used on it.

ANOTHER SERVICEABLE WINDMILL FROM SCRAP

This sketch is of a mill built by one farmer from scrap. Two oil drums are cut in half vertically to provide the vanes, which are mounted on a wooden frame to rotate on a horizontal plane. The frame was centred and securely fastened to a car wheel by means of U-bolts, and the wheel was then keyed to the end of a driveshaft on a rear-axle assembly, which was rigidly fastened on a tower made of poles and old timber.

With this arrangement, it was

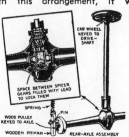

CAR WHEEL KEYED TO DRIVE-SHAFT

SPACE BETWEEN SPIDER GEARS FILLED WITH LEAD TO LOCK THEM

WOOD PULLEY KEYED TO AXLE

SPRING

PIN

WOODEN PITMAN

REAR-AXLE ASSEMBLY

necessary to make both axles of the rear end work as one, and therefore the space between the spider gears was filled with lead to lock them. On the end of one axle, a wood pulley was keyed, this being provided with an eccentric pin to drive a wooden pitman, the lower end of which was connected to the pump.

USEFUL HOME-MADE FARM FOOTBRIDGES

The first sketch is an arched bridge, made in two sections of equal length, made by nailing 3 ft. lengths of 1 in. board to two pieces of 2 x 6 in. plank. The total length of the two sections,

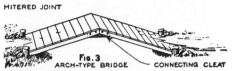

MITERED JOINT

Fig. 3
ARCH-TYPE BRIDGE   CONNECTING CLEAT

Two Simple Footbridges for Spanning a Small Ra-
vine or Stream That can be Made from Readily
Available and Inexpensive Materials

when laid end to end, should exceed the width of the place to be bridged by several feet. Two posts are solidly planted at each end of the bridge site so that the distance between them will be from 1 to 1½ ft. less than the width of the sections. When the shore ends of the sections are made to butt against the two pairs of posts, the ends at the centre will be somewhat higher, as shown.

Heavy cleats behind the planks are used for securing the sections together at the centre. Such a bridge will support itself and will bear a remarkable amount of weight.

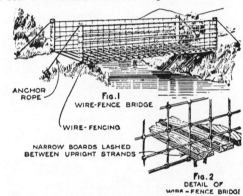

ANCHOR ROPE

Fig. 1
WIRE-FENCE BRIDGE

WIRE-FENCING

NARROW BOARDS LASHED BETWEEN UPRIGHT STRANDS

Fig. 2
DETAIL OF
WIRE - FENCE BRIDGE

The second is made of heavy galvd. wire and narrow boards. Four posts, 2 at each end, are set into the ground at the desired distance apart, usually about 3 ft. These should be securely anchored to the anchor posts, a few feet to the rear. Wire fencing is stretched across the space and made fast to the posts on opposite sides, care being taken to have the bottom strand of each strip parallel with the other. One inch boards for the floor should be drilled at each end and secured to the bottom strands of the fencing with wire (as shown in detail 2).

The third is made from discarded rails which make an excellent footbridge. A log is buried on each bank of the creek and the ends of the rails spiked to them. The floor (2 in. hardwood planks) rest in the lower flanges. When spiking down the rails, care should be taken to get them parallel, so that the deck

SPIKES   OLD RAILS   2" PLANKS   4" X 5" TIMBER

planks, a neat fit, will slide into place from one end. A couple of stout pegs driven into the ground on each bank at the ends of the planks, where they will be out of the way of traffic, will prevent the deck from shifting.

WATER CONSERVATION AND OTHER HINTS

WATER LEVEL INDICATORS FOR TANKS

A Long-distance Tank Level Indicator

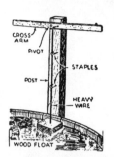

This device will enable one to know when a tank supplied by a mill is full and so save going any distance.

The indicator is a wooden cross arm pivoted to a post, which is set in the ground so as to project above the tank. A stiff wire, running through staples placed in the side of the post, is fastened to the arm and to a wooden float inside the tank, the wire being of such length that the arm is almost vertical when the tank is empty, and horizonal when full.

This can be adapted to any form of tank or trough for stock, showing at a glance the height at which the water stands.

A Level Indicator for a Concealed Tank

This can be fitted to almost any tank. The float, in this instance, is a tightly stoppered varnish tin, attached to one end of a hinged wooden arm, as shown. The opposite end of the arm is provided with an eye screw, to which one end of a stout board or flexible wire is attached.

The indicator dial is made of wood or sheet metal, and is supported on a pipe standard as shown, the lower end of the pipe being split and spread at right angles to form feet, which are bolted to the top of the tank. The indicator is made of polished tin or brass, and is attached to one end of a light shaft, to which a wooden spool or drum is secured, behind the dial, a sheet metal strap supporting the rear end of the shaft as shown.

The cord or wire from the float arm is brought up through the pipe and is given two turns around the spool. The free end of the cord has a suitable counterweight attached to it which is concealed inside the pipe standard.

Another Simple Tank Gauge

This is another simple gadget that will indicate the amount of water in a distant tank. All that is required is a forked stick and a long light pole with the long end in the tank and a float attached. The float can be light wood, cork, or a

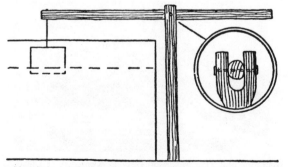

soldered tin. Adjust so that the pole is level when the tank is full, and it is then easy to gauge the water level by the angle of the pole as the float sinks downward.

EMERGENCY REPAIRS TO SPLIT PIPES

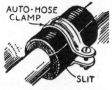

These are two good ways of effecting temporary repairs to damaged pipes. **The first** is more of a temporary nature in which a piece of garden hose (say about 2 in.) is used, slit along one side and clamped down over the leak with either one or two clamps.

The second is almost a permanent job, which can be further tightened if necessary. It is a special clamp of round iron rod, threaded on each end previous to winding it round the pipe.

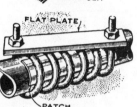

A flat plate is drilled to receive the ends of this clamp and it is then screwed down tightly, as shown. Before applying the clamp, a patch of rubber or packing and a metal plate bent to the contour of the pipe is placed over the break.

USEFUL WAYS OF BENDING PIPES (see also page 20.)

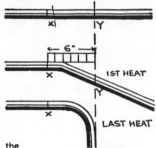

These hints might be useful where unorthodox bends are required or where no fittings are available. **In the first,** a plug is inserted in the lower end of the pipe, which is then stood on end and filled with sand. The sides are then hammered so as to pack the sand, more being added until no more can be put in. This tightly packed sand prevents kinking when bending.

A plug is then put in the top end. The pipe is then heated to a red heat, where it is to be bent—the larger the pipe the greater should be the radius of the bend—do not attempt short bends with large pipe nor expect to finish the bend with one heat.

The second shows a very useful procedure when bending either with or without a sand filling; it will also save a lot of cutting, threading and use of fittings.

First, in order to ascertain where the bend should commence, mark a position, say, 6 in. short (see x) of the line to which the pipe is to be bent (y); this ensures that the bend finishes in the right place. It should then be heated at "x" and quenched with water on each side, leaving only, say, 2 in. red hot.

Only a slight bend should be made at first; then, reheating and repeating the process several times (each time taking care that only the small portion to be bent remains red hot) till the bend is gradually completed. Do not overdo the bending.

A USEFUL PIPE BENDING POST

A post bored with holes of various sizes is a convenient one to have handy. Pipe can then be put into whichever hole it fits and the bend can be made easily with the use of a vice. In time, the edges of the holes may become burned, but roundness of edge does not matter.

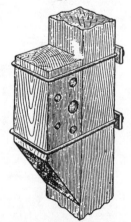

WATER CONSERVATION AND OTHER HINTS

REMOVING RUST FROM PIPING

This is one good method of cleaning rusty piping — the scraper shown being in every way as good as a steel brush.

It is made by riveting several rows of bottle caps to the inside surface of a piece of old tyre casing. Each cap is held in place by a single split rivet and is used in the manner shown at the bottom of the sketch.

CONNECTING PIPES TO TANKS

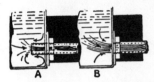

For best results, pipe connections to tanks should not project inside them as the projecting ends cause considerable friction against the flow of liquid (as indicated at "A."

When the connection is made as at "B," the resistance to the flow is less than half of that when the pipe projects inside. The idea shown here is therefore one method of doing this, although the same fault to a lesser degree is apparent.

ANOTHER METHOD OF CONNECTING PIPE TO TANK

This is one improvised method when there is no tap available, but is not so good as the above. It is done by threaded rings from a pipe fitting and gives best results if the projection inside the tank is no more than the width of the threaded ring.

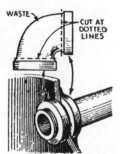

Any pipe projecting further can be filed off.

In this sketch an elbow is also used by sawing off the end. After screwing one of the rings so made over the pipe on each side of the tank, and drawing them tight, molten solder is brushed over the outside ring to help make the connection watertight.

HOW TO PREVENT A DRAIN PIPE FROM CLOGGING

In this instance, the idea of inserting an elbow into the tank has a different purpose. Where pressure is not needed and where the tanks in question are apt to get dirty, this arrangement is a good one.

Instead of using a screen to prevent drain pipes from getting clogged up by floating debris in the tank, add an elbow to the intake end of the pipe and turn it down. The opening of the drain pipe is then always below the level of the water flowing out of the pipe.

A TILE GATE FOR A SMALL DAM

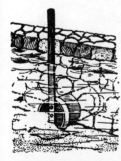

Trouble is often caused by a leaky gate in a dam. A square gate may stick just at the time when it is to be raised. Such difficulties can be avoided by using a simple gate made of a piece of tile pipe.

Put the tile through the dam with the collar side inside the dam. Bolt a pole to a round wooden disc which will fit the collar of the tile. The pole is long enough to project above the waterline. When the gate thus formed is in position, some dirt is thrown against it to hold it in place.

This closes the outlet through the dam. When it is to be opened, remove the cover from the end of the tile by using the pole as a lever.

MAKING A CONCRETE TILE OUTLET

Very often a drainage system is spoilt by its outlet, caused by dirt washing down the bank and stock tramping down loose dirt and stones in front of the mouth of the tile. The only way to prevent this occurring is to build a concrete wall around the mouth of the tile in order to hold the dirt back and to prevent the tile from caving in.

These illustrations show how to make a concrete retaining wall that will be quite effective. The wall should be at least 6 ft. long and 8 inches thick. The height will depend upon the height of the ditch bank. An entire height of 4 feet is usually sufficient, one foot of which is below the surface. This leaves three feet above ground.

The form is made of boards of 4 x 2 material.

The form needs only to be built for that part of the wall that extends above the surface as shown in the section view.

Stakes and braces are used to hold the form in place. A 1-2-3 mixture should be used, and care taken to work the concrete well under the tile into the corners of the form.

REPAIRING LEAKS IN UNDERGROUND PIPES

A drain pipe which is laid underground can be repaired in the manner shown here. After digging down to the pipe, a half tile is placed under it and the pipe is wrapped with a couple of layers of tape to cover the hole.

Sheet metal is then bent around the pipe to give a half inch clearance all round and to provide a form. Dirt is then banked at both ends of the form, after which junk babbit and lead is poured around the pipe.

A SIMPLE CONTROL VALVE

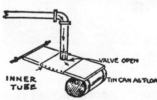

This is a simple way to make a valve to control the flow of water from tank to trough. It is another use for the well-known inner tube. A bit of board is hinged as shown. To it is attached an empty tin, say, 1 gal. capacity. This presses the rubber against the end of the pipe and shuts off the water when the trough is full. The sketch will show the manner of construction which is quite effective.

HINTS ON MAKING EXCAVATIONS SYMMETRICAL

With Aid of Rod and String

In excavating for a cistern or tank, or for any other purpose, it will be found that the opening can be kept symmetrical as the work progresses by measuring with a string from a rod driven into the ground on the centre line of the excavation.

The measurements are taken at regular intervals, and the rod is driven down as the soil is removed.

WATER CONSERVATION AND OTHER HINTS

AERATING STALE WELL WATER

When water is allowed to stand for some time in a well or underground tank without being used, it becomes stale and often has a bad odour. This can usually be dissipated by aerating the water.

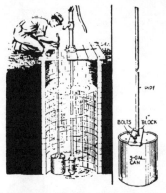

The simplest way to do this is to attach a kerosene tin or a 5-gallon oil drum to a long rod or piece of pipe. One end of the drum is removed, and four or five holes punched in the other end. A bar of wood fastened across the closed end and held by screws or small bolts serves to fix the handle to the drum, as shown in the annexed sketch.

A pipe flange, if obtainable, is useful for this purpose, especially if the handle is made from pipe.

To operate the device, the drum is pushed to the bottom of the well by means of the handle and raised above the surface again. This process is repeated a number of times. The air trapped in the drum at the surface is slowly released as the drum is forced downwards, and is thus distributed all through the water, the air bubbles carrying away the bad odour as they float to the surface.

FLOAT IN WELL OR TANK PROVIDES CLEAN WATER

Many wells or tanks have so much sediment in the bottom that the water pumped from them is muddy and hardly fit to use. While the condition may be remedied by cleaning, this is no permanent cure.

One man solved the problem as shown in the sketch. One end of a piece of hose was attached by wire to a short length of 2 x 4 in. timber, the other end of the hose being attached to the lower pipe connection of the pump cylinder. This block, floating upon the water in the cistern, holds the free end of the hose above the sediment at all times. The water pumped from a cistern equipped in this manner is always clear, and contains a minimum of dirt.

NOVEL WAY OF TIPPING BUCKET WHEN BALING FROM TANK OR WELL

This is an idea well worth knowing, although there are, of course, other equally useful and ingenious ways of doing this job.

When water is to be bailed from a tank, cistern or well, it will not be necessary to jerk the bucket about to fill it if a long hook is knotted loosely in the rope at the point indicated.

The hook will engage the bottom rim of the bucket when it is lowered to the surface of the water, holding it in position to be submerged quickly. A slackening of the rope from above releases the hook so that the bucket can be lifted.

ANOTHER SELF-TIPPING BUCKET

One farmer got over the difficulty of tipping a bucket by using the simple clip shown here. This consists of a short piece of hose, which is shaped as indicated in the small inset, and slipped over the rope above the bail of the bucket.

Before lowering the bucket into the cistern, it is inverted and held in this position by slipping the lip of the hose over the rim around the bucket bottom.

When lowered into the water, a quick jerk on the rope releases the clip and permits the bucket to fill. It can then be raised in the ordinary manner.

NOVEL METHOD OF SAMPLING WATER FROM DEEP WELL

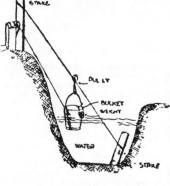

If it is desired to obtain a sample of water from the bottom of a deep well for testing purposes, the following idea of one farmer is well worth knowing.

A small bottle or vial is used, which is weighted with a fishline sinker. First the bottle is corked lightly, after which a long string is tied to the cork, then around the neck of the bottle and finally to a sinker.

This arrangement prevents water near the top of the well from entering the bottle as it is lowered to a position near the bottom. A firm jerk of the line pulls the cork and allows the bottle to fill, after which it can be pulled up.

A HANDY WATER ELEVATOR

This device should interest anyone with a creek frontage.

A length of No. 8 fencing wire is stretched from a post at the top of the bank to a stake driven into the creek bed, in such a position that the lower end of the wire will be completely under water. A bucket is suspended from the wire by means of a pulley and snap hook. A weight must be attached to the side of the bucket in order to sink it. The bucket is operated by a rope, either with the hand or a small windlass.

NOVEL WAY OF DRAWING WATER OVER A STEEP BANK

A 5-gal tin, with the top removed and a square hole cut in the side, is mounted on one end of a trough, which is pivoted between

two upright pieces at the edge of the bank. There is a slight recess at the end to facilitate filling the tin. The other end of the trough is fitted with a handle and is counterweighed to balance the tin.

WATER CONSERVATION AND OTHER HINTS

ANOTHER METHOD OF MENDING LEAK IN WATER PIPE

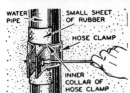

This is another way of mending water pipes which may have developed a leak. They can be quickly stopped by first placing a piece of inner tube over the hole to be mended, setting a piece of sheet metal on top of the rubber, and fastening it in place, as shown. The sheet metal should be bent to take a small bolt which is then tightened.

Another way to utilise an inner tube is to wrap a strip of it tightly stretched around the pipe and over the break, fastened on with friction tape, heavy cord or soft wire. This will hold till a permanent repair can be made.

A HANDY WATER TROUGH FROM TYRE

This is a very handy type of home-made trough which can be used for conveying water from a pump or mill to any place where it may be required. It is made from a discarded tyre.

First cut off the beading and nail the tyre to a length of 4 x 1 timber. Leave about 10 inches unnailed at one end and put on a wire fastening so that it can be slipped over the spout of the pump.

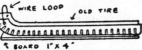

Such an arrangement can be used in connection with small water channels to the vegetable plot, etc.

A NOVEL WATER FLASHLIGHT

This is a novel way in which one farmer found an article he was looking for in rather deep water.

The sketch shows a flashlight inserted into a fruit bottle with the light turned on. The lid is screwed down tightly, and the jar lowered into the water. It should show up any articles quite easily.

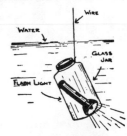

WATER DIVINING

This is one method used quite successfully with ordinary fencing wire. The wire is bent and held with the bent part upwards, as shown. The operator then walks along slowly, holding the wire tightly, and when water is located, the wire will commence to pull downwards.

Many a novice has found water in this fashion without knowing he is able to do it, but, of course, before going to any expense in well-digging, it is much better to call in an expert to confirm your findings.

Some say that when the wire turns away from the body, the chances are that the water is fresh, but if it turns towards the body, it may be inclined to be salty, whilst the strength of the turn will probably indicate the pace of the stream and not the quantity of water.

SUGGESTED METHOD OF COVERING DAMS

As a substitute for iron, bush timber, forks and poles, with ti-tree scrub for thatching, is a good cover. Wire and netting are not so good, as sooner or later the roof will sag.

When covering the dam with bush timber, the important thing is to widen the forks so that the bearers are down on the centre of the forks and not riding on the sides. If this is not done, the weight of the roofing will split the forks and let a part of the dam cover into the water. Saw level on the inside of the fork, then trim straight with axe, as shown.

When the forks are in and bearers on, the light poles and scrub can be put on. Start from the outside and work towards the centre, using a long plank.

When you have covered a dam, it is a good idea to put another dam down alongside the covered one. This extra dam is to keep the covered dam full until wanted, say at end of summer. This will ensure plenty of water.

When the two dams are down alongside each other, erect windmill and tank on the dump between the two dams and fit up as per sketch. A 6 ft. windmill is big enough, and you can use 1¼ inch pipes. Pump from the uncovered dam into the tank which supplies your stock. Leave the mill pumping all the time, and the overflow runs into the covered dam, which will keep that dam full to the top until wanted. There is always some evaporation and soakage during summer, even when your dam is covered.

When the uncovered dam is empty, just undo the socket-union near the pump, turn the short piece of pipe round towards the covered dam, screw the union-socket together on the piping running into the covered dam; let your mill go and it fills your tank from the full dam, and there is no waste, as the overflow runs back into the covered dam. The scheme works very well, and the actual cash outlay is only for the mill, tank and piping. Once they are paid for, you have an asset and fewer water worries. By putting the mill and tank on the dump your mill is 6 ft. higher in the air, and you get a better pressure from the tank.

A hint on erecting the mill. The earth in the dump is not as tight as ordinary ground, so when you assemble the mill tower, bolt two good sleepers to the feet of the tower, then dig two trenches in the dump, and as you pull your tower up, the sleepers will slip into the trenches.

Don't forget to use the spirit level to get your tower level, or the mill-head will not swing true to the wind.

When making the tank, put an extra ¾ in. socket in the bottom, screw a bend and plug in this socket; then, when you want to clean the sediment out of the tank, just unscrew the plug and most of it will drain out.

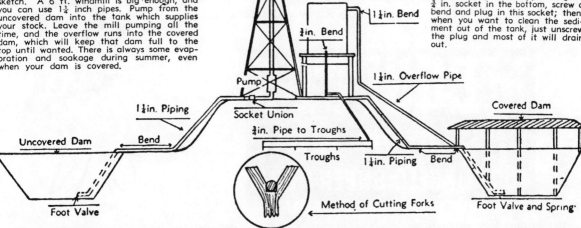

Uncovered Dam · 1¼in. Piping · Bend · Foot Valve · Pump · Socket Union · ¾in. Pipe to Troughs · Troughs · 1¼in. Piping · Method of Cutting Forks · 1¼in. Piping · 1¼in. Bend · ¾in. Bend · 1¼in. Overflow Pipe · Bend · Covered Dam · Foot Valve and Spring

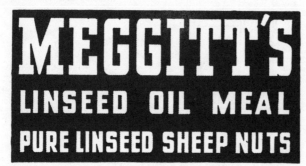

USEFUL HINTS   WITH SHEEP

THE MAIN POINTS

1, Face. 2, Horn. 3, Poll.
4, Scrag. 5, Wither. 6, Girth.
(white line).   7, Back.
8, Loin. 9, Rump. 10, Tail.
11, Twist. 12, Inner Flank.
13, Outer Flank. 14, Hock.
15, Stifle.   16, Pastern.
17, Underline.   18, Elbow.
19, Knee. 20, Brisket. 21,
Shoulder. 22, Apron. 23,
Throat. 24, Muzzle.

OF A SHEEP

Aim for a flock of large-framed sheep. Character is denoted by crimp (the waves seen on wool fibres); the more crimps to the inch, the finer the wool. Sheep should be strong, robust looking, body long and level on top, good depth at girth, well sprung ribs, wide deep chest and legs set well apart.

TELLING THE AGE

The teeth are the best guide, although, of course, that somewhat depends upon the country on which the animal feeds. Rough and stony ground means greater wear and tear than on grass country.

TELLING THE AGE

A sheep has 8 incisors and 24 molars, the former in the lower front jaw, and the latter in both jaws at the back—the upper front jaw, being a rubber-like pad only. The following sketches give appearance at various ages.

At 3 weeks, the 8 incisors usually appear; these are only temporary.

At 12 to 15 mths. the 2 central ones come out, and the first 2 permanent incisors appear. It is then called a two-tooth.

At 2 years, the next tooth on each side of the first pair are replaced. It is then a four-tooth.

At 3 years, the next 2 permanent teeth appear, one on each side of the two-year-old teeth. It is then a six-tooth.

At 4 years, the last two permanent incisors are seen; it is then a full-mouth sheep.

After 4 years, age is more difficult to gauge; when 5 years old, the 2 central incisors will show signs of separating in the middle. At 6 years, the next two will separate and the first two may be broken. It is then termed broken-mouthed.

BLADE SHEARING—SOME IMPORTANT POINTS FOR THE BEGINNER

In quite a number of cases it may be necessary for the small sheep-owner to do his own shearing or he may have someone on the place who may not be an expert, and as such work will probably be done with blade shears and not by machine, these notes and illustrations showing the most important points to be observed may be of interest and assistance in this respect.

The methods given may not, of course, be those used by every expert, but the general principles given are those which, if adopted, will give satisfactory results.

Illustration No. 1 shows how a sheep should be caught in the pen. The left arm should be placed around the neck with the hand on the brisket; the right arm placed around the flank and well up against the right foreleg; the right knee being well under the sheep. Undue gripping of the wool should be avoided in order not to bruise the sheep itself.

To lift the sheep, the right hand then takes hold of the sheep's off foreleg as shown in

Figure 2 (next column). This is the correct procedure for carrying the sheep to the point where it is to be sheared; the right hand gripping the off foreleg so that the sheep can be lifted just clear of the floor. It should then be carried and placed quite gently on the board; the shearer's right foot usually being

used to lever the sheep to the correct position. On no account should a sheep be caught by the hind leg and dragged out of the pen in that fashion. This is a point which should be remembered at all times.

The importance of placing the sheep in the correct position in shearing cannot be over-emphasised and therefore the illustrations and notes given on the following pages should be of assistance in this direction, but before explaining them, we first of all give a list of "DON'TS," which, if borne in mind at all times, will help considerably in shearing.

Don't knock the sheep about.

Handle them gently. Animals will respond to kindness.

Fight them and they will fight you.

Don't lost your temper if the sheep kicks. It is probably your own fault.

Don't put undue strain or weight on the sheep.

Don't cut off their breath by putting your hand across their nostrils.

Don't lean on the sheep. Let your own legs hold you up. The sheep is quite uncomfortable enough without carrying your weight.

Don't endanger your penmate by holding your shears low while the sheep is kicking. Hold them high above your head. Don't have your spare shears standing on the floor. Keep them high up; they are not then dangerous to anyone or anything.

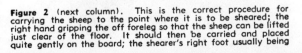

USEFUL HINTS WITH SHEEP

Don't shear in hobnail boots, and don't try to shear too fast.

Take things quietly until you are expert.

DON'T MAKE SECOND CUTS— THEY MEAN WASTE WOOL.

The general principles of shearing procedure are as follow:

Figure 3. With a quick forward movement of the right knee press back the fleece wool just under the shoulder. You can now pick up your shears and get busy.

Clear the brisket and part of the belly, then run the shears down and open up as shown in fig. 5, then clear the remainder; great care being taken when clearing the udder, as it is a serious thing to cut off a teat. The sheep's right foreleg is under the shearer's left armpit.

Figure 4. This illustration indicates the starting of the shearing at the brisket, and when that is cleared off:

Figure 5. Proceed to start shearing the belly. To open up the belly, cut downwards as shown in this sketch.

Figure 6. DO NOT START to open up the belly like this. Cutting across the wool in this fashion means wool not cut right down on the skin; in other words the staple is cut in half, and at the end of the day a surprising amount of wool would be spoilt.

Figure 7. The belly wool having been taken off, you next prepare to clear out the crutch.

The left foot is drawn back to just to the left of the sheep's backbone, and the sheep's body is held back, resting between the shearer's legs, with a firm grip, as is the case in ordinary crutching.

Figure 8. Here we see the crutch cleared out and the left hind leg being shorn. Pressing down the left hand on the sheep's stifle joint will make the leg kick out stiffly, so that it can be shorn easily. Shearing starts at the

hock and cuts up towards the sheep's body.

Figure 9. Shearing down over the tail and clearing the rump. The left hind leg of the sheep is grasped in the left hand of the shearer and the rump is lifted up as the shearing proceeds.

Clear well down under the tail, and with a quick movement of the closed shears fold the shorn wool well under the sheep's rump.

Figure 10. The rump completed, the closed shears are used to sweep the wool under the rump and tuck it out of sight for the time being.

Figure 11. With the right foot in between the sheep's hind legs and its body gripped between the shearer's legs, the neck is pulled straight and bent round the shearer's left knee preparatory to opening up the neck.

Take care not to cut off the sheep's breathing by gripping it tightly round the nostrils; this is what makes a sheep kick.

Figure 12. Having cut up the neck from the brisket to the right of the sheep's lower jaw, pull the wool open—don't draw back the shears and cut the neck wool.

The shearer in this sketch is shown having "broken open" the neck by an outward thrust of the hand with the closed shears in it.

Whether the shearer opens up to the jaw or to behind the sheep's ear is immaterial, it is well to take the line of least resistance here. Don't just chop your way up to the neck; if so, you will be cutting a lot of the best fleece in half.

USEFUL HINTS WITH SHEEP

When shearing down the first side, do not go too far over the backbone because you may spoil a lot of wool by what is known as cutting out into the fleece.

Some do this part of the job in haphazard fashion but if not done cleanly it may be the cause of grass seeds, etc., collecting and sore legs resulting from same.

Figure 15. The sheep is then made to recline on its right side and long sweeping blows are taken with the shears right from rump to neck, this being called clearing the backbone. Note the shearer is carrying his own weight;

Figure 13. The sheep's head having been shorn together with the top-knot, if any, the shearer comes down the left side of the neck and body. Shearing the foreleg is a trifle tricky, but by a quick movement of the left hand, press down the wool on the forearm, and the shears will have it right away. Clear the shoulder, then trim the leg.

Figure 14. If the elbow is grasped as shown in the sketches and squeezed firmly the foreleg will be thrust stiffly out and can be shorn with comparative ease. Never grip the sheep's foot, because it is dangerous. You may get badly cut, and it makes the sheep kick.

he is not kneeling on the sheep's flank as is often done.

Figure 16. Here we see the last ribs being shorn and the right hind leg being approached. The shearer is now about to bring the sheep's head up in front of him to a sitting position.

Figure 17. Just starting to shear the last hind leg. The skin is being pulled up taut by the shearer's left hand, and, later, he will press down on the sheep's stifle joint to stiffen out the hind leg and make it rigid.

The shears are used here with an outward rolling motion; care must be taken, however, as this is a place on the sheep which is easily cut.

HANDY HOME-MADE WOOL TABLES

These are two suggestions which might be of interest. In both, a good, strong frame should be made using 4 x 2 if possible, whilst the frame itself is also bolted throughout as indicated in the sketch even though not shown, each end of the bolt should be countersunk. **The dimensions** of the table are also important, as they should be at least 10 ft. long, 5 to 6 ft. wide (preferably the latter) and 3 feet high. As shown, it is also a good idea to design the legs so that, for economy's sake, they can be folded up and placed against the wall when not in use.

It is also a good idea to nail a piece of timber to secure both legs when the table is in use, which can then be removed to allow them to be folded when shearing is completed.

When in use, the table should be kept away from the wall so that one can have access to it from all sides otherwise the fleece is often incorrectly classed if the classer has to lean right over the table to do the job.

The first table shown below is one of a very strong and useful type of home-made table which is made with laths rounded on top and slotted as shown in the smaller detail. These should be about ¾ in. wide and about 1 in. deep, spaced not less than 1 in. apart. To place these laths in position, countersinking will be necessary, as indicated in the sketch. Do not countersink the full depth of the lath, as a clean and attractive finish can be made by planing the end of the laths down to the level of the frame after they have been fixed in position. Pine or other timber which is easily planed smooth is recommended but timber such as stringy bark, which would splinter easily is not recommended, for obvious reasons.

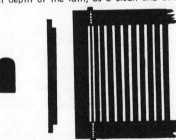

In the second type of table (see below), wooden rollers are used (broomsticks or other material) and these should be placed in positions say ¼ to ½ in. below the level of the top of the framework at a distance between each of approximately ¾ in. (see smaller detail), and inserted into the frame in such a way that they will revolve quite easily.

Holes about ½ in. deep should be bored in the positions as indicated, and these holes should be a little larger than the rollers themselves and should not be bored right through the framework. Naturally, if broomsticks are used the last side of the frame would be fixed after all the holes had been fixed and the slats in position.

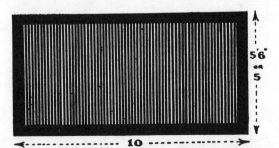

USEFUL HINTS WITH SHEEP

CLASSING A FLEECE AND PREPARING WOOL

These notes are mainly for the beginner and indicate the difference between fine, medium and strong quality wools. Clips marketed with mixed qualities do not attract like even quality wools.

For those that are new to classing, it is a good idea to take a good sheep skin, dry it out carefully, spread it and compare the wool on it with this sketch. Then take a live sheep and examine it and the difference in the character of the wool will be seen. This indicates the general position of the wool.

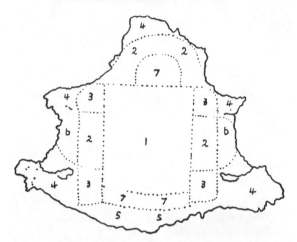

No. 1 is the main fleece, well skirted. No. 2 are the first pieces. No. 3, the second pieces. No. 4, the third pieces. No. 5, stained wool. No. 6, bellies. No. 7, broken wool (shoulders and rump).

Good classing is essential as prices are usually based on the lower value wools in the bale. With small flocks it is not usually necessary to make more than two lines of fleece wool, but the following information may assist those who class their own clips.

The coarser the quality the wider the crimp is apart. All that is really necessary is for a grower to keep the wide crimps apart from the medium, and the medium from the narrow.

QUALITIES

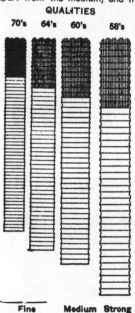

70's 64's 60's 58's

Fine   Medium Strong

These sketches (although not accurate as to quality, will do for purposes of comparison) represent four qualities of merino wool, mostly grown, i.e., fine, medium fine, medium strong and strong.

The shaded portions are shown thus to give the illustrations the appearance of wool, while the unshaded portions are to allow of a comparison of the width of the crimp.

Upon looking at these, it will be found that the lines drawn to represent crimps are wider apart in No. 2 than in No. 1. No. 3 is wider apart than in No. 2, and No. 4 wider than in No. 3.

It will also be noticed that the wider the crimps are apart, the longer the staple and also that the staple is wider across.

A suggestion for branding the various qualities is given in the following:

AA. The finest quality, the longest and most even in length (narrow crimps). If possible, show the difference by adding E for ewes, H for hoggets, W for Wethers, Lbs. for lambs, MO for merino, and Xbd for cross-bred.

AA Comb. Medium quality (or medium crimps).

BB Comb. Strong quality (or wide crimps).

A. The shorter and heavier fleece wools. Do not include any strong or discoloured fleeces.

Pieces. Pack in two lines if possible; the longest and brightest being marked A pieces.

Bellies. After removal of stained pieces.

Stained Pieces. These should be dried and packed quite separately.

Locks. These should be free from dags and stained pieces and packed separately.

Lambs' Wool should be classed according to length.

BRAND EVERY BALE ON TOP IN ADDITION TO THE FRONT, WITH BRAND, DESCRIPTION AND NUMBER. AVOID MIXED BALES. SKIRT LIBERALLY

USEFUL HINTS WITH BLADE SHEARS

Most shearers like some adjustment to this type of shear before using them. **In the first sketch,** a pair of new shears are shown but the experience of a number of farmers show that the following adjustments will improve them.

The first operation is rather a drastic one and consists of the actual bending back of the blades in their grips—this makes them open out wider with a smaller opening of the hand, making it easier for the operator. However, this bending back upsets the blades for closing and to get them to shut properly, the "knockers" (KK in the sketches) should be filed away to allow the points of the blades to close properly. This bending back is usually done by hand, with a piece of sacking wrapped round the sharp edge, but a home-made tool, such as that shown at the foot of this column, will do the job.

Such a tool will slip along the grip of the shears until it is in its correct position, when the screw is turned which will gradually force the blade back on its grip, i.e., backwards. Each blade is done until the necessary degree of alteration is attained.

The illustration shows the clamp in just about the correct spot and it should not be any nearer the blade.

In any alterations on new shears, it is important not to upset the "set" of the blades. To gauge the "set," the shears should be closed and looked at edge on. The "set" means the angle at which the two cutting edges meet each other. This should not be disturbed.

In the second illustration, it shows how two cork knockers have been put on to prevent the shears clashing when they are closed. The strap "D" is also an advantage. The right hand is pushed through this and obtains a good grip and purchase for pushing the blades through the wool.

Some bind a shaped piece of flax stick at the point where shown, this being called a jockey, the idea being to lift the heel or butt of the right hand; some thinking this desirable but not necessary.

Shears should be ground on a grindstone with water and not on an emery or any dry grinding material; this latter causes the metal to lose its temper. When in use, they should be ground at least once per day.

USEFUL HINTS WITH SHEEP

A SHEEP CHAIR FOR TREATING FOOT AILMENTS, ETC.

PADDING

This idea comes from England and is a very useful contrivance for holding sheep whilst their feet are being treated for such things as foot rot, etc. It comprises a box, say, 20 x 13½ x 9½ in., the bottom of which is shaped and padded for the sheep to sit upon.

A chain or rope is fastened to the post and passed round the sheep under the forelegs as shown, where it is hooked up. This arrangement can be used in any part of the yard or made portable by means of a strong upright securely fastened to one end of the box.

A HOME-MADE JETTER FOR SMALL NUMBERS

This is an idea based on somewhat similar ideas to others shown in this book—it involving the use of an oil drum and a motor valve.

The sketch will explain itself—a hole is bored in the side of the drum where indicated, into which some ¾ in. pipe is placed and secured.

Some hose is then clamped on one end and a nozzle on the other.

Then solder a motor valve into the small bung. Both bungs should be screwed up tightly after the dipping solution has been put in.

A HOME-MADE TEMPORARY WOOL PRESS

This is quite a good arrangement for a small flock, and it will turn out neat square bales of between 2 and 3 cwt., the wool being trampled into the bale. It

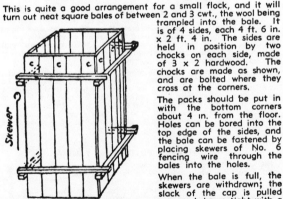

Skewer

is of 4 sides, each 4 ft. 6 in. x 2 ft. 4 in. The sides are held in position by two chocks on each side, made of 3 x 2 hardwood. The chocks are made as shown, and are bolted where they cross at the corners.

The packs should be put in with the bottom corners about 4 in. from the floor. Holes can be bored into the top edge of the sides, and the bale can be fastened by placing skewers of No. 6 fencing wire through the bales into the holes.

When the bale is full, the skewers are withdrawn; the slack of the cap is pulled over and drawn tight with a 4-ply stitch. When this is done, two bolts are withdrawn from the chocks and the bale is released and then sewn up.

ANOTHER HANDY HOME-MADE PRESS

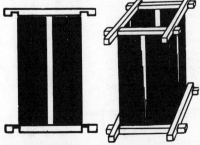

This is another type of home-made wool press which is easily made. The inside dimensions are 4 ft. 6 in. high and 2 ft. 3½ in. square. Steel hooks keep the bale in position while it is being filled and if 4 levers each having 4 hooks are used, it will then be easy to release the bale.

A NOVEL HOME-MADE DRENCHER FOR SHEEP

This is a simple but very effective home-made drencher, which is the idea of Mr. A. C. Duval of Morphett Vale, who has many novel ideas and arrangements on his farm. It is very useful to have on hand for emergencies.

It is merely a five-ounce bottle with a hole bored in it to correspond with the dose required. If, say, a 2 oz. dose is required, the quantity is measured and a hole bored in the bottle to take exactly that amount. A piece of rubber tube is then cut and fitted into the bottle neck in order to give the sheep something to bite on.

In use, the bottle is dipped into the liquid, when any surplus over and above the required dose will run out through the hole, leaving the exact amount in. The thumb is then placed over the hole, the tube inserted in the sheep's mouth, when it will bite on the tube, and as it bites, the thumb is lifted and the sheep will automatically swallow the dose. It is a very quick method and, being of glass, one can see when the animal has taken the full dose.

A NOVEL HOLDER FOR SHEEP LICK

With Automatic Lid to Keep Weather Out—Yet Easy of Access

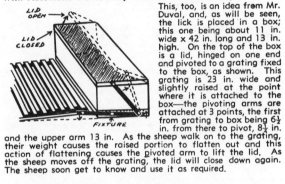

LID OPEN

LID CLOSED

FIXTURE

This, too, is an idea from Mr. Duval, and, as will be seen, the lick is placed in a box; this one being about 11 in. wide x 42 in. long and 13 in. high. On the top of the box is a lid, hinged on one end and pivoted to a grating fixed to the box, as shown. This grating is 23 in. wide and slightly raised at the point where it is attached to the box—the pivoting arms are attached at 3 points, the first from grating to box being 6½ in. from there to pivot, 8½ in. and the upper arm 13 in. As the sheep walk on to the grating, their weight causes the raised portion to flatten out and this action of flattening causes the pivoted arm to lift the lid. As the sheep moves off the grating, the lid will close down again. The sheep soon get to know and use it as required.

ANOTHER USEFUL LICK BOX

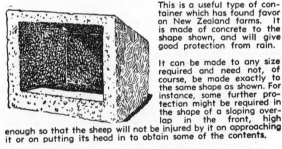

This is a useful type of container which has found favor on New Zealand farms. It is made of concrete to the shape shown, and will give good protection from rain.

It can be made to any size required and need not, of course, be made exactly to the same shape as shown. For instance, some further protection might be required in the shape of a sloping overlap in the front, high enough so that the sheep will not be injured by it on approaching it or on putting its head in to obtain some of the contents.

A COLLAPSIBLE CRATE FOR LIVESTOCK

For forwarding livestock, this crate will be of much use. The sides and bottom are hinged together so that it is collapsible.

Hinge the sides together on 3 sides and provide the fourth with hooks to engage with screw-eyes. The top and bottom of the crate are also hinged and hooked to the sides. When the crates are empty, it is an easy matter to fold them up so that they will occupy very little space.

USEFUL HINTS WITH SHEEP

HOME-MADE HAND FEEDERS FOR LAMBS

This is one idea in which several lambs can be fed at the one time from the one bucket. Drill holes in the bottom of the bucket in the position shown; solder on short lengths of pipe, with a slight rim or bulge at the other end over which a nipple could be slipped without being pulled off.

A frame can be made and this can then be set where the lambs can help themselves. It works well and the lambs soon learn to drink.

The second idea. All that is necessary is a cork to fit the bottle to be used, and a piece of thin rubber tubing about 2½ in. long, together with a piece of thick wire. Heat the wire till red hot, and with it bore a hole through the centre of the cork. Push the tubing through the hole, leaving about 1 in. out of the top for the lamb to suck.

Do not make the hole too big, or the tubing will slip out. The milk may come too quickly for a very young lamb, but the flow is easily regulated by pressure of fingers.

ANOTHER METHOD OF FEEDING MOTHERLESS LAMBS

This idea from New Zealand is worthy of consideration as it has been tried with success there. Make some pegs, as shown, about 18 in. long, pointed at one end, with a curved ring on top, to which is attached a dog chain. On the other end is a swivel attached to a short length of strap, with buckle tongue removed to form a running noose. This is placed over the ewe's front leg, just above the hoof, and pulled tight.

Tether the ewe just where she is found—her first action is to pull back on the noose, and she will hang back for some time in this position, being so occupied in doing so that the lamb has every opportunity to approach from the rear and drink. Once the lamb has succeeded in drinking once or twice, the ewe will usually mother it. The ewe can then be released the same day. It is a good idea to carry several of these round so that they can be put down wherever a ewe is found.

A HOME-MADE FOOTBATH FOR TREATING INFECTED SHEEP

This is of cement and easily made, say 20 ft. long x 20 in. wide and 10 in. deep. Fences or hurdles are placed on each side with a forcing pen at one end and a good draining pen at the other.

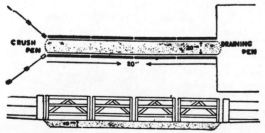

The sheep should not run straight through, but should be checked in batches and not allowed to go into a muddy yard or wet pasture before the solution has had time to act on the infected parts. The depth of solution should be 4 in. and sheep should be handled quietly to avoid splashing, especially if bluestone is used, as the latter will stain the wool. Straw in the bottom of the bath will help in this respect.

FARM BUTCHERING—KILLING A SHEEP

This information is for the amateur and should be found useful.

First, keep the sheep without food for at least 12 hours, but give it water. Tie forelegs and right-hand hind leg together. Lay sheep on left side, draw head back, and insert a sharp knife through neck just behind the jaw. Cut through the neck outward. Bend head back with a jerk to break neck. When blood ceases to flow, untie legs and skin. Put sheep on its back and place left leg between your knees. Make an incision just above

knee and run knife down towards the brisket point, then along neck to head. When this is opened up skin round the leg and down the neck and repeat on the other fore leg. To open hind legs, turn round after doing the second fore leg, and make an incision at the hock. Open the skin down to the tail, and repeat on other side.

Place a gambrel in the hind legs as shown in the diagram, and hoist the carcase to a convenient height. Split the skin that has been opened out between the hind legs and keep opening it down the belly to the brisket end. When the belly skin is opened out, the skin is usually worked off with fist or butt end of knife.

Dressing the Carcase. The skinning completed, take out the intestines, open the belly right down and through the brisket.

Before removing entrails, cut round the rectum and see that the entrail is loose; also the gullet pipe is knotted; as this assists to keep the carcase free from discharge from the entrails.

The heart and lungs, etc., are removed down through the split brisket, after the diaphragm has been cut round. If a sheep is dressed cleanly, little washing is necessary, and the less water used the better, as excessive washing often causes the meat to go bad. It is necessary that the carcase should be thoroughly cold and set before being cut up, if a clean job is to be made.

Joints. The sketch shows the number of joints. When a saddle of mutton is required, the legs are cut short, as marked on the right side. The large leg is indicated on the left side with a dotted line. The right side, between the leg and the level of the fore-quarter, are the full loin and rib chops, from which the flank can be cut any width desired. Many cut the flank full on both sides. The fore-quarter shown consists of shoulder, ribs and brisket.

A HANDY FARM BUTCHERING BARROW

This will be found useful for many jobs and especially when any killing is to be done. Length, 6 ft.—the sides are of timber about 2 ft. apart at the handle and 18 in. at the other end—legs and other fittings as shown.

The sides are joined by lengths of round iron or other material; these being curved in the form of a trough and covered with netting. At the wheel end there is a piece of tin placed so that it will convey the blood into something provided for it underneath.

So that the animal killed will not slip down when the arrangement is stood on end, a short length with a light hook attached is connected to the handles to act as shown in the sketch.

The axle for the wheels should be in a position a short distance from the ends (the actual position depending upon the diameter of the wheel used), in order to allow the barrow to be stood

on end with the front ends of the frame touching the ground.

USEFUL HINTS WITH SHEEP

HOME-MADE HAY RACKS FOR SHEEP

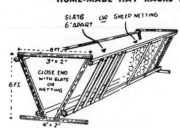

There are several very good and useful home - made hand feeders to be seen, but these ideas may be of interest to some.

The sketch combines two different types— one being made of slats nailed about 6 in. apart and built in the manner shown at the front end of the illustration. These are a good type and will last a long time. At the other end of the sketch a similar idea is shown except that the slats are wider apart and netting used to keep the food in. For the former the measurements would be about 6 ft. across and 6 ft. high and for the latter perhaps 4 ft. high or a little lower. 8 or 9 feet long would be a convenient length.

A HANDY HOME-MADE SHEEP FEEDER FOR SMALL NUMBERS

For such things as chaff, this is very useful. The dotted lines show the essential features—an inverted "V" inside—this extends upwards from the bottom for about 18 in. so that the chaff will slip down over it into the trough (see No. 2). An opening

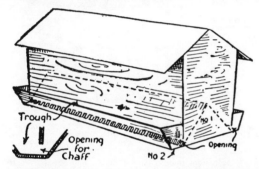

on each side of the feeder between the "V" and the troughs allows the feed to flow freely into the trough as the sheep eat.

The trough is 4 in. wide at bottom and 6 in. at top—7 to 8 in. deep. Walls 3½ to 4 ft. high; width 2 ft. 8 in. at top sloping to about 2 ft. 4 in. at the opening (bottom). Roof should extend beyond the sides to protect food in troughs from weather—iron being better than wooden roofs. If built on two heavy sledge-like timbers, it can be attached to a horse for transport. With strengthening stays, it could be enlarged for larger flocks.

HOME-MADE GRAIN TROUGHS FOR SHEEP

This shows a small inner section (without ends) of a home-made trough (either iron bent to shape or bags) affixed to wire. Good strong posts (about 15 in. dia.) should be embedded firmly in the ground, with 3 ft. above ground—50 or 100 yards apart, and two plain wires are fastened one on each side of the posts, about 14 in. from the ground, to which are affixed the sides of the trough. If bags are used, the latter are joined end to end and

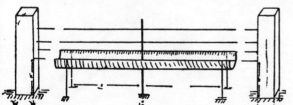

wires are laced through the sides and strained tightly. To support the troughing, hardwood posts are also placed 8 to 10 ft. apart on both sides.

To prevent sheep from jumping over, two wires 6 in. apart above trough level, supported by iron droppers 16-18 ft. apart, driven through the trough, are used, whilst to keep the bottom down in windy weather, stones or wire can be put in the bottom.

ANOTHER HOME-MADE FEEDER FROM CORNSACKS OR SUPER BAGS

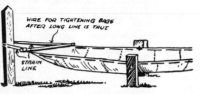

These are efficient and easy to make, whilst they can be hitched to trees or posts as desired — preferably at brisket height. When the bags are sewn together, they are threaded with wire along the edges and are kept open by spacing bars bored to take the wires. Spacing posts are also needed, as shown, say, about 10 feet apart. The wires can be strained as indicated, being eased around the post in order to get an even tension, with extra wires running from the spreader round the trees to maintain the bags at a proper tension.

ANOTHER IMPROVISED RACK FROM NETTING

The following are two other types of netting feeders (both somewhat similar), but finished off in different ways.

In the first, you take a roll of ordinary big gauge netting and fold it in half (length-wise). Fix two stakes in the ground and the top of the netting to the stakes (the width apart depending upon the height of the netting) ; put down stakes on both sides about every 10 yards, this making a trough. Sheep will not bite through the wire.

The second is another cheaply made hay feeder. Take some 3 ft. netting and 10 gauge wire and build it as follows:—Cut 4 posts for each section, say 7 in. thick and 6 ft. long. Measure off the side for the rack and erect the 4 posts, 10 ft. apart and about 2 ft. 6 in. between—the post being 2 ft. in ground. Then bore a

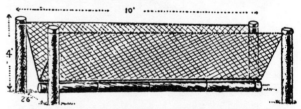

hole through the upright a few inches from the top. Cut netting into 10 ft. lengths, thread the wire through the netting and through the holes in the posts and secure the wire tightly.

Iron or logs can then be used for the bottom as shown. The top of the feeder can be covered by a 12 ft. sheet of iron. The width at the top could be wider to carry more hay. Keep the feeder clear of the ground and yet not to the extent of encouraging the stock to crawl under it.

A PORTABLE WHEELBARROW TYPE OF SHEEP-FEEDER

It often happens that one wishes to run sheep or other animals on several different pastures, or perhaps give them special food,

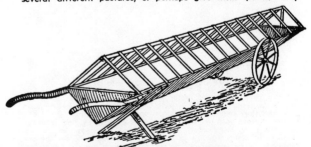

PORTABLE RACK FEEDER

and this arrangement will help. It is simply mounted on a pair of wheels at one end, having handles affixed at the other or, if it is a large one, it can be attached to a waggon.

USEFUL HINTS WITH SHEEP

HOME-MADE FARM SHEEP DIPS

It should be essential for practically every property carrying sheep in districts where dipping is necessary to be equipped with a suitable dipping bath and the following illustrations will give some good and varied ideas in this direction.

These have all been well tried out and found very satisfactory, so perhaps one idea among them might be found useful to any who contemplate building. Space in this issue does not permit of the inclusion of all the ideas we have, but others will appear in any other book which we might later on have the opportunity of publishing.

The first sketch is of a straight out design recommended by one manufacturer of sheep dips and the others are of dips made by various farmers, etc. This particular design is one adaptable for small and medium size flocks, and its construction will be found self-explanatory. In making one of this type, the following materials, in addition to the gates and fences, would be required.

Concrete Mixture—A mixture of 1:2:4 is very suitable.

The Bath—6 cubic yards of metal; 3 cubic yards of sand, and 39 bags of cement, each 94 lbs., will be needed.

Draining Yards—For this (4 in. concrete), 5 cubic yards of metal, 2½ cubic yards of sand, and 31 bags of cement would be required.

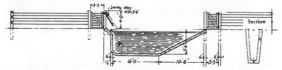

As regards the cement plaster, a 2:1 mixture should be used and 10 cubic feet of sand, while 5 bags of cement will be needed for the bath. 16 cubic feet of sand and 18 bags of cement would do for the draining yards.

If bricks are used instead of concrete, there would be 2,000 bricks (9 in. walls) and a cement mortar would be required, containing 2 cubic yards of sand and 21 bags of cement.

The draining yards would take 1,500 bricks, with 1 cubic yard of sand and 9 bags of cement for the cement mortar.

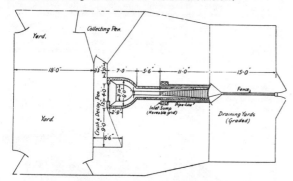

SOME USEFUL HINTS ON DIPPING

Dip big sheep first and lambs last. Sheep should not be overheated or thirsty prior to dipping. Yard some time before dipping and they should not be full of food when dipped. Don't dip in the hottest part of the day. Avoid dipping in cold weather or when rain is indicated. Allow dipped sheep to dry in the shade and cease dipping in time to allow them to dry before nightfall. Sheep should not be rushed through the dip but given time to become thoroughly saturated. Heads should be immersed once. Allow sheep to drain properly before removing from pens.

Do not drive immediately before or after dipping. Keep the bath thoroughly mixed and use soft water with powder dips.

ONE NOVEL DESIGN FOR THE SMALL FLOCK OWNER

This is from the Queensland Agricultural Journal, and is a good type of circular dip. It is 7 ft. 10 in. in diameter and 4 ft. 6 in. deep; great care being taken to keep the sides perpendicular.

When this is excavated, sink a hole about 2 ft. deep in the centre of the hole to set in concrete a strainer post; 6 ft. 6 in. x 12 in. dia.; then rough cement all the bottom of the excavation about 3 inches thick and allow same to set.

Cut both the top and the bottom out of an old 1,000 gallon tank 7 ft. 4 in. x 4 ft. 2 in., and place it in the excavation. If, however, say a 2,000 gallon tank is available, with 8 ft. 3 in. diameter, it can be used if it is cut down to reduce the height.

If the excavation is true, there should be a space of 3 in. between the tank and the sides. Mark off a width of 4 ft. where you require your walk-in-and-out, and pack and ram concrete all the rest of the way round between the tank and the sides.

Then give the bottom a final coat of fine cement about 1 in. thick, and allow it to set. Cut a part of the tank away from the 4 ft. space left for the walk-in-and out to

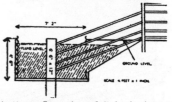

within 1 ft. from the bottom. From about 6 ft. back, slope a cutting 3 ft. 6 in. wide down to about 6 in. from the bottom of the hole and round the corners off back to where the tank has been cut away.

Concrete both sides and bottom of the cutting about 6 in. thick and then cement inside the tank. From the centre strainer post, run a fence back, through the middle of the cutting, thus utilising one side for the walk-in and the other for the walk-out; this side being battened to facilitate an easy exit.

When small flocks have to be dipped, two small draining pens of 7 x 6 ft. will be found sufficient, while a small ramp along the entrance race will prevent dirt being carried into the tank. As many as 300 sheep could pass through this dip in an hour. They have a swim of approximately 21 feet. For larger numbers a bigger tank would, of course, have to be made.

A PORTABLE DIPPING PLANT

This would be quite useful for small numbers; it takes the dip to the sheep; it avoids manhandling as there is no lifting and turning required. It also assists penetration of the dip as it is claimed that the lowering action has the effect of raising the wool, thus making it easy for the dip to penetrate. The sheep walk up a wooden track into a metal crate which is lowered into the bath by a windlass, guide tracks being fitted on either side of the tank. Round bars at the bottom of the crate serve to open the clays for the treatment of foot rot. Foothold in the 10 ft. drying pen is afforded

by wire-netting on the wood, the wire being detachable for easier cleaning up of droppings, etc. This also speeds up drainage because sheep shake themselves more thoroughly when sure of their footing. Portability is enhanced by building this arrangement to fit on to a motor truck chassis, thereby enabling the dipping apparatus to be taken to the sheep. This can be enlarged to dip 20 or more at one dipping.

USEFUL HINTS WITH SHEEP

ANOTHER EXCELLENT FARM DIP
Capable of Handling up to 2,000 Sheep Easily

This is a very handy home-made dip, made and used with success by Mr. A. C. Duval, of Morphett Vale, to whom we are indebted for a number of these ideas, the sheep being able to pass in and out easily. Its capacity is 450 gallons, and it has a good automatic slip-in device, which has proved very advantageous.

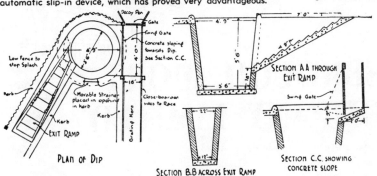

The essential features are a circular pit 4 ft. 9 in. in diameter at the top, sloping down to 3 ft. 6 in., with an overall depth of 5 ft. 6 in. At one side there is a concrete slope, made slippery with floor polish, on to which the sheep walk from a race. Their hindquarters go from beneath them, and they drop into the dip, their fall being eased by means of a swing gate (as shown in the smaller detail).

The sheep are then rump first as they go in and the operator, standing on the lip of the dip, can duck them again if thought necessary.

pen. They pass down the race quite readily, and are checked where necessary by a man standing at the side.

As the swinging door is loose, as soon as the weight of their rump pushes against it, they slip down; the fall being easy, the dip being filled with liquid almost to the top. The swing door falls back of its own accord, and provision should be made to stop it at the right position and not allow it to swing into the race.

A low fence of galvanised iron fixed upright and bedded in concrete protects the dip and the exit ramp on the sides shown, and confines the splash. An optional swing gate is shown in the crush pen. This will be found useful when handling small lots of stud sheep.

This dip is very simple in design if the drawings are followed: "AA" shows the measurement and construction of the dip itself, with exit. The ramp starts 18 in. from the bottom. "BB" shows the cross-section of ramp at its lowest point.

As the bottom of the ramp comes up the slope and approaches the top, it widens out, until eventually it dies out on ground level at 22 inches wide. The ramp steps are easily made with a trowel, but the steps themselves should NOT go right to the wall, but a narrow channel should be left, down which the liquid can run when the dip is emptied. The sheep, of course, are fully immersed in the liquid until more than half-way up the ramp.

The drawing will illustrate the arrangement, but space will not permit of our showing the rather good type of swinging gate through which the sheep slip into the bath, but it has been found very effective indeed. The fall is an easy one, and the sheep should become completely immersed.

Space also does not permit of our showing several other very good types of home-made dips, but we will endeavour to show more of these in later books.

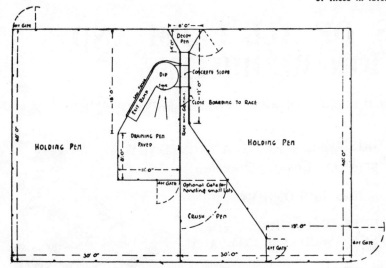

This dip will hold 5 average merinos. When immersion is complete, they walk out of their own accord up the exit ramp on a series of steps.

The drainage pen is paved, and the liquid runs back across the graded paved area to a moveable sieve which is fixed in the curb protecting the dip. The curb goes all round the draining pen, so that no liquid can go back into the dip without going through the sieve.

Working the Dip. When entering the dip from the crush pen, the sheep pass down a narrow closed boarding race, at the end of which they can see the decoy sheep. The race has a timbered grating, on which the dirt adhering to their hoofs is knocked off. This helps keep the dip clean and the crush pen itself could be paved.

The race is also close boarded so that the sheep have no view, either of the dip or of any other sheep except those in the decoy

A HOME-MADE CONTRIVANCE FOR EMPTYING A DIP

This idea comes from a farmer as a suggestion for places where the dip is not fitted with waste pipes or any other means of emptying.

If the task of emptying by hand has to be done, an arrangement such as this will lighten the labour. Put a tall post in at the side of the dip, and on this, by means of a chain, hang a free moving beam. To one end of the beam hang a sack of stones and to the other end a drum. The rest is simple.

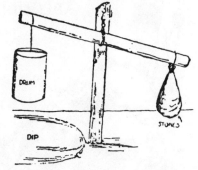

USEFUL HINTS ON EMPTYING A DIP

If a dip is on high ground, it can be emptied by siphoning with a hose or with any type of pump in which valves will not clog too readily.

It is an advantage to form a small saucer-like depression as a sump in the bottom of the dip, from which the last dregs can be drained. Mud will collect at the bottom, and this should be bailed out or flushed out and pumped up with more water.

Do not dispose of the dip anywhere where animals or children can have access to it, or run it into a watercourse but dig a pit and fill it with stones which will absorb the dip.

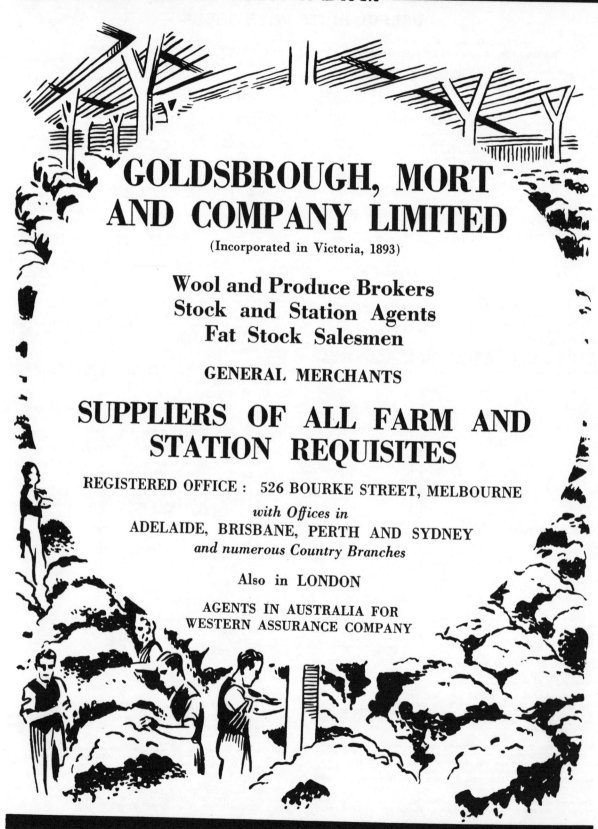

GOLDSBROUGH, MORT AND COMPANY LIMITED

(Incorporated in Victoria, 1893)

**Wool and Produce Brokers
Stock and Station Agents
Fat Stock Salesmen**

GENERAL MERCHANTS

SUPPLIERS OF ALL FARM AND STATION REQUISITES

REGISTERED OFFICE : 526 BOURKE STREET, MELBOURNE

with Offices in
ADELAIDE, BRISBANE, PERTH AND SYDNEY
and numerous Country Branches

Also in LONDON

AGENTS IN AUSTRALIA FOR
WESTERN ASSURANCE COMPANY

USEFUL HINTS WITH HORSES

THE MAIN POINTS

1, Muzzle; 2, Nostril; 3, Forehead; 4, Jaw; 5, Poll; 6, Crest; 7, Windpipe; 8, Shoulder Blade; 9, Point of Shoulder; 10, Breast; 11, True-arm; 12, Elbow; 13, Forearm; 14, Knee; 15, Cannonbone; 16, Back Sinew; 17, Fetlock; 18, Coronet; 19, Hoof; 20, Heel; 21, Withers; 22, Back; 23, Ribs; 24, Girth; 25, Loins; 26, Croup; 27, Hip; 28, Flank; 29, Root or Dock of Tail; 30, Hip Joint Round, or Whirl Bone (should actually be shown just above 28); 31, Stifle Joint; 32, Lower Thigh or Gaskin; 33, Quarters; 34, Hock; 35, Point of Hock; 36, Curb Place; 37, Cannon Bone; 38, Back Sinew.

OF A HORSE

Based on the Clydesdale, the jaw should be broad; nostrils, large and open. Eyes, full and vigorous, but mild. Forehead, broad. Head, well set on neck. Neck, well arched over shoulders and of good length. Shoulders, deep and sloped well back. Legs, good and sound. Knee, flat and broad. Cannon Bone, flat when looked at from side. Back, medium length, strong across loins. Body, deep. Ribs, close together. Hindquarters, broad, low set. Thighs, muscular. Hocks, well developed with muscles strong and firm. Legs, from hock to ground should be long, broad and flat, inclined slightly forward. Horse should stand evenly and firmly on feet.

TELLING THE AGE

The usual method is to judge by the condition of the teeth, chiefly the incisors (front teeth). The change in shape and appearance which the teeth undergo is important from an age point of view.

TELLING THE AGE

There are 6 incisors, the two in the centre being called " central," the one on each side of these being termed " laterals," and the two outside ones, the " corner " incisors.

The following is a summary of the dental change in Horses :

1 yr   2 yrs   3 yrs   4 yrs

At Birth (or a few days after)—2 central temporary incisors in each jaw, and 12 temporary molars.

At 6 to 8 weeks—2 more lateral incisors in each jaw.

At 9 months—4 more molars appear.

At 12 months (or very shortly after)—the temporary corner incisors.

At 1 year he should have 6 temporary incisors in each jaw.

(see illustration). They can be recognised as temporary because of their white milky appearance, small size and narrow neck.

At 2½ years, the permanent central incisors appear, being fully up at 3 years (see sketch).

At 3½ years, the permanent laterals appear (see sketch, 4 years).

At 4½ years, the permanent corners appear (see sketch 5 years).

5 yrs   6 yrs   7 yrs

These diagrams show how to judge a horse's age from the incisor teeth from 1 to 7 years, after which other things must be taken into consideration.

A fairly accurate estimate can be obtained from the above, but there is another appearance which gives a further guide. On the wearing surfaces, there are cavities or marks which are caused by a central core of dark material tapered in shape, as shown in the accompanying figure 1.

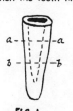

FIG 1.

When the tooth first appears these dark marks are largest, but as the tooth grows out and wears down, the size of the mark gradually diminishes, as the tooth is worn down to sections indicated by AA or BB in figure 1. In fact, lower down the dark mark disappears from the tooth altogether. This happens when the tooth itself is about 4 years old.

Thus the illustrations will show that the central incisors at 3 years have large dark marks in the centre, which practically disappear at 6 years, and almost entirely so at 7 years. At 8 years of age, they will have disappeared from all teeth, but, as this is a negative guide, there is nothing to say whether the horse is only 8 years or more.

There is another indication, however, in that the teeth at 7 or 8 years commence to wear with a groove similar to that shown in fig. 2, and this naturally increases up to a certain limit as the horse gets older. Furthermore, as the dark marks in the centre of the

teeth wear away, the smaller dark marks that remain are surrounded by a slightly discoloured mark, which clearly shows in the illustration of a 7-year-old set of incisors.

In addition to the development of the incisors, the canine teeth or tushes appear in stallions and most geldings, but never in mares, at about 4½ years of age, and are generally fully up at 5 years. These never appear except as permanent teeth, and sometimes appear later in the upper than in the lower jaw.

Although after 7 years of age it is hard to tell the exact age of a horse by its teeth, there is another mark which can be followed, i.e., a triangular mark which appears in the upper corner incisors at about 7 years, but this is not very reliable.

A puzzle is sometimes presented by a horse which may be 4 years old on the offside and 5 years on the near side—a condition which may be caused by a slight deformity in the mouth or some temporary disability, or anything which causes him to use one side more than he does the other.

FIG. 2

Horses, however, develop other signs of age, and these marks may be accentuated by hard conditions but the above are fairly reliable indications of the value of a horse.

USEFUL HINTS WITH HORSES

HINTS ON BUYING

There is an old saying, " No foot, no horse." It is wise to first of all look at the feet. (1) Pick up the feet and look over the bottoms of them carefully. If they are dirty, clean them off so that you can really see them. Have they an unhealthy look?

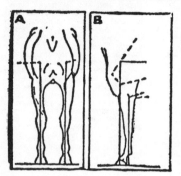

Is there any foul odour indicating the possibility of thrush? Are the heels contracted? "Yes" to these questions means "No" when buying.

(2) Are the walls of the hoof straight? Any rings or ridges or convexities in the walls indicate previous as well as future troubles.

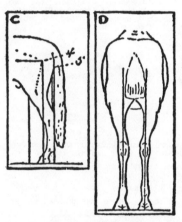

(3) Look at the feet and legs from the front, side and rear. Does the horse stand squarely on them or is too much of the weight borne on either side, on the heel, or on the toe? If so, the horse may be an interferer, a stumbler, or, if not already afflicted with some unsoundness of legs, is likely to develop same following hard work.

Further points on buying are also shown in these illustrations, viz.:

(A) A vertical line from the point of the shoulder should fall on the centre of the knee, cannon, pastern and foot. Defects are toes pointing out or in, causing interference, knees too close, feet toeing in or out, and knees too wide apart.

(B) A vertical line from the centre of the elbow joint should fall on the knee and pastern and back to the foot, and the centre of the foot should be directly under the point illustrated in the drawing. Defects include legs too far under the body, too far advanced, legs that are knee-sprung, and calf legs.

(C) The centre of the foot should be directly underneath the hip-joint and the line joining them should divide the gaskin. A vertical line from the point of the buttock should hit the back of the cannon. Avoid horses with hind legs too far under the body and too far back of the body.

(D) A vertical line from the point of the buttock should cross the centre of the hock, cannon, pastern and foot. Hind legs wider apart than this produce a sprawling gait. Also avoid horses with cow-hocks or pigeon-toes.

JOCKEY STICK BETWEEN BRIDLES QUIETS QUARRELSOME TEAM

This team is kept from quarrelling by a length of broom handle snapped between their bridles.

Experiencing considerable trouble by having his team of horses fight and bite each other when hitched, a farmer eliminated the difficulty by keeping their heads spread apart with a length of broomstick.

A harness snap is attached to each end of the stick by means of short straps, and the snaps are hooked on the inside ring of each horse's bridle bit.

A HOME-MADE TOOL FOR CLEANING HOOFS

This little easily made tool will be found handy for cleaning horses' hoofs or the lugs on tractor wheels and it can be made as follows :

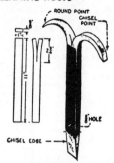

A length of iron, 11 x 1 x 3-8 in. is split at one end and bent to the shape shown, one end being ground to a round point, and the other end to a chisel point.

A 3-8 in. hole is drilled through the tool so that it can be hung up in the stable ready for use.

SHOEING A ROUGH HORSE

To shoe a rough horse, put him in a stall, tie his head short, tie a neck rope round a hame strap, and strap the buckle round the horse's fetlock. Tie the other end to an overhead beam, as shown in the sketch, so that when the loose end of the rope is

pulled, the knot will come undone.

Tie the knot tight. It will be seen that it resembles a "clove hitch" with the end brought back.

If trouble arises, or it is desirable to give the horse a rest, the loose end of the rope is pulled; it can easily be tied again when wanted. For safety, it is best to do this when standing in the next stall.

A rope might also be tied as suggested by the dotted line, from the horse's foot to a post at the rear. To get the hind legs into the forward position, move the rope forward as far as necessary along the beam. The forelegs may be managed in the same way.

AN ADJUSTABLE NOSE BAG

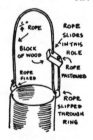

This is a very handy adjustable arrangement for attaching the nose-bag according to the feed in the bag itself.

The slide shown in the sketch makes it possible to adjust it for any horse after placing the nosebag on its head.

The wooden block will grip wherever it is placed. Horses' heads vary in size and with this arrangement their nosebags do not need to be kept separate. Instead of a wooden block a piece of some other softer material might, however, be preferable so that it will not worry the horse unduly.

A NOVEL NOSE GUARD FOR HORSE

A simple guard that will keep insects from bothering the nose of a horse working in a field, and also prevent the animal from constantly nibbling at growing crops, can be made from a piece of inner tube as indicated.

The large holes cut in the rubber should coincide with the horse's nostrils so that its breathing will not be impeded. The guard will also tend to discourage a horse that has acquired the habit of nipping at another when they are hitched together.

USEFUL HINTS WITH HORSES

AN IDEA FOR KEEPING HAY IN MANGER

Most cows and many horses have a tendency to push hay out over the top of the manger, making it necessary to put it in again or let them go without sufficient hay. There is also more or less waste of hay and silage.

This trouble is practically eliminated by putting a 6 x 1 board the entire length of the manger, nailing it flat on the top edge of the manger.

When the hay is pushed up against the board, it simply drops back into the manger, and the waste is prevented. For concrete mangers, a 4 x 2 could be bolted to the manger and the board nailed to it.

PROTECTING THE EDGES OF FEED BOX OR MANGER

This is a novel and handy way of preventing stabled horses from damaging the edges of their feed boxes and mangers by gnawing away portions of the soft wood.

In this instance, some lengths of heavy smooth wire are stapled to the top edges as shown in the sketch.

As an alternative to wire, some strips of flat iron could easily be used.

A FEED BOX—EASY TO CLEAN

This is another rather useful type of feed box which has been found very handy and easy to clean by those who have made them. It is a very simple arrangement of hinges as shown in the sketch.

A lot of people are often satisfied to nail a small case or similar article on to the wall of the stable in a corner or some other such place to serve as a feed box.

If it is fixed in a permanent position chaff and rubbish will accumulate in the box and, as it is troublesome to clean, it is usually left dirty for a long time.

If the box is hinged in the manner shown, it is a matter of only a second or so to tip the box up and empty its contents on to the floor, whence it can be swept up in the ordinary course.

A PORTABLE FEED BOX

A very good idea in order to provide a portable feed box for horses or cattle is shown here. This can be merely hung over any fence at a moment's notice and it is ready for use.

A 5 to 10-gallon oil drum makes a very handy feed box for this purpose if cut down as shown. Just cut the drum as indicated in this sketch by the dotted lines, one half of each end being removed, and the longer side of drum then bent to hook over the fence or other support. The shorter end is rolled to give a smooth edge.

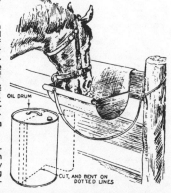

Such a feed box is everlasting. Kero tins can also be used, but they are scarcely strong enough and need reinforcement.

A NOVEL FEED BOX ANCHOR FOR OUTDOOR USE

When an animal is fed from an open box outdoors, it can be kept from upsetting the box by using a horse-shoe pivoted at one end to a post as shown in the accompanying illustration.

This permits of the box to be removed easily for cleaning, yet keeps it securely in place when turned over the box edge.

Such an arrangement would be found very convenient and it can be transported from place to place easily.

A PAD FOR SADDLE

For an ordinary size saddle, get about two feet two inches of sugar or other bag. Sew two rows of stitching down the centre about 3½ inches apart.

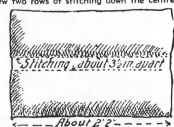

Fill the two sides up with chaff, with no oats in it, or enough hair to make a pad of medium thickness on each side as shown.

This saddle pad is easy to make and it will be found economical and serviceable, whilst it will help avoid many sore backs.

HANGING AND HANDLING HARNESS

A method of hanging heavy work harness, to make it easier for the farmer to take off and put on again, is shown here. This plan was worked out by a farmer who had injured himself so that carrying and lifting heavy harness hurt his back.

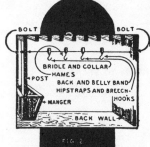

The arrangement for removing harness easily.

The drawing illustrates a cross section of the barn, from the manger to the back wall; as usually in any barn construction, there is a support post in front of the manger.

Four pulleys, with hooks, are slipped on a length of ¼ in. cable or heavy wire, and one end fastened to the wall of the barn with an eye-bolt as shown, while the other end is fastened to a manger support.

The cable should be drawn tightly, by tightening the nuts on the eyebolts. The cable should be stretched so that it will come directly over the horse when in the stall, but high enough not to interfere with the feeding and handling.

For ease, the snaps and buckles are loosened in the regular manner.

The hip straps, breeching and tugs are hooked over the first hook as shown; the back band, carrying the lines, comes on the second hook, and the hames on the third.

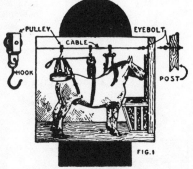

How parts of the harness are lifted and attached to the hooks.

Now the whole bunch of hooks are slipped back to the wall and the harness is away from the horse and hung with no great effort. The fourth hook may then be used for collar and bridle.

USEFUL HINTS WITH HORSES

A GOOD METHOD OF PROTECTING HORSES FROM INJURY

This is a method used on many occasions throughout one Remount Depot in order to make everything as comfortable as possible for the horses which they have to handle—the idea being to lessen the chance of injury which might possibly be caused by the use of bare ropes.

The chaff or other bag is rolled lengthwise and tied at the ends in the manner indicated with binder twine. It is then used either by placing it round the neck with the tied portion under the throat, or round the fetlock as the case may be for the job on hand.

If a rope is used under similar circumstances it might result in chafed necks or injured fetlocks, heels, etc. USE SUCH AN ARRANGEMENT ON EVERY OCCASION POSSIBLE RATHER THAN THE BARE ROPE.

TYING UP A COLT

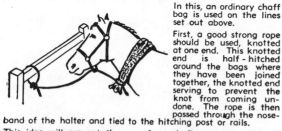

In this, an ordinary chaff bag is used on the lines set out above.

First, a good strong rope should be used, knotted at one end. This knotted end is half - hitched around the bags where they have been joined together, the knotted end serving to prevent the knot from coming undone. The rope is then passed through the noseband of the halter and tied to the hitching post or rails.

This idea will prevent the rope from chafing and it will help avoid such things as " rope galls " and possible " kinking " should the colt be inclined to hang back on the rope.

Also, the rope passing through the halter ensures that the bag does not get twisted around the neck as it should always remain in the correct position. The horse cannot therefore harm itself, no matter how much he pulls and moves his head about.

TEACHING A HORSE TO STAND

This is quite a good method of teaching a horse to stand quietly.

Merely take a short length of rope and tie the near foreleg to the near hind leg—for the first lesson use about 3 feet of rope and gradually reduce the length as the horse becomes accustomed to the rope. The idea in the first place is merely to let the horse know the rope is there.

He will soon learn to stand naturally and quietly.

The legs should, of course, be secured by two hobble-straps and the length between altered to suit.

A GOOD HALTER ROPE

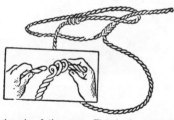

This illustration is of a very easy to make rope halter which can be adjusted to any size required to fit anything from a young calf to a large horse.

In the first place, bind both ends of the rope, then use a punch or some other pointed object to form loops in the strands of the rope. This is shown in the smaller detail of the illustration. The rope is then run through the loops as indicated.

QUICK RELEASE KNOTS

It may often be necessary to get a horse free in a hurry, say, in case of fire or some other trouble, and therefore a hitch such as this is a handy one to know.

The sketches are self-explanatory. "S" represents the standing part of the rope and "F" the free end.

1. Pass the free end over a bar or ring and make a single twist and loop (b) in the standing rope.

2. Bring the free end under the twist and behind both the free and standing parts. Make a loop as at (a).

3. Pass the loop "a" through the loop of "b" and pull on the standing rope. To release, a sharp pull on the free end is sufficient. With practice, these will be found easy.

A NOVEL HITCHING POST

This is an excellent idea. The top is quarter slotted, as shown, the slots running to a depth of about 6 in. from the upper end.

The halter rope can be drawn through these slots quickly and pulled to hold the animal with a long or short hitch as required.

No tying or knotting of the rope is necessary as the double looping through the slots holds it securely in place.

A DOUBLE LOOP HALTER TIE

This halter-tie is actually better than a knot in the rope.

When a horse is tied to a manger or other place, there is always a possibility that the knot employed may become so tight from the animal pulling at it that it will be difficult, if not sometimes almost impossible, to loosen.

If a long slot is sawed in the manger, or other place where it is customary to tie the animal up for any period, to receive the looped rope, and the end (knotted) is dropped through this, as shown in the illustration, the tie will hold against all ordinary pulling, yet it may be loosened and released instantly.

MAKING A STUBBORN HORSE PULL

This is quite a good idea in cases where any stubborn horse refuses to pull.

Simply get a length of twine; wet the twine and pass the ends through the loop twice, then slip the loop over the horse's ear and pull it tight.

Let him stand for a minute or two until he begins pawing and shaking his head a few times, after which he will be quite willing to go along quietly.

This method has been successfully tried a number of times and very rarely known to fail.

USEFUL HINTS WITH HORSES

ONE IDEA FOR A LEAD ROPE

This is a handy method used in one quarter which acts very well. The user states that if you have any horses or other animals which have to be led around for any reason at all on any occasion, a rope fixed like that shown here will come in handy.

In use, the rope is looped over the animal's neck, after which a short piece of hose is slipped up to keep the looped portion in place.

The hose should be of a size to be a snug sliding fit over the rope. The rope can then be quickly slipped off and, if the other ends are tied together, it is always ready to be hitched to a post or vehicle as the occasion may demand. It is a very simple arrangement but quite effective.

AN IDEA FOR A SHY LEADER

This is a very easy and effective method of leading a shy horse. It is a somewhat similar arrangement to that shown under the heading of "effective cures for the horse that pulls back" as it works in the same manner.

In this the rope is formed into a sort of lasso in the same way as described in that article, and carried on through the head collar in the same way.

Both this rope and the reins from the halter are then carried by the person leading the horse, the reins being held a little shorter than the rope from the hindquarters, but, if he shows any signs of sticking up, then the weight can be taken on the quarter rope when he will move along as required.

ANOTHER METHOD OF SHOEING A ROUGH HORSE

This is another occasion on which the chaff bag idea can be used to advantage (see page 216) as it will help to avoid any possible injury which may be caused by a rope.

First, a neck-rope is placed around the neck, to which a ring is attached where shown. Side-lines, to which have been attached a chaff bag tied in the usual way, are then run from the fetlock through the ring and back through the bag on the leg. Then, in order to get a stronger purchase, pass the rope back through the ring again—take up the side lines to the length required in order to obtain the most comfortable position to shoe the horse and tie the rope with two half-hitches over the side lines close to the ring.

The horse cannot then snatch his leg across and if he does happen to kick, he would only throw the man aside. This is specially useful where a lively or rough horse is concerned.

PROTECTING TRACE CHAINS

This is one good way of affording protection to trace chains, besides making it easier for the horse. For this purpose, one farmer slips lengths of inner tube over the chains of his harness traces.

Besides holding the traces in place on the single-tree hooks the tubes also protect the horses' legs if they happen to rub against the chains.

AN IDEA TO PREVENT ACCIDENTS

You can avoid accidents resulting from your team running away in the field because one of the horses may have got his line caught under the mower or wagon tongue in such a way that you might not be able to manage or guide them, by an arrangement such as this.

Merely tack a piece of discarded bicycle tyre over the end of the tongue, as indicated in the accompanying sketch. It has been tried in many parts with success and safety.

ANOTHER METHOD OF KEEPING THE REINS UP

This is another simple but effective way to avoid having the reins get under the tongue of a wagon.

It is merely the hanging of a chain over the end of the tongue in the manner shown in the sketch. This may save many stops to untangle them.

MAKING A SUITABLE HORSE DIP

In many centres, public horse dips are in use for the treatment of animals suffering from irritation by external parasites on the legs. Some owners have erected horse dips on their properties and the accompanying diagram will show the plan and side elevation of a horse dip erected on a well known stud property, together with the following specifications which should prove of use to any one desirous of building a suitable dip, say 2 ft. 6 in. wide.

Concrete Specifications. The mix should be $3\frac{1}{2}$ parts of clean, well-graded coarse aggregate, either stone screenings or gravel, say, from $\frac{1}{4}$ inch up to $1\frac{1}{4}$ in. in size; two parts of clean, sharp sand, graded from "fine" up to the size of a pea, and one part of cement. The water should be clear and drinkable, carefully measured, and should be in the proportion of about $5\frac{1}{2}$ gallons to the paper bag of cement. Avoid a sloppy mix. A close dense concrete will be obtained by carefully mixing, placing, and ramming the mixture.

The approximate quantities for the dip specified above would be 26 bags of cement, 2 cubic yards of sand, and $3\frac{1}{2}$ cubic yards of screenings or gravel.

Method of Mixing. Spread the sand required for a batch in a layer about 4 in. deep, then spread the necessary quantity of cement evenly over the sand. Mix thoroughly three times. Again spread out and cover evenly with the screenings or gravel. Mix thoroughly at least two or three times.

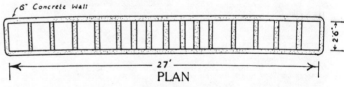

PLAN

Form the mixture into a heap and scoop out a hole in the top, sufficiently large enough to hold the required amount of water for the batch. Pour water into the hole and allow it to soak through the heap, then turn the lot over vigorously three times and use immediately. Mix sufficient only at a time to ensure of its being placed and rammed within the hour.

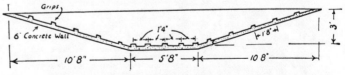

SIDE ELEVATION (Sectional)

Showing the plan and side elevation of a suitable Horse Dip. NOTE: Feet grips on the slopes are 1 ft. 8 in. between centres, 4 in. wide, and 2 in. high, tapering to 1 in. Grips on the bottom are 4 in. wide and 2 in. high.

All inside edges of grips are rounded.

When the job is finished, cover with wet bags within a few hours, and keep covered for at least seven days or longer if possible, say, from 14 to 21 days. One should then have a very satisfactory job.

USEFUL HINTS WITH HORSES

PROTECTING HORSES FROM POISON

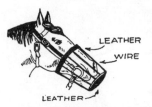

One who has had long experience with stock and poison advises the use of a muzzle as shown in the illustration as a preventative instead of relying upon antidotes.

The sketch is self-explanatory, being made from leather and good, strong fencing wire which can be slipped on over the winkers. Such an arrangement should not interfere with driving, and, as it is only a very light thing, it should not inconvenience the horse. It is far better to make some little arrangement like this rather than take risks.

STABLE DOORS WITH SPECIAL FEATURES

The sketches given here are of double doors made by one farmer which have some special features. The best way to arrange the ledges on a door with two heights is shown in figure 1.

It will be seen that the top ledge of the lower door (indicated by letter A) stands up above the top edge of the door about an inch, forming a rebate for the top door to fit in as in figure 2, and thus preventing draughts coming at the joint as is often the case when the battens or boards are simply bevelled as shown in figure 3, and the ledge kept below the top edge of the bottom door.

It is an advantage to have a small hit-and-miss ventilator in the upper part of a stable door, and the simplest method of forming this is illustrated in the sketches.

A slit or narrow opening should be cut in each of the four or five centre boards of the door B in figure 1, this being done by boring a hole at the top and bottom of each as in figure 4, and cutting out the intervening piece of wood as indicated by the dotted lines.

A frame, as figure 3, must then be made of ¾ in. thick wood, the widths of the bars and open parts being so arranged that when the frame is moved backwards and forwards at the back of the slits cut in the door it entirely closes up or uncovers the openings as may be required.

The various members forming the frame should be halved together, as shown in figure 6, and grooves be formed at the top and bottom of the ventilator for the frame to slide in as shown in figure 7.

ANOTHER NOVEL IDEA FOR THE STABLE

The annoyance of matted straw and other refuse becoming impaled in the fork may be overcome by nailing a section of a discarded broom on to the side of the stall as indicated.

It just takes a moment to draw the prongs of the fork through the projecting bristles of the broom in order to clean them thoroughly.

If desired, flat-iron brackets can be attached to the stall so that the broom pieces can be inserted or removed without the use of hammer and nails. This idea is not only applicable to stables but may be used in connection with other jobs round the place. Old brooms can also be fixed in position as boot wipers just outside the stable door.

HOW TO MAKE A STITCHED HARNESS SPLICE

In repairing harness, it is often necesary to make a stitched splice. Tools needed are a knife (preferably round) a finishing wheel, a marking wheel, a sewing awl, waxed and needled harness thread, and a clamp.

Cut the ends of the straps square as shown at A. Skive off or taper the ends on the flesh or rough side of each piece for about 1½ in., as at B. Lap the straps about 2 in., and mark off the stitches the full length of the splice as at C.

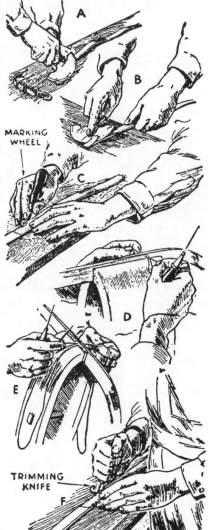

Place the splice in the clamp with the marked side and end nearest you facing right, and the marks close to the jaws of the clamp as at D.

Make the first hole in the single strap farthest away from you (beyond the splice). Place the thread in the hole and draw the ends even. The awl is kept in the right hand.

Make the second hole and place the left needle in it, and draw it about 1 ft. through with thumb and index finger of right hand.

With the awl and both needles in the right hand, pass the right-hand needle through the hole, draw it through with left hand, and pull the stitch up tight as at E. Continue this until the last stitch has been made through the two straps.

Make one hole beyond the splice, and pass the right needle through.

Remove the work from the clamp, cross the threads, replace the work in the clamp end for end with the other edge up, and continue the stitching.

Finish the stitching by placing the left needle and thread in the last hole, which is beyond the splice; then, when the right needle is in the hole, the left thread is wound twice round the right needle, and the threads are drawn tight. This ties and locks the thread.

How the ends of the straps are skived, and steps in stitching and trimming the splice.

The right thread is then passed through another small hole about 1-8 in. below the next to the last stitch, and the threads are cut off close to the strap. The stitching is then smoothed down with the finishing wheel, and the edges are trimmed smooth with an edging tool or knife, as shown at F.

USEFUL HINTS WITH HORSES

HINTS ON THROWING HORSES

A few short notes on this subject may be of some interest to those who may have occasion to put a horse down for some purpose or other and who may not have had very much experience in this direction.

In the first place, always see that some soft ground is chosen for such work in order to avoid as much discomfiture as possible to the horse and so lessen the chance of injury.

Illustration No. 1. As will be seen, the folded chaff-bag idea is again used round the fetlock in order to avoid any possible injury which might otherwise be occasioned should a rope only be used for the purpose. A good, strong hobble-strap could, of course, also be used.

First, a neck-rope is placed around the neck with a ring attached and the side-lines are placed in position for use. The leg is then strapped up as indicated in the sketch.

The arrangement of the side-lines is similar to that explained under the heading of "Shoeing a rough horse," page 248; and, if a bag is used, they are attached to it as indicated in "Tying up a colt," page 217. The side-line is passed from the bag or hobble-strap round the fetlock, up through the ring on the neck-rope, back to the bag or hobble-strap and returned through the ring as indicated and operated as follows:

By holding the halter or halter rope with one hand and gently exerting a pull on the loose end of the side-line, the horse should go down quite gently. It is merely a combination of strapping up a front leg with the use of side-lines as indicated.

The second illustration is one which can be used should the horse be one which will not let one touch his legs.

A good strong rope with a noose on the end is laid on the ground and the horse manoeuvred until his fore-foot is in the loop. This is then worked up into position on the horse's leg and tightened sufficiently. The rope is then passed over the back when the hoof can be lifted by hauling on the rope. When the foot is off the ground, secure the rope by, say, passing it round the base of the neck or round the body and tying it in some convenient manner.

The horse can then be thrown by any of these methods and if the following one is used, then, of course, the head should be pulled down from the opposite side as indicated.

The third sketch shows another way to throw a horse when working single-handed; it being a very effective and easy method of doing this job.

Work from the opposite side to that on which it is desired that the horse should fall. The fore-leg on that side is first strapped up in any convenient way. A strong rope is then taken from the head of the horse on the opposite side to the strapped up leg and passed through a ring on the surcingle to the person standing on the opposite side, and the horse's head is then drawn round as shown in the drawing, when it should go down very nicely and easily on the side required—the illustration will clearly show the method.

It is necessary, of course, that the legs be secured when the horse is down, whilst his head can be kept down by placing a super bag or cornsack half filled with sand across his neck.

HOW TO MOUNT A DIFFICULT HORSE

First, take a small strap with a ring on the end and buckle it on to the girth just below the saddle flap, as shown.

Then take a short piece of rope with a spring hook attached to one end and fix it on to the bit. Then pass this rope through the ring and pass the loose end over the horse's neck as for riding.

Then hold the rope and reins together in the left hand—the rope being held the tighter of the two, when it will tend to draw the horse's head down and towards the person mounting. When mounted, the rope can be released.

HOW TO SUBDUE A BOLTING HORSE

The following are some good methods of obtaining control—the idea being that there is then a direct purchase on the mouth.

The first sketch shows how a piece of rope can be looped and inserted into the horse's mouth in the same way as a bit gripping it firmly round the lower jaw.

For preference, it is really better to have the loop (or a bowline knot) on the end of the rope when the loose end should be passed **under the horse's neck** from the offside, then over the neck and back through the loop in somewhat the same manner as shown in the lower sketch (which is really the Indian war bridle)—the one difference being that the war bridle is fixed with a running knot whereas in the other the rope is merely threaded through the loop then on to the point of control. If in harness, the rope can be passed back through the ring in the saddle to the vehicle and the horse controlled from there.

The Indian War Bridle. As mentioned, this is somewhat similar to the above idea, but the rope is fixed with a running knot which can be quickly loosened by pulling on the free end of the rope. However, while this is in operation, it can be rather painful, but it can be released quite easily when its purpose is complete.

OTHER CONTROL METHODS

The use of some hitches, as sometimes seen and which are painful to the horse, should be avoided if possible, but if they are necessary, the methods shown here should be found almost as good as any, although, of course, there may be others better. Some vicious horses need some control, and if some short, sharp lesson can be taught, it is far better than inflicting any pain which might be harmful.

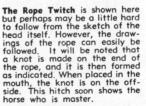

The Halter Twitch. The sketch on the right indicates how the rope is attached to the halter and looped to go round the jaw, then over the head and down through the mouth. A slight pull on the rope will cause it to tighten and will soon teach the horse to stand still when required.

The Rope Twitch is shown here but perhaps may be a little hard to follow from the sketch of the head itself. However, the drawings of the rope can easily be followed. It will be noted that a knot is made on the end of the rope, and it is then formed as indicated. When placed in the mouth, the knot is on the off-side. This hitch soon shows the horse who is master.

Another method is the "Noose Twitch," which, although not shown here, is a simple noose which is placed behind the horse's ear and under the top lip only, where it comes into contact with a nerve centre, when a slight pull will command attention.

USEFUL HINTS WITH HORSES

CURING HEAD TOSSING HORSES

This is an idea used with success in Scotland. A small weight or ring is attached to the harness as indicated in the sketch.

The cord on which it is threaded should be such as to make certain that the small weight does not come into contact with the horse's eye as it moves. This weight will hit the horse on the forehead every time he tosses his head and it will teach him in a very short time to overcome this habit.

This little gadget can be used on any horse, no matter where it is in the team, and has rarely been known to fail (a ring is actually the better article to use), and it is certainly better than some of the remedies one sees at various times.

HINTS ON STRAPPING THE FRONT LEG

Sometimes in handling a horse, it is necessary to strap up a front leg. This can be done by using hobble, or hame straps.

That shown in the first sketch shows how the strap is passed over the foreleg, and under the pastern and tightened. When moving, this often slips. This can be rectified by merely passing straps between pastern and fore-arm, through a small suitable ring.

The other illustrations give details of other ways of doing the same job. For instance, a pole-strap is a good thing for strapping up a horse's leg as it already has a " D " in the required posi-tion.

Where a pole strap is not available, an ordinary stirrup leather makes a good substitute if used as indicated in the accompanying illustration.

For throwing, or for perhaps any lengthy operation, it is a good idea to suspend a leg to a surcingle.

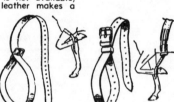

RING

RAISING A HORSE WITHOUT PULLEYS

If it is desired to lift a horse up and there is no other means available, this should answer the purpose well. Two poles are

pushed under the recumbent animal across the long axis of the body, one a hand's breadth in front of the hind limb and the other a similar distance behind the fore limb.

The poles must be 3 to 4 yards long so that they project 6 to 9 inches beyond the length of the limb and 2 to 3 feet the other side.

A rope is knotted on to the poles, as shown, and firmly tied above and below the body. The lifting up is accomplished by a man being stationed at the shorter ends of the poles to prevent these slipping, while two men lift at the longer ends. A man is also at the horse's head. A heavy horse can thus be lifted without any great exertion.

EFFECTIVE CURES FOR THE HORSE THAT PULLS BACK

Some good ways of tying a horse up with the object of teaching him not to pull back are shown here. Always use good, strong ropes because, if once a horse breaks one when trying to get away, he will continue to try for a long time to come.

The first is a very simple idea and is somewhat similar to that shown under "An idea for a shy leader on page 217."

A rope is taken in the form of a lasso and passed over the hindquarters, through the headstall to the post. As soon as the horse tends to move backwards, he feels the rope round his hindquarters, and at once steps forward again.

Both the quarter and head ropes should be made fast to the hitching post, ensuring that the quarter rope is tied a little shorter than the head rope so that should the horse hang back, the first strain is on the quarter rope. This is a very simple method which may not, of course, be as quickly effective as the last method shown here where a very lively horse is concerned; nevertheless, it will teach most horses to stand still.

The second sketch show another simple cure for the horse which persists in pulling back. In this instance, a rope in the form of a noose is put around the body in the manner shown, and is then passed through a ring in the halter before being tied to the post.

The end of the rope which is round the body should have rather a large loop in it so that when the horse goes forward after backing, the rope will at once slacken and the horse will not therefore remain uncomfortable.

The third drawing is that of another method very commonly used; it being known as the "crupper" idea and its application is well illustrated in the sketch.

First get a rope sufficiently long for the purpose, then double and twist it in the manner shown to form what is known as the "crupper." This is placed under the tail and along the back of the horse as indicated.

The two ends of the rope are then passed round, one on each side of the horse, and tied at the chest as shown.

The rope from the halter is then attached to or passed round the hitching post and then returned to the horse and tied to the crupper rope at the chest. It will therefore be seen that as soon as he pulls back the crupper rope tightens and forces him to move forward again.

There is also a somewhat similar idea used by some horsemen and that is to pass the loose ends of the crupper rope forward through the halter and tie them to the post instead of tying across the chest. The neck rope is then left slack.

A good way to teach the horse quickly not to pull back is to tie him up by one of these methods, using only good, strong rope, and then cause him to back suddenly by waving something in front of him. After a few times he will learn to stand quietly.

To cure a horse which already has this bad habit and is hard to cure, try the crupper idea with the addition of a weak cord tied from post to bit. Make him draw back suddenly and when the cord breaks it will bring the crupper into action suddenly with such a jolt that he will leap forward thoroughly scared. Be sure good rope or gear is used so that he cannot break it.

USEFUL HINTS WITH HORSES

THE DIAMOND HITCH FOR SECURING PACK LOADS

This is one way of securing a pack load on a horse and the following hints on " how to go about arranging it " might be useful.

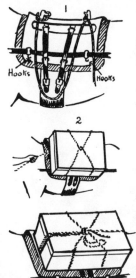

Figures 1, 2 and 3 will show the procedure to be adopted. It first of all needs a length of rope, say, 25 ft. long. This is doubled at the centre and the loop so formed is passed through the "D" of the front arch of the pack-saddle, the two ends then being passed through the loop and drawn tight; one end then falling on each side of the horse.

The rope is then secured to the front loading hook with two half-hitches and tied close to the portion of the rope which passes through the front arch "D."

A loop of the rope is then made and hung as indicated in fig. 1, the size of the loop, of course, being in accordance with the size of the pack to be carried. When the size of this loop has been fixed, the rope is attached to the rear loading hook with two half-hitches, the spare end being left for the time being.

The pack is then placed in position on the saddle and the loop mentioned in the previous para. is brought up round the bottom of the pack, reaching just half-way up the pack, as shown in figure 2.

The spare end of the rope which is hanging from the rear loading hook is then passed through the top of the loop and back to the front arch and drawn tight. Figure 2 will show the movement—the hand showing the action of drawing the rope tight.

After having been drawn tight, this loose end is then passed right round the load horizontally from front to rear, through both arches of the pack-saddle from rear to front and secured with a hitch in the centre of the pack (see fig. 3).

The same procedure is then adopted on the other side in order to balance the load, when both loads are then secured by a surcingle in the usual manner.

The illustrations given show quite a good procedure which, if done with a certain amount of care, should result in a nice firm pack which will stand plenty of movement without becoming loose or uncomfortable in any way.

Some, however, prefer to arrange the pack on the ground and then fix it on by merely hooking same on to the saddle on special hooks placed there for the purpose.

ANOTHER NOVEL HORSE FEEDER

This is an idea recently seen on one of the remount farms which has been found very effective and economical as it eliminates to a great extent a certain wastage of chaff from wind, etc.

They are made from 40 gallon drums, cut with a wide cutter—the edges then being hammered round in order that there will be no

sharp edges on which the horse might scratch itself.

The ideal cut is to take not more than one-third of the drum out, which then means that the top edges curve inwards, this being the idea that eliminates wastage from wind as very little is then blown out. On the day the writer saw this idea there were other types of feeders on the place, from which the fine chaff could be seen blowing out, but none was escaping from these particular feeders. Usually they are about half filled with chaff.

The method of construction is shown—the length of timber being about 3 ft. 6 in.—made from any scrap. This height is ideal as otherwise, if higher, the horses would have a tendency to use them to rub their hindquarters on.

HINTS ON SHOEING YOUR OWN HORSES

Although the following may not make one a fully fledged smith, it may prove useful. It is not wise to make horses go without re-shoeing for months — some authorities state that shoes should not be left on for more than 2 months. As the hoof grows at the rate of 1/3rd of an inch per month, some of the hoof should be removed before re-shoeing.

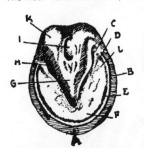

These sketches show some common types of horses' feet. In NARROW FEET the heels are higher than those of the normal horse and the toe and quarters more upright.

The walls are usually strong and hard but careful shoeing is necessary.

(1) A sound, strong foot. (2) A narrow foot. (3) A flat foot. (4) A dished foot.

FLAT FEET usually have large frogs and open, low weak heels. Such feet are liable to corns and bruises and may be troublesome to shoe. DISHED FEET are feet with hollow walls and rounded soles, akin to flat feet, only the trouble is more marked, prone to bruises and disease.

The hoof consists of wall, sole and frog, the walls continuing inwards to form the "bars." Between the bars is a mass of elastic tissue called the " frog," which takes the jar of contact. Between the frog and the wall is the arched sole, above which is a sensitive sole.

(a) Ground surface of wall at toe, (b) at quarter, and (c) at heels where it turns and forms the bars; (d) the bar; (e) white line or junction of the wall and sole; (f) the sole; (g) the frog; (h) the commissures; (i) the cleft of frog; (k) the bulb of heel; (l) the seat of corn.

attempt to cut the bars out. The outer edge of the bearing surface should be bevelled by

Tools. A hoof cutter, a rasp about 16-18 in. long, and a drawing knife, the latter to complete the bevelling of the bearing surface and to remove flakes from sole and flaps of tissue from the frog. In using the rasp, be careful not to over-reduce the wall.

The foot is prepared with the rasp, both sides of the wall must be the same height and the heights of the heel and toe must be in proportion to one another. Do not over-reduce the foot.

The sole should not be cut. If there are any flakes, they may be removed, which also applies to the flaps which, however, should not be pared. Do not using the file.

Making the Shoes. The bar iron is measured, heated to a red heat and then manipulated on the anvil to conform to the foot. The toe, quarters and heel of the shoes should be of even thickness. It should then be tested for fit.

If testing to a " hot " fit, the shoe is heated to an even dull red heat and then applied to the foot. The parts in contact with the shoe will char, and show up any irregularities in the bearing surface. When the shoe fits, some then press it on to the foot till a level bearing surface is obtained by burning.

The fewer nails used the better—usually 4 on the outside and 3 on the inside. Make sure not to drive nails into the sensitive parts or to press on them. The nail holes in the shoe are usually made so that the nails are driven slightly inward, particularly at the toe, so as to keep in line with the angle of the hoof, while the quarter and heel nails are more vertical.

Section of hoof showing position and direction of the two front nails. The right side of shoe shows the clinches turned over.

Whatever you do, do not rasp the walls of the hoof after nailing the shoe. This will tend to make the hoof brittle and liable to break off where the nails are clinched. **Use the knife and rasp sparingly and never rasp the hoof above the clinches.**

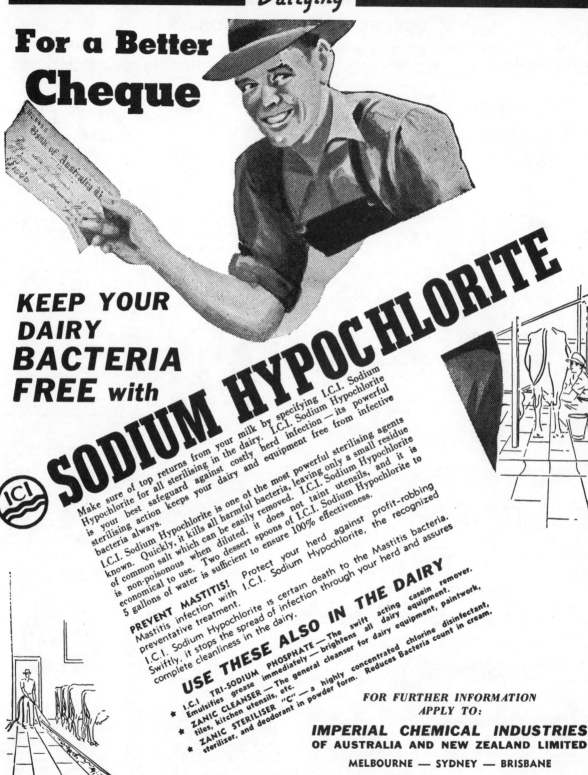

DAIRYING HINTS

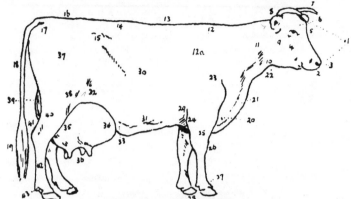

THE MAIN POINTS

1. Head
2. Muzzle
3. Nostril
4. Face
5. Eye
6. Forehead
7. Horn
8. Ear
9. Cheek
10. Throat
11. Neck
12. Withers
12a. Crops
13. Back
14. Loins
15. Hip Bone
16. Pelvic Arch
17. Rump
18. Tail
19. Switch
20. Chest
21. Brisket

OF A COW

22. Dewlap
23. Shoulder
24. Elbow
25. Forearm
26. Knee
27. Ankle
28. Hoof
29. Heart Girth
30. Side or Barrel
31. Belly
32. Flank
33. Milk Vein
34. Fore Udder
35. Hind Udder
36. Teats
37. Upper Thigh
38. Stifle
39. Twist
40. Leg or Gaskin
41. Hock
42. Shank
43. Dew Claw

TELLING THE AGE OF CATTLE

Any one with experience of cattle can determine the age, especially if one works along the lines of these diagrams given herein. The teeth of an ox number 32, comprising 8 incisors and 24 molars.

The former are broad at the crown and narrow at the neck. These are on the lower jaw only. The upper jaw has a dental pad against which the lower incisors play.

Fig. 1. The incisors at one month. Temporary incisors and molars are up soon after birth.

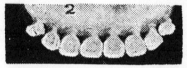

Fig. 2 are the incisors at 1 year old.

Fig. 3, 1 yr. 10 months. At 1½ to 2 yrs. the central permanent incisors come up.

Fig. 4, at 2¼ to 2½ years. At this age the internal laterals appear.

Fig. 5, at 2½ to 3 years. At about 3 years the external laterals appear.

Fig. 6, incisors at 3 to 3¼ years. At 3½ years the corners are right up.

Fig. 7, incisors at 4¾ years.

Fig. 8, incisors at 10 years.

The first molar appears at 6 months and they are all up at 3 years. Another guide to age is the horns of cattle. Generally allow 3 years for the top and a year for every ring on the horn.

Dairymen, when buying cows, generally judge the number of calves the cows have had by the rings on the horns.

HOW TO ESTIMATE THE WEIGHT OF CATTLE

There are several methods by which one can obtain an approximate idea as to the weight of cattle, and these notes give two ways of doing it by measurement in a very simple manner.

The first idea is that of squaring the girth and then multiplying that by 5 times the length (both measurements in feet) then dividing the answer by 21, which should give the dead weight in stones (14 lbs.).

In the second, the girth is squared and multiplied by the length (both measurements in inches) and the result divided by 7,344—the answer being the dead weight in stones again.

The girth should be taken round "1-2" just behind the forelegs, keeping the tape pretty tight. When obtaining the length, feel for the top and bottom of the shoulder blade, and fix position "5" which is one-third of the distance down the bone. The length is from "4," a point just above "5," straight along the back to the square of the rump at "3."

FARM BUTCHERING—BEEF JOINTS

No. 1—Ox Cheek: Splendid entree; can be braised or stewed.

No. 2—Neck: Suitable only for beef tea, soups or stews.

No. 3—Chuck: Pot roast, free from fat. **No. 4—Back Ribs:** Roast.

Nos. 5 and 6—Prime Ribs: Roasting joint, rolled or with bone.

No. 7—Wing Rib: Roasting joint, free from surplus fat.

No. 8—Middle loin: Roast.

No. 9—First Cut Sirloin: Roasting joint with undercut.

No. 10—Rump: Steak meat, selvidge fat.

No. 11 — Shoulder: Tender beefsteak.

No. 12—Bolar: Boiling joint.

No. 13—Brisket: For corned beef.

No. 14—Brisket: Middle cut, corned with bone, streaky fat.

No. 15 — Brisket: Thin end, corned with bone; streaky fat.

No. 16—Thin Flank: Corned and rolled, extra quantity of fat.

No. 17—Thick Flank and Topside: Prime beef steak.

No. 18—Silverside: Corned round, prime corned joint, free of fat.

No. 19—Shin: Suitable for soups and potted meats

No. 20—Leg: Suitable for soups and potted meats.

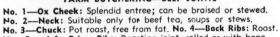

Showing the various parts of the ox.

[W. Anglia.

DAIRYING HINTS

HINTS ON THROWING CATTLE

It is sometimes necessary to throw a cow or bullock and these notes give details as to two or three ways in which this can be done in a quiet and easy manner and without having to tie their legs and so perhaps bring them down in a way which might injure.

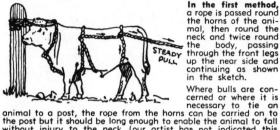

In the first method, a rope is passed round the horns of the animal, then round the neck and twice round the body, passing through the front legs up the near side and continuing as shown in the sketch.

Where bulls are concerned or where it is necessary to tie an animal to a post, the rope from the horns can be carried on to the post but it should be long enough to enable the animal to fall without injury to the neck (our artist has not indicated this sufficiently in the sketch, but it should be borne in mind).

The second sketch is slightly different inasmuch as the rope is passed round the horns, then around the neck and twice around the body direct from the neck.

All that is necessary to bring them down in all these methods is a steady pull from behind—they should go down easily and gently and if pressure is maintained on the rope they should remain down as long as required.

The third is another effective method — the rope is tied round the neck and not the horns, then wound two or three times round the body as shown. The rope is again merely pulled, and if the animal starts forward, the rope action will bring it down just the same. When he or she is down, one person should hold the head whilst the other operates. If the rope is held firmly in each instance, the animal is not likely to struggle and it should not actually be necessary to tie their heads, whilst when once down it should not be necessary to hold their legs either, one person holding their heads should be sufficient.

A QUICK TIE-UP FOR BRANDING STOCK

This is a very convenient way of securing cattle in order to brand them. It is a method used quite a lot with success—one advantage being that one can manage quite a large number of stock with only one assistant, whilst if there are large numbers to be branded and one has several men to do the work, it can be done at various parts of the yard at the same time.

As shown, the animal is taken up to the rails and roped over the horns or neck to the post. Another rope is fixed to the fence hip

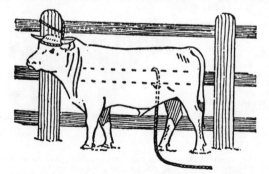

high and placed on the ground as shown, and when the animal is brought alongside the fence, the rope is thrown over the top rail and pulled taut. The job can be done quickly and satisfactorily.

A USEFUL COW TIE

This is a method used by one farmer who finds it very convenient. It is an adaptation of an old idea in which two chain links are used.

The free end "B" is long enough to go round the cow's neck. The knot passes through the loop "AA."

Do not make the loop "A" big enough to go round the cow's neck or you would simply have a slip knot and perhaps a dead cow in the morning.

The loop is to hold the knot in the end of the rope.

KEEPING THE BULL AT HOME

This is a device which has been used with success by many, and, although it might seem rather a heavy contraption for the animal to carry round, it need not be made of heavy material. However it will certainly teach him a lesson, and is an excellent idea for the purpose.

It will keep a bull from going through a fence as the notches shown will catch on the wires.

A piece of strap iron an inch wide and 12 or 14 inches long would be quite sufficient. With a hacksaw, make three notches in one edge and then give the upper end a half turn and fasten it to the bull ring.

A PRACTICAL BULL YARD

This idea is from England from Mr. H. Hale, who has won many prizes in stock management. It enables a herd bull to be kept in such a way that it allows the animal to obtain exercise which is so necessary to him and yet he is safe as far as human beings are concerned.

Each of Mr. Hale's bulls has a 12 ft. square box made from second-hand material, roofed with curved galvanised iron. Out of each box leads a run of about 45 ft. in length and 16 ft. wide. A passage at the back of the box permits the animal to be tied up or fed without entering his quarters. Down the centre of the run and box passes a flexible steel cable, secured at each end to stout posts by means of thread eye-bolts to permit the tension to be adjusted. A steel chain, free to run up and down the cable secures the bull.

The chain has two branches with spring snaps on each, one of which is fixed direct to the nose-ring, the other secured to a chain halter which runs through the ring. Spare chains at each end of the cable serve to tie up the bull either in the run or in the box.

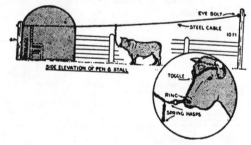

In the box the cable is 6 ft. from the ground, and the chain is of such a length that the bull can lie down without becoming entangled. At the end of the run, the cable is 10 ft. from the ground, allowing the bull to serve without interference.

This arrangement was commented upon very favourably by a representative of the "Farmer and Stockbreeder" as the bulls appeared to be contented and in excellent condition. They were able to get plenty of exercise and yet be under perfect control.

By means of a pole, the chain, and therefore the bull, could be moved up and down the cable to any portion of the run without entering the bull-yard.

DAIRYING HINTS

CALF TROUBLES

The following are some of the ways of leaving a calf in the field with its mother, and, at the same time, weaning it.

The first is made from a piece of tin and some wire and is not painful to the mother as some ideas are, whilst the calf can feed comfortably. The tin is cut U-shaped and bent back where shown. Sharpened wire is then threaded through it and the calf's nostrils at the same time.

The second is also from a strip of sheet metal 9 x 10 in. This is bent to fit the calf's muzzle and holes are punched in the tin, with the jagged ends outwards. This makes it uncomfortable for the mother but enables the calf to breathe. The weaner extends about 2 in. past the calf's mouth.

The third is a method used by one farmer. It is made from 2 ft. of No. 8 gauge wire which fits into the nostrils of the calf. Any cow would repel the advances of a calf armed with this. Measurements are given.

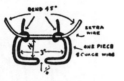

ANOTHER HOME-MADE CALF MUZZLE

Some forms of calf muzzle (perhaps somewhat similar to some of the above) and which consist of sheet iron bent over into a roll at one edge with a short piece of wire pushed into the roll from each end, and projecting over a gap in the rolled edge, may cause the nose of the calf to chafe.

One good plan is to use two wooden pins, rounded off smoothly at the inner ends, in lieu of the wire. Ordinary cotter or split pins passed through holes drilled in both plate and pegs will hold the wooden pegs firmly in position.

Only one of these holes should be drilled at first, the other being marked when the plate is tried on the calf's nose and drilled afterwards. If the muzzle grips too tightly, the pegs can be cut back as far as necessary by filing.

This is quite a good idea

FOUR METHODS OF CURING SELF-SUCKING COWS

1. Put a surcingle and head stall on cow with 2 x 1 dropper fixed between legs by rings to each (see sketch). 2. Put a piece of plain galvd. iron, 12 in. wide, long enough to go round neck.

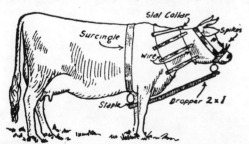

Punch some holes in bottom and lace with light wire (not tightly). 3. Staple half a dozen 2 x 1 slats on 2 lengths of fencing wire round cow's neck. 4. Fix three sharp nails on a nose-band of the head stall.

A FALSE TEAT FOR CALF

One dairyman had a calf which would not take the fingers held in the pail. It was becoming weak, so it was decided to make an artificial teat such as that shown here, and it worked.

He took a piece of poplar branch about 3 ins. long which was smoothed down to the shape of a

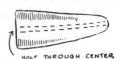

cow's teat. Then a hole was made through the centre. Around the large end was fastened a large wire, allowing at least 12 inches upright for the handle. When feeding the calf, the teat was held by the wire handle. It saved the calf's life, considering the condition it was in beforehand.

TEACHING A CALF TO DRINK

This sketch shows a very handy gadget for weaning any calves that refuse to drink from a bucket without the aid of fingers.

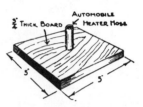

Use a 5 in. square piece of light ¾ in. board with a 3½ in. piece of motor heater hose inserted in a hole in the centre. The hose may be tacked in with small nails at the bottom edge. This will float on the milk and works like a charm.

STOPPING A COW FROM STRAYING

This is one plan which can be adopted with a cow that habitually strays out of the pasture.

It is a cow chain and a pole about 4 ft. 6 in. in length, a little stronger than a fork shaft, as shown in the sketch.

The cow will be able to eat comfortbaly but is not likely to try and get out of the paddock.

SUPPORTING A PENDULOUS UDDER

To prevent a cow which has a pendulous udder from damaging the delicate blood vessels and tinting the milk, obtain a piece of calico two yards by one; split up the centre and in each piece pierce four holes to allow the teats to protrude, as in the sketch.

Wrap it round the cow and secure as shown. By using alternately, this support can be kept clean.

AN ECONOMICAL CALF HOUSE

One can make a very cosy and snug calf house from straw as shown in this sketch, one which costs very little to build.

To make this house, all that you need is a supply of saplings of various sizes, some old fencing wire, and some netting and straw.

The saplings are used for posts (these want forks at top), rafters, top plates, ridge pole, battens, etc. The wire is run on both sides of the posts and is tightened by placing whip-sticks at short intervals. The straw is then laced horizontally between the whip-sticks and the wire. The roof is first covered with netting and then thatched with straw. The sketch will show the finished house.

DAIRYING HINTS

A HOME-MADE MILKING STOOL FROM BUSH TIMBER

The first is one made from bush timber which might be on the place and is one of the simplest possible.

The legs are merely made from a three-pronged fork of a tree and the top is a piece of wood or cross section of a tree approximately round spiked into position.

It is strong, easily moved and should last for years.

A HANDY MILKING STOOL ACCESSORY FROM SEPARATOR STAND

This is rather a useful and convenient idea. In this instance, the milk-stand from an old separator is bolted to one of the legs of the milk stool and thus serves as a rest for the milk pail.

It is not necessary, of course, to wait until the cream separator is finished with, but some other useful article around the place could be used in a similar way.

USEFUL MILKING STOOL
Always Ready to Use

A handy stool is made from a circular piece of thick wood or 2 thin pieces nailed together, fitted with a leg about 12 in. long and 2 in. square. The leg may be fastened to the seat with a long screw or with a bolt with the nut notched in as shown in the sketch.

The strap nailed to the underside of the seat is buckled round the body, so that the milker can move from one cow to another without bothering about the stool.

ANOTHER EVER-READY STOOL

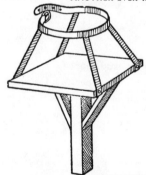

This is also a very convenient stool for milking in yard or field. It is merely a one-legged stool to which is attached four straps connecting with a broad strap buckled around the waist. The stool is quickly fastened to the milker, and is always in position so that one can sit down anywhere.

Such a stool with a short leg would also be useful in the garden, or, if preferred, it could have 4 legs, but experience proves that the one-legged stool serves best.

A HANDY PAIL HOLDER

This sketch will give details of an arrangement which will fit comfortably over the legs and which will hold the pail snugly between the knees, thus easing leg strain and making it unnecessary to keep up a pressure against the pail. It also reduces the possibility of the pail being tipped over.

It is made from a piece of heavy wire, bent round the pail near the top with large loops twisted on the ends as shown. The loops are curved to the contour of the legs so that the pressure is evenly distributed.

A USEFUL MILKING HINT

This handy little arrangement will serve a double purpose, as it will act as a support for the milking bucket and it will also have a controlling effect on the tail of the cow.

The device is merely a bent piece of wire shaped so that the milking bucket will fit into it, as in the sketch—this wire can, if necessary, be shaped to take the milker's knees as indicated in other sketches. The tail of the cow is then arranged as shown, and the wire support is then hooked to the belt of the person milking. The weight is then distributed between the belt and the legs, and if the milker is not wearing a belt, a piece of strong cord tied in the same way will do.

A HANDY STRAINER FOR MILKING BUCKET

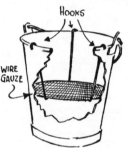

This is quite a useful idea—easily made—and consists of a piece of wire made into a circle to fit closely into the bucket at whatever part of the bucket is desired. This should then be covered over with fine gauze attached to the wire in some way (soldered for preference). The addition of 3 or 4 hooks, as indicated, long enough to hook on to the bucket, is an advantage.

Milking is then done through the sieve and it will prevent any outside matter from getting into the milk and it will also prevent the milk from splashing.

AN IMPROVISED CREAM GAUGE FROM BOTTLE

By keeping a record of each cow's production of cream, one is able to ascertain the productive animals of the herd. In the absence of other means of testing, a satisfactory cream gauge can be made from a tall bottle, or test tube, which should be 7 or 8 in. long. A strip of paper is cut about 1 in. wide and long enough to reach the shoulder of the bottle. An open slot, 1-8 in. or $\frac{1}{4}$ in. wide, is cut in the centre of the strip, as shown.

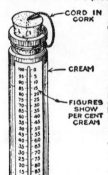

Beginning at the top on one side, the open space is divided into 100 equal parts, marking them 5, 10, etc. On the opposite side of the slot, the same number of graduations is made, but beginning at the bottom.

To use the tester, the milk (as fresh as possible from the cow) is thoroughly stirred, and the bottle filled with it level to the top marks.

The bottle is then tightly corked, placed upright in a jar of cold water, and allowed to stand in a cool place for about 10 hours, when the proportion of cream to milk is easily read off. The scale beginning at the top gives the percentage of cream, and the opposite graduations the amount of milk.

SOLDERING INITIALS ON MILK OR CREAM CANS

Some dairymen have trouble with labels becoming detached, resulting in loss. To make letters on the sides, the part where they are to be placed should be carefully cleaned, and the letters marked on the patch, which is then dressed with soldering fluid.

The soldering iron is then brought into play and the solder gradually built up over the letters, until they stand in some relief. It is better for the beginner to practise on something.

DAIRYING HINTS

AN IDEA TO PREVENT COWS FROM KICKING

This diagram shows one method used by one dairyman to stop cows from kicking the bucket over. His idea is that many punish their cows by tying their legs with chains, but such cows should be handled with care.

His method is to tie a rope round her neck and draw it snug into the stanchion. So tied, the cow is not able to kick, because to kick she must move forward, and she is already as far forward as she can go. Do not tie her so closely that she cannot get air. Just do this a few times and she will then stand without kicking.

ANOTHER PREVENTATIVE DEVICE FOR KICKING COWS

There are various devices for leg roping cows in order to prevent them from kicking the milk bucket over, and this is quite a good one.

It is a piece of wood 15 or 16 inches long with straps inserted as shown. This is then attached to the cow's leg, which will not then be able to kick forward and therefore the milk bucket will be safe.

Usually the animal will get over the habit of kicking after she has had this arrangement attached to her leg for a little while, when it should not be necessary to continue with such an arrangement.

A USEFUL METHOD OF STAKING OUT STOCK

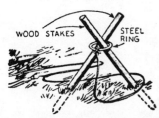

WOOD STAKES   STEEL RING

This is one very useful way of staking out stock. In this the tangling of the tether is avoided by the double stakes shown.

The illustration shows how the two stakes are driven into the ground at certain angles. The rope will not then tangle, regardless of the number of times the animal encircles the anchorage.

The tether should be made fast to the stakes by a loose loop or large ring which is indicated in the accompanying sketch.

ANOTHER USEFUL METHOD OF TETHERING OUT STOCK

This method is simple and effective. The sketch shows how two stakes are driven into the ground several feet apart with a rope or wire stretched between them on which a ring is placed.

To this ring a halter strap is fastened as shown. The animal can graze up and down on both sides without inconvenience. The stakes can then be easily moved from place to place without much trouble and quite a large area of ground can be grazed at the one time.

COW TIED OUT TO FEED

TAMING A COW'S TAIL

It is very often unpleasant to be hit about the head and face by a cow's tail whilst milking is in progress, but this may be easily averted by throwing a loop of heavy rope over the cow's hips and tail as shown in this sketch.

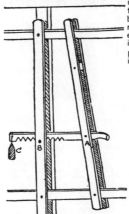

HEAVY ROPE

A USEFUL TYPE OF COW BAIL

COW·BAIL

This sketch illustrates a type of cow bail with a ratchet or saw edged latch instead of a pin and hole in the top bar.

This can be worked with one hand and one movement, instead of three or four movements and two hands for the pin method.

The ratchet is made with a piece of 3 x 1 hardwood with a small weight on "C" and hingeing on bolt "A," the end at "A" making a handle.

To open or shut, simply press on "A" and push backward or forward as required. "B" is a bolt running through to the stud to catch the teeth of the latch. Make it work fairly loose and easy.

AN AUTOMATIC BAIL—COW LOCKS HERSELF IN

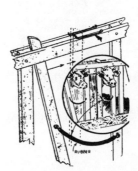

Cows may be made to lock themselves in the bail by attaching an automatic latch, as shown.

The movable bar of the bail is connected with the opposite standing post by means of a spring made from a length of inner tube twisted into a cable and fixed with staples at both ends.

When the cow goes into the bail and puts her head down to get at the feed manger, her neck presses on the cable and draws the moving bar inwards until it slips under a wire latch fixed on the top cross-bar, locking it into position. The top of the moving bar is bevelled off and the latch correspondingly bent upward to give a smooth action.

ANOTHER COW BAIL HINT

This is one which costs very little to make, holds the animals securely and allows a certain amount of movement sideways, thereby giving greater comfort. The stanchion poles are spiked with 6 in. spikes in a channel formed by 4 x 2's at the bottom.

The spike serves as a pivot. The top of the stanchion poles swing free from A to B in a channel formed by 5 in. poles, which, contrary to most homemade poles, gives plenty of room for movement of head and shoulders.

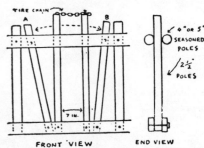

FRONT VIEW   END VIEW

Between each stanchion 3 pieces of pole are spiked upright to hold the feed back. The distance between the centres of the stanchions is 33 in. and between the poles at the bottom, inside faces, 7 in., while 50 in. from the floor to above the animal gives ample standing room.

DAIRYING HINTS

A USEFUL DEVICE FOR SUSPENDING CREAM CAN

A handy device for suspending cream cans on a wall or other place is illustrated here.

Two iron rods with hooks at ends are fastened on to an iron ring at one end to the handles of the cream cans as shown. This will be found to be a very convenient arrangement, and, of course, could be used in conjunction with the "flying fox" idea shown on these pages.

AN IDEA TO SEPARATE MILK FROM CREAM

Although a complete separation of milk and cream is not made by this device, it is useful when the milk is wanted before  the cream is skimmed off. Punch a hole in the bottom of the dish used for setting the milk, and plug it with a stopper cut from cork or wood.

Fill the dish, and when the cream has partly risen, there will be no difficulty in draining the milk from the bottom of the dish without disturbing the cream.

USEFUL WAYS OF HANDLING MILK OR CREAM CANS

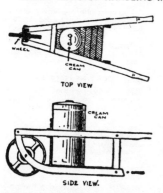

TOP VIEW

SIDE VIEW.

The illustrations indicate some very useful ideas in connection with the handling of milk or cream cans—all of which are the ideas of various dairymen and which have been found very efficient indeed.

The first shows how a very useful barrow can be built from scrap and which is of extra value when cans have to be taken down hill and the ground might be very wet or slippery.

The load can then rest on the two bottom runners, which act like a sledge.

The second illustration is one indicating a trapdoor let into the floor of a wheelbarrow in order that the can is able to be set in such a way as to lower the centre of gravity of the load and so minimise upsetting.

The cut-out section of the floor is hinged so that it can be dropped back into place, and a steel bracket is suspended beneath the wheelbarrow in order to hold the can.

When not in use for milk or cream, this barrow can then be used for other purposes by replacing the hinged portion.

The third shows how a useful but somewhat similar milk and cream cart can be made by using an old motor wheel for easy running.

In this, any of the foregoing ideas can be used in conjunction.

KEEPING CREAM CANS UPRIGHT ON LORRY

Those who haul cream cans and similar containers will find that an old inner tube stretched across the body of the truck as indicated will hold the cans so that they will not bounce around and tip over.

Heavy wire rings on the ends of the tube engage hooks placed at intervals in the truck sides which permit the tube to be adjusted for a few cans or a full load.

A USEFUL HOME-MADE CHURN FROM CREAM CAN

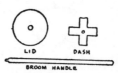

A very useful small churn can be made from an ordinary cream can. The end of a box is cut round and bevelled to fit to make a good top.

For a dash you can use the handle from an old broom and two pieces of wood 2 ins. wide nailed together in the form of a cross. Make the cross pieces long enough so that they can be just passed through the neck of the can at an angle.

A HANDY OUT-OF-THE-WAY WEIGHING HOOK

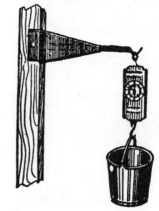

This is a handy mounting for a hook on which to suspend a spring scale for weighing cream or any other commodity.

A large heavy "T" hinge is obtained, and the small end formed into a hook, or a hook fastened on it if the hinge is not long enough.

The butt plate of the hinge is screwed to a convenient post, so that the hook may be turned back out of the way when not in use.

This idea would be quite suitable for a number of purposes in addition to that mentioned above, and for such it might be also well worth while putting one in the workshop.

A HOME-MADE "FLYING FOX"

This is a real labour saver for carrying milk buckets or other objects from place to place. It can be made by twisting 3 fence

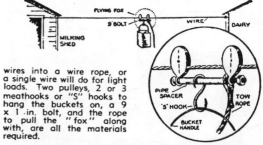

wires into a wire rope, or a single wire will do for light loads. Two pulleys, 2 or 3 meathooks or "S" hooks to hang the buckets on, a 9 x 1 in. bolt, and the rope to pull the "fox" along with, are all the materials required.

Before the milk is put into the buckets, the contraption should be secured with rope to a strong post. The wire should be taut when erected, as the load will tend to bring it lower.

DAIRYING HINTS

A USEFUL BEEF HANGING DEVICE

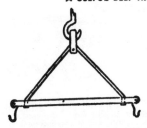

This can be made from any material on hand—this one being from the front axle and radius rods of an old Ford car. If you take off the steering knuckles but leave the bolts, then hang on good hooks, it makes a great way of hanging up beef whilst you are butchering it.

A clevice is put at the ball and socket end and hung on a chain hoist.

AN IDEA FOR A TAIL SWITCHER

This is another and rather a good idea to adopt in order to counteract the nuisance one is often subject to when a cow has the habit of switching her tail at milking time.

An old battery clip is used, and a piece of halter chain or small rope together with a block of wood are all that is necessary for this cow tail holder. The chain is attached to the block with a staple and the clip, a large one, is snapped to a bunch of hair on the cow's tail before beginning to milk.

AN ELECTRIC " PERSUADER "

This home-made electric livestock prodder can be used for touching up stubborn cows, pigs, or other animals when they object to going up loading chutes or into trucks, etc. This one is a model T Ford coil clamped to an old billiard cue and actuated by a 3-cell flashlight battery and a simple push button switch.

Insulated wires leading from the coil out to the end delivers a hot spark where it will do the most good. This is also much more humane than a club or pitchfork and does not bruise or damage.

A NOVEL DAIRY BROOM

This novel broom has a two-fold purpose as it will wash down the floor of the dairy at the same time as it sweeps the floor.

It is merely the usual yard broom with a handle of ¾ in. piping inserted into it in the usual place. The length of piping can be made to suit the particular user, the end of which is screwed to take an ordinary hose fitting. A pin or nail of some sort should be driven through a hole previously bored in the piping at the lower end so that it can be held in the broom securely.

The hose is then attached to the tap which is turned on just sufficiently for the water to percolate through the broom. This should enable dirt to be quickly washed off the floor without the necessity of scrubbing and cleaning separately.

ANOTHER USEFUL COW-HOUSE GADGET

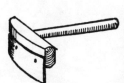

This is a useful tool to scrape the rainwater from the backs of cows when they come in for milking after heavy rain.

Once the water is off their backs they dry in a very short time. The scraper consists of a blade, made of zinc or other non-rusting material with a curved edge, screwed to a wooden head (with curved face also). A wooden handle about 12 in. long and 1 in. wide completes it.

ANOTHER HOME-MADE HOE AND COW YARD SCRAPER

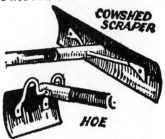

Some very serviceable home-made hoes and scrapers can be made from the curved pieces of steel which fits above the comb of an old harvester, or one can easily improvise some other piece of steel to do the same job.

For a ferrule, use a 2 in. length of 1 in. pipe bored with two holes at the end.

These have ¼ inch holes tapped to take two short lengths of five-sixteenths round iron threaded at one end and flattened at the other. The flattened ends and the curved steel are bored for rivets, and the result is a very useful scraper for cleaning out the yards or cowsheds.

When the two pieces of iron are curved as shown, a short length of steel makes a splendid hoe (see illustration No. 2).

AN ADJUSTABLE FLOOR FOR LOADING STOCK

This adjustable loader is a very convenient one for transferring stock to trucks at various heights.

First make the bottom or platform of 2 inch planking, laying the boards lengthwise, and then nail cleats across the top surface to prevent the stock from slipping.

The posts are 6 x 3 set in concrete, a vertical row of holes being drilled in the front and centre posts to receive lengths of heavy pipe, which support the platform at various heights.

The two front posts are also drilled to take a winding crank, made of heavy iron rod and bent as shown. Two lengths of wire Cable or strong rope, fastened to the platform, are run over 2 pulleys mounted on the front posts, and are then wound on the crank.

The sides of the loader are nailed to the inside of the support posts in the usual way. It is a good idea to nail a metal or wooden strip vertically over the side boards at each post, to prevent the platform from catching on them when it is raised or lowered.

In use, the platform is adjusted to the desired height by turning the crank, and the pipes are then inserted in the holes to support it in this position.

Some other types of home-made loading chutes are also given in a later section of this book, any one of which might suit the particular circumstances desired.

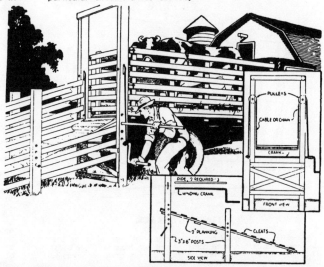

DAIRYING HINTS

A SIMPLE GUARD FENCE FOR HAYSTACK

Instead of going to all the work of setting posts and stretching wire to fence a haystack temporarily, one idea is to merely lean poles against the haystack and nail the barb wire to them as shown in this drawing.

The poles must be long enough so that the animals are not able to reach the hay. This guard fence can be quickly erected and easily taken down whenever desired.

A HANDY CALF-FEEDING DEVICE

To feed half a dozen calves at once is possible if one uses the device shown here. A man who has one reports no more trouble with calves since he commenced using it. He rattles a couple of buckets together, the calves come running up to the fence, and soon have all their heads through the stanchions, to which they are easily fastened by throwing down lever (a), which

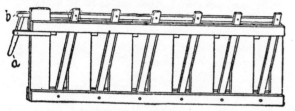

STANCHIONS FOR CALVES

draws the bar (b) into position. Then one may feed each calf without difficulty.

Leave a 4-inch space for the calves' heads. Make the rack of 1-inch timber, and it can be moved from one pasture to another and attached to the fence or a couple of posts. It can also be used for holding ewes at lambing time.

A NOVEL FEED RACK FOR SHEEP OR CALVES

An overhead feed manger, as shown in this illustration, is an excellent one for sheep or calves. It should hang just high enough so that they will pass under without rubbing their backs.

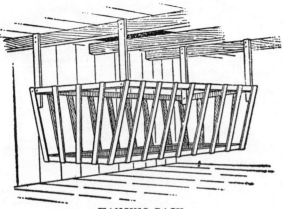

HANGING RACK

When filled with hay from above, they will eat of it at their pleasure, and at the same time, it will not take up floor space. This, of course, would not be suitable for grain or fine cut fodders, as too much would be wasted.

A USEFUL WATERING TANK FROM TRACTOR WHEEL

This tank would have to be permanently placed. The wheel is a large drive wheel from an old tractor. The hub and spokes are first removed and then it is laid on its side on a strong reinforced concrete foundation. A rich mixture of concrete is then made and placed on the floor, both inside and outside the wheel, to make it water-tight.

If there are any leakages in the rim, the cement may be brought up inside it almost to the top. To get a good shape for this lining a template should be made. It is fastened in the centre at at the bottom, with the upper part resting on the upper edge of the rim. Then the template can be turned round and round to shape the concrete lining.

ASSURING WATER SUPPLY TO CALVES

This is quite a good way of ensuring that calves are always able to reach water for drinking purposes.

First, get an old oil drum and cut it in half and set the lower part inside the regular stock tank near one edge, then anchor it in place by setting large stones against it on the outside or by some other means.

A pipe from the pump or a hose (not shown in this illustration) can then be run directly into this smaller tank, which overflows into the larger tank. In this way the smaller vessel always has the most water in it and the calves should always be able to reach it and they will soon get the habit of going straight to it.

A USEFUL SUPPORT TO CALF-FEEDING BUCKET

NAIL KEG

This is a good labour-saver, as the calf will be able to eat or drink quite comfortably without anyone having to hold the bucket. As shown, the bucket is set in an empty barrel so that it fits in at a convenient height.

One end is knocked out of the barrel, which is then set on the ground and tied to a post with wire.

The arrangement should ensure that the food or drink is not knocked over by the calf. Several of these attached to several posts round the cow yard should be a convenience as the food buckets could then be carried around and dumped into the respective places and each calf would be well separated from the others.

A HOLDER FOR ROCK SALT

Cattle can be kept from pushing rock salt from the platform which may have been provided in order to keep the salt off the ground, in this manner.

First of all provide a peg, as shown, into the centre of the platform and then slip the salt block over the peg in the way suggested.

An old augur will serve for making the hole in the salt so that it can be placed on the peg. This will be found a very convenient arrangement.

DAIRYING HINTS

A SIMPLE DRAIN FOR COWSHED FLOORS

This sketch shows a simple type of drain for the cowshed. By providing a double channel as shown, any liquid is allowed to pass

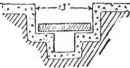

down under the board which divides the gutter and it should always flow freely.

This has the added advantage that one can clear up the dung much more easily than the slush which forms in the single channel. The construction of the gutter is obvious from the sketch, and would present no difficulties in practice. It would be well to tar the planks thoroughly to prevent rotting and to facilitate cleaning.

CONCRETE FLOORS FOR DAIRIES

Concrete floors are ideal for such things as dairy floors, etc., being clean, hard, and able to stand rough wear.

To begin with, a foundation must be prepared and the forms fixed in position, the latter being well greased with soft soap or crude oil. Clean the forms after use in readiness for the next job.

All concrete floors should rest on a good, sound base. Prepare the foundation by digging out to the depth needed, and after levelling the area with pegs, a straight-edge and level, cover the earth wtih a light layer of sand and cinders. This should be tamped down well before beginning the work of concreting.

Allow for drainage towards one corner, and do the whole surface in lesser sizes so as to form slabs which allow for expansion and contraction due to climatic conditions (see 1). Strips of timber will form the framework for these squares, the usual size of which is about 4 ft. square for each, although smaller slabs have a better appearance.

A two-course floor is usually used, i.e., one having a base of heavier material with a top course of lighter finishing mortar.

The upper drawing will illustrate this. The proportion of the first course is usually 1 of cement, 2½ clean sand, and 4 of gravel or screenings. Put this down to a depth of 2½ inches for ord-

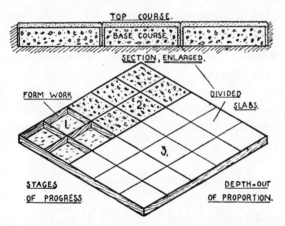

inary duty floors, and level off. For heavier service, increase the thickness in proportion up to 5½ inches for vehicular traffic. Give the base course about two hours at least to set (No. 2).

The form timbers can then be removed, and the finishing mortar prepared, i.e., 1 of cement and 2 of sand. Apply this to a depth of 1 inch and work well down into the spaces made by the timbers.

This is then levelled with a straight edge, and when beginning to harden, finish with a wooden float. Separate each division to allow for expansion by making a cut through the mortar in the timber space with a knife or the trowel edge, and then finish the knife cuts with an edging tool to give a better appearance (No. 3)

Curing or drying is the last stage, i.e., keeping the surface damp with clean bags or sand for a period of from 7 to 10 days until hardening has taken place uniformly.

A CATTLE-PROOF RAMP

Particulars of one very useful home-made ramp is given under another section of this book, i.e., "Gates and Fences," but that shown here is of a slightly different type. It is, however, very effective; the centre sections being raised just as much as desired or left level if necessary.

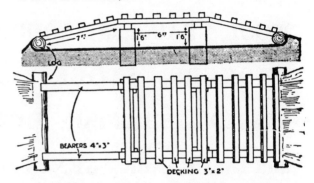

In this particular ramp, sleepers are used and therefore any such timber should be strong enough for the purpose. The construction of the ramp is sufficiently illustrated in the diagram and it should be all that is necessary to prevent cattle from straying from one place to another.

ANOTHER NOVEL AID FOR WASHING DAIRY FLOORS, ETC.

This sketch is of another very useful type of home-made article which will be found very useful.

It shows how a piece of hose can be pushed on to the prongs of an ordinary garden rake, or something similar, and how it can be used in the role of a squeegee for washing dairy and cowshed floors.

AN IDEA TO PREVENT BUCKETS FROM SLOPPING OVER

Those who carry pails of milk, water or other liquids any distance often find it very annoying to have the contents slop out on their feet and clothing.

A pail can be made almost slop-proof by spreading the eye of the bucket bail as shown at "A" in order to slip off the ears. Then get a link from any light chain and clip the link in the ear of the pail as at "B," also on the eye of the bail. The link is then closed as shown. This does away with the pail getting in step with those carrying it.

A CONCRETE IDEA FOR COWSHED OR STABLE DOORS

A concrete inclined runway over the sill at the entrance to the doors will make it possible to run the wheelbarrow inside for manure removal, and thus save time and the labour of removing the manure by single trips with the pitchfork.

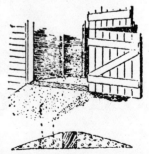

By banking the concrete flush with the top of the sill as shown, it will also make access for the stabled animals better and prevent them from tripping on any high sill.

PIGS

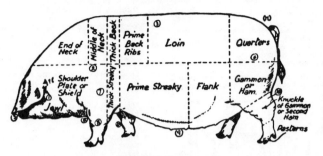

THE MAIN POINTS OF A PIG AND

Points other than those set out: 1, Head. 2, Forequarters. 3, Back. 4, Hindquarters. 5, Snout. 6, Knee. 7, Shoulder. 8, Foreleg. 9, Belly. 10, Hock. 11, Rump. 12, Chest.

Head should be well proportioned, medium length, wide and clean between ears. Ears, long, thin and well inclined over face. Jowl, cheek, medium size, strong under jaw. Neck, medium length

CLASSIFICATION
For Market Purposes

and smooth. Chest, wide and deep. Shoulders, Fine and in line with ribs. Back, long and level. Ribs, well sprung. Loin, broad. Sides, deep. Belly and flank, medium and well developed. Hams, large and well filled to hock. Quarters, long, wide and not drooping. Tail, set high, of large size. Legs, well set, straight and flat. Pasterns, strong. General movement, active. Skin, fine and soft.

CLASSIFICATION

Age	Approx. Weight	Age	Approx. Weight
Sucking Pig—6 weeks	15 lb. dressed	Heavy Porker—5½/6 months	75 lb. dressed
Weaner—8 weeks	25 lb. alive	Light Baconer—6/6½ months	90/100 lb. dressed
Slip—10 weeks	32 lb. alive	Medium Baconer—6½/7 months	100/120 lb. dressed
Store—12/16 weeks	45 lb. alive	Heavy Baconer—9/10 months	120/135 lb. dressed
Light Porker—4 months	50 lb. dressed	Choppers—Up to 2 years or more	Up to 3 cwt. dressed or
Medium Porker—4½ months	60 lb. dressed		heavier

A USEFUL CRATE FOR WEIGHING PIGS

This sketch will be valuable to those who watch their animals closely and desire to know whether they are making headway on the food supplied.

In addition to being used to weigh the pigs, it will be found handy when they have to be loaded on to a cart.

¾ in. hardwood is preferable for the job. The pigs are placed in crate when on the ground, and by pulling the chain at the long end of the lever, the crate is raised and the weight registered on the scales.

Such a crate will be found handy also when young pigs are being ringed or earmarked, or their feet have to receive attention. It can also be put to other uses.

A PIGGERY SWING DOOR

The principle of the swinging door before the pig trough so that the pigs can be kept back while it is being filled, is familiar to every pig farmer, but the open construction is not so common and particulars may be worth while to someone.

This little sketch will give details as to how it is made. It is suspended from the top bar by strap hinges. The bottom of the door strikes against the outside edge of the trough, which acts as a stop.

The trough is of reinforced concrete, the inside measurements being 7 in. in depth, 10 in. wide at the top, and 8 in. at the bottom.

A SWINGING PIG PEN DOOR

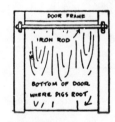

This is a handy hanging door for the pig house. It is simply made, and needs no additional explanation to that shown in the illustration.

Hang the door on a rod so that it will swing both ways. The pigs then simply root the door and it will swing either way in order to let them in or out as they wish. It should also keep fowls, etc., out of the sty.

A PIG-PROOF FENCE—HOW TO BEAT THE ROOTER

This is also a very useful fence as regards dogs. Dogs and pigs, especially the latter, burrow their way under a wire-netting fence but this little idea will help beat them.

If the fence is anchored at short intervals in the manner suggested, the most industrious pig will find himself baffled. Wood blocks, large stones or bricks, are buried a foot or two in the ground, which serve for anchors, to which the netting is tied

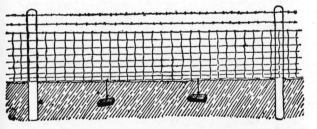

EXTENSION FENCE KEEPS CATTLE FROM PIG TROUGH

When cattle and pigs are kept in the same yard, the latter can be fed without having to drive the cattle away, by the use of an extension fence. Horizontal bars are attached to the fence posts, near which the troughs are located. At the ends of these bars a single barb wire is attached, this being anchored at either end to the fence. This will permit the pigs to have access to the trough, while the other animals are kept at a distance.

with strong fencing wire. Two or more anchors will be required between each pair of posts. This is a much better plan than pegging the fence down with long wire "hairpins," which are easily drawn out of the ground. No amount of pulling will draw the anchors mentioned above.

PIGS

FARM BUTCHERING—PIG KILLING AND DRESSING

First, stun the pig by hitting it on forehead with heavy instrument. Then stick it and bleed it. It should then be scalded, all the hair scraped off, the head, ears and feet properly cleaned, and the toenails removed with a hook. To enable the dirt, hair, etc., to be removed easily, add 2 oz. of caustic soda or 1 lb. of washing soda to each 20 gallons of water. The hair, etc., will come off easily if the carcase has been well soaked.

A gambrel is inserted through each hock, and the carcase hoisted to convenient height. Then, with a keen-edged knife, the opera-

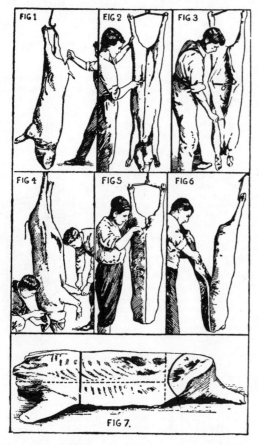

FIG 1 FIG 2 FIG 3
FIG 4 FIG 5 FIG 6

FIG 7.

tor cuts all round the head of the back passage (as in Fig. 1) to release it from the surrounding tissue. After splitting the skin between the hindlegs, a free incision is made through the skin only right down the centre of the belly, along the breast bone, terminating at the jaw (Fig. 2).

Next, open the body high up, and place the fingers of the left hand inside the flesh to guide the knife point and prevent it perforating the bowels, continue cutting down through the breast bone (as shown in Fig. 3).

Grasp the intestines just below the bladder, pass the knife blade in a circular fashion upwards around the bony structure, and release all the back passages and bladder, drawing them forward and outwards. The kidneys, which are attached to the backbone and kidney fat, are thus exposed. At this stage leave them. Then make a cross cut to the backbone under the kidneys and around the diaphragm, or partition retaining the intestines, and remove the whole of the entrails, including the large and smaller intestines, spleen, liver, gall bladder, stomach, heart and lungs, right down to the tongue, including the windpipe and gullet. Leave the tongue in the head until a later stage. Insert (as in Fig. 3) a spreader about 1 foot long, to keep the carcase open for cooling and draining, and place a small block between the teeth to release the drainage through the mouth.

Wash Thoroughly.—The interior of the carcase should be washed throughout with clean, cold water, the edges trimmed, and the body left to drain and cool in a dust-free, cool atmosphere for 24 hours. Next day, providing the flesh is firm and set, the cutting up can be done.

Cut off the four trotters at the fetlock. Remove the head by inserting the knife deeply round the neck, half an inch behind the ears (Fig. 4). The operator then seizes the head, the attendant firmly grips the forearms, and both simultaneously make sudden movements in opposite directions, with the result that the head is screwed off. Take out the tongue, split the head, remove the membranes of the nostrils and brains, and then put the head with the trotters and tongue into the brine tub to be pickled.

To divide the carcase, make a deep incision with the knife into the backbone from the tail to the poll (as in Fig. 5). Then saw down through the centre of the backbone (Fig. 6). Lay the sides flat on the table or bench with the fleshy portions exposed.

Commencing near the flank, seize the layer of the leaf lard, and gradually peel it away from the back, taking the kidney with it on each side. The strip of lean meat under the loin is inferior and difficult to cure. Hence it is best to remove it. Saw the backbone off at an angle that will take it all, with as little flesh as possible. Remove all rough edges, blood or stained pieces.

If it is intended to cure the complete side, no further cutting is required. When it is desired to cure the side in three pieces, cut off the ham in a slightly circular bevel shape, beginning at the flank. The shoulder, which also can be made into ham, is cut through between the middle and fourth ribs (see Fig. 7). The side is now ready for curing in three pieces. This necessitates free trimming and shaping. All trimmings are useful for sausages.

The cavity of the joints in both shoulders and hams are receptacles for point oil. This, if left, is liable to decompose, and it is best released, and well washed out with brine. In each case the joints will require to be punctured. If the pig is to be used for roasting, pickled pork, chops, etc., it should be cut up according to the dotted lines in Fig. 7. The belly generally is salted for pickled pork; the leg and shoulder end are roasted, and the loin and the first few ribs make good chops.

A USEFUL CARCASE HOIST

This is a really good butchering hoist with which one man can raise the heaviest pig or beef with ease. The ¾ in. rope must be long enough to reach the animal when the two ends are tied to the beam.

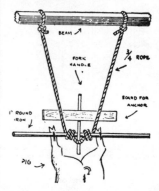

BEAM
¾ ROPE
FORK HANDLE
BOARD FOR ANCHOR
1" ROUND IRON
PIG

Insert an inch-round iron rod through the cords of the animal; bring the rope around under the rod, and with a piece of fork handle, twist the rope round and round the rod. This raises the animal.

When it is high enough, drop a piece of board in behind the fork handle to anchor it. However, do not let the fork handle slip. That would be dangerous.

A HANDY PIG-WEIGHING OUTFIT FOR RAPID WORK

Where pig raising is practised on a large scale, it pays to weigh the pigs at regular intervals and this sketch is of a plan of a special weighing race in use at the Wye Experimental Station in England. Here the pigs are kept in litters until they reach certain stages when they are sorted into pens of 5 to enable even lots to be formed.

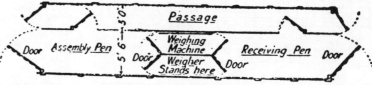

Passage
Door Assembly Pen Door Weighing Machine Weigher Stands here Door Receiving Pen Door

With this arrangement it is possible to weigh a pig a minute.

The construction is not expensive, but the weighing machine, of course, would be an item and it would only be profitable to instal one where the piggery is on a big scale.

PIGS

HANDY PIG CATCHERS

These are quite use-ful gadgets with which to catch pigs.

In the first, fasten a wire on the end of a pipe, push the other end through the pipe and put a ring in it, as shown. This leaves a loop at the other end of the pipe.

When you want to catch a pig, slip the loop in the pig's mouth around the upper jaw and pull on the ring to tighten and hold. A rope can be snapped into the ring and tied to a post. One man can then ring a pig in five minutes with this catcher.

The second sketch comprises a 7 ft. loop of baling wire put through an ordinary cotton reel of suit-able size, slip-knot fashion. Wrap the other end of the wire securely in the centre of a foot and a half length of broom handle. Just slip the loop over the upper jaw, and push the spool down tight.

A PORTABLE PEN FOR PIGS

The following idea from England is a useful description of a type of portable pen for pigs, etc., which is easily made.

It is from 8 to 9 ft. long, with rails about 6 x 1. The spaces between the horizontal rails should vary, beginning with a 2 in. space at the bottom, then a 3 in. one, and a 4 in. space at the top. The vertical strips are 4 x 1 in.

The side hurdles should be made in pairs. In making up the end hurdle, if the length of the two middle rails is 9 ft. the top and bottom ones will be 8 ft. 4 in. Two vertical strips 2 ft. 9 in. long are nailed to the 4 rails, and the position of these in rela-tion to the short rails is 8 ft. 2 in. over, thus allowing the top and bottom rails to project 1 in. on either end past the vertical parts; the two middle rails having an equal projection on each end.

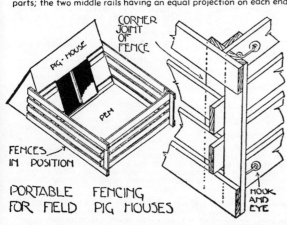

CORNER JOINT OF FENCE

PIG-HOUSE

PEN

FENCES IN POSITION

PORTABLE FENCING FOR FIELD PIG HOUSES

HOOK AND EYE

The side fencing is made up in much the same way. The length of the rails, if the pen is made as shown, is 8 ft. 7 in. for the two inner ones, and 9 ft. for the top and bottom ones. In this case the vertical piece next the pig-house is kept flush with all the rails. Where the joint is formed with the end hurdle, the first vertical piece is kept flush with the ends of the long pieces. The other vertical strip is flush with the ends of the short rails. Remember there should be a space sufficient to allow the end hurdle to pass into between the two vertical strips.

The joint is fastened together with a top and bottom hook and eye, as shown in the sketch of the joint. To fasten the ends of the fence to the pig-house, the best arrangement is to nail a piece 2 ft. 9 in. long and 2 in. x 2 in. on the framing of the house, and so that it will butt against the end of the fence. On the top of that nail a piece of 3 in. x 1 in., make it project on the pen side of the 2 x 2, so that a pocket is formed, and fasten the hurdle to the house with a pair of hooks and eyes.

Make sure that the joints of the fences are well nailed together.

By the undoing of eight hooks and eyes, the pen is lying on the ground ready to be shifted to another part of the field.

RINGING PIGS

This is a very useful type of pig ring which should prove successful in preventing the worst of pigs from rooting up the pasture. It is made from a small piece of piping, say 3-8 in. diameter, the width being in accordance with the size of the pig.

A piece of soft wire is threaded through the pipe, the ends are flat-tened, sharpened and bent, as shown, and then inserted through the cart-ilege of the nose. The pointed ends are then rolled after hav-ing passed through the snout. This arrangement will then act as a roller should the pig make any effort to root up the pasture.

ANOTHER USEFUL TYPE OF PIG RING

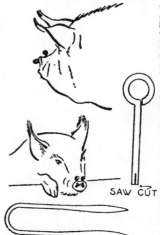

SAW CUT

To make home - made rings, take a piece of heavy gauge wire about 4 or 5 in. long and turn it into a staple, and flat-ten the two long ends out very thin like knife blades so that they can be twist-ed round very easily.

Make a hacksaw cut about $\frac{1}{2}$ in. down the end of a piece of $\frac{1}{2}$ in. round iron for a key. Use an old $\frac{1}{2}$ in. eye-bolt, which an-swers very well.

Force the staple through the pig's nose from the front and curl up the thin ends with the key.

The rings are put through the top of the snout. The idea of ringing the pigs is as mentioned in the top para. and not as a means of control as in the case of a bull.

HOW TO MAKE CONCRETE PIG FEEDING FLOORS

The same principles as outlined in a previous section relating to dairy floors can also be applied to the above, but in these cases, very often only first course work is necessary so that the finish will not be too slippery.

The following illustration gives a good idea as to the work, show-ing how it is advisable to erect the forms, do the work in alternate squares, and allow for a slope for drainage purposes.

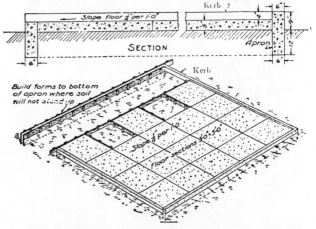

Slope floor $\frac{3}{4}$ per 1·0"

Kerb

SECTION

Apron

Build forms to bottom of apron where soil will not stand up

Kerb

Slope $\frac{3}{4}$ per 1·0

floor sections 10 · 50

There will also be a kerb round it which protects the food, as the pig will be unable to nose his food off the eating surface. Con-crete floors also prevent them from trampling food into the ground.

PIGS

A HANDY BARREL BARROW FOR CARTING ANIMAL FOODS, etc.

This is excellent for carrying pig and other foods and for other purposes as well.

Two disused plow handles are attached to an old plow wheel using a 16 in. hardwood axle.

The ends of the handles are reinforced with heavy gauge sheet iron nailed firmly over the ends.

Cleats are bolted to the side of the barrel to help carry the weight when the barrel is heavily loaded. This will be found extra useful when there are a large number of pigs, etc., to be fed.

AN AUTOMATIC PIG WATERER

This is an automatic water fountain that can be made from an oil drum and a few pieces of old timber. The pipe that runs

from the drum to the trough must be plugged when filling the drum. The top cap is screwed up to make it airtight just before the plug is removed.

A large funnel is necessary if it is to be filled from a bucket. A funnel with a bent spout can be made to fill with if the screw cap is on the end of the drum. This will then keep the water supplied to the trough. This type of fountain should be useful with poultry.

CONCRETE PIG TROUGHS WITH GROUND AS MOULD

Trough mould in ground.

If there are not many to make and a rough and cheap finish is good enough, troughs can be cast in the ground. Dig a trench of the required size in a level piece of ground (as shown in the sketch). The middle should be shaped so that when the concrete is poured in, it will come three inches over the top of the ridge. A round shape like this prevents food from lodging in the corners. Reinforce. Cure the concrete for a week before turning out, and keep full of water for another week.

HOW TO MAKE STANDARD CONCRETE FEEDING TROUGHS

These are easily made. A 1:2:4 mixture should be used—coarse aggregate not more than ¾ in. with sides at least 2 in. thick at top. Reinforcements as in fencing posts; at least 3 in. base, one of which should be bent round the end to encircle the trough, overlapping a little and wired together. A section showing a simple method is shown, showing shape of form with clamps or

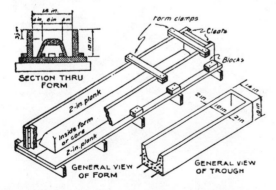

braces together with shape and method of inserting the "core" to give space for food and water. These troughs turn out better if made upside down (as in sketch)—they give a level finish.

Oil forms before using.

USEFUL WOODEN PIG FEEDING TROUGHS

Where wooden troughs are concerned, a very good flat-bottomed one for feeding young pigs can be made from 2-inch timber as illustrated. They are portable and easily cleaned.

A Flat-bottomed Trough for Young Pigs.

A shallow depth is necessary for young pigs, say, about 10 or 12 in. wide and 4 to 6 in. deep. Food can be placed in these at three weeks and should also be accessible to sow. In this way the smaller pigs are encouraged to feed themselves.

ANOTHER TYPE OF WOODEN TROUGH

To construct a "V" shaped trough, nail two pieces of timber together as shown, to be 6 or 8 in. deep. To get the same depth

on either side, it is necessary to have one piece of timber 2 in. wider than the other, if 2 in. material is used. They then fit underneath. The trough can be made to any length, but should be divided off into sections as shown.

ROUND PATTERN PIG TROUGHS

These useful types are easy to make and a number of pigs can be fed at the same time without interference with each other.

The smaller sketch is somewhat the same as the larger, but naturally not with the same finish. A space is left underneath the sides of the central storage bin for the food to automatically fall into the "outer" as it is consumed.

It is made from an old oil or petrol drum with a galvd. corrugated iron trough round same, affixed and apportioned off with small iron bars.

Similarly, a watering trough can be made along the same lines. A screw is let into the top of the drum and a plughole also let into the bottom; the latter, say, ½ in. in diameter and 1½ in. from the bottom. It is plugged and the screw on top of the drum opening for filling. The screw is then replaced and the plug removed to keep the trough full of water.

The larger drawing is of iron and consists of a single container, divided into a dozen or more feeding compartments by radiating iron bars, which keep the pigs well apart. It is portable and

yet can be fixed firmly into ground by driving stakes in on each side of the legs. The bottom is shaped so that the food runs down to the outside edge.

PIGS

A PIG TROUGH ANCHOR TO MAKE IT STAY IN PLACE

Some trouble is very often experienced through pig-troughs being knocked over when the pigs are feeding, but this one cannot be upset so easily.

The illustration shows how, at the ends of the trough, stakes having large eyes at the upper ends to serve as handles, are slid through large staples or screw-eyes driven into the ends of the troughs.

These should be made long enough to allow one end of the trough to be raised for the insertion of small blocks when levelling it. It is an arrangement well worth while.

AN AUTOMATIC PIG FEEDER FROM OLD DRUM AND WHEEL

This will provide an all-metal feeder with plenty of weight to prevent tipping. It consists of an oil drum with both ends removed and fastened to the centre of a large implement wheel.

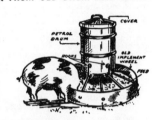

Hooks bent from iron rods are slipped over the wheel spokes and bolted to the drum to keep it in place. It is a good idea to set the feeder on a concrete platform.

PIG FEEDER FROM TRUCK TYRE

Handy pig troughs can be made from old tyres as shown here. The tyre is split all round and, according to one user, is a very useful type.

There would, however, be less waste of food if some sort of disc were fitted into the centre so that the food cannot be pushed over the edge. Several of these feeders could be placed here and there around the place.

A USEFUL FRAMEWORK TO KEEP PIGS OUT OF TROUGH

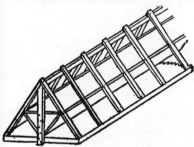

This is self-explanatory. It allows each pig to feed separately and it keeps them from stepping into troughs. Each pig will also receive its share.

It is simply made—the trough being a V section of any length.

Side uprights are 2 x 1 and top bar 3 x 2.

End supports are of the same material.

ANOTHER TYPE OF SELF-FEEDER

Pigs are wasteful feeders and one such as this will remedy that. It is a simple hay rack, made to any size.

Any small pieces that may fall from the rack falls into the trough below from which it is eaten by the pigs. This is also a good idea for fowls, too. It provides a hinged top so that it can easily be filled and fastened down.

A HINGED GUARD RAIL FOR FARROWING PEN

The farrowing pen in every piggery should be protected by a guard rail on each side.

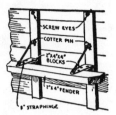

This sketch shows a practical type that will keep the sow from crushing the little pigs against the sides of the pen when lying down. The rail should be approximately 9 ins. from the floor. When it is not needed, it can be hooked up out of the way.

A BREEDING CRATE FOR SOWS

This is one useful type. The dimensions of the box shown are:—Length, 5 ft. 6 in.; width, 2 ft., and height 3 ft. The length of the short box, which may be made by moving the end board J into the slot K is 3 ft. 6 in. The corner posts are 4 x 2 and the sides 4 x 1. A, A, A, are joists for nailing the floor to B, B extra board to which the joists are nailed to stiffen the sides of the box. C, C are boar supporters, which hold the boar's weight.

The boar supporter on the left is stationary; that on the right is adjustable to the size of the sow and should fit up tight against her side.

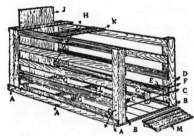

D is a piece used to adjust the right-hand support; E is a pin which holds the support in place; F is a strip to hold D in the groove. The G's (six of them) are pieces that hold the supports solid and are 13 in. in length; H is a wooden screw to hold the front end of the adjustable support in place. I is a 7-8 in. rod which is placed behind the sow to keep her from backing out of the box; J is a movable end board which is used to adjust the box to different length sows.

When long sows are to be bred, the board is placed in the end of the box as shown, and when the short sows are bred the board is removed and placed in the slotted board K. LL are cleats holding the bottom end of the board J in place; M is a platform used to raise a small boar high enough to service a large sow.

AN AUTOMATIC WATER FOUNTAIN ON RUNNERS

Mounted on a pair of runners, this fountain can be pulled to the well, filled and then returned to the field by team or tractor.

It consists of a large oil drum for a reservoir, and an old car crankcase for a fount in which a certain water level is maintained by the vacuum principle. Water runs from the drum to the pan through an assembly of pipe elbow and two nipples screwed into the end bung. When the water level in the pan reaches the end of the nipple the flow stops. The drum must be airtight, of course, a gasket being used at the filler hole, which is hung on the side of the drum.

PIGS

A HOME-MADE DRENCH FOR PIGS

This is the experience of one farmer whose sow fell sick after farrowing. It needed a drench and difficulty was experienced in administering it. Usually a pig will squeal when caught and there is a danger of choking.

The difficulty was overcome in the following way. They got a piece of water tubing, 18 in. long with one end slightly bent.

A rope was placed in the pig's mouth and carried over a beam in the sty to keep the mouth open. They then placed the iron tube in the mouth to the root of the tongue and poured the medicine steadily into the tube. The plan was simple and effective.

OILING POSTS FOR PIGS

Pigs, if troubled with lice, look for something to rub against and if anything placed around posts is kept oiled, the parasites will soon disappear. With this idea, sacks are wrapped round the post and are thoroughly saturated with oil—the post being 5 ft. long and 4 to 5 in. in diameter—set well into the ground.

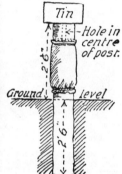

A constant supply of oil is obtained by boring a ¾ in. hole in the centre of the post about 8 in. deep and on top of this, nail a gallon tin with a small hole leading through its bottom to the ¾ in. hole bored in the post. At right angles, bore ¼ in. holes to meet the centre hole —this enables the oil to soak into the bags round the post, which are wired on.

If waste oil is placed in the tin it wil seep down and keep the bags saturated. The pigs will do the rest and will soon be free.

The second idea is somewhat similar with the exception that the post is set at an angle—some saying the pig is then able to scratch its back as well as its side—angle about 45 degrees.

OIL CONTAINER

WRAPPING REMOVED TO SHOW PERFORATED PIPE

Some sort of arrangement can be fixed to the top of the post to supply the oil, and another idea is to insert some perforated pipe or rubber tubing under the wrapping on the topmost edge so that the oil will penetrate fairly evenly.

If parasites are very bad and many pigs are in trouble herd them all into a small enclosure where they will be crowded and where there is a good floor. Apply a thick emulsion made from two parts of oil and one part water, to which a few drops of cattle dip or carbolic has been added, to the backs of the animals through a watering can. Keep them there for an hour and they will rub themselves together and oil each other.

HANDY METHOD OF KEEPING ANIMALS CLEAN WHEN DRINKING FROM WATER HOLES, etc.

This illustration shows a very useful method of providing access to streams or water holes for any pigs or other animals.

This will prevent mud wallows and will help keep the pigs or other animals clean.

It is merely a race built from old timbers, running down to the water with space at the end just sufficient for the animals to obtain a drink and fenced off to stop them from getting into the water itself. The idea is sufficiently illustrated and needs no further description.

A HOME-MADE MOVABLE SWILL BIN

In this English idea, the trouble of moving waste from the boiling tanks to the pens is eliminated. It is simple in operation and consists of two long handles fixed near one end along the edge of two triangular plates, the opposite corner of the plates being secured to the axle.

An iron frame, approx. 3 ft. 6 in. x 1 ft. 6 in. is slung from the corner of the plates opposite to that from which the long handles project. This frame rises and falls as the handles are lowered or raised, but, at the same time ,it moves on a pivot and retains a perpendicular position. It is wheeled up to a drum or barrel previously raised at one side on a piece of wood. The handles are raised on one side so that the bottom of the frame now touching the ground slips under the edges of the barrel or drum.

A hook attached by chains to both handles is dropped over the top of the barrel and as the handles are pressed down the barrel is pulled back into the frame, which at the same time is being raised from the ground.

PIG PROOF GATES WHICH ALLOW FREE PASSAGE TO HORSES, ETC.

These sketches represent various types of pig-proof gates which will allow cattle and horses to pass over, but which will prevent pigs from going through.

The first is made from a storage tank or other cylindrical obstable, in the manner shown here. It is necessary only to run a shaft through the centre and fasten it to the two posts and the tank will rotate on the shaft.

The following ideas are a little different to the above, but are for narrow and wide gates both based on the same idea as each other.

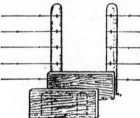

Pig-proof gateway

Two low fences across any gateway should stop any pig but allow horses and cattle to pass. The boards should be solid and about 18 in. high.

About 18 in. from each gatepost and inside where the pigs are confined, a short post is driven. Long boards nailed from one to the other of these posts make another panel of board fence, 18 in. high and parallel with the boarded up gate, with an 18 in. space between the two low walls. When a pig comes to this detached panel, it will go to the end, and pass round into the narrow passage between the two board walls, continuing on through and out at the other end till it tires of the performance. No wide cracks offering footholds should be left between the boards. Pigs that are short enough to turn in the 18 in. passage are too small to climb over the boards and one that cannot turn is unable to face the wall and make the attempt.

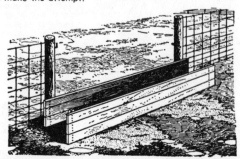

SUNDRY HINTS WITH STOCK

A SPECIAL GATE FOR THE DOG

If your yard is fenced in and you want to give your dog the run of the farm and of the enclosed yard as well, cut a hole 10 in. x 10 in. the wire or other gate.

Then cut a board to fit the hole; drill two holes about an inch from the top of the board, run wires through the holes, and hang the board to the wires of the fence.

If the dog is put through the hole two or three times, he will readily catch on to the idea and will then go in and out without someone having to open the gate for him.

A "SLAPPER" FOR STOCK

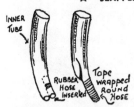

This little idea wil be found very useful when loading stock and when driving them also. The advantage is that it will make plenty of noise and the animal will not be injured in any way.

Such a gadget should help lessen the number of badly bruised carcases which are caused by the use of whips and other things when loading, etc.

It is made from old motor tube, each about 3 feet long, with several slits cut in one side so that a short length of rubber hose can be inserted. When the hose is worked through the slits it is wrapped round tightly with the tube and then bound with tape to make a firm handgrip.

PORTABLE TROUGHS FOR SHEEP, PIGS, ETC.

A few of these are very handy.

Two "A's" are made, each leg being 4½ feet long. 4 inch material will do. Two cleats are used on each A, and a 4 x 1 or 6 x 1 is placed between the four upper ends.

This latter is usually 6 ft. long. The trough is then built of 4 in. material for the sides and a 6 x 2 or 8 x 2 for the bottom.

This is placed as shown and the two units are then nailed fast. Several of these feed troughs can be used to good advantage in the sheep, pig or calf paddock, and because of their portability can be moved as soon as mud and muck begin to accumulate about them.

A USEFUL STOCK CART

This is a handy transfer cart made from old implement wheels (motor tyres if preferred) in which pigs, calves or sheep can be transported from one place to another very easily.

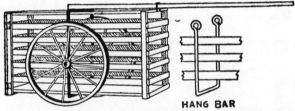

HANG BAR

TRANSFER CART FOR SMALL ANIMALS

Raise the tongue, which lets the rear end on ground, then drive in the animal; shut the gate, pull the tongue down, and you have your load ready to fasten on to a wagon.

A USEFUL STOCK LOADING CHUTE

This is a very useful chute for loading stock or goods on to a lorry—it can be either stationary or portable—if the latter is preferred, one need only add a set of small wheels near each end to enable it to be moved about easily.

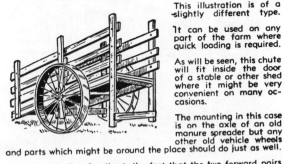

The bottom can be of suitable boards and cleats for stock to get a footing on and it can be lowered or raised to any height desired by the manipulation of a short length of water pipe inserted through holes in the post. Also, if entrance to the shed for stock is desired, the outer end can be lowered right down to the ground.

ANOTHER TYPE OF LOADING CHUTE

This illustration is of a slightly different type.

It can be used on any part of the farm where quick loading is required.

As will be seen, this chute will fit inside the door of a stable or other shed where it might be very convenient on many occasions.

The mounting in this case is on the axle of an old manure spreader but any other old vehicle wheels and parts which might be around the place should do just as well.

One thing worthy of notice is the fact that the two forward pairs of uprights project below the bottom of the runway with crosspieces nailed on in order to keep them in a vertical position.

ANOTHER HOME-MADE LOADING CHUTE

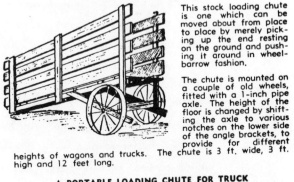

This stock loading chute is one which can be moved about from place to place by merely picking up the end resting on the ground and pushing it around in wheelbarrow fashion.

The chute is mounted on a couple of old wheels, fitted with a 1-inch pipe axle. The height of the floor is changed by shifting the axle to various notches on the lower side of the angle brackets, to provide for different heights of wagons and trucks. The chute is 3 ft. wide, 3 ft. high and 12 feet long.

A PORTABLE LOADING CHUTE FOR TRUCK

Time which is often wasted in looking for a suitable place to load stock where regular chutes are not available can be eliminated by a home-made arrangement like this.

It can then be carried on the truck at all times and will always be ready for use.

It is really a portion of the end of the truck hinged so that it merely drops down to form a ramp, and detachable sides are built to fit this ramp, stoke pockets being built into the side of the ramp to take them when required. Either side pockets are built on to the lorry to hold them in place when not required or they can be carried under the truck bed.

See also page 263 under heading Motor Trucks

CHEMISTRY
IN THE FOWL-YARD

SUCCESSFUL poultry farming, like any other business, requires intelligent fostering. . . . The hen can only eat about 6 ounces of food a day, so, if it is to produce an egg as well as keep itself alive, this food must be rich in all the essential nutrients. In addition to being well fed, the health of the hen must be watched, and it is here that the work of the research chemist is of utmost importance to the poultry farmer.

Liming the runs, cleaning houses with sodium carbonate (washing soda), and sterilising the drinking water with hypochlorites should be among the routine precautions for keeping away disease. Insecticidal powders are used to rid birds of lice, fleas or ticks. Solutions of nicotine are necessary as perch paints. Special ointments are sometimes required to treat scaly leg and fungus diseases, quinine sulphate for colds and sulphate of iron as a tonic. The production of an egg **needs** the help of the research chemist.

IMPERIAL CHEMICAL INDUSTRIES OF AUSTRALIA AND NEW ZEALAND LIMITED

ICI

ALL CAPITAL CITIES AND WELLINGTON, NEW ZEALAND

POULTRY

THE MAIN POINTS OF A BIRD

1, Beak or Mandible. 2, Eye. 3, Face. 4, Wattle. 5, Earlobe. 6, Tuft Covering of Ear. 7, Comb. 8, Spike or Serration. 9, Neck Hackle. 10, Back or Saddle. 11, Breast. 12, Wing Bow. 13, Wing Bar or Coverts. 14, Thigh. 15, Shank. 16, Toes.

THE MAIN POINTS OF A BIRD

17, Hocks. 18, Back Toes. 19, Spur. 20, Abdominal Fluff. 21, Wing Bay or Secondaries. 22, Saddle Hackle. 23, Sickles. 24, Tail Coverts or Hangers. 25, Stiff or Hen Tail. 26, Keel. 27, Primaries or Flight Feathers, folded out of sight when not in use.

A LOW COST POULTRY FENCE

A useful poultry fence that is non-sagging, can be made from a plasterer's lath and some 19 g. galvd. wire.

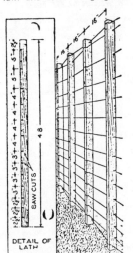

DETAIL OF LATH

A pattern lath should first be cut so that all are alike.

To do this, a common 48 in. lath is marked off as shown.

The two notches near the ends, on the same side, are for the selvedge wires; those on the opposite edge for the intermediate wires.

At each of the points shown, the lath should be sawn about one third through. For 100 ft. of fence, about 75 such laths will be required, which can be notched in lots of several at a time by using the pattern as a guide.

Two posts, 100 ft. apart, should be set in the ground, and 15 wires strung between them, spaced to correspond with the pattern.

These should be left somewhat slack, and the laths put in place, 16 in. apart, with the slots in adjacent ones on opposite sides of the fence. When all laths are in place, the wires should be tightened and stapled to the intermediate posts.

A VERMIN PROOF POULTRY FEEDER

One useful way to keep feeders vermin proof and so that the fowls cannot climb into them is shown here. It is made out of cake tins and funnels and mounted on wooden stakes.

The tins are of a type having a hollow spout projecting upward from the centre.

BRAD
FUNNEL
CAKE PAN
BRAD
WOODEN STAKE

When the tins and funnel are mounted, stakes are driven into the ground in order to elevate the tins a few inches to prevent mice from getting at the contents. The funnels prevent the fowls from getting into the tins and also shield the feed from chaff and litter.

A SWINGING FEED HOPPER

SLITS CUT IN EACH SIDE AND METAL ABOVE BENT IN.

This is another good idea for a mouse-proof self-feeder for poultry. As indicated in the previous drawing, in order to keep mice from the mash fed to poultry, shallow tins are suspended a few inches above the floor, but, often being open at the top, the fowls scratch litter into the food.

This idea is one that will keep out mice and, at the same time, it will act as a self-feeder. It is made by cutting long slits in opposite sides of a bucket an inch or so above the bottom of the container, as shown. The metal above the slits is bent in as shown, to provide two openings from which the mash is accessible to the poultry.

A SIMPLE AUTOMATIC FOUNTAIN FROM DRUM

This will provide a good supply of fresh water. An ordinary 5-gal. drum (40-gal. for large flocks) is laid on its side and a trough soldered on at one end. A small hole punched in the end of the drum just below the level of the top of the trough makes the fountain automatic, and ensures an ample supply at all times.

ANOTHER AUTOMATIC WATER FOUNTAIN

This is another, but more complicated idea. A large automatic water fountain can be made from an oil drum mounted on a sturdy wooden stand.

Two pipe nipples and an elbow are assembled to fit the opening near the edge of one end of the drum as shown. The outlet pipe is extended into a suitable trough and must be plugged or inverted when filling, after which the filler opening is closed with a plug and a rubber gasket to make it airtight. A bucket for filling the drum is shown in the detail.

A POULTRY FEEDER AND WATER CONTAINER ON FENCE TO SAVE WORK

WIRE HOOKS
FILL HERE
WATER
ON
ROLLED
WOOD
LEAVE TROUGHS FOR FEED

Suspended from the exterior of the fence, feed and water containers made from large tins and old troughs not only save many steps, but prevent scattering of feed and contamination of water.

Old paint tins with portions of the backs cut out serve for water containers. The supply may be replenished through the opening in the top.

The feed troughs have curved pieces of wood nailed to the ends. Cut openings in fence.

POULTRY HINTS

INVERTED CHIMNEY CAP OR CONE PROVIDES VERMIN PROOF FEEDER

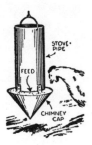

This is a very useful idea for a clean, vermin proof automatic feeder for poultry, especially where there are mice about, as it should make it impossible for them to reach the food; at the same time, it prevents the fowls from polluting the food.

Fitted to a length of large stove-pipe and inverted as shown, a sheet metal chimney cap provides the main idea for this purpose. The assembly can be hung from some other overhead arrangement, in any convenient spot. One need not have a spare chimney cap about the place, as a similar arrangement could be made from any old scrap, and shaped as shown.

A HANDY CHICKEN WATERING TROUGH FROM OLD TYRE

This is another use for an old tyre, and it makes a very handy article.

The illustration shows how pieces can be cut out in order to make it into an excellent chicken watering trough. When doing the cutting, see that a keen edged pocket-knife is used as it will make a better job.

One tyre will provide drinking accommodation for quite a large flock of birds and if one wishes to go further and make something to prevent pollution of the water, it would only be necessary to put some tight fitting object inside it with an overlap low enough to prevent the birds from standing on the tyre.

CAR RIM ROUND FOUNTAIN WILL HELP KEEP WATER CLEAN

This is another way of keeping water clean. Large motor car or truck rims placed round poultry water fountains, as shown in this sketch, will prevent the fowls from scratching chaff and other litter into the water. The rim also prevents the water from being splashed into chaff or food.

This idea can also be used in conjunction with many of the other water fountains one sees used in various parts and with some of the other ideas appearing on these pages.

A DRINKING FOUNTAIN FROM OIL DRUM

Here is another simple self-watering device for fowls, which, although it may appear a little complicated, is not so. All that is needed is a 44-gal. drum together with a smaller 10-gal. drum.

First, cut off the bottom of the larger drum 4 in. from the edge for the trough.

Then punch two small holes in the smaller ones (one on each side of the drum), say, 1½ in. in from the bottom, using, say, a 2 in. nail for the purpose.

Then put the small drum in the centre of the bigger part which has been cut from the big drum. This completes the arrangement. Then fill the small drum with water, and screw back the plug tightly, as the whole thing depends upon the smaller drum being airtight.

A GUARD FOR POULTRY FEEDER

This is a simple way to keep chickens from roosting on and dropping into the feeders. Take some empty tins with the tops still on; punch a hole in each end just large enough to fit over an iron bar or brake rod which is just long enough to reach the length of the feeder. Slots for this bar are cut in the ends of the feeder. When chickens attempt to get on top of the feeder, the tins revolve and they soon learn to leave it alone.

ANOTHER POULTRY TROUGH WHICH SAVES FEED

One of the simplest and most reliable feed troughs for keeping hens from soiling the feed is shown here.

It resembles an ordinary feed trough except that there is a strong wire fastened across the top, running from end to end.

This simple device prevents the hens from getting their feet into the trough and thereby wasting or contaminating feed.

ROOSTING ON FOUNTAIN PREVENTED BY FUNNEL

This is another way of preventing poultry from perching on the water fountain and thus polluting the water.

The idea is to place a small tin funnel over the top of the chickens' water fountain if they show any signs of roosting on it.

If a number of fountains are to be protected, coil springs from old motor cushions or the like could be used in a similar way.

A COMBINED RAISED POULTRY STAND AND FEEDER

These combined hoppers and stands are very convenient and all danger of soiled mash is removed by such a hopper. The fowls cannot get into it for the strip or reel at the top and they cannot roost on the reel as it is on a pivot.

The buckets rest on a cross board attached to the ends of the water stand.

Both stand and hopper can be made with only one slat on each side. The size is 22 x 36 in. and of the mash hopper 24 x 60 in. in all. The hopper is 12 in. across. The stands are removable and the water cannot be spilled or mash wasted, whilst the entire floor space is also available.

ANOTHER TYPE OF RAISED POULTRY WATER STAND AND HOPPER

This is easily made and takes up no floor space.

One end is nailed to the wall under the window and the other end is suspended from the ceiling by a piece of 4 x 1, leaving all the floor space for the hens.

The two 4 x 1 in. running boards are a little longer than the feed hopper and are placed close enough together for a pail of water to fit in between.

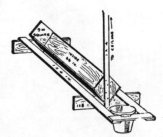

Keep it about 16 or 18 inches off the floor. This is a very efficient and clean arrangement and well worth while making.

POULTRY HINTS

CHICKEN FEEDERS FROM OLD TINS AND TUBES

Instead of using wire or other guards for food and water containers, one poultryman uses the lids of tins around which he stretches wide rubber bands cut from old inner tubes.

Each piece is serrated along the upper edge as shown. The contents of the tins are thus readily accessible to the chicks, and there is no danger of them getting their heads caught in the rubber bands.

ANOTHER USEFUL CHICKEN FEEDER

This is a useful feeder for the small poultry yard—it is one into which the mash can be put and which will remain clean.

Just take an old tin, and about 6 in. from the bottom cut four pieces about 7 in. long and 3 or 4 in. apart around the can. With a hammer bend the edge of each place in, so that the hen can get her head in to eat. Then put your feed in and put the lid on and you will have a good feeder.

A POULTRY TROUGH FROM KEROSENE TIN

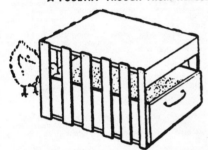

Cut a kero tin in half lengthwise and turn over the raw edges. The case is then stripped of a little more than a half of each end, the top and bottom removed and split into 2 in. slats which are nailed across 2 in. apart in place of the top and bottom. The half tin is then slid into the case—it is then well protected against fouling, and shaded from the sun.

A NOVEL DRY FEED MIXER

This is a very useful mixer for dry feed.

It is merely an ordinary wooden barrel mounted between two posts on an iron rod, which is bent at one end to form a crank.

A door is cut in the side of the barrel and fitted with hinges and a hook to hold it tightly shut. This idea might also be suitable for home-made wheat and grain picklers, etc.

ANOTHER USEFUL MASH MIXER

From Old Motor Fan

Where many fowls are kept and much mash has to be mixed, the task is made less tedious by rigging up this device.

The fan of an old motor is attached to a wooden or iron shaft with a crank handle fixed on the other end. This shaft works through a strong wooden bar which rests on the top of the barrel or drum in which the mash is mixed.

Turning the crank causes the fan to mix the mash thoroughly. The handle must, of course, be turned so that it pushes the food upwards and not downwards.

CATCHING FOWLS BY CROOK OR BY NET

One of the best plans to catch fowls is to use a hook or a long handled landing net, the former for large fowls and the latter for chickens. With the hook, all that is required is to quietly round up a few birds in the corner of the yard, and then slip the hook over the leg of the one required. It will then be captured with the minimum of excitement for the flock.

With the net the chickens are gathered in close and the net is slipped over the doomed one, which is quickly turned upside down.

ANOTHER USEFUL METHOD OF CATCHING CHICKENS

A hinged panel covered with wire netting makes it a simple matter to catch fowls. In this instance the panel is 5 to 7 feet one way and 2½ to 3 feet the other, both of the same height (30 to 36 in.), hinged together as shown.

Panel frames are 4 x 1 timber covered with 1 in. netting. With a light weight portable panel like this, chickens of any age can quickly and easily be held in a corner for culling, etc.

A HOME-MADE EGG CLEANER

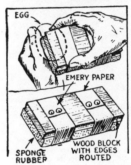

This is quite a good home-made cleaner for those with small flocks. It consists of a wood block about 2½ in. wide and 6 in. long faced on one side with sponge rubber around which is wrapped two strips of emery paper, one fine and the other coarse.

This is secured with thumb-tacks and is placed near the ends of the block. In using the cleaner, any heavy dirt can be removed quickly by the coarse emery paper and the cleaning finished with the fine paper, after which dust can be wiped off with the sponge rubber.

MARKING EGGS (a simple recording method)

A simple way of marking eggs with the date or other particulars was devised by one poultryman who perforated the inscription on a strip of waxed paper and glued it over an ordinary rubber stamp ink pad.

As each egg was removed from the nest the end was pressed against the masked pad and received an imprint of the design. To facilitate the work he soldered a safety pin on the bottom of the pad container, so that it could be attached to his sleeve. His hands were thus left free for gathering and markign the eggs.

The ordinary paper used in offices for mimeograph work furnishes the waxed paper required and the stencil may be cut on a typewriter or drawn with a dull steel point, the paper being placed over a fine flat file while doing so.

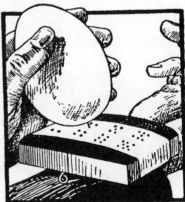

Stamp-pad Marker for Eggs.

POULTRY HINTS

CHICKEN COOPS FROM OIL DRUMS

HALF OF OIL DRUM

An old oil drum will provide two economical coops for small chickens when it is cut in half lengthwise.

The coops are weather and vermin proof and will last indefinitely if painted.

A door is cut in one end, and a number of $\frac{1}{2}$ in. holes are drilled in the end near the rim to assure ample ventilation.

A PORTABLE PEN FOR HEN AND CHICKS

A good portable pen that is convenient for moving a hen and chicks about the yard is easily made from a piece of chicken wire rolled into a cone and tacked to a sharp stake.

It is an easy matter to pull the stake and move the pen along to a new spot without allowing the hen to escape, and, while the hen is kept inside, the chicks can pass in and out freely.

A portable and larger chicken pen could also be made with a view to keeping chickens within certain bounds, and so that they could be put on different grass from time to time merely by using smaller wire and using a bigger stick and making a larger cone.

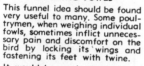

CHICKEN WIRE

STAKE POINTED

SCALES

FUNNEL

USEFUL METHOD OF WEIGHING FOWLS

This funnel idea should be found very useful to many. Some poultrymen, when weighing individual fowls, sometimes inflict unnecessary pain and discomfort on the bird by locking its wings and fastening its feet with twine.

It would be much simpler, and would save time as well, to roll a sheet of tin, or some heavy cardboard, into an open-end cone, and suspend this from the hook of the scales, as shown in this illustration.

The fowl, lowered head first into this cone, will not struggle, and its weight may thus be readily ascertained.

RUBBER SHOCK ABSORBERS
For Egg Transport

All egg farmers do not live on a bitumen road, and eggs carried to market in carts or trucks are frequently subjected to such jolts and jars that a number of them often get broken in transit. This simple little arrangement will help to make such journeys very much safer. Four short pieces of garden hose about 3 in. long are nailed on the bottom corners of the carrying case, leaving each piece protruding about an inch at right angles to the side.

The result can be described as 'pneumatic' egg carrying boxes — the hose forming excellent shock absorbers.

MOVABLE COOPS FOR FOWLS ON GRASS

Where grass land is available near a poultry run, but it is not desired to allow the birds to run at large on it, a simple way of giving the fowls the benefit of the grass is to construct a light portable run that can be moved about from place to place with ease.

The run may be made in the form of four batten frames covered with wire netting and joined at the corners with light iron brack-

ets. The roof may be made of palings, tarred felt, strong cotton sheeting (oiled), or even old linoleum. Four small wooden wheels, attached with bolts at the corners, make it possible to push the run about easily.

Drinking fountains may be attached at two corners and food hoppers at the other two corners. The coop should be moved to a fresh position every day, otherwise the birds will eat down the grass too closely and injure the sod. Repeating this process will serve the double purpose of keeping the grass trimmed and furnishing the birds with fresh green feed. The contrivance is made of the size necessary to accommodate the number of birds to be confined in it.

ANOTHER "POULTRY YARD" ON WHEELS WHICH IS EASILY MOVED

For those who wish to keep chickens apart from the rest of the fowls, or grown fowls apart from the others, and yet wish to move them about from place to place where there is grass, this movable coop would be ideal.

It is a combination coop and wire-enclosed run, is mounted on two small wheels, and by lifting one end of the run to clear the ground the whole thing is easily moved about.

It is framed of $1\frac{1}{2}$ by $1\frac{1}{2}$ in. pine, and is covered with 4 in. lap siding. This is broken at one joint on three sides, and the top section is hinged so that it lifts for cleaning. The frame of the run is joined to the coop, and all corners are stiffened with metal brackets. Fine poultry wire covers the top, sides and one end.

A small trap-door is framed into the top, and is hinged so that it can be lifted for feeding. The 6 in. wheels are mounted on brackets made from $\frac{1}{4}$ in. flat iron.

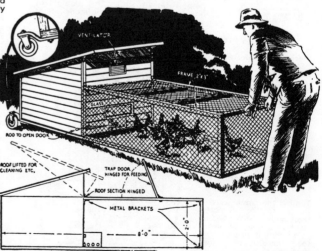

POULTRY HINTS

DISCOURAGING BROODY HENS

Unable to settle down comfortably on a nest, a broody hen wearing this leg clamp is soon discouraged and returns to profitable egg laying.

The clamp is a strip of sheet metal 1½ in. wide and 5 in. long drilled and bent to the shape shown.

A piece of felt or rubber is used as a cushion between the clamp and the leg to prevent injury. The clamp will not interfere with the regular habits of the bird.

CATCHING MICE IN POULTRY HOUSE

Setting traps in some fowlhouses endangers the fowls, and, of course, should not be done.

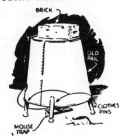

One way of getting over this danger is to turn a bucket upside down over a trap, as shown. Four clothes pegs slipped over the rim of the bucket will serve as legs to raise the bucket above the floor so that the mice can enter, and the fowls cannot. A brick is also placed on top of the bucket in order that the fowls will not upset it.

MAKING HENS LAY

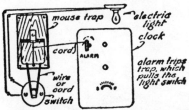

This is one way in which one farmer improvised an alarm and light for the fowlhouse in order to make his hens lay, thus giving them longer feeding hours.

In this way he turned the light on in the fowlhouse between 4 and 5 in the morning. It was done by remote control with the aid of an alarm clock and mousetrap arranged as shown.

USEFUL METHOD OF HANDLING EGGS

To speed the work and decrease the loss, one poultryman uses a rubber finger-stall which will allow the eggs to be lifted with the least possible fumbling, thus automatically speeding up the job, and, at the same time, decreasing breakages.

AN IDEA TO COMBAT FOWL TICK

Tick are usually active at night, so besides applying the usual disinfectants, the perches should be made tick-proof.

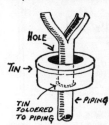

This is done by perch supports made of piping, as indicated, the pipe being inserted through a tin soldered at the bottom end. A hole in the top is made so that the kero or other liquid can be poured into the tin.

AN IMPROVISED EGG TESTER

This is quite a good tester, easily made and easy in operation. All that is needed is some stiff paper for a cone which is cut according to the pattern shown. The top opening is large enough to hold an egg without permitting it to drop through. A 2-cell flashlight provides the illumination.

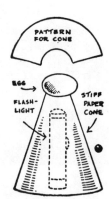

ANOTHER IMPROVISED TESTER

An emergency light for testing can be made by wrapping some stiff paper round the end of a torch.

This should extend an inch or more above the lens. A strip of tape or a rubber band will hold it in place.

ANOTHER TYPE OF HOME-MADE EGG TESTER

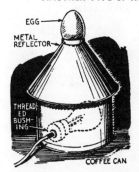

Made from a 1 lb. tin and a metal light reflector, this will give quick and accurate grading. In use the reflector is set over the open top of the tin, as shown.

The lamp socket is attached to the side of the tin by first punching a hole and inserting a threaded bushing of the proper size to screw into the socket cap.

After the cord has been drawn through the bushing and the socket re-assembled, a nut turned on to the outer end of the bushing holds the assembly in place.

Another tester can be made by using a lamp shade and light bulb on the end of an extension light.

ONE METHOD OF TEACHING CHICKENS TO ROOST

This type has been found very successful—the size is, of course, governed by requirements, but it is advisable to allow 3 or 4 feet of floor space between the foot of the ramp and the end of the building so that the chickens have room to run in the compartment without having to go on to the ramp in the daytime. If chicks are well reared in the brooding stage and not removed from brooders before 6 weeks of age, there should be very little mortality afterwards, and by having suitable arrangements in the second stage, rearing losses can be avoided.

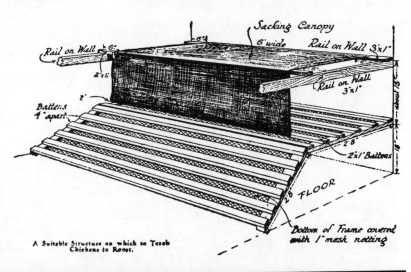

A Suitable Structure on which to Teach Chickens to Roost.

POULTRY HINTS

EXTERMINATING VERMIN IN POULTRY HOUSE

Lice and other parasites can be killed by filling the fowlhouse with carbon monoxide gas. It can be directed into the house through a pipe or hose connected with the exhaust from a car.

First, remove all poultry from the house, and then seal the doors, windows and cracks as tightly as possible in order to retain the gas.

Then set the carburettor to produce a rich fuel mixture, and let the motor run for several minutes.

The gas will impregnate all parts of the building and kill everything. As this gas is very poisonous when inhaled, open all doors and windows after the job is complete and leave them so for at least an hour or so before entering it.

AN IDEA TO KEEP NESTS CLEAN

Hens standing on the edges of the laying boxes cause dirty eggs, but this can be prevented by fitting free-turning rollers on the edge of the nests, as shown here.

These rollers, about the thickness of a broom handle, should have headless nails driven into the ends as pivots, so that they will turn easily.

They do not prevent the hens from entering or leaving the nests but they cannot perch on them. Soiled eggs bring a lower price and therefore something like this is well worth while.

HOME-MADE BROODERS

We have details and drawings of a good many types of useful home-made brooders, but space does not permit of their inclusion so we are therefore only including hints on the making of one electric type and one ordinary.

The electric brooder shown is one for, say, 50 chicks, the material necessary being two batten holders for the lamps, 2 wooden blocks, about 5¾ in. square, a length of flex, and an adaptor or plug for connecting up with the lighting circuit. A cylindrical screen of perforated zinc completes the equipment.

The practice in this is to insert one 32 and one 16 c.p. lamp before the chicks are put into the brooder and thus get the temperature up to the required degree.

When the chicks are in, the 16 c.p. lamp is replaced by an 8 c.p., the 32 c.p. remaining in place.

After the first week only one bulb, the 32 c.p. is left in and the lower c.p.'s are used to replace it as the weeks go by and less heat is required for the job.

USEFUL HOME-MADE BROODERS
A HOT AIR BROODER FOR 100 CHICKS TO THREE WEEKS

The maker of this claims an advantage over the hot-water circulating and other brooders, in that the heat does not vary, and one does not have to sit up at night to stoke up, also there is no danger of the chicks becoming overheated no danger on windy nights of the lamp being blown out or catching fire.

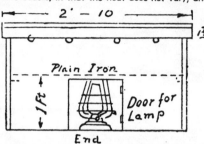

Instructions are as follow: Place the hurricane lamp in the centre of the iron underneath with a good sized frame, and keep ½ inch depth of sand on top of iron, which is the floor of the warm compartment; confine chicks to brooder for a couple of days until strong enough to run up and down the ramp, and, for a few nights, as it gets towards bedtime for the chicks, throw a sack over the glass window, or they may pile up against the glass, and should they take to a corner, fill a jam tin with sand and stand in the corner.

There is no need to trim lamp other than, say, once every two weeks, when properly set, but, of course, it needs filling daily. Should lamp not quite fit underneath, scratch out a little earth until low enough. The brooder can be used out in the open, or in a shed, and will rear 100 chicks up to three weeks old.

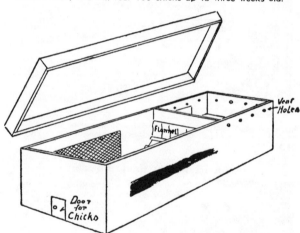

Cut boards 5 ft. 10 ins. and 2 ft. 10 ins., then a sheet of 6 x 3 ft. flat iron will fit nicely on top for keeping out the wet and rain. The warm compartment is made by nailing a piece of flat iron 1 ft. high to battens on the sides, and is 2 ft. 6 ins. wide, and on top of ramp is a cleat of wood to stop the sand sliding out.

The roof is made by nailing the boards crossways to 1½ in. battens on their edge, and with a piece nailed on each end, makes a lid to drop on, which will slide either way for feeding, but

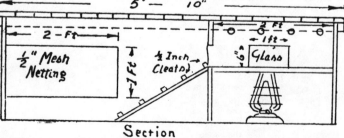

which cannot blow off, and with a sheet of 6 x 3 ft. flat iron, nailed on top, completes the job, except for a coat of red oxide paint.

DOGS

DOES YOUR DOG CHASE CARS?

The habit of a dog to chase cars not only endangers the animal, but may result in a serious accident if a motorist swerves the car or becomes confused in trying to avoid hitting the dog.

Such a habit can often be stopped by a small rubber ball attached to one of the dog's front legs as shown. The ball is not likely to hurt the dog and it will not keep it from getting plenty of exercise, but it hinder it from running fast.

RUBBER BALL

PREVENTION OF DOG BITE

This idea is well worth keeping in mind, as so many lambs are rejected for export because of dog bite.

This guard is simply made, and appears to be much preferable to a wire or leather muzzle, being cooler and costing nothing

FINE COPPER WIRE WINDING

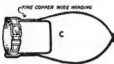

to make. "A" shows the device in use; "B" the method of bending the wire; and "C" the wire attached to the collar.

A USEFUL SLIP COLLAR FOR DOG

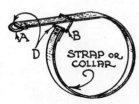

STRAP OR COLLAR

This suggestion comes from one who has found this type of collar successful.

Take an ordinary dog collar and cut the tongue out of the buckle at "B," then thread the strap or collar through the buckle at "B," and cut to length required, then get a circular ring and rivet it to the end of the strap or collar at "A," and the collar is complete.

The metal D at "A" should be large enough to prevent it from slipping through the one at "B." Put the collar over the dog's head and hook up the chain at "A"—this arrangement has held dogs when nothing else has.

ANOTHER DOG COLLAR THAT HOLDS

Cut the collar in half, putting a D at "A" and "B." Connect a piece of pliable leather through the two D's and place another D at "C," leaving the D at "C" loose. Pull the chain "E" and it will draw together "A" and "B," tightening the collar

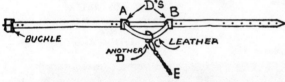

BUCKLE   A D'S B   LEATHER
ANOTHER D   E

round the dog's neck, and as the dog slackens off, so does the collar.

One who has been an old shepherd vouches for the above, as it will hold the best of dogs who have the habit of slipping their collar.

NOVEL METHOD OF PREVENTING DOG FROM TEARING BANDAGES OFF

If your dog has his leg bandaged (or foot), and perhaps has the habit of tearing off the bandage with his teeth and you wish to cure him, just wet a cake of soap and rub it over the bandage as indicated in this sketch.

A dog does not usually like the taste of soap and usually will not bother about the bandage when he has once realised that there is soap on it. He soon learns to leave it alone.

TIE BACK OVER FOOT LOOSELY

PLACE DOG'S PAD

<-- 3½ INCHES ACROSS -->

HERE

LACE AROUND FETLOCK.

USEFUL BOOTS FOR DOGS

Protection from damage to feet and legs can be obtained by the use of a boot made as per the accompanying illustration. This has been tried by several farmers with distinct success.

It is specially useful where easy travelling is concerned, but even on hills and sea cliffs, it has proved its worth.

It is easily made: an old boot upper will sometimes provide the material or perhaps an inner tube or some other thick material. It will protect against thistles, shingly country, sunburn and road soreness.

Discretion should be used as to the size and tightness of the lacing. The completed boot may look a little sloppy but it will protect the dog from anything which tends to aggravate the dog. The length of the pattern is 8½ in.

HOW TO TELL THE AGE OF A DOG

The following diagrams indicating one method by which the approximate age of a dog can be told, might be of interest.

Key to Drawings

A: Pincher incisors.

B: Intermediate incisors.

C: Corner incisors.

D: Tushes.

1 year   1½ Yrs

At 1 year, the teeth are usually pure and white and the incisors are intact and shaped somewhat like a fleur-de-lys, the tushes being fresh and unworn.

At 15 months, they commence to wear—this is first seen in the inferior pinches as at 1½ years, the tushes still being fresh and white. At 2½ years, the intermediate incisors in the upper jaw are becoming worn down and all teeth begin to lose their freshness. When over 3 years, all the incisors are becoming worn and are followed by the wearing of the superior intermediate teeth—the tushes are yellow and dirty in appearance and after 4 years it is difficult to tell the age at all, all incisors and tushes being much worn.

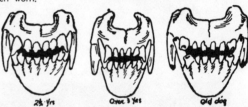

2½ Yrs   Over 3 Yrs   Old dog

Old dogs become grey around nose, eyes and forehead—noses become larger and the skin over the whole face wrinkled. Of course, the teeth depend on food, etc., and whether the dogs are taught to bring back hard objects, in which case they will wear quicker.

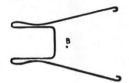

USEFUL IDEAS IN THE GARDEN

DEPTH (IN INCHES) AT WHICH VEGETABLE SEEDS SHOULD BE PLANTED

The following sketch should be useful to the amateur gardener; it being intended to convey an idea as to the various depths at which various seeds should be sown—the inch measure being shown on the right hand side of the illustration.

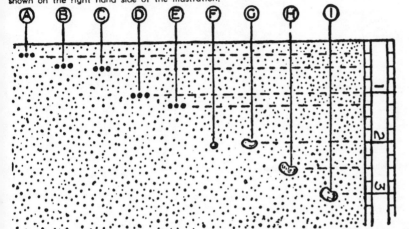

(A) Lettuce and Onion. (B) Carrot. (C) Cabbage, Cauliflower, Brussels Sprouts, Broccoli, Radish, Turnip, Parsley and Parsnip. (D) Spinach and Beet. (E) Asparagus. (F) Peas. (G) French Beans. (H) Runner Beans. POTATOES—4 to 5 in. deep.

Seed Required for Sowing

Beans (Broad)—1 quart to 4 rows, each 15 ft. long.
Beans (French)—1 quart to 9 rows, each 15 ft. long.
Beet—1 oz. to 3 rows, each 15 ft. long.
Broccoli—1 oz. broadcast will sow a bed 4 ft. x 13 ft.
Brussels Sprouts—1 oz. broadcast will sow a bed 4 ft. x 13 ft.
Cabbage—1 oz. broadcast will sow a bed 4 ft. x 13 ft.
Carrot—1 oz. to 4 rows, each 25 ft. long.
Cress—1 oz. broadcast to bed 4 ft. x 20 ft.
Kale—1 oz. broadcast to bed 4 ft. x 12 ft.
Leeks—1 oz. to 4 rows, each 25 ft.
Lettuce—1 oz. to 4 rows, each 30 ft. long.
Mustard—1 oz. broadcast to bed 4 ft. x 36 ft.
Onions—1 oz. to 10 rows, each 10 ft. long.
Parsley—1 oz. to 10 rows, each 8 ft. long.
Parsnip—1 oz. to 10 rows, each 15 ft. long.
Peas—1 quart to 8 rows, each 15 ft. long.
Potatoes—14 lbs. to 100 feet of rows, set 1 ft. apart.
Radish—1 oz. broadcast will sow a bed 4 ft. x 30 ft.
Spinach—1 oz. to 6 rows, each 10 ft. long.
Turnips—1 oz. to 10 rows, each 15 ft. long.

AN ADJUSTABLE DIBBLE

Sets Plants at Uniform Depths

The problem of setting plants or bulbs at uniform depths can be solved by making an adjustable dibble as shown in this sketch.

This differs from the usual type, which is nothing more than a pointed stake, with holes drilled through it near the pointed end to take a short dowel which will serve as an adjustable gauge. With this handy little tool, it is a simple matter to go over the ground very quickly, and at the same time to make sure that the holes of the right depth are made.

MIXING SEED FOR DISTRIBUTION

Small seed should be mixed with sand or dry sifted soil to facilitate distribution and the two methods given below indicate some useful ways of doing this.

Plants of Broccoli, Cabbage, etc., from seed sown broadcast have to be transplanted when large enough. This is the invariable plan, but culture and transplanting will be facilitated if the seeds are sown in line and not broadcast. The latter only saves time in the initial stages.

Two Methods of Sowing Fine Seed

Even distribution of seed is necessary in seed sowing.

The first sketch indicates one way in which seed may be mixed with fine dry sand for distribution; care of course being taken to ensure that it runs evenly from the hand.

The other method is that of tearing off the corner of the packet to emit a few seeds at a time, or some other such receptacle could be used in which one could mix fine sand with the seed and then emit same evenly in the same way. There are, of course, other such ideas, and the regular gardener may have better ones, but these should be found very useful to the amateur.

SYSTEMS FOR PLANTING THE FRUIT GARDEN

Some like the " square " and some the " hexagon " method, but in the latter there are 3 ways of working against only two ways in the other method. Given the same distance between trees, more are accommodated in a given area by the hexagon method, but it is wiser to base the number of trees per acre on the carrying capacity of the land and other conditions. For instance, if it has been found under certain conditions that certain trees are satisfactory when planted 24 ft. apart on the square system (approx. 75 to the acre) and it is intended to plant more of such trees under similar conditions but on the hexagon system, then

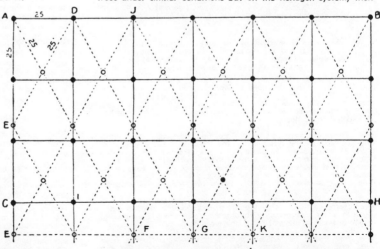

it is better to space them at a distance that will approximate the same number per acre, which means they will be 25 ft. 9 in. apart.
Headlands of at least 30 ft. should be allowed between the fence

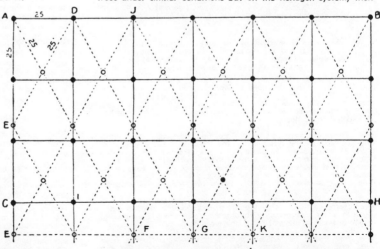

USEFUL IDEAS FOR THE GARDEN

and the first row of trees, to allow the easy turning of horse teams.

The square and hexagonal methods of marking out are both shown in the drawing on the previous page. The figure shows the principle, though to save space it is abbreviated, and the distances between A and C or A and F only allow for 4 and 5 trees respectively. In actual practice, of course, this line is usually extended.

When the pegging out of the rows is done with a stretched rope and marking pole, provided the ground is fairly level (or even if it is steep, provided the slope is fairly even) the distance between the lines AB and CH can be 700 to 800 feet if necessary and yet be conveniently operated.

PLANTING TREES

In any scheme of planting trees, either for shelter, appearance or garden, there are several important points to be observed, particular attention being given to the texture of the soil. If the trees are for windbreak purposes, it is well to try a mixture, say, three rows of tall trees, flanked on each side by two rows of small trees and perhaps some small shrubs on either side again.

Having selected the types of trees and shrubs, it is necessary to prepare the soil. In the case of isolated trees it is necessary to dig holes about 4 feet square and three feet deep. With hard subsoils it may be necessary to dig slightly larger holes and even to resort to gelignite to loosen the subsoil, since in such soils waterlogging may occur, which is in some cases fatal to the young plant.

The first 10 to 12 inches — the surface soil — should be removed and placed on one side and the removed sub-soil kept apart. In the case of a poor sub-soil it may be wise to add extra well-rotted manure, soil, should be placed mixed with surface in a shallow cone, in soil; on the top of the bottom of the should be placed in this the surface soil

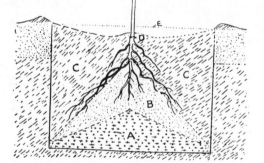

**The correct method of planting a young tree.
A, the replaced topsoil mixed with stable manure;
B, replaced topsoil; C, sub-soil; D, soil level of
tree when in pot; E, ground level.**

the form of a cone, the apex of which comes practically to the surface of the hole. On this cone the young trees should be placed, and the roots spread radially outwards and downwards (if the plant possesses a tap root this should be placed vertically within the cone.

The sub-soil may now be placed in position, working it downwards and outwards in the direction of the roots, and firmly consolidated. It is important to place the plant in a position in which the soil level is maintained with reference to the top of the hole, that is, that the surface soil level in respect to the tree is the same both when in the pot and after planting. In filling in the hole a depression should be left so that the trees can be watered without loss through overflow.

The accompanying sketch will explain these points. A good soaking with water is necessary immediately, which should be repeated in the absence of rain at least one week later.

The trees should be staked, and, if necessary, protected from wind and animals. Apply water liberally. Where trees are planted together and in large numbers it is not practicable to dig so many holes. The necessary cultivation may be achieved by ploughing and removing the surface soil to a depth of 10 inches and then ploughing the subsoil again as deeply as possible.

HINTS ON PRUNING FRUIT TREES

The first three years is all important. Careful pruning for the first three years has a large bearing on its success not only as regards shapeliness of the tree, but the cropping and freedom from disease is also largely affected.

In pruning deciduous trees, the aim is to produce an even, well balanced tree, open in the centre to admit light and air, and with most branches growing in a horizontal direction rather than upright.

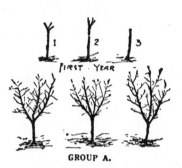

GROUP A.

Most deciduous trees which are dense produce poor crops, as the spur growths, which bear the fruit, must have light and air to mature the fruitings spurs and buds. This applies more to apples, apricots, pears and plums than to peaches, which produce fruit on younger wood than the former.

Do not try to produce fruit too soon, but concentrate first on building up a strong tree which can carry the subsequent wood and fruit in future years. This restraint for the first few years will pay big dividends later. Being in too much of a hurry for crops is the ruin of more young trees than any other cause.

The sketches on this page will illustrate the procedure to be followed: Taking group "A" as the procedure for pruning when planting young trees, figures 1 and 2 show trees which carried 3 or 4 evenly spaced branches when received from the nursery; while figure 3 illustrates a tree which was either without side growths or the growths available were so badly spaced as to be better removed.

When receiving the trees from the nursery, cut back as suggested, and then the following summer they will grow into trees as illustrated.

Second winter. The second winter pruning after planting consists of cutting back the main branches again, leaving them 9 to 18 in. long according to their strength. All

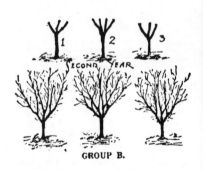

GROUP B.

other branches should be cut out close to the trunk, except when dealing with plums, apples and pears, which can have a few small spurs left on the branches.

Always select the branches with a horizontal tendency. Discard those with an upward growth, as they usually produce all growth and no fruit; and always cut to a bud pointing outward.

The second summer is important, as then the branches are selected for the secondary arms, and all others removed. This tends to force the growth into the main branches and strengthens them ready for the following winter pruning.

If you study the sketches in group "B," you will follow which branches are to be retained for future use. Those in group "C" (next column) show how to proceed with **the third winter** pruning after planting, and the resultant growth in the following summer, when the tree has been properly formed and can be allowed to settle down to serious cropping.

Future pruning must be governed by the growth of the trees.

When the trees are well furnished and are carrying stout main

USEFUL IDEAS FOR THE GARDEN

stems, it is only necessary to top the main leaders lightly for a year or two. After a few years, the trees increase in size and the main branches lengthen, but if horizontally inclined growths are retained and the main leaders kept topped, the trees can be kept within bounds.

Always aim to keep the branches within reasonable distance from the ground, as high trees are a nuisance when gathering the fruit and also make effective spraying and summer thinning much more difficult.

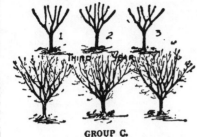

GROUP C.

To help those with older trees to distinguish the difference between fruiting wood and leaf wood, there is another diagram on this page showing the characteristics of each.

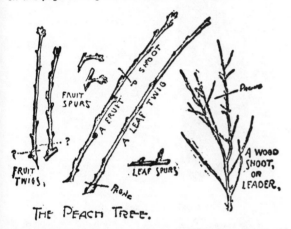

THE PEACH TREE.

Fruiting wood should be retained where possible, but leaf wood must not be cut too hard, as this will only force on extra growth and defeat the object.

PRUNING CITRUS TREES

Generally this is much simpler than the pruning of deciduous trees and consists mainly of shaping the young tree for the first few years, bearing in mind the necessity of allowing plenty of

light and air to penetrate. Also, any dead wood should be cut out. The trees should be compact and reasonably low to facilitate picking the fruit, and spraying. Unlike deciduous trees, the centre must not be kept too open, and the various branches should protect one another from too much sun; but at the same time they must be open enough to allow air to pass freely through the tree.

The subject of pruning is a large and interesting one, of which only the main principles can be mentioned here, but there are several excellent books on this subject.

BUDDING FRUIT TREES

This consists of the removal of a bud with a portion of the bark attached, and inserting it beneath the bark of another plant, the main principle being the same as in grafting. It should be done when the bark separates readily from the wood, which is at the time when growth is most active, warm weather being best. What is known as shield budding (see sketch) is quite easy. A shoot is taken with the buds of the right character, and the buds are sliced off as shown at C, the bark being then removed

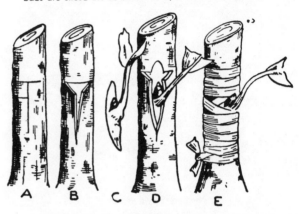

from the portion of wood attached. A slit is then made in the bark of the stock, and a transverse notch enables the operator to slip the handle of a budding knife under the bark so as to raise it.

The bud is then forced down wedge end first until the whole of the bark is underneath that of the stock and lying flat against the wood. The operation must be quickly performed or the bark will dry. After the bud has been inserted, it should be bound round with fine matting or worsted, not too tightly, but with just sufficient pressure to hold the whole together. Of course, the binding must have the bud itself lying at the axil of the leaf-stalk quite free. In a month or six weeks a union will have been effected, when the binding can be removed. With fruit trees a good time to bud is when the sap is flowing freely.

CORRECT WAY TO PLANT FROM POTS

There is a mistaken idea prevalent amongst some amateur gardeners to the effect that plants which have been grown in pots should have their roots disentangled when being planted in a garden but this is wrong. Many plants resent having their roots disturbed, and plants are grown in pots so that their roots will not be disturbed and so receive a check on being transferred to the ground.

The correct method of planting is to leave the ball of soil intact, merely carefully removing the drainage material at the bottom of the ball of soil. The plant should be placed about

3 in. lower than the surface of the prepared hole, fine soil filled round, and firmly pressed down until the plant is firm. Tie the plant to the stake and water well, filling in the rest of the soil after the water has drained away.

A mulching of dry leaves, grass and such-like material will stop evaporation, and a few twigs stuck in the ground will shelter the plant from the hot sun if planted in summer, or from frost in winter. The initial good watering of any newly-planted plant goes a long way towards its success. All tender evergreens should be planted when the ground is warm.

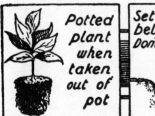

Potted plant when taken out of pot

Set plant 3 ins. below soil level. Don't disturb roots

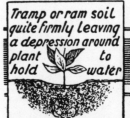

Tramp or ram soil quite firmly leaving a depression around plant to hold water

Shelter from frost with ferns or twigs arranged tent-wise

USEFUL IDEAS FOR THE GARDEN

ANOTHER HOME-MADE GARDEN WEEDER

This is a very useful tool and easily made. This particular one is made from a discarded mower section (but other types of metal will do) bolted on to a wooden handle.

It is specially handy to use when weeding around plants, and takes very little time to make.

A HOME-MADE WHEEL HOE

The knife for this cultivator was made from an old car spring, shaped and tempered. The handles were made from 2 x 2 stock. The braces are ordinary band iron.

When laying out the garden have the row of vegetables a little wider than the cultivator blade so that you will only need to go down each row once for each cultivation. This is simply made and a real time saver.

A HOME-MADE HEDGE SLASHER

When one cuts hedges with a slasher it is often necessary to pull out the cut pieces by hand, but with this device this is eliminated and hastens up the job. The device does not interfere with the use of the slasher.

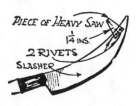

As shown, fit a piece of heavy saw with two holes drilled in it so as to correspond with two holes in the slasher so as to rivet the two. The hook needs to be about 1¼ in. long from the back of the slasher. Do not make it too heavy or it may affect the balance.

A FOOT-REST FOR SPADE

Spadework is often hard on boot soles and continued pressure often causes sorenes under the arch of the foot. Some spades have this rest, whilst various other remedies such as slitting a piece of garden hose or water piping and clipping it on top are used.

However, a piece of angle iron makes a better and more stable attachment, as it can be riveted on. The iron may be in one piece, notched to fit around the handle, or two short pieces can be used, one on each side. **Another way** is to fit a small length of pipe or old tyre where the angle iron is shown in this drawing.

A USEFUL PLANT SUPPORT

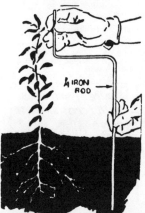

A good idea of supporting plants so that the roots are not injured by the support is given here. Instead of driving a stake into the ground close to the plant, a length of heavy wire, No. 8 or stouter, is driven into the ground several inches from the base of the plant.

The wire is then bent over at ground surface, and upwards, so that it lies parallel and close to the stem of the plant, which may then be tied to the upright portion at several points if needed. If preferred, the first bend may be made higher up, to support the plant at the top only, as shown in the sketch.

AN IMPROVISED FRUIT PICKER

This is a device for picking apples, oranges or other fruit which may be so high up on the top of the tree or so far out on the limbs that they are hard to reach from picking ladders, etc.

It is very easily made from stiff wire arranged as shown, and fixed on a bamboo pole or other light stick. The basket framework is shown, i.e., three or four rings of wire connected by a number of uprights, whilst the pole can be made to any length required.

Soft cloth sewn on the inside of the wires will assist careful handling and, under ordinary conditions, the fruit should not bruise if picked in this way. Hooks can be added, as shown, in order to hang the arrangement upon any convenient bough.

ANOTHER NOVEL PICKER

This home-made contrivance is very useful for getting out-of-the-way apples at the top of the tree. It is a frame cut out (see inset) from three-ply with a fret saw. The exact size or shape does not matter, providing the opening is large enough to take the fruit.

An old stocking is passed through the hole and its top edge fixed to the frame by tacks, and when attached to a long pole by a couple of screws, the picker is complete.

In action, the picker is manoeuvred so that the fruit rests inside the opening, when a downward pull dislodges the apple into the stocking.

A HOME-MADE SPRAY PUMP

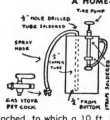

A simple pressure type sprayer for plants and trees can be made at little cost from a small drum, a tyre pump and some fittings.

Near the top of the drum mount a valve stem from an old inner tube. Clamp the tyre pump to the side of the drum, attaching the hose to the valve stem. A ½ in. copper tube which extends within about ½ in. of the bottom of the drum is next soldered in position and a coupling attached, to which a 10 ft. length of garden hose can be coupled. At the outer end of the hose attach a gas stove cock and it wlil be all complete.

A HOME-MADE SPRAY TOWER

This should be useful where there are a number of trees sufficiently spaced to permit of it being used—more efficient spraying would result.

The main feature is a tower which enables the operator to work at a convenient height, and so spray every branch. Any old pair of wheels can be used, with a platform built as shown. One can work with either a knapsack or any other spraying outfit. If a petrol driven type is used, this can be placed on the lower platform whilst other types can merely be strapped to the back as usual.

The arrangement can be made so that the spraying outfit can be taken off so that the vehicle can then be used for fruit picking.

USEFUL IDEAS FOR THE GARDEN

PROTECTING YOUNG TREES FROM DAMAGE BY RABBITS

These are two novel and effective ways of protecting trees from such damage.

In the first, all you need is some old screen wire. Form it into sleeves as shown here and place it around the tree to keep the rabbits from gnawing the bark. Such protection can be used from year to year and is much handier to put on and take off than cloth or paper which are often used for the same purpose.

The second method consists of painting the butt of the tree with some sort of fish oil. One orchardist states that liberal coatings of this is quite sufficient for the purpose — it is best applied in cool weather, when it is thicker.

PAPER MULCH TO AID YOUNG TREES

When a small tree is transplanted, much of the success in saving it depends upon keeping plenty of moisture around the roots for the first few months.

One way to ensure this is to mix plenty of peat moss with the soil and then place a large square of tar paper on top of the ground around the tree. This helps to slow up evaporation of the moisture from the soil.

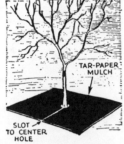

A USEFUL GARDEN LINE MARKER

Pointed at the ends and pivoted together with a small bolt, 2 lengths of broom handles provide a handy stake with which a garden row marker can be tightened and anchored easily.

The line is wrapped round one stake, which is then pushed into the ground — the other stake serving as a handle to turn the one in the ground tighten the line, after which the handle is tilted to engage the ground and prevent the assembly from turning to loosen the line.

A METHOD OF MAKING DUPLICATE FURROW SEED ROWS IN ONE OPERATION

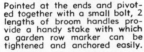

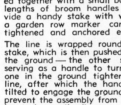

This is one way to save work in the garden and it will space the rows and furrow them at the same time.

In this way small seeds are spaced properly and can be covered to a uniform depth.

The marker is simple to make. It has two runners affixed to a board as shown, which are adjustable to the spaces required. The method of adjustment is also simple and is shown in the smaller detail.

PROTECTING SEEDS FROM BIRDS

One method of checking birds is to criss-cross black cotton in all directions over the sowings, held in position by short twigs puhed into the ground.

Old newspapers may also be used. Spread out the sheets, cut them lengthwise in half and then fold them so that they may easily assume a tent-like shape along the rows of the newly planted seed. Pegs are driven in to keep the paper in position.

Make the edge of the second and subsequent pieces overlap the first. The pieces pegged on the ground should be doubled under to give a better hold against the wind; dry soil may be heaped up on the folded edge to give greater resistance.

This idea will serve to protect from sun as well as from birds, and the sowing will be forced along because of the warmth and moisture retained beneath the paper. With iceland poppies, stocks and other sowings made in drills, this paper protection may be tried for benefits other than that of the bird pest.

A HANDY ARRANGEMENT FOR FORCING PLANTS

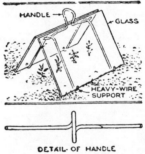

It is often necessary to force seedlings under glass. Old photo negative glasses are useful for such a purpose — the larger, of course, the better.

Two glasses are required for each forcing screen, held together in the form of a V by three pieces of stiff wire, bent as shown. The loop in the top piece serves as a handle. When no longer required, the screens are easily dismantled and stored away.

Such an arrangement can also, of course, be made from other things and one's own ingenuity will no doubt suggest something along somewhat similar lines to the above and which will be quite as effective.

A USEFUL ORCHARD LADDER ON WHEELS

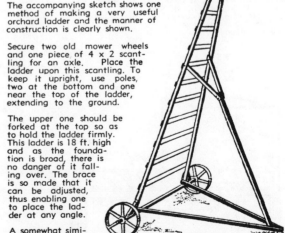

The accompanying sketch shows one method of making a very useful orchard ladder and the manner of construction is clearly shown.

Secure two old mower wheels and one piece of 4 x 2 scantling for an axle. Place the ladder upon this scantling. To keep it upright, use poles, two at the bottom and one near the top of the ladder, extending to the ground.

The upper one should be forked at the top so as to hold the ladder firmly. This ladder is 18 ft. high and as the foundation is broad, there is no danger of it falling over. The brace is so made that it can be adjusted, thus enabling one to place the ladder at any angle.

A somewhat similar arrangement can also be made with a pair of wheels on the support and not on the ladder uprights, in which case of course it should be built square with the ladder and not to an angle as indicated.

USEFUL IDEAS FOR THE GARDEN

A SIMPLE IRRIGATING SYSTEM FOR THE HOME GARDEN

These are good labor savers for the home garden as, by using some form of an irrigating system, a small piece of ground will produce good crops. However, the system described here is not designed for a large area.

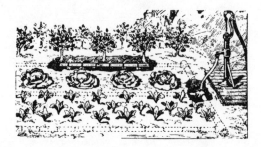

Near a source of water pressure, such as a hydraulic ram, windmill, or hydrant, a line of 6 in. glazed tile, with T-connections every 6 ft., is laid 1 ft. below the surface. From each connection are laid parallel lines of 3 in. unglazed tile.

The joints of the glazed tile are cemented, but the unglazed tiles are merely placed end to end, allowing the water to percolate into the soil more rapidly than it would be merely soaking through the tile. The fall need not be more than 1 in. in every yard. When the trenches have been filled in, the system is ready to use, water being supplied by a pump, or hose from the hydrant to the glazed tile. A tomato patch, 20 ft. x 30 ft., with the plants set 3 ft. apart each way, and irrigated for a few minutes night and morning by 3 lines of tile, will produce a crop which will more than pay for the tile and labor in one season.

ANOTHER SIMPLE IRRIGATING SYSTEM FOR GARDEN

By using this simple system, you not only save time, but you also save water as there is less evaporation than there is when you sprinkle with a hose. Also, sprinkling requires your constant attention, which is not necessary with this.

To instal the system, all you need is a suitable length of $\frac{3}{4}$ in. pipe, which is capped at one end and provided with a fitting at the other to take a garden hose. Wood blocks support the pipe, which has 1-8th inch holes drilled in one side to direct the water into trenches between the rows. After irrigating, fill the trenches immediately with soil to keep the sun from drying out the wet ground.

AN IMPROVISED SPRINKLER

If you happen to have no regular sprinkler or if the one you have is out of order and you do not have the time to stand and water the garden, just twist the hose in the manner shown in this drawing.

It will make a very good substitute and will not need moving so very often from place to place or it can easily be moved by simply drawing it along to the next spot to be watered without the usual procedure of stopping the tap first.

IMPROVISED FERTILISER SPREADERS FOR GARDENS AND LAWNS

Fertiliser can be spread evenly over the lawn or garden or any other small area with the assistance of either of the home-made contrivances shown here.

The first sketch shows a handy device, the container for which is made from a 2-gal. tin (or a larger one if desired), the side being perforated with $\frac{1}{4}$-inch holes. A detachable handle is made of twisted wire, as indicated, the ends of which fit into holes punched through the centres of the top and bottom of the drum.

To elevate the drum a sufficient distance above the floor to allow the compound to sift through and also to provide silencers, rubber tyres made from cross sections of old inner tubes, are slipped over the ends. To fill the cylinder with fertiliser, the handles and one end cover is removed. The other end cover can be a fixture.

This will ensure an even distribution.

The second is somewhat similar in design but different in the method of filling. In this the fertiliser is put into the container through a capped opening in one of the wheels as shown in the inset drawing. It sifts through the perforations as the many sided drum turns.

In this instance, the container is made from strips of tin fastened together, or, of course, it could be made from a drum as in the other illustration.

Heavy cardboard can also be used for this type of spreader and the wheels can be made of lightweight metal. A handle attached to a wire frame completes the job, and this is used for pushing the spreader. The ideas shown may also suggest something else or a combination of both ideas in some shape or form might be used by those who may have use for such a machine.

A HOME-MADE GRADING TABLE FOR POTATOES AND OTHER PRODUCE

A very useful home-made grading table is described here—it is a New Zealand idea and one which has been found very efficient and well worth while.

The type illustrated is one fitted with a hopper or wooden box at one end and built to a size suitable for holding a quantity of the potatoes or other produce to be sorted. From there the potatoes pass out on to an apron, made on the principle of a narrow binder or canvas, in the manner indicated.

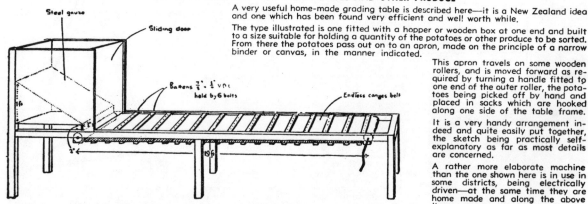

This apron travels on some wooden rollers, and is moved forward as required by turning a handle fitted to one end of the outer roller, the potatoes being picked off by hand and placed in sacks which are hooked along one side of the table frame.

It is a very handy arrangement indeed and quite easily put together, the sketch being practically self-explanatory as far as most details are concerned.

A rather more elaborate machine than the one shown here is in use in some districts, being electrically driven—at the same time they are home made and along the above lines.

USEFUL IDEAS FOR THE GARDEN

HOME-MADE WATERPROOF KNEE PADS FOR THE GARDEN

CUT OUT OF OLD INNER TUBE

This is useful for working in the garden as it is often necessary to remain in a kneeling position for some time. A pair of pads cut from an old inner tube will be found waterproof and will protect your knees against damp ground. It also eases the strain on the knees.

All that is necessary is to cut a section of the tube as shown and if it is too tight, a piece can be spliced in with rubber cement.

RUBBER BAND HELPS KEEP LEGS DRY ON WET GROUND

This is quite a good idea for quite a number of purposes; it even being an excellent substitute for a cycle clip, etc.

However, the idea shown here is to keep the trousers fastened down over the boots by the use of rubber bands cut from inner tubes.

The band should be split on one side as shown and will be found to be an excellent and comfortable method of keeping the legs dry when the garden or fields are muddy and sloppy.

PIECE OF INNER TUBE

NOVEL WAY OF USING PERFORATED TINS TO WATER YOUNG TREES SLOWLY

This is an idea which has often been used with success. Newly planted trees require frequent watering, but quantities of water dashed around the roots will often flow away before thoroughly soaking into the soil.

To avoid this, obtain a number of discarded paint or other tins and perforate each one on the bottom with a small hole, or holes. One or more is set at each tree, and the water poured into them trickles out slowly into the ground and will then keep the soil damp much deeper and much longer than the ordinary method of watering will do.

NOVEL IDEA TO PREVENT BREAKING OF MARKING LINE

This illustration explains itself inasmuch as it shows how the addition of a length of tubing to the end of the marking line will

STRIP OF INNER TUBE

Strip of Inner Tube Prevents Breaking of Line for Marking Garden Rows

make it pliant and help prevent it from breaking by the strain sometimes put upon it when using the hoe or other implement. It will give to the hoe and come back into place itself.

HOW TO MEASURE A TREE'S HEIGHT

Two well-planed pieces of wood are fastened together at an angle of 45 degrees. A thick piece of wood is prepared for use as a post, and the angle is placed on this so that its base is parallel with the ground. A sight is then taken along the upper arm of the angle-piece and the stand is then moved backwards or forwards until the top of the tree just touches the line of sight. Then the angle-piece is continued backwards in an imaginary line to the spot where it touches the ground. Then the distance from this point to the trunk is measured and this represents the approximate height of the tree.

A SMALL INCINERATOR OF WIRE-NETTING FOR LEAVES, ETC.

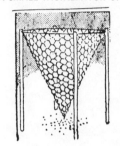

Light garden rubbish may be burned in an incinerator made in the following manner. Shape a couple of yards of wire-netting into a wide-mouthed cone as shown.

Drive three or four metal stakes, about 3 ft. high, into the ground for supports, and place the cone so that the pointed end is about 4 inches above the ground.

Rubbish burns readily in this incinerator, as the ashes fall through and may be collected into the garden.

A USEFUL WHEELBARROW GARDEN PLOW

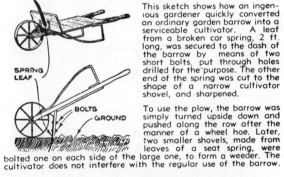

SPRING LEAF

BOLTS

GROUND

This sketch shows how an ingenious gardener quickly converted an ordinary garden barrow into a serviceable cultivator. A leaf from a broken car spring, 2 ft. long, was secured to the dash of the barrow by means of two short bolts, put through holes drilled for the purpose. The other end of the spring was cut to the shape of a narrow cultivator shovel, and sharpened.

To use the plow, the barrow was simply turned upside down and pushed along the row after the manner of a wheel hoe. Later, two smaller shovels, made from leaves of a seat spring, were bolted one on each side of the large one, to form a weeder. The cultivator does not interfere with the regular use of the barrow.

NOVEL WAY OF SUPPORTING OVERWEIGHTED LIMB

SECTION OF OLD AUTO TIRE

PROP

This is an excellent method of propping up the boughs of a fruit tree which might have become overladen with fruit and in danger of breaking.

It has two distinct advantages. The piece of old tyre will prevent the chafing of the bark and will give the limb a secure grip, thus avoiding any sudden fall of the limb in windy weather which is often caused by the bough slipping off the prop.

Here is a tree-limb prop that will not chafe the bark, and the wind cannot blow it down

USEFUL IDEAS FOR THE GARDEN

SEMI-RUSTIC GARDEN FURNITURE

These few hints should be useful to those who desire to make this type of furniture. As it has to stand the wear and tear of exposure, it must be solidly constructed, so use a fairly massive timber, otherwise it is apt to fall to bits early. Use bush timber for the larger sections and sawn hardwood, usually jarrah, for the smaller, and a more lasting job will result.

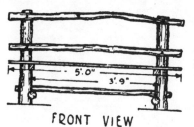

FRONT VIEW

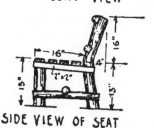

SIDE VIEW OF SEAT

The timber usually used is red gum. Sugar gum is also good for straight pieces, as when dry it makes light and strong timber. Most Australian hardwoods, however, deteriorate fairly quickly on the outside layers, which become pithy, so that when making joints give preference to those fixings when heartwood comes against heartwood.

If buying your timber with the bark on, bark it by hammering along the piece all round, when the bark should come off cleanly. Then put the timber aside in the shade to dry.

The garden seat and table shown here are on the semi-rustic principle. For the seat the bearers and the seat are of sawn jarrah, and for the table the bearers and the top are jarrah also. For both articles, $3\frac{1}{2}$ inch diameter timbers are required for main sections; for the rails $2\frac{1}{2}$ to 3 in. are large enough. For the seat back supports select bent pieces as shown with about 4 inches of springback.

The seat bearers are cut out of 2 x 2 in. jarrah, and the seat out of 3 x 1 jarrah, screwed to the bearers. For bolts use 5/16th BRH or carriage bolts, with washers under all nuts, and vaseline the threads so they will not rust up and may be tightened later.

When building up the frames of the seat it is a good plan to lay one out full size on the floor, and fit the available timber to it as nearly as possible. As you cannot reverse the second frame very well, after building the first, make another layout by reversing it, and build the second frame to the new layout. This will become quite clear as you proceed. For the table top, bearers are made of 3 x $1\frac{1}{2}$ in. jarrah, and the top by 3 x 1 in. slats, set $\frac{1}{2}$ in. apart, to allow water to run through and avoid excessive buckling.

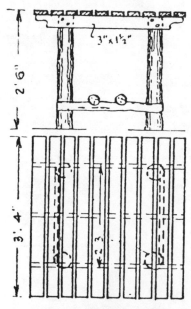

SIDE VIEW

PLAN OF TABLE

ANOTHER TYPE OF RUSTIC GARDEN SEAT

Only good timbers should be used as it has to withstand all weathers. Jarrah is best, not painted but coated with hardwood oil. Redgum is good, but karri is not so suitable. Joints should not be put together with glue but with thick white lead, to which a trace of red lead can be added, sufficient to give it a faint pink tinge.

Timber should be barked and cleaned when green, and when preparing it all ends should be cut off square with a saw. Cart the timber to the spot in as large sections as possible—branches with forks still on, and so on, as these can then be worked into the designs.

As an example, as to how to work out a rustic design, look at figure 1, which shows an armchair. Note how the main stem forms the front legs, and a branch in the natural position the arm rests. Some ingenuity has to be exercised in balancing two sides of a design as nearly as possible.

Comfort is a special consideration. Seats may be built up with round timbers longitudinally (fig. 2), or if transversely (as in fig. 3) they should be butted into round pieces as shown in figure 3 (side view fig. 4). In this case it is usual to fix the slats by nailing them right through the front and back pieces.

Avoid clumsy joints and any flattening of timbers. Nails as big as 6 in. can be used, but for the main joints, 5/16th bolts are best. Backing underneath the nuts with many washers should be avoided. When using nails, holes should be bored.

It is sometimes done, but is really incorrect, to paint rustic work—hardwood oils should be used, although they do not, of course, stand the weather like paint.

As rustic work is of a free and easy type, it is not possible to give exact details of any articles, so much depends upon the materials available. The beginner is not advised to put much labor into making articles of wattles or of light saplings as they cannot be expected to last.

ANOTHER LAWN-TYPE SETTEE

This is made entirely from inch timber. The curved edges are cut with a key-hole saw. Some of the major measurements are given here, from which the rest can be judged.

The front standards are 23 in. high and $46\frac{1}{2}$ in. from outside to outside. The front support is $46\frac{1}{2}$ in. long and 6 in. wide, and is let into the front standard its own thickness.

The arms are 27 in. long and $4\frac{1}{2}$ in. wide, and curved on the inside. The runners are three in number, one to support the seat in the middle, and are curved to make the hollow in the seat.

The two end ones are bolted to the front standards whilst behind they rest on the ground. The highest pieces of the back are $33\frac{1}{2}$ in. long and 5 in. wide, and the other somewhat shorter, as shown. Note that there is a cross-piece, to hold the back together near the top. It is $2\frac{1}{2}$ in. wide and $43\frac{1}{2}$ in. long. The arms are supported at the rear by another cross-piece $2\frac{1}{2}$ in. wide and 51 in. long.

USEFUL IDEAS FOR THE GARDEN

HOW TO MAKE ONE TYPE OF ROCKERY POND

Showing Inlet and Outlet Pipes, which can also be fitted into the Brick and Concrete Pool below.

A rockery pond is made by lining the floor and sides of a hole in the ground with large pieces of stone, cemented in with a mortar of sand and cement. It should not be less than 6 ft. x 4 ft., with depth of water at least 1 ft. 6 in.

First, decide the position and outline the shape with a length of

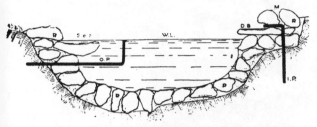

Section of a suggested rocky pond, showing R, rocks; M, mortar; IP, inlet pipe from water supply; OP, outlet pipe to drains; WL, water level; SBB, submerged bird bath; DP, drip bowl.

rope, and then mark the outline with the spade. Allow 6 in. to 8 in. for the lining, i.e., make the excavation that much wider and deeper than the finished measurements. One big point is to get the mortar well packed in to prevent leakage.

The illustration will show the best method of placing the stones and packing them with cement (1 part cement to 2 parts clean sand) mixed to a stiff consistency. The last paragraphs of the following article on "A Brick and Concrete Pool" will also apply here.

MAKING A BRICK AND CONCRETE GARDEN POOL

ARRANGEMENT OF BRICKS

CONCRETE

The details in this sketch have a twofold object in that it is shallow enough for children to climb out of if they accidentally fall in, and yet it has a deeper section, covered by a grating, for deeper growing plants.

A ledge around the parapet makes the outside of the pool shallow. The construction is simple and inexpensive if used bricks are laid in the walls with a mortar consisting of clean, dry sand (5 parts) and 1 part of cement.

The concrete is poured with a mixture of 2 parts sand, 2 parts gravel and 1 of cement. The concrete is kept moist by means of wet sacks until it has set, after which the entire surface of the pool is painted with waterproof cement mixed to the consistency of thin cream.

A rich soil well mixed with manure should be laid at the bottom

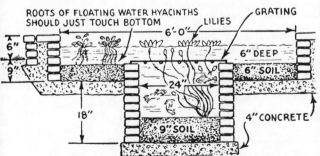

ROOTS OF FLOATING WATER HYACINTHS SHOULD JUST TOUCH BOTTOM
LILIES
GRATING
6'-0"
6" DEEP
6" SOIL
24"
4" CONCRETE
18"
9" SOIL

as indicated. When the plants have been set out and the pool filled, the water should be drained out after 2 or 3 days. Then refill it and the job is done for the summer.

HOME-MADE GARDEN WHEEL CULTIVATORS

Either one of these two types of useful garden cultivators will be found quite easy to make. That shown here (with 5 prongs) can be made or taken from an old hand cultivator.

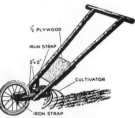

A bicycle wheel is then used in the manner shown. Panels of ½ in. plywood join the frame members and support the tool rigidly. With a smaller wheel as shown below the force is applied in a direct line to the cultivator prongs.

Assemble all parts with bolts and nuts. Strap iron extensions support the axle. Two braces make a rigid unit of the handle members and the lower frame.

It will be noted that the **second illustration** is of a different type fixture for both handles and forks.

The dimensions in both will depend upon the size of the wheel, but the handle should come about elbow height. Always use bolts and nuts in assembling the parts as something strong and durable is needed. The illustrations in both cases will show the whole arrangement of wheel and tynes.

SHARPENING AND ADJUSTING GARDEN TOOLS

Sharpening should be done on the grindstone or with a carborundum hone and the original cutting angles should be retained where possible.

With shears "A," the blades are bevelled on opposite sides as shown by the enlarged section at "B." The inner surfaces of the shears must be perfectly flat, as the slightest amount of bevel on these surfaces will spoil the cutting action. There are two bevels, the one on the side of the blades lopes considerably, but it is not considered, it is the slight bevel on the edge that is important.

Grass or reaping hooks are also sharpened on one side only, the upper surfaces only being honed. In these, there is only one angle, and care should be taken to keep it as flat as possible, as shown in the enlarged section at "D." The point of the blade is very liable to become blunted. It should be kept sharp and the greatest care is needed when using it.

Spring shears "F" have usually only one angle, due to the thinness of the blade. Care should be taken in sharpening to see that the hone is rubbed completely along the blade. The blades should be opened out by placing a suitable block of wood just below the spring. Like the shears, one side only of each blade is sharpened. Secateurs are also sharpened similarly to shears.

Cutting tools, such as axes and edging knives, indicated at "J" and "H" and at "K" and "L," should be ground without a second cutting angle as shown in the sections and the surfaces should be kept smooth and bright.

The blades of shears should not be allowed more play than is necessary for free movement and attention should be given to the pivot. Tightening is carried out by a turn on the nut or, in the case of riveted joints, by a slight tap or two with a hammer. If the handles of shears work loose, bind the tang with twine and drive the handles on again, taking care to avoid splitting the wood.

USEFUL HINTS FOR THE MOTORIST

A SIMPLE GAUGE FOR OIL OR OTHER DRUMS

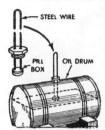

Provided it is a drum which does not have to be returned to any firm, and if you desire to keep a careful check on oil supplies, it can be done in this way.

First drill two holes in the drum cap to take the ends of a U-shaped wire. These wire ends are then soldered to a small tin box, which has already been sealed by flowing solder along the edge of the lid. With the cap in place, the box will float on the surface of the oil, leaving the loop end of the wire exposed to indicate the fuel level in drum.

A HANDY DEVICE FOR LIFTING PETROL DRUM

This handy device makes the lifting of petrol drums unnecessary. With 4 x 4 material, a stand is made to keep the drum 8 in. off the ground. A 2½ in. nipple is then screwed on a ¾ in. pipe into the small end of the drum. To this is connected a ¾ in. elbow and 20 in. of ¾ pipe, threaded at both ends.

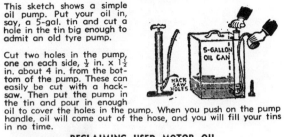

A cap screwed to the end of the pipe keeps it airtight. When petrol is wanted the screw cap is removed, the pipe is turned to the left until the petrol runs into the pail. To shut off, lift the pipe upright again and replace the cap. The outlet pipe could, of course, have a downward slant if necessary.

A HOME-MADE VALVE FOR DRAINING OFF PETROL

For those who keep petrol in large drums, this simple home-made valve should be just the thing for venting the barrels when removing contents. The valve will always stay closed except when compressed and there is then no chance of its staying open and allowing the contents to evaporate, which often happens when the bung cap is loosened to vent the barrel.

This valve is made from the regular bung, which is counterbored on the threaded end to take a small rubber ball. The bung is drilled through for the insertion of a wood screw which is driven into the ball. A coil compression spring under the head of the screw to bear against the bung completes the job. In use, just press on the head of the screw, which pushes the valve away from the bottom of the bung and allows air to enter the barrel as the contents are drained out.

A SIMPLE HOME-MADE PETROL PUMP

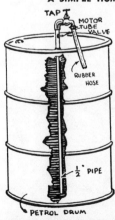

This is rather a novel idea for drawing kerosene or petrol from a drum. The first thing is to bore a hole down through the large bung of the drum and then insert a length of pipe (say ½ in.) long enough to reach practically to the bottom of the drum.

As most drums have to be returned to the makers, one can merely keep a regular sized bung already bored on hand and this can be fitted to the new drums as they arrive.

In this a tap and short length of hose is fitted to the pipe as shown, whilst a motor car valve is also soldered into the side of the pipe just below the tap, as indicated in the illustration. Everything must be airtight, of course. When this is ready, a tyre pump can be fitted and a few strokes will create sufficient pressure of air to make the contents flow when the tap is turned on.

A NOVEL OIL PUMP

This sketch shows a simple oil pump. Put your oil in, say, a 5-gal. tin and cut a hole in the tin big enough to admit an old tyre pump.

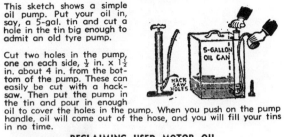

Cut two holes in the pump, one on each side, ½ in. x 1½ in. about 4 in. from the bottom of the pump. These can easily be cut with a hacksaw. Then put the pump in the tin and pour in enough oil to cover the holes in the pump. When you push on the pump handle, oil will come out of the hose, and you will fill your tins in no time.

RECLAIMING USED MOTOR OIL

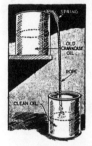

This is a useful method of reclaiming old motor oil for other uses as it will come out clear and free of carbon or other foreign particles.

Just put the used oil in a container on a shelf, box or table. Then hang a rope over the edge of the container with one end in the oil and the other in a second container underneath. A spring or coiled wire over the rope where it contacts the edge of the upper container will keep it in place. Capillary action will cause the oil to rise in the rope and run down into the lower container.

AN INEXPENSIVE HOME-MADE BATTERY FILLER

This handy distilled water container for filling storage batteries is easily made from a bottle, a rubber stopper and a length of small rubber tubing.

The stopper is drilled lengthwise to take the tube tightly, and one side at the upper end is cut away as indicated.

This permits the user to close the tube with the thumb in order to stop the flow of water as desired.

A COMPASS TEST THAT WILL REVEAL CRACKED BATTERY WALL

A sudden jar may crack the separator between the cells and cause trouble in starting. The battery might not reveal this but a compass will. Just place it on the lead strap connecting first one set of cells and then the other.

If cracked, the compass needle will be deflected at right angles to the connecting strap between the cells. If you do not get this reaction, the trouble is elsewhere.

MAKING DISTILLED WATER FOR BATTERY USE

Take a saucepan and an earthenware basin to fit inside. Put sufficient water in saucepan to reach half-way up the basin. Then place the saucepan lid in position upside down and fill the inverted lid with cold water. The lid should be an enamelled one. As the water in the pan commences to boil, it will condense on the lid and run into the basin. Only allow the water to simmer or it is liable to boil up over the edge of the basin. Put cold water into the lid at intervals.

USEFUL HINTS FOR THE MOTORIST

CIGARETTE SMOKE FINDS LEAK IN INNER TUBE

If it is not possible to dip the tube into water, the smoke from a burning cigarette will guide you.

The cigarette is moved round the surface of the inflated tube, until the air jet from the leak deflects the rising smoke.

Make sure, before using this method, that there is no strong air current where it is being done.

The second idea will also help get over the above trouble if you happen to have a glass available. All you need is to put a puff of smoke into the glass and then pass the inverted glass over the tube, when the air current from the puncture will show up at once.

A NOVEL METHOD OF CLEANING FUEL LINES

A length of speedometer cable is ideal for cleaning clogged oil or fuel lines. It will follow the bends without catching and is much better than wire or compressed air, as the latter may possibly burst the line.

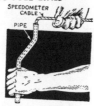

Compressed air can, of course, be used after the line has been opened by the cable in order to remove any loose particles.

A USEFUL TYRE CHANGING HINT

The use of a clothes peg can be a great help in tyre changing or repairing as it can merely be slipped over the valve stem after the latter has been pushed through the hole in the rim.

This will prevent the valve from slipping back inside while the tyre is being mounted.

HANDY METHODS OF RAISING WHEELS TO ATTACH CHAINS

HUB CAP

(1) Using a Hub Cap. Carry a deeply cupped hub-cap in your car, as it will be handy to raise a wheel when necessary. Just lay the chain over the cap and move the car so that the tyre rests on the cap.

It is better if the tyre rests a little off centre on the cap—this will allow you to stretch the chains tightly and fasten them in place without using a jack.

(2) A Portable Ramp. Tyre chains can be put on your car wheels in good time by using this simple portable ramp. Three blocks,

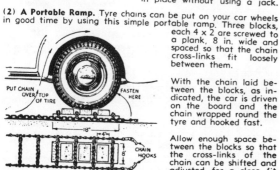

PUT CHAIN OVER TOP OF TIRE

FASTEN HERE

CHAIN HOOKS

TOP VIEW

each 4 x 2 are screwed to a plank, 8 in. wide and spaced so that the chain cross-links fit loosely between them.

With the chain laid between the blocks, as indicated, the car is driven on the board and the chain wrapped round the tyre and hooked fast.

Allow enough space between the blocks so that the cross-links of the chain can be shifted and adjusted for a close fit around the tyre casing.

A PORTABLE BENCH TO HOLD PARTS WHEN WORKING ON MOTOR

An arrangement like this to straddle the car on which work is being done will save time and steps.

Also, with this bench handy to hold the parts, one is not tempted to place them on the fenders or other places where they mar the paint, or may be lost.

If equipped with castors, this bench can be moved about easily.

A USEFUL METHOD OF ROTATING TYRES

One of the recognised methods of securing longer mileage is to even up tread wear by the rotation of tyres. And yet this system, so well known in theory, has until recently not been reduced to an exact practical operation.

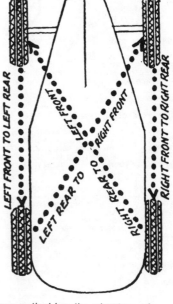

LEFT FRONT TO LEFT REAR

LEFT REAR TO

RIGHT REAR TO

LEFT FRONT

RIGHT FRONT

RIGHT FRONT TO RIGHT REAR

However, after a long period of trial, a new method has been evolved which has proved best to even up the tread wear and increase the average mileage. The new method is :

Change from right front to right rear, left front to left rear, right rear to left front, left rear to right front, both front tyres being moved straight back to the rear on the same side, while the rear tyres are moved diagonally to the opposite position.

Changes are made by transferring wheel without dismounting tyres. However, if tyres are removed from rims, they should be re-applied so that the same side of the tyre will face outwards as before. This new method has the advantage of :

1. Reduction of noise from rear tyres. 2. Better average non-skid traction during the life of the tread design; and 3. Better average mileage per tyre.

The tyres should be rotated every 2,500 to 3,000 miles.

SPRING SQUEAKS STOPPED BY TINFOIL

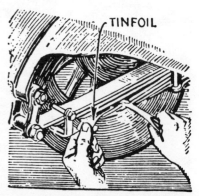

TINFOIL

Motorists are often annoyed by squeaking noises coming from the springs of a car.

According to one authority these squeaks can be eliminated by inserting a strip of tinfoil about 4 inches long between the leaves of the springs near the ends.

USEFUL HINTS FOR THE MOTORIST

SPARE WHEEL AS SHOCK ABSORBER IN EMERGENCY

This is a good idea when perhaps the use of a tow-rope may result in damaged fenders whilst it will also give control over both cars. Merely lash the spare tyre and wheel between the two bumpers, first letting out some of the air so that the tyre will absorb the shocks.

The front car brakes will serve for both cars.

A HANDY TOWING DEVICE

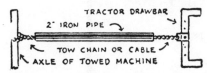

For towing a vehicle from a truck or tractor, the plan shown here of running the towing chain or cable through an iron pipe, 6 or 8 ft. long will admit of either pushing or pulling and will prevent the towed machine from running into the other on the down grade.

HOME-MADE GADGET TO PREVENT CAR FROM TOPPLING OFF LIFTING JACK

One often has the annoying experience of one's car toppling off the jack at an awkward moment, especially when it might have been found necessary to use the jack in an awkward place.

This can be overcome by the use of cross-pieces of steel threaded through the jack at right angles in the manner shown in this illustration. The jack cannot then incline either way and should not therefore fall over.

A USEFUL AID IN GETTING CAR OUT OF SAND OR MUD

This is simple and effective, and a good thing to carry in districts where one is liable to get stuck at any time.

It consists of a strip of canvas sewn around a piece of timber in the manner shown here, the timber being about 3 feet long. When the wheel touches the canvas it will draw it down and the timber will then give the wheel a good grip and so make getting out very much easier.

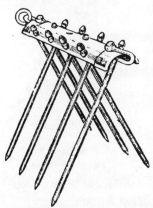

A USEFUL EARTH ANCHOR —A MOTORIST'S STANDBY

This gadget provides a good means of obtaining a quick hold on the ground for attaching hauling tackle of any kind. It is sunk into the ground to the saddle and the prongs should hold it so firmly that it will bear a considerable pull before it will give way.

The hauling tackle is hooked on to the shackle at one end.

The ring at the opposite end serves to attach the device to a small tree that might not be strong enough in itself to hold the tackle, but would be of use to reinforce the anchor. The saddle is fixed end on to the line of the pull.

A SUBSTITUTE FOR SUN GLASSES

This idea is worth knowing. People with eyes sensitive to strong light and who find they have gone driving without their sun glasses, may make a very good substitute by placing a pencil over their regular glasses so that it rests between the spectacles and the forehead.

It is a very simple idea but a very effective one and one which will save a good many headaches on very bright days.

AN IDEAL PLACE FOR ROAD MAP IN CAR

The sun visor in front of the driver's eyes is an ideal spot to keep the road map. It can then be studied at a glance without taking the eyes from the road for more than a second or so.

Fold the map so that the portion required can be seen; a couple of rubber bands will keep it in place.

AN AUTOMATIC LATCH FOR SLIDING DOOR

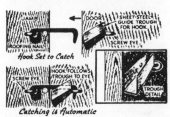

This is useful for those who have sliding doors which hook on the inside, it being a nuisance to have to lock the hook and screw-eye from the inside and then leave by the side door. A sheet metal track screwed to the door guides the hook as the door shuts, dropping it into the screw-eye and a large nail holds the hook so that it enters the track properly.

A HOME-MADE RAMP FOR CAR

When there is no pit available, wooden ramps will be found useful. They are about 3 ft. 6 in. long, formed of 9 x 1¼ in. wood with strong supports at the end, in order to raise the car 7 or 8 in. off the ground. The ramps must be splayed outwards to prevent their being pushed sideways in use.

Shorter supports can be put in at the middle to prevent springing. There must be stops at the upper ends and guides along the sides. Scotch the wheels and apply the brake when the car is on the ramp.

A SIMPLE RAMP FROM SANDBAGS

An easy way to raise wheels is to run them up on sacks filled with sand. It is easier, safe and quicker than resting the car on jacks. Chocks should be placed under the rear wheels, as shown.

The bags should be tightly filled, but not so tight that they will burst under the weight of the car.

SHELL
IN THE HOME
A Product for Every Purpose.

AeroShell Engine Oils, Fluids, Greases and Compounds

Automotive and Tractor Oils and Greases

Diesel Engine Oils and Greases

Marine Oils and Greases

Industrial Oils and Greases

Agricultural Machinery Oils and Greases

Specialised Cutting Fluids

Tanning and Textile Oils and Greases

Corrosion Preventives

Pennant Lighting Kerosine for all types of kerosine burning equipment

Shellite for petrol stoves, irons, lamps, etc.

Mineral Turpentine

White Spirit

Petroleum Solvents

Chemical Solvents

Naphthenic Oil Residue

Paraffin Wax

Aviation Gasolines

Motor Spirits

Cross Power Kerosine

Diesoline

Diesel Oil

Fuel Oil

Furnace Oil

Bitumen

Bituminous Paints

Flintkote

Colas

Colasmix

Terolas

Malariol

Shelltox

Household Oil

Lighting and Cleaning Fluid

Teepol

Spraying Oils

Defiance Blowfly Oil

Weevil Oil

Sheep Branding Oils and Marking Crayons

HEAD OFFICE: 163 WILLIAM STREET, MELBOURNE

BRANCHES: SYDNEY BRISBANE ADELAIDE PERTH HOBART

YOU CAN BE SURE OF SHELL

THE SHELL COMPANY OF AUSTRALIA LIMITED (Incorporated in Great Britain)   G 51

USEFUL HINTS FOR THE MOTORIST

A HANDY STOCK HURDLE FOR A TRUCK MADE FROM PIPE

Quite a useful design is shown here which is made of welded pipe.

It can be removed holus-bolus by means of a pulley and a rope to the top rail, and it should not be difficult to put a removable floor into a frame such as this. Doors could be sliding ones made on the principle of one pipe sliding into another.

This little idea should result in quite a saving of petrol, as a wooden frame can make a big difference owing to the extra wind resistance. Another thing is that a high wooden frame has a tendency to make the centre of gravity too high and causes sway.

MAKING A HURDLE FOR THE MOTOR TRUCK
An Easily-constructed Type

This small sketch might be of use to anyone wishing to construct some collapsible hurdles for carting hay and chaff, and at the same time enable him to cart sheep, pigs and cattle.

The hay frames can be made from bush timber in an hour or two.

Four fairly stout poles are used for the base, and a bolt at each corner holds them to the body of the truck. The length of these depends on the carrying capacity of the vehicle, as any desired amount of width can be given by adding extra side rails.

The hurdles can be made from gimlet or mallee poles, bolted or twitched together. When running empty, the hurdles can be lifted out and laid flat on the truck, although it is more convenient to make the front hurdle a fixture by adding two stays as shown by the dotted lines. Pine, from the point of view of lightness, would be a suitable timber for the sheep hurdles.

A good method would be to have the side hurdles fitting into

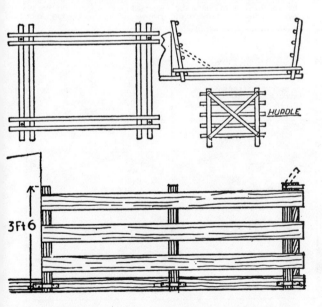

sockets or staples attached to the side of the truck with a loop of hoop-iron fitting over the end upright to hold the back hurdles in position. If it is necessary to carry cattle frequently, higher hurdles could be fitted, but if the animal's head is tied down to the floor, a cow can be carried safely even with the low hurdles.

A HOME-MADE COMBINATION RAMP AND RACE FOR LOADING TRUCKS

This has two advantages. It will combine a loading ramp for solid material, such as drums of petrol, oil, etc., and also a loading race for sheep and lambs.

It has the advantage in that it can be carted anywhere on the back of the truck, and it only takes two men to erect the whole thing in a very few minutes.

The sketch shows all the necessary details with the exception of the floor. That is made 16 in. wide from any suitable material, with cleats on top to provide a foothold for the sheep. This is simply laid on the ramp.

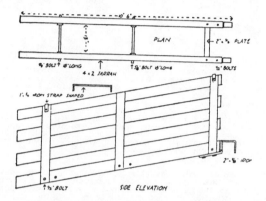

The two sides are held on with three $\frac{1}{2}$ in. bolts, and the two straps at the top provide them with the necessary rigidity. Any timber will do for the sides. The 18 x 5-8 in. bolts are made from broken harvester spokes, and the other bolts and plates are made from the scrap iron that can be found on any farm.

A HANDY METHOD OF FASTENING FLOOR OF STOCK TRUCKS

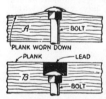

When the floor of the stock truck becomes worn, the boltheads are often left projecting as shown in the illustration at (A), which makes it difficult to clean the floor, since the shovel will continually catch on the bolt-heads projecting.

A good way to avoid this difficulty is to lay the planks as at "B" with the bolts countersunk considerably below the surface and then fill the holes with molten lead.

This provides a floor that remains comparatively smooth because the lead, being quite soft, wears down with the wood.

PROTECTING THE BACK OF TRUCK CABIN

This is an idea for the protection of the truck cabin when timber or any such article is carried and which might bump against the cabin and injure same.

In this case, pieces of old garden hose are used and are spaced about 6 in. apart and nailed or bolted horizontally to the back of the cabin as shown.

The hose cushions the back of the cabin so that when any part of the load jams against it, the cabin is neither broken nor damaged as it might otherwise have been.

USEFUL HINTS FOR THE MOTORIST

HINTS ON REPAIRING DENTED MUDGUARDS AT HOME

Few think of repairing a dented mudguard yet it is not very difficult if a little patience is exercised, and these few notes might therefore help someone who might be a little distant from an experienced man.

First of all, the tools needed are shown here, i.e., "A," a bumping hammer for heavy work, "B," a dinging hammer for light work, and "C," a half-hammer for use where space is limited.

Then get several dolly blocks "D," and an assortment of dinging spoons as at "G" and E." The former are used for raising low metal during the dinging process, whilst the latter act as pads between hammer and metal in transferring the force of the blow to the mudguard without marring its surface. A file completes the list, preferably an adjustable one as shown. These tools are all worth having as they are also useful for other purposes.

The first step is to remove all dirt from the top side of the mudguard, and then scrape the underside free of tar or other clinging particles with a wire brush. Next, spread a thin film of oil over both sides of the guard. It will reflect light on to hidden indentations, and also protect the paint while the fender is being repaired.

A basis rule of repair is that the dent must come out the way it went in. Though no two damaged fenders look alike, they are nothing more than a differently patterned series of ridges and valleys. Therefore, determine the path of the force that caused the pattern.

In repairing, work the last buckled ridge back to the point of the first contact. The larger dents are then removed first. This process is called bumping. Never try to bump out small dents. If the part to be repaired is folded into tight accordion" layers, bring these out by pulling on the mudguard or by prying the folds open with a dinging spoon.

Place a dinging spoon on the first ridge and strike the spoon a sharp blow with the bumping hammer. Never hammer at an angle; bring the hammer squarely down on the ridge. This starts the high metal down. Then start on the next high ridge and go through the same process until all the high metal has been beaten to the contour of the fender.

The general rule for using a **dolly** is to hold it against the low spot while you hammer at the high spot (see illustrations). Hammer off the dolly rather than squarely on it to prevent the metal from stretching.

In the case of a deep, narrow dent, remember to place the dolly directly underneath, exerting a vertical pressure, while you hammer at the rim of the dent.

When the dent is broad and shallow, place a dolly block opposite the side on which the dent was made and bump at the outer edges, working in towards the centre. Always use a dolly block having the same contour as that of the fender before it was damaged. Be sure your hammer and dolly surfaces are free of scratches and nicks to avoid scarring the fender surface.

When the high metal has been backed down to normal, the low metal can be sprung into position. It will go quite easily because the removal of the high metal has eliminated most of the strains on the fender. All you have to do is to bump lightly from underneath with a dolly block. If you fail to bump systematically, you may bring the high metal down further than it should go. A few careless blows may mean extra hours of work.

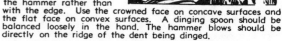

After all the larger dents have been smoothed out, dinging to remove the smaller dents is next (see illustrations). The principle behind it is similar to working metal on an anvil, the dolly block being the anvil. A dinging hammer should not be gripped too tightly, but it should be swung with enough flexibility so as to rebound to the starting position. Strike with the entire head of the hammer rather than with the edge. Use the crowned face on concave surfaces and the flat face on convex surfaces. A dinging spoon should be balanced loosely in the hand. The hammer blows should be directly on the ridge of the dent being dinged.

After bumping and dinging processes have brought the guard into normal shape, it is ready for finishing and painting. **Sight** across the back or front of the car to see if the guards line up evenly. If both have been damaged compare them with a car of similar make. You may bring a fender that is out of line back to its original position with a fender jack or by heating the brace.

Though the job may now seem perfectly smooth, slight irregularities will probably exist, but the finishing operation will take care of this.

The defects may be detected by holding a long piece of chalk flat against the damaged portion and rubbing it up and down. The high spots will be white while the low spots will be dark. The fingers alone are not sensitive enough to find the irregularities.

The correct way is to lower the elbow, lay the palm and fingers flat against the fender, and rub the hand up and down over the damaged area. Remove the small dents with a hammer and dolly.

Then use the file to smooth the surface.

Be careful not to file away too much metal. Pulling the file evenly along the contours will remove the tops of the high spots,

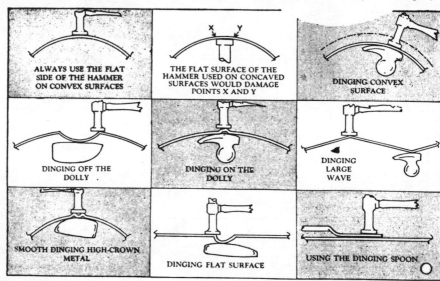

ALWAYS USE THE FLAT SIDE OF THE HAMMER ON CONVEX SURFACES

THE FLAT SURFACE OF THE HAMMER USED ON CONCAVED SURFACES WOULD DAMAGE POINTS X AND Y

DINGING CONVEX SURFACE

DINGING OFF THE DOLLY .

DINGING ON THE DOLLY

DINGING LARGE WAVE

SMOOTH DINGING HIGH-CROWN METAL

DINGING FLAT SURFACE

USING THE DINGING SPOON

thus revealing the final dents to be dinged away. Use the file again to prepare the surface for sanding. Wetting the sandpaper with petrol will clear the surface of dirt. When it is shiny it is ready for painting. First comes a coat of primer, then brush or spray on 3 or 4 coats of lacquer about 20 minutes apart, and when the final coat is dry, sand it with fine-grained sandpaper. Then apply a good body polish.

USEFUL HINTS FOR THE MOTORIST

HANDY RACKS FOR TRUCKS FROM PIPING, ETC.

This suggestion is a useful one to enable the carriage of tubing or timber on the truck. It is the use of piping, angle iron or other material for this purpose.

It need not, of course, be built on the top of the cabin and something could be fixed to the side but in this way it will make more room on the truck. If such an arrangement is placed on the side of the truck, it could, of course, be made removable so that it need not be carried on the truck all the time.

MAKING KEYS EASILY IDENTIFIABLE

DROPS OF SOLDER FOR IDENTIFICATION OF KEYS IN DARK

This is a very useful method of ensuring that one can easily find the right key in the dark.

It is often annoying to try every one but the right key, especially if it is desired to lock the car from the outside and it happens to be raining.

It is merely a few drops of solder put on the keys as shown—one drop for one particular key, two drops for another, and so on.

AN EASY METHOD OF LIFTING A BOGGED CAR

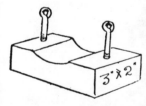

A simple set of gadgets to help lift a car out of a bog may be made from a piece of 3 x 2 hardwood and eight eye-bolts.

Each driving wheel should have two lifters, fixed in position with fine rope, as the knots can then be cut after use. If using wire to fix on, wire in such a way that the ends do not puncture covers. When the lifters are in position, get 4 stout saplings and lay them under the wheels if going forward, or behind if backing. The wood should be longer for a truck and there should be enough clearance under the mudguards. Before using lift the car with jack or pole and fulcrum, and put a little packing under the wheels.

It is a well-tried idea and very useful to a man who may be bogged when by himself. If the first lift is not enough take the car out, move the saplings forward one at a time and repeat the lift.

A SIMPLE LATCH TO ENGAGE GARAGE DOORS

This is a useful arrangement: a pair of latches such as shown here, attached to the sides of the garage will automatically engage the doors when they are opened.

The circular inset shows the latches which can be shaped out of a piece of flat iron.

These slip through slots cut in the doors, the slots being faced with pieces of flat iron to provide long-wearing surfaces for the latches to bear against.

PIPES SET IN GARAGE FLOOR TO ENGAGE DOOR BOLTS

When laying the garage floor, it is a good idea to leave holes for the door bolts, but these often have a tendency to chip away, leaving too much play to hold the doors snugly.

It is therefore better to set small lengths of pipe in the floor when it is laid, to take the bolts. This makes a neat job which will last indefinitely.

If possible, make the pipes project a little (if not in the way) so that dirt from the floor level will not clog them up.

FLEXIBLE GARAGE DOORSTOP FROM RADIATOR HOSE

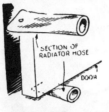

A good flexible door-stop can be made from old radiator hose as indicated here. Each piece is flattened and riveted at one end to make an elastic wedge and when the doors are slammed on to them, they make quite a good catch and hold them firmly.

It is then only necessary to push the doors in the opposite direction when necessary to open them. This is a very convenient and efficient arrangement.

TYRE BUFFERS IN GARAGE PROTECT MUD GUARDS, ETC.

With the increasing length of the motor car, the old garage is often very little longer than the car itself.

When this is the case, the front bumper not infrequently comes into contact with the end of the garage.

The result is a jolt to the garage. To avoid this, mount two halves of an old tyre on the wall as shown in the diagrams. The heavier the construction of the tyre the better.

If placed at convenient points in the garage they will save quite a lot of unnecessary damage.

MARK ON GARAGE WALL SHOWS BACKING LIMIT.

One sometimes uses the space against the wall of the garage for storing things, and it is then difficult to judge the correct distance when backing.

A vertical line painted on the side wall opposite one's head as one sits in his seat will overcome this, or a tennis ball can be suspended to just touch some part of the car when the desired point is reached.

BAG AS WARNING MARKER

This is another type of warning, as it will show the driver when his bumper bars are close to the wall. Suspended from the ceiling located so that it just touches the top portion of the wind shield, will give fair warning to the effect that the bumpers are within a few inches of the wall.

AFTER THE WAR . . . your very own home
with many conveniences to take the drudgery
out of housework . . . all your pet ideas in
interior decoration . . .

And on all the floors

FELTEX

*Insist on
Genuine Feltex
Look for the name*

FELT AND TEXTILES OF AUSTRALIA LTD.
Manufacturers of Plain and Marbled Feltex

INVEST IN COMMONWEALTH LOANS

HOME-MADE FURNITURE

From Packing Cases and Scrap Timber

FURNITURE FRAMES FROM ODD TIMBERS AND PACKING CASES

Good strong packing cases and other timber can be put to good use as frames for upholstered furniture of various sorts. When

designing a frame, especially for larger articles like armchairs and settees, it is best to err on the side of strength.

This class of furniture has a massive look after upholstering and is therefore subjected to heavier use than is accorded ordinary furniture, i.e., the arms of padded chairs are often made to do duty as seats, etc.

When making joints, adhere as far as possible to the conventional methods, such as mortises and tenons, because these are strongest. But joints using halving and screwing can be used where it would not be permissable in ordinary furniture, and reinforcing blocks can be used liberally.

All joins should be put together with glue, and all blocks should be screwed in position as well. In long pieces of furniture, such as seats, the longitudinal bracing can be done with blocks in the corners.

A few simple frames which can be easily made and covered at home are suggested here. A footstool (fig. 1) can be built up out of 1 in. board, with battens screwed underneath to prevent

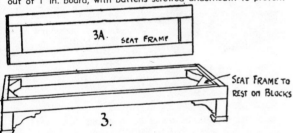

warping, and four turned legs or castors. The top is padded with flock or fibre, and covered with hessian before the final covering is tacked on.

Another footstool can be made with an open frame (fig. 2) with webbing tacked across to hold the stuffing. It may be upholstered with or without springs.

A simple fender stool or long footstool with a lift-out frame for taking the seat upholstery (fig. 3a) is shown in fig. 3. The rails are mortised into the short legs and further strengthened with blocks, which are set down 1 in. so as to form a sort of rebate on which the seat frame rests. The main frame of this is exposed, and should be of blackwood or similar timber.

The framework of a simple barrel seat for a child is shown in fig. 4. This can be built up very cheaply out of narrow boards with circular frames (fig. 5).

The frame for the seat should come down about 1 in. so that a loose frame, holding the actual upholstery, can be slipped into position. This is a very simple and effective piece of furniture.

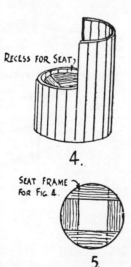

All these need only a remnant of shadow tissue or cretonne on top of the necessary padding and hessian to be made presentable enough for any room in the house, and many similar articles can be devised from any old timber by any handyman.

A KITCHEN DRESSER MADE FROM PIANO CASE

A very useful dresser may be made from a piano case with very little difficulty. A shelf, which is really the "table" part of

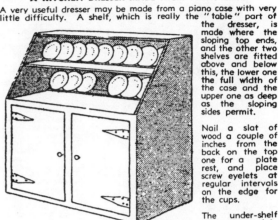

the dresser, is made where the sloping top ends, and the other two shelves are fitted above and below this, the lower one the full width of the case and the upper one as deep as the sloping sides permit.

Nail a slat of wood a couple of inches from the back on the top one for a plate rest, and place screw eyelets at regular intervals on the edge for the cups.

The under-shelf will accommodate saucepans which may be hidden by doors, or a cretonne curtain. The whole may be painted white or any light colour, to tone with the colour scheme of your kitchen.

A HANDY CABINET FROM BUTTER BOXES

A very handy cabinet can be made from five butter boxes complete with lids, five lengths of light pine batten, and the necessary hinges, screws and nails.

Take one box apart and with two sides subdivide two other boxes in order to form two shelves in these boxes. Next, nail the four boxes together to form the body of the cabinet, which will now have two cupboards below and two compartments above, each complete with shelf. The lids of the cases are hinged to the sides, thus forming four doors.

Furniture knobs are now required for the doors, but if they are not available, cotton reels with one end sawn off and fixed by means of a round-head wood screw through the hole in the reel will serve the purpose.

Now take the four lengths of batten and nail to the corners of the cabinet flush with the front and back, making the legs for the cabinet about 6 inches in length, and the remainder of the uprights extending beyond the top of the cabinet to carry the table top to be added next.

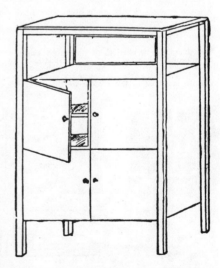

The remaining length of pine is cut into 4 lengths, suitable to be checked into or nailed between the uprights flush with the tops.

This forms a support for the top, which is constructed from the remaining two sides of the first butter box.

The cabinet is now complete from the constructional point of view.

These cases are generally quite smooth and clean and a rich dark varnish stain may next be applied. Two coats will give the cabinet a really smart appearance, and when finished, it will be found quite an artistic piece of furniture, suitable for many uses.

HOME-MADE FURNITURE FROM PACKING CASES

A HANDY MIRROR STAND

A handy stand for a small mirror to be used for shaving or on a dressing table can be made from a piece of 4 x 2 with a slanting cut made near one end and large enough for the mirror to fit into. It can be made decorative if sanded smooth and painted to match the mirror.

The illustration will show the arrangement suggested.

A USEFUL DRESSING TABLE FROM BOXES

A very commodious and yet quite good looking table can be made from kerosene cases or other such boxes.

These can be arranged in various ways.

This illustration gives one way of making such an article, showing the bare cases only, but a 3-ply top and sides (stained and polished) with a curtain over the front makes a big difference. The lower cases shown in the drawing have doors fitted in the ends.

ANOTHER HOME-MADE DRESSING TABLE FROM PACKING CASE

An attractive dressing table can be made from a large packing case as shown here. The first illustration gives an idea as to its finished appearance. A case about 28 in. wide, 30 in. high and 12 in. deep will be found suitable, but these measurements can be modified if necessary.

The top, front and bottom are removed. The bottom is replaced 4 in. above the floor and the bottom edges of the ends are cut to a simple ornamental shape, as shown. The front is cut up to make a partition and two or more shelves, which are nailed inside the case. A strip may be nailed along the upper edge of front.

A piece of wood, 3 in. wide, is nailed along the front edge of the top, thus making it 15 in. wide, and the corners are cut off. The top is then replaced, and strips of ornamental beading are pinned around the edges.

Two doors will be needed, and these are easily made from pieces of plywood, 26 in. x 14 in. Wooden strips 2 in. wide and $\frac{1}{4}$ in. thick are tacked around the edges as shown in fig. 2. These doors are hinged to the front edges of the ends and a small ornamental handle is fitted in the middle of the inner edge of the doors.

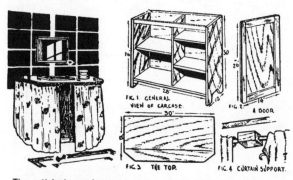

FIG. 1. GENERAL VIEW OF CARCASE.

FIG. 2. A DOOR

FIG. 3. THE TOP.

FIG. 4 CURTAIN SUPPORT.

The article is sandpapered at this stage and is then given two coats of quick drying enamel in a light shade of grey, blue or green. Curtains of some floral material are fitted along ends and front. Fig. 4 shows details of front curtains which are the only ones that are movable.

ENLARGING A TABLE

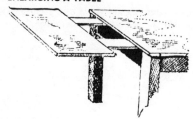

Procure two 5 ft. lengths of 3 x 1 hardwood or 3 x 1½ oregon. Cut two slots in one end cross-bearer of the table as close to the top as possible, so that the 2 lengths of timber will slide neatly to the extent of 2½ feet.

Nail to the protruding ends some flooring boards the width of the table top, and finish with a coat of stain or paint. This extension, if made accurately as above, may be slipped in as the occasion arises, and will be quite firm.

KNEE-HOLE DESK MADE FROM PACKING CASES

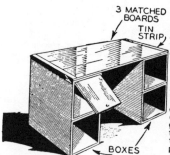

3 MATCHED BOARDS

TIN STRIP

BOXES

This type of desk will make quite a good study table, yet it costs very little more than the price of the paint. Apart from the packing cases, which can usually be found about the place, only a little spare time work is needed.

Three wide boards will do for the top or, for preference, some good matched boards, as they will give a good smooth surface, but almost any material such as metal, or plate glass can be used.

Apart from the top, all that is needed is 4 boxes of about equal size, say around 26 in. x 15 in. x 12 in. wide; then nail the boxes together as indicated, then neatly fit strips of tin to the top edges. Finally, sandpaper and enamel carefully.

CLOTHES PEG HEADS MAKE GOOD KNOBS FOR SMALL DRAWERS

CUT

This idea should be useful for quite a number of things. In making a small cabinet like the one illustrated to be used in the kitchen or workshop or for small tools, screws, etc., or for keeping sugar, flour, tea, etc., a good idea is to use the heads off some clothes pegs as shown.

They provide neat and easily made drawer pulls. Screws from inside, screwed through the drawer front, will attach these knobs.

FURNITURE FROM PETROL CASES OR PETROL BOXES

With 6 petrol cases, a dozen petrol tins, and a pot of paint, a useful piece of furniture can be made. Nail the cases together side by side and 3 deep, then cut one side completely off the tins, and knock the rough edges down.

By placing the tins inside the cases, taking care that the handles are on the outside, the cabinet is complete. The names of the contents can be painted on and the top can be used as a table. This would be good for either kitchen or workshop.

HOME-MADE FURNITURE FROM PACKING CASES

A KITCHEN STOOL FROM BOX

This is a useful and handy type of stool which can be quickly and easily put together for use in either kitchen or workshop.

The illustration will show its construction—it is 12 inches across, whilst the support for the seat is a box about 4 inches square made from some $\frac{3}{4}$ inch material about a foot or so long.

The legs are made from 2 x 1 in. of strong, straight-grained timber screwed on to the box with $1\frac{1}{2}$ inch screws. It would be particularly adaptable for the workshop as the round seat makes it very convenient.

A HOME-MADE TABLE LAMP FROM SCRAP WOOD

A length of flex and an electric globe is all that is needed to make this handy lamp. The wood can be of any scrap and the material for the shade (about 1 yard) can be made from any left over from other jobs around the place.

Dimensions will, of course, vary according to requirements, but for a guide, the following measurements of the wooden support are given:

Two slats of wood 1 in. x 1 in. x 14 in.; two blocks of wood 1 x 1 x 6 in.; two blocks of wood 1 x 1 x 3 in.; and one block of 1 in. x $\frac{1}{2}$ in. x $\frac{1}{2}$ in. Inch nails are used to join the blocks and slats.

Nail the ends of the long slats to the middle of the 6 in. blocks. Stand on the table a quarter of an inch apart and nail the three inch blocks on to the six inch blocks, and bring the flex between the two slats.

The Shade. With a sharp knife, cut 8 strips of fairly stout cardboard, 8 in. long and 1 in. wide.

Score them lengthwise down the middle, and bend them into a right angle. Fasten four together at the end with paper fasteners to form a square.

Cut a piece of cardboard 2 in. square for the top, and fasten a strip from each corner, to the corners of the base. Cut a heavy piece of cardboard to be fixed across the middle of the base, with a hole cut in it to take the neck of the globe.

Paste a covering of cloth or parchment over the frame, and paint, lacquer or stain the wooden parts as desired.

A VEGETABLE RACK FROM BUTTER BOXES

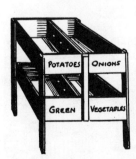

This is a very useful addition to kitchen equipment and is something which can be easily and quickly made.

The materials needed are — two boxes with lids will do, about 14 ft. of 2 x 1 battens, cut into 4 lengths 2 ft., and six 1 in. countersunk screws.

First cut the butter boxes in halves and screw them together as shown, using countersunk screws.

The longer battens are nailed to the ends of the boxes as indicated in the drawing (for a stronger job, screws could be used). The two shorter lengths are nailed down over the centre joints of the boxes to act as cover strips. Care should be taken before joining the boxes to plane off all brands. Finish with a coat of white enamel and label divisions.

A USEFUL COUCH OF OLD INNER TUBES

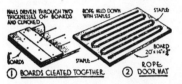

This is simply made. The frame is of wood and the inner tubes, partially inflated, take the place of the springs.

The cover can be made by using wool or other filling and if a valance is attached, to come down nearly to the floor, this could be made an attractive piece of furniture as well as a comfortable one. The idea is clearly shown in the sketch.

A DOORMAT FROM ROPE

This makes quite a serviceable doormat. Select a piece of wood, say 20 in. x 14 in. x $\frac{3}{4}$ in. If nothing else is available, a number of 3-8 in. narrow-width boards cleated together as in fig. 1 will do.

The nails should be long enough to go right through the two thicknesses of wood, and the projecting points of the nails can be clinched over to prevent their withdrawal. Then select some thick rope to fix on the top of the board with wire staples, metal brackets, or long nails bent over, see fig. 2. If $\frac{1}{2}$ in. rope is used, a 1 in. space can be left between the rows, but thicker rope can be spaced further apart. When the mat requires cleaning it is easy to take the dirt out, and if necessary it can be cleaned by scrubbing with soap and water.

A COMBINATION WRITING TABLE, BOOKCASE AND LINEN PRESS FROM PETROL CASES

This is a useful home-made article from petrol cases. It comprises 14 cases, 1 sheet of 3-ply, 6 x 4 ft.; 5 yards of cretonne; 2 drawer-pulls, two drop handles, 4 pairs of hinges, $\frac{1}{4}$ yard of baize, some lacquer or stain. Fancy beading will enhance the appearance but it is not really necessary.

The measurements of the finished article are: height, 5 ft. 3 in.; length, 7 ft.; writing table, $3\frac{1}{2}$ ft. long x 14 in. wide.

Procedure: Arrange 6 boxes as shown on the left; decide what shelves will be required and use box ends for some. Nail all boxes securely in position. Repeat this process for right-hand side of combination. Then cut one box in half for the table. To fit as in diagram this can be done only in one way as will be seen when working. Nail these halves end to end, and place battens of box-wood on open sides to support drawers. Make two drawers to fit halves and attach drawer-pulls. Nail table in position, thus joining the two ends of the combination.

Brackets can be used to add strength. Cut out shaped back and make small shelves to hold pens, ink, etc. Nail in position.

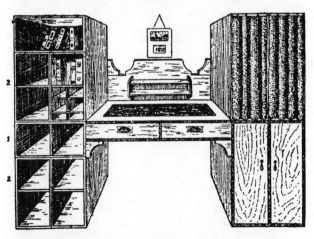

Glue $\frac{1}{4}$ yard (9 in. x 37) of baize on to table. From plywood cut out two doors, fix drop handles and hinges and attach to boxes, as diagram. Lacquer or stain combination.

HOME-MADE FURNITURE, ETC.

HINTS ON MAKING PICTURE FRAMES AT HOME

One often has things worth framing and if one can use a saw and hammer, a frame can be made at very little cost. Suitable mouldings can be purchased, whilst the only other things needed are a piece of glass the same size as the picture, a piece of cardboard for the back, and some small nails.

A mitre box or block on which the corners of the frame sides are cut will also be needed but one can easily be made (fig. 1) from two scraps of wood. The upper piece is about half as wide as the lower one to which it is securely nailed. Two saw cuts are made at angles of 45 deg. to the front edge, making sure that they are quite perpendicular.

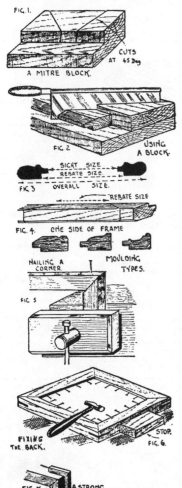

FIG. 1.
CUTS AT 45 Deg
A MITRE BLOCK.

FIG. 2.
USING A BLOCK.

SIGHT SIZE
REBATE SIZE
FIG. 3 OVERALL SIZE.

REBATE SIZE
FIG. 4. ONE SIDE OF FRAME

NAILING A CORNER.
MOULDING TYPES.

FIG. 5

STOP.
FIXING THE BACK.
FIG. 6.

FIG. 7.
A STRONG CORNER

Next, choose some suitable mouldings— a simple, fairly narrow one usually being the most suitable.

Before starting to measure and cut the sides, the various measurements to be considered should be studied (see fig. 3).

The space between the inner edges determines the amount of the picture that will be seen; the rebate size will be the same size as the picture, and the overall size gives the outside measurements of the frame.

The rebate size must be carefully marked on the back of the moulding, which may then be put on the mitre block, and sawn to size (fig. 2), though it is advisable to put the moulding on the block with back uppermost, so that any sawcuts may be made exactly on the marks, or at least not inside them.

Saw a little on the outside of the marks as a side may be shortened if too long, but cannot be lengthened. The sides should be assembled with the glass in place to see if the corners fit before being finally nailed together.

A little trimming with chisel or sandpaper may be necessary to make a perfect corner fit.

Fig. 5 shows the best way to nail corners together. One side is clamped in a vice with only a small part of the end showing. An other side is placed against it with the mitred faces in contact, but with the upper edge a little higher than its final position. A little glue between the faces as they are fixed will make a stronger joint.

Fig. 7 shows another method of strengthening the corners. A saw-cut is made through both pieces at the corner and a thin piece of wood is glued in this cut, the edges afterwards being made flush with the edges of the frame sides.

Nothing now remains but to assemble the picture and the glass in the frame, and fix in the cardboard backing piece. This piece of cardboard is the same size as the glass, and should be fairly thick. The glass must be cleaned on both sides before being put in the frame, and the frame is held against a stop as the nails are driven in (fig. 6). The stop is merely a block of wood fixed to the bench.

The frame is finished by putting in two small screw-eyes to hold the wire or cord which supports the frame on the wall.

MAKING A FOLDING TABLE FROM BOXES

The convenience of this lies in the fact that it can be folded up and, at the same time hold a number of utensils.

Two shallow boxes are hinged together to form the top, and the legs are bolted at the four corners, as shown, so that they can be folded within the top. Suitable straps or hooks and screw-eyes hold the two boxes together when closed. It is best to make the sides and ends of the boxes of 1 in. stock, about $2\frac{1}{2}$ or 3 in. wide.

The bottom is made of 3-8 in. plywood or other thin timber. The legs should be made of 1 in. material, preferably hardwood, 28 in. long. They should be tapered from a width of 3 in. at the top to 1 in. at the bottom. The top end of the legs must be rounded to prevent binding when they are folded inside the top. When bolting the legs in place, do not shut them tight up in the corners; they should be set back about $\frac{1}{4}$ in. from the corners, so that when the table is set up, they will project outward at the bottom.

HOME-MADE BOOKCASE WITH CORRUGATED BACK TO KEEP BOOKS ERECT

CORRUGATED CARDBOARD

The problem of keeping books neatly erect in a bookcase, especially when the shelves are not entirely filled, can be solved by strips of corrugated cardboard or iron fastened to the back of the case.

The books are pushed against the corrugations to prevent them from tipping.

Where the depth of the bookcase is greater than that of the books which are aligned with the front edge of the shelves, only the last book need be pressed against the corrugated backing.

Books will not tip when one is removed if corrugated cardboard is glued to the back of the case

SIMPLE AND ATTRACTIVE BOOKCASE MADE FROM BRICKS

Ordinary bricks make quite a good bookcase, especially when colours are used which harmonise with the room.

Take five boards of any desired length, and as wide as your bricks are long. Place one brick on each end for the base, three bricks between shelves and two on top. A coat of paint on the boards completes the job and the bricks can be given a coat of shellac or varnish.

BOARD
ROUGH BUILDING BRICK

HOME-MADE BENT TUBE FURNITURE

How to Make Useful Articles from Conduit or other Tubular Material

These useful ideas from an overseas source may be found of interest to any who may desire to make things of this nature from materials on hand or easily acquired as any of the very attractive designs shown here can be easily and inexpensively made by any average 'handyman.'

The Bending Jig. This is, of course, the first thing required and a simple arrangement made on the above lines would be quite sufficient. The illustration explains itself, there being two rectangular blocks of wood and a turning disc placed in the position as set out in the sketch.

It is advisable to turn a groove in the disc to avoid flattening the piping on the bends, and, as an added precaution, it is also advisable to fill up the tubes with sand and plug the ends before trying to bend them. It is also a good idea (as shown in the sketch) to bend the material a little more than the angle required to allow for any spring in the material.

Size of Material. Experience has taught that $\frac{1}{2}$ in. material may be heavy enough for such things as children's furniture, but it is a little light for most things and therefore $\frac{3}{4}$ in. material would be better for heavier work and wear.

The illustrations given show a fair range of articles which can easily be attempted by anyone and the drawings should also provide a good method of going about the work.

The particular models shown were actually made from conduit, as it is a material soft enough to bend in a cold state, yet it will remain sufficiently rigid to withstand quite a lot of work.

Tables and chairs are quite simple propositions for the beginner and the illustrations shown will be found almost self-explanatory with regard to the method of shaping and forming the different articles.

In this latter connection it is a good idea to draw a full-size plan to scale along the lines indicated alongside two or three of the sketches before starting to bend the material, and then lay the plan down on the floor as a pattern to work on. This will make for greater accuracy and will help avoid mistakes.

As an instance we point out the two different types of chairs shown in the previous column, together with the scale alongside each. If the necessary scale is drawn and the shape of the article drawn on that scale, the tubular material can then be bent to the exact shape needed for the particular furniture that it is desired to make.

There can also be different designs of legs as is indicated in the drawing at the foot of this column.

Each leg is formed from a single piece of piping bent to any shape provided the bends to represent the bottom of the legs are all uniform and enable the table or chair to stand perfectly square and level.

It can be arranged that one portion of the tube fits into the other where it crosses and fixed by means of screws through the tubing or other such way.

To fix such legs to the tops of the table or chair, wooden plugs can be driven into the tops of the legs. One type of suggested plug is shown in the lower illustration. The top can then be secured by screwing into these wooden plugs and the table or chair top can then be finished off with lino or other material as desired.

The seat bearers shown in the lower illustrations can also be secured by plugging at the ends, which are then filed concave and secured by means of long screws, or full length rods pinned over the ends.

There is not space in this article to enlarge upon the construction of each article, but, if the methods indicated above are followed and the drawings and scale carefully studied, a very good job can be done and when one gets into the swing of the thing, the rest will become easy.

Several suggestions for chairs and tables are given in these illustrations and by combining these ideas with one's own requirements, some very attractive sets of furniture can be made. One of the main things necessary is to take a little care and make a good bending jig along the lines of that shown in para. 1. It will help considerably in effecting good work.

HOME-MADE FURNITURE, ETC.

A COMBINED TROUGH AND TABLE

A very handy table can easily be made which can be fitted over the wash or other trough in washhouse or workshop. It will be found very useful indeed.

The trough can be made from an old oil drum, cut in two lengthwise. One-half will make the trough and by using both halves a longer trough can be made.

The framework is made of old angle iron and the lid of old timber.

The finished article should be about 26 inches in this particular instance but measurements will have to be made to suit.

NOVEL FOLDING SHELVES FOR CAMPING OR OTHER USES

This novel idea is one which might be very useful on a number of occasions, the shelves being collapsible and made in such a manner that they can be folded into a very small space and thus assist easy transport from place to place.

They are easy to construct and require only plain hand tools, whilst old packing cases would be quite sufficient as far as the timber is concerned, although, of course, other finished timber will make a better job.

The only other things needed are 5 steel or brass rods of the length indicated in the sketch.

One end of each rod is bent over as a stop when the rod is dropped into position—this is clearly shown in the drawing. When assembled the shelves will stand sturdily or, if necessary, they may be hung from a tree or other convenient object.

When taken apart, they make a very compact bundle for stowing away in a convenient place for transport.

The illustration shows the general overall dimensions and assembly details but the dimensions may, of course, be altered to suit individual requirement. However, the size given here should be very convenient for all-round use.

Standard 8-inch boards are used throughout (7¾ milled) into which are inserted the shelf-slots on both the sides and back as illustrated.

The shelves have metal tabs screwed to their undersides which fit in the slots which have been cut through the back and side planks. Holes in the outer ends of the tabs accommodate the rods, which lock the whole business together when slid into place.

The shelves may be assembled and fixed as shown in the smaller detail. They can be stained and given two coats of spare varnish. Protected thus, they will be easy to clean and will last indefinitely, barring, of course, any breakages.

This is quite a novel idea and might suggest itself as something worth having on hand, as, in addition to keeping them for any camping out trips which might be necessary, they can easily be moved about on the farm or station to places where they are wanted from time to time.

FLY-PROOFING HOUSES

The following notes are the experience of one country house owner and they might be of interest to those who have had little experience in this respect and who might wish to do this type of work. The notes include a useful extending screen which is particularly useful to some types of windows.

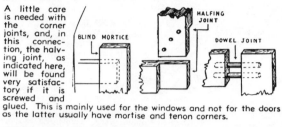

A little care is needed with the corner joints, and, in this connection, the halving joint, as indicated here, will be found very satisfactory if it is screwed and glued. This is mainly used for the windows and not for the doors as the latter usually have mortise and tenon corners.

With regard to the latter, it is better to use the "blind" mortise, as shown in the left-hand side of the above illustration, i.e., one that does not show the outside edge.

The other joint shown above is the dowel and this may be used if a jig is available to ensure accurate drilling. As regards the timber to be used, it is best in all cases, to have a good straight-grained pine rather than woods such as jarrah, as it is easier to work and better in most respects.

The sketches shown above will give the amateur a good selection of the joints to use and how to make them, whilst the sketches at the foot of this column give several ideas with regard to the many and various patterns for doors which may be made; for instance, if making doors for a house where there are children, or perhaps a dog, it is a good idea to use panels of 3-ply wood for the bottom section.

The extending screen shown at left is from one journal and is a very good idea; it can be made either as indicated here or to open and shut upwards. Its construction is clearly shown and indicates how strap metal runners are fixed on each section, so that they can slide across or up and down as desired.

Some care is needed when it comes to nailing the netting on as it should be done nice and tightly, and the following procedure might therefore be helpful to some.

The first thing is to cut the netting to the approximate size, leaving, say, ¾ in. for a turnover on each side, top and bottom.

Then pull the wire tight and put a tack in each corner, without actually driving it home. Then nail along the shortest side, seeing that the tacks are only partially inserted into the wood on a slant, and they are gradually straightened up as they are firmly nailed in. Each tack will then tighten the wire a little.

Next, take one of the long sides, and proceed in a similar manner—then do the other long side, and finish on the second short side. It only needs a little practice to find that the job can be easily and successfully done.

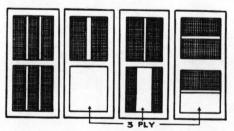

When finishing off, turn the surplus wire in and put some tacks through the two thicknesses, covering it with beading. Do not overstrain the wire or it may later on give way.

USEFUL IDEAS ROUND THE HOME

A NOVEL STEAM HEATER FOR THE STOVE

Keeping meals hot for several people if they are delayed at work can be solved by a steam heater operated from a kettle. It will need the minimum of fire and attention.

A good butter or other box is required. Remove the lid, which is used for a door, hinged to the side. Cut a hole 6 inches in diameter in the top of the box for a saucepan. Nail 3 cleats on

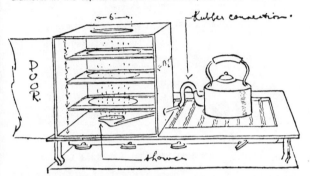

the inside of each side of the box, using, say, 1 x ½ pine, the first one to be 3 inches from the bottom and the other two 3 in. apart. On these cleats put two pieces of 1 x ½ in. wood cut to size for shelves. Fix a shower spray on the open bottom facing upwards. To this fix a small length of piping, which should project about 3 in. outside the box. This pipe is joined to the spout of the kettle by a piece of hose-pipe. A small jet or fire will keep the kettle boiling and the dinner hot. Our illustration shows a gas stove in operation, but one can easily convert a wooden stove to the same use.

AN EASILY MADE PLATE DRAIN RACK

This is one simple design, the cost being lessened by having 1 row of rods instead of the customary two. There are 3 rails at the back and 2 at the front, cut from 1½ x ¾ material, sawn and squared to length. In the 3 back rails 3-8 in. holes are bored for the rods, right through the top 2 rails and 1 in. into the bottom.

The holes for the rods are bored at 1½ in. from centre to centre. Start each hole with a bradawl. Make the two uprights at each end 2 x ¾ in. They are held together by 3 short cross-pieces 1 x 1¾ in. and 8½ in. long respectively, fixed to the uprights with brass screws, this being shown in the side view. An overlap will be noticed on the bottom and second of these cross-pieces.

Unless round-head screws are used, it will be necessary to countersink the screw heads into the wood.

To facilitate screwing the back rails to the end frames, the front uprights at each

SIDE

end are unscrewed. On the inner top edges of the two front rails small notches must be cut to provide places for plates to rest. Two cuts at 45 deg. will answer the purpose.

Bore holes at each end and screw the front rails in place. By lengthening the timber in the cross-rails 1¾ x ¾ in. for strength.

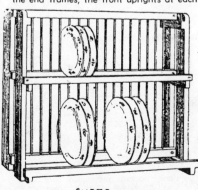

SKETCH

ANOTHER TYPE OF HOME-MADE PLATE DRAINER

Whilst on the subject of handy kitchen aids, the following design for another handy plate drainer might be found useful.

In this illustration (which is really one of a portable type), the plates are held by the notches in the bottom and they rest against the central handle, which enables the drainer and plates to be bodily moved about from place to place.

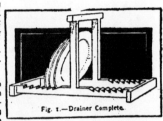

As indicated, the drainer will hold a dozen plates and the length may be increased if more accommodation is desired.

Figures 2 and 3 show the dimensions to which a dozen size drainer should be framed.

Material required is 1 in. thick, the following being required: Two sides 1 ft. 9 in. long x 1¼ in. wide; two ends 9 in. long x 1½ in. wide; two uprights 1 ft. 1¼ in. long x 1 in. wide; and a handle 9 in. long x 1 in. wide.

The parts are framed up with mortise-and-tenon joints secured with wooden pins, the sides being framed into the ends, the uprights into the sides, and the handle to the ends of the upright.

Fig. 1.—Drainer Complete.

The notches in the sides may be cut after the framing is complete, but before the joints are fixed. A depth of ½ in. is sufficient for the notches. They are spaced as shown in fig. 4, and may easily be cut with a tenon saw and chisel.

COOKING "CLOCKS" FOR THE STOVE

This is a handy thing to make for the stove. It is very often difficult to remember how long certain foods have been cooking when several of them are on the stove together.

If so, a set of clock dials, one for each burner, painted on a strip of cardboard or metal and attached to the back of the stove

When you put the food on the stove just set the dial to indicate time for removal

will help avoid this trouble. Each dial is provided with two pivoted hands just like a clock. When the food is put on the stove, the hands are set to indicate the time it should be removed.

SUNDRY OTHER HOME-MADE ARTICLES FOR THE HOME

A NON-SAGGING CLOTHES LINE

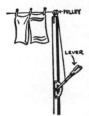

There are several ways of keeping the clothes line from sagging, and this is one of them, whilst it is, at the same time, a good and easy method.

In this, a lever from an old farm machine is used to apply the pressure. As will be seen, the end of the line is then attached to it and the line runs up over a pulley in the top of the post.

By pulling or releasing the lever, the line is easily tightened or lowered as required and needs only a moment's adjustment.

ANOTHER CLOTHES LINE HINT

Sagging clothes line will not slide off props and thus let their burdens become soiled if slotted props, such as the one shown here, are used.

Bore two holes first to form the ends of the slots; then, with a fine saw, cut the V-shaped notch in from the edge and saw out the stock between the holes. It is a very efficient arrangement.

ELEVATING A CLOTHES LINE

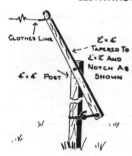

In order to keep your clothes high and out of reach of anything, try this method of elevating it. It is a great help in keeping long pieces of laundry from dragging on the ground and is a convenient way of tightening a line also.

The idea is simply to attach the clothes line to levers which are bolted to each post. By pulling down on the levers, the line is elevated. The ropes are used to pull down the levers until the line is tight and then are wrapped round the post and fastened.

ANOTHER NOVEL METHOD OF TAKING SLACK OUT OF CLOTHES LINE

When the clothes line sags under the weight of hanging clothes which might be wet, it can be "lifted" up with little effort if you

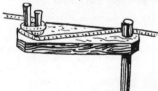

have a wooden tightener that twists the line round its two fingers as shown in this sketch.

You simply insert the line between the prongs and give the tightener one, two or three turns as the case may be until the rope is taut, then use a projecting section of the handle to keep it from unwinding. As will be seen, it is easily made and will be a boon on occasions when the weather is inclined to be windy.

A SIMPLE SHOE CLEANER

This is a useful idea for the home, i.e an economical shoe scraper. All you do is to cut an old worn out broom in the manner shown here, fastening the butt of the handle into a bit of wood and nailing it on to one of the steps when you will have a handy article which will help keep the house clean of dirty marks from muddy shoes.

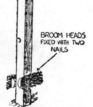

BROOM HEADS FIXED WITH TWO NAILS

The second idea is shown on the right. Again, when the broom gets worn, drive in a post about 4 ft. high and nail two old broom heads to this and you will have an excellent gadget for removing soil from boots before going into the house. Both are quickly and easily made and will be found well worth while.

A HOME-MADE STOVE-PIPE CLEANER

All that is required for this handy kitchen aid is an old scrubbing brush and a strip of wood for a handle.

The handle is screwed on to the back of the brush as shown. It will make a cleaner job than pounding the pipes, and, furthermore, the job is not so messy if done with this type of cleaner.

A KITCHEN KNIFE RACK FROM COTTON REELS

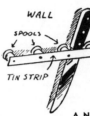

Special knives for different jobs are often wanted at odd times and this method of keeping them always at hand is a useful one. The idea can also be used in the workshop for the various tools there.

This rack is made with four or five spools and a strip of tin a foot or so long. The nails hold the tin against the spools and the spools to a suitable place on the wall.

A NOVEL TIGHTENER FOR JAR LIDS

All you need in order to make a jar tightener is a piece of wood and a strap as shown in this illustration.

The strap is nailed to the handle, as shown. It is quite a good idea to have two of these, one to hold the jar and the other to tighten the lid. It can also be used for loosening tight lids.

HOW TO OPEN STUBBORN JAR TOPS

When the top of a sealed jar becomes obstinate and persistently refuses to yield to all the pressure that can be applied in the ordinary way, this simple method may turn the trick and the top.

Use part of an old belt or strap with the buckle on it in the manner shown in the accompanying sketch.

A NOVEL ADJUSTMENT FOR WINDOWS

This is a useful idea when the sash cord of a window may become broken and difficulty is experienced in keeping it open.

This shaped stick is cut from a piece of common board and can be made to hold the window at various heights.

Several of them can be used, one at each window. Measurements are given in the illustration and they are very simple and easy to make.

A HOME-MADE LAWN SWING

This is a good swing, easy to make. The seat is an old couch spring. The ends are of light, but strong, metal, and the whole is suspended in light chains, with hooks to go in the holes of the end pieces.

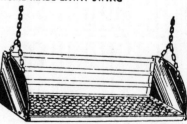

By hooking the chains in different holes, the seat can be tipped back to any comfortable angle. Placed in a shady spot this will be a real luxury and well worth the making.

SUNDRY OTHER HOME-MADE ARTICLES FOR THE HOME

A USEFUL LIGHT CLOTHES DRIER

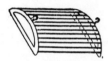

This is a handy little arrangement for drying light things like handkerchiefs, stockings, etc.

Just take two ordinary wooden clothes hangers and attach pieces of strong wire, about 16 or 18 inches long, between them. It can be hung up near the kitchen fire.

NOVEL SEWING COMPANION

This novel sewing stand enables one to keep several reels of cotton, needles, pins and thimbles within easy reach and is quite easy to make.

The base consists of two parts, the lower one 3-8 in. thick, so that the stand will be firm. The upper one is 3-16ths thick. Variations to suit can, of course, be made, but it is advisable to mark out patterns first on paper. Clean up the edges of both bases with sandpaper.

Besides having a circular tray and an oblong one cut into it, the upper part of the base has two slots at the sides into which the tenons at the bottom of the upright pieces fit.

These uprights are cut from ¼ in. wood, and are glued in place. Each piece has 3 holes drilled in it to take the lengths of thin dowel rod, which hold the reels of cotton. The rods are 6 in. long, and small, round wooden knobs are glued on the ends.

The stand has a plain top 5½ in. x 1¾ in. x ¼ in., with its edges rounded off with fine and coarse sandpaper. It is held on top of the uprights with glue and fine nails.

When the rods are pushed through the first holes and the reels threaded on, they should fit the second set of holes just tightly enough to hold them in place. The completed stand is cleaned up with fine sandpaper, and stained and polished.

PORTABLE SEWING STAND FOR ALL ARTICLES

Any part of your home can be converted into a sewing nook with this folding screen, the back of which is equipped with pockets and shelves to accommodate sewing materials.

When not in use, the screen can be folded and set away. One panel is provided with small hooks at the top for hanging up unfinished garments, sewing apron or frock, clothes-hangers, etc.

FOLDING SCREEN

The centre panel is equipped with three or more pockets sewed on to a strip of oilcloth or cotton.

The outside panel has narrow spool shelves near the top. Below this is a series of pockets to take care of the smaller articles needed in sewing.

In the centre is a deep pocket for scissors; on either side are shallow pockets to hold such articles as tape measure, thimble, cards of fasteners, needlebooks and other miscellaneous items.

A square pin cushion, flat at the back, is hung at one side on a drapery hook. At the bottom of the panel a large bag serves as a waste-basket. Holes punched at one side slip over small hooks on the panel, so that the bag can be removed for emptying.

A USEFUL HINT FOR THE POWER PLUG

This is a useful hint for the electric light plug should it be found too tight fitting for easy manipulation. One can assist withdrawal by taping it in the manner shown.

This will ease the strain on the cord and will allow the plug to be pulled from the power point very much easier than would otherwise be the case.

WIND FRICTION TAPE AROUND WIRE

ONE WAY OF PROTECTING FURNITURE SURFACES

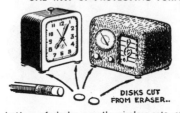

DISKS CUT FROM ERASER..

Very often mantlepieces or other furniture surfaces become scratched or damaged by other articles being placed on them and subsequently moved.

To protect against this, cut some small rubber discs, say from a pencil eraser and glue such discs to the bottom of clocks, mantle wireless sets, etc., as shown here. They will act as vibration dampers and will prevent many scratches.

PROTECTING WALLS AND WALLPAPER FROM BACKS OF CHAIRS

RUBBER-HEADED TACKS

Walls and wallpaper are often damaged by the backs of chairs and other furniture coming into contact with or rubbing against them.

This can be avoided to a certain extent by inserting some rubber or cushion tacks into the backs of the chairs, as shown here. They can protrude sufficiently to take the bump against the wall should the chair be suddenly moved or if people sitting in them should force the chairs against the wall. Rubber strips could also be tacked along the top of the chairs for the same purpose.

AVOIDING MARKS ON WALLS FROM PICTURE FRAMES

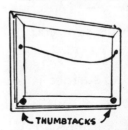

THUMBTACKS

This is a somewhat similar idea to the above. Rubber thumb tacks or other somewhat similar articles can be inserted or put on to the lower corners of the back of a picture frame for the purpose of providing an air space between the frame and the wall.

This will keep a dust line from marking the wall, and will avoid possible damage when putting the pictures back on the wall after spring cleaning or when one may find it necessary to change them around.

RUBBER HOSE AS TEMPORARY WHEELS FOR CHILDREN'S PRAMS OR TOYS

This is quite a good idea for replacing worn out rubber wheels on prams or on children's toys, such as tricycles, carts, etc. Take some fairly heavy ½ in. or other suitable size hose, and four ordinary door or other similar springs and fit them as shown.

Cut the lengths of hose one inch longer than the circumference of the wheel and **stretch** the spring through each length of hose as shown at 2, then join the end loops with strong wire as at 3. Force the hose ends as tightly together as possible—the spring, if it has been stdetched, will do this. A clip can also be used if necessary on the sides to keep it together. The hose can be turned occasionally in order to obtain a new wearing surface.

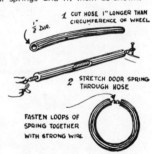

1 CUT HOSE 1" LONGER THAN CIRCUMFERENCE OF WHEEL

½ DIA.

2 STRETCH DOOR SPRING THROUGH HOSE

FASTEN LOOPS OF SPRING TOGETHER WITH STRONG WIRE

HOUSEWIVES

CIGARETTE

PIPE

& CIGAR SMOKERS

ALL AGREE ...

the best Matches

are made by **BRYANT & MAY**

What's the first item on your shopping list today — Matches? Then be sure you get Bryant & May's. The  striking surface is now not only on both sides of the box . . . but it is improved. And the match itself is improved. With those straight grained, steady burning sticks, the heads never fly off, and there's no waste at all. So always insist on Bryant & May's.

EVERY STRIKE A CERTAIN LIGHT!

POINTS FOR PICNICKERS AND CAMPERS

BOILING THE BILLY

A good working knowledge as to how to boil the billy is well worthwhile, as many do not know how to make a good job of it.

BUILD FIRE 'UNDER HERE

The first idea shown is a very good and complete one. Two good sized logs are placed parallel to each other and the fire is built in between them. The pots can then be hung either with wire or with some good strong green sticks shaped as shown in the sketch.

When the wood has burned down to hot embers, some smaller green sticks can be placed across them, as shown, for the frying pan, as the embers underneath form a perfect frying fire. You must watch and see that the sticks do not burn through and let the frying pan fall, but if they do burn, just replace them with new ones.

All that is then needed are two strong uprights and a crosspiece when boiling and frying can be done at the same time. Dinner will then be ready in no time.

Two other useful methods are also shown in the accompanying illustrations. One of them shows a tripod arrangement with a small length of chain (or other material such as wire) to hold the billy in position.

This is quickly and easily made and is quite sufficient for occasions when there is only one billy to boil.

The third idea is merely that of a sapling resting against a log in such a manner that it will hold the billy over the fire. This, too, is a quick and easy arrangement.

In building a fire of any sort, it is good practice to always clear a good space all round the site first of all and see that the fire is completely extinguished before leaving the locality.

A SIMPLE CAMP STOVE

A very handy camp stove for use when camping or out harvesting, etc., can be made as shown.

Merely take four pieces of light strap iron, two of them 2 ft. long, and the other two 22 in. long. In each end of each piece, drill a small hole and rivet them together. Mark the 2 ft. pieces 6 inches from the corners and bend them down to form the legs.

Then drill two holes in the centre of the top cross-pieces and rivet a piece of sheet metal upside down to the frame. When using, dig a hole in the ground over which to place the stove.

PROVIDING WARMTH FOR TENT OR IN OPEN AIR

This is a very useful idea for both heating and cooking as well as providing warmth.

The sketch illustrates the idea which consists of two stout logs from 12 in. to 2 feet apart driven into the ground propped against two or more stout posts, the arrangement leaning back against such props at the angle shown.

A fire built like this will burn all night and will throw the heat forwards into the open end of the tent or wherever it is desired to have heat.

To keep the fire going all night, cover it with ashes and it will then burn slowly for hours.

If the fire is also required for cooking or boiling the billy, some other such arrangement as indicated above can be added as the occasion arises.

A NOVEL COLLAPSIBLE PICNIC TABLE

This handy picnic tray is easily made and very convenient.

All you have to do is to cut a piece of plywood, 12 in. square and get a piece of broomstick about 22 in. long. Sharpen one end of the latter so that it can be pushed into the ground. The top of the broomstick is made to fit into the centre of the plywood square, either as a fixture or so that it can be taken to pieces easily.

USEFUL HOME-MADE TENT SHELTERS

These sketches indicate two useful types of simple home-made shelters, both of which can be improvised at short notice, inasmuch as forked sticks and a log can be secured at almost any camp site.

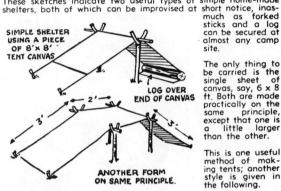

SIMPLE SHELTER USING A PIECE OF 8' x 8' TENT CANVAS

LOG OVER END OF CANVAS

ANOTHER FORM ON SAME PRINCIPLE.

The only thing to be carried is the single sheet of canvas, say, 6 x 8 ft. Both are made practically on the same principle, except that one is a little larger than the other.

This is one useful method of making tents; another style is given in the following.

ANOTHER HANDY HOME-MADE TENT

The only framework needed is two light poles and two pegs. The poles are pressed into the ground about 8 or 10 feet apart and are brought together and fastened at the top with a joint as shown, or by passing a string through two screw-eyes placed one on each pole.

The tent is made from 4 triangular sheets of duck or drill, one being cut up the centre and hemmed to form a doorway (see fig. 2). These pieces are sewn together at the edges, the corners and apex being reinforced with stout canvas. Cords are stitched to the corners by which to attach them to the pegs.

To erect the tent, put up the two poles in the shape of an inverted V, and draw the tent cloth over them with the opposite seams and corners fitting over the poles. Draw out the other two corners and tie them to stout pegs, as shown. It is a good idea to hem a strong light cord all round the bottom of the tent for strength and especially across the door side (leaving the flaps free of the cord). This will not be in the way, as it will lie across the opening on the ground, but it will greatly strengthen the tent.

This type of tent can be made large or small as desired, but it is suggested that the sides be made with an 8 ft. base. If

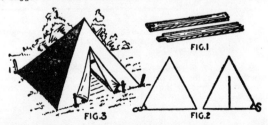

FIG.1

FIG.3   FIG.2

each side of the triangle is made this length, the tent will be almost 7 feet high at the peak. First draw the plans carefully to scale before actually cutting up the material.

HOW TO DESTROY DOMESTIC ANIMALS

OTHER USEFUL IDEAS IN CONNECTION WITH STOCK

The information given here is taken from the instructions issued by the Royal Society for the Prevention of Cruelty to Animals and included here in order that the information might be at hand in case such a job might be necessary at a moment's notice.

However, if an animal is badly wounded, contact should be established as quickly as possible with the nearest veterinary authority but if the beast is obviously beyond hope, and delay would entail cruelty, the following are the directions given for their destruction. This is given, of course, as a last resort and so that the job will be done with the least pain and to avoid needless suffering on the part of the beast concerned.

The directions show the spot on an animal's head where the instrument should be placed or pointed, and the angle at which it should be held, in order to obtain the best results.

HORSE. Draw an imaginary line from the base of each ear to the opposite eye, the intersection of the lines being the centre, which, if hit, ensures instant loss of consciousness.

When using a revolver, place it within a few inches of the head; with either rifle or shotgun, a short range of a couple of feet is best.

If absolutely impossible to aim at the centre of the forehead (i.e., if the horse is down in a confined spot), shoot into the base of the ear across the brain. The marked position is better if it is at all possible.

COWS OR LARGE CATTLE. "C" is the brain. Fire towards the same spot aimed at when pole-axing. Point slightly towards the top of the head.

INSTRUCTIONS FOR DESTROYING DOMESTIC ANIMALS

PIG. "C" is the brain. Fire about a finger's width above the level of the eyes. To avoid the risk of firing into the snout instead of the brain, give the instrument a slight tilt as shown by the arrow in the illustration.

CALF. "C" is the brain. Aim at the forehead "A" rather lower than for large cattle, as the upper part of a calf's brain is often undeveloped. Or place the instrument at the back of the skull near the ears and point it towards the nose and snout. (See arrow "B".)

CATS. Failing the lethal chamber or chloroform, if A CHEMIST IS AVAILABLE, hydrocyanic acid is sudden and effective.

If the animal is nervous or vicious, a swab of cotton wool on a wire and soaked in the acid is seized by the cat through a small aperture in its container, and death is then immediate.

A small lethal chamber is easily made where coal gas or exhaust gas from a car is available, by leading the gas by a tube into an airtight receiver, such as a kerosene tin placed open end down on the ground, and weighted or held in order to prevent it being upset. Painless asphyxiation is rapidly brought about.

Shooting Cats, except by a marksman, is not recommended on account of the smallness of the vital organs exposed, but in cases of **great emergency** and to save suffering, dislocation of the cervical vertebrae, as in the case of a rabbit, may be resorted to.

Also, one may resort to drowning, if it is properly carried out, the cat being

DOG. Shoot at the point indicated at the back of the head, as the dog is less suspicious, and the medulla and cerebellum are then totally destroyed.

If this position is impossible, shoot in the centre of the head above the eyes at the spot marked, pointing the instrument downward and backward so that the charge will destroy the spinal cord as well.

SHEEP. "AB" is the skull under the wool. "C" is the brain. Aim at the top of the head between the ears, and tilt to point slightly forward, as shown by the arrow.

placed in a bucket of water QUITE FULL, with a well-weighted board on top.

These latter methods, however, SHOULD ONLY BE RESORTED TO IN CASES OF EMERGENCY, and where other means of destroying an injured cat are impossible.

By including these notes, we hope that we will be able to help further the good work which is being done by the Royal Society for the Prevention of Cruelty to Animals, because in a book such as this, the information is at hand just when wanted and so be the means of preventing any undue suffering which might otherwise be the case.

FIRST AID

This section is included in this book in order that the information might be useful at some time or other just when it is perhaps wanted, especially by someone who may be some distance from medical attention.

Although the publisher cannot, of course, accept any responsibility in connection with same, readers can rest assured that the information is compiled from reliable sources.

Acknowledgment. Quite a number of the illustrations on page 325 and on are taken from the book " First Aid in Pictures," by Mr. David J. Farrell, of Sydney, which book we think is one of the best available on the subject. It is one containing many more illustrations that we have shown here, and can be thoroughly recommended. To Mr. Farrell we extend our thanks for permission to reproduce such illustrations in order to benefit Blinded Soldiers, etc.

WHAT TO DO UNTIL THE DOCTOR COMES

Articles to keep ready for use. These should be in some place readily accessible and out of the way of children. A pair of scissors, 3 or 4 large needles (threaded), at least 4 triangular bandages (cut from a 40 in. square of calico), 3 or 4 rolls of bandage; some gauze or clean linen for dressings; some lint; oil silk; cotton-wool for padding; olive oil; some safety pins; enamel basins; and a small quantity of boracic acid in powder; a small bottle of iodine; some adhesive plaster and 2 or more large handkerchiefs. Some bottles of other home-made antiseptic lotion can also be kept.

Useful Home-made Lotions. A bottle of bicarbonate of soda lotion can be made by dissolving 1 teaspoonful of bicarbonate of soda in ½ pint of boiling water. Use this strength for **burns.** For **eye-baths,** reduce this lotion with 4 parts of boiling water. Allow the lotion to cool before using.

A second bottle of solution can be prepared by dissolving ½ teaspoonful of salt in ½ pint of boiling water, i.e., **Saline Solution.** Use as a mild antiseptic, a lotion for bathing and swabbing wounds, and as a gargle. Reduce with 2 pints boiling water for eye-baths.

Sterilising Dressings. One way is to immerse in boiling water a selected tin to hold the dressings, and then allow to dry by evaporation. Line the tin with a piece of clean cloth, and place the strips of gauze or clean linen in the tin. Cover with the cloth, put on the lid, and bake in a fairly hot oven, but not so hot that the dressings will scorch. Leave the tin in the oven for about an hour. On removal from the oven, seal down the lid with sticking plaster to prevent the entry of air and germs. Dressings treated in this way should be quite free from germ infection.

A USEFUL FIRST AID CABINET

This useful article has a convenient drop door, a shelf for medicine bottles, and 2 drawers for bandages, etc. Planed 3-8 in. wood

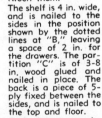

can be used for the sides, which are 15 in. long and 7 in. wide, shaped at top and bottom as indicated. The bottom and top parts, also of 3-8 in. wood, are each 14½ in. long and 6¾ in. wide. These are screwed to the sides, as in diagram "A," allowing a space of 11 in. between them.

The shelf is 4 in. wide, and is nailed to the sides in the position shown by the dotted lines at "B," leaving a space of 2 in. for the drawers. The partition "C" is of 3-8 in. wood glued and nailed in place. The back is a piece of 5-ply fixed between the sides, and is nailed to the top and floor.

Each drawer can be made with 5 pieces of planed ¼ in. wood glued and screwed together as shown at "B." A small knob can be screwed into the front of each drawer.

To make the door, plane up some strips of wood, 1½ in. wide x ¼ in. thick, and saw off two pieces each 11 in. and 11½ in. Glue and screw these to a plywood backing to give a panel effect, as shown at "E," and fix a small knob and catch. Cut two slots

"FF" for the hinges and fix these to the door and floor with brass screws.

Two lengths of chromium-plated chain, attached to screw-eyes, can be used for supporting the door in its position. Give the finished cabinet 2 coats of white enamel.

A USEFUL HOME-MADE FIRST AID BOX

A square-shaped one, such as that shown here, is best, as it will not fall over easily and it will allow any bottles to stand upright. Its construction is very simple.

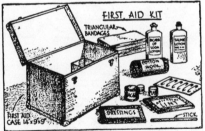

In this, you will have space for most of the articles shown in the opposite column as being necessary to have on hand, the large handkerchiefs mentioned being very handy in case it is necessary to apply a tourniquet (see article on precautions to be taken in this connection).

HOW TO SECURE A SPLINT

Learn how to apply splints properly and practise to keep your hand in. Never try to force a bone which has protruded through the skin. Apply cotton-wool and a light bandage to exclude germs and air.

The first-aider should always remember that the patient is relying implicitly on the assistance given, so that it is more than ever necessary to be competent to give that assistance.

WHAT TO DO TILL THE DOCTOR COMES

FIRST AID TO THE INJURED

HOW TO MAKE A SET OF SPLINTS

A suitable set of splints for average requirements can be made with 3-8 in. wood of the dimensions given in this diagram, but if you wish, additional splints can be prepared.

The splints for the arm should be 3 inches in width, while the leg splints should be 4 inch. It is advisable to round off all corners and the sharp edges with a rasp, and then all surfaces can be smoothed with sandpaper.

When a bone is broken, it is referred to as a fracture, and the first-aider's obligation is merely to provide a support in the form of splints in order to prevent complications developing.

Since shock is always increased by pain, most people who break a limb suffer from shock. Splints are used to immobilise the limb so that the broken pieces of bone will not rub on each other and the surrounding tissue, and thus cause needless suffering.

Splints should be fitted firmly, and should be long enough to extend above and below the joints on either side of the fracture. Always place the splints on the limb, and never the limb on the splint. If necessary, they can be fitted over the top of the clothing.

If no splints are available in an emergency, you can use such articles as broom handles, walking sticks, pieces of wood, an umbrella, tightly folded newspaper, cardboard, or anything that is firm and long enough to provide adequate support.

If no splints are available, place a broken arm in a comfortable position against the body and bandage it firmly in this position; tie a broken leg firmly to the good leg. If a patient is seriously injured do not waste time tinkering with him. Place him gently on a stretcher and get him to hospital quickly.

HOW TO BLANKET A STRETCHER

The "blanketing" of a patient on a stretcher should be done in certain definite ways. The larger of the two diagrams given below shows how to use 2 blankets and the other one 3 blankets

and the blankets cannot then be very easily disarranged.

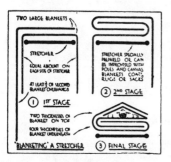

We will explain the larger one of the two : If you fold the two large blankets into 3, it will be an easy matter to arrange them on the stretcher. The middle third of the first blanket should be placed on the stretcher with one-third hanging down over each side. The second blanket has one-third over the stretcher and two-thirds hanging down one side.

Then the free one-third of the first blanket is folded back over the stretcher (fig. 2), and then the second blanket is folded over.

The patient can be lifted on to the stretcher and covered with the 3 free ends of the blankets as shown in fig. 3.

The usual method of lifting a patient on to the stretcher is for 3 bearers to kneel on the left side of the patient, and then to carefully raise the patient on to or up to the height of the knees.

Another bearer pushes the stretcher under the patient, so that he can be gently lowered on to it.

HOW TO TIE A REEF KNOT

This knot is important and, with practice, is simple to apply. It will not slip when strain is applied, and it is in contrast to the "granny" (shown here), which will not hold.

The usual explanation of tying right over left, then left over right, can be easily misunderstood, but a study of these sketches will assist.

"Reef" Knot   " Granny "

Using a piece of cord, go through the stages shown, watch each movement carefully and you will soon be able to do it blindfolded.

Note the way the light portions of the

 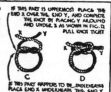

cord, as well as the dark portions, come out on the same side of the loops in the knot. Practice with bandages.

HOW TO LIFT HEAVY WEIGHTS

This illustration depicts an excellent idea that may be the means of saving a life. If a person is pinned under a heavy weight, such as the wall of a building, or a slab of concrete, it is possible to raise that heavy weight by means of a long pole and a block of wood.

Push the end of a long pole, or an iron bar, under the object to be lifted, place a large block of wood under the pole as near to the object as is possible and exert pressure or your full weight on the free end of the pole. Usually the object can be easily raised, but if it is impossible to make a movement, you must either push the block nearer to the object or obtain a longer pole.

With the object raised sufficiently, a block of some description can be placed under it by another person to hold it in that position until the rescue is effected.

HOW TO PREPARE TRIANGULAR BANDAGES

The triangular bandage is one of the most important items of equipment and every farm or station should see that one of its number has a working knowledge of its application.

The main uses of bandages are to hold dressings in place; to protect the injured part; to keep splints firmly in position; to afford support to an injured limb, and to make pressure and thus prevent or reduce swelling. You can make two triangular bandages by cutting a 40-in. square of clean cloth, such as linen or calico from corner to corner. You should have 4 of these bandages. The long edge is called the base, the opposite corner

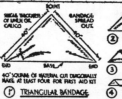 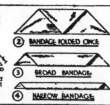

is the point, and the two other corners are called ends.

Sometimes, as in the case of a sling, the bandage is used open, whilst for certain other purposes, the point of the bandage is brought down to the centre of the base (see 2) and is folded over again to form the broad bandage (3). A narrow bandage (4) is made by folding the broad bandage once.

WHAT TO DO TILL THE DOCTOR COMES

FIRST AID TO THE INJURED

BLEEDING, ETC.

For bleeding other than arterial bleeding, just bandage a dressing firmly over the wound. If the bleeding is from the leg, or arm, make the patient lie down and raise the limb.

For bleeding from the nose. Make the patient lie down on his side with the head on a high pillow. Apply cold, wet cloths to the back of the neck.

Internal Bleeding. If anyone is hurt internally, there may be indications as to where the injury might be. For instance, if blood is coughed up and is bright red and frothy, it will indicate that the LUNGS have been injured.

If the blood is at all coffee-coloured, it will probably be vomited up from the STOMACH and if the BLADDER is injured, the patient may not be able to pass water, or if he can, it will probably be stained with blood. The latter might also indicate injury to the KIDNEYS.

Injury to the LIVER and INTESTINES do not bring up blood but it will cause swelling.

The latter are usually accompanied by signs of severe shock—a cold, clammy skin, pale-faced, and shallow breathing, possibly yawning. The patient should be kept as quiet as possible. Keep him lying as comfortably as possible, loosen clothing at the neck and waist, and wrap him warmly in rugs. Give nothing at all to drink. Call for a doctor or get him to hospital as soon as possible.

PRESSURE POINTS YOU SHOULD KNOW

With simply acquired knowledge, a little care, and a cool head, you can easily stop bleeding that might otherwise result in loss of life within a couple of minutes.

If the bleeding is bright red; if it spurts out to correspond with the pulsations of the heart, and flows from the side of the wound nearest the heart, you will know that AN ARTERY has been severed, and it must be stopped at once. Some direct pressure should be applied on a pressure point between the wound and the heart to stop the bleeding. This illustration shows the pressure points —that is, the points where an artery can be pressed with the thumb or the fingers against a bone or cartilege to cut off the supply of blood This may allow a clot to form and thus stop bleeding; a dressing firmly bandaged over the wound will then be sufficient.

If an artery has been severed **in or above the throat,** the pressure should be at the throat, pressing from the front against the spine just to one side of the windpipe. A second pressure can also be effected above the bleeding point to stop the blood from flowing from the jugular vein.

Three pressure points are most important.

1. To control bleeding from the shoulder or arm, press deeply downwards behind the centre of the collarbone with the thumb.

2. To control bleeding from the lower part of the arm, grasp the upper arm from behind with the fingers on the inner side, press the flat not the tips of the fingers firmly against the bone of the arm.

3. To control bleeding from the leg, pressure should be placed on the centre of the groin against the pelvis with one thumb over the other and the injured leg should be raised as shown in another illustration. Keep the pressure up without ceasing till the doctor comes.

MAIN ARTERIES OF THE BODY

ALSO SHOWING PRESSURE POINTS

HOW TO DRESS A SURFACE WOUND

This is quite simple, but it is important not to touch with the fingers any part of the wound, or any portion of the dressing that will make contact with the wound. Unless previously washed in an antiseptic solution, the fingers are usually contaminated with germs.

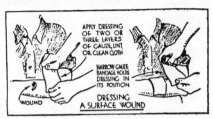

DRESSING A SURFACE WOUND

Be careful also to remove foreign bodies from the wound and if the wound is very dirty, wash with sterilised or fresh boiled water, an antiseptic or a saline solution (see page 279). Always wash away from the wound. If there is any possibility of contamination with tetanus germs, seek medical advice at once regarding an anti-toxic injection.

Over the wound you should place 2 or 3 layers of perfectly clean gauze (sterilised for preference), lint, or a folded handkerchief, which should be held in place with a few turns of gauze bandage or another handkerchief. If you wish, an antiseptic lotion can be applied to the wound, but you should not apply ointment because of likely germ infection. Try to avoid exposure to the air longer than is necessary.

Clean dressings can be prepared by washing and boiling pieces of soft cloth for at least 20 minutes, then wash the hands thoroughly, and iron the cloths with as little handling as possible.

HOW TO APPLY A TOURNIQUET

Firstly and most important, a tourniquet should NOT be applied at all unless as a last resort—one should become familiar with pressure points in order to keep blood back, but if this is not possible and the wound is of a serious nature, it can then and then only be applied. However, **it is very important not to use it unless it is imperative.** More harm than good is often done in this way.

The above diagram shows the first stages of application. A bandage should be rolled tightly to form a compact pad. Place it right on the pressure point on the limb near to the wound and on the heart side. Secure the pad there with a second bandage, which is tied with a half reef knot on the opposite side of the wound; lay a stick on the half-knot, and complete the reef knot.

It has been shown how a pad should be placed on the pressure point with a bandage to hold it in position. As the reef knot is being tied, a short stout stick is inserted in the knot, and this is twisted until sufficient pressure is applied to hold up the flow of blood from the wound. Do not twist more than is necessary.

You should then place a turn of another bandage around the free end of the stick, and tie the bandage around the arm to prevent the stick from twisting back.

It is important to release the tourniquet every 10 to 15 minutes to prevent damage to the nerves and structure of the limb. Do not leave a person unattended while a tourniquet is on, in case fainting should develop. If the bone in the limb is not broken, elevate it until bleeding ceases and then, in the case of an arm wound, the limb can be placed in a sling. If the wound is on the head, you must rely on finger pressure at the pressure points.

APPLYING PRESSURE WITH A TOURNIQUET...FINAL STAGES

PLACE ARM IN SLING

Usually a dressing held very firmly on a minor wound will cause the blood to clot and thus arrest bleeding, but this method cannot be relied upon if the flow of blood is strong.

WHAT TO DO TILL THE DOCTOR COMES

FIRST AID TO THE INJURED

BANDAGES AND BANDAGING

THE ROLLER BANDAGE AND ITS APPLICATION

The following notes and accompanying illustrations may be helpful to those who are not very conversant with the manner in which the roller bandage should be used for various injuries.

The drawings show by arrows the direction in which the roller should be unwound and placed on the arm, leg or body as the case may be.

For the fingers the bandages should be ¾ in. wide, but for other purposes wider bandages usually are used.

The top left-hand illustration shows the Capeline Bandage for **the Head,** the method of applying being clearly shown by the small arrows indicated on each fold.

On the right is the simple Spiral Bandage for **the Fingers** (No. 2).

No. 3 indicates the procedure to be followed in bandaging various injuries to the hand, arm, wrist and thumb, viz.: The top gives details of the bandage for the **Forearm and Hand** — the centre sketch indicates the figure 8 bandage for **the Hand** only and the lower one shows the spica bandage for **the Thumb.**

No. 4 is the figure 8 type of bandage which is used for the **Elbow,** and its method of application is clearly shown.

No. 5 is another view of the spiral bandage for the **Forearm** and **Hand.**

No. 2

No. 3

No. 4

No. 6

No. 5

No. 6 shows the method of bandaging the **Leg** from knee to the instep. This is done on the figure 8 principle.

One or two other types of bandage are also given at the foot of this page.

With a little practice and care, one can soon master this useful art as it may prove very useful at any unexpected time. The sketches given are from a competent authority, and should enable one to become quite efficient.

Figure 8 bandage for Foot or Ankle

Spica Bandage for Groin or Hip

The Spica Bandage for Shoulder

HEAD BANDAGES

These sketches show how to apply bandages to the Head, all dressings being completely covered by the bandages to prevent them from moving.

For the Scalp. It is easy to protect the scalp or to keep a dressing in place, if it is done in this way. First, make a 1½ in. fold along the long base of the triangular bandage. Place the middle of the folded edge across the forehead just above the eyebrows, and allow the remainder of the bandage to rest across the top of the head with the point hanging down the back of the neck as shown. Then bring each of the two free ends right on round the back of the head above the ears as shown in the first sketch, tying them together in the centre of the forehead with a reef knot.

The point of the bandage hanging down the back can then be lifted up over the top and fixed to the bandage with a safety pin.

Face and Head (the Bridal Bandage). For a wound in the head or face, it is generally necessary to apply over the wound a dressing and then a bandage to keep it in place. If injuries are on certain parts of the forehead, cheek, chin, top of head, or back of head, a face and head bandage can be applied. This requires a fairly narrow bandage.

The middle third of the bandage should rest on the injured side of the face and then the free ends on the sound side can be crossed (see first sketch) and carried round the head. They are then tied where they cross each other at the side of the head—this is the most comfortable place for the injured person. The bandage then serves as a pad for the knot, and it will keep dressings on various parts of the head.

Eye Bandages. If the eyes are injured and it is necessary to bandage them, first place a pad or dressing over the injured eye, and then fold the bandage as indicated in the drawing—tying it over the dressing. See that it is firmly fixed without causing any inconvenience.

Other Useful Head Bandages. There are a number of other bandages which can be applied for various parts of the head, some being on similar lines to the eye bandage already shown. For instance, there is one for the side of the head, as shown here on the left, whilst that on the right is on similar lines to the four-tailed jaw bandage given

in the next sketch, and can be used for any part of the head.

The illustration of what is known as the four-tailed bandage is self-explanatory and it provides a very secure and excellent support for such things as broken jaws. Each of the 4 tails are brought together and knotted in the places shown.

The last four illustrations comprise the following :

Top Left: Bandage for fracture of **Lower Jaw,** in which two bandages are needed.

Top Right: Bandage for **Forehead,** which is somewhat similar to others shown here.

Bottom Left: A ring pad used to relieve pressure where a fracture or a foreign body is suspected.

Bottom Right: A bandage for the **Ear.**

WHAT TO DO TILL THE DOCTOR COMES

FIRST AID TO THE INJURED

BANDAGING OF THE ARM, ETC.

THE LARGE ARM SLING

This sling is to support the arm when the injury is below the elbow. It is easy to apply and allows the injured arm to relax.

A large triangular bandage is spread over the front of the patient as shown. He should bend his injured arm at right angles, and support it across the body.

Then place one end of the bandage over the shoulder on the sound side, and pass it around the back of the neck to rest on the shoulder of the injured side.

The lower corner of the bandage is pulled up over the arm to the shoulder, where the two corners are tied together with a reef knot. The knot should rest in the hollow just above the collar bone. The surplus bandage at the elbow can be tucked in between bandage and elbow, and fixed there with a safety pin.

It is important that the tips of the patient's fingers should be free beyond the edge of the bandage. In the event of a bandage not being available, the coat sleeve in which the injured arm is placed can be pinned to the coat, or else the lower edge of the coat can be turned up and pinned above the forearm, or the hand can be pushed into an unbuttoned portion of the vest.

THE SMALL ARM SLING

This is made along somewhat similar lines to the above, except that it is made by folding the bandage broad as in fig. 3 of the sketch on page 280, under "How to prepare triangular bandages." It supports the wrist, and at the same time, allows the elbow to hang freely. First, place one end of this bandage over the shoulder and then pass it round the neck. Then place the wrist over the centre of the bandage and raise the other end in order to tie same near the neck as shown.

THE ELEVATED SLING FOR FOREARM AND HAND

This type of sling is intended to keep the hand well raised, more or less as indicated in the left-hand illustration. When a collar-bone is broken it is advisable to also insert a rolled pad of material, say 4 in. x 2, and place it in the armpit on the injured side. Then complete the bandage, allowing the knot to rest in the hollow just above the collar-bone.

Injuries of this nature should receive early medical attention for the purpose of setting the bone in its correct position.

For fractured collarbone or shoulder blade or severe hand bleeding.

THE CHEST BANDAGE

Place the bandage firmly over the dressing with the point over the shoulder on the same side; then fold a hem along the base of the bandage; carry the ends around the waist and tie them, leaving one end longer than the other, then draw the point over the shoulder and tie it to the longer end. The sketch will show the finished bandage. **For the back** the bandage is applied in the same way except that it is begun at the back.

ELBOW AND KNEE BANDAGES

Elbow   Knee

These bandages fold over both knee and elbow and yet allow for a little movement. When commencing, bend the elbow and knee a little so that this movement can be allowed for.

FRACTURED BONES

The actual setting of fractures should be left in the hands of the Doctor, as unskilled handling can do much harm, but it is important that a fractured limb should be secured in splints before the injured person is lifted.

A simple fracture is one where the bone has a clean break; a compound one is where the broken bone protrudes through the skin or a wound leads down to the fracture. General symptoms are indicated by pain and tenderness, swelling, loss of power in the limb, deformity, an unnatural movement or position of the limb, or the bone may be felt just underneath the skin. All breaks should be splinted on the spot, care being taken to prevent further injury.

Fractured Elbow. This requires great care and serious complications may be saved if correctly applied.

A fractured elbow will swell at the joint. Use a 24 in. strip of cloth material at least 1 in. wide; bind a 15 x 3 in. and a 12 x 3 in. splint together at right angles to form an L shape. The 12 in. upright should reach to the armpit and extend below the elbow, while the 15 in. horizontal should reach beyond the elbow and the finger tips. The splint can be placed on either the inside or outside of the arm, depending on which side is least injured.

Pad the surfaces which make contact with the arm, especially over the bony parts. Then fix the splint in position with three bandages. Place one round the upper arm, and two round the forearm, leaving the finger tips free. A large arm sling can then be put on to support the arm and a cold compress placed over the fractured part to reduce the swelling.

Fractured Wrist. A well-padded splint, 3 in. wide, should be applied to the forearm, so that it goes well under or overlaps the elbow at one end and the fingers at the other. The splint is then secured with 2 bandages, one to hold the splint to the upper part of the forearm, and the other forming a figure 8 around the hand. The ends are tied with reef knots. The arm should then be supported in a large sling, and a broad bandage fastened around the arm and the chest in order to minimise movement.

A Broken Leg. If both bones of the lower leg are fractured, there will be no doubt about the injury, but often when only one bone is broken, the deformity is not so noticeable. When the smaller bone is broken, the patient may be able to stand fairly well, because the other bone serves as a splint, and, if the break occurs near the ankle, it is easy to mistake it for a sprain. There may also be considerable discolouration of the skin over the fracture.

If a third person is present have him steady the leg by holding the ankle and the foot, and then gently draw the foot into its natural position. The leg should not be allowed to slip into any other position while the splints are being applied.

If no actual splints are available, use a walking stick or some other stout piece of wood or iron, or, if nothing is available, both legs could be tied together at the thighs, ankles and feet.

Showing single-handed treatment

If only one splint is available, bandaging can be done as shown on the left, or, if working single-handed, all bandages can be tied round both legs as indicated. If two splints can be used, they should be applied to the outer and inner sides of the leg, and extend from above the knee to beyond the foot. Tie the bandage first above the fracture and then one just below the fracture; one around the ankle; one over the knee; and then the others can be arranged to suit.

I Fractured Leg

WHAT TO DO TILL THE DOCTOR COMES

FIRST AID TO THE INJURED

A FRACTURED FOOT

This injury is indicated by pain, loss of power, and swelling of foot. First, remove the boot and sock (perhaps by cutting away),

and apply a well-padded splint to the sole of the foot by means of two bandages as shown in the sketch.

The first bandage should be taken around the ankle and the splint in the form of a figure 8, and then brought to the side of the foot, or the back of the splint, where the ends are tied with a reef knot.

Fractured Foot

The other bandage is taken two or three times around the toes and the splint before tying. The splint should be a little longer than the foot, and the foot should be raised slightly on a low pad or cushion.

A BROKEN ANKLE

A splint is fixed to the sole of the foot in the same manner as described for a broken foot, and then supported by two splints, which should extend from below the foot to beyond the knee (in the same style as outlined for a broken leg). This can be secured with four bandages, two around the lower leg, one around the ankle to hold the foot firm, and one above the knees.

A FRACTURED KNEECAP

Indications are great pain, helplessness of the limb, irregularity, and swelling.

Allow the patient to lie face upwards, on a high pillow, and

then carefully push a long splint under the limb to reach from beyond the heel to the buttock.

Fractured Knee-cap

Place a good size pad in the natural hollow under the ankle, to raise the heel, as shown. Fasten the splint around the thigh and lower leg. Tie where shown, one being tied on the upper surface of the splint just under the bottom of the foot. A cold compress placed over the fracture will reduce swelling.

A FRACTURED THIGH

Indications of a fractured thigh will be pain, loss of power swelling and discolouration, irregularity of the bone, the foot will lie on its outer side, the limb may be slightly shorter than the other limb, and the patient, when lying on the back, cannot raise the heel from the ground.

Have someone to steady the limb at the ankle, while you pass the seven bandages under the natural hollows of the limb and the body by means of the flat stick.

Then carefully pull the bandages into positions indicated in the illustration; apply a splint on the outside of the body and the leg to extend from the armpit to beyond the foot, and a second splint the full length of the leg on the inside surface.

As you tie the leg bandages, have an assistant gently draw the foot down to the same level as the other foot, and be most careful that the leg is not allowed to slip back into its former position.

The lowest bandage makes a figure 8 around the foot and the splint, and the ends are tied with a reef knot under the foot.

Two broad bandages should be fixed around the body or they could all be tied right around as indicated.

Fractured Thigh Bone

Do not attempt removal of the patient until splinting has been completed and some form of stretcher is available, and even then take particular care to prevent movement of the injured part.

FRACTURED UPPER ARM

First, support the forearm across the chest at right angles to the upper arm and apply a narrow sling. You can use either 2 or 3 splints, and they should extend just beyond the elbow joint and beyond the shoulder. The splints should be padded especially over the bony prominences.

In addition to the bandage round the forearm, there should be another (or two) bound round the splints

Fractured Upper Arm

as shown, one section above the injury and the other below.

A reef knot is used to tie the ends. If it is not possible to obtain a splint of any sort, tie the arm to the side of the body with two bandages.

FRACTURED FOREARM

Fractured Forearm

First of all, place the arm across the chest and then make either one or two splints, and tie as shown in this illustration.

It can then be completed by the addition of a large sling. When tying the splint to the forearm, try and do so on either side of the fracture. This makes it firmer and keeps the arm in place.

FRACTURED COLLARBONE

Fractured Collar Bone

This is generally indicated by the patient supporting the elbow with his hand, inclining his head towards the injured side.

Take off the coat and as much of the clothing as possible, then place a pad in the armpit and secure firmly to the side, as shown here. See that the circulation of the arm is not interfered with by feeling the pulse; if it cannot be felt, relax the bandage round the body a little.

FRACTURED RIBS AND SHOULDER BLADE

A break in the ribs can usually be told by sharp, cutting pain and difficulty in breathing easily. If the lungs are hurt, frothy bright red blood will be coughed up.

In this case do not bandage, but lie the patient down with his body turned towards the injured side, and then support him in that position.

Fractured Ribs

Loosen his clothing and place the arm on the injured side in a sling and apply cold compresses to the seat of the injury.

Fractured Shoulder Blade

WHAT TO DO TILL THE DOCTOR COMES

FIRST AID TO THE INJURED

TRANSPORTING INJURED PERSONS

The Fireman's Lift

This is an excellent idea for carrying an unconscious person, who must be moved without delay. It is a method often used during the last war, and only one carrier is necessary.

As one arm is free, it is possible to carry the patient along a narrow passage or down a ladder with safety.

The patient should lie face downwards, and the bearer stoops opposite the patient's head to raise the patient to a kneeling position. Then the bearer places his own shoulder against the patient's body near the waist, and carries the patient's arm over his neck, as shown in the first sketch.

The bearer should then rise slightly, place his right arm around or between the patient's thighs; grasp the patient by the right wrist, and rise to a standing position.

Then the patient's right arm can be held as illustrated. The bearer's left hand will be free to grip a ladder or to steady himself as he goes.

Hand-Seat Methods of Transporting the Injured

The Two-handed Seat. There are often times when it is necessary to rapidly transport an injured person from one place to another place of safety and comfort, and it is at such times that hand-seat methods can be adopted. If you have sufficient practice, you will not then hesitate as to what should be done at a critical moment.

(1) THE HOOK-GRIP used for THE TWO-HANDED SEAT

The two-handed method is generally used when two carriers are available to carry a patient who has injured both arms, and thus cannot assist to support himself. The carriers, one on each side of the patient, face each other, and then stoop. They place their nearer fore-arms across the patient's back just below the shoulders, and on raising the patient into a sitting position, they pass their free arms under the patient's knees. Here both hands are gripped together as shown in the above sketch.

The carriers rise together, and step off with opposite feet, so that jolting movements are reduced to a minimum. If a folded handkerchief is placed between the gripped fingers, the strain will be reduced.

The final carrying position is as indicated in the sketch on the left.

The Three-handed Seat. The three-handed seat is an alternative method to replace the four-handed seat (both of which are illustrated at the head of the next column), but it has an added advantage for the person with an injured leg, or who can support himself with only one arm.

In this, the free hand of one of the carriers can be placed around the back to steady the patient (as shown on left) or else an injured leg or arm can be supported to reduce strain. The method of clasping hands is very similar to the four-handed idea, except that the carrier on the injured side of the patient uses only one arm for the seat. The carriers should stand face to face behind the patient, and then clasp three hands on to the wrists as shown in the illustration at top of next column.

As the carriers stoop down the patient should, if the arms are not injured, place them around the shoulders of the carriers,

and help to lift himself on to the hand-seat. The carriers then rise together and step off with opposite feet.

If necessary a pad or cushion can be placed on the carriers' hands before the patient settles down.

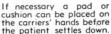

(2) Grip for THE FOUR-HANDED SEAT   (3) Grip for THE THREE-HANDED SEAT

The lower left-hand drawings in the previous column show the three-handed seat from the back. It indicates how one of the bearer's arms supports the patient from the back.

This, like the four-handed seat, is a very simple and effective one and it is also quite comfortable to the patient.

The four-handed seat. This is one of the simplest methods of carrying a person who is able to be transported in the sitting position. This seat can be resorted to when a person can place both arms around the shoulders of the carriers to help support himself.

The carriers face each other behind the patient; they join hands on to wrists (as shown above) and then stoop down. The patient is then instructed to place his arms over the shoulders, so that he can assist to raise himself. The carriers rise together and step off with opposite feet.

The illustration given here shows the front view of the four-handed seat; giving the position of the patient and the manner in which the carriers transport the patient and the way in which he makes himself comfortable by putting his arms around their necks.

Of course, these methods are mainly useful for carrying up to 100 yards or so, but for longer distances a stretcher of any improvised type is the recognised method of transport, or of carrying patients who are seriously injured.

The last four illustrations on this page show various other positions of transport, each of which is effective.

The Human Crutch. If the injured person is able to walk to some extent, you can assist by taking one of his arms over your own shoulder, grasping him around the waist with your other arm.

Incline your body a little away from the patient so that you can take as much weight as possible off his legs.

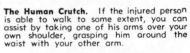

The legs nearest each other should be kept in step and walking should be slow. It is also best to stand on the injured side of the patient.

Pick-a-back Style. This explains itself, but a heavy person is rather a strain on the carrier, and cannot be kept under observation, therefore only use it under certain circumstances.

The Cradle. This is a lift suitable only for carrying children or very light persons. In this, the arms must be passed well under the patient before commencing to lift.

The last method shown here is only used when space does not permit of a hand seat. In this, the bearers should walk in step. One carrier places himself between the patient's legs and takes one leg just above the knee in each arm, the other carrier placing his hands under the armpits.

WHAT TO DO TILL THE DOCTOR COMES

FIRST AID TO THE INJURED

OTHER USEFUL GENERAL INFORMATION

ANOTHER ANTISEPTIC SOLUTION (see also page 279)

Two teaspoonsful of boracic powder, added to a pint of water, makes a mild antiseptic solution, useful in any wound or inflammation. The powder dissolves best in hot water. It may also be used dry, as a dusting powder.

BROKEN BONES

See illustrations and information on previous pages.

BRUISES AND SPRAINS

If a bruise can be treated at once, apply cold water and keep the part at perfect rest; otherwise apply relays of hot fomentations, still keeping the part at rest. Later apply warmth and very gentle friction, with cottonwool and bandage.

Sprains require perfect rest and support. Immediate plunging in cold water may prevent swelling, but warm applications are necessary to remove it; with cottonwool and bandaging for some days. A day's absolute rest at the time of the accident is worth a month's afterwards, therefore, never neglect a sprain.

BURNS AND SCALDS

Put out any burning clothes by smothering flames with rug or anything available. Remove or cut away any clothing from the injured part.

Put a cover over any burnt skin to keep air out. Do not break blisters, but place burnt part in lukewarm water, to which a small amount of boracic acid, salt, or baking soda has been added. When the dressing is ready, bandage tightly. "Tannafax" is very good to cover the injured part with. Do not use butter or carron oil in the wound. Give plenty to drink.

Severe burns produce great shock and stimulants may be necessary. If your dress catches fire, throw yourself at once flat on the ground and roll over.

SHOCK

Indications: Shallow breathing, weak pulse, pale face and lips, beads of cold sweat, skin clammy, and falling temperature.

The patient should be covered all round with rugs or coats and lie down, clothing should be loosened, and, if no internal injury, plenty of sweetened tea or coffee given to drink.

No alcohol should be given. Hot water bags should be placed against sides of body and between legs.

FAINTING

Sprinkle face with water, loosen clothing around neck and waist, put hot-water bottles over heart and stomach; rub legs and arms upwards, and give smelling salts. Lie patient down and raise feet. If patient's face is flushed raise head and lower feet. Give plenty of air.

CONCUSSION

Indicated by pale face, cold skin, quick and weak pulse, shallow breathing, slightly dilated pupils, and patient in a stupor. Clothing should be loosened, patient laid down in darkened place and kept warm. Apply cold-water compress to head.

COMPRESSION OF BRAIN

Is indicated by flushed face and heavy breathing, and blood may ooze out from nose and ear. The pupil of one eye may also be larger than the other. Treatment: Same as for concussion; if ear bleeding, incline patient towards that side and apply soft dressing. No stimulants or smelling salts.

CHOKING

Open the mouth, and with one or two fingers hook out or displace the foreign body. Slap the back between the shoulders. If necessary, a child may be held upside down for a few seconds.

CONVULSIONS IN INFANTS

Place the child at once in a warm bath about a 100 degrees, and leave for 10 minutes if necessary, at the same time applying an iced cloth to the head. Give a dose of castor oil afterwards.

FITS IN ADULTS

If you are sure it is a fainting fit only, as from fright, fatigue, bleeding, etc., **keep the head low.** Neglect to do this has caused many deaths. Later on give warm tea. **In all other fits raise the head slightly,** prevent self-injury, see that breathing is easy, keep warm, and do not give anything by mouth.

FOREIGN BODIES IN THE EYE

Don't rub. Bathe eye well. If in upper lid, turn lid over a pencil by pulling eyelashes upwards and brush it off gently with a handkerchief. Afterwards drop some oil between lids and keep eye closed.

FOREIGN BODIES IN THE EAR

Don't meddle unless it is near surface and can be seen, otherwise you may do mischief. Pour some oil in and cover gently with cotton wool.

ONSET OF COLD, RHEUMATISM, ETC.

Try a hot mustard foot bath until feet are reddened, or general hot bath, with a hot drink and sleeping in the blankets.

INSECT STINGS

Apply vinegar at once, baking soda or weak ammonia solution.

SUFFOCATION

Fresh air at once, clear throat, loosen clothing around chest, dash cold water in face, apply smelling salts.

SUNSTROKE

Generally occurs from over-exertion or over-drinking in hot weather. It may come on without exposure to sun's rays. Remove to a cool place, apply cold water freely to the head, and if skin is hot and flushed, sponge it with cold water. Spirits or other stimulants should **not** be given. All drinks should be cold.

POISONING

Except where mouth and throat are corroded, produce vomiting by giving one or two tablespoonsful of mustard or common salt, in a cupful of warm water.

(1) If pain and purging, give two teaspoonsful of chalk, whiting or magnesia in a tumbler of milk or water, repeating from time to time.

(2) If sleepy, keep awake by walking, and give strong coffee; keep warm, and, if necessary, promote breathing artificially as described in drowning.

An emetic (i.e., something to make the patient vomit) should be given for poisons which do not stain the mouth, such as Arsenic, Phosphorous, Strychnine, Prussic Acid, Belladonna, Ptomaine or Alcoholic poisoning, Opium, Morphia, Laudanum, Paregoric, Chlorodine, etc. AN EMETIC SHOULD NOT BE GIVEN FOR POISONS WHICH BURN OR STAIN THE MOUTH :

Acids. i.e., Nitric, Sulphuric, Hydrochloric, Muriatic (Spirits of Salts), Carbolic, Oxalic, etc., or Caustic Potash, Caustic Soda and Ammonia. In the case of acids, give magnesia or common whiting with milk or water. In the case of Caustic, etc., give lemon or lime juice or vinegar with water. Strong tea is always a good neutraliser.

ANTIDOTES FOR POISONS

CARBOLIC ACID—Give milk with $\frac{1}{2}$ oz. of Epsom salts to pint.

PRUSSIC ACID—(1) Place patient in open air; (2) dash cold water on head and spine continuously; (3) apply artificial respiration; (4) hold smelling salts to nose.

POISONOUS MEAT, FISH, AND FUNGI—Give an emetic, and when emetic has acted then give castor oil.

STRYCHNINE—Give an emetic; (2) apply artificial respiration.

ALCOHOL—Give an emetic if patient can swallow.

ARSENIC—Stomach pump or give an emetic and cause vomiting.

WHAT TO DO TILL THE DOCTOR COMES

These hints are not intended to do instead of the Doctor.

Send for him at once if anything serious is the matter.

WHAT TO DO TILL THE DOCTOR COMES

FIRST AID TO THE INJURED

WOUNDS AND CUTS

Wash wounds thoroughly with cold boiled water (after own hands have been thoroughly cleansed) containing a little boracic acid. See that bleeding ceases; and bandage.

When the bleeding has stopped, wrap a little piece of cotton wool round the stick of a match and dip it in a mild tincture of iodine or methylated spirits. Put a few drops into the cut. Then apply a piece of boracic lint to the cut, put a piece of wool on the top of the lint, and wool round the stick of a match and dip bandage. (See also page 281 on "How to treat a surface wound.")

If bleeding be severe :

(1) Raise the limb and apply pressure directly over the wound, either by clean finger or rolled up clean handkerchief.

(2) If bleeding continues bright scarlet and in spurts, press with the fingers or tighten a bandage around the limb on the side nearest the heart, if necessary, after direct pressure over the wound and elevation on the limb.

(3) If dark and in a stream, tighten the ligature round the limb on the side away from the heart.

(4) See also previous hints on pressure points and tourniquets.

After treating the wound as above, keep at rest. Remember that profuse bleeding may be fatal, and the bleeding must be stopped before the wound is bound up.

Scratches and Scrapes. Use a few drops of iodine. Then put on a piece of boracic lint spread with boracic ointment—like butter on bread. Apply wool and bandage.

SNAKEBITE

Tie a ligature near the bite, between it and the heart, tight enough to stop all circulation. Best effected by passing a stick underneath ligature and twisting, then securing (see tourniquet).

Cleanse the wound thoroughly. Do not leave ligature on for more than 30 minutes, undo for five minutes then tie again.

Where ligature cannot be tied (face, neck or body) pinch up bitten part between finger and thumb and cut it out with a clean knife.

After tying ligature promote free bleeding by numerous little cuts over and around bites for half an inch and suck by mouth freely. This can be done without danger to anyone if the mouth is free from cracks or abrasions. If available, permanganate of potash can be rubbed into parts.

Effect of poison. Venomous bite can be distinguished by depression in early stages—nausea, coughing or spitting of blood, dilations of pupils of eyes, ultimately paralysis of limbs and finally suffocation from paralysis of respiratory organs. Many symptoms often follow from simple fright.

Persevere, no matter how unfavourable the symptoms appear to be. After treatment, do not walk patient round while waiting for a doctor.

Keep him warm and cheerful, give strong, hot tea or black coffee, use alcoholic stimulants with discretion; these can be given in small quantities if patient be faint.

If medical assistance cannot be obtained and if grave symptoms supervene (adults rarely die within three hours of bite) let some competent person inject strychnine with a hypodermic syringe in the following manner.

Cleanse the needle and the inside of the syringe with some spirit, draw up into the syringe five drops of the recognised strychnine solution (obtainable from chemist), pinch up the skin of the forearm, introduce the needle and inject the contents into the skin.

Especially watch the respiration throughout, and if the breathing becomes weak or irregular, perform artificial respiration as recommended in dealing with the apparently drowned.

DROWNING

Act promptly and energetically. (1) First loosen clothing, stripping patient to waist, clear the throat, and turn over on to face so as o get rid of water, mud, etc. (2) Excite breathing by slapping on chest, smelling salts, etc. (3) If these means fail, place patient's face to ground with head turned to one side. Put a folded coat or something under lower part of chest. Then apply artificial respiration.

ARTIFICIAL RESPIRATION (The Schafer Method)

Artificial respiration, or the restoring of natural breathing, is used in cases where breathing is seen to be failing or has ceased, examples of which are drowning, hanging, choking, inhalation of gases, electrocution, pressure on chest, smothering, etc.

Commence treatment immediately. Lay the patient in the prone position as shown, with the arms extended above the head. Turn the patient's head on one side, so as to keep the nose and mouth away from the ground, making sure that the air passages are clear by inserting a finger into the mouth and sweeping it deep into the throat to remove possible obstruction, such as weeds or false teeth, etc.

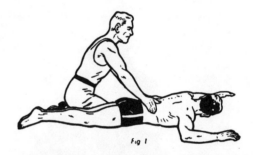

Fig. 1

First, kneel on one side facing his head. Take up the position shown, feel for the lowest ribs, and place the hands over them, wrists nearly touching, fingers circling the loins on either side, and pointing to ground, but not spread out. (Fig. 1.) Then swing body forward slowly, keeping arms straight, so that your weight is conveyed directly downwards. (Fig. 2.) This presses air and water in the lungs out through the mouth. Then swing your body

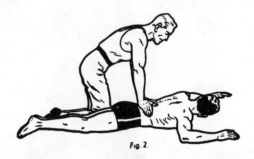

Fig. 2

slowly backwards to first position, removing the weight from the hands, which are kept in position. The releasing of the pressure induces air to pass back into the lungs.

Do these movements at the rate of: **Pressure**, 2 seconds; **relaxation**, 3 seconds; and so on. When natural breathing begins, regulate movement to correspond with it, and promote circulation by rubbing vigorously towards the heart and by applying warmth.

WHAT TO DO TILL THE DOCTOR COMES
These hints are not intended to do instead of the Doctor. Send for him at once if anything serious is the matter.

THOMAS HARDY & SONS LTD., ADELAIDE, SYDNEY, MELBOURNE ; MAKERS OF
TINTARA GOLD LABEL PORT, AMONTILLADO SHERRY, GOLD LABEL MUSCATEL ;
THE TINTARA SPARKLING WINES :—CHAMPAGNE, HOCK, MOSELLE, BURGUNDY,
AND TINTARA OLD BRANDY

A. M. L. & F. Co. Ltd.

WOOL BROKERS
STOCK & STATION AGENTS

Selling Brokers for

FURS, SKINS, HIDES & TALLOW

PURE STOCK & PROPERTY SALESMEN

AUSTRALIAN, MERCANTILE, LAND & FINANCE CO. LTD.
(Inc. in England)

VICTORIA	NEW SOUTH WALES	QUEENSLAND
Offices :	Offices :	Offices :
122 WILLIAM STREET, MELBOURNE	4 BLIGH STREET, SYDNEY	129 CREEK STREET, BRISBANE

Offices also at:

LONDON, BUENOS AIRES, SYDNEY, NEWCASTLE, MOREE, WAGGA, HAY, HENTY, BRISBANE, CHARLEVILLE, TOWNSVILLE

OTHER GOOD IDEAS WORTH KEEPING

If you should see any other good idea which you would like to keep before you for future use,
make a note of it or paste it in here

An Efficient and Courteous

Banking Service

An account with The Bank of Adelaide will place at your disposal an efficient and courteous personal banking service—a service that incorporates every facility to suit your personal or business requirements. The Manager at any of our many Offices will be pleased to explain the numerous services which are available to you.

The Bank of Adelaide

Established 1865

(Incorporated in South Australia with Limited Liability)

Head Office :   King William Street, Adelaide, South Australia

98 Branches and Agencies in South Australia

Branches also at BRISBANE, SYDNEY, MELBOURNE, PERTH, FREMANTLE, and at LONDON

AGENTS THROUGHOUT THE WORLD

INDEX TO CONTENTS (Sectionised)

WORKSHOP IDEAS AND GADGETS

Index

Index

CEMENT AND ITS USES

HANDYMAN JOBS AROUND THE HOME (Home Repairs, etc.)

HANDY HINTS and Novel Devices for FARM AND STATION

Co-operation -
the Keystone of **NATIONAL EFFORT**

Modern banking includes much more than accepting deposits and granting loans. It makes available a wide range of services and facilities, which are not only useful, but are essential for the conduct of modern business. The protection of its customers' deposits is one of the main duties of the Bank, and in carrying out that duty, the Bank makes loans to trade and industry, and invests in Government bonds. In so doing it assists business, encourages sound enterprise, and helps to provide means for carrying through community efforts.

THE NATIONAL BANK
of Australasia Limited
(Incorporated in Victoria.)
88 years' experience of Australian Banking.

HANDY HINTS and Novel Devices for FARM AND STATION (continued)

GATES AND FASTENERS (Home-made)

FENCING HINTS

KEEP THEM HEALTHY...
AND *Worm-free* ALWAYS!

Drench with ... PHENOVIS

Stop flock losses and keep your sheep in top condition always by drenching with **PHENOVIS** — the effective gastro-intestinal worm remedy. **PHENOVIS** contains phenothiazine — the only successful treatment for nodule worm and is deadly against large stomach, small intestine or black scour, and other intestinal worms in sheep and domestic animals.

PHENOVIS is non-toxic and harmless to sheep when used as recommended, and is supplied ready to use in handy powder form. Mix with water and administer as directed.

*PHENOVIS — registered trade mark

Available in
1 LB. TINS — 7/-; 7 LB. TINS — 6/8 PER POUND
Freight and postage extra

Supplies available from
STORES, MERCHANTS AND PASTORAL HOUSES

AN I.C.I. ANIMAL REMEDY

Index

FENCING HINTS (continued)

WATER CONSERVATION and Other Hints

SHEEP (Some Useful Hints)

HORSES

Index

DAIRYING HINTS

PIGS

DOGS

ANIMAL DESTRUCTION

POULTRY HINTS

Index

THE GARDEN—SOME USEFUL HINTS

FIRST AID TO THE INJURED

How to Make a Useful First Aid Box
How to Make a First Aid Cabinet
Articles to Keep Ready for Use
How to Make Temporary Splints
How to Make Temporary Bandages
How to Apply Bandages, etc.
How to Secure Splints
How to Make Reef Knots
Hints on Bandages and Bandaging

Pages 279 to 287

How to Blanket a Stretcher
Some Useful Home-made Lotions
How to Cope with Bleeding, etc.
How to Treat Fractured Bones
How to Treat Surface Wounds
Hints on Artificial Respiration
How to Transport Injured Persons
How to Find Pressure Points
And many other Useful Hints which may be Useful in an Emergency

Australia's Quality Radio

COMBINING the experience of precision radio manufacture, gained over the past twenty years, with engineering far-sightedness in assessing your peace-time radio requirements, Astor brings you a comprehensive range of models.

Tonal perfection, split hair selectivity, and modern, beautifully finished cabinet design are the natural attributes of a radio range by Astor — an organisation with vast technical and manufacturing resources.

Individual needs are completely catered for by the production of vibrator, battery and electric models, designed to outmode all existing standards of radio listening.

Get the complete story from your nearest Astor Radio retailer.

ASTOR

Precision RADIO

A PRODUCT OF RADIO CORPORATION PTY. LTD
(A   Division   of   Electronic   Industries   Ltd.)

A Job Well Done....

AFTER five years of mounting difficulties there is a community tribute due to the vast numbers of Australians who have played their part in this war from atop the tractor and beside the harvester, who have ploughed and sowed and reaped their unspectacular way through the seasons and the years, that the soil might produce, that the Allied nations might be clothed and fed, that life might continue in a battle-broken world, towards a brighter horizon.

Theirs is a job well done — with plough and pruning hook, with shaft and shearing blade, in daylight and in darkness, through defeat to triumph, in faith and in hope ....

To them all honour and the gratitude of a Nation.

RURAL BANK
OF NEW SOUTH WALES
HEAD OFFICE: MARTIN PLACE, SYDNEY

Commissioners:

C. R. McKERIHAN (President)   H. ROGERS   P. KEARNS

New South Wales
and
Queensland Wool

SHEEP, LAMBS, CATTLE, PROPERTIES

WINCHCOMBE, CARSON
Ltd.

WOOL BROKERS, STOCK AND PROPERTY SALESMEN

have a well equipped organisation for the conduct of business throughout both States.

They have Wool Stores with spacious, perfectly lighted showfloors in—

SYDNEY, NEWCASTLE AND BRISBANE

The ramifications of their stock and property business are most extensive.

They have offices at—

Winchcombe House, Bridge Street, Sydney.

10 Watt Street, Newcastle—99/101 Eagle Street, Brisbane.

N. S. Wales—Yass, Orange, Forbes, Bourke, Armidale.

Queensland—Longreach, Emerald, Hughenden, Charleville, Dalby, Miles, Tara, Goondi- windi, St. George.

Post Office Communications

- The ends of the earth are at your nearest Post Office.

- Progress and communications have always been notable for their inter-dependence, and the many services provided by the Australian Post Office have played an impressive part in the development of the Nation.

- Today the Post Office forms an integral part of the comprehensive international organisation of communications encircling the globe and linking together peoples of all civilised nations.

- In war years, the Post Office has served the Nation loyally in providing reliable communication facilities both for the fighting forces and on the home-front. Throughout these years there has been an unprecedented increase in the volume of traffic handled in all branches of the Department, but with a depleted staff, long hours of duty and the assistance of our women folk, the motto has been " carry on."

- This huge organisation of plant and personnel, affords a practical demonstration of the commercial and social application of modern scientific discoveries to the complex problems of the communication needs of mankind. Keeping in touch . . . in the cities . . . in country towns and settlements . . . in the far-outback. Wherever two or three people are gathered together, there also is the Post Office . . . maintaining a communication service; keeping the city in touch with the country and the rural dweller in touch with the town.

- The Post Office steadfastly pursues a policy ensuring that the latest world advances in communications practice are incorporated in all its technical services for the benefit of the Nation and the individual alike. Modern and progressive are the Australian Airmail, Postal, Telephone, Telegraph and Wireless Services. The watchword is " Speedy, courteous and reliable service."

VAST TO SERVE THE NATION — PERSONAL TO SERVE YOU !

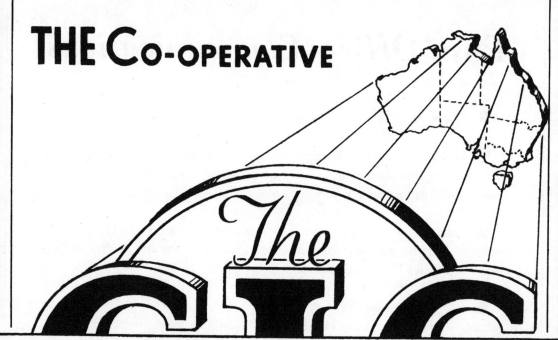